Beyond Notes

Improvisation in Western Music of the Eighteenth and Nineteenth Centuries

Specvlvm Mvsicae

Edendum Curavit
Roberto Illiano

Volume XVI

Publications of the Centro Studi Opera Omnia Luigi Boccherini
Pubblicazioni del Centro Studi Opera Omnia Luigi Boccherini
Publications du Centro Studi Opera Omnia Luigi Boccherini
Veröffentlichungen der Centro Studi Opera Omnia Luigi Boccherini
Publicaciones del Centro Studi Opera Omnia Luigi Boccherini
Lucca

BEYOND NOTES

IMPROVISATION IN WESTERN MUSIC OF THE EIGHTEENTH AND NINETEENTH CENTURIES

EDITED BY

RUDOLF RASCH

❧

BREPOLS

TURNHOUT

MMXI

D/2011/0095/132

ISBN 978-2-503-54244-7

CONTENTS

PREFACE   ix

TO BEGIN WITH…

RUDOLF RASCH
   The Volatility of Musical Composition   1

THE EIGHTEENTH CENTURY: THEORY

MARTIN KALTENECKER
   The «Fantasy-Principle». Improvisation between
   Imagination and Oration in the Eighteenth Century   17

CARMELA BONGIOVANNI
   Testimonianze sulla prassi improvvisativa
   dei musicisti italiani tra Sette e Ottocento   35
   English Summary   48

MARIATERESA DELLABORRA
   «L'orecchio più che 'l tempo dee servire di guida».
   L'improvvisazione nella trattatistica italiana del secondo Settecento   49
   English Summary   66

THE EIGHTEENTH CENTURY: PRACTICE

ROGÉRIO BUDASZ
   Harmonic Patterns and Melodic Paraphrases
   in Eighteenth-Century Portuguese Music for the Five-Course Guitar   67

SIMONE CIOLFI
   Formule e improvvisazione nei recitativi
   delle Cantate di Alessandro Scarlatti   83
   English Summary   96

GREGORIO CARRARO
   Natura e arte nell'improvvisazione di Giuseppe Tartini   97
   English Summary   109

John Lutterman
«Cet art est la perfection du talent».
Chordal Thoroughbass Realization and Improvised Solo Performance
on the Viol and Cello in the Eighteenth Century   111

The Nineteenth Century: Keyboard Instruments

Rohan H. Stewart-MacDonald
Improvisation into Composition. The First Movement
of Johann Nepomuk Hummel's Sonata in F-sharp Minor, Op. 81   129

Valerie Woodring Goertzen
Clara Wieck Schumann's Improvisations
and Her 'Mosaics' of Small Forms   153

Martin Edin
Cadenza Improvisation in Nineteenth-Century Solo Piano Music
According to Czerny, Liszt and Their Contemporaries   163

Steven Young
Practical Improvisation. The Art of Louis Vierne   185

The Nineteenth Century: Bowed Strings

Philippe Borer
Paganini's Virtuosity and Improvisatory Style   191

Renato Ricco
Charles-Auguste de Bériot e l'improvvisazione virtuosistica per violino   217
English Summary   237

Csilla Pethő-Vernet
The Advantages and Drawbacks of Notation, or How to Face Improvisatory
Elements in Nineteenth-Century Hungarian Popular Music   239

The Nineteenth Century: Vocal Music

Damien Colas
Improvvisazione e ornamentazione
nell'opera francese e italiana di primo Ottocento   255
English Summary   276

Laura Moeckli
    «Abbellimenti o fioriture». Further Evidence of Creative
    Embellishment in and beyond the Rossinian Repertoire   277

Naomi Matsumoto
    Manacled Freedom. Nineteenth-Century Vocal Improvisation
    and the Flute-Accompanied Cadenza
    in Gaetano Donizetti's *Lucia di Lammermoor*   295

Raffaele Di Mauro
    Improvvisazione popolare e urbana a Napoli nel primo Ottocento.
    Dai canti del molo a «Io te voglio bene assaje»   317
    English Summary   343

...and to End with

Vincenzo Caporaletti
    «Ghost Notes». Issues of Inaudible Improvisations   345

Contributors   375

Index of Names   379

PREFACE

IMPROVISATION IS A WORD, a term, a concept, which everybody assumes that they know and understand. However, when it comes to devising a precise definition of improvisation, it is less easy than it may at first have seemed. Literally, it means 'that which is not foreseen', in the sense of 'not seen before'. It may designate the action of producing such unforeseen things, as well as the results of such actions. How does this relate to music?

If I tune my violin and I play a short melody on it to check the tuning, or some scales or arpeggiated triads, without much preconception, I may call it an improvisation. In the historical literature this action so is called 'preluding', and I produce a Prelude before the main performance. The next day I may do it again, but probably differently, so it remains improvisation. After some time I may find certain passages genuinely useful, so I start to repeat them, literally or not. Is that still improvisation? Or have I entered into the field of unwritten composition?

There are, of course, more important improvisations than my little preludes on the violin. Pianists may add improvised cadenzas and interludes to their recitals, they may add something to a concerto they perform. Singers may add embellishments to their arias which are not notated in their scores. Pianists may also conclude their recitals by playing compositions composed on the spot, on themes handed to them by the public. Jazz musicians are accustomed to including a great deal of unwritten music in their performances; improvisation is their core business, as it were. In all these cases we listen to these improvisations as if they were compositions. For the listener, then, it does not make very much difference whether or not what he hears is improvised or composed.

In mentioning the word 'composition' I have introduced the antonym of improvisation: both terms imply the creation of musical structures, but improvising means creating them while performing, composing means committing them to paper. Both improvisations and compositions are realisations of musical structures, so they must both obey at least an overlapping set of musical rules. One commentator has said that improvisation is quick composing, and composition is slow improvising, because, indeed, in order to compose something on paper, it must also be thought of first and be unforeseen, in the sense of not yet existing.

Now, where do all these musings bring us? Not very far, I am afraid, and they may be nothing more than just a kind of improvisation in writing. But it at least makes us realize that between the poles of absolute improvisation and absolute composition there is a gradual transition, a large field in between, including phenomena that some person will call improvisation, another one not. To give a few examples: Is the addition of ornaments to a piece in a style where those ornaments are expected or even required improvisation, or is it rather part of the interpretation, along with the choice of instrument, the tempo, many of the dynamics, and so on? What is to be said about basso continuo, notated as a bass line with figures, but performed as three- or four-part harmony (or counterpoint)? Are cadenzas added to sonatas and concertos really improvisations? They might have been prepared, or exist as a logical consequence of what has preceded. In any case, an improvisation must fit, must be suitable in the context of its environment, it cannot be just anything.

The improvisation which is praised the most is the one which cannot be distinguished from a written composition when one hears it. Here the improviser shows that he is a real master of the art: he can do at once, without preparation, what others can do only with preparation, taking their time, and applying a considerable amount of trial and error. To ensure that an improvisation is really an improvisation, it is sometimes required that it be based on themes given to the improviser by the public at the moment of the improvisation.

Therefore, the perfect improvisation should be indistinguishable from a written composition; this leads to a strange paradox, however. There is a genre of written compositions which is supposed to resemble improvisations, especially those entitled Improvisation, Fantasy, Impromptu, Prelude, and so forth. These compositions should be, when one listens to them, clearly distinguishable from standard written compositions due to a lack of clear structure, unexpected, sometimes strange turns, a lack of consequence and consistency, fantasy, the unexpected and the unforeseen in general. Therefore, whereas an improvised improvisation should sound like a written composition, a written improvisation should sound like anything but a written composition.

This little sample of remarks makes clear that improvisation is anything but a well-defined concept, apart from the fact that the term denotes both a process and the outcome of that process. If we look up an encyclopedia article on 'Improvisation', like the one in the *New Grove Dictionary*, Second Edition, 2001, we find a number of subjects treated, among them 'ensemble improvisation' in early music history (the *ex tempore* addition of unwritten parts to a written part); ornamentation (as additions to existing compositions); free improvisation (of preludes, and so forth) and continuo realization. This is as far as Western art music is concerned. Improvisation in jazz is discussed separately, as are equivalents in non-Western music. It is interesting to see to which other articles are referred to for further reading: Aleatory, Cadenza, Continuo, Division, Jazz, Notation, Ornament, Performing Practice, Prélude non mesuré. Improvisation is not a single subject, it is a cluster of subjects, or perhaps a key concept with manifold ramifications.

Improvisation is not a process limited to music alone. Within the arts it is conspicuously present in the theatre (think of the famous *Commedia dell'arte*) and to a lesser extent in poetry. Outside the arts improvisation can be part of a broad range of human actions, from a holiday trip to dealing with disasters. We could say that improvisation is a natural element in the life of mankind and that it is therefore only natural to find it in music[1].

The essays brought together in this volume do confirm the problematic aspect of the concept of improvisation and the wide range of approaches that can be taken to it. Because of the collective nature of this volume, the approaches do indeed vary greatly. A Dutch proverb says 'Two know more than one' and a fortiori one could then say 'Twenty know much more than one', meaning here that a much wider range of topics and treatments is available in a collective volume than a single author alone could provide. Some contributions deal with improvisation from the conceptual point of view: what really *is* improvisation. Others deal with certain repertoires, or with specific examples. Some deal with improvised additions, others with improvisational aspects of written compositions.

One recurrent theme in the articles brought together here is that of improvisation as a typically Italian art form, especially in relation to singing and violin playing. But here again is a paradox: although organ improvisation was practiced throughout Europe, in the nineteenth century it was considered a French art, at least in France. Several historical texts are referred to time and again in the essays brought together in this volume, especially Carl Philipp Emanuel Bach's discussion of the free fantasy in his *Versuch über die wahre Art das Clavier zu spielen, Zweiter Theil* (1762), Francesco Galeazzi's *Elementi teorico-pratici di musica, Tomo secondo* (1796), and Carl Czerny's *Systematische Anleitung zum Fantasieren auf dem Pianoforte* (1829). Diverse as the subject is, the presence of some common ground cannot be denied.

Dealing with improvisations from times preceding the recording of sound is a difficult enterprise. We have to use verbal descriptions of improvisations or transcripts testifying to their transcribed nature. Perhaps the article on Louis Vierne (Young) is the only one dealing directly with recorded improvisations. The article on the flute-cadenza in Donizetti's *Lucia di Lammermoor* (Matsumoto) encompasses recorded material, but this was rather semi-improvisational, prepared certainly, but not necessarily notated and not necessarily performed identically every time. Then we move to contemporary descriptions of improvisations: we find them in the articles on Italian music theorists (Dellaborra), on Italian musicians in general (Bongiovanni), on Hummel (Stewart-MacDonald), Paganini (Borer), Bériot (Ricco), Clara Wieck Schumann (Goertzen) and Czerny, Liszt and Henselt (Edin). Compositions in improvisatory style are discussed in several of these articles and in one on nineteenth-century Hungarian or so-called 'Gypsy' music (Pethő-Vernet). Analogous to the concept of the sonata-principle one could speak of a fantasy-principle (Kaltenecker). *Ad libitum* ornamentation is discussed in relation to Tartini's violin sonatas (Carraro) and nineteenth-century operatic arias (Moeckli, Colas). Other contributions

---

[1]. See PETERS, Gary. *The Philosophy of Improvisation*, Chicago, University of Chicago Press, 2009; *Menschliches Handeln als Improvisation. Sozial- und Musikwissenschaftliche Perspektiven*, edited by Ronald Kurt and Klaus Näumann, Bielefeld, Transcript, 2008.

discuss the instability that is a property of nearly all music (Rasch) or the migration of motives and schemes from one composition to another (Budasz, Ciolfi, Lutterman, Rasch), processes that pave the way for improvised additions. Caporaletti's study provides a theoretical reflection on the subject of improvisation.

This book is not the first to deal with improvisation in music. Actually, one could fill a complete library with books dealing with improvisation in one way or another. There are books on improvisation in Western art music, both historical and contemporary[2]. Nearly every book that deals with jazz music also deals with improvisation, which is seen as one of the basic characteristics of the genre. Improvisation is also an element of popular music and exists in nearly every non-Western musical culture. Books have been written about the role of improvisation in all these areas; and books have been written about the role of improvisation in musical education. Furthermore, there are textbooks on how to learn to improvise on a great variety of musical instruments. The ones cited in the footnotes to this paragraph are just few samples from a large corpus.

The present book grew out of an international conference held at La Spezia, Italy on 15-17 July 2010, organized by the Centro Studi Opera Omnia Luigi Boccherini (Lucca) and the Società dei Concerti (La Spezia). During this conference twenty-four papers were presented, of which twenty found their way, generally in a revised form, into the present volume. These twenty articles are by authors residing in seven different countries: France, Italy, the Netherlands, Sweden, Switzerland, United Kingdom, and the United States. The conference was bilingual. Consequently, several contributions are in Italian, with English summaries provided.

The editor wishes to thank all the contributors for their efforts in providing valuable articles for this volume, for their patience with his many questions and requests during the editing process, and for their willingness to consider all of these questions and requests. Rohan H. Stewart-MacDonald and Valerie Woodring Goertzen were kind in providing a final check of the English written by not-native writers. Thanks are also due to Roberto Illiano, general editor of the series 'Speculum Musicae', for all his help, advice and inspiration. 'Improvisation in Western music' has proven to be a subject worthy of the efforts of all of us.

Rudolf Rasch
Utrecht, Netherlands

---

[2]. See the collective volumes *Musical Improvisation. Art, Education, and Society*, edited by Gabriel Solis and Bruno Nettl, Urbana, University of Illinois Press, 2009, and *In the Course of Performance. Studies in the World of Musical Improvisation*, edited by Bruno Nettl and Melinda Russell, Chicago, Chicago University Press, 1998, to name but a few. In Italian: CAPORALETTI, Vincenzo. *I processi improvvisativi nella musica. Un approccio globale*, Lucca, LIM, 2005, and the collective volume *Sull'improvvisazione*, edited by Claudio Toscani, Lucca, LIM, 1998.

THE VOLATILITY OF MUSICAL COMPOSITION

Rudolf Rasch
(UTRECHT)

AT FIRST SIGHT IMPROVISATION AND MUSICAL composition seem to be very distinct phenomena. Improvisation in music is what is produced on the spot, without any premeditation. Musical compositions are written down on paper after careful thinking and correcting. When one examines these two processes a little more closely, however, the distinction is not as absolute as it may first appear. Improvisation is usually based on certain melodic material or on some kind of pre-existing model, and follows all kind of rules, according to which it is certainly not totally 'new'. Composed music may leave ample space for liberties in performance, with respect to many parameters: tempo, dynamics, ornamentations, instruments, cuts or additions, and so on. In other words: parts of an improvisation may have been composed, a composition will be supplemented by improvised elements when performed.

The improvised component of a further written composition necessarily facilitates variability in the performance of this composition. But the variability goes deeper. The history of musical composition and the publishing of music teach us that the same composition only rarely reappears in a totally identical form if it is written down or published again. Different periods in the history of music notate music in different ways, which means that if we continue to republish works from earlier periods every new edition will look different from its predecessors. This brings us to the realisation that there will never be a definitive notation of the pieces of music which we study. This is why we can speak of the volatility of music: a piece of music will not allow an unambiguous, definitive form.

In this essay I will discuss this volatility or, more fundamentally, the variability of the musical text on several different levels. Firstly there are the differences between performances when the same piece of music is performed again by the same or by other musicians. The argument of the flexible relation between score and performance can be extended to include that between the score and what there was before it became a score. If we explore that relationship, we will see that even a score, a palpable, fixed object at first sight, is also something which is constantly subject to changes and transformations in the hands of those who use it and those who transmit it from one generation of users to the next. If one studies the way in which a piece of music has been written down through the centuries, one will discern continually new notational methods. The publication history of Corelli's Violin Sonatas Op. 5 will serve as an example. Finally there may be the difficulty of establishing an initial text for a piece of music. This aspect will be illustrated with reference to the Trios Op. 1 of Luigi Boccherini.

THE VARIABILITY OF PERFORMANCE

When music is being performed, and that is certainly its goal, the written form only partially defines the resulting sound. We all know that when we hear music performed by a computer which takes the notation literally the result may give us some impression of the type of music, but it brings us little aesthetic satisfaction. To obtain that, it is necessary to add something to the written score and that is necessarily something that is unwritten.

We know, for example, that we must change the tempo of the performance here and there a little, that we must not take all the dynamic indications literally. Articulation is often determined to a great extent by the performer. Especially with early music — and the more so the earlier the music — performers have to take many decisions about the unwritten aspects of the music they are performing. Instrumentation is another source of variability. Which instruments do we choose to perform the music, how many of each instrument in an orchestral performance? There is virtually no musical style where the notation of music is so precise that every performance is exactly the same as every other, with the possible exceptions of mechanical music (on *Flötenuhre*, musical boxes and player pianos) and pre-recorded electronic music. They are characterized by the absence of a musician, which may make us think that it is the presence of the musician which is all-decisive in the obviously omnipresent variability in the performance of music.

When we listen to a performance that we do not yet know, live or recorded, and follow the notation of the music in a score, it is often surprising to observe the relation between what we hear and what we see. We hear many things we do not see, even if everything we see is heard. Can we call the things we do not see in the score 'improvisation', which literally means 'things not seen before'? Perhaps, but perhaps preferably not. During a performance the musicians do not proceed haphazardly, rather they work according to certain existing traditions, traditions which determine the choice of instruments, the tempo, the articulation, and so forth, everything that must be done to make music out of the written notes. Musicians follow a certain system of rules that converts the notation into sound. The first aim of this system is to create a performance that is aesthetically satisfying. When a performance is repeated the result will be more or less the same, it may be difficult to distinguish the repetition from the original.

Of course, there is not a single system of rules for the performance of music. Instead, there are many, perhaps even an infinite number. Every musician or ensemble will have his, her or their own rules, often with characteristic traits, to be recognized for them. Ideas about how to perform the same music may vary quite a bit, both among musicians living contemporaneously and when we consider these things throughout history. To give a very simple and trivial example: Beethoven's sonatas may sound very different if performed by different pianists; if we study performances of these sonatas throughout history, there will be considerable diversity.

However, as said above, one should be very reluctant to call these differences improvisations. They are interpretations, and fall within a range of variability in a way already foreseen by the composer: he must have known that his music would not always be performed the same way and certainly not for ever. Composers of the seventeenth and eighteenth centuries must have known that their figured basses would be realized in many divergent ways, to give a single example.

Things become different if musicians do something or add something that is not within a generally accepted system of rules. They may add ornamentation not hinted at in the score, they may vary a melody when repeated; they may change instrumentation, add cadenzas, and so on. We could say that interpretation has to do with those aspects of the performance where the performers are expected to do something and then improvisation is not what is expected but is permitted.

At this point, things get complicated. How do we know that something we hear is interpretation and not improvisation, or improvisation and not interpretation? This is only possible if we know the score, and know the rules of interpretation. However, very often — perhaps it is the normal state of listening — we do not know the score, or not precisely enough to judge whether something we hear is interpretation or improvisation. Perhaps we can hear consistency: are those interpretations and improvisations in line with the basis of the composition, the notes that are written down in the score? I will not explore this point further here.

What is important to realize is that a single piece of music may sound very different on different occasions. A piece of music is, when it is composed and leaves the composer's desk, not a final product, it rather is a semi-manufactured article, to be finished during performance. This process we could call the volatility of music in relation to performance: we do not know what will come out of it, and every time it will emerge somewhat differently.

The Variability of Tradition
The Sonatas Op. 5 by Arcangelo Corelli

No autograph score is known of Corelli's Op. 5, a set of twelve sonatas for violin and figured bass. What we have is a first edition that was clearly authorized by the author[1]. It is an edition consisting of a series of beautiful engravings made by Gasparo Pietrasanta, who certainly did his work under the eyes of the composer (see Ex. 1). The edition was published in Rome, by the composer himself, with the date of 1 January 1700 — certainly not a coincidence — under the dedication to the Electress of Brandenburg, Sophia Charlotte. The engraving, and therefore the printing, can be seen as a faithful copy of the composer's manuscript, so that we have, with it, a text bearing a high level of authority.

If we study the 1700 edition of Corelli's sonatas, we see that it is very accurate, that it is almost totally unambiguous, that it is practically devoid of errors, and that it is

Ex. 1: first page of music in the first edition of Arcangelo Corelli's *Sonate a violino e violone o cimbalo* [...] *Opera quinta*, Rome, [Author], [1700].

[1]. Corelli, Arcangelo. *Sonate a violino e violone o cimbalo* [...] *Opera quinta*, Rome, [Author], [1700].

very consistent in its notation. Nevertheless, the edition is not in any way a replica of the performances that can be based on it. It leaves a great deal of space between its notation and the resulting sound, a space that we may call the interpretation. The violin player must add bowing and fingering, ornamentation, articulation, dynamics, tempo, and so forth. The accompaniment may adopt a great number of formats. The title page says it is for 'violone o cembalo', which is sometimes interpreted literally. Even if not taken literally, there is almost endless variation. The bass line can be played by the cello, the viola da gamba or even the bassoon, or only by the harpsichord (or any other keyboard instrument). For the realization of the figures, harpsichord, organ or theorbo are only the most obvious choices. Furthermore, it is impossible to know exactly which notes are going to be played as accompaniment.

The Amsterdam edition of 1702 consists of a score with two partbooks, violin and violoncello, thus strongly implying both a melodic and a harmonic accompaniment[2]. That edition also adds continuo figures to those already present in the Roman edition. Another variation occurs when the notation with two-stave systems with treble and bass clefs is not interpreted as a score for violin and bass, but as keyboard music. Nothing prevents someone from playing these pieces on a harpsichord, organ or pianoforte, and there are a number of editions which suggest this.

Corelli's Op. 5 sonatas belong to that category of works which, immediately after their 'birth', acquired further lives, in the form of arrangements and adaptations. The first of these are the arrangements for recorder published in London by John Walsh in 1702[3], the best known, concerti grossi by Francesco Geminiani (1725, 1729)[4]. Are these arrangements still compositions by Corelli, or should we consider the arranger as a composer? Or should we leave this question open and recognize two layers in the arranged composition, each one with its own composer? We all know that the history of music is full of arrangements and that some pieces circulated so widely in arrangements that it may be difficult to establish its original format. These observations show that a composition that leaves the composer's desks is not only a semi-manufactured product that can be completed in a performance by interpretation; it may also be processed further to give rise to compositions of a quite different nature. Not only were compositions arranged by other composers, it is also not unusual that the original composer himself re-used his compositions or material taken from it for later works. The history of music is full of this re-use of musical material by the composer himself.

---

[2]. ID. *Sonate a violino e violone o cimbalo* [...] *Opera quinta*, Amsterdam, Estienne Roger, [1702].

[3]. ID. *Six sonatas for a Flute an a Bass* [...] *Being the Second Part of His Fifth Opera*, London, John Walsh, [1702].

[4]. GEMINIANI, Francesco. *Concerti grossi* [...] *Composti delli sei soli della Prima parte dell'Opera quinta d'Arcangelo Corelli*, London, William Smith & John Barret, [1725]; ID. *Concerti grossi* [...] *Composti della Seconda parte del Opera quinta d'Arcangelo Corelli*, Amsterdam, Michel-Charles le Cène, [1729].

Corelli also occupied himself with the Opus 5 sonatas for a second time, when in 1710 the Amsterdam publisher Estienne Roger issued an edition of the sonatas with added ornaments for the slow movements (see Ex. 2)[5]. On the title page we read that these ornaments were «composed as Monsieur Corelli plays them» (*composez comme M. Corelli les joue*), and so far we do not have a valid reason to doubt this statement. The embellishments clearly represent a part of the 'interpretation space', but due to the word 'composed', they can hardly be called improvisations. Of course, they could have been composed as improvisations, and indeed, they are rather irregular in structure and contain many recurrent formulas, both elements often ascribed to 'improvisational style'. In addition, their notation uses minims, crotches, quavers, and so on, but is not metrical: the note values usually greatly exceed that of a normal bar. Therefore, they cannot be performed as written, thus creating their own space for interpretation. They probably will sound different with each performance.

Ex. 2: fragment of the first movement of the Sonata Op. 5 No. 1, with an embellished version of the violin part, according to the edition published in Amsterdam by Estienne Roger in 1710.

---

5. CORELLI, Arcangelo. *Sonate a violino e violone o cimbalo* […] *Opera quinta, Troisième édition ou l'on a joint les agréemens des Adagio de cet ouvrage, composez par M. A. Corelli comme il les joue*, Amsterdam, Estienne Roger, [1710].

Everything we have said so far about Corelli's Opus 5 concerns the early eighteenth century, a period that still had direct contact with Corelli's performance practice through the circulation of early editions and the influence of Corelli's pupils. Perhaps they can be called 'authentic variations' of the original text. The editions of Corelli's Opus 5 of the second half of the century largely repeat what was already to be found in the first half.

The nineteenth century saw a sustained interest in Corelli's Sonatas Opus 5. However, if we look at editions published in the second half of the century we see something quite different from the original edition of 1700. In a typical nineteenth-century edition the sonatas have been transformed from a sonata for violin and figured bass into a sonata for violin and pianoforte. The violoncello has disappeared; the figuring has been used to compose a fully written-out piano accompaniment. There are bowings and fingerings in these additions, and many added interpretational indications and remarks. It is impossible to identify the eighteenth-century basis. We could say that these editions made the interpretation space explicit and visible. In fact they adapted the notation of Corelli's sonatas to what was in their time necessary to perform them. They made the interpretation space explicit rather thoroughly, but in doing so they removed the possibility of ever looking for and finding other ways to fill this space. Today these editions are not valued very highly. But we should not be too critical, because we cannot reprove a period for having its own ideas about how to present, publish and perform music, either that of its own time or of earlier times.

The nineteenth-century manner of presenting Corelli's sonatas as pieces for violin and pianoforte was employed until well into the twentieth century. After editions prepared by George Piggot (1849), Arnold Dolmetsch (1881) and Gustav Jensen (1893), all produced in Great Britain, came the Italian editions by Ettore Pinelli (1906; see Ex. 3), Alceo Toni (1919) and Enrico Polo (1935)[6].

Other formats for presenting Corelli's sonatas arose in the late nineteenth and twentieth centuries. Friedrich Chrysander published the compositions as part of his complete edition of the works of the composer[7]. It is what is now called an *Urtext* edition: it transcribes the original source, in the notational format of the time, but refrains from further additions. Recently (2006) a new critical edition was published, which basically

---

[6]. ID. *Twelve Solos for the Violin, [...] with an Accompaniment for the Piano Forte*, edited by George Pigott, London, Pigott, 1849; ID. *Six Sonatas for the Violin [...] (Op. 5)*, edited by Arnold Dolmetsch, London, Novello - Ewer & Co., 1881; ID. *12 Sonatas for Violin with Figured Bass*, edited by Gustav Jensen, London, Augener, 1892; ID. *12 Sonate a violino e cimbalo Op. 5a*, edited by Ettore Pinelli, Milan, Ricordi, 1906; ID. *Sonate per violino e pianoforte*, edited by Alceo Toni, Milan, Istituto Editoriale Italiano, 1919 (I Classici della Musica Italiana, 9); ID. *12 Sonate per violino e pianoforte*, edited by Enrico Polo, Milan, Ricordi, 1935.

[7]. ID. *VI Sonate a violino solo e violone o cembalo, Opera quinta: parte prima / Preludii, Allemande, Correnti, Gighe, Sarabande, Gavotte, e Follia a violino solo e violone o cembalo, Opera quinta: parte seconda*, edited by Joseph Joachim and Friedrich Chrysander, London, Augener, 1891 (Oeuvres, Book 3).

Ex. 3: the Gavotta of Corelli's Sonata for Violin and Bass Op. 5 No. 11 set for violin and piano by Ettore Pinelli, Milan, Ricordi, 1906.

follows the same principles[8]. These editions are hardly suitable for practical use. They leave the interpretation space completely open. For musical practice, since the middle of the twentieth century, there have been what one could call the historically informed editions, as an analogue to the expression 'historically informed performance'. The basis

---

[8]. ID. *Sonate a violino e violone o combalo Opus V*, edited by Cristina Urchuguía, Laaber, Laaber-Verlag, 2006 (Historisch-kritische Gesamtausgabe der musikalischen Werke, 3).

for such editions are the texts of 1700 and 1710, but proposals have been put forward for the filling-in of the interpretation space, mostly by realizing the figured bass and by carefully adding bowing and fingering to the violin part. I can mention four of such editions: those by Bernhard Paumgartner (1948), Michelangelo Abbado (1961), István Homolya (1982) and Bernhard Moosbauer (2003)[9].

All the editions mentioned so far present or pretend to present the same music, Corelli's Sonatas Op. 5, but they look continually different. That means that there is not a single form of these works. There may be a common structure behind all the different editions, but this common structure is abstract. None of the existing editions should be identified with this abstract background structure.

The Variability of the Basic Text
The Trios Op. 1 by Luigi Boccherini

In the case of Corelli's Opus 5 we still had the first edition of 1700 as a point of reference, as a kind of basic text or Original Version. Fortunately, for many works in the history of music we have such an authoritative source to serve as such: a composer's autograph, an authorized first edition, a corrected later edition, and so on. What if we do not have such a source to begin with? Then we must work only with 'later sources' and we must work backwards towards the Original Version. We have seen in the previous section that, as a rule, later sources alter the original version at least in some respect, so that this backward journey is not without risk.

A case in point are the six Trios for Two Violins and Violoncello Op. 1 by Luigi Boccherini, apparently the composer's first works, written in 1760[10]. No autograph is known, nor any copy of which can be said that it was directly derived from it. The first edition, published in Paris by Antoine Bailleux in 1767, as Op. 2, was certainly not authorized, but rather based on a circulating manuscript in which the composition had already undergone serious alterations[11]. All other early editions are based directly or indirectly on the Bailleux edition, so that they do not help us in our search for the basic text[12]. We can equally exclude from further study the manuscripts of the works which are clearly derived

---

9. ID. *Zwölf Sonaten für Violine und Basso continuo Op. 5*, edited by Bernhard Paumgartner, 2 vols., Mainz, Schott, 1953; *12 Sonate per violino e pianoforte Op. V*, edited by Michelangelo Abbado, 2 vols., Milan, Ricordi, 1961; *12 Sonate per violino e basso continuo Op. 5*, edited by István Homoloya, 3 vols., Budapest, Musica, 1983; *Sonaten für Violine und Basso continuo Op.5*, edited by Bernhard Moosbauer, 2 vols., Mainz, Schott, 2006.

10. The author of this contribution is preparing a critical edition of these works for the Opera Omnia Luigi Boccherini, Bologna, Ut Orpheus Edizioni, forthcoming.

11. BOCCHERINI, Luigi. *Sei trietti per due violini e basso [...] Opera II*, Paris, Antoine Bailleux, [1767].

12. Editions published in London by Robert Bremner (1769), in Amsterdam by Johann Julius Hummel (1771), in Paris by Jean-Jérôme Imbault (c. 1810) and Janet & Cotelle (c. 1824).

from one of the editions[13]. What is left is a group of nearly fifty manuscripts with one to six works, which are independent of the Bailleux edition. This independence must mean that they were derived via an unknown number of intermediary steps from Boccherini's now lost autograph or Original Version[14]. Manuscripts of this type are found in libraries all over Europe, but especially in Italy, France, Central-Europe, further German-speaking areas and Scandinavia. Their ubiquitous existence points to a dissemination that had started before the edition and which was apparently ample.

In order to arrive at the Original Version of Boccherini's Trios Op. 1 a detailed study of the works as they are found in the manuscripts is inescapable. The first outcome of such a study is that no two manuscript sources are exactly identical, be it that some come very close; but this is an exception. Variants may concern the musical text, but also the general titles (Trio, Sonata, Divertimento), the name of the bass instrument (Violoncello, Violoncello Obbligato, Basso), tempo-indications, time signatures, and sometimes even the order of the movements.

The differences between the manuscripts can be classified in several categories, the intervening boundaries not always being equally well-defined. We can in principle distinguish between: (1) errors; (2) non-essential variants; (3) essential variants; (4) revisions; and (5) arrangements. In our search for the basic text, these categories have varying degrees of relevance. Errors (wrong notes, missing accidentals, missing bars, and so forth) may occur in sources of every kind, they must be corrected but do not have further significance, except for an assessment of the quality of source. Arrangements, for other instruments, must be ruled out for further study: they have nothing to do with Boccherini's Original Version[15]. The revisions are interesting, because they show that some contemporaries were not content with the pieces as they found them, but thought it necessary to recompose them partially, to improve them. The source material of Boccherini's Trios Op. 1 contains three examples of such revisions[16]. It is interesting to note that, in fact, we recognize the revision via statistical means, via the observation that in just one source the piece is quite different from how we find it in all the other sources. There is no reason to suppose that any of the revisions have anything to do with Boccherini himself.

We come, then, to the variants, the nightmare of every editor. We have divided them into two categories: essential and non-essential variants. The latter category includes

---

[13]. See the Critical Commentary of the forthcoming edition (see note 10). These manuscripts can be called 'post-publication manuscripts'.

[14]. See the Critical Commentary of the forthcoming edition (see note 10). These manuscripts can be called 'pre-publication manuscripts'.

[15]. The Violoncello part of all six trios has been rewritten for double bass in I-Nc, Mus. Str. 439. The two violin parts of the Trio in A major have been set for flute in I-Gc, Ms. SS.A.1.8. The manuscript CH-EN, Ms. A 231, with the Trio in F major, has an extra part probably for a viola da spalla or a viola pomposa.

[16]. The Trio in F major is found in a revised version in I-AN, Ms. mus. 3; the Trio in B-flat major, in I-Mc, Ms. Da Camera 3/12; the Trio in G major, in CZ-Pnm, Ms. XXIII.A.506.

the variants that do not really change the musical text: an octave displacement of a bass note, the division of a longer note in shorter ones or vice versa, a different composition of a double- or triple stop, different rhythmical figures, and so on. They might go unnoticed in performance. The essential variants are more pervasive. They do not recompose the piece but produce a quite noticeable variation in the musical text. Exs. 4 and 5 can serve to illustrate this notion.

Ex. 4: sample bars from the Allegro of Boccherini's Trio Op. 1 No. 1 in C major. The upper system presents the reading of the Central-European and First Italian Groups, the lower the reading of the Second Italian Group.

Ex. 5: sample bars from the Tempo di Minuetto of Boccherini's Trio Op. 1 No. 6 in A major. The upper system presents the reading of the Central-European Group, the lower the reading of the First and the Second Italian Group.

The study of variants appears to be of importance because it makes it possible not to deal any longer with all manuscripts individually, but instead with groups of manuscripts. A group is ideally characterized by the simultaneous presence of a number of essential variants, which are not found elsewhere. In practice a number of non-essential variants may follow the occurrence of essential variants. Working along these lines makes it possible to establish three basic groups of manuscripts of Boccherini's Trios Opus 1, which we may call (1) the Central-European Group, (2) the First Italian Group, and (3) the Second Italian Group. The names follow the locations of the majority of the manuscripts contained in the group. Manuscripts of the Central-European Group are found in Vienna, Graz, Prague and Neckarzimmern (Southern Germany), manuscripts of the Italian groups are found in Ancona, Bologna, Florence, Genoa, Montecatini Terme, Montecassino, Naples, Rome, Venice (but also outside Italy). Within the First Italian Group some small groups of manuscripts form subgroups defined by the occurrence of common variants.

It is disconcerting to have to state that the establishment of groups of sources does not automatically bring us information about which group must be considered as being nearest to Boccherini's Original Version. If two groups differ by certain variants, we do not know which variant came first and which variant is an altered version. To establish this we require additional, external information. Knowledge of the dates of the sources would help greatly, but these are normally unknown. Another problem is that we do not know how many sources must once have existed, in addition to ones of which we are now aware.

Fortunately, in the case of Boccherini's Trio's Opus 1, there are two indications that can help in establishing which one of the three groups most likely represents, or comes nearest to, Boccherini's Original Version. The pieces were composed in 1760 in Vienna and this suggests that the Central-European Group of manuscripts, which is at least geographically the closest, represents more or less the Original Version. This is confirmed by the order in which the pieces occur in the manuscript now in Vienna, an order not found in any other manuscript (nor in any printed edition)[17]. The order

---

17.   The manuscript A-Wm, Ms. IX-2020.

of the Vienna manuscripts appears to be entirely identical to that of Boccherini in the catalogue he retrospectively drew up in 1796, including the earlier works[18]. It is true that 1796 is 36 years later than 1760, but Boccherini must have had either still his autograph or notes providing this order.

We can therefore say that the version of the Trios Op. 1 to be found in the Central-European manuscripts probably comes closer to Boccherini's Original Version than any other manuscript, but it is difficult to go any further than that. There are differences among the various Central-European manuscripts themselves, and in addition the Vienna manuscript itself, although without doubt the main source, is not without its problems: it contains a number of errors, and is quite inconsistent as far as ornamentation, dynamics and articulation are concerned.

This all means that, with the source material that we have at our disposal today, it is impossible to reconstruct Boccherini's original version faithfully and reliably. We can use the Vienna manuscript as the basis of a new edition, but the text of this manuscript has to be edited in a number of ways to make it suitable for performance. Examination of the other Central-European manuscripts does not establish whether or not the Vienna manuscript brings us Boccherini's reading. The Vienna manuscript is not yet Boccherini's Original Version. No other choice of basic source will solve this problem. One of the consequences of this is that a certain amount of subjectivity is introduced into even the most accurate critical edition. It is the subjectivity of the editor, and were the same works to be prepared by another editor, the outcome could be quite different. That makes every edition of musical works an approximation at best.

For Boccherini's Trios Op. 1 the actual situation is in fact worse than as sketched above. If we include the so-called secondary elements of the score in the discussion, that is, articulation, dynamics and ornamentation, the sources do not present even the lowest conceivable level of completeness and consistency, not within individual sources and certainly not when sources are compared. Every source seems to follow its own logic (or lack of logic) in this respect, and, as just observed, internal consistency is also missing or limited at best: dynamic indications may be conflicting between instrumental parts, articulation and ornamentation of passages may not return in parallel passages. To illustrate this point one might view and compare the first bar of the Trio in C major as found in the Vienna manuscript (Ex. 6) and in Bailleux's first edition (Ex. 7).

---

[18]. The original catalogue has not been preserved. Recently the copy once in possession of Pierre Baillot was discovered in the Bibliothèque national in Paris under no. Vma 1074 R.74707. See PASCOE, Keith. 'La reaparición del catálogo de Baillot. Un eslabón perdido en la transmisión temprana de los catálogos de la música de L. Boccherini', in: *Luigi Boccherini. Estudios sobre fuentes, recepción e historiografía*, edited by Marco Mangani, Elisabeth Le Guin and Jaime Tortella, Madrid, Biblioteca Regional d Madrid Joaquín Leguina, 2006, pp. 77-90. The page with the six Trios Op. 1 is reproduced on p. 83.

Ex. 6: opening bars of Boccherini's Trios Op. 1 No. 1 in the manuscript A-Wm, IX.2020.

Ex. 7: opening bars of Boccherini's Trios Op. 1 No. 1 in the first edition, *Sei trietti per due violini e basso* [...] *Opera II*, Paris, Bailleux, [1767].

Although there are certain correspondences between the two versions regarding articulation, dynamics and ornamentation, there are as many differences. For a critical edition one has to choose one pattern, but that choice will always contradict other potential patterns. That means that adaptations are unavoidable, making this an inevitably subjective process.

THE VOLATILITY OF MUSICAL COMPOSITION

The reasons for presenting the above observations are simple: they show that in the 'life' of musical compositions processes of change are continually active. In the transmission of musical works there is no standard version. All versions actually come into existence as the result of an interaction between the previous versions and the requirements of the consumers of the new one. Since the users, or the consumers, of the musical work change continually (or may be very different at one point of time), the outcome of the interaction process, the new version, will be correspondingly different. All versions of a musical work are way-stations between a previous and a later version.

Another consequence is that for a musical composition of the past a single, complete and unequivocal notation does not exist. Every notation is bound to be just one from a large, perhaps infinitely large, collection of possible notations. Therefore, no edition will last for ever. As time proceeds, the users of the music will change their habits and their wishes, and in doing so they will create the need for new editions.

What is, then, the true form of a piece of music if it is not possible to record this form on paper? Perhaps the answer is that, after all, a musical composition is an abstraction, an abstract entity, for which the composer is only the first person to choose a manner of notation. Later on, users, copyists, editors and publishers will constantly provide and invent new ways of notating the same music onto the paper, and create new versions. But abstractions are not real things, they exist only in our minds, although the musical abstractions in question are transferred from one person to another by notations on paper, or by sound. It is no wonder that in these renotations changes can be and are introduced, which may in turn affect the reconstructed underlying abstractions. Because of the uncertainty that is inherent in these processes it is impossible to speak any longer of the true form of a composition. Instead, musical compositions are elusive and volatile.

The «Fantasy-Principle»
Improvisation between Imagination and Oration in the Eighteenth Century

Martin Kaltenecker
(Paris)

In 1739, among the qualities of the perfect *Kapellmeister*, Johann Mattheson included «musical sensibility», or otherwise «a brain more alike wax than stone»[1], which had to be trained by free improvisation (*fantasieren*). In this paper, I shall consider the free fantasy in the second half of the eighteenth century as the musical representation of such improvisational techniques. This means, on the one hand, that I shall neither deal with the practice of ensemble improvisation (especially via 'heterophonic' ornamentation)[2], nor with basso continuo realization, practices locally applied to pre-existing scores. On the other hand, I shall consider the scores of fantasies as a global image of what improvisation was thought to be, without further distinguishing between these two realms, the notated fantasy and the ephemeral improvisation, as other scholars do[3]. Following Peter Schleuning[4], I try to describe something like a 'fantasy-principle' which would subsume the (always legitimate) distinctions between genres or practices such as *préludes non mesurés*, free introductions, *Eingänge*, *partimenti*, cadenzas, capriccios, and fantasies, either written down or not.

---

[1]. Mattheson, Johann. *Der Vollkommene Kapellmeister*, 2 vols., Hamburg, Christian Herold, 1739, vol. II, Chapter 2, §§ 51 and 52, p. 107. I should like to thank Jean-Charles Beaumont for his linguistic advice.

[2]. See Spitzer, John - Zaslaw, Neal A. *The Birth of the Orchestra. History of an Institution, 1650-1815*, New York, Oxford University Press, 2004, p. 383.

[3]. See Kaden, Christoph. *Des Lebens wilder Kreis. Musik im Zivilisationsprozess*, Kassel, Bärenreiter, 1993, pp. 48ff. For Czerny's typology, see Czerny, Carl. *Systematische Anleitung zum Fantasieren* Op. 200, Leipzig, Breitkopf & Härtel, 1829, § 5, p. 4. For a recent one, see Carew, Derek. *The Mechanical Muse. The Piano, Pianism and Piano Music, c. 1760-1850*, London, Ashgate, 2008, pp. 443-455.

[4]. Peter Schleuning in the catalogue of the exposition *Das Capriccio als Kunstprinzip* at the Kunstmuseum Wien, 1997, quoted by Sità, Maria Grazia. 'Modi dell'improvvisazione per tastiera tra Sette e Ottocento. Il 'Principio artistico del capriccio', in: *Sull'improvvisazione*, edited by Claudio Toscani, Lucca, LIM, 1998, pp. 63-85.

'Free fantasy' is a term introduced by Carl Philipp Emanuel Bach and Friedrich Wilhelm Marpurg in the 1750s[5]. During the second half of the eighteenth century free fantasy dealt with form, with communication between the composer/performer and the listener, and with the link between form and communication. While reflecting on form as process and displaying an image of its gestation, the free fantasy did not only refer to terms and techniques inherent in the realm of music (as the 'sonata-principle' does), but also in external discourses: one dealing with imagination, a major philosophical topic of the time[6]; the other with oration, a rhetorical interpretation widely applied to music in the Baroque era, though not always providing an exhaustive or precise description of it. The fantasy as a result of the free play of imagination tends towards a solipsistic production during which the performer may forget his audience, while its rhetorical orientation aims at a permanent contact with the listener, a contact of which form, or *dispositio*, is the warrant. I shall try to show that the fantasy-principle draws on both discourses and on their possible conflicts, and how it seems to disappear in the 1830s along with these two.

IMAGINATION AT WORK

Within the philosophical tradition, imagination holds an intermediate position between sensation and judgement[7]. Sensation is dependent on the presence of an object, while imagination is able to create representations of absent objects, their mental images. Therefore, imagination may be synonymous with memory. In the eighteenth century, however, theorists frequently underscored the active element of imagination (as compared to passive memory): imagination is, Étienne de Condillac said, «memory having reached all the vividness of which it is capable»[8]. Imagination, furthermore, is the capacity to assemble the elements it has memorized in a new way. David Hume wrote:

> Nothing is more free than the imagination of man; and though it cannot
> exceed that original stock of ideas, furnished by the internal and external senses,
> it has unlimited power of mixing, compounding, separating, and dividing these
> ideas, in all the varieties of fiction and vision. It can feign a train of events,
> with all the appearance of reality, ascribe to them a particular time and place,
> conceive them as existent and paint them out to itself with every circumstance,
> that belongs to any historical fact, which it believes with the greatest certainty[9].

5. See LÜTTEKEN, Laurenz. *Das Monologische als Denkform der Musik zwischen 1760 und 1785*, Stuttgart, Metzler, 2000, p. 415.

6. This point has already been suggested by LÜTTEKEN, Laurenz. *Op. cit.* (see note 5), p. 421.

7. See for instance ARISTOTLE. *De anima*, III, 3.

8. CONDILLAC, Étienne de. *Traité des Sensations* [1754], Paris, Fayard, 1984, p. 30.

9. HUME, David. *An Enquiry Concerning Human Understanding*, critical edition by Tom L. Beauchamp, Oxford, Clarendon, 2006, p. 40.

For Voltaire, imagination was a *combinatoire*, and thus «the only means which allows us to assemble our ideas, even the most metaphysical ones»[10]; active imagination seems «to create more than merely to arrange»[11].

At the end of the century, Kant would return to the distinction between reproductive and productive imagination: famously, he held that productive imagination (*produktive Einbildungskraft*) invented a scheme of reality, as a kind of preparatory sketch for judgement[12]. In the *Critique of Judgement* he elaborates on the free play of the creative imagination which «enlarges our concept of an object in an unlimited manner», by adding «aesthetical ideas» (that is, revealing new, unknown aspects of it). Imagination, Kant claims, creates «so to speak a second nature with the materials supplied by nature»[13]. It is, furthermore, especially related to genius, that is «the innate mental aptitude (*ingenium*) through which nature gives the rule to art»[14]. There is, however, concerning genius, a special variety of imagination, called *Laune* ('mood', 'moodiness'), a more capricious or fanciful imagination, that is the state of the mind in which «things appear otherwise than (or even contrary to) normally, though still being judged by rational rules»[15].

The philosophical prestige of this faculty of the mind explains the general interest in the manner by which it proceeds, for imagination at work, and thus the direct observation of the interplay between fixed rules and fancy, which coincides with the struggle between talent (who thoughtfully observes the existing rules) and genius (who invents and dictates new ones)[16].

Before turning to music, lets us mention some testimonies about the Italian *improvvisatori* and their public declamation of poems on topics suggested by the audience. Always accompanied by a keyboard instrument or a guitar, such performances were mentioned in several musical dictionaries and formed a kind of subgenre equally concerning music and poetry[17]. In 1739, Charles de Brosses reported the performance of such an *improvvisatore* in Siena, elaborating the theme of the *aurora borealis*:

---

[10]. Voltaire. *Dictionnaire philosophique*, London, 1764, quoted by Cannone, Belinda. *Philosophies de la musique*, Paris, Klincksieck, 1990, p. 146.

[11]. *Ibidem*, article 'Imagination' (which includes the article on the same subject in the *Encyclopédie*), Section 1.

[12]. Kant, Immanuel. *Kritik der reinen Vernunft*, Riga, Hartknoch, 1781, A 137/B 176-A 147/B 187.

[13]. *Ibidem*, B 152; Id. *Kritik der Urteilskraft*, Berlin-Libau, Lagarde und Friederich, 1790, § 49, B 193-195.

[14]. Abrams, Meyer H. *The Mirror and the Lamp. Romantic Theory and the Critical Tradition*, New York, Oxford University Press, 1971, p. 207.

[15]. Kant, Immanuel. *Kritik der Urteilskraft, op. cit.* (see note 13), § 54, B 230.

[16]. *Ibidem*, § 46, B 181.

[17]. The *improvvisatori*, Koch writes, perform «im Recitativstyle unter eigner Begleitung einer Guitarre. [...] Die lebhafte Einbildungskraft solcher Personen ist allerdings zu bewundern, und zeugt von einem glücklichen Genie, obwohl sehr leicht einzusehen ist, daß in Gedichten von solcher Geburt viel Schlechtes und Zusammengerafftes mit unterlaufen müsse». See Koch, Heinrich Christoph. *Musikalisches Lexikon*, Frankfurt/Main, August Hermann, 1802, p. 777.

He dreamt a while, his head down, during a large quarter of an hour, to the sound of a harpsichord which improvised a prelude *mezza voce*. Than he stood up and began to declaim softly a succession of stanzas in *ottava rima*, while the harpsichord, playing chords as he spoke, began to improvise again, filling out the intervals between each stanza. They succeeded each other rather slowly at the beginning, but little by little his verve got more and more inspired, as the harpsichord got louder. At the end, the poet declaimed like a man full of enthusiasm. [...] His sketch (*canevas*), poetically designed, full of harmonious sentences, and swiftly uttered, soon dazzled the listeners and made them part of the poet's enthusiasm. You will believe however that all this contains more words than things. It is impossible for the syntax not to be often violated and for the stuffing not to consist in a pompous gibberish (*galimatias*)[18].

In 1827, during his stay in Rome, August von Platen heard «the famous Sgrizzi [...] improvise an entire tragedy in five acts about the Death of Turnus at the Argentina Theatre», after picking out his topic from an urn containing more than a hundred suggestions, and the equally famous Rosa Taddei, who produced «epical-lyrical poetry to the soft accompaniment of a piano, playing behind her, in a slow measure, to an extremely simple melody, though enchanting to the ear, probably an extremely old one»[19]. Georg Sievers, critic of the magazine *Caecilia*, talked more pungently about Taddei, whom he heard her three years later: her melodies were actually vulgar tunes everyone whistled in the streets, and their repetition about twenty times was intolerable to the ear of a non-Italian, as were the slips she made on purpose, her scratching of the head, all devices she used to make her improvisation more plausible. «It was very difficult», Sievers writes, «to believe in the second nature produced here before us»[20].

---

[18]. BROSSES, Charles de. *Lettres d'Italie du Président de Brosses*, Paris, Mercure de France, 1986, vol. I, pp. 404-406: «Il rêva, tête baissée, pendant un bon demi-quart d'heure, au son d'un clavecin qui préludait à demi-jeu. Puis il se leva, commençant à déclamer doucement strophe à strophe en rimes octaves, toujours accompagné du clavecin qui frappait des accords pendant la déclamation, et se remettait à préluder pour ne pas laisser vides les intervalles au bout de chaque strophe. Elles se succédaient d'abord assez lentement. Peu à peu la verve du poëte s'anima, et à mesure qu'elle s'échauffait, le son du clavecin se renforçait aussi. Sur la fin, cet homme extraordinaire déclamait comme un poëte plein d'enthousiasme. [...] Ce canevas, tourné poétiquement, rempli de phrases harmonieuses, déclamées avec rapidité; jointes à la difficultée singulière de s'assujettir aux strophes en rimes octaves, jette bien vite l'auditeur dans l'admiration et lui fait partager l'enthousiasme du poëte. Vous devez croire néanmoins qu'il y a là-dessous beaucoup plus de mots que de choses. Il est impossible que la construction ne soit souvent estropiée et le remplissage composé d'un pompeux galimatias».

[19]. PLATEN, August von. *Tagebücher*, Zürich, Manesse, 1990, p. 443.

[20]. SIEVERS, Georg. 'Die Improvisatrice Taddei', in: *Caecilia*, XI/43 (1830), pp. 218-220. Note that Sievers uses Kant's expression «second nature».

In an extensive description published in 1840, Karl August Mayer added some further details about the improvisers who appeared at the Teatro Fiorentino in Naples[21]. The scenery, a room in a palace adorned with statues of ancient gods standing in niches and a table supporting candles, evoked a supernatural space as well as the closet of a writer. The *improvvisatore*, after having chosen one of the topics collected in an urn, remained with his head resting on his hand while the pianist began to play «a very simple melody. Soon the Spirit took hold of him: he jumped up, went to and fro in a violent pace, then advanced towards the edge of the stage and began his poem 'At the Grave of a Young Woman', performing it as a recitative softly accompanied by the music». Thus the inspirational process itself was staged (or mimicked), the audience being able to observe the body seized by inspiration. The improviser then passed over to a comic subject, this time without any music, while he and the public in turn suggested the missing rimes: the final product was the result of a collaboration. During some poems «only the sublime passages were declaimed to music», while at other times, «being disturbed by the melody, he demanded another one, which instantly proved to be more efficient»[22].

When, in 1802, Heinrich Christoph Koch defined the three meanings of the word 'improvisation', the first one referred to the play of the composer's imagination expressed in sounds and so to speak immediately jotted on the paper; the second to a special kind of performance; and the third one to a particular form that does not respect any model. The first meaning seems to be illustrated by an anecdote about Jean-Joseph Cassanéa de Mondonville who, having received the commission for an opera from the Académie Royale de Musique, asked a friend to write the libretto for him. Inquiring repeatedly about the progression of the work, the friend, after two years, visited the composer and asked him to play it.

> «I'm done», Mondonville ascertained, «here is the poem, I can do without now». For a moment he pretended to be looking for his score, but couldn't find it. Anyway, he said, I know it by heart, you will hear it. Then he sat at the piano and improvised the whole work from the beginning to the end, without overlooking one single verse. The enthusiastic librettist ran to the Opera to break the news; everyone was glad, and Mondonville was urged again, and was then compelled to compose. But no longer challenged as he had been the day of his improvisation, he could not rekindle his fire; it was even said that this work was among his weakest[23].

---

[21]. On Mayer see also the contribution by Raffaele Di Mauro, in this volume, and, on the *improvvisatori*, the recent volume by Esterhammer, Angelica. *Romanticism and Improvisation, 1750-1850*, Cambridge, Cambridge University Press, 2009.

[22]. Mayer, Karl August. *Neapel und die Neapolitaner*, 2 vols., Oldenburg, Schulze, 1840-1842, vol. II, Letter 70, pp. 179-182.

[23]. I have not been able to trace the origins of this anecdote, which is reported in *La France Musicale*, 8 January 1840: «J'ai fini, voici le poème dont je puis me passer maintenant». Il feignit quelques instants de

More important, perhaps, than the veracity of the anecdote is the fact that it has been reported and quoted, circulating until 1840 at least. The interest in the imagination or the *ingenium* at work aimed at seizing it from the onset, seizing the very first energy and impetus, as expressed in those first drafts that one might compare to sketches. In his *Allgemeine Theorie der schönen Künste* (1771-1774) Georg Friedrich Sulzer wrote:

> The fantasies of the great masters, especially those played with a certain abundance of feeling and the fire of enthusiasm, are very often like the first sketches of the painters, full of extreme beauty and power, impossible to obtain in a more tranquil state of mind[24].

Sulzer here mentioned the famous machines conceived by Creed (1747) and Hohlfeld (1752), where every sound (that is: every pressed key) was transmitted to lead pencils which inscribed small strokes on paper scrolls — a kind of Morse which had to be transcribed afterwards into the usual notation, machines which Charles Burney, while staying in Berlin, describes in detail[25], while Friedrich Wilhelm Marpurg was more ironic:

> When the most ingenious mechanic Hohlfeld from Berlin [...] went around with an improved version of his a machine for fantasies, two organ players came to see him and asked him if they could try it. After improvising for a while in turns, they were keen to see what their ideas looked like printed on the paper scroll. They began to read, shook their heads, flabbergasted, for they could not believe their eyes. And neither was willing to admit that he was the author of what was printed there. They laughed much about each other[26].

---

chercher sa partition, et ne la trouvant pas : 'N'importe, continuât-il [*sic*], je la sais par cœur, et je vais vous la faire entendre'. Il se mit alors au piano, et improvisa d'un bout à l'autre l'ouvrage, sans omettre un seul vers. L'auteur enthouisiasmé courut porter cette bonne nouvelle à l'Opéra; on s'en réjouit, et l'on pressa de nouveau Mondonville qui fut bien obligé de s'y mettre tout de bon, et d'écrire; mais il ne trouva plus ce feu du dépit qui l'avait si bien servi le jour de l'improvisation; on prétend même que ce fut son plus faible ouvrage».

[24]. Sulzer, Johann Georg. *Allgemeine Theorie der schönen Künste*, 4 vols., Leipzig, M. G. Weidmanns Erben, 1771, article 'Fantasieren, Fantasie', vol. I, pp. 368-369: «Die Fantasien von groszen Meistern, besonders die, welche aus einer gewissen Fülle der Empfindung und in dem Feuer der Begeisterung gespielt werden, sind oft, wie die ersten Entwürfe der Zeichner, Werke von ausnehmender Kraft und Schönheit, die bey einer gelassenen Gemüthslage nicht so könnten verfertigt werden». The image of the sketch was also used by de Brosses (*op. cit.* [see note 18] p. 405) and Carl Maria Junker; see Lütteken, Laurenz. *Op. cit.* (see note 5), p. 420.

[25]. Burney, Charles. *Voyage musical dans l'Europe des Lumières*, Paris, Flammarion, 1992, pp. 440-442.

[26]. Marpurg, Friedrich Wilhelm. *Legende einiger Musikheiligen*, Cologne, Peter Hammer, 1786, Art. IX, pp. 97-98: «Als der geschickte Mechaniker Hohlfeld zu Berlin, [...], mit der Verbesserung seiner Fantasirmaschine umgieng, kamen zwey Organisten zu ihm, und baten sich die Erlaubnis aus solche zu probieren. Nachdem sie eine Zeitlang wechselweise darauf fantasiret hatten, waren sie neugierig den Abdruck ihrer Ideen auf den abgerollten Papier zu lesen. Sie lasen, stutzten, schüttelten den Kopf, und keiner wollte sich zu seinem Machwerk bekennen. Einer lachte über den andern».

ORDER AND DISORDER

At their worst, improvisers produced trash in *ottava rima*, stanzas only filled with common-place phrases, or unprintable *horrenda*. At their best, they displayed a wondrous and paradoxical combination of liberty and constraint, of free invention and respect for the rules. The fascination aroused by imagination at work was due to the fact that it was a challenge to order, an order for which theorists in the eighteenth century could rely on various descriptions: the philosophical one concerning variety and unity (as analyzed for instance in Francis Hutcheson's *Inquiry into the Origin of Our Ideas of Beauty and Virtue*, 1725), the discourse about the hierarchy of harmony and melody (the latter considered as the guiding element by Rousseau, Sulzer, and Johann Friedrich Agricola), or the rhetorical approach, to which we will turn later. Still predominant at the beginning of the century, the latter allowed one to find out strict equivalents for every literary trope or to equate the seven parts of an ideal speech (*exordium, narratio, confutatio*, and so on) with the different sections of an aria or instrumental movement.

To stress the activity of imagination at work meant to depart from, or at least to question, these models. The fantasy-principle is contemporaneous with what Hans Heinrich Eggebrecht once called a general shift from «music expressing something» to «expressing oneself in music»[27], or what Catherine Kintzler described as the «victory of an aesthetics of the sentimental (*touchant*) over the aesthetics of the exemplary»[28]. Mocking more often than not the direct imitation of affects or images[29], theorists and musicians have, since the 1770s, fantasized about something like the seizure of 'pure' emotion. In 1786, Joshua Reynolds seemed to express a common view when he held that architecture «applies itself, like Musick [...], directly to the imagination, without the intervention of any kind of imitation»[30].

Hence the importance of the *genius*, who breaks the rules, thanks precisely to the free play of his imagination or, as Diderot wrote, its greater force: the man of genius remembers better, and more things, he takes a more vivid interest in them, and is

---

[27]. EGGEBRECHT, Hans Heinrich. 'Das Ausdrucks-Prinzip im musikalischen Sturm und Drang', in: ID. *Musikalisches Denken*, Wilhelmshaven, Heinrichshofen, 1977, pp. 69-111: 81.

[28]. KINTZLER, Catherine. *Introduction* to ROUSSEAU, Jean-Jacques. *Essai sur l'origine des langues*, Geneva, s.n., 1781; reprint Paris, Flammarion, 1993, p. 12.

[29]. See for instance KRAUS, Joseph Martin. *Etwas von und über Musik aus dem Jahr 1777*, Frankfurt/Main, Eichenbergsche Erben, 1778, p. 12, or BOYÉ. *L'expression musicale mise au rang des chimères*, Amsterdam-Paris, Esprit, 1779, pp. 14-24.

[30]. REYNOLDS, Joshua. *Discourses Delivered at the Royal Academy*, 1769-1791, *Discourse* XIII, 1786, quoted by GERHARD, Anselm. *London und der Klassizismus in der Musik*, Stuttgart, Metzler, 2002, p. 99. For a defi-nite refusal of the necessity to imitate in music, see SMITH, Adam. *Essays on Philosophical Subjects*, London, Cadell-Davies, 1795, Part II, § 'On the Nature of that Imitation Which Takes Place in What Are Called the Imitative Arts'.

affected by everything with greater intensity: «He does not merely see, he is touched; in the silence and the obscurity of his closet, he enjoys a lovely and fertile country-side; he is iced by every whistling wind, burnt by the sun, and frightened by the tempest»[31]. For Johann Gottfried Herder, imagination is no longer that ancillary faculty defined by Kant which decodes reality in order to prepare the conceptual definition, but the name of «the profound confluence» of sensations, sounds, images and feelings within our soul «which common language is unable to define»[32]. Imagination is «the sea of our inner sensibility», and its activity is essentially synaesthetic, combining every vibration captured by our nerves[33].

While challenging the rules, imagination may rely on the 'sublime' and its techniques. As early as 1712, Joseph Addison had linked the imagination to the sublime:

> I shall first consider those pleasures of the imagination which arise from the actual view and survey of outward objects; and these, I think, all proceed from the sight of what is *great, uncommon,* or *beautiful.* There may indeed, be something so terrible or offensive, that horror or loathsomeness of an object may overbear the pleasure which results from its *greatness, novelty* or *beauty*; but still there will be such a mixture of delight in the very disgust it gives us, as any of these three qualifications are most conspicuous and prevailing[34].

The literary genre that offered the playground both for pure imagination and sublime effects was the *ode,* and this would, in turn, as Laurenz Lütteken has suggested, serve as a model for the free fantasy[35]. The ode, Edward Young wrote,

> as it is the Eldest kind of Poetry, so is it more Spirituous, and more remote from Prose than any other, in *Sense, Sound, Expression,* and *Conduct.* Its thoughts should be uncommon, sublime, and moral; its numbers full, easy, and most harmonious; Its expression pure, strong, delicate, yet unaffected; and of a *curious felicity* beyond other Poems; Its conduct should be rapturous, somewhat abrupt, and immethodical to a vulgar Eye. That apparent order, and connection, which gives form, and life to *some* compositions, takes away the very Soul of *this.* Fire,

---

[31]. DIDEROT, Denis - D'ALAMBERT, Jean Lerond de. 'Genie', in: *Encyclopédie ou Dictionnaire raisonné des sciences, des arts et des métiers,* mis en ordre et publ. par M. Diderot, [...] et quant à la partie mathématique, par M. d'Alembert, 35 vols., Paris, Briasson-David-Le Breton-Durand, 1751-1780.

[32]. HERDER, Johann Gottfried. *Vom Erkennen und Empfinden,* Riga, Hartknoch, 1778, in: *Werke in fünf Bänden,* 5 vols., Berlin, Aufbau, 1964, vol. III, p. 27.

[33]. *Ibidem,* vol. III, p. 28, and vol. IV, pp. 200-201.

[34]. ADDISON, Joseph. *The Spectator,* No. 412, Monday, 21 June 1712, further developed in *The Spectator,* No. 418, Monday, 30 June 1712.

[35]. For the application of the sublime to symphony, see BEY, Henning. ''ein Mensch, der wachend träumt und mit Verstand raset». Symphonie und Ode. Musik als schöne Kunst im ausgehenden 18. Jahrhundert', in: *Musicologia Austriaca,* XXIII (2004), pp. 29-56.

elevation, and select thought are indispensable; a humble, tame, and vulgar Ode is the most pityful error a pen can commit[36].

Thus the essential technical feature of the ode is the elimination of transitions. Moses Mendelssohn explained in the 1760s:

> As within the enthusiastic imagination the notions follow one another [...] thus they must appear in an ode [...]. The link words [*Mittelbegriffe*] connecting the different members but do not themselves possess the highest degree of liveliness, are here omitted by the poet; hence the apparent disorder generally ascribed to the ode[37].

This rhapsodic character was ascribed again in 1801 by Christian Friedrich Michaelis, a follower of Kant, to the sublime in music, which consists for him in a «rapid alternation of the impressions», in

> everything that is surprising, brief and vigorous, and takes us off with vivacity, either in the realm of harmony or in the realm of melody. [...] Our imagination is thus transported by means of a few notes, which fill up a brief moment, into new and far-off regions, the regular exploration of which would require a much wider space of time: everything that would have needed a long preparation suddenly confronts us with all its perfection[38].

The Fantasy

The innumerable definitions of the fantasy in the eighteenth century usually refer either to imagination or to improvisation, in order to define its apparent disorder. According to Peter Schleuning, the idea of the free fantasy (*freye Fantasie*) emerges with Carl Philipp Emanuel Bach[39], who famously described it in 1753 as «arousing various affects in a quick succession, and calming them down», taking hold over «the soul of the listeners» by «a speaking character» (*das Sprechende*), and the masterful display of «surprises»[40]. In the free fantasy, which can do without any division in bars, one modulates more than in normal

---

[36]. Young, Edward. 'On Lyrick Poetry', in: *Ocean. An Ode*, London, Thomas Worrall, 1738, pp. 14-30.

[37]. Mendelssohn, Moses. *Briefe die neueste Literatur betreffend*, No. 275, quoted by Gerhard, Anselm. *Op. cit.* (see note 30), p. 174.

[38]. Michaelis, Friedrich Christian. 'Ueber das Erhabene in der Musik', in: *Monatszeitschrift für Deutsche*, No. 1 (1801), pp. 42-52.

[39]. For controversial discussions about the ode and their influence upon C. Ph. E. Bach, see Lütteken, Laurenz. *Op. cit.* (see note 5), pp. 418-422.

[40]. Bach, Carl Philipp Emanuel. *Versuch über die wahre Art das Clavier zu spielen*, Berlin, Selbstverlag, 1753, pp. 123ff.

pieces, though the modulations are «reasonable treacheries»[41], meaning order dissimulated under harmonic extravagance. In his *Dictionnaire de musique* (1768) Rousseau has separate entries for 'Caprice' and 'Fantaisie': the former is «a kind of free music where the author unbounds his genius and gives himself entirely up to the fire of composing», a «collection of singular and disparate ideas assembled by the enthusiastic imagination», while the latter may be «a regular piece» but is «invented while being performed and does not exist anymore once it is over»[42]. The point of the *caprice* lies in the nature or quality of the ideas, the point of the *fantaisie* in the swiftness with which they shoot up; consequently, if you write down a fantasy, it merely becomes an «ordinary piece».

We have already mentioned that, in 1802, Koch distinguished between three different meanings of the word 'fantasy'. The first one designates the free play of the imagination «entirely abandoned to itself», the second one an improvised piece «where the player doesn't bother about form, a principal tone, a regular metre, or a fixed character, but represents the succession of his ideas by the means of connected or loosely lined up melodic phrases, or else with different kinds of broken chords». The third one refers to a particular form reminiscent of a painters sketch, «which contains more striking and characteristic features […], as is the case with the drawings preceding a painting, where the more subtle features of the ideal, which is still present, appear»[43].

At the end of the period we are dealing with, Peter Lichtenthal's *Dizionario della musica* (1826) still draws upon the *Leitmotive* associated to the fantasy by most of the authors of the previous century[44]. Improvising, or «composing or performing a piece of music, either vocal or instrumental, is more genuine to music, defined as a natural and perfectly regular language», than to poetry. In order to improvise, the musician needs to master the foundations of his art, especially counterpoint (this in stark contrast to Mattheson and the German *freye Fantasie*[45]), he is perfectly skilled on his instrument, and owns «furthermore a soul prone to exaltation and a spirit ever-present, warranting the unity of the thoughts which form a piece created in this manner». As to the *fantasia*, Lichtenthal also distinguishes between the active or creative imagination and sheer memory. «One might say that the composer of vocal music who only endows poetry with sounds has imagination, while the one who writes instrumental music has much fantasy». The improviser, either as a composer or as a performer, is the real «sovereign» of the realm of sounds. Lichtenthal's characterization of the fantasy (in which he includes the cadenza) does not add any new feature to those enumerated by C. Ph. E. Bach or by Koch. When they appear in print, he

---

[41]. SCHLEUNING, Peter. *Die Fantasie II. 18. bis 20. Jahrhundert*, Cologne, Arno Volk, 1971, p. 11.

[42]. ROUSSEAU, Jean-Jacques. 'Caprice', in: *Dictionnaire de musique*, Paris, Veuve Duchesne, 1768, p. 74, and 'Fantaisie', p. 215.

[43]. KOCH, Heinrich Christoph. 'Fantasie', in: *Musikalisches Lexikon, op. cit.* (see note 17), pp. 554-555.

[44]. LICHTENTHAL, Peter. 'Fantasia', in: *Dizionario della musica*, 4 vols., Milan, A. Fontana, 1826, vol. I, pp. 270-271.

[45]. SCHLEUNING, Peter. *Op. cit.* (see note 41), p. 6.

adds, fantasies are more regular, «making some further step toward musical compositions that are well written (*ben condotti*)».

All these definitions provide us with a satisfactory description of the fantasy-principle, which transcends the different subgenres. It pertains to a reflection upon form and disorder, upon imagination and instantaneous invention, and it has a self-reflective ('transcendental', as Kant would say) character. The fantasy, as one critic wrote about Schubert's 'Wanderer-Fantasie' in 1823, is a «mirror» reflecting «those feelings that animated the composer while he composed it»[46].

One might try to classify the figures of disorder, of heated imagination and quasi-improvisation within the category of experimentations with sheer 'quantity', that is 'material' effects. The fantasy experiments with durations: Cherubini's 'Caprice ou Étude pour le pianoforte' (1789) alternates, as Maria Grazia Sità has shown, either with too long or too short sections[47]. Other fantasies avoid a poised conclusion, finishing abruptly or too lightly, as the one in B-flat major (1785) by Ernst Wilhelm Wolf and another by C. Ph. E. Bach in F-sharp minor, entitled 'C. Ph. E. Bach's Empfindungen' (1787)[48]. The exploration of remote harmonic regions (E minor in Wolf's B-flat major fantasy, A-flat minor in C. Ph. E. Bach's fantasy in G minor)[49], the number and quick succession of effects that within the 'normal' form would have to be counterbalanced give us the impression that the form vacillates, and the same might be said of modulations going into the 'wrong' direction (Mozart's C Minor Fantasy K 475 goes to B minor after ten bars). Harmonic hesitations produce the image of disorientation, of form before purification, which seems to be the very topic of Johann Wilhelm Hässler's Fantasia Op. 17 (ca. 1803)[50]. Sometimes, remote keys appear 'just for nothing', entering like a breeze, as the E minor (one measure) or F-sharp major (four bars) in Johann Christoph Kellner's extraordinary 'Fantasia con espressione' (1784)[51]. And finally, if the fantasy, like the ode, can be described as the form of the missing link, of omitted transitions, it also frequently consists *only* of transitional material, like those written by Vincenzo Manfredini[52], Johann Gottfried Müthel (a whole page for the sole left hand) or Wolf again (endless scales in the right hand)[53]. Such formulas — alike to the «pompous gibberish» De Brosses moaned about while listening to his *improvvisatore* — devoid of any quality, draw on the vocabulary of the toccata and call to mind the grip on the keyboard, the hand warming up, sheer tactility.

---

[46]. *Ibidem*, p. 11.

[47]. Sità, Maria Grazia. *Op. cit.* (see note 4), p. 80.

[48]. See the remarkable collection of fantasies assembled by Schleuning, Peter. *Op. cit.* (see note 41), especially pp. 38 and 48.

[49]. *Ibidem*, pp. 28 and 48 (bar 13).

[50]. *Ibidem*, pp. 79-84.

[51]. *Ibidem*, p. 52 (bars 24 and 27-30).

[52]. Reproduced in the annex of Sità, Maria Grazia. *Op. cit.* (see note 4).

[53]. Schleuning, Peter. *Op. cit.* (see note 41), pp. 41 and 47.

On the one hand, this attraction by quantitative effects coincides with the one for isolated effects in the last third of the eighteenth century, for noises[54], with Herder's representation of sound as gesture or sublime call[55], or the fascination for isolated sounds, summed up by the writer Joseph Joubert: «One sound is more beautiful than a long discourse»[56]. All these effects pertain to an *anti*-structural stance (and pleasure). On the other hand, the accumulation of such effects within the fantasy introduces the listener into a laboratory or a studio. The fantasy appears as the preparatory sketch of a possible work and thus illustrates an *ante*-structural stance (and pleasure).

Judging from the traces left in the free fantasies published at the end of the eighteenth century, improvisation was conceived as 'reflective', perhaps as a musical counterpart to philosophical theories about of artistic creativity, as exposed by Novalis or Friedrich Schlegel: every poem was considered to be a construction made with other poems, and the artistic 'irony' was defined as a reflection on the work within the work itself. Improvisation meant questioning the process of imagination and the virtual work; improvising and composing (which both pertain to what Voltaire called a *combinatoire*) represented similar kinds of the same species — an idea, I suppose, that Schumann or Eduard Hanslick would have vigorously rejected. During the eighteenth century, imagination at work never lost its reflective character, akin to reason and judgement, though trying to free itself from them. The genius is not yet the inspired romantic poet traversing the anxious nights of E. T. A. Hoffmann's *Nachtstücke* (1816-1817): he questions and rediscovers the rules, he does not subvert or destroy the old rules, nor does he invent new ones. John Ogilvie asserted in 1774 that «originality obviously results from the manner in which objects are selected and put together, so as to form upon the whole an unusual combination»[57]. However, to recombine elements is not exactly destroying the code. Even Kant's *Laune* means to see things in a new light, not making out new things. The *ingenium* is linked to a kind of circular activity: far from creating extravagant objects, it heats up the existing code, gives new force to it, sometimes overheats it.

Oration

The rules challenged by the fantasy-principle were especially the rhetorical ones. Not understood in the strict sense, as exposed by Joachim Burmeister, Mattheson, or

---

54. See Kaltenecker, Martin. *L'Oreille divisée. Les Discours sur l'écoute musicale aux XVIIIᵉ et XIXᵉ siècles*, Paris, Editions MF, 2011, pp. 191-218.

55. Herder, Johann Gottfried. *Op. cit.* (see note 32), vol. II, pp. 115-118.

56. Joubert, Joseph. *Pensées*, Paris, Union générale d'éditions, 1966, p. 218. Note that the sketch is the reverse of the ruin, a major fascination in the eighteenth century, both converging in the capriccio.

57. Abrams, Meyer H. *Op. cit.* (see note 14), p. 162.

Johann Nikolaus Forkel, but in a more general way, the rhetorical approach tried to introduce whatever techniques of persuasion into a musical composition, and claimed that these techniques are central. For instance, Francesco Geminiani held in *The Art of Playing on the Violin* (1751) that «all good Musick should be composed in imitation of a Discourse», and James Beattie repeated in the 1770s: «Music is like an oration delivered with propriety, but in an unknown tongue»[58]. However, a speech, an oration, is not a text. Introducing rhetorical devices means to anticipate or integrate a special *context* within the text. Music conceived in this way aims at immediate appraisal or assent; one holds that the communicational process must never be put at risk. Music is always addressed to a present (not a future, absent or hypothetical) community. When Johann Joachim Quantz[59] or Giuseppe Maria Cambini[60], among others, applied the rhetorical categories and devices to the art of performance, it was in order to suggest that the performer must never lose contact with his listeners.

Since at least the triumph of the 'galant style', this concern about a successful communication with a present audience is something like an *idée fixe* in the eighteenth century. Music has to be understood instantly, as there is little chance to hear it again, with the exception perhaps of opera; success, assent is vital, for there may be no second chance. Even the theorist's definitions of order and the interplay between variety and unity are always dependent on psychological criteria, taking the listener's soul into account[61].

Now, the free fantasy may precisely appear as the solipsistic genre *par excellence*: the listener, so to speak, is introduced into a private studio where he may observe in silence the creative imagination at work. For Laurenz Lütteken, the free fantasy offers precisely a striking example for what he calls the «monologue-principle» (*monologisches Prinzip*), predominant at the end of the century, and we know that composers such as Haydn, Johann Wilhelm Hertel[62] or Beethoven[63] used to progress into composition after improvising on the pianoforte. One must, however, be attentive to the context of other performances, which seemed to imply quite frequently almost *one* listener as a necessary

---

[58]. *Ibidem*, p. 94.

[59]. QUANTZ, Johann Joachim. *Versuch einer Anleitung die Flöte traversière zu spielen*, Berlin, Johann Friedrich Voß, 1752, p. 100.

[60]. See the commentary on Cambini's *Nouvelle méthode théorique et pratique* (ca. 1800) in GÉRARD, Yves. 'Musique instrumentale et expression. De l'imitation contestée à l'autonomie rêvée', in: *De la rhétorique des passions à l'expression du sentiment*, Les Cahiers du Musée de la Musique, IV (2003), pp. 110-115.

[61]. See HUME, David. *Op. cit.* (see note 9), Section III, or SULZER, Johann Georg. *Op. cit.* (see note 24), articles 'Anordnung' and 'Hauptton': the artist must guide the imagination of the listener, combining order (for example, a principal topic or theme) and distractions (for example, digressions, modulations).

[62]. See the testimony quoted by LÜTTEKEN, Laurenz. *Op. cit.* (see note 5), p. 423.

[63]. See the various testimonies quoted in SCHRAMOWSKI, Herbert. 'Bemerkungen zu zwei Funktionsarten der Klavierimprovisation im Schaffen Beethovens', in: *Bericht über den internationalen Beethoven-Kongress 10.-12. Dezember 1970 in Berlin*, Berlin, Verlag Neue Musik, 1971, pp. 395-404.

condition for a successful improvisation. Remember Charles Burney listening to the inspired C. Ph. E. Bach[64], or the connection between the free fantasy and a chosen circle of connoisseurs[65]. Johann Nepomuk Hummel's methodical learning of improvisation allowed him first to perform before small audiences and before progressively larger ones, up to one to two thousand listeners. «I ventured to extemporise before a few persons only, some connoisseurs, others unacquainted with the science, and while so doing, observed quietly how they received it, and what effect my Fantasia produced on both portions of my little, assembled, and mixed public»[66].

In 1805, Heinrich von Kleist was to produce a genuine theory about the «progressive elaboration of the thoughts while speaking»: *l'idée vient en parlant*, as he writes. In order to find the new thought, we may improvise even without having any precise idea of what is coming next, and we must never interrupt the flow; we may produce inarticulate sounds, stretch the linking elements, perhaps add an apposition where it is not really necessary. Furthermore, one most important element is the presence of another person, «an enthusiastic face», in this case, his sisters', «and nothing is more helpful than a movement of hers, as though she would interrupt me, for this attempt from outside [...] to snatch the speech from me stirs up my spirit all the more»[67].

If communication remains the plausible frame of reference for a great number of free fantasies, this explains the permanence of rhetorical categories: the fantasy is a form which is not destroyed, not subverted, but only *under strain*. Improvisation may still be compared in one breath to an ode and to an oration, to an epic and a disputation, as Johann Samuel Petri suggests in 1781[68]. The rhetorical categories provide for a parallel analysis or description, exactly as Peter Lichtenthal still links in 1828 the cadential movement from the dominant to the tonic to the voice of the orator which sinks a fifth at the end of a period[69]. Thus, as Johann Nikolaus Forkel explains, the musical tropes related to the imagination of the composer coincide for a large part with those meant only to keep alive the attention of the listener, and all of them cover the techniques of the fantasy: interruptions, ellipses,

---

[64]. BURNEY, Carles. *Dr Burney's Musical Tours in Europe*, London, Oxford University Press, 1959, p. 219: «During this time he grew so animated and *possessed*, that he not only played, but looked like one inspired. His eyes were fixed, his under lip fell, and drops of effervescence distilled from his countenance. He said, if he were to set to work frequently, in this manner, he should grow young again».

[65]. SCHLEUNING, Peter. *Op. cit.* (see note 41), p. 7. For Hummel's views about improvisation, see Ulrich Mahlert's Introduction in CZERNY, Carl. *Systematische Anleitung zum Fantasieren auf dem Pianoforte Op. 200*, Vienna, 1829, facsimile edition edited by Ulrich Mahlert, Wiesbaden, Breitkopf & Härtel, 1993, p. vi. Hummel still uses the comparison with the orator (p. ix).

[66]. CAREW, Derek. *Op. cit.* (see note 3), p. 437.

[67]. KLEIST, Heinrich von. 'Über die allmähliche Verfertigung der Gedanken beim Reden', in: *Heinrich von Kleists Werke*, Stuttgart, Bergland, 1960, p. 992.

[68]. SCHLEUNING, Peter. *Op. cit.* (see note 41), p. 8.

[69]. LICHTENTHAL, Peter. 'Cadenza', in: *Dizionario della musica, op. cit.* (see note 44), vol. I, pp. 107-109.

insisting repetitions[70]. As to sudden interruptions and unexpected digressions, Muzio Clementi explicitly referred to the classical treatise by Quintilian and his maxim: «If there is no door, break through the wall» (*Si non datur porta, per murum erumpendum*)[71].

Even the techniques of the sublime show the same ambiguity. While Edmund Burke links the sublime to solitude (while beauty is a 'social quality'[72]), for Herder, at the end of the century, the sublime is always a *call*, everything that figures as an «announcement», emitted by the trumpet, the thunder, the distant horn, solemn choirs or overtures[73]. Every isolated sound is a vibration seeking communication and response. The sublime may thus be understood as a strain on normal communication, a filtering of amiable transitions helpful to the amateur, whereas the connoisseur can do without them. The sublime is elliptical, yet not erratic, and its sound effects are the atoms of communication. In consequence, formal symmetries appear within free fantasies, though distorted by figures of imagination or sublime jolts. The harmonic labyrinth at the centre of C. Ph. E. Bach's F-sharp minor fantasy may be analyzed as the imitation of a torment, of melancholy, of a lament; as an allusion to the development in a sonata form[74]; or as the field of harmonic turbulences that Mattheson links to the *confutatio* of an ideal speech[75]. The first and slow section of Wilhelm Friedemann Bach's Fantasia in C Major offers a regular repetition of the material on the dominant, before being swept away by a Prestissimo reassuring order and regularity. Kellner's already mentioned 'Fantasia con espressione' and Christian Gottlieb Neefe's 'Fantasia per il cembalo' (1797) clearly depart from the 'fantastic' order and the fragmentary style: their horizon is now the sonata form.

Czerny, Beethoven, and beyond

In Czerny's *Systematische Anleitung zum Fantasieren* Op. 200 (1829) the category of oration is still applied: «As soon as the improviser sits down as to extemporize, he can compare himself to an orator, aiming at expanding his topic clearly and exhaustingly if possible». As the orator masters his mother tongue, the improviser masters his instrument; as the orator must be well read in every domain of culture (needing many anecdotes to furnish the *narratio* in order to illustrate his case with famous examples) the improviser must

---

[70]. FORKEL, Johann Nikolaus. *Allgemeine Geschichte der Musik*, 2 vols., Leipzig, Schwickert, 1788-1801, §§ 107-119, pp. 54-59.

[71]. As reported in CRAMER, Carl Friedrich. 'Nachricht von dem Clavierspieler Clementi. Bern im Oktober 1784', in: *Magazin der Musik*, II (1786), pp. 365-373.

[72]. BURKE, Edmund. *A Philosophical Enquiry into the Origins of Our Ideas of the Sublime and the Beautiful*, London, Dodsley, 1757; reprint Oxford, Oxford University Press, 1990, p. 39.

[73]. HERDER, Johann Gottfried. *Kalligone*, Weimar, Hermann Böhlau, 1955, p. 229.

[74]. SCHLEUNING, Peter. *Op. cit.* (see note 41), p. 31.

[75]. MATTHESON, Johann. *Op. cit.* (see note 1), Part II, Chapter 14, §§ 1-12, pp. 235-236.

know all the excellent and outstanding productions of the great masters of all times. The orator has to avoid dryness and boredom, thanks to grace, clarity, choice images and ornate language; the improviser must seek fine expressions, elegance, appropriate ornaments, all this taking the understanding capacities of his audience into consideration. The same reflexivity is to be found in both performances: speaking freely is no dreaming, although not every sentence is necessarily prepared in advance; and the musician must avoid being terse, rhapsodic, unintelligible, or prone to digression[76].

These remnants of a discourse more typical of the eighteenth century evolve in parallel to Czerny's obsession with form as 'the whole', and a new stress on unity in a Beethoven-like manner[77]. For instance, «the talent and art of fantasy» consists in weaving «some kind of musical composition which, though in a much freer form, must build up a well-ordered whole, as far as necessary to be intelligible and interesting»[78]. Improvisation is not an edifice, Czerny holds, but like an English garden, apparently not obeying any rule, but showing plenty of surprising variety, achieved in a reasonable, sensible and planned-out way[79], a garden which may remind us of Kant's 'second nature' produced by imagination. For Czerny, the fantasy on one theme only is a «regular whole», where the main theme must reappear many times, being the basis of the construction; thus Bachs 'Art of Fugue' is «a kind of fantasy»[80].

Beethoven's improvisations clearly represent Czerny's point of reference, though the latter was less loquacious about the composer's «off-handed moodiness in performance» (as Ferdinand Ries put it[81]) than about the new species of unity Beethoven wanted to realize through composition and improvisation alike. «Everyone knows», Beethoven once said to Václav Jan Křitel Tomášek, «that the greatest virtuosos on the piano were the greatest composers as well. [...] The true virtuosos, when they played, produced something connected, something forming a whole; once written down, it can be considered as a well elaborated (*durchgeführtes*) work»[82]. Czerny's *Über den richtigen Vortrag der sämtlichen Beethoven'schen Klaviermusik* supplies us with more information about the formal aspects of Beethoven's improvisations than about the style of his performance. His improvisations, Czerny writes, were different whether he chose his own themes or those of others, and they fell into three categories. First, a sonata form with an exposition in which the composers invents a second theme in a related key and finishes it in a regular manner, while in the

---

76. CZERNY, Carl. *Systematische Anleitung zum Fantasieren* [...], *op. cit.* (see note 3), p. 36.

77. *Ibidem*, p. 2. See also the commentary by ESTERO, Andrea. 'L'improvvisazione pianistica a Parigi intorno al 1830. Permanenze ed innovazioni', in: *Sull'improvvisazione, op. cit.* (see note 4), pp. 97-103.

78. CZERNY, Carl. *Systematische Anleitung zum Fantasieren* [...], *op. cit.* (see note 3), p. 36.

79. *Ibidem*, p. 3.

80. *Ibidem*, pp. 43 and 63.

81. BARTH, George. *The Pianist as Orator. Beethoven and the Transformation of Keyboard Style*, Ithaca (NY), Cornell University Press, 1992, p. 54.

82. SCHRAMOWSKI, Herbert. *Op. cit.* (see note 63), p. 397, after Thayer.

development, he «abandons himself to his enthusiasm in a free manner, using the motive in different guises, and the virtuoso passages were still more difficult than those we find in his works». The second form consisted in 'free variations', like those to be found in his 'Chor-Fantasie' Op. 80 or the finale of the Symphony No. 9 (to which we might add the 'Fantasie' Op. 77[83]), and the third one a 'mixed genre', akin to the pot-pourri[84].

Meanwhile, Beethoven's constant and experimental elaboration of sonata form(s) seems to have absorbed the fantasy-principle. Antoine Reicha remembered a remark about his decision, circa 1800 and in a «sudden mood [...] to compose from now on as he improvised, that is to transcribe immediately on the paper everything valuable that his imagination suggested to him, without caring for the rest»[85]. Beethoven's sketchbooks show that this was never the case, though 'the rest' he no longer wanted to bother about (transitions and connective elements), were exactly what the amateurs would miss in his music until the late 1860s at least and what explains its numerous descriptions as 'sublime' by the specialists[86].

Now, if the sonata itself is affected by the fantasy-principle, the face-off between imagination and oration disappears. The horizon of improvisation is no longer free imagination putting on strain the reasonable communication of precise affects or ideas but experimentation with sonata form, or a respect for its established models. This shift coincides with the progressive replacement of the rhetoric paradigm by the organicist one. The predominance of the sonata model (akin to Beethoven's first type of improvisation, as described by Czerny) is illustrated by such works as Johann Nepomuk Hummel's Fantasie Op. 18 (ca. 1805), Ferdinand Ries's 'Grande sonate' Op. 26 (1807/08), Ignaz Moscheles's 'Fantaisie héroïque' (ca. 1822) or Frédéric Kalkbrenner's 'Effusio musica' (1823)[87]. It is attested as well by descriptions of public improvisations,

---

[83]. See RINK, John. 'The Rhetoric of Improvisation. Beethoven's Fantasy Op. 77', in: *Secondo convegno europeo di analisi musicale*, edited by Rossana Dalmonte and Mario Baroni, Trento, Università degli Studi di Trento, 1992, pp. 303-317.

[84]. CZERNY, Carl. *Über den richtigen Vortrag der sämtlichen Beethoven'schen Klaviermusik*, Vienna, Universal, 1963, p. 21.

[85]. REICHA, Antoine. *L'art du compositeur dramatique, ou Cours complet de composition vocale*, 2 vols., Paris, A. Farrenc, 1833, vol. II, p. 283. After SCHRAMOWSKI, Herbert. *Op. cit.* (see note 63), p. 397.

[86]. The technical features of the sublime defined by Michaelis reappear for instance in Hoffmann's description of the Overture *Coriolan*. See HOFFMANN, Ernst Theodot Amadeus. *Schriften zur Musik. Singspiele*, Berlin, Aufbau Verlag, 1988, pp. 99-101. See also the following remark by Ernst Ludwig Gerber, hostile to Beethoven: «Unsere Sonaten sind Phantasien, unsere Ouvertüren sind Phantasien, und selbst unsere Sinfonien, wenigstens die von Beethoven und Konsorten, sind Phantasien». See SCHLEUNING, Peter. *Op. cit.* (see note 41), p. 15.

[87]. For the commentary of these *fantaisies-sonates*, as opposed to *fantaisies-caprices*, see BARTOLI, Jean-Pierre. 'Réflexions sur l'évolution de la fantaisie pour piano au début du XIXᵉ siècle en France', in: *Musique, Images, Instruments*, XI (2009), pp. 191-203.

such as one by Moscheles, consisting of different themes combined in a central section as in a development[88]. This standardisation is deplored by François-Joseph Fétis[89] but acclaimed by a critic in *Le Pianiste* in 1834:

> In general, a fantasy is a work more important (*capital*) than a theme with variations; the fantasy is to the sonata what a concertino is to a concerto, a piece in three movements: it is the piece of our time. The form admits an introduction, or prelude, and even asks for it. A first recapitulation as in a sonata, well carried out; a large *cantabile* and a finale forming a shorter rondo — that is the fantasy as we conceive it, as it has been treated by [Charles] Chaulieu, Henri Herz, [Ferdinand] Hérold, [Franz] Hünten, [Frédéric] Kalkbrenner, and [Johann Peter] Pixis, and it most certainly allows any author to show his skills[90].

88. See the description in *Revue et Gazette Musicale*, 24 January 1836.

89. Fétis wrotes in *La musique mise à la portée de tout le monde* (Paris, Mesnier, 1830): «Mais depuis environ vingt ans, rien n'est moins libre que la fantaisie; on ne le fait plus que sur modèle donné qui est toujours le même, et dans lequel l'imagination n'est pour rien». Quoted by ESTERO, Andrea. *Op. cit.* (see note 77), p. 360.

90. *Le Pianiste*, 8 June 1834, pp. 117-118, quoted by BARTOLI, Jean-Pierre. *Op. cit.* (see note 87), p. 200.

Testimonianze sulla prassi improvvisativa dei musicisti italiani tra Sette e Ottocento

Carmela Bongiovanni
(Genova)

Sul frontespizio de *Il tempio dell'armonia*, coro a quattro voci con accompagnamento di pianoforte o arpa di Ferdinando Paer, pubblicato a Parigi verso il 1820, leggiamo che «questo coro è stato improvvisato dal Signor Paer ed eseguito dagli allievi del Signor Massimino»[1]. È una delle numerose occasioni in cui abbiamo una testimonianza concreta della diffusione della prassi improvvisativa in ambito musicale tradizionale, anche se questa testimonianza è un poco diversa da quelle che più solitamente si riscontrano a proposito di improvvisazioni alla tastiera o altri strumenti, ovvero legate a cantanti o virtuosi di diverso genere. Il testo di questo coro in italiano era dello stesso Paer; la composizione vocale improvvisata era un prodotto didattico destinato agli allievi di Frédéric Massimino, vale a dire l'italiano naturalizzato francese Federico Massimino (1775-1858), professore di canto e di solfeggio, celebre didatta di musica, a capo di una scuola il cui metodo di insegnamento è stato definito da François Lesure 'mutuo' (*mutuel*)[2]. Sappiamo che nella sede parigina della *Institution de Massimino* si organizzavano concerti. Effettivamente, le testimonianze biografiche su Ferdinando Paer, compositore italiano trasferitosi a Parigi, attestano che quest'ultimo fu musicista abilissimo nell'improvvisazione melodica, oltre che eccellente cantante lui stesso. E d'altronde la stessa prassi del canto di primo Ottocento ha una forte connotazione improvvisata. Questo esempio, ancora, segnala la stretta congruenza tra l'arte dell'improvvisazione e il mestiere del compositore.

Ho voluto iniziare con una testimonianza d'improvvisazione per uso didattico, al di fuori dell'alveo elitario del virtuosismo del tempo e quindi di teatri e accademie ove di preferenza i modelli del virtuosismo improvvisativo si esplicano, per sottolineare la straordinaria diffusione della prassi improvvisativa nella vita artistica del primo Ottocento.

---

[1]. Paer, Ferdinando. *Il tempio dell'armonia (Le temple de l'harmonie). Choeur à 4 voix avec accompagnement de piano ou harpe, Paroles et musique de Ferdinand Paër, Dédié à son ami Fréderic Massimino*, Parigi, l'Auteur, [ca. 1820]: «N.^ta Ce choeur a été improvisé par M^r. Paer et exécuté par les Elèves de M^r. Massimino».

[2]. Lesure, François. 'Introduction', in: *La musique à Paris en 1830-1831*, a cura di François Lesure, Parigi, Bibliothèque Nationale, 1983, p. 11.

In Italia in particolare, numerose fonti e testimonianze di differente grado indicano una certa predilezione quasi trasversale in campo culturale per la estemporaneità nelle arti.

L'improvvisazione, è difficile non riconoscerlo, ha costituito un tema estremamente dibattuto nella musicologia internazionale degli ultimi decenni. Sono state studiate le molteplici forme dell'improvvisazione in musica nei modi più differenti e nelle culture più lontane, dalla musica tradizionale colta di oriente e occidente alle forme del canto popolare delle più diverse latitudini. Interessanti studi comparati sono stati svolti per analizzare le diverse interpretazioni che i tempi, i luoghi e le culture hanno dato dell'arte dell'improvvisazione. È lo stesso concetto dell'improvvisare che assume una molteplicità di significati: esso presuppone tuttavia un apprendimento mnemonico di formule e passaggi, la cui didattica risulta viva ancora nell'Ottocento.

Tra i virtuosi estemporanei in campo diverso dalla musica segnalo i poeti improvvisatori italiani che tra Sette e Ottocento ebbero un notevole successo di pubblico. Su di essi abbiamo numerose testimonianze; ad essi non solo possiamo collegarci per stabilire tratti d'unione con la prassi improvvisativa ed estemporanea in musica (la loro abilità improvvisativa può essere paragonata alla capacità da parte dei musicisti di effettuare variazioni estemporanee sulla base di temi musicali forniti all'istante), ma anche per considerarne la pervasività nella cultura italiana; perfino il giovanissimo Pietro Metastasio fu poeta estemporaneo! Al di là del fenomeno Metastasio, alcuni poeti improvvisatori fornirono testi per musica o comunque furono legati alla musica; è il caso della celebre poetessa estemporanea lucchese Teresa Bandettini (1763-1837), autrice di testi per musica musicati da Paer e non solo, e inoltre della poetessa improvvisatrice e musicista dilettante Corilla Olimpica (1727-1800) alias Maria Maddalena Morelli, incontrata da Charles Burney a Firenze durante il suo celebre viaggio italiano[3]. Come ricorda Umberto Monti a proposito di uno degli innumerevoli poeti estemporanei tra Sette e Ottocento, il genovese Gian Carlo Di Negro (1769-1857), quella del poeta improvvisatore era una vera e propria attività artistica, del tutto parallela al virtuoso solista di musica: si esibivano entrambi in accademie pubbliche e private, talora nella stessa serata[4].

In sostanza: improvvisare un coro con intenti didattici e inventare all'istante una lunga sequenza di strofe su tema dato sono entrambi parte della cultura dell'estemporaneità,

---

[3]. BURNEY, Charles. *The Present State of Music in France and Italy* (1771), traduzione italiana a cura di Enrico Fubini *Viaggio musicale in Italia*, Torino, EDT, 1979, p. 225. Giuseppe Bertini la segnala allieva di violino di Pietro Nardini: «Ella improvvisava de' versi sopra ogni sorta di soggetti, suonava la sua parte di violino in un concerto, e cantava con moltissima grazia e talento». Si veda BERTINI, Giuseppe. *Dizionario storico-critico degli scrittori di musica e de' più celebri artisti di tutte le nazioni si' antiche che moderne*, Palermo, Tipografia Reale di Guerra, 1814-1815, Tomo II, p. 80. Per una rapida disamina sui poeti improvvisatori italiani in campo dotto e popolare si veda GENTILI, Bruno - CATENACCI, Carmine. 'La riscoperta della voce', in: *Manuale di letteratura italiana*, a cura di Franco Brioschi e Costanzo Di Girolamo, vol. IV, Torino, Bollati Boringhieri, 1996, pp. 285-296.

[4]. MONTI, Umberto. *Gian Carlo Di Negro*, Genova, F. Ceretti, 1950.

e dimostrano la diffusione del modello dell'improvvisazione nel dominio artistico anche a livelli propedeutici e non solo virtuosistici; l'arte dell'improvvisazione è tesa a nascondere il metodo, la tecnica, dietro una parvenza di istinto improvvisativo e virtuosistico.

Un problema strettamente correlato con la prassi dell'improvvisazione è quello del ruolo del testo, vale a dire della musica scritta, notata, nel periodo tra Sette e Ottocento in rapporto all'atto performativo, vale a dire la relazione tra esecuzione (ed esecutore) e testo musicale scritto.

È indubbio che il rapporto tra interprete e testo musicale notato dal Novecento in poi rispetto ai secoli in esame sia totalmente dissimile, e ciò non solo perché i virtuosi vissuti tra Sette e Ottocento erano in maggioranza essi stessi compositori o quanto meno padroni delle cognizioni armoniche; d'altra parte in ogni tempo, al di là di qualsiasi prassi esecutiva, è ovvia la ferma volontà del compositore di affermare le proprie scelte artistiche e compositive a discapito dell'arbitrio dell'esecutore. Non sembri banale ripetere che l'essere compositore per questi virtuosi (e il virtuoso è quasi sempre anche compositore tra Sette e Ottocento) è in stretta relazione con le metodiche dell'improvvisazione, ma anche, in modo differenziato, con l'arte dell'ornamentazione e della variazione. Effettivamente, secondo il celebre trattato di Francesco Galeazzi della fine del Settecento, 'Virtuoso' è un titolo «che solo compete a chi possiede il genio inventore, e lo stile, che forma il carattere proprio delle belle arti»[5]. Dunque, virtuosismo e arte della composizione alla fine del Settecento vanno a braccetto. In particolare, il concetto di virtuosismo porta con sé, in modo spontaneo e pressoché naturale, anche quello d'improvvisazione più o meno libera (secondo canoni talora di rigore). Se il virtuoso non è lo stesso autore di quanto esegue, è comunque uno stretto collaboratore del compositore (a volte mal tollerato), in quanto è chiamato ad integrare e completare l'opera altrui.

Tra Sette e Ottocento la parola 'improvvisazione' sembra essere prevalentemente associata con l'aggiunta di abbellimenti estemporanei e in particolare con l'arte della variazione per evitare la ripetizione pedissequa della stessa linea melodica. 'Variare' e 'improvvisare' sono quindi due aspetti strettamente connessi tra loro, figli del virtuosismo.

Il diaframma che separa una vera e propria improvvisazione da una gradazione più o meno accentuata di variazione e diminuzione di un testo musicale dato è quanto mai sottile[6]. Il gusto per la variazione continua di ciò che si suona, che presuppone una tecnica ferrea sia in campo virtuosistico che per quanto attiene la conoscenza dell'armonia e del

---

5. GALEAZZI, Francesco. *Elementi teorico-pratici di musica*, Tomo II, Roma, Michele Puccinelli, 1796, p. 261. Lo stesso Galeazzi dedica l'Articolo XXI, alle pp. 237-239, al tema 'Del Suonare all'Improvviso'.

6. Ma è ancora più importante sapere che «tutto ciò che è scritto non è esente dall'oralità e dall'impre-visto. Nessuna notazione, infatti, è capace di trascrivere tutti gli elementi di un brano: a un buon interprete si chiede di leggere 'al di là delle note'». Si veda SIRON, Jacques. 'L'improvvisazione nel jazz e nelle musiche contemporanee. L'imperfetto del momento attuale', in: *Enciclopedia della musica*, a cura di Jean Jacques Nattiez, vol. V: *L'unità della musica*, Torino, Einaudi, 2005, pp. 737-756: 741.

contrappunto, è quanto si evince ad esempio dalle testimonianze circa le esecuzioni di Paganini. Come suonava le proprie composizioni Paganini? C'è da ritenere in modo sempre diverso di volta in volta; è la libertà del compositore virtuoso che sconfina nella improvvisazione, come abbiamo potuto osservare. Questa impressione coincide con le parole di Carl Friedrich Zelter che ebbe occasione più volte di ascoltare Paganini. In una sua lettera a Goethe, Zelter afferma che la musica suonata da Paganini «è sempre nuova ed interessante»[7]; noi invece dai programmi dei concerti di Paganini sappiamo quante volte in realtà il virtuoso ripetesse in concerto le stesse composizioni (almeno sulla carta). È questa prassi interpretativa della musica scritta — che va al di là dell'arte del diminuire, una interpretazione che noi oggi potremmo definire come una vera e propria rielaborazione o variazione a partire dallo stesso testo — che forma l'oggetto della presente comunicazione. Si considerino i celeberrimi precetti di Galeazzi sui vantaggi del contrappuntista suonatore e sulla possibilità di variare in modo competente passi troppo complicati o comunque non consoni alla propria tecnica[8]. Insomma: l'originalità diviene sistema. La questione relativa all'improvvisazione, sapiente rielaborazione in sintonia con prassi esecutiva e stile della composizione, è naturalmente connessa, come si ribadirà più oltre, anche con la metodologia della didattica tra Sette ed Ottocento.

La tradizione degli studi sulla prassi esecutiva, in particolare per quanto attiene agli abbellimenti e alle diminuzioni aggiunte ad arbitrio del musicista, ma anche l'esame delle personalizzazioni che ciascun interprete-virtuoso compositore apportava al repertorio che eseguiva, è ormai piuttosto nutrita. Legato al tema di questo intervento è la figura di sicuro affascinante e oggi pressoché scomparsa del virtuoso-compositore. Questo binomio, come noto, nascondeva una profonda conoscenza nell'arte dell'improvvisazione.

Variazioni, abbellimenti estemporanei, fantasie e preludi introduttivi alla tastiera e al violino, cadenze e capricci a mo' di cadenze, composizione ed esecuzione di virtuosi sono i diversi aspetti di una prassi che vede impegnati in prima persona compositori, strumentisti e cantanti tra Sette e Ottocento. Le testimonianze sono numerose, sia dal lato dei cronisti e memorialisti e degli stessi musicisti che dal lato dei teorici, senza limiti per quanto concerne gli strumenti musicali (dal flauto, alla tastiera, agli strumenti ad arco, al canto, ecc.) e soprattutto senza confini.

Gli studi potranno ancora chiarire il passaggio da una interpretazione del testo in senso moderno a una vera e propria rielaborazione sostanziale secondo i canoni delle

---

7. Riportata in *Niccolò Paganini. Epistolario 1810-1831*, a cura di Roberto Grisley, Milano, Skira, 2006, p. 530, nota 1. Su Paganini si vedano anche i saggi di Philippe Borer e Renato Ricco nel presente volume.

8. GALEAZZI, Francesco. *Op. cit.* (si veda nota 5), p. 261: «Altro non men pregevole vantaggio gode il Contrappuntista Suonatore, ed è che in caso che gli si presentino all'improviso de' passi difficili, e della di cui netta esecuzione possa egli dubitare, può sul fatto rimediarvi mutandoli, ed addattandoli alla propria abilità, senza uscir d'armonia, in guisa che non possa verun uditore, anche Musico, accorgersi dell'ingegnoso stratagemma».

scuole vocali e strumentali dell'età classica e viceversa. Non sembri inutile tornare a soffermarsi qui su alcune testimonianze di musicisti e ascoltatori: mi riferisco a quella del celebre musicografo-viaggiatore-musicista Charles Burney[9] e anche a quella meno nota del violinista virtuoso e direttore Nicola Petrini Zamboni (1785-1849), le cui memorie e scritti costituiscono un preciso contraltare di provincia al contemporaneo dispiegarsi della carriera del virtuoso internazionale per eccellenza, Nicolò Paganini[10].

Il vocabolo 'improvvisazione' è usato più volte da Burney durante i suoi viaggi musicali europei: ora è lui stesso chiamato a improvvisare alla tastiera (secondo una prassi riconducibile all'alveo del preludiare alla tastiera, ma non solo)[11], ora sono piccoli e grandi compositori a improvvisare, come nel caso dell'episodio significativo di Johann Adolf Hasse durante il suo soggiorno viennese. Hasse improvvisa così bene che non si distingue l'improvvisazione dalla composizione realizzata razionalmente[12]. L'improvvisazione è così diffusa all'epoca di Burney che si è inventata una macchina «creata» — come dice lo stesso Burney — «per registrare le musiche improvvisate»[13].

I protagonisti della musica e i tempi cambiano, ma il giudizio degli ascoltatori sulle capacità improvvisative dei virtuosi sembra ripetersi quasi con le stesse parole: lo studioso Jeffrey Kallberg ad esempio, ci ricorda che anche Chopin improvvisava, e che le sue improvvisazioni erano considerate, da chi ebbe la ventura di ascoltarle, forse ancor più profonde ed espressive dei suoi lavori scritti[14].

---

[9]. BURNEY, Charles. *The Present State of Music in France* [...], *op. cit.* (si veda nota 3); ID. *The Present State of Music in Germany, the Netherlands, and United Provinces* (1773), traduzione italiana a cura di Enrico Fubini, *Viaggio musicale in Germania e Paesi Bassi*, Torino, EDT, 1986.

[10]. PETRINI ZAMBONI, Nicola. *Memorie di un violinista cesenate (1785-1849)*, a cura di Franco Dell'Amore, Cesena, Comune di Cesena, [1995].

[11]. Sull'arte del preludiare al violino e sul preludio scritto come 'improvvisazione al quadrato' si veda ad esempio STOWELL, Robin. *Violin Technique and Performance Practice in the Late Eighteenth and Early Nineteenth Centuries*, Cambridge, Cambridge University Press, 1985, pp. 354-355. Qui Stowell afferma tra l'altro che il preludio serviva a una quantità di propositi, sia a beneficio dell'esecutore che dell'ascoltatore, vale a dire il controllo dell'intonazione del violino, un richiamo a fare silenzio, a sciogliere le dita in previsione del concerto, testare la propria padronanza della tecnica dello strumento e stabilire per l'ascoltatore la tonalità e il modo della musica principale che stava per essere eseguita. Sull'arte del preludio alla tastiera si veda SITÀ, Maria Grazia. 'Suonare prima di suonare. La prassi del preludio improvvisato nella trattatistica per tastiera tra Settecento e Ottocento', in: *Rivista Italiana di Musicologia*, XXXI/2 (1996), pp. 303-326, e inoltre: CARRER, Pinuccia. 'La didattica preludiante. Alessandro Rolla interprete di una tradizione', in: *Alessandro Rolla (1757-1841). Un caposcuola dell'arte violinistica lombarda*, a cura di Mariateresa Dellaborra, Lucca, LIM, 2010, pp. 267-275.

[12]. BURNEY, Charles. *The Present State of Music in Germany* [...], *op. cit.* (si veda nota 9), p. 120: Hasse «improvvisò per me una Toccata o Capriccio con dei passi veramente meravigliosi, ma egli possiede un gusto troppo sicuro per sciupare in circostanze di scarso rilievo ciò che deve essere riservato ai momenti eccezionali».

[13]. *Ibidem*, p. 214. Su questa macchina confronta il saggio di Martin Kaltenecker nel presente volume.

[14]. KALLBERG, Jeffrey. 'Chopin and the Aesthetic of the Sketch. A New Prelude in E♭ Minor?', in: *Early Music*, XXIX (2001), pp. 408-422.

Anche la moglie di Hasse, l'italiana celebre cantante Faustina Bordoni, secondo la testimonianza di Burney, «era dotata di un'ottima memoria per gli abbellimenti e i mutamenti che apportava arbitrariamente alla partitura»[15]. A costo di apparire banale vorrei ricordare — a fianco dell'esperienza di Faustina che rientrava di fatto nella quotidianità del cantante virtuoso[16] — il celebre passo di Burney (durante il suo viaggio italiano) sull'altrettanto famoso castrato Farinelli: tra le quattro arie che questi intonava ogni sera per Filippo V re di Spagna, vi era un minuetto «che egli variava a suo piacere»[17]. Anche questo rientra nella sfera dell'interpretazione come variazione del testo musicale. Gli esempi sono innumerevoli; nei pressi di Roma, Burney incontra un'abile cantante dilettante e pittrice, la Bacchelli detta Mignatrice:

> Possiede una perfetta padronanza della musica e sa abbellire e mutare qualsiasi passaggio a suo piacimento con grande facilità e destrezza come non mi è mai accaduto di notare in alcun'altra cantante. Insomma, il suo canto non è tanto nello stile di una regina dell'Opera, ma possiede tutti i requisiti che sarebbero desiderabili in una signora alla moda o in una gentildonna[18].

La costruzione all'improvviso dei periodi e delle frasi musicali si fonda su alcuni modelli armonici variati con l'aggiunta di inventiva melodica; questo tipo di composizione estemporanea, alla pari della prassi italiana del partimento, era probabilmente un quotidiano esercizio per molti musicisti contemporanei.

Burney non è solo ascoltatore ma anche lui stesso padrone della tecnica dell'improvvisazione: a Venezia, in casa Grimani, dietro insistenza generale — come dice Burney —, il viaggiatore inglese deve suonare: «Eseguii un brano improvvisato poiché non ero in grado di vedere né di ricordare alcunché, tanto ero emozionato»[19]. Burney evidentemente con questa espressione di 'brano improvvisato' fa riferimento preciso ad una tecnica di organizzazione dell'armonia e della melodia basata su un metodo appreso; anche il conte Antonio Torre Taxis, dilettante e prolifico compositore, «improvvisò» al clavicembalo davanti a Burney «dimostrando non comune abilità nella modulazione»[20].

Ovviamente l'arte dell'improvvisazione è diffusa in modo capillare per tutti gli strumenti; essa quindi è una prassi condivisa e metodica. Le testimonianze molteplici dell'abilità dei violinisti nel variare all'improvviso sono davvero tantissime, così come

---

[15]. BURNEY, Charles. *The Present State of Music in Germany* [...], *op. cit.* (si veda nota 9), p. 205.

[16]. Testimonianza di come non sempre improvvisare sia sinonimo di originalità. Si improvvisa infatti usando schemi fissi appresi e rielaborati secondo una metodica di scuola. Si veda in proposito la relazione di Damien Colas sull'improvvisazione in ambito vocale nell'Ottocento nel presente volume.

[17]. BURNEY, Charles. *The Present State of Music in France* [...], *op. cit.* (si veda nota 3), p. 189.

[18]. *Ibidem*, p. 266.

[19]. *Ibidem*, p. 166.

[20]. *Ibidem*, p. 166.

numerose d'altro canto sono le testimonianze del rigore esecutivo richiesto da alcuni dei maggiori compositori del Settecento agli esecutori: ricordo a puro titolo esemplificativo Handel, Mozart, Haydn con svariati aneddoti, ma anche compositori italiani come Niccolò Jommelli. I principali virtuosi tra Sette e Ottocento sembrano eccellere in queste abilità improvvisative[21]; tra questi il violinista e compositore Felice Giardini (1716-1796), maestro nell'uso della variazione all'improvviso, che fu a sua volta protagonista di un celebre aneddoto insieme al compositore Jommelli, narrato dallo stesso Burney in *A General History of Music* e ricordato successivamente da musicografi antichi e studiosi moderni. Poiché Giardini da giovane era un po' troppo avvezzo ad infiorettare e variare la musica, secondo la prassi della scuola italiana, si prese per questo malvezzo un bello schiaffo in pieno viso da Jommelli (voleva fare il virtuoso davanti al compositore, pasticciando a propria fantasia la musica di questi)[22]. Giardini aveva la reputazione di un grandissimo virtuoso di violino. I contemporanei parlano di un suono dolce e insieme potente. Ma non basta: Giardini sapeva variare all'improvviso, senza cambiare una nota, in pratica usando solo gli abbellimenti (secondo la testimonianza di Burney)[23]. Resoconti diversi indicano che la prassi dell'improvvisazione di abbellimenti da parte di musicisti italiani era fiorente nell'ultima parte del Settecento e all'inizio dell'Ottocento[24]. Gli italiani effettivamente

---

[21]. STOWELL, Robin. *Op. cit.* (si veda nota 11), pp. 337 e segg., ove l'autore segnala come il tardo Settecento/primi Ottocento sia il periodo della massima fioritura dell'improvvisazione (in particolare alla tastiera) sia in forma di cadenza melodica, che di ornamentazioni, preludi, realizzazioni del continuo, ecc. Sulla prassi della ornamentazione improvvisata in area italiana e sulle peculiarità che la distinguono si veda SMILES, Joan E. 'Directions for Improvised Ornamentation in Italian Method Books of the Late Eighteenth Century', in: *Journal of the American Musicological Society*, XXXI (1978), pp. 495-509.

[22]. 'Giardini, Felice', in: CHORON, Alexandre - FAYOLLE, François-Joseph-Marie. *Dictionnaire historique des musiciens, artiste et amateurs, morts ou vivans*, 2 voll., Parigi, Valade, 1810-1811, vol. I, p. 271; BERTINI, Giuseppe. *Op. cit.* (si veda nota 3), Tomo II, p. 176. Bertini, che traduce pedissequamente Choron & Fayolle, così si esprime a proposito di Felice Giardini: «nelle orchestre divertivasi sommamente di far de' preludj, e di variare i passaggi che doveva eseguire». Sullo schiaffo di Jommelli si veda anche il saggio di Gregorio Carraro nel presente volume. L'episodio di Giardini e Jommelli è citato in MCVEIGH, Simon. *The Violinist in London's Concert Life 1750-1784. Felice Giardini and His Contemporaries*, New York, Garland, 1989, p. 148, e inoltre in SPITZER, John - ZASLAW, Neal. 'Improvised Ornamentation in Eighteenth-Century Orchestras', in: *Journal of the American Musicological Society*, XXXIX (1986), pp. 524-577: 559, nota 86, che datano l'episodio al 1747 o 1748 e lo commentano come testimonianza dell'uso italiano, ma non solo, di infiorettare con abbellimenti improvvisati le linee delle parti superiori dell'orchestra. Nel caso riportato tuttavia, Giardini non si limitava solo a diminuire, ma inventava pezzi a mo' di preludi e inoltre variava quelli esistenti della sua parte.

[23]. Citato da MCVEIGH, Simon. *Op. cit.* (si veda nota 22), p. 197.

[24]. È il caso del violoncellista Bigati la cui voce appare nel già citato *Dizionario* di Giuseppe Bertini (si veda nota 3), Tomo I, pp. 117-118: «Questo artista può considerarsi come uno de' migliori accompagnatori del suo tempo: egli improvvisava seguitamente, e con la più grande facilità, sopra tutti i pezzi che sentiva, o di cui se gli offeriva la parte recitante: Boccherini essendo ad Avignone, Bigati lo accompagnò ne' suoi primi *quintetti*, quivi eseguiti per la prima volta. Quel celebre compositore avendo inteso vantare la facilità che aveva Bigati nell'improvvisare, levogli d'innanzi la parte del basso di accompagnamento, e rimase assai soddisfatto di quello che gli sostituì».

avevano la fama di essere improvvisatori molto solerti e di arricchire con abbellimenti eccessivi le composizioni da loro eseguite[25]. Naturalmente l'abilità e la consuetudine con l'improvvisazione non escludono per contro la capacità di lettura e interpretazione rigorose del testo musicale; sulla fedeltà al dettato della composizione abbiamo in effetti altri esempi che ci confermano la consapevole scelta di prassi da parte dei musicisti: improvvisazione sì, ma a suo tempo e luogo.

Per venire a Nicola Petrini Zamboni, violinista del quale ci sono rimaste memorie e scritti intorno ai violinisti ripubblicati alcuni anni fa[26], sappiamo che questi fu in relazione con Paganini; quest'ultimo infatti gli indirizzò alcune missive; di lui inoltre Paganini fa cenno in altre lettere[27]. Le memorie di Petrini Zamboni per la loro spontaneità possono servire come testimonianza della condizione del violinista tra Sette e Ottocento, ma anche della prassi esecutiva su questo strumento e del sistema di apprendimento, basato sull'imitazione del maestro. Dunque, Petrini Zamboni, nel narrare della sua formazione, racconta di un suo giovane maestro piemontese di passaggio a Cesena, Domenico Giorgis, e così lo descrive:

> Abbondava anche troppo di trilli, trilletti, gruppi, mordenti, ecc. Intuonazione perfetta! Mano agile, occhio franchissimo, per cui gran suonatore all'improvviso! […] Scriveva pure qualche cosa; ma soprattutto riusciva maravigliosamente nel suonare delle estemporanee Variazioni a qualche Tema gli fosse dato. Il Cantabile non era da lui conosciuto [si legga: infiorettava qualsiasi melodia con andamento moderato][28].

Quindi, afferma Petrini Zamboni, Domenico Giorgis non era espressivo, ma virtuoso sì. Più oltre prosegue nel descrivere il metodo didattico di Giorgis, che tuttavia si inquadra nella prassi violinistica della scuola italiana, vale a dire l'apprendimento tramite l'imitazione del maestro:

> Non mi faceva suonare nulla di scritto, ma m'insegnava a mente dei passi di concerto, dei capricci, infinite scale ascendenti e discendenti, arpeggi modulati, e cose simili, sempre passeggiando per la camera dopo la mezzanotte[29].

Ancora Petrini Zamboni, che sul problema dell'improvvisazione e dell'esecuzione variata ha taciuto per tutte le sue memorie, nel trattare 'De' violinisti più celebri d'Italia' ribadisce che proprio il Giorgis si distingueva «per la facilità che aveva di comporre

[25]. SMILES, Joan E. *Op. cit.* (si veda nota 21).

[26]. PETRINI ZAMBONI, Nicola. *Op. cit.* (si veda nota 10).

[27]. *Niccolò Paganini. Epistolario* […], *op. cit.* (si veda nota 7), *passim*.

[28]. PETRINI ZAMBONI, Nicola. *Op. cit.* (si veda nota 10), p. 29.

[29]. *Ibidem*.

estemporanee variazioni sopra un tema che gli fosse dato»[30]. Non a caso un altro violinista abilissimo improvvisatore citato da Petrini Zamboni, Giuseppe Miliolli di Cremona, i cui «capricci estemporanei facevano sbalordire», suonava tutto a orecchio; effettivamente non sapeva leggere una nota[31].

Il problema dell'improvvisazione non è legato solo alla prassi della composizione e quindi dell'apprendimento dell'armonizzazione del basso continuo (il violoncellista per esempio improvvisava gli accompagnamenti aggiungendo accordi arpeggiati e abbellimenti)[32] e delle competenze di contrappunto, ma più direttamente e ampiamente è inerente alla prassi della metodologia della didattica dello strumento (tastiera, arco, fiato o altro).

Come ho già osservato, al tema dell'improvvisazione è strettamente connessa l'abitudine ugualmente diffusissima tra i virtuosi della rielaborazione all'improvviso di pezzi altrui: è celebre il caso della lettura rielaborata con aggiunta di abbellimenti, insieme all'esecuzione del tema all'ottava alta in armonici doppi, della Sonata in fa maggiore 'La primavera' di Beethoven per violino e pianoforte da parte di Paganini, le cui licenze nell'esecuzione lasciano sbalordito il testimone Wilhelm Speyer, che poi ne fa parola per iscritto a Louis Spohr, in una lettera datata 7 settembre 1829[33]. Madame de Genlis, in un

---

[30]. *Ibidem*, p. 146. Sul rapporto tra variazioni e improvvisazione si veda il breve contributo di SCARPETTA, Umberto. 'Quanto della musica è in grado di trasmetterci la tradizione musicale scritta?', in: *Affetti musicali. Studi in onore di Sergio Martinotti*, a cura di Maurizio Padoan, Milano, Vita e Pensiero Edizioni, 2005, pp. 15-21.

[31]. PETRINI ZAMBONI, Nicola. *Op. cit.* (si veda nota 10), p. 149. Immagini leggermente diverse ci trasmette la testimonianza delle esecuzioni dei capricci da parte del violinista Antonio Lolli, trascritta da Giuseppe Bertini nel suo *Dizionario* (si veda nota 3), Tomo III, p. 33: «La destrezza, che egli aveva acquistata sul suo strumento, era del tutto sorprendente; egli saliva più al di là di qualunque altro suonatore; i suoi capricci talmente lo trasportavano negli *a solo*, che il più esercitato accompagnatore poteva appena seguirlo: egli medesimo non poteva accompagnare il canto, perché difficilmente andava in misura». Fino a questo passaggio Bertini traduce fedelmente Choron & Fayolle (si veda nota 22). Bertini prosegue tuttavia con un ricordo personale di un concerto di Lolli a Palermo nel 1793: «La prima volta che Lolli fecesi sentire in un suo concerto sul teatro di Palermo nel 1793, mi sovviene d'aver inteso sgridar in pubblico il Sig. Blasco primo violino dell'orchestra, che non aveva uguale nell'arte di dirigerla, perché non si erano trovati insieme in misura, ma lo sbaglio era piuttosto del Lolli, che affrettava sempre il tempo, ed andava avanti». E per questo motivo, dice Bertini, ricusava di suonare gli adagi.

[32]. Sull'arte dell'accompagnamento al violoncello *cfr.* tra gli altri: WALDEN, Valerie. *One Hundred Years of Violoncello. A History of Technique and Performance Practice, 1740-1840*, Cambridge, Cambridge University Press, 2004, pp. 241-269; WATKIN, David. 'Corelli's Op. 5 Sonatas: 'Violino e violone o cimbalo'?', in: *Early Music*, XXIV (1996), pp. 645-663; BACCIAGALUPPI, Claudio. 'Primo violoncello al cembalo: l'accompagnamento del recitativo semplice nell'Ottocento', in: *Rivista italiana di musicologia*, XLI/1 (2006), pp. 101-134. La testimonianza più significativa è tuttavia quella fornita da Giuseppe Bertini citata alla nota 24, e inerente al violoncellista Bigati. Si veda anche il saggio di John Lutterman nel presente volume.

[33]. Ecco come conclude Speyer: «A dispetto degli abbellimenti in biscrome e semicrome, mai in vita mia udii uno che suonasse così in tempo». Come si vede, se Antonio Lolli abbelliva all'improvviso la propria linea melodica, senza tuttavia mantenere il tempo di battuta, Paganini invece riusciva a fare entrambe le cose ottimamente. L'episodio è riportato in GAMBERINI, Leopoldo. *La vita musicale europea del 1800. Archivio musicale genovese*, vol. I, *Introduzione. Opera lirica e musica strumentale. Documenti e testimonianze*, Siena, Università di Siena - Facoltà di Magistero in Arezzo, 1978, p. 138. Sull'aggiunta di variazioni alle composizioni altrui da parte di Paganini, si veda STOWELL, Robin. *Op. cit.* (si veda nota 11), p. 347:

suo trattato d'arpa dell'inizio dell'Ottocento, afferma che le diminuzioni servono a 'coprire' la musica mediocre[34]: non sembra che Paganini fosse dello stesso avviso. D'altra parte, gli episodi di lettura variata e improvvisata su composizioni altrui da parte di Paganini sono numerosi e celebri; alcuni di questi sono segnalati in calce alle lettere dello stesso Paganini apparse nella recente edizione dell'epistolario a cura di Roberto Grisley: è famoso quello relativo al concerto tenuto insieme al violinista Charles-Philippe Lafont l'11 marzo 1816, durante il quale Paganini negli 'a solo' improvvisò secondo la sua «fantasia d'italiano» (vale a dire, secondo la prassi tutta italiana dell'esecuzione variata dei pezzi)[35]. Proprio a Paganini un critico della *Gazzetta Piemontese* in data martedì 17 febbraio 1818 rimproverava l'eccessivo uso di 'ricami'[36]. L'abitudine di Paganini di ornamentare il canto delle composizioni altrui da lui eseguite, secondo le modalità della scuola violinistica italiana, è attestata a più riprese, in diversi tempi e sedi[37].

Quanto all'aggiunta di 'ricami' alle composizioni di primo Ottocento in ambito italiano, una testimonianza singolare per il repertorio coinvolto è quella del giovane compositore Otto Nicolai, che nel 1837 a Roma ebbe modo di ascoltare la Cappella Pontificia:

> Nell'esecuzione del canto solistico i cantori sistini si prendono quelle libertà massime, di cui è difficile farsi un'idea considerando le partiture nelle

---

«Paganini evidently could scarcely ever resist the opportunity of giving free rein to his flight of fancy, especially when playing the works of others».

[34]. La citazione è tratta da JEROLD, Beverly. 'How Composers Viewed Performers' Additions', in: *Early Music*, XXXVI (2008), pp. 95-109: 107, nota 17. Secondo Madame de Genlis, composizioni di autori scarsamente abili possono e debbono esser diminuite per coprire la mediocrità. Quindi i maggiori compositori meritano il più gran rispetto proprio perché la loro musica non necessita né di abbellimenti né di inutili guarnizioni a una melodia già bella di per se stessa. La testimonianza è interessante nonostante provenga da una musicista d'oltralpe.

[35]. La testimonianza di Paganini stesso, riportata in FÉTIS, François-Joseph. *Notizia biografica intorno a Nicolò Paganini*, Milano, Ricordi, 1875, p. 36, è citata da PAVOLINI, Claudio. 'Fonti di ispirazione del violinismo paganiniano', in: *Paganini divo e comunicatore*, a cura di Maria Rosa Moretti, Anna Sorrento, Stefano Termanini ed Enrico Volpato, Genova, SerEl International-Eeditrice.com, 2007, pp. 299-358: 339, nota 135. Sul medesimo concerto, si veda la testimonianza di Pierre Lafont, riportata in *Nicolò Paganini. Epistolario* [...], *op. cit.* (si veda nota 7), pp. 80-82, nota 3.

[36]. *Nicolò Paganini. Epistolario* [...], *op. cit.* (si veda nota 7), Lettera n. 34, p. 114, nota 1, ov'è trascritto il resoconto giornalistico apparso sulla *Gazzetta Piemontese*, n. 21, martedì 17 febbraio 1818, del secondo concerto dato da Paganini a Torino, il 15 febbraio 1818, a firma di Paolo Luigi Raby: la critica è favorevole, tuttavia il recensore deplora con tono piuttosto contenuto le variazioni virtuosistiche fatte sulle note della musica, aggiunte o ricami che vengono a storpiare le note stesse: «la giudiziosa *cadenza* fatta alla fine dell'*Adagio* del concerto, ci ha fatto argomentare che egli ne eseguirebbe maestrevolmente uno di *Viotti*, se, rinunziando al lusso dei tanti ricami, si attenesse severamente alle note». Si tratta di una critica alla volontà di alterare il testo musicale, improvvisando con lo scopo di mettere in mostra il virtuosismo.

[37]. Sempre nel primo Ottocento e per quanto attiene alle orchestre italiane e alla prassi di abbellire a prima vista si veda SPITZER, John - ZASLAW, Neal. *Op. cit.* (si veda nota 22), p. 567, ove sono segnalate testimonianze da parte di visitatori stranieri di passaggio in Italia.

quali leggono [...] Inoltre i cantori, a loro discrezione, inseriscono nella melodia una moltitudine di abbellimenti, di note di passaggio e di ritardi [...] Questa aggiunta di ghirigori d'ogni specie porta nella Sistina a numerose distorsioni, e bisogna ammettere che oggigiorno molte composizioni vengono deturpate da un'ornamentazione inadeguata[38].

Per ritornare ancora una volta a Paganini, la sua abilità di improvvisatore si esplica anche sulla chitarra: davanti a Karol Lipiński, violinista polacco ammiratore di Paganini, quest'ultimo improvvisa alla chitarra un accompagnamento di uno studio per violino solo composto e eseguito dallo stesso Lipiński (p. 125): «ora provavo per lui una sconfinata ammirazione come virtuoso di chitarra e per l'enorme talento dimostrato nel rendere lo spirito della mia composizione e nell'improvvisare un così stupendo accompagnamento»[39]. I fatti narrati nell'aneddoto si svolsero nella città di Piacenza nel 1818, anche se la narrazione di Lipiński è piuttosto confusa. Ancora in altra occasione, Paganini improvvisa questa volta a Bologna, con Rossini seduto al cembalo in casa Pegnalver[40].

L'arte virtuosistica di Paganini, come è stato più volte sottolineato, scaturisce in parte da questa lunga tradizione di improvvisazione di abbellimenti italiana, la cui principale derivazione è stata individuata nella 'Scuola delle Nazioni' di Tartini e che è stata tramandata in alcuni importanti trattati, come quello di Johann Joachim Quantz e quello di Leopold Mozart[41]. Essa proviene inoltre da una prassi di variazione e rielaborazione estemporanea il cui metodo è parte della didattica dello strumento in Italia, almeno da quanto possiamo arguire dalle testimonianze dei violinisti contemporanei e precedenti a Paganini.

[38]. Kantner, Leopold - Pachovsky, Angela. *La cappella musicale Pontificia nell'Ottocento*, Roma, Hortus Musicus, 1998 (Storia della Cappella Musicale Pontificia, 6), cap. ii: 'Prassi esecutiva', p. 69. Ancora nell'Ottocento, la prassi esecutiva della Cappella Pontificia era tenuta gelosamente riservata. In effetti Pachovsky dice che i documenti tacciono in proposito e che pertanto le principali fonti per noi sono i «racconti dei viaggiatori coevi» (p. 65). A p. 66 aggiunge Pachovsky: «Caratteristico della prassi esecutiva sistina era l'uso di diverse forme di improvvisazione sia nel canto fermo ('contrappunto alla mente', 'falsobordone', 'girelli') sia nel repertorio polifonico ('abbellimenti')». Tra le diverse improvvisazioni, i cantori della Cappella Sistina avevano l'abitudine di aggiungere sulle note finali dei canti gregoriani degli ornamenti, che potevano essere mordenti, appoggiature, trilli, gruppetti; erano i cosiddetti 'girelli'. A proposito del 'contrappunto alla mente' in uso presso i cantori pontifici, lo stesso padre Giovanni Battista Martini, nel suo *Saggio fondamentale di contrappunto*, testimonia di averlo ascoltato nel 1747 a Roma nella Basilica Patriarcale di S. Giovanni Laterano. La citazione è tratta dalla voce 'Contrappunto alla mente' in Lichtenthal, Pietro. *Dizionario e bibliografia della musica*, Milano, Antonio Fontana, 1836, p. 199. Alla voce 'Improvvisare', pp. 327-328, Lichtenthal aggiunge: «Per improvvisare però con successo nella musica, bisogna essere iniziato a fondo nell'arte, e particolarmente in tutte le specie del Contrappunto, essere padrone assoluto dello strumento su cui si improvvisa, aver inoltre un'anima che s'esalti facilmente ed uno spirito sempre presente, acciò vi sia dell'unità ne' pensieri che compongono un pezzo creato di questa maniera».

[39]. *Niccolò Paganini. Epistolario [...]*, *op. cit.* (si veda nota 7), p. 125.

[40]. *Ibidem*, p. 137, nota 4.

[41]. Quantz, Johann Joachim. *Versuch einer Anweisung, die Flöte traversiere zu spielen*, Berlino, Johann Friedrich Voss, 1752; Mozart, Leopold. *Versuch einer gründlichen Violinschule*, Augusta, Johann Jacob Lotter, 1756.

Un altro aspetto strettamente correlato alla prassi della improvvisazione è quello della lettura a prima vista, abilità nella quale sappiamo eccelleva lo stesso Paganini.

Sull'abitudine del suonare all'improvviso tra Sette e Ottocento — su cui si veda l'ultimo capitolo del trattato sopra l'arte del suonare il violino di Francesco Galeazzi — abbiamo numerose testimonianze: è lo stesso Burney ad informarci ad esempio che a Roma fu costretto a suonare a prima vista una sonata di Gaetano Pugnani, mentre qualche giorno dopo, sempre a Roma, gli toccò la lettura a prima vista di alcuni trii manoscritti del medesimo compositore[42].

Una traccia significativa del lavoro improvvisativo di Paganini virtuoso e compositore sarebbe forse desumibile dalle note vicende relative all'introduzione delle 'Variazioni sulla quarta corda' sul *Mosè* di Rossini, dello stesso Paganini. È forse possibile che la parte introduttiva venisse ogni volta improvvisata (o meglio variata estemporaneamente) dallo stesso Paganini come era da sempre prassi, e che pertanto questi non abbia ritenuto il caso di fermarne e divulgarne una versione definitiva sulla carta?

Nulla come il concetto di 'improvvisazione' acquista in musica una pervasività così ampia, senza confini di spazio, genere e tempo. Dalle forme di musica popolare fino ai livelli più diversi della musica colta nelle più diverse aree geografiche è possibile riscontrare l'improvvisazione. La musica, nel suo nucleo più profondo è arte dell'improvvisazione per eccellenza[43]. Possiamo rilevarlo ad ogni livello del far musica; qualsiasi periodizzazione dal Medioevo ai nostri giorni ne è interessata. In particolare, nel periodo oggetto di studio di questo convegno, l'improvvisazione costituisce il *trait d'union* tra composizione ed esecuzione virtuosistica. Ma il concetto di improvvisazione, così ampio nel suo significato per quanto attiene il periodo e il genere di musica qui considerato, implica anche altre possibili chiavi di lettura e nodi problematici: in particolare mi riferisco al tipo di approccio nei confronti del testo musicale da parte del musicista contemporaneo a Paganini.

Sto cercando di chiarire i modi della lettura del testo musicale da parte del musicista di due secoli fa, certamente dissimili da parte del musicista interprete dei medesimi testi oggi. Se l'approccio odierno al testo musicale scritto è ben diverso rispetto a quello di primo Ottocento, di questa differenza il compositore, nell'atto di porre per iscritto le proprie musiche, doveva per forza di cose tenere conto. È noto che il testo scritto non era quanto in realtà veniva effettivamente eseguito e non solo per l'uso sapiente ed energico di abbellimenti e diminuzioni, ma anche per la ricerca di varietà nelle ripetizioni e per il concetto di 'variazione' (secondo quanto afferma il Galeazzi) quale banco di prova per il musicista delle sue effettive conoscenze in materia di contrappunto.

---

[42]. BURNEY, Charles. *The Present State of Music in France* [...], *op. cit.* (si veda nota 3), pp. 349, 353.

[43]. JANKÉLÉVITCH, Vladimir. 'Dell'improvvisazione', traduzione di Alessandro Arbo, in: *Nuova Rivista Musicale Italiana*, XXVII (1993), pp. 227-253, p. 231: «l'improvvisazione è il primo passo dell'invenzione creatrice a partire dal nulla, dal foglio bianco».

L'improvvisazione come arte della variazione brillante nella musica colta del secondo Ottocento giunge ad assumere un connotato negativo, come qualcosa di superficiale, scadente «concessione al cattivo gusto della folla», come afferma Giuseppe Depanis nel 1879 a proposito di certa musica di Giovanni Bottesini[44]. Come si vede, il gusto per l'improvvisazione e soprattutto certa tinta improvvisativa in musica sono ormai pervenuti a netta decadenza anche in Italia.

---

[44]. Citazione da Martinotti, Sergio. *Ottocento strumentale italiano*, Bologna, Forni, 1972, p. 315.

CARMELA BONGIOVANNI

ENGLISH SUMMARY

EVIDENCE OF THE PRACTICE OF IMPROVISATION BY ITALIAN MUSICIANS
IN THE EIGHTEENTH AND NINETEENTH CENTURIES

Carmela Bongiovanni

The practice of improvisation has a long and extraordinary tradition in Italian music of the eighteenth and nineteenth centuries. The practice of musical improvisation developed in Italy simultaneously with a successful practice of extempore poetry, by poets who were acclaimed as virtuosos by contemporary audiences. Two kinds of sources are available for the study of the practice of improvisation by Italian musicians during the two centuries mentioned. Firstly there are contemporary texts on music history and theory, nowadays often studied and cited, for instance, the travel accounts by Charles Burney and the celebrated treatise by Francesco Galeazzi, perhaps the most important text regarding improvisatory practice on the violin. These reports are complemented by the direct affirmations of virtuosos in their double role as interpreters and composers; the memoirs of Nicola Petrini Zamboni are just one example. Other sources of great importance are chronicles and letters which gather and convey the reactions of listeners and music critics to public and private performances of Italian composers and virtuosos. The study of these sources brings to light a wide practice of improvisation by musicians of different kinds, from the musician-composer (as, for example, Nicolò Paganini, but also Ferdinando Paer) to the local virtuoso player. These practices lead to various results, each with its own characteristics, depending on the circumstances. Later on in the nineteenth century improvisation would develop into a superficial show of technical ability.

«L'orecchio più che 'l tempo dee servire di guida» L'improvvisazione nella trattatistica italiana del secondo Settecento

Mariateresa Dellaborra
(Pavia)

Relativamente al tema dell'improvvisazione, i trattati di autori italiani sia manoscritti sia editi nel secondo Settecento formalizzano, in modo pressoché sistematico e costante, alcune soluzioni anche se destinate a strumenti differenti. La disamina cercherà di evidenziare la varietà degli atteggiamenti e di fornire nel contempo un quadro quanto più possibile vasto e approfondito degli argomenti: suggerimenti per meglio rendere concretamente 'affetti' e specifici passaggi; riferimenti al repertorio contemporaneo o del passato come paradigma da seguire o evitare; buoni e cattivi maestri, compositori autorevoli nonché differenze o eccezioni nella realizzazione di certi procedimenti pratici a riprova ulteriore della discrepanza tra teoria e prassi.

La necessità dell'improvvisazione nasce, secondo Francesco Galeazzi, da un motivo ben preciso, da una contingenza legata alla natura stessa della scrittura musicale:

> Scrivesi la musica in un modo purtroppo sì complicato e confuso, che non permette al compositore di notare tutto ciò appuntino, che gli sta in mente, e deve necessariamente per non rendere ineseguibili le sue carte, lasciar molto all'arbitrio dell'esecutore; tocca dunque a questi il supplire di suo capriccio, a ciò che non ha espresso il compositore; richiedesi però a quest'effetto l'arte più fina, il più savio discernimento, e qui principalmente campeggia il suo buono, e cattivo gusto, in una parola il suo genio musicale[1].

L'imperfezione o meglio la complessità della grafia musicale porta inevitabilmente l'autore a lasciare campo all'esecutore che, secondo il suo gusto personale, può completare il pensiero originario. Ma per compiere in modo appropriato tale operazione, occorre possedere doti musicali che vengono dettagliate nel momento in cui il teorico si prefigge di definire il

---

[1]. Galeazzi, Francesco. *Elementi teorico-pratici di musica […] Tomo secondo*, Roma, Michele Puccinelli, 1796, Articolo XV, Comma 230, p. 190.

virtuoso: «titolo che non si acquista se non si possiede il genio dell'arte, ciò che in pratica dicesi lo stile. Un suonator senza stile è un materiale accozzator di suoni, che non sa dar anima, e sentimento a ciò che eseguisce, e che per conseguenza non può sperar mai di recar diletto, e dar piacere agli ascoltanti»[2]. I due cardini dello stile sono «l'ornamento, e l'espressione»[3].

Precisato dunque che il momento creativo è indispensabile per l'interprete del Settecento, è altresì indubbio che la lezione tramandata sulla carta deve essere rivissuta appieno dall'esecutore e dunque 'completata', arricchita con estro estemporaneo.

Innanzitutto può essere interessante riferire come il termine 'improvvisazione' venga definito in due testi autorevoli che si potrebbero considerare come *terminus a quo* e *terminus ad quem* dell'indagine: il *Dictionnaire de musique* di Jean-Jacques Rousseau (del 1768) e il *Dizionario e bibliografia della musica* di Pietro Lichtenthal (del 1836). Nel primo:

> Improvvisare è fare e cantare estemporaneamente canti, arie e parole, che si accompagnano comunemente con una chitarra o un altro strumento simile. Non c'è niente di più comune in Italia che vedere due maschere incontrarsi, sfidarsi, attaccarsi, contrattaccarsi in questo modo, con delle strofe sulla stessa aria, con una vivacità di dialogo, di canto, d'accompagnamento, di cui bisogna essere stati testimoni per comprenderla. Il verbo 'improvvisar' è specificamente italiano, ma, poiché riguarda la musica, sono stato costretto a francesizzarlo, per far intendere cosa significhi[4].

Nel secondo:

> Improvvisare comporre ed eseguire *ex tempore* un pezzo di musica vocale o strumentale. Essendo la musica un linguaggio naturale, perfettamente regolare e conforme alla nostra organizzazione, egli è più facile d'improvvisare in questo linguaggio che in quello di cui le parole sono di convenzione. Per improvvisare però con successo nella musica, bisogna esser iniziato a fondo nell'arte, e particolarmente in tutte le specie del contropunto, essere padrone assoluto dello strumento su cui si improvvisa, aver inoltre un'anima che s'esalti facilmente ed uno spirito sempre presente, acciò vi sia dell'unità ne' pensieri che compongono un pezzo creato di questa maniera[5].

---

[2]. *Ibidem*, Comma 229, p. 190.

[3]. *Ibidem*.

[4]. ROUSSEAU, Jean-Jacques. *Dictionnaire de musique*, Parigi, Veuve Duchesne, 1768, p. 252: «Improviser c'est faire & chanter impromptu des chansons, airs & paroles, qu'on accompagne communément d'une guitarre ou autre pareil instrument. Il n'y a rien de plus commun en Italie, que de voir deux masques se rencontrer, se défier, s'attaquer, se riposter ainsi par des couplets sur le même air, avec une vivacité de dialogue, de chant, d'accompagnement dont il faut avoir été témoin pour le comprendre. Le mot *improvisar* est purement italien: mais comme il se rapporte à la musique, j'ai été contraint de le franciser pour faire entendre ce qu'il signifie». Questo passo, al pari di tutti quelli trascritti segue la grafia originale, ad eccezione delle maiuscole uniformate all'uso moderno.

[5]. LICHTENTHAL, Pietro. *Dizionario e bibliografia della musica*, 4 voll., Milano, Antonio Fontana, 1836, vol. I, pp. 307-308.

Rousseau indica un contesto preciso e un repertorio particolare in cui fare pratica di improvvisazione: fa riferimento a brani vocali e specificamente accompagnati da chitarra o da altri strumenti che possano provvedere a un sostegno ritmico e armonico simile. E sottolinea parimenti che si tratta di una pratica tipicamente italiana, sconosciuta all'ambiente francese, probabilmente derivata dal teatro, in quanto allude a un dialogo tra maschere in cui si inserisce anche il canto e l'accompagnamento, tutti rigorosamente creati estemporaneamente. Lichtenthal invece estende la pratica dell'improvvisazione anche alla musica strumentale, sottolineando il fatto che risulti semplice improvvisare nella musica più che in ogni altra disciplina o arte. Perché si possa procedere con logica ed efficacia è tuttavia indispensabile padroneggiare le regole di composizione e di contrappunto e conoscere a fondo la tecnica dello strumento che si sta suonando. Scopo dell'improvvisazione, o meglio, riuscita perfetta dell'improvvisazione si avrà soltanto se il prodotto finale sarà unitario e logico in tutte le sue parti, dunque se produrrà un effetto compiuto, paradossalmente quasi di brano scritto. Il critico però si spinge anche oltre nel momento in cui definisce la fantasia:

> Attiva e vivace facoltà della mente, la quale crea nuove idee ed immagini alla composizione d'idee e di immagini già avute. Essa differisce dall'immaginazione, la quale non è altro che la facoltà di richiamare alla mente idee già avute: la prima è dunque produttiva e creatrice e l'altra riproduttiva. [...] ma l'artista nel sonar e cantar estemporaneamente è vero creatore e sovrano nel regno de' suoni. Quindi la parola fantasia significa nella musica una cosa inventata a piacere, e nella quale si ha seguito piuttosto il capriccio che le regole dell'arte; oppure un componimento che non è soggetto né a misure fisse, né a ritmi decisi, né ad una disposizione e condotta regolare, né ad un carattere determinato; ma in cui l'artista rappresenta le immagini della sua fantasia senza piano notabile ed in certo grado d'irregolarità, or in frasi sconnesse ed interrotte, or in semplici accordi ec. Di siffatta qualità è fra le altre quella *fantasia* che ordinariamente si chiama *cadenza*, avendo luogo al fine del pezzo di musica, immediatamente innanzi la cadenza[6].

Il musicista che improvvisa è un vero creatore in quanto sbriglia la propria fantasia nel momento finale della cadenza — una delle tante accezioni previste per il termine — sia per richiamare pensieri già noti ed espressi nel corso del brano sia per librare le proprie idee secondo un istinto personale. L'improvvisazione ovviamente può riguardare sia l'accompagnamento sia la parte principale[7].

---

6. *Ibidem*, pp. 270-271. I corsivi sono originali.
7. I trattati consultati sono elencati in appendice.

Improvvisazione dell'accompagnamento

Almeno tre settori sono coinvolti nell'improvvisazione dell'accompagnamento: (1) il ruolo dell'accompagnatore; (2) le regole per condurre il basso continuo; e (3) le tipologie di repertorio, su due filoni: musica strumentale *versus* vocale e pochi *versus* tanti strumenti.

Francesco Manfredini nelle sue *Regole armoniche* (1775) prospetta tre tipi di accompagnamento del basso, il terzo dei quali si pratica «allorquando il basso è solo e senz'alcun numero, nel qual caso s'accompagna, regolandosi secondo l'andamento, o sia movimento del medesimo, o coll'ascoltare attentamente quello, che nello stesso tempo esprimono le parti»[8]. E in nota aggiunge: «Quest'ultima maniera di accompagnare è la più difficile, soprattutto per chi non è pratico abbastanza».

Nella realizzazione del basso, quando non ci siano vincoli fissati dal compositore, è possibile dunque improvvisare, ma per farlo nel modo più puntuale e in linea con l'idea originaria, è indispensabile cogliere il carattere e l'andamento del brano nella sua totalità e verificare il movimento delle voci che si accompagnano. Nell'esecuzione estemporanea, inoltre, il continuista non dovrà coprire le restanti sezioni, ma rimanere in subordine[9], scegliendo la tipologia di realizzazione più consona. L'improvvisazione consisterà pertanto nel creare scarne armonie, evitando di introdurre abbellimenti o altre linee melodiche che raddoppino quella principale[10].

Auspice del medesimo atteggiamento è Giovanni Battista Rangoni quando sottolinea, nel suo *Saggio sul gusto della musica* (1790), che l'accompagnamento deve essere «semplice ed ingenuo» e chi accompagna deve «dimenticare se stesso per far risaltare e trionfare colui che è accompagnato». Introdurre ornamentazioni, dunque, farcire a dismisura la parte, potrebbe risultare addirittura controproducente perché distoglierebbe l'attenzione dell'ascoltatore dalle parti fondamentali e contrasterebbe con la natura stessa della composizione. L'improvvisazione con «ornamenti superflui e a capriccio come variazioni, grazie ed arpeggi», dettata solo dal desiderio di ostentare la propria bravura e per «sciocca vanità», getterebbe di conseguenza l'interprete «nella derisione e nel disprezzo del pubblico»[11].

---

[8]. Manfredini, Francesco. *Regole armoniche*, Venezia, Guglielmo Zerletti, 1775, p. 30.

[9]. *Ibidem*, p. 63: «Il termine solo di accompagnare denota abbastanza quali sieno i doveri dell'accompagnatore, cioè d'esser soggetto, e non di comandare».

[10]. *Ibidem*: «Deve dunque chi accompagna sonare il basso come sta scritto, e non sempre gli accordi, né raddoppiarli colla mano sinistra, se non quando vi ha bisogno di far molto rumore; come p.e. in una grande orchestra, o in una musica ecclesiastica a più cori; ma accompagnando un cantante solo, o un sol sonatore, deve colla sinistra mano eseguire il basso solo, o al più aggiungergli l'ottava, e con la destra, far poca armonia. Deve ancora tralasciar di esprimere certe galanterie, o sieno adornamenti: e molto meno deve compor sopra il basso un canto, invece di dargli solamente gli accordi più necessari, il quale essendo lo stesso di quello, che eseguisce il sonatore, ovvero il cantante, farà cattivo effetto il sentirlo duplicato; e non essendo il medesimo arrecherà una discordanza insoffribile».

[11]. Rangoni, Giovanni Battista. *Saggio sul gusto della musica*, Livorno, Tommaso Masi, 1790, p. 69: «Ogni ornamento, capace di distrarre l'orecchio del cantore e dividere l'attenzione dello spettatore, è

Secondo Antonio Tonelli tuttavia, nel trattato manoscritto *Teorica musicale* (ante 1760), un valido e interessante sistema di «rinvigorir l'armonia» è introdurre «acciaccature (e queste sono ottime per li cembalisti)», mentre per «infiorire l'accompagnamento s'adoprino degli arpeggi, contrattempi, trilli, appoggiature, mordenti ed altri ornamenti di buon gusto e maniera»[12]. Se invece fosse un violino ad accompagnarne un altro, il quale, solo, deve «eseguire all'improvviso francamente, e senza esitare la propria parte», secondo Galeazzi «bisogna proscrivere ogni ornamento e diminuzione, e suonare liscio, e schietto; solo si permette qualche appoggiatura dove sia necessario per unir l'espressione»[13]. Nell'invenzione estemporanea conta dunque molto il tipo di composizione che si sta eseguendo. Se infatti si tratta di recitativo secco, «è d'uopo regolarsi sempre alla parte cantante»; se invece si dovesse suonare solo saltuariamente «dopo il cantante, questo si fa solo dopo avere sentito l'ultima sillaba, col dovuto movimento e tempo», stando al parere di Antonio Lorenzoni nel *Saggio per ben sonare il flautotraverso* (1779)[14].

Inoltre, secondo un anonimo settecentesco, nel recitativo sono spesso presenti molte modulazioni non condotte sulla base delle regole dei manuali, ma allineate con l'unico scopo di «esprimere la varietà degli affetti, che richiedono le parole»[15]. Qualunque sia la lezione scritta dall'autore, nell'improvvisazione occorre però, secondo un altro anonimo, «procurare che sempre le mani vadino di moto contrario, cioè se una và in su l'altra venga in giù, come pure sonare il più unito che si puole cioè in slontanarle gran cosa una mano da l'altra, et osservare di sonar sempre nel mezzo del istrumento, delle consonanze imperfette se né possono fare una dietro l'altra quanto uno vuole»[16].

La questione della padronanza della materia, prima di procedere a qualunque improvvisazione, è sostenuta da diversi teorici. Tra i più strenui va annoverato Padre Francescantonio Vallotti, che propugna anche la necessità di introdurre «figure diverse» ottenute con il «vario movimento delle parti», da farsi anche in modo non ortodosso, sia nella melodia che nell'armonia «per sfuggire la nauseosa monotonia»[17]. Tuttavia la varietà

---

inopportuno, ed in una voce o in un sono a solo, sarebbe contrario all'indole della composizione, e ne guasterebbe l'effetto».

[12]. TONELLI, Antonio. *Teorica musicale ordinata alla moderna pratica*, Manoscritto, I-Bc, L.54, fol. 36v.

[13]. GALEAZZI, Francesco. *Op. cit.* (si veda nota 1), Articolo xx, Comma 304, p. 228.

[14]. LORENZONI, Antonio. *Saggio per ben sonare il flautotraverso*, Vicenza, Francesco Modena, 1779, § 85, p. 49.

[15]. ANONIMO. *Regole per accompagnare*, Manoscritto, I-Bc, I.37, fol. 9v, anche MARTINI, Giovanni Battista. *Regole per accompagnare*, Bologna, 1761, Manoscritto, I-Bc, I.51, fol. 9v, Regola 95. Lo sostiene anche l'anonimo autore delle *Regole per sonare il cembalo*, Manoscritto, I-Bc, P.132, fol. 79r: «molte volte li compositori, si pigliano delle licenze che non si possono insegnare se non con una lunga pratica». È per questo che si deve «guardar sempre alla parte che canta per poter antivedere gli accompagnamenti».

[16]. ANONIMO. *Regole per sonare il cembalo*, Manoscritto, I-Bc, P.132, fol. 79v. Tale concetto è assicurato anche in ANONIMO. *Regole per accompagnare la scala*, Manoscritto, I-Bc, H.71, fol. 88r.

[17]. VALLOTTI, Francescantonio. *Trattato della moderna musica*, Manoscritto, I-Pca, edizione moderna a cura di Giancarlo Zanon, Padova, Biblioteca Antoniana-Basilica del Santo, 1950, Libro III, Cap. XXXVI, p. 373. Parimenti CAMPAGNOLI, Bartolomeo. *Nuovo metodo della mecanica progressiva per suonare il violino*, Firenze,

non deve mai essere disgiunta dall'invenzione logica e unitaria e quindi deve creare un effetto omogeneo. Suggerisce quindi alcuni procedimenti da considerare utilmente al fine di improvvisare: «motivi proposti da strumenti devono essere continuati non sempre in identità ma spesso in rassomiglianza»; introdurre varietà dei tempi, tenendo tuttavia in conto il loro adattamento al senso delle parole.

Altro elemento legato alla pratica improvvisativa potrebbe ritrovarsi nell'impiegare diversi timbri strumentali cui affidare a turno l'esecuzione, oppure nel ricorrere all'uso di effetti speciali quali «pizzicati e sordini», dai quali devono tuttavia fuggire i compositori di chiesa. «Per ogni conto introdur conviene una varietà maschia e modesta che insieme con l'unità del modo formi un composto dilettevole, ragionato e maestoso», come indica Vallotti[18]. Galeazzi ribadisce che nell'improvvisazione occorre fare in modo che «tutto ciò che si fa riesca polito, e sensibile, né si perda cosa alcuna, e di evitare le noiose ripetizioni introducendo sempre una piacevole varietà, senza però dipartirsi mai da quella bella unità, che forma il più prezioso carattere di tutte le belle arti»[19].

Per poter improvvisare degnamente è comunque indispensabile, secondo Tonelli, «suonare in partitura, poiché da quella s'ottiene la guida più certa, e sicura d'un più fino, e valido accompagnamento»[20].

In generale la regola aurea è che «l'orecchio più che 'l tempo dee servire di guida» (Lorenzoni[21]) ed è l'esercizio, la pratica che aiuta a procedere nel modo opportuno[22],

---

Ricordi, [1797], p. 36, prescrive che chi ornamenta conosca le leggi dell'armonia e controlli il movimento del basso. In generale è indispensabile imparare a ben leggere prima di darsi agli abbellimenti e Galeazzi sollecita lo studio del contrappunto, «studio troppo necessario e troppo negletto, senza del quale è quasi impossibile il giungere alla perfezione in qualunque parte della musica». Tra gli altri vantaggi esso assicura di «non uscir d'armonia nel diminuire, e rivestire specialmente i Larghi, come pur troppo accade a molti anche classici professori». Si veda GALEAZZI, Francesco. *Elementi teorico-pratici di musica* [...] *Tomo primo*, Roma, Pilucchi Cracas, 1791, Articolo XIV, Comma 131, p. 61.

[18]. VALLOTTI, Francescantonio. *Op. cit.* (si veda nota 17), Libro III, Cap. XXXVI, p. 374.
[19]. GALEAZZI, Francesco. *Op. cit.* (si veda nota 1), Articolo XVI, Comma 259, p. 119.
[20]. TONELLI, Antonio. *Op.cit.* (si veda nota 12), Comma 5, fol. 36v.
[21]. LORENZONI, Antonio. *Op. cit.* (si veda nota 14), p. 49.
[22]. Lo sostiene ad esempio TOMEONI, Pellegrino. *Regole pratiche per accompagnare il basso continuo*, Firenze, Anton Giuseppe Pagani, 1795, p. 39, § 'Delle imitazioni, Dialogo sesto': «Siccome l'imitazioni sono varie, così non le potrete concepire se non coll'atto pratico», lo ribadiscono l'Anonimo estensore delle *Regole per accompagnare* (si veda nota 15), Regola 95, fol. 9v, quando afferma che alla conoscenza delle regole si deve aggiungere la riflessione e «con l'esercizio, e la pazienza, si avrà il compimento dell'opera» e MANCINI, Giambattista. *Riflessioni pratiche sul canto figurato*, Milano, Giuseppe Galeazzi, 1777, Articolo XI, p. 181, 'Delle cadenze': «Sarà un gran vantaggio l'esser dotato di una mente creativa (e questi sono quei tratti dell'estro inaspettati ed improvvisi, parti della mente creatrice, che fanno in un punto distinguer l'uomo, e portarlo coll'evviva alle stelle). E per questo richiedesi un retto giudizio, ch'è necessario per formarne un perfetto ammasso. Ognuno è in grado d'acquistare tutte queste necessarie qualità collo studio. E benché la mente creatrice sia ordinariamente puro dono della natura, pure, combattendo con lo studio, si può ottenere per acquisto a tal segno, che basti a non far lo studioso cattiva comparsa».

facendo comprendere con precisione che «nulla è più difficile da cogliere quanto il vero movimento e lo spirito dei brani che si stanno eseguendo; spesso hanno un carattere, una fisionomia particolare la cui espressione dipende da una differenza sottile nella celerità ovvero la lentezza dell'esecuzione», secondo le parole di Florido Tomeoni, nella sua *Théorie de la musique vocale* (1799)[23], tenendo anche in debito conto lo stile che si vuole seguire. La maniera italiana, in generale, prevede una ricca e animata realizzazione; quella francese invece più rada ed essenziale[24].

IMPROVVISAZIONE DELLA PARTE PRINCIPALE

Relativamente alla parte principale, l'improvvisazione è concentrata nelle cadenze e nell'introduzione degli abbellimenti se si intende variare una sezione. La cadenza infatti è il luogo deputato all'invenzione estemporanea. Lo conferma Rousseau quando ne offre la definizione:

> *Cadenza*, parola italiana, con la quale si indica una fermata (*point d'orgue*) non scritta, e che l'autore lascia alla volontà di colui che esegue la parte principale, affinché faccia, in merito al carattere dell'aria, i passaggi più adatti alla sua voce, al suo strumento ovvero al suo gusto. [...] Si chiama anche 'arbitrio', a causa della libertà che vi si lascia all'esecutore nell'abbandonarsi alle proprie idee, e nel seguire il proprio gusto. La musica francese, particolarmente quella vocale, che è estremamente servile, non lascia al cantante alcuna simile libertà, di cui perfino sarebbe imbarazzato a servirsi[25].

---

[23]. TOMEONI, Florido. *Théorie de la musique vocale*, Parigi, Charles Pougens, [1799], p. 83: «Rien en effet n'est plus difficile à saisir que le vrai mouvement et l'esprit des morceaux que l'on exécute; ils ont souvent un caractère, une physionomie particulière dont l'expression dépend d'une différence légère dans la vitesse ou la lenteur de l'exécution». Prosegue ponendosi in linea con i teorici precedenti (nota 17) affermando che «L'aplomb de la phrase musicale fait l'excellence du chant; mais c'est une qualité que donne seule la pratique, et que l'on ne peut acquérir que par une grande habitude».

[24]. ID. *Méthode qui apprend la connoissance de l'harmonie et la pratique de l'accompagnement selon les principes de l'école de Naples, dédiée aux amateurs*, Parigi, Vanglenne, [1798], p. 19: «Dans les mouvements lents on frappe souvent l'accord sur chaque note; dans les mouvements vifs on fait de même, et c'est selon la manière italienne; la manière française consiste à frapper l'accord plus rarement, c'est-à-dire au commencement de la mesure ou à chaque temps; mais tout cela dépend du goût». Su questo argomento offre il suo contributo, che si allinea con le affermazioni riferite, ROUSSEAU, Jean-Jacques. *Op. cit.* (si veda nota 4), p. 13.

[25]. ROUSSEAU, Jean-Jacques. *Op. cit.* (si veda nota 4), p. 69: «cadenza s.f. mot italien, par lequel on indique un point d'orgue non écrit, & que l'auteur laisse à la volonté de celui qui exécute la partie principale, à fin qu'il fasse, relativement au caractère de l'air, les passages les plus convenables à sa voix, à son instrument, ou à son goût. [...] Il s'appelle aussi *arbitrio*, à cause de la liberté qu'on y laisse à l'exécutant de se livrer à ses idées, et de suivre son propre goût. La musique française, sur tout la vocale, qui est extrêmement servile, ne laisse au chanteur aucune pareille liberté, dont même il seroit embarassé de faire usage». Corsivo originale.

E lo ribadisce Lichtenthal:

> Cadenza, s.f. fantasia libera che il suonatore di concerto o il cantante
> fanno sentire al termine del pezzo musicale, ove la cadenza nella tonica viene
> fermata sull'accordo di quarta e sesta mediante una così detta corona, o fermata.
> Il compositore dà con ciò occasione al cantante, e particolarmente al sonatore di
> concerto, d'improvvisare il contenuto principale del componimento dietro il suo
> individuale sentimento a guisa di fantasia, tenendo sempre in mente l'idea principale
> del pezzo, ovvero concatenando il più breve possibile le sue idee principali[26].

Le due definizioni presentano un fondamentale tratto comune: è indispensabile che
l'invenzione del solista, sia esso cantante o strumentista, prosegua idealmente il carattere e lo
stile del brano originario. Secondo Lichtenthal sarebbe altresì opportuno che l'invenzione
non si prolungasse a lungo; Rousseau invece rimarca che si tratta di una prassi tipicamente
italiana, essendo i francesi più ligi alla lezione autoriale.

L'atteggiamento degli esecutori, secondo i trattatisti, dovrebbe differenziarsi sulla
base del repertorio strumentale e vocale. Nella pratica invece ciò non avviene e i teorici
lo rilevano con grande disappunto non soltanto perché i cantanti si comportano come
strumentisti, ma anche perché si improvvisa senza la minima intelligenza e buon gusto. Per
Galeazzi «è più difficile il cantare che il sonare» anche se il cantante già dal frontespizio vede
quale passione dovrà trarre dal brano[27]; per Giuseppe Tartini «gli strumentisti possiedono più
libertà e più facilità dei cantanti, perché ci sono molti modi e andamenti che convengono
agli strumenti e che la voce non può eseguire, e questi passaggi producono sempre un
buon effetto»[28]. L'autore fornisce quindi un'abbondante casistica di situazioni[29].

Francesco Algarotti, nel suo *Saggio sopra l'opera in musica* (1755), rimprovera i cantanti
non solo per l'incessante introduzione di passaggi fioriti, ma anche perché «adattano le
stesse grazie musicali ad ogni sorta di cantilena; e co' loro passaggi, co' loro trilli, e colle
loro spezzature fioriscono, infrascano, e disfigurano ogni cosa»[30]. La qual cosa equipara,
secondo il teorico, in un modo non condivisibile, il repertorio strumentale a quello
vocale. «Il qual vizio volea rimproverare a un suo scolare quel maestro dicendo: "Tristo
a me, io t'ho insegnato a cantare, e tu vuoi sonare"»[31]. Sarebbe preferibile addirittura

---

[26]. LICHTENTHAL, Pietro. *Op. cit.* (si veda nota 5), vol. I, p. 109.

[27]. GALEAZZI, Francesco. *Op. cit.* (si veda nota 1), Articolo XVI, Comma 254, p. 197.

[28]. TARTINI, Giuseppe. *Traité des agrémens de la musique*, Parigi, Pierre Denis, [1771], p. 86: «les joueurs
d'instruments ont plus de liberté et de facilité que les chanteurs, parce qu'il y a beaucoup de modes ou de
traits qui conviennent aux instruments et que la voix ne peut exécuter, lesquels traits produisent toujours un
bon effet».

[29]. *Ibidem*: «Ces modes artificiels de bon gout consistent dans les échelles montantes et descendantes
qu'on peut varier presque à l'infini». Gli esempi si estendono a pp. 86-94.

[30]. ALGAROTTI, Francesco. *Saggio sopra l'opera in musica*, [Venezia, G. Pasquali, 1755], p. 19.

[31]. *Ibidem*. Nella seconda edizione Livorno, Marco Coltellini, 1763, p. 46, la frase è pronunciata da
Francesco Antonio Mamiliano Pistocchi a Antonio Bernacchi.

non «lasciare al musico libertà nel cantare», ma adottare la «pratica dei Franzesi, che non permettono a' loro musici quegli arbitrj, de' quali troppo sovente sogliono abusare i nostri; e gli riducono ad essere, quali pur esser debbono, meri esecutori». A pochi interpreti infatti «dovrebbono esser permesse le mutazioni nelle arie; come a quelli che possono ben entrare nella intenzione del maestro, e non sogliono aver dispareri, come si dice, col basso, e coll'andamento degli strumenti»[32]. E prosegue sottolineando che «per le stesse ragioni non si vorrebbe abbandonare al musicista la cadenza, che d'ordinario riesce di tutt'altro colore che non l'aria. Ella sembra, dice il Tosi, la girandola di Castel San Angelo, a cui i nostri virtuosi dan fuoco in sul fine dell'aria. E la cadenza non dovrebbe essere altro in sostanza, che la perorazione dell'aria medesima». Si rimarca ancora una volta una differenza sostanziale tra prassi francese e italiana: nella prima non sono ammesse interferenze da parte degli esecutori, nella seconda sì, pur correndo il rischio di produrre qualcosa di poco consono allo spirito dell'autore e non in linea con le caratteristiche del brano.

Molto pragmatico Lorenzoni che innanzitutto definisce cosa intenda per cadenza: «quell'adornamento arbitrario, che si dà della parte principale, secondo la volontà e fantasia di colui ch'eseguisce, alla quinta del modo, nel quale il pezzo è composto, accompagnata dalla quarta, e sesta»[33]. Peculiarità della cadenza è di non «avere alcun riguardo al tempo»[34], e su questo punto trova conforto nel passo di Tartini a proposito delle «cadenze artificiali sulle quali il cantante o lo strumentista si ferma ad arbitrio e senza riguardare la misura»[35]. Lorenzoni inoltre si preoccupa di rimarcare che «le cadenze debbono essere dedotte dalla passione che regna principalmente nel pezzo. Imperciocchè come si confarebbe una cadenza mesta in un pezzo allegro, un'allegra in un pezzo mesto?»[36]. In sostanza l'improvvisazione nella cadenza dovrebbe proporsi come una «ripetizione, per così dire, della melodia contenuta nel pezzo»[37], ma senza eccedere «per non cagionare tedio»[38], soprattutto mantenendo lo stesso carattere[39], e senza vagare per modi diversi da quello primigenio, nel caso fosse di breve estensione; in caso contrario potrebbe peregrinare secondo una certa regola[40].

---

[32]. Fa riferimento esplicito a «tra' i comici [Giovanni] Garelli e [Giuseppe] Campioni; tra' musici [Giuseppe Appiani detto] Appianino e [Felice] Salimbeni». *Ibidem*, p. 20.

[33]. LORENZONI, Antonio. *Op. cit.* (si veda nota 14), § 133, pp. 64-65.

[34]. *Ibidem*, § 134, p. 65.

[35]. TARTINI, Giuseppe. *Op. cit.* (si veda nota 28), p. 82: «cadences artificielles sur lesquelles le chanteur ou le jouer d'instrument s'arrête à volonté et sans avoir égard à la mesure». Il violinista inoltre precisa che «cette sorte de cadence est à present plutôt un caprice qu'une cadence».

[36]. LORENZONI, Antonio. *Op. cit.* (si veda nota 14), § 135, p. 65.

[37]. *Ibidem*, § 136, p. 65.

[38]. *Ibidem*, § 137, p. 65.

[39]. *Ibidem*, § 136, p. 65, e precisamente: «una cadenza nell'Adagio dee essere composta d'intervalli gli uni agli altri vicini; nell'Allegro di grandi salti, di passaggi vivi, di triplette con de' trilli frammischiati».

[40]. *Ibidem*, § 138, p. 65, e precisamente: «si potrà passare, o al modo maggiore, o minore (secondo il modo nel quale è la cadenza) della dominante, o della sottodominante; o al modo minore dello stesso suono, se il

Se però l'interprete fosse particolarmente fantasioso e ferrato nella teoria (cioè, con le parole di Lorenzoni: «provvisto non solo della cognizione delle regole dell'armonia, ma eziandio possedere invenzione, e facilità d'esecuzione sul momento») potrebbe intraprendere «grandi variazioni arbitrarie» da intendere come «diversa combinazione delli suoni dell'accordo nell'armonia del pezzo supposto, coll'aggiunta di alcune note di gusto»[41]. Pur richiedendo queste soltanto «facoltà d'invenzione, e prontezza d'esecuzione», sarebbe importante attenersi a sei precetti di massima:

> 1. non dovrà fare alcun adornamento arbitrario, prima d'essere in caso di sonare la composizione come è scritta. 2 non farà variazioni se non quando suona una parte principale nudamente accompagnata, come un solo di concerto 3. Non farà variazione, se non quando ch'esse sieno per rendere migliore la melodia; in caso diverso sarà meglio sonare quello che è scritto. 4. Non farà variazioni, che dopo aver fatto sentire la semplice melodia: senza questo chi ascolta non potrà nemmeno giudicare se sieno variazioni. 5. Nel variare si regolerà sempre al numero delle parti dalle quali è composto il pezzo. 6. Se le parti hanno la stessa melodia l'una contro l'altra, andando o in sesta, in terza, o in ottava; in tal caso non farà alcuna variazione, quando non fosse convenuto per lo avanti colle altre parti.

I principi portanti e imprescindibili di qualunque forma improvvisativa sono qui sintetizzabili in tre punti chiave: il brano originario dovrà essere enunciato nella sua interezza prima di iniziare qualunque forma di improvvisazione. Si dovrà trattare sempre e comunque di una parte principale, di un assolo di concerto, e sarà opportuno verificare che il tema che si intende elaborare non venga esposto contemporaneamente da altri strumenti. La variazione che verrà condotta estemporaneamente si dovrà commisurare al numero delle parti che accompagnano e dovrà avere come esclusivo scopo quello di ingentilire e abbellire la melodia originaria.

A questi dettami può aggiungersi l'aurea idea di Tartini che, mentre sostiene come al suo tempo «ogni cantante, o ogni strumentista si permette allungare tutto e con delle espressioni così differenti», subito aggiunge che, nonostante «oggigiorno agli ascoltatori piace sentire questa sorte di cosa sebbene irregolare e poco adattata, si deve sapere farla [...] con qualche genere di ragione»[42].

---

modo del pezzo sarà maggiore; o al modo maggiore della terza minore, se il modo sarà minore; o al modo minore della sesta maggiore, se il modo sarà maggiore; o al modo minore della seconda maggiore, se il modo sarà maggiore; ma sempre brevemente, e con gran circospezione, a fine di poter ritornare di buona grazia al modo principale».

[41]. *Ibidem*, § 191, p. 83.

[42]. TARTINI, Giuseppe. *Op. cit.* (si veda nota 28), p. 82: «tout chanteur, ou joueur d'instrument, se permet d'allonger tout et avec des expressions si differentes», p. 93: «comme les auditeurs se plaisent à présent à entendre cette sorte de chose quoique irregulière et peu convenable, il faut sçavoir la faire [...] avec quelque espèce de raison».

Nondimeno preziose sono le prescrizioni tramandate da Giambattista Mancini il quale precisa nelle sue *Riflessioni pratiche sul canto figurato* (1777) che «giudiziosi posson chiamarsi quelli, che non eccedono certamente mai su questo punto, ma regolati dal sapere e dall'arte, conducono al suo fine la cadenza, senza mai oltrepassare quei limiti, che sogliono apportar noia»[43]. E Galeazzi di rimando: «la natura, più d'ogn'altri, dev'essere in questa parte la maestra, e chi non l'ha avuta per tale, invano cercherà di farsi uno stile, o d'intendere cosa egli sia»[44]. Infatti «l'espressione è l'anima della musica» e non «è già il più valente, e bravo suonatore quello che fa più note, che più riempie e diminuisce, e sfioretta [...] anzi è bene spesso il più sciocco, il più inabile»[45]. Galeazzi è convinto che «coloro che fanno lunghe cadenze, o capriccio a solo, e senz'alcun accompagnamento, dan prova del loro cattivo gusto, e a tutta possa si affaticano per annojar l'udienza, e per far sbadigliar i circostanti»[46]. E prosegue: «furono le cadenze ne' tempi addietro inventate, per iscoprir meglio il buon gusto, e la fantasia del suonatore, ma al presente, che s'infrascano ne' concerti tante comuni, riprese, fermate, e che so io? Le cadenze son quasi inutili». In effetti l'autore si vanta di aver composto dei concerti senza cadenza, incoraggiando «ad abolire questa, direi quasi, gotica usanza, o almeno parcamente usarne».

Vige dunque la norma che «il buono unito alla proporzionata brevità, procura a chi se ne sa prevalere stima universale» (Galeazzi)[47] e l'esecutore che saprà «prender dal motivo, o sia dal corpo del ritornello di quell'aria quel tal passo, che frammischiato con giudizio più s'accorderà col resto di sua invenzione, ne riporterà lode, e particolare applauso» (Mancini)[48]. Se, ad esempio, si facesse improvvisazione creando una cadenza «in fine di un primo allegro, ed in tal caso corta, anzi cortissima: praticarvi corde doppie, ed arpeggi, e soprattutto farla estemporaneamente, e all'improvviso, mentre non vi è cosa più cattiva, che una cadenza studiata» (Galeazzi)[49].

È inoltre indispensabile, per Giuseppe Aprile, nel suo *The Modern Italian Method of Singing* (1795), «che gli ornamenti ed abbellimenti di brani vocali derivino dal carattere

---

[43]. MANCINI, Giambattista. *Op. cit.* (si veda nota 22), pp. 182-183.

[44]. GALEAZZI, Francesco. *Op. cit.* (si veda nota 1), Articolo XV, Comma 231, p. 191.

[45]. *Ibidem*, Articolo XVI, Comma 253, p. 197, e Comma 257, p. 198.

[46]. *Ibidem*, Articolo XX, Comma 315, p. 235, non dopo aver precisato che «se l'armonia senza melodia non parla, né esprime cosa alcuna, la melodia senz'armonia è un linguaggio in vero, ma sì debole e snervato, che non fa veruna, o almen ben poca impressione nell'uditorio».

[47]. *Ibidem*.

[48]. MANCINI, Giambattista. *Op. cit.* (si veda nota 22), p. 184, e GALEAZZI, Francesco. *Op. cit.* (si veda nota 1), Articolo XX, Comma 315, p. 235, di rimando «formare con essa [cadenza] un tutto unito, e di una sola idea». CAMPAGNOLI, Bartolomeo. *Op. cit.* (si veda nota 17), Osservazioni 190-192, p. 35: «Il buon gusto prescrive che s'impiegano gli ornamenti con saggezza e sopra tutto che sian tolti dalla natura stessa dell'espressione del canto».

[49]. GALEAZZI, Francesco. *Op. cit.* (si veda nota 1), Articolo XX, Comma 315, p. 235.

dell'aria e dalla passione delle parole»[50], e che, in generale la musica conservi «la sua prerogativa essenziale, la melodia, e non snaturarla fino al punto di rendere i suoi effetti impercettibili sia al fisico sia al morale» (Tomeoni)[51].

Un'ultima ma non trascurabile considerazione di Galeazzi sulla tipologia di improvvisazione è costituita dall'analisi del luogo in cui si sta suonando:

> Devesi poi aver in somma considerazione il sito, ove suonar si deve in pubblico. Ne' luoghi ristretti, ed angusti (e specialmente se appartati) ove le più delicate melodie riescono sensibili, si possono dare molti ornamenti, diminuire molto, acciò non ne risultino de' vuoti, che facciano languir l'effetto. [...] Si vede quindi evidentemente, quanto male la pensino coloro, che studiando un concerto, si limitano ad un sol modo di suonarlo; il gran professore sa variarlo sul momento a seconda del luogo ove si trova, intimamente persuaso, che suonato in un modo più piacerà v.g. in camera, che in teatro, o in chiesa, ed in altro farà più effetto in tai vasti luoghi, che in altri più angusti, e ristretti[52].

L'annotazione più importante da rimarcare riguarda l'assoluta necessità per lo strumentista di conoscere a priori il luogo in cui avverrà la sua performance; in caso contrario, saranno doti indispensabili prontezza e duttilità nel saper creare la propria esecuzione *ad hoc*, specificamente per quel contesto.

ALTRE TIPOLOGIE DI IMPROVVISAZIONE

Forma di improvvisazione può essere considerata altresì la pratica di preludiare un poco prima di iniziare un'esecuzione vera e propria, secondo quanto consiglia Manfredini: «un'altra attenzione che deve avere il bravo sonatore si è quella di preludiare un poco, ossia sonar qualche cosa di capriccio, e far la cadenza nel tono principale prima di eseguire qualsivoglia sonata, o concerto; e prima di accompagnare qualunque pezzo di musica»[53].

Parimenti va considerata forma di estemporaneità anche quella che induce lo strumentista a variare la propria esecuzione, se in difficoltà: «in caso che gli si presentino all'improvviso de' passi difficili, e della cui netta esecuzione possa egli

---

[50]. APRILE, Giuseppe. *The Modern Italian Method of Singing*, Londra, Goulding, D'Almaine, Potter & Co., [1795], § XXI, p. 2: «that the ornaments and embellishments of songs should be derived from the character of the air, and passion of the words».

[51]. TOMEONI, Florido. *Op. cit.* (si veda nota 23), p. 89: «sa prérogative essentielle, la mélodie, et ne pas la dénaturer au point de rendre ses effets insensibles au physique comme au moral».

[52]. GALEAZZI, Francesco. *Op. cit.* (si veda nota 1), Articolo XX, Comma 313, p. 233.

[53]. MANFREDINI, Vincenzo. *Regole armoniche* [...] *Seconda edizione*, Venezia, Adolfo Cesare, 1797, p. 25.

dubitare, può sul fatto rimediarvi mutandoli, ed adattandoli alla propria abilità, senza uscir d'armonia, in guisa che non possa verun uditore, anche musico, accorgersi dell'ingegnoso stratagemma» (Galeazzi)[54].

Conclusioni

L'improvvisazione secondo i trattatisti è dunque auspicabile, ma deve essere condotta secondo il buon gusto che Francesco Geminiani definisce così nel suo *The Art of Playing on the Violin* (1751):

> Molti pensano che il vero buon gusto non possa in alcun modo venir appreso per mezzo di qualsiasi regola o artificio; costoro credono che il buon gusto sia un particolare dono di natura, conferito soltanto a coloro i quali dispongono di un buon orecchio, e dal momento che la maggior parte di essi si lusinga di avere tali qualità, ne deriva che chi canta o suona non pensa ad altro che ad introdurre continuamente passaggi e volani o altri abbellimenti, credendo in tal modo di essere considerato un buon esecutore, senza invece comprendere che suonare con buon gusto non significa caricare la melodia con passaggi continui, ma esprimere con decisione e delicatezza le intenzioni del compositore. Tale espressione rappresenta ciò che ognuno dovrebbe sforzarsi di acquisire, e può pervenirvi chiunque non sia eccessivamente invaghito delle sue opinioni e non resista ostinatamente alla forza dell'evidenza[55].

Oltre alla sensibilità individuale e all'intelligenza nel saper affrontare un brano, il perfetto improvvisatore dovrà ancora far proprio il consiglio elargito da un teorico anonimo: «aggiungasi alle sudette regole la riflessione, con l'esercizio, e la pazienza, e si avrà il compimento dell'opera»[56].

---

[54]. GALEAZZI, Francesco. *Op. cit.* (si veda nota 1), Articolo XXI, Comma 322, p. 235.

[55]. GEMINIANI, Francesco. *The Art of Playing on the Violin*, Op. IX, Londra, [Autore], 1751, Esempio XVIII, p. 6: «It is supposed by many that a real good taste cannot possibly be acquired by any rules of art; it being a peculiar gift of nature, indulged only to those who have naturally a good ear: And as most flatter themselves to have this Perfection, hence it happens that he who sings or plays, thinks of nothing so much as to make continually some favourite passages or graces, believing that by this means he shall be thought to be a good performer, not perceiving that playing in good taste doth not consist of frequent passages, but in expressing with strength and delicacy the intention of the composer. This expression is what every one should endeavour to acquire, and it may be easily obtained by any Person, who is not too fond of his own opinion, and does not obstinately resist the force of true evidence». Al termine dell'affermazione elenca una serie di abbellimenti con le relative caratteristiche espressive.

[56]. ANONIMO. *Op. cit.* (si veda nota 15), Manoscritto, I-Bc, I.51, fol. 24v.

Appendice

Elenco cronologico dei trattati consultati[57]

Le tabelle che seguono, frutto di una ricerca focalizzata sul periodo 1750-1799, riportano un essenziale elenco di testi teorici fioriti durante il Settecento specificamente relativi all'argomento del presente saggio. La prima tabella contiene i trattati pervenutici in manoscritto. La seconda tabella elenca i trattati stampati. Per offrire un quadro quanto più esaustivo, non si sono trascurati i trattati anonimi nonché gli scritti che non è stato possibile collocare in una porzione temporale specifica. Non sono invece stati inseriti i testi di autore noto o di anonimi per i quali si conosce con sicurezza la datazione precedente la metà del secolo. Per i trattati manoscritti si indicano autore, titolo, datazione e segnatura. Come da siglario internazionale, l'abbreviazione XVIII corrisponde all'intero secolo XVIII nel caso in cui non sia stato possibile precisare l'ambito; XVIII/m si riferisce alla seconda metà del secolo XVIII; XVIII/t indica l'ultimo quarto di secolo. Per i trattati stampati si indicano autore, titolo, luogo della pubblicazione, editore e datazione.

Trattati Manoscritti

Autore	Titolo	Datazione	Collocazione
Anonimo	*Regole per sonare il cembalo*	XVIII	I-Bc, P.132
Anonimo	*Regole per il basso*	XVIII	I-Bc, P.134
Anonimo	*Vera regola, e modo d'imparare a suonare sopra la parte*	XVIII	I-Bc, P.134
Anonimo	*Regole del sonare*	XVIII	I-Bc, P.134
Anonimo	*Alcune regole per ben sonare il basso continuo*	XVIII	I-Bc, P.135
Anonimo	*Regole per sonare organi regolatamente con gravità e leggiadria*	XVIII	I-Bc, P.135
Anonimo	*Regole per imparare a sonare il cimbalo o organo*	XVIII	I-Bc, P.135
Anonimo	*Regole per accompagnare su l'organo. Dialogo*	XVIII	I-Bc, P.139
Anonimo	*Regole per sonare il cembalo sopra la parte del basso continuo*	XVIII	I-Bc, P.140
Anonimo	*Regole per sonare su la parte*	XVIII	I-Bc, P.140
Anonimo	*Esercitio per imparar di sonar sopra la parte*	XVIII	I-Bc, P.140
Anonimo	*Modo pratico facilissimo per sonar la parte*	XVIII	I-Bc, P.140
Anonimo	*Regole del sonare*	XVIII	I-Bc, P.140

---

[57]. La ricognizione è stata possibile all'interno del progetto ITMI (Indici della Trattatistica Musicale Italiana) ospitato presso la Fondazione Franchescini di Firenze e il cui gruppo di lavoro è coordinato da Piero Gargiulo. Si veda <http://www.itmi.it>.

Autore	Titolo	Datazione	Collocazione
Anonimo	Regole d'accompagnamento	XVIII	I-OS, Mss. Teoria B 28
Francescantonio Vallotti	Trattato della moderna musica	XVIII	I-Pca
Anonimo	Regole per sonare cadenze	XVIII/m	I Bc, P.120
Anonimo	Regole per sonare sopra la parte / Regole per accompagnare il basso continuo	XVIII/m	I-Bc, P.134
Anonimo	Regole per sonare organi	XVIII/m	I-Bc, P.135
Anonimo	Regole generali per saper accompagnare	XVIII/m	I-Bc, P.140
Anonimo	Regole per l'accompagnatura	XVIII/m	I-Fn, Rostirolla, Ms. Mus. 603
Anonimo	Principi per cembalo o organo	XVIII/m	I-MOe, Ms. Mus. F 1774
Carlo Cotumacci	Principi e regole di partimenti con tutte le lezioni	XVIII/m	I-Rsc, A-MSS-535
Domenico Gherardeschi	Metodo teorico pratico per il b[asso] cantante	XVIII/m	I-PS
Alessandro Rafaele	Regole per ben sonare il cembalo	XVIII/m	I-SSVcap, Ms. 487
Giuseppe Tartini	Libro de regole ed esempi necessari per ben suonare	XVIII/m	US-BE, It. Ms. 987
Giuseppe Tartini	Regole per arrivare a saper ben suonare il violino	XVIII/m	I-Vc, Ms. 323
Carlo Cotumacci	Regole e principi di sonare, e lettioni di partimenti con tutte le sue regole spiegate	1751	I-Rsc, A-MSS-535
Guglielmi	Trattato del moderno contrappunto	1756	I-OS, Mss. Teoria B 1
Antonio Tonelli	Teorica musicale ordinata alla moderna pratica	Ante 1760	I-Bc, L.54
Giovanni Battista Martini	Regole per accompagnare	Bologna, 1761	I-Bc, I.51
Giovanni Battista Martini	Regole per accompagnare su'l cembalo o organo	[1763]	I-Bc, I.50
Giovanni Battista Martini	Regole per accompagnare su'l cembalo	[1767]	I-Bc, I.37
Filippo Dalla Casa	Regole di musica ed anco le regole per accompagnare sopra la parte per suonare il basso continuo	1769	I-Bc, EE.155/1-2
Anonimo	Metodo musicale	1777	I-Gsl, A/9
Pietro Tulli	Regole per il contrappunto	1777	I-Fn, Rostirolla, Ms. Mus. 57
Pietro Tulli	Regole facilissime per apprendere l'accompagno del cembalo	1795	I-Fn, Rostirolla, Ms. Mus. 247
Vincenzo Benatti	Il filarmonico prattico	1797	I-OS, Mss. Teoria A 4
Giuseppe Sarti	Trattato del basso generale	XVIII/t	I-Bc, L.20

TRATTATI STAMPATI

AUTORE	TITOLO	LUOGO / EDITORE / DATAZIONE
FRANCESCO GEMINIANI	*The Art of Playing on the Violin*, Op. IX	Londra, [Autore], 1751
FRANCESCO GEMINIANI	*L'art de bien accompagner du clavecin*	Parigi, [Autore], 1754
FRANCESCO ALGAROTTI	*Saggio sopra l'opera in musica*	[Né luogo né editore], 1755
FRANCESCO GEMINIANI	*Arte di accompagnare col' cimbalo*	Parigi, Mad. Boivin, [1756]
FRANCESCO GEMINIANI	*The Art of Accompaniment*	Londra, John Jonson, [1756-1757]
CARLO TESSARINI	*Nouvelle méthode pour apprendre par théorie dans un mois de tems à jouer du violon*	Liegi, Desoer, [ca. 1760]
CARLO ZUCCARI	*The True Method of Playing an Adagio*	Londra, Bremner, [1762]
PIETRO GIANNOTTI	*Méthode abregé d'accompagnement à la harpe et au clavecin*	Parigi, Durand, 1764
CARLO TESSARINI	*An Accurate Method to Attain the Art of Playing Violin*	Londra, Peter Welcker, [1765]
PIETRO LEONE	*Methode raisonnée pour passer du violon à la mandoline et de l'archet à la plume*	Parigi, Mme Vendôme, [1768]
GIUSEPPE TARTINI	*Traité des agrémens de la musique*	Parigi, [Pierre Denis], [1771]
GIAMBATISTA MANCINI	*Pensieri e riflessioni pratiche sopra il canto figurato*	Vienna, Ghelen, 1774
FEDELE FENAROLI	*Regole musicali per i principianti di cembalo*	Napoli, Vincenzo Mazzola-Vocola, 1775
VINCENZO MANFREDINI	*Regole armoniche*	Venezia, Guglielmo Zerletti, 1775
P. SIGNORETTI	*Méthode contenant les principes de la musique et du violon*	L'Aja, Williams, 1777
GIAMBATTISTA MANCINI	*Riflessioni pratiche sul canto figurato*	Milano, Giuseppe Galeazzi, 1777
ANTONIO LORENZONI	*Saggio per ben sonare il flautotraverso*	Vicenza, Francesco Modena, 1779
GENNARO CATALISANO	*Grammatica armonica fisico-matematica*	Roma, San Michele a Ripa, 1781
GIOVANNI BATTISTA RANGONI	*Saggio sul gusto della musica, col carattere de' tre celebri sonatori di violino i signori Nardini, Lolli, Pugnani*	Livorno, Tommaso Masi, 1790
FRANCESCO GALEAZZI	*Elementi teorico-pratici di musica […] Tomo primo*	Roma, Pilucchi Cracas, 1791
ANONIMO	*Armonici erudimenti nei quali si contengono le regole e suoi esempi per imparare accompagnare sul cimbalo il basso continuo*	Firenze, Anton Giuseppe Pagani, 1790
PELLEGRINO TOMEONI	*Regole pratiche per accompagnare il basso continuo*	Firenze, Anton Giuseppe Pagani, 1795
FRANCESCO GALEAZZI	*Elementi teorico-pratici di musica […] Tomo secondo*	Roma, Michele Puccinelli, 1796

«L'ORECCHIO PIÙ CHE 'L TEMPO DEE SERVIRE DI GUIDA»

Autore	Titolo	Luogo / Editore / Datazione
Vincenzo Manfredini	*Regole armoniche*	Venezia, Adolfo Cesare, 1797
Bartolomeo Campagnoli	*Nuovo metodo della mecanica progressiva per suonare il violino*	Milano, Ricordi, [1797]
Florido Tomeoni	*Méthode qui apprend la connaissance de l'harmonie et la pratique de l'accompagnement selon les principes de l'école de Naples*	Parigi, Autore, [1798]
Florido Tomeoni	*Théorie de la musique vocale*	Parigi, Charles Pougin, 1799

MARIATERESA DELLABORRA

ENGLISH SUMMARY

«IT IS RATHER THE EAR THAN TIME THAT MUST SERVE AS GUIDE»
IMPROVISATION IN ITALIAN MUSIC TREATISES OF THE
SECOND HALF OF THE EIGHTEENTH CENTURY

Mariateresa Dellaborra

Studying Italian music theory of the second half the eighteenth century, it becomes soon clear that improvisation was viewed as an important element of performance. In general, it was considered impossible to include in the musical notation all the necessary nuances of a performance. Rousseau (1768) and Lichtenthal (1836) provide insightful definitions of 'improvisation'. Improvisation of the accompaniment is, of course, closely related to figured bass, which allows for a great variety of realizations. Theorists such as Tonelli (before 1760), Vallotti, Manfredini (1775) and Rangoni (1790) discuss the various ways in which the accompanist must adapt his 'improvisations' to whom and what he is accompanying. Improvisation takes entirely different forms in the solo parts. One of them is the cadenza, which is on the one hand 'free', but more effective if is it connected with the musical material already presented. Another method is the addition of ornamentation to solo melodies. Many theorists warn the performers that, in this case, they must make sure the original melody is not lost entirely. Theorists dealing with these problems are, among others, Algarotti (1755), Tartini (1771), Mancini (1777), Lorenzoni (1779) and Galeazzi (1796). Common to all theorists studied is the emphasis on good taste in improvisation. The essay concludes with a detailed list of the most important treatises consulted.

Harmonic Patterns and Melodic Paraphrases in Eighteenth-Century Portuguese Music for the Five-Course Guitar

Rogério Budasz
(Riverside, CA)

In Portugal, as in many parts of Southern Europe and Latin America, the guitar was for centuries the preferred instrument for the accompaniment of singing and dancing. It was only during the nineteenth century that the *viola* — as the five-course guitar was known in that country — was replaced in urban areas by the so-called Portuguese guitar, an adaptation of the cittern-derived English guitar, or *guittar*. Even so, the *viola* remained an important instrument in rural areas of Portugal, the Azores and Madeira, as well as in Brazil, Portugal's largest former colony. The *viola*, henceforth guitar, was less expensive than most string or wind instruments of similar quality, but it also owed its popularity among amateurs to an alternative type of music training that developed alongside the instrument's evolution, a kind of musical subculture that did not rely on traditional staff notation, but rather on tablature and cyphering.

Until the late eighteenth century, tablature was the standard form of notation for the guitar, lute, and numerous other plucked string instruments, even for types of music we may call 'learned', or 'scholarly', such as ricercares, fantasias, variations and more stylized and elaborated dance suites. Tablature can be a complex system, and in many cases more precise than staff notation. Although the type of tablature most commonly found in eighteenth-century Portuguese sources is fashioned on Italian models, with horizontal lines for the strings and numbers for the frets, it lacks rhythmic indications, bringing us to the paradoxical situation that what made music accessible then makes it elusive now. The presence or absence of rhythm, or duration signs, in a specific source is an important factor in determining the level of formal musical training of its creators and users. Likewise, it poses some interesting questions concerning the level of autonomy enjoyed by the performers in matters such as variation, embellishment and improvisation.

Nicolau Doizi de Velasco, a Portuguese musician who lived in Naples, published a treatise on guitar notation in that city in 1640. Three early or mid-eighteenth-century manuscripts in tablature for the five-course guitar or *viola* are about all that remain of the Portuguese repertoire for that instrument before Manuel da Paixão Ribeiro's book published in Coimbra in 1789. TABLE 1 lists these sources.

TABLE 1
SOURCES OF SEVENTEENTH- AND EIGHTEENTH-CENTURY
PORTUGUESE GUITAR MUSIC

PRINTED BOOKS			
AUTHOR	TITLE	PLACE AND PUBLISHER	YEAR
Nicolau Doizi de Velasco	*Nuevo modo de cifra para tañer la gvitarra con variedad, perfección, y se muestra ser instrumento perfecto, y abundantíssimo*	Naples, Egidio Longo	1640
Manoel da Paixão Ribeiro	*Nova arte de viola que ensina a tocalla com fundamento sem mestre*	Coimbra, Real Officina da Universidade	1789
MANUSCRIPTS			
AUTHOR	TITLE	LOCATION	DATING
Joseph Carneyro Tavares Lamacense	*Cifras de viola por varios autores*	Coimbra, University Library, M.M. 97	Early 18th century
Unknown	No title	Lisbon, Calouste Gulbenkian Foundation, Music Division, no shelf mark	Early 18th century
Unknown	*Livro do Conde de Redondo*	Lisbon, National Library, F.C.R. Ms. Ne 1	mid-18th century

The absence of earlier Portuguese printed books for the guitar or related instruments before 1789 does not mean that there was no national tradition. Well-known sixteenth-century Spanish *vihuela* players such as Miguel de Fuenllana and Luys de Milán lived in Portugal and/or dedicated books to the Portuguese king. And there were notable Portuguese *viola* players during the sixteenth and early seventeenth centuries: Peixoto da Pena, Luiz de Victoria and Nicolau Doizi de Velasco, to name but a few. No music of these early Portuguese guitar players has survived, however.

Nicolau Doizi de Velasco's instruction book mentioned above, the *Nuevo modo de cifra*, is almost exclusively theoretical. It presents a few examples of cadences and intervals in staff notation. Two musical fragments, a 'Chacona' and a 'Passacaglia', are written down using Velasco's own system of ciphering, by far the most complex to be found in the complete guitar literature before the twentieth century. His system comprises 228 chords, nineteen for each of the twelve semitones, including major and minor triads in root position and first inversion, as well as several dissonant chords. Although comprehensive — or, in fact, because of that — the system was not adopted by later generations of guitar players. Gaspar Sanz considered Velasco's system ingenious, but too complicated, precisely because of the great number of chords that must be memorized: it was much more practical to keep using the simpler Italian *alfabeto* notation for the easiest chords and to combine it with Italian tablature for the more complex passages[1].

Velasco's system is, above all, a system of transposition. The author makes that clear in the most important section of the book, where it is shown how the same piece of music can be played sequentially in each one of the twelve 'letters', or keys. Sixteen 'musical circles' are presented to the reader, each one passing through a number of keys and returning to the starting point. Velasco explains that these *vueltas*, or 'round trips', may be accomplished by twelve ascending fifths, twelve descending fifths, an alternation of major and minor thirds, or six major seconds. It is not difficult to understand that by using this system, the guitar player could introduce some variety in a series of dances or short songs, by easily passing through several different keys and then returning to the original harmony. Because of its fretted neck, the guitar was one of the few instruments suitable for this type of transposition, as theorist Francisco Valls observed in 1742: «One will also find musical circulation in most organ keyboards, and with better approximation in the Spanish guitar, in which all the semitones are equal»[2].

Players of fretted instruments, and for that matter also viola da gamba players, obviously knew that they could adjust the temperament by carefully sliding the frets of their instruments according to the key of the piece they were about to play. This is not the place for a discussion of that aspect; it is enough to say that early theorists paid attention to the advantages of fretted instruments when it came to tonal versatility.

The chronological boundary of this article is 1789, when Manuel da Paixão Ribeiro published his *Nova arte de viola* in Coimbra. The book marks the definitive adoption of modern staff notation for guitar music, while still presenting the last traces of the old-fashioned traditions of figured bass and tablature. Although Ribeiro's book is mostly instructional, it does present two minuets and two *modinhas* (a Luso-Brazilian art song type), in staff notation. On the other hand, when explaining accompaniment formulas and the formation of chords, Ribeiro still resorts to tablature notation and the centuries-old practice of drawing the guitarist's left-hand positions on a stylized fretboard. One of the plates is particularly noteworthy in that it uses a single set of five parallel lines as a staff

---

[1]. SANZ, Gaspar. *Instrucción de música sobre la guitarra española*, Zaragoza, Dormer, 1674, fol. 8r.

[2]. VALLS, Francisco. *Mapa armónico práctico*, E-Mn, Ms. M 1071, fol. 252r: «Hallaráse también la circulación Musical según los más de los teclados de los Organos, y más proximamente de la Guitarra Española, donde todos los semitonos son iguales».

to notate the bass notes and simultaneously as a tablature to indicate arpeggiated chords[3]. To a certain degree it is fair to say that systems of notation based on linear tablature and fretboard drawings were transferred to the realm of urban popular music, where they still are used today in songbooks and instruction books.

Ribeiro's book is invaluable to an understanding of the later developments of the five-course guitar in Portugal, especially issues such as stringing and construction. But for more interesting insights on improvisatory practices one needs to look back at the eighteenth-century tablature manuscripts. These sources present a variety of examples of harmonic patterns, some of them of Portuguese origin or further developed in Portugal. In addition, they shed light on practices of composing over melodic-harmonic modules, on local paraphrases of foreign melodies, and on local and idiomatic practices of ornamentation and diminution.

Probably compiled during the early decades of the eighteenth century, the 'Coimbra Codex', the manuscript Coimbra, University Library, M.M. 97, is written in Italian tablature throughout, rarely including any rhythmic indication. It contains 267 pieces for guitar, 13 for bandurria, and 43 for violin, among them fantasias, *batalhas*, *rojões*, *chácaras* and other Iberian genres commonly found in guitar books of the period. It also features a section of French and Italian dances, and some settings of Afro-Iberian pieces, such as *arromba*, *gandum*, *cubanco*, and *sarambeque*. Most of its contents are anonymous, but some works are ascribed to Abreu, Barros, Gomes, Diogo Doria, Frei João, Pepo Licete, Marques, Monteiro, Sylva or a certain Cavagliero Mascarelli. Among these, the only composer whose biography is somewhat known is Antonio Marques Lésbio (1639-1709), master of the Portuguese Royal Chapel and famous for his villancicos. A close examination of the repertoire shows that some of the anonymous pieces are actually works by Ennemond Gaultier, Domenico Pellegrini, Francesco Corbetta, Robert de Visée or Gaspar Sanz.

The 'Gulbenkian Codex', a manuscript without shelf mark in Lisbon, Calouste Gulbenkian Foundation, Music Division, and compiled a few years after the Coimbra Codex, has a similar distribution of musical forms. It is somewhat smaller though, with 67 pieces for guitar, 33 for bandurria, and 28 pieces notated in a particular system called *cifras aritméticas*, intended to be played on the guitar, bandurria, or harpsichord. Some authors are identified: Abreu, Denis de Barros, David, Manuel de Mattos and Antonio Marques [Lésbio]. Works by Sanz, Corbetta, and Visée also appear, but without proper attribution.

The 84 guitar pieces in the 'Redondo Codex', the manuscript Lisbon, National Library, Fundo Conde de Redondo, Ms. Ne 1, are examples of a later repertoire, which still includes fantasias and batalhas, but has a larger number of *oitavados*, *gigas*, and above all, minuets. Although most of the manuscript seems to contain original guitar music, it also includes some transcriptions of works by Corelli and Scarlatti — identified as Corely and Escarlate — and

---

[3]. RIBEIRO, Manuel da Paixão. *Nova arte de viola que ensina a tocalla com fundamento sem mestre*, Coimbra, Na Real Officina da Universidade, 1789, plates 1-8.

some other pieces without indication of authorship, but probably drawn from Raoul-Auger Feuillet's *Recueil de contredances* (Paris, author, 1706) or an intermediary source.

HARMONIC AND MELODIC-HARMONIC PATTERNS

The harmonic structure of the majority of the *rojões* in Portuguese sources leaves no doubt that these belong to the musical genre known everywhere else in Europe as *passacaglia*. The most important *rojão* scheme found in Portuguese sources is a descending harmonic bass in minor mode. In most cases the descending tetrachord is implied in the harmonic progression rather than being explicitly stated (see Ex. 1 and 2). Comparisons with concordant *passacaglie* in other guitar sources suggest triple meter[4].

Ex. 1: harmonic scheme of the *rojão*.

Ex. 2: first measures of the 'Rojão 10 tom de Marques'. Coimbra Codex, fol. 26v.

One of the *rojões* in the Coimbra Codex (fols. 36v-37r) is the 'Passachaglia sopra X'[5], a work also found in Francesco Corbetta's guitar book of 1643[6]. Whereas the first page of the printed version is found in the Coimbra Codex with only a few changes, the material of the second page is reassembled and suffers several cuts. In addition, the last eight measures are replaced by a different six-measure ending, and a four-measure ritornello that modulates to A major (in order to connect with the following item in a series of *passacaglie*)

---

4. Barring and rhythm in the music examples drawn from the Portuguese manuscripts are reconstructed by the author.

5. The *alfabeto* capital X denotes the chord of B minor.

6. CORBETTA, Francesco. *Varii capricii per la ghittara spagnuola*, Milan, s.n., 1643, pp. 32-33.

is suppressed in order to finish the piece in the key of B minor, thereby transforming it into a self-contained work.

In some *rojões* in the Coimbra Codex and in the majority of those in the Redondo Codex, the descending tetrachord formula in triple meter is abandoned in favor of another, harmonically simpler one in duple meter. This simpler pattern resembles, although with some passing harmonies, the *a compasillo* formula I IV V I, an Iberian rhythmic-harmonic variant of the *passacaglia*, conspicuously found in Santiago de Murcia's manuscript guitar books.

Like the *passacaglia*, the *rojão* is both a functional genre — serving as an instrumental ritornello in strophic songs or as a connection between pieces of different keys — and a ready-made harmonic basis for variations, which could be extemporized on the spot or written down. Corroborating this versatility is the fact that in Portuguese sources *rojões* are found in all eight *tons*, or keys, of the harmonic system then in use in that country.

A less versatile harmonic scheme is the *magana*, of which the Coimbra Codex contains the only known extant examples. Early mentions of a dance called *mangana* are found in Garcia de Resende's 1516 *Cancioneiro Geral*[7]. In the *Coplas a los negros y negras* by Rodrigo de Reynosa, printed around the same time, the *mangana* is compared to the African-Iberian *guineo*[8]. Some decades later, Luís de Camões referred to the *mangana* as a vocal piece[9]. However, given the large time span that separates these references and the Coimbra Codex, it is not very likely that the *magana* in the latter source is in any way related to the dances and songs mentioned in the sixteenth-century sources quoted above. Interestingly, however, around 1620 Diogo de Sousa described the *mangana* as a song accompanied by a small guitar:

> Sabe cantar, mas sempre está mui rouco;
> Na guitarrinha põe sua mangana,
> toca as teclas de um cravo, mas é mouco[10].

> (He knows how to sing, but always very croaky;
> on a small guitar he plays his *mangana*,
> and touches the keys of a harpsichord, although he is a little deaf.)

---

[7]. RESENDE, Garcia de. *Cancioneiro Geral*, Lisbon, Hermã de Câmpos, 1516, fol. 164v. The following lines place the *mangana* in the category of popular *bailes*, rather than courtly *danças*, such as the *alta* and the *baixa*: 'Se m'a mim não mente Aixa, / se me Comba não engana, / sei bailar melhor mangana / que dançar alta nem baixa' (If to me Aixa does not lie, if Comba does not deceive me, I know better how to dance the *mangana* than to dance the *alta* or the *baixa*).

[8]. REYNOSA, Rodrigo de. *Comiençan unas coplas a los negros y negras*, Burgos, Juan de Junta, c. 1520, fols. 1-2.

[9]. CAMÕES, Luís de. *Cartas (4-795). Obras completas*, Lisbon, Sá da Costa, 1972, Vol. III, p. 262: 'Aonde, com triste som, / lhe cantaram a mangana / e, com esta dor profana, / gritos daba de passion / aquella Reina Troyana' (Where, with sad music, they sang to her the *mangana* and with such profane pain, she cried out of passion that Trojan Queen).

[10]. SOUSA, Diogo de. *Jornada às Cortes do Parnaso*, edited by Valeria Tocco, Bari, Adriatica, 1996, p. 136.

The Coimbra *maganas* are set on the first four *tons,* roughly corresponding to the keys of D minor, G minor, E minor, and A minor. The harmonic scheme i VII III V, exemplified in the 'Magana 10 tom' (see Ex. 3), bears some similarity to schemes of some *chácaras,* especially those that present passing harmonies between i and V. The pattern can be expanded to a six-measure scheme (i VII III iv-VI V V), as for example in the 'Magana ou Chacoina 4°.

Ex. 3: first measures of the 'Magana 10 tom'. Coimbra Codex, fol. 48v.

The Coimbra Codex has six settings of the dance-type or instrumental form called *sarao,* three in a major and three in a minor mode. Besides sharing motivic material, all these settings clearly are based on a single harmonic pattern, the first half of which seems to derive from the *magana,* in minor mode: i II III V V / i VII iv V i; in major mode: I VII III-IV V V / I IV V I (see Ex. 4). Although the two extant guitar settings of the *sarao* in Spanish and Mexican sources follow a different harmonic progression[11], Luis de Briceño's 1626 version, printed in France, bears some similarity to the minor-mode intabulations in the Coimbra Codex[12].

Ex. 4: first measures of the 'Sarao 4o tom de Sylva'. Coimbra Codex, fols. 44v-45r.

[11]. 'Sarao de la Comedia del Retiro', in E-Mn, Ms. M 811, p. 129, and 'Sarao o Bailete de el Retiro', in the manuscript Mexico City, Collection Saldivar, No. 4, fols. 71r-72v, attributed to Santiago de Murcia.

[12]. BRICEÑO, Luís de. *Metodo mui facilissimo para aprender a tañer la guitarra a lo español,* Paris, P. Ballard, 1626, fol. 13v: 'Dança o Entrada de Sarao Español'.

Chácaras are among the most numerous pieces in the Coimbra Codex: there are thirteen for *viola* and three for bandurria, making this collection the most important source for this musical form. The number of settings is smaller in the Gulbenkian Codex: four for *viola* and two for bandurria; the dance is completely absent in the Redondo Codex. The *chácaras* in the Coimbra Codex are also the best examples of the form, with settings mainly in first *tom* (roughly D minor), but also in fourth (A minor) and second (G minor) *tons*. As in the Spanish *jácaras*, these pieces follow a process of recomposition based upon two short melodic-harmonic formulas or clichés that are reassembled according to principles of modular composition typical of Iberian traditional music (see Ex. 5). The modules play the roles of refrain and variation material at the same time and appear consistently in settings to be found in Portuguese, Spanish and Mexican sources (see Ex. 6)[13].

Ex. 5: Main melodic-harmonic formulas of the Iberian *jácaras*.

Ex. 6: Some opening statements of Portuguese *chácaras*. Coimbra Codex.

---

[13]. Not only *chácaras/jácaras*, but also Afro-Iberian guitar pieces and dance types such as the *gandum*, *cumbe*, *cubanco*, and the *arromba* display similar modular structures. See Budasz, Rogério. 'Black Guitar-Players and Early African-Iberian Music in Portugal and Brazil', in: *Early Music*, xxxv/1 (2007), pp. 3-21.

Paraphrases of Foreign Melodies

The Redondo Codex features three settings of André Campra's air 'Aimable vainqueur'. The original music was written for the opera *Hésione* (1700), where the aria is followed by an instrumental setting of the same music, danced to a choreography prepared especially for the occasion. The dance eventually found its way into ballrooms everywhere thanks to French dancing-masters Louis-Guillaume Pécour and Raoul-Auger Feuillet, who exported it to the rest of Europe and beyond.

The air 'Aimable vainqueur' was not introduced in Portugal in its original form, that is, as part of Campra's *tragédie lyrique*. The Portuguese probably knew the melody from Feuillet's *Recueil de contredances* (Paris, 1706)[14]. The guitar settings probably contain clues about the practice of improvised guitar accompaniment in Portugal. They are not realizations of a continuo line, but paraphrases of the melody. In the first 'Amable' in the Redondo Codex (fols. 3v-4r), the paraphrase accompanies the voice that is singing the main melody, oddly suggesting a heterophonic texture, since different versions of the melody — not diminutions — are heard simultaneously (see Ex. 7). The Portuguese text is not based on Campra's text, although it displays similar affects. All other Iberian 'Aimable vainqueur' arrangements are instrumental, and they are all based on the dance that follows the aria[15]. Even the vocal setting in the Redondo Codex is based on material from this

---

[14]. Feuillet, Raoul-Auger. *Recueil de contredances*, Paris, L'auteur, 1706, pp. 17-24.

[15]. For a detailed study of this dance see Hilton, Wendy. 'Aimable Vainqueur or The Louvre', in: *Dance and Music of Court and Theater*, selected writings of Wendy Hilton, New York, Pendragon Press, 1997, pp. 437-446. For some concordances see Russell, Craig. *Codice Saldivar No. 4. A Treasury of Secular Guitar Music from Baroque Mexico*, Urbana, University of Illinois Press, 1997, pp. 182-183.

dance, evidence that strengthens the hypothesis that *Hésione* as a whole was unknown in Portugal at the time the setting was made.

Ex. 7: André Campra's 'Aimable vainqueur' compared to a Portuguese 'Amable'. (a) The main melody, as found in *Hésione*, Act 3, Second Air, entracte; (b) The Portuguese text, as found in the Redondo Codex, fols. 3v-4r (text); (c) The guitar setting, *ibidem*, in tablature and modern transcription.

The reworking of vocal pieces into dances and vice versa was a fairly common practice in the seventeenth and eighteenth centuries, as illustrated by a great number of cases, among them the 'Aria di Fiorenza', the 'Ballo di Mantova', and a large number of sung minuets. The 'Ballo di Mantova', or 'La Mantovana', was a very popular tune, with many arrangements published for lute, keyboard, and instrumental ensemble throughout the seventeenth century. Its probable source is Giuseppe Cenci's canzonetta 'Fuggi, fuggi da questo cielo'[16].

In spite of the ensemble settings by Gasparo Zanetti and Giuseppe Giamberti in the first half of the seventeenth century, 'La Mantovana' was mostly available in *alfabeto* notation, printed in many Italian guitar books without its melody or lyrics. In the Iberian Peninsula, the 'Baile de Mantua' or 'Mantuana' appears in Gaspar Sanz's 1674 guitar

---

[16]. CENCI, Giuseppe. 'Fuggi, fuggi, fuggi da questo cielo', I-Fn, Ms. Barbera 158, fol. 82v. Transcription in HILL, John Walter. *Roman Monody, Cantata, and Opera from the Circles Around Cardinal Montalto*, Oxford, Clarendon Press, 1997, vol. II, p. 396.

instruction book[17] and in the Coimbra Codex. Sanz's setting is notated in the *alfabeto* system and is virtually identical to the setting Carlo Calvi published in Bologna in 1646[18], apart from Calvi's major chord ending. Unlike most guitar settings, the two Coimbra versions are notated in tablature. Both follow the standard harmonic pattern closely, and one of them features elaborate diminutions. Although further evidence is yet to be found, these settings seem to provide clues to a rather common practice of paraphrasing songs through extemporized ornamentation and variation.

SOME THOUGHTS ON TRANSMISSION

Many of the works in the eighteenth-century Portuguese manuscripts for the guitar are *unica*. Among the works for which concordances have been identified, there are significant modifications. A comparison of the various settings (and their probable sources) gives us important insights into the process of transmission and the ensuing reworking of this repertoire.

The 'Alemanda' on fols. 92rv of the Coimbra Codex poses an interesting problem (see Ex. 8). We find the piece in Domenico Pellegrini's guitar book of 1650[19]. Apart from the fact that the last eleven measures are missing in the Coimbra version, there is only one mistake: the *alfabeto* capital R was taken as a C major, rather than a B major chord. However, this piece is marked in Pellegrino's book as a 'Corrente, detta La Savellina', not an *alemanda*. This is a major issue, for the player should make rhythmic choices that would conform to the ternary division of the *corrente*. Since this piece appears in a group of *alemandas*, and not in the section of *correntes*, the Coimbra compiler probably replicated a mistake he found in an intermediate source.

Ex. 8: (a) the 'Alemanda' in the Coimbra Codex, fol. 92r, and (b) Domenico Pellegrini's 'Corrente detta La Savellina', in his *Armoniosi concerti*, 1650, p. 50. The cross and the capital B are *alfabeto* signs, representing an E minor and a C major chord respectively.

17. SANZ, Gaspar. *Op. cit.* (see note 1), fol. 19r.
18. CALVI, Carlo. *Intavolatura di chitarra e chitarriglia*, Bologna, G. Monti, 1646, p. 15.
19. PELLEGRINI, Domenico. *Armoniosi concerti sopra la chitarra spagnvola*, Bologna, Giacomo Monti, 1650, p. 50.

Another unintentional reworking appears in the 'Corrente del Cavagliero Mascarelli', on fol. 97r of the Coimbra Codex (see Ex. 9). The first part of this piece is actually an 'Alemanda' by Pellegrini included in his 1650 book, whereas the second part is the *corrente* found on the following page of the same publication (both pieces are in D minor)[20]. In addition to identifying the dance incorrectly, the copyist had some trouble determining the *alfabeto* chords, reading the capitals O and I as figures 0 and 1 on the third course, rather than G minor and A major chords. In addition to misinterpreting several other chords, the copyist does not seem to have been aware of the meaning of the little strumming signs on the lower line, which are mostly ignored, but sometimes identified as the figure 1. The results must have sounded a little strange to early eighteenth-century ears.

Ex. 9: (a) a fragment of the 'Corrente del Cavagliero Mascarelli' in the Coimbra Codex, fol. 97r, and (b) Domenico Pellegrini's 'Alemanda', in his *Armoniosi Concerti*, 1650, p. 39.

There are many cases of intentional reworking of original works by well-known authors, sometimes in the form of a *pasticcio*, a new piece created by joining together sections from different pieces by one or more composers. Other types of liberties that one could call improvisatory include changing the texture by providing chords to melodic passages or adding new sections in diminutions or *glosas*. A section of diminutions added to the famous 'Pavana Italiana' is an example of writing that is at once very idiomatic to the guitar and stylistically appropriate, even for a piece that should seem fairly old-fashioned by the early eighteenth century (see Ex. 10). But in most cases, these sections of diminutions fail to conform to the style of the piece to which they are attached, thus giving clues to local tastes and practices. Gaspar Sanz's 'Matachín', for example, printed in his 1675 book[21], has interspersed diminutions consisting of ascending and descending scales, and the 'Minuete' by Robert de Visée[22], is followed by glosas exploring repeated notes and open strings in a type of tremolo or pedal point (see Ex. 11). This technique of added diminutions is widely used in the three manuscripts under consideration.

---

[20]. *Ibidem*, pp. 39-40.

[21]. SANZ, Gaspar. *Libro segundo de cifras sobre la guitarra española*, Zaragoza, Dormer, 1675, fol. 2v.

[22]. VISÉE, Robert de. *Livre de pièces pour la guittarre dedié au roy*, Paris, A. Letteguine, 1686, p. 16.

Ex. 10: 'glosas', or diminutions on the 'Pavana Italiana'. Coimbra Codex, fols. 45v–46r.

Ex. 11: diminutions on a 'Minuete' by Robert de Visée. Gulbenkian Codex, fol. 26v.

In other passages, the handwriting seems to show the performer/composer caught in the act of writing down extemporizations. In one such example in the Gulbenkian Codex, an experiment on *falsas*, or dissonances, the performer slides the notes of a chord one by one, creating and resolving harmonic tension. In the process, the calligraphy becomes increasingly sloppy, until the exercise is abandoned before it is finished (see Ex. 12).

Ex. 12: an unfinished passage of *falsas*. Gulbenkian Codex, fol. 22v.

CONCLUSION

One or more stages of written, or in some cases oral transmission might separate the reworked pieces in the Portuguese sources from their original models. It seems logical that the performer for whom, or by whom these manuscripts in tablature without rhythmic indications were written was expected to have prior knowledge of the rhythm of the standard dances; after all, there were not so many. In other cases, such as the accompaniment or paraphrase of a song, the tune could have been known to many, and the remaining parts supplied with more or less precision by filling the rhythmic spaces and paying attention to the barring. However, the large number and considerable length of the fantasias in the Portuguese manuscripts — 33 of them in the Coimbra Codex alone, out of a total of 267 guitar pieces — make it difficult to imagine that an average performer could have learned and memorized the minute rhythmic details of all these works and kept them in his or her memory for life. Of course, some notion of rhythm could have been obtained from an instructor or fellow guitar player, but it is logical to think that even when dealing with unknown pieces a good performer would have been able to recognize dance patterns, cadential and ornamental formulas, diminutions, and counterpoint passages, and perform them in a rhythmically convincingly way, even when using a different configuration each time. In addition, the ability to extemporize passages was something expected of good players, but extemporizations were rarely, if ever, written down.

These guitar sources bring us a great amount of information on how the authority of a received text was subject to changes by local performers, according to factors such as local taste and practices, a wish for modernization, the ability and musical proficiency of the performers, and the change of medium. They also give us a glimpse of performance practices that were closer to the everyday life of the average eighteenth-century Portuguese than to the sophisticated music heard at the Court. Improvisation was as important to an obscure guitarist playing at a tavern or a brothel as it was to celebrated court musicians such as Carlos Seixas and Domenico Scarlatti. But unlike the carefully copied scores or printed music of court composers, manuscript tablatures like those in the early guitar codices examined here, full of mistakes, second thoughts, and incomplete passages, are invaluable windows on a dynamic musical life that prized the ability to improvise passages and thus transform old pieces of music into something new, so that they could remain functional for decades or more after they were composed.

FORMULE E IMPROVVISAZIONE NEI RECITATIVI DELLE CANTATE DI ALESSANDRO SCARLATTI

Simone Ciolfi
(ROMA)

PARLARE DI IMPROVVISAZIONE per prodotti COSÌ ricercati e bizzarri come i recitativi delle cantate di Alessandro Scarlatti (1660-1725) può suonare strano. Additati per tutto il Settecento e oltre come pezzi eccentrici e stravaganti, tali recitativi sembrano invece proprio il prodotto di una lunga riflessione creativa[1]. Il discorso, tuttavia, vale anche per noti improvvisatori come Mozart, Clementi, Beethoven o Liszt, i cui lasciti sono spesso altrettanto ricercati e complessi. Alla base della fluidità e dell'efficienza di queste opere c'è sicuramente una prolungata dedizione creativa, ma vi giace anche lo strumentario di un malleabile mestiere, riconoscibile nella velocità di scrittura, nella ricorrenza di certi archetipi formali, di certe 'idee tipo', per usare un termine di Max Weber e Carl Dahlhaus, che si rinnovano nell'epifania di usuali progressioni armoniche combinate a soluzioni ritmiche e timbriche sempre nuove[2].

Questo argomento è particolarmente appropriato per il recitativo: quasi tutti gli studiosi, anche in riferimento a Scarlatti, hanno parlato di un sistema di formule ricorrenti, sia armoniche che melodiche[3], e alcuni ottimi studi generali sono stati dedicati ad

---

[1]. BURNEY, Charles. *A General History of Music from the Earliest Ages to the Present Period*, 4 voll., Londra, 1789, vol. IV, p. 170: «The cantatas of Scarlatti are much sought and admired by curious collectors. [...] His modulation, in struggling at novelty, is sometimes crude and unnatural, and he more frequently tried to express the meaning of single words than the general sense and spirit of the whole poem he had set in Music». *Ibidem*, p. 175: «Scarlatti's recitative is, in general, excellent; for in that, bold modulation is wanted. And he seems to have expressed the words with peculiar felicity». RAGUNET, François. *A Comparison between the 'French' and 'Italian' Musick and Opera's, Translated from the French, with Some Remarks*, traduzione attribuita a Ernest Galliard, Londra, printed for William Lewis, 1709, p. 16, nota 12: «the recitative in Scarlatti's cantatas, where he makes use of all sorts of dissonance to express the force of the words, and afterwards resolves 'em so well that indeed the most beautiful concords are hardly so sweet and harmonious as his discords».

[2]. William E. Caplin cita Carl Dahlhaus e Max Weber in riferimento al concetto di 'idea tipo' e dà un'utile definizione di questa definendola «abstractions based on generalized compositional tendencies». Si veda CAPLIN, William E. *Classical Form*, New York, Oxford University Press, 1998, p. 4.

[3]. Michael Talbot parla di «much-used fragments» e «recombinations of simple formulas» per lo stile recitativo delle cantate. Si veda TALBOT, Michael. 'Patterns and Strategies of Modulation in Cantata Recitatives',

approfondire, per esempio, le soluzioni interrogative o quelle cadenzali[4]. Tuttavia, mi preme aggiungere: se si parla di formule si parla anche di un livello neutro che le rende riconoscibili nel repertorio di uno o più autori, e si parla anche di come essi hanno voluto personalizzarle. E ancora: se si parla di formule si parla del loro mascheramento, della sorpresa che deriva dal loro tradimento, si parla di scrittura veloce o, al limite, anche di improvvisazione.

Oltre che dall'analisi del repertorio, l'esistenza di soluzioni ricorrenti si può secondariamente osservare anche ricercandone la teorizzazione a livello didattico. La produzione teorica e didattica di Scarlatti è contenuta in cinque manoscritti, due dei quali autografi:

Biblioteca	Manoscritto	Titolo	Data
GB-Lbl	Add. Ms. 14244	*Principj della musica*	[1715-1716]
GB-Lbl	Add. Ms. 31517	*Regole per principianti* [due versioni]	Senza data
I-MC	Ms. 126 D. 4	*Regole per principianti*	Senza data
I-MOe	Campori App. 2404-y.L	[*Regole*] *Per accompagnare il cembalo, ò pure Organo, ò altro strumento in consonanza*	[1730-1740]
US-NH	Misc. Ms. 164 (Ms. Higgs)	*Regole per principianti*	[1724 circa]

La British Library conserva sotto la segnatura 'Additional Manuscript 14244' un manoscritto parzialmente autografo dal titolo *Principij di musica*. Le poche pagine di *Regole per principianti* contenute nel 'Manoscritto Higgs' e collocate all'inizio di una collezione di Cantate sono a mio avviso, e secondo l'opinione di Reinhard Strohm, autografe[5]; il loro

---

in: *Aspects of the Secular Cantata in Late Baroque Italy*, a cura di Michael Talbot, Farnham, Ashgate, 2009, pp. 255-271, p. 256. Costantino Maeder parla di «molteplici convenzioni musicali e notazionali che riguardano formule melodiche e cadenzanti». Si veda Maeder, Costantino. *Metastasio, L'*'Olimpiade' *e l'opera del Settecento*, Bologna, Il Mulino, 1993, p. 98. Roger Freitas, riguardo ai recitativi delle cantate di Atto Melani, fa riferimento a «the almost formulaic use of certain compositional gestures». Si veda Freitas, Roger. *Portrait of a Castrato. Politics, Patronage, and Music in the Life of Atto Melani*, Cambridge, Cambridge University Press, 2009, p. 243.

4. Alcuni studi sulle formule cadenzali: Monson, Dale. 'The Last Word. The Cadence in *recitativo semplice* of Italian *opera seria*', in: *Studi pergolesiani / Pergolesi Studies*, 1 (1986), pp. 89-105; Hudson, Richard. *Jumping to Conclusions. The Falling-Third Cadences in Chant, Polyphony, and Recitative*, Aldershot, Ashgate, 2006; Hostrup Hansell, Sven. 'The Cadence in 18th-Century Recitative', in: *The Musical Quarterly*, LIV/2 (1968), pp. 228-248; Westrup, Jack Allan. 'The Cadence in Baroque Recitative', in: *Natalicia musicologica Knud Jeppesen*, a cura di Bjørn Hjelmborg e Søren Sørensen, Hafniae, Hansen, 1962, pp. 243-252.

5. Strohm, Reinhard. 'Scarlattiana at Yale', in: *Händel e gli Scarlatti a Roma, atti del convegno internazionale di studi (Roma, 12-14 giugno 1985)*, a cura di Nino Pirrotta e Agostino Ziino, Firenze, Olschki, 1987, pp. 113-152: 119.

contenuto è *grosso modo* simile a quello delle varie *Regole per principianti* contenute nelle altre fonti in elenco. Se il Manoscritto Higgs e le altre *Regole* suggeriscono alcuni elementi di analisi pertinenti alla risoluzione del basso continuo nei recitativi e nelle arie, nell'Add. Ms. 14244 due recitativi di una cantata lasciata in abbozzo ricevono particolare attenzione. Sebbene saltuariamente citato, il volume non è stato in realtà mai analizzato né descritto in alcuno studio. Non è esplicitamente dedicato all'arte di suonare il cembalo, anche se tale finalità, reperibile negli altri manoscritti, adombra sempre un'intenzione più ampia che va dall'accompagnare il canto all'apprendere alcuni processi basilari della composizione. Mi accingo a farne qui una breve descrizione: essa risulta funzionale alla finalità di questo scritto perché mostra alcuni agili strumenti utilizzati nella pratica della composizione e dell'improvvisazione nel Settecento. Il volume è composto di 72 fogli, e nei primi lo scritto contiene una serie di formule cadenzali man mano sempre più complesse, quasi totalmente autografe di Scarlatti e talvolta chiamate 'clausole' in altri trattati[6], nonché porzioni della Regola dell'Ottava, la scala armonizzata che originò diffusi *pattern* contrappuntistici all'inizio del Settecento[7]. Gli esempi sottostanti mostrano una selezione del materiale di questo tipo contenuto nell'Add. Ms. 14244.

Es. 1: tre clausole e una porzione della Regola dell'ottava ascendente; da *Principj della musica* di Alessandro Scarlatti, GB-Lbl, Add. Ms. 14244, foll. 4v, 6r, 10v e 18r.

6. Emerge dai trattati scritti tra il periodo rinascimentale e il periodo classico che 'clausola' e 'cadenza' erano talvolta usati come sinonimi. Nel repertorio polifonico prearmonico il termine 'clausola' sottolinea la relazione tra la terminazione del verso e il modulo cadenzale che la sottolinea. Nel genere recitativo è appropriato usare il termine 'clausola' proprio perché questo rapporto sussiste e sottolinea la stretta relazione tra l'unità verso, il basso continuo e la declamazione. Tale relazione può essere realizzata tramite clausole risalenti alla pratica del vecchio stile polifonico (①②①, ①⑦①, ecc.), porzioni della Regola dell'ottava o moderne 'cadenze'. In ogni modo, è molto importante non confondere la moderna concezione di cadenza autentica o semicadenza con la varietà di 'cadenze' codificate tra il Settecento e l'Ottocento, una categoria di formule dal potere di chiusura variabile (spesso apparentato ai vari gradi della punteggiatura) ordinata in GJERDINGEN, Robert. *Music in Galant Style*, New York, Oxford University Press, 2007, pp. 139-176.

7. CHRISTENSEN, Thomas. 'The 'Régle de l'Octave' in Thorough-Bass Theory and Practice', in: *Acta Musicologica*, LXIV (1992), pp. 91-117; SANGUINETTI, Giorgio. 'La scala come modello per la composizione', in: *Rivista di Analisi e Teoria Musicale* (*Composizione e improvvisazione nella scuola napoletana del Settecento*, a cura di Gaetano Stella), XV/1 (2009), pp. 68-96; HOLTMEIER, Ludwig. 'Heinichen, Rameau, and the Italian Thoroughbass Tradition. Concepts of Tonality and Chord in the Rule of the Octave', in: *Journal of Music Theory*, LI/1 (2007), pp. 19-22.

Es. 2: uso parziale della Regola dell'ottava: ①②③ e ③②①; da *Principj della musica* di Alessandro Scarlatti. GB-Lbl, Add. Ms. 14244, fol. 40v. I numeri cerchiati indicano il grado melodico della scala nel basso.

Es. 3: uso parziale della Regola dell'ottava ⑤④③②① e ①②③④⑤, da *Principj della musica* di Alessandro Scarlatti. GB-Lbl, Add. Ms. 14244, fol. 41r.

All'interno del manoscritto seguono poi una lunga serie di bassi numerati e non numerati. Sono 'partimenti', cioè bassi da realizzare a fini di studio, schemi che avranno grande successo nella didattica dei conservatori napoletani del Settecento. Anche questi sono in gran parte autografi di Scarlatti. Tra questo materiale si trovano saltuariamente stesure delle *Toccate* reperibili nei manoscritti di Modena, Montecassino e New Haven (Yale)[8]. Vi si trova accennata anche la grafia di un copista che redigerà anni dopo la serie delle *Regole per principianti* e delle *Toccate* contenute nel manoscritto Campori di Modena edito in facsimile da Luigi Ferdinando Tagliavini per Forni[9].

Ma quello che più ci interessa è che nelle ultime pagine del volume, con molta probabilità sempre autografe di Scarlatti, è abbozzata anche una cantata intitolata 'In su la piaggia aprica'. Tale cantata possiede due recitativi: il primo è interrotto da una serie di progressioni fondamentali I-V-I; il secondo è interrotto da sequenze di basso numerato chiamate 'arpeggi di cembalo' (si veda Es. 4). Riassumendo, il primo recitativo è interrotto per cominciare a realizzare una sequenza di semplici formule cadenzali, mentre il secondo è interrotto da sequenze più complesse definite 'arpeggi di cembalo': la grafia per semibrevi e le saltuarie legature fra i suoni, il fatto che siano 'arpeggi' e quindi facciano riferimento alla pratica dell'accompagnamento o dell'intonazione e che le loro sequenze armoniche siano facilmente reperibili nei recitativi della stessa cantata, ci fanno certi che questi siano bassi 'tipo' per recitativi.

La presenza dell'armatura di chiave non deve sorprendere: la maggior parte dei recitativi di Scarlatti la posseggono. Ciò non significa che questi recitativi abbiano una tonalità precisa: è semplicemente un mezzo per evitare di scrivere continuamente le alterazioni e circoscrivere più facilmente un ambito di triadi in cui muoversi. In

---

[8]. Si veda la griglia iniziale con le collocazioni.

[9]. SCARLATTI, Alessandro. *Lezzioni. Toccate d'intavolatura per sonare il Cembalo. Riproduzione del manoscritto della Biblioteca Estense di Modena*, a cura di Luigi Ferdinando Tagliavini, Bologna, Arnaldo Forni, 1999.

Es. 4: tre «arpeggi di cembalo» da *Principj della musica* di Alessandro Scarlatti. GB-Lbl, Add. Ms. 14244, folia 66r-71v. Le parentesi sotto i pentagrammi sottolineano la tonicizzazione di alcune zone e non sono presenti nell'originale.

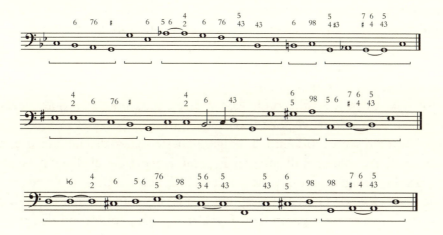

essi poi ritroviamo anche alcune formule cadenzali viste nell'Es. 1, come l'inizio con la nota di volta (clausola ①⑦①) o il tetracordo discendente, tanto usato da Scarlatti nell'apertura dei suoi recitativi. Era comunque materiale condiviso, reperibile anche in altri trattati che toccano direttamente il tema del recitativo e connettono le formule suddette a questo stile: per citarne solo alcuni si pensi alle parti dedicate al recitativo ne *L'armonico pratico al cimbalo* di Francesco Gasparini (1708), che opera nello stesso periodo di Scarlatti, e a *Li primi albori* di Lorenzo Penna, stampato quarant'anni prima. Nel suo trattato, pubblicato per la prima volta nel 1672, Penna mostra cinque 'affetti dissonanti' tipici del recitativo (si veda Es. 5); il quarto e il quinto sono simili alle formule osservate in Scarlatti e, in generale, alle clausole contrappuntistiche del periodo polifonico che sono alla base di questi moduli[10].

Es. 5: i cinque 'affetti dissonanti' dello stile recitativo e quattro battute di 'ruota delle cadenze' del quarto affetto, da *Li primi albori della musica figurata* di Lorenzo Penna (1672).

---

[10]. Penna, Lorenzo. *Li primi albori musicali per li principianti della musica figurata*, Bologna, Giacomo Monti, 1684, pp. 185, 186, 178, 181. Anche Georg Muffat nelle sue *Regulae concentuum partiturae* pubblicate nel 1699, usò la terminologia di 'affetto' in connessione ai processi armonici dello stile recitativo. Si veda Carchiolo, Salvatore. *Una perfezione d'armonia meravigliosa*, Lucca, LIM, 2007, p. 292.

La 'ruota delle cadenze' che Penna illustra in connessione a ogni affetto (poche battute ne sono mostrate nell'esempio precedente), testimonia due importanti elementi: (1) l'esempio mostra come sia necessario fare esercizio in ogni tonalità per divenire agile nell'uso delle formule suddette, sia per l'esecuzione del basso continuo che per l'improvvisazione; (2) queste formule si costituiscono come unità tonali discrete e indipendenti, utilizzabili come elementi singoli nel tessuto musicale del recitativo.

La datazione del materiale contenuto nell'Add. Ms. 14244 ce la dà il manoscritto stesso: al fol. 38v, dove Scarlatti comincia a redigere una nuova seconda versione delle *Regole*, si legge in alto a destra «A. S. 1715».

Perché Scarlatti sente il bisogno di redigere questo materiale che, in parte, condivide con altri autori alcune soluzioni didattiche? *In primis* a beneficio di allievi presenti e futuri. *In secundis* perché redigere detto materiale avrebbe apportato, a suo vedere, ulteriore prestigio: la stessa strategia era stata perseguita da maestri come Bernardo Pasquini, con il suo *Esemplare*, e Francesco Gasparini, con *L'armonico pratico*, conoscenti diretti di Scarlatti. Manca all'appello un altro noto conoscente romano, Arcangelo Corelli, ma è assente solo in apparenza, perché con le sue *Sonate* e i suoi *Concerti grossi*, a ben vedere, Corelli ha realizzato l'opera didattica più nota e diffusa del Settecento. Un'altra ragione per redigere delle 'regole' è sicuramente dovuta al momento storico: questi autori sentirono, con l'avvento del Settecento, l'esigenza di razionalizzare i metodi di insegnamento e di composizione per comunicare un pensiero musicale più moderno e attento alle nuove tendenze culturali. La stessa esigenza coinvolgeva la poesia, settore cardine dell'ambito culturale tardo barocco e primo settecentesco: si pensi solo alle teorie poetiche dell'Arcadia[11].

Ma c'è un'altra probabile ragione per cui Scarlatti ha scritto i *Principij*, le *Regole* e le *Toccate*: quella per cui li abbia scritti per sé, come teorico, compositore e clavicembalista. Scrivere velocemente, accompagnare con abilità, erano requisiti richiesti dai circoli culturali dell'epoca, in parte perché soddisfacevano le esigenze di mecenati e occasioni varie, in parte poiché avere queste doti significava essere in contatto diretto con la 'natura' intesa come fonte di ispirazione e di imitazione, un concetto estetico essenziale all'inizio del Settecento: è in virtù di questo contatto diretto, di questo dono 'naturale', che l'improvvisazione sorge.

Quanto si possa parlare di improvvisazione in un brano con un organico minimo di due esecutori come un recitativo è difficile a dirsi. Alcune fonti citano questa possibilità, specialmente alla fine del Settecento: nel momento in cui la tradizione va declinando alcuni teorici sentono cioè il bisogno di fissarne le caratteristiche. A proposito del recitativo, Carlo Gervasoni nella sua *Scuola della musica*, pubblicata nel 1800, scrive:

---

11.   MORELLI, Giovanni. 'Et in Arcadia ego et Rex et Regina mea. Sulle pratiche musicali romane dei primi anni dell'Arcadia', in: *L'invenzione del gusto. Corelli e Vivaldi: mutazioni culturali a Roma e Venezia nel periodo post-barocco*, a cura di Giovanni Morelli, Milano, Ricordi, 1982, pp. 32-41.

> Colla perfetta intelligenza delle regole e precetti in queste lezioni
> indicati, dopo tre anni circa di esercizio continuato […], si giugne a cantare con
> fondamento ed anche all'improvviso[12].

Per il recitativo sicuramente si può parlare di estemporaneità, cioè di una composizione seduta stante che prevedeva un minimo di accordo precedente con la controparte, poeta e cantante che fosse. La famosa citazione tratta da *L'Arcadia* di Giovan Mario Crescimbeni e riguardante l'estemporizzazione di una cantata di cui Scarlatti realizza la musica e Gian Felice Zappi il testo, testimonia l'apprezzamento per questo genere di 'spontanea' creatività, abbondantemente praticata dai poeti e dai musicisti dell'epoca[13].

Certo l'improvvisazione poteva essere svolta senza incertezze dall'esecutore o dal poeta in esibizioni individuali; con un organico di due persone, in effetti, la cosa riesce più difficile. Ma un metodo per favorire l'estemporaneità o l'improvvisazione in un recitativo poteva essere quello di avere una strategia per collocare le formule nella sequenza corrispondente alle caratteristiche del testo da musicare[14]. L'analisi del repertorio dei recitativi delle cantate di Scarlatti ha infatti messo in evidenza che tale recitativo realizza, differentemente dalle forme chiuse o cicliche, una musica basata quasi interamente sul testo poetico, sulla sua punteggiatura e sulla sua struttura, una musica impegnata a seguire il periodo con caratteri ricorrenti.

Il problema, dunque, è quello di capire quanto le formule possano accordarsi ad altri elementi, principalmente a possibili 'formule' poetiche, e se le clausole e le porzioni di Regola dell'ottava compaiano con una funzione armonica parallela alla concatenazione dei versi, acquisendo così anche delle funzioni formali più o meno precise nel tessuto 'atonale' del recitativo. Il recitativo scarlattiano ha rivelato avere una struttura funzionale al testo nella organizzazione dei materiali formulaici: ovvero certi moduli compaiono prima di altri, e mai viceversa, così come certi altri seguono a loro volta altre formule. Insomma vi si può reperire un ricorrente 'ordine' di comparizione degli elementi simile a quello della sintassi

[12]. Gervasoni, Carlo. *La scuola della musica*, Piacenza, Niccolò Orcesi, 1800, p. 208, § 'Maniera di esprimere il recitativo'.

[13]. Crescimbeni, Giovan Mario. *L'Arcadia*, De Rossi, Roma, 1711, Libro VII, Prosa V, pp. 288-290. Si veda Rinaldi, Mario. *Arcangelo Corelli*, Milano, Curci, 1953, pp. 268-273.

[14]. Vincenzo Caporaletti evidenzia una differenza tra improvvisazione ed estemporizzazione: egli sostiene che la pratica del basso continuo debba costituirsi come 'estemporizzazione' perché realizzazione di un 'modello'. Tuttavia, c'è qualcosa di totalmente inaspettato anche nella realizzazione di un modello, per esempio nella distribuzione degli accordi o degli arpeggi durante l'accompagnamento, oppure nella realizzazione della condotta delle voci, che può essere modificata tramite processi di scambio tra la voce principale e le voci secondarie implicite nella linea contrappuntistica. Sebbene la differenziazione tracciata da Caporaletti sia fondata, i contemporanei di Scarlatti davano a questi elementi il nome di 'improvvisazione' e qui si sceglie di continuare a usare questo termine. Si veda Caporaletti, Vincenzo. *I processi improvvisativi nella musica*, Lucca, LIM, 2005, pp. 98-99 e 231.

linguistica, un ordine nel quale clausole e porzioni di Regola dell'ottava ricoprono, all'interno delle sequenze che realizzano, diverse funzioni formali in rapporto al periodo sintattico della poesia, come fossero frasi del discorso musicale. Tale rapporto si basa sulla connessione tra verso e formula, rapporto che costituisce la caratteristica principale dello stile recitativo. La struttura musicale di tale stile può essere analizzata percorrendo all'indietro la distribuzione dei suoi moduli a partire dalla cadenza perfetta. Alcune formule funzionano da esordio, altre hanno funzione di narrazione, altre sono invece adatte alle chiuse funzionando da epilogo. Questa struttura retorica giunge al recitativo dal tardo madrigale, spesso considerato da teorici e musicisti di inizio Settecento come il modello dello stile recitativo dell'epoca[15], nonché dalla pratica barocca d'organizzare il testo poetico, lirico e sacro, in distinte sezioni, pratica adoperata e insegnata nel sistema didattico gesuitico[16].

Nel recitativo di Scarlatti, dunque, clausole e porzioni di Regola dell'ottava compaiono in rapporto a versi e a sequenze periodiche dalle precise caratteristiche, facendo sì che la sintassi e il valore semantico della poesia facciano da binario alla scelta di alcune formule, le quali, a loro volta, si organizzano in un discorso formale e funzionale ricorrente.

Alcuni esempi: se un recitativo di Scarlatti inizia con un'esclamazione contenente un verso in cui si evoca la bellezza o i pregi dell'amata o dell'amato, vengono preferite al basso le formule ①②①, tonica-sopratonica-tonica, oppure ①⑦①, tonica-sensibile-tonica, sia per il valore statico e contemplativo sia per l'armonia che realizza una sorta di 'guscio' musicale intorno alla figura amata. Si vedano gli Ess. 6, 7, 8.

---

[15]. Arcangelo Spagna scrisse nel 1706 che «in una virtuosa accademia che si adunava una volta al mese in casa del Signor Antonio Maria Abbatini, famoso contrappuntista del secolo passato, dove mi ritrovai più volte, fra le altre materie ivi discusse e ventilate fu riconosciuto che i nostri recitativi erano succeduti in luogo di quei madrigali che furono posti in musica dal principe di Venosa e dal Monteverde, de' quali è propria la totale osservanza delle rime sopradette». Si veda SPAGNA, Arcangelo. *Oratorii overo melodrammi sacri con un discorso dogmatico intorno l'istessa materia*, Roma, Buagni, 1706, p. 2.

[16]. Si veda CECCHI, Paolo. 'Il rapporto tra testo letterario e intonazione musicale nei teorici italiani di fine Cinquecento', in: *Claudio Monteverdi. Letture e prospettive*, a cura di Paola Besutti, Teresa M. Gialdroni e Rodolfo Baroncini, Firenze, Olschki, 1998, pp. 565-566: «La complessa trattazione zarliniana del rapporto tra musica e parola deriva anche [...] da alcune tendenze della teoria poetica coeva che — partendo da alcuni assunti dell'umanesimo letterario, in particolare da una rilettura della retorica oraziana e ciceroniana — sviluppa un'organica e precipua trattazione della prassi poetica, con una specifica attenzione per la poesia lirica». Il testo della *Ratio studiorum*, il manuale basilare che regolava l'insegnamento nelle scuole gesuitiche, riporta abbondanti tracce del tipo di analisi e di strutturazione retorica del testo che veniva praticata durante l'insegnamento. Si vedano: *La 'Ratio studiorum'*, con testo latino a fronte e traduzione italiana, introduzione e traduzione dal latino di Giuliano Raffo S. I., Milano, Garzanti, 1989, pp. 136-137, 163 e 269; ZANLONGHI, Giovanna. 'Il teatro nella pedagogia gesuitica. Una scuola di virtù', in: *I Gesuiti e la Ratio Studiorum*, a cura di Manfred Hinz, Roberto Righi e Danilo Zardin, Roma, Bulzoni, 2004, pp. 180-181.

Es. 6: Alessandro Scarlatti, Cantata 'Liete, placide e belle acque', secondo recitativo, bb. 1-3. I-Nc 34.5.9, fol. 18r.

Es. 7: Alessandro Scarlatti, Cantata 'Filli che del mio core', primo recitativo, bb. 1-3. I-Nc, Cantate 29, fol. 29r.

Es. 8: Alessandro Scarlatti, Cantata 'Dimmi Clori superba', primo recitativo, bb. 1-3. I-Nc 33.3.10, fol. 17r.

Se invece i versi di un recitativo cominciano senza una frase cornice, preferibilmente con le congiunzioni «così», «ma» «dunque», l'accordo in rivolto origina un inizio in *medias res*, generalmente preferito per il recitativo interno di una cantata. Si vedano gli Ess. 9-10.

Es. 9: Alessandro Scarlatti, Cantata 'Ho una pena intorno al core', secondo recitativo, bb. 1-3. GB-Lbl, Add. Ms. 31512, fol. 28r.

Es. 10: Alessandro Scarlatti, Cantata 'Piangi la tua sventura', secondo recitativo, bb. 1-4. I-Nc, Cantate 256, fol. 68r.

L'inizio in forma di 'lamento' è invece realizzato con un tetracordo discendente, spesso cromatico, in corrispondenza di versi che collocano il verbo all'inizio e dissipano l'energia espressiva scivolando sul quinto grado. Lo si ritrova all'inizio di celebri cantate come 'Andate o miei sospiri al cor d'Irene', 'Al fin m'ucciderete o miei pensieri' e 'D'altr'uso serbate quest'amaro mio pianto'.

Tutto questo si chiarisce anche in rapporto al fatto che lo stesso Scarlatti aveva doti più o meno navigate di poeta: non si dimentichi che fu ammesso all'Arcadia anche come rimatore e che a lui si deve l'adattamento se non la creazione di alcuni testi delle sue cantate[17].

Sicuramente egli doveva avere un repertorio armonico da connettere a particolari elementi poetici. Non dico certo una cosa nuova, molti autori si sono soffermati su questo come Caraci o Roger Freitas[18]: non poteva essere che così per un autore che ha scritto più di 600 cantate talora al ritmo di più di una alla settimana, come dimostra il famoso diario contenuto negli autografi di Yale[19]. La paura che le formule possano rivelarsi noiose o ripetitive è assolutamente fugata in Scarlatti: il recitativo mantiene, come detto, un rapporto strettissimo con la poesia realizzandosi, nella composizione scritta, in modo stravagante, libero e spesso espressionistico. Cioè, tenendo ferma l'architettura di base, egli mette in opera delle tecniche per arricchirla. Gli Ess. 11-13 mostrano vari esordi in regola dell'ottava ascendente ①②③④⑤: la tonicizzazione di ③ per mezzo dell'inserzione di un Sol diesis (una piccola clausola ⑦①) in corrispondenza delle parole «caro Fileno» (Es. 12), o l'eliminazione della tonica per rendere udibile la distanza tra il felice passato e l'infelice presente (Es. 13, sulle parole «mi ricordo»), con la conseguente differenziazione del primo accordo rispetto alla rimanente porzione della scala ascendente, sono due delle numerose possibilità per arricchire semanticamente la formula.

---

[17]. IACONO, Sarah M. 'Una raccolta di cantate di Alessandro Scarlatti', in: *Fonti Musicali*, XI (2006), pp. 93-95.

[18]. CARACI, Maria. 'Le cantate romane di Alessandro Scarlatti nel fondo Noseda', in: *Händel e gli Scarlatti a Roma*, op. cit. (si veda nota 5), pp. 93-112. FREITAS, Roger. Op. cit. (si veda nota 3).

[19]. STROHM, Reinhard. 'Scarlattiana at Yale', in: *Händel e gli Scarlatti a Roma*, op. cit. (si veda nota 5), pp. 134-139.

Es. 11: Alessandro Scarlatti, Cantata 'O voi di queste selve abitatrici', primo recitativo, bb. 1-4. I-Nc 34.5.8, fol. 27r.

Es. 12: Alessandro Scarlatti, Cantata 'Appena chiudo gli occhi in breve sonno', primo recitativo, bb. 1-4. I-Baf 1417.14, fol. 50r.

Es. 13: Alessandro Scarlatti, Cantata 'E pur il gran tormento', primo recitativo, bb. 1-3. I-Nc, Cantate 264, fol. 22v.

Anche l'arioso può spesso essere considerato un'altra formula recitativa. Contrariamente a quanto si crede l'arioso non occupa solo la fine di un recitativo, ma può occupare la fine di un singolo periodo interno ad esso, ovvero prendere il posto di una cadenza autentica, permettendo poi al recitativo di continuare indisturbato con note di valore lungo. Nel repertorio di Scarlatti si trovano anche recitativi che iniziano con un accenno di arioso, quasi sempre legato a parole come 'lamento', 'pianto' 'tormento', 'lontananza'.

Se c'era dunque una percentuale di materiale standardizzato, se c'era un ordine in cui questo poteva essere collocato, la libertà dall'andare a tempo e le esigenze di certi tempi drammatici, attestati da molti trattatisti a proposito del recitativo, potevano forse aiutare quando un'improvvisazione si rendeva necessaria, così come il compositore poteva guidare armonicamente il cantante suonando l'accordo prima dell'entrata della voce o il cantante poteva guidare l'esecutore nella chiusura anticipandone l'andamento, per esempio, in una 'cadenza tronca'. Sulla 'libertà' dall'andare a tempo ecco alcune osservazioni di Carlo Gervasoni:

> Non è il recitativo sottomesso alle leggi del canto rapporto alla durata dei suoni; ma indifferentemente si può esprimere la durata di più note ancora d'un eguale valore, tenendo alcune di queste più o meno brevi o lunghe; cosicché né la misura né i tempi particolari di esse non conservino alcuna rigorosa eguaglianza; e l'espressione del sentimento è quella sola che dee dirigere la maggiore o la minore durata dei suoni[20].

Giuseppe Liverani attesta un simile procedimento nella sua *Gramatica della musica* (1798):

> È bene di far qualche parola sui Recitativi, che per l'ordinario non sono obbligati al Tempo, ma rimessi all'arbitrio del cantante. […] Si richiede in questi, quasi più che nelle composizione obbligate, una esatta obbedienza al sentimento della parola, perché senza misura di Tempo[21].

Certo il momento della cadenza era di primaria importanza e in parte riconoscibile per via del suo corrispondere quasi sempre al punto grammaticale. Ciò che traspare poi dai trattati dell'epoca era che il recitativo non era cantato nel senso in cui intendiamo noi il canto. Si avvicinava di più a una sorta di 'melologo' dalla declamazione guidata. Un altro fatto che poteva certo aiutare, se non togliere di impiccio, al momento dell'improvvisazione: sui pannelli musicali del compositore il cantante poteva prendersi alcune licenze nell'intonazione in nome dell'imitazione del discorso parlato.

In ogni caso (e prima di tutto quando era impossibile provare o quando non c'era tempo per studiare), era importante che il cantante desse prima uno sguardo al brano per conoscere il susseguirsi delle tonalità nel quale il basso muoveva (e dopo questo, possiamo ipotizzare, poteva anche improvvisare una linea melodica). Sostiene infatti Gervasoni:

> In qualsivoglia recitativo poi egli è necessario altresì che il Cantore vegga il Basso continuo che vi si rapporta, affinché più chiaramente conoscer possa i toni in cui tratto tratto si fa passaggio[22].

---

[20]. GERVASONI, Carlo. *Op. cit.* (si veda nota 12), p. 207.

[21]. LIVERANI, Giuseppe. *Gramatica della musica*, Roma, Cracas, 1798, pp. 48-49.

[22]. GERVASONI, Carlo. *Op. cit.* (si veda nota 12), p. 208.

Era assai utile procedere così anche per un'altra ragione: ogni formula ha la propria condotta vocale che il cantante poteva usare come semplice schema per ulteriori diminuzioni. La triade del momento poteva essere realizzata come un arpeggio; il cambiamento di formula poteva esser segnato con l'immissione *ex abrupto* nel canto della sensibile della seguente triade; la declamazione di molte formule aveva quasi sempre una fase iniziale ascendente e una fase discendente realizzata tramite figure cadenzali più o meno codificate e da figure retoriche terminanti su consonanze perfette e imperfette. Molte di queste soluzioni appaiono anche nelle linee vocali delle arie: in questa sede è impossibile approfondire la comparazione delle formule nelle arie, ma si può ipotizzare con una certa sicurezza che sussistevano anche in quella forma una serie di strategie, legate al testo, alla pratica del basso continuo e a quella del 'partimento', che potevano guidare gli esecutori anche nell'improvvisazione un'aria.

Formule, condotte vocali standard o diminuite, sistema armonico funzionale correlato al testo (e quanto fosse 'formulaica' l'espressione poetica della lirica arcadica è fatto noto), libertà nell'intonare e nel tenere il tempo, sono chiare tracce di una pratica improvvisativa che potremmo definire come una sorta di oralità artificiosa. Infatti ciò che, al di là di ogni analisi, connette il recitativo all'idea dell'improvvisazione è la sua struttura armonica volutamente aperta, la sua apparente rapsodicità, la scioltezza ritmica dell'accompagnamento. Il recitativo è una creatura musicale che risponde a regole formali finalizzate a non creare forti legami tra le parti. È una creatura artistica che intende sembrare spontanea, non costruita, quasi sorgesse nuova ad ogni battuta, completamente asservita alla forma del testo. È una forma musicale, insomma, che tramite un sistema artificiale riesce a proporsi sempre inattesa e, potremmo dire, improvvisata. Se il recitativo scarlattiano ancora tiene il punto su una ricca descrizione degli affetti, sulla differenziazione delle sezioni con un arioso, sulle minime sezioni melismatiche o sulla pittura madrigalistica di alcune parole, il recitativo operistico settecentesco farà di questa architettata naturalezza il cavallo di battaglia del genere.

SIMONE CIOLFI

ENGLISH SUMMARY

FORMULAS AND IMPROVISATION IN ALESSANDRO SCARLATTI'S CANTATA RECITATIVES

Simone Ciolfi

Perhaps the recitatives in the cantatas of Alessandro Scarlatti do not come to mind as examples of compositions based on improvisation. However, closer scrutiny reveals many passages that follow certain formulae or modules, and one could then conceive of composition as a process of assembling these formulae in a more or less improvisatory way, in order to retain the required degree of spontaneity. Scarlatti has produced a 'treatise' on music theory and composition, preserved in various manuscripts in various versions, entitled *Principi di musica* or *Regole per principianti* or similar. Here we find cadential formulas and harmonized scales, which can be used as the building-blocks of larger structures. They are comparable to the examples found in Lorenzo Penna's *Li primi albori della musica figurata* (1672). In the recitatives of Scarlatti's cantatas the formulae described in the treatises are easily recognized, and they appear to be applied in close correspondence with the meaning and character of the text. Texts containing an evocation of the beauty of the beloved are often set to a simple cadential formula based on tonic-supertonic-tonic or tonic-leading note-tonic. Texts beginnings with a conjunction such as «ma», «dunque», «eppure», etc. followed later by a conclusion are often set to a held sixth chord on the leading tone before resolving to the tonic. Notwithstanding these rules, all theorists allow the singer a large amount of freedom in the performance of the recitative. Both singer and accompanist must, however, know what the other does to achieve a fully satisfactory performance.

Natura e arte
nell'improvvisazione di Giuseppe Tartini

Gregorio Carraro
(Padova)

Cosa vuol dire *beyond notes*? Il virtuoso Felice Giardini avrebbe potuto rispondere che significa buscare un vero e proprio schiaffo da Niccolò Jommelli, «in premio de' ricami che egli aggiungeva alla sua parte [violinistica] di accompagnamento»[1]. Da questo punto di vista, *beyond notes* significa aggiungere un testo (improvvisato dall'esecutore) ad uno preesistente (scritto dal compositore). In altre parole, il termine identifica un tipo particolare di improvvisazione in stato di minorità, tra parentesi, che se da un lato va 'oltre le note' di un testo musicale — spesso con grande potere metamorfico —, dall'altro rimane confinata rigorosamente entro gli intervalli scritti dal compositore.

A ben vedere, ogni epoca (pur con vistose differenze di approccio) dà una sua lettura di che cosa significhi andare *beyond notes*: dal Quattrocento del *Buxheimer Orgelbuch* e del *Codex Faenza*[2], al Cinquecento della *Fontegara* di Sylvestro Ganassi[3], dei trattati di Diego Ortiz, Girolamo Dalla Casa e Giovanni Bassano (senza dimenticare Giovanni Battista Bovicelli)[4], dal Seicento di Francesco Rognoni[5], al Settecento dei trattati di Johann Joachim Quantz, Leopold Mozart e Giuseppe Tartini[6].

---

[1]. Bertini, Giuseppe. *Dizionario storico critico degli scrittori di musica e de' più celebri artisti di tutte le nazioni sia antiche che moderne*, Palermo, Tipografia Reale di Guerra, 1814, p. 176. Sullo schiaffo di Jommelli si veda anche il saggio di Carmela Bongiovanni nel presente volume.

[2]. Per un'edizione moderna del Buxheimer Orgelbuch (Monaco, Bayerische Staatsbibliothek, Ms. Mus. 3725), si segnala quella a cura di Bertha Antonia Wallner, Kassel, Bärenreiter, 1958; per il Codex Faenza (Biblioteca Comunale Manfrediana, Ms. 117) si veda Plamenac, Dragan. 'Keyboard Music of the 14th Century in Codex Faenza 117', in: *Journal of the American Musicological Society*, IV (1951), pp. 179-201; Memelsdorff, Pedro. 'New Music in the Codex Faenza 117', in: *Plainsong and Medieval Music*, XIII (2004), pp. 141-161.

[3]. Ganassi, Sylvestro. *Opera initulata Fontegara*, Venezia, [Autore], 1535.

[4]. Ortiz, Diego. *Trattado de glosas sobre clausulas*, Roma, Valerio Dorico, 1553; Dalla Casa, Girolamo. *Il vero modo di diminuir*, Venezia, Angelo Gardano, 1584; Bassano, Giovanni. *Ricercate passaggi e cadentie*, Venezia, Giacomo Vincenti & Ricciardo Amadino, 1585; Bovicelli, Giovanni Battista. *Regole, passaggi di musica*, Venezia, Giacomo Vincenti, 1594.

[5]. Rognoni, Francesco. *Selva de varii passaggi secondo l'uso moderno*, Milano, Filippo Lomazzo, 1620.

[6]. Quantz, Johann Joachim. *Versuch einer Anweisung, die Flöte traversiere zu spielen*, Berlin, Johann Friedrich Voss, 1752; Mozart, Leopold. *Versuch einer gründlichen Violinschule*, Augsburg, Johann Jacob Lotter, 1756; Tartini, Giuseppe. *Traité des agréments de la musique*, a cura di Pierre Denis, Paris, Autore [=Denis], 1771.

Vista nel suo insieme, dunque, l'improvvisazione 'tra le note' (più che 'oltre le note') è un aspetto centrale nella fruizione della musica, legato a schemi mentali e culturali che hanno prodotto un vero e proprio paradigma. Mutando lungo la linea del tempo, diversificandosi in strati stilistici, esso è tuttavia rimasto omogeneo nel suo obiettivo operativo: modificare un testo musicale dato. Il cuore del problema sta nel definire correttamente questo paradigma, collocando il gesto improvvisativo (ogni tendenza metamorfica del testo, ogni sua modificazione) nel contesto storico-stilistico nel quale accade ossia dal quale ha origine. Va da sé che questo risulti un approccio particolare all'improvvisazione[7].

Tanto più se si riflette su un dettaglio significativo: da un certo momento in poi (dal Quattrocento, come indicato poc'anzi) l'arte di modificare un testo musicale dato è stata tramandata per iscritto. Se non ci sono supporti audio che testimoniano direttamente le improvvisazioni dei cornettisti di San Marco, o dei grandi virtuosi del Settecento, esistono testi che mostrano in base a quali schemi (mentali e musicali) questi improvvisassero. O, più precisamente, come imparassero ad improvvisare[8]. Nel caso particolare del Settecento, l'improvvisazione 'tra le note' si definisce 'ornamentazione', erede della precedente tecnica cinque-seicentesca della diminuzione[9], in tutto e per tutto simile ad essa.

Beyond notes significa, riassumendo, aggiungere una sovrastruttura ad una struttura. In questo senso, lo studio dell'ornamentazione nella musica strumentale del Settecento riguarda i rapporti che intercorrono (o che non intercorrono) tra queste due categorie. Che senso ha un simile approccio? Lo scopo ultimo è quello di stabilire quale ruolo abbia l'ornamentazione nell'«essenza artistica di un brano musicale»[10]. In che modo si stabilisce? È necessario porre alcune domande. Qualora sia scritta, in che modo l'ornamentazione è utile ad un testo base? È qualcosa che ne arricchisce la linea melodica, o ne sottolinea l'affetto desiderato dal compositore? Oppure è un semplice esercizio di scuola che, per così dire, mummifica le possibilità e le scelte improvvisative di un esecutore? Si proceda con ordine.

Il Settecento fornisce numerosi 'luoghi' dell'ornamentazione scritta. In particolare, ne esistono due di privilegiati: i trattati, dove l'argomento viene discusso con precisione chirurgica, dove si spiega ogni singolo dettaglio con dovizie di esempi. In secondo luogo,

---

[7]. A differenza di quanto sostenuto nell'interessante lavoro di CAPORALETTI, Vincenzo. *I processi improvvisativi nella musica*, Lucca, LIM, 2005.

[8]. Certo, una simile argomentazione porta al limite del paradosso: cosa significa 'improvvisazione scritta'? Qual è il limite (se c'è è davvero sottile) tra diminuzione, ornamentazione, improvvisazione? Caporaletti parla di 'estemporizzazione' (*ibidem*, pp. 98 e segg.), ma la natura pratica di questo intervento impedisce ogni ulteriore digressione semantica, che si rinvia ad altra sede.

[9]. Una melodia viene diminuita quando le note che la compongono *ab origine* vengono sostituite da note di valore inferiore (di ornamento), che nell'insieme (proporzionalmente) ricoprono la medesima durata delle note originali.

[10]. NEUMANN, Frederik. *Ornamentation in Baroque and Post Baroque Music, with Special Emphasis on J. S. Bach*, Princeton (NJ), Princeton University Press, 1983.

solo per articolare l'argomentazione in due punti, non perché meno importanti, ci sono i testi musicali, dove la mano del compositore in persona, o quella di un copista, propone la versione ornata alternativa (per esempio, di un movimento di sonata).

Al fine di esemplificare questa astratta suddivisione tipologica, si propongono alcune considerazioni sul *Traité des agrémens de la musique* di Giuseppe Tartini (1692-1770), e su alcuni esempi da sonate per violino del piranese, materiale autografo e manoscritto oggi conservato presso l'Archivio Musicale della Cappella Antoniana di Padova.

Il *Traité des agréments de la musique*
e *Le regole per arrivare a ben suonare il violino* di Giuseppe Tartini

Il *Traité des agrémens de la musique* si chiama *Traité*, ma in realtà non è un trattato nel senso classico del termine. Innanzitutto perché non l'ha scritto Tartini di suo pugno, né è dimostrabile (come sua) la volontà di organizzarlo così come appare strutturato. Ne esiste una versione a stampa del 1771, pubblicata a Parigi da Pierre Denis appena dopo la morte del Maestro delle Nazioni, ma, come sottolinea Pierluigi Petrobelli, l'«originale italiano ci è pervenuto in almeno tre manoscritti che presentano lievi, e pur significative varianti nella lezione del testo»[11]. Tali lezioni nascono dalla mano degli allievi di Tartini che, raccogliendo e razionalizzando gli insegnamenti del Maestro riguardo l'arte del violino (e dell'ornamentazione), avevano dato vita ad uno dei più esaustivi compendi di prassi esecutiva del loro tempo. In questo modo, si è fissato per iscritto quello che Tartini spiegava oralmente durante le sue lezioni. Risultato: tramite esempi scritti, si può risalire a quale soluzione musicale il Piranese ritenesse migliore nell'ornamentazione di precisi spunti melodici. Insomma: il trattato fissava per iscritto 'cosa fare', 'dove farlo', e soprattutto 'come farlo'.

La stesura manoscritta di riferimento è quella dell'allievo Giovanni Francesco Nicolai, conservata a Venezia nella biblioteca del Conservatorio di Musica 'Benedetto Marcello', oggi facilmente accessibile nell'edizione anastatica di Erwin Jacobi[12]. Il manoscritto intitola: «*Regole | per arrivare a ben suonare il violino, col vero | fondamento di saper sicuramente tutto quello che si fa | buono ancora | a tutti quelli ch'esercitano la musica | siano | Cantanti o Suonatori | date in luce dal celebre Sig.r | Giuseppe Tartini | per uso di chi avrà volontà di studiare | copiate da Giovanni Francesco Nicolai | suo Scolaro*». D'ora innanzi, per brevità si parlerà di *Regole*.

---

[11]. PETROBELLI, Pierluigi. 'Giuseppe Tartini', in: *Storia della musica al Santo di Padova*, a cura di Sergio Durante e Pierluigi Petrobelli, Vicenza, Neri Pozza, 1990, pp. 195-196.

[12]. TARTINI, Giuseppe. *Traité des agréments de la musique*, a cura di Erwin R. Jacobi, Celle, Moeck, 1961, Supplemento. Si veda anche JACOBI, Erwin R. 'G. F. Nicolai's Manuscript of Tartini's *Regole per ben Suonar il Violino*', in: *The Musical Quarterly*, XLVII (1961), pp. 207-223.

Continuando con il citato Petrobelli, il trattato tartiniano «offre un'importante delucidazione della tecnica degli ornamenti nella prassi italiana (non solo strumentale) alla metà del Settecento ma deve essere letto e valutato nel quadro complessivo delle idee del suo autore[13], e della sua produzione strumentale, per essere correttamente compreso»[14]. Le *Regole* copiate dal Nicolai rappresentano «il primo lavoro ad essere esclusivamente rivolto alla materia delle ornamentazioni. L'autore appartiene a quella risma di musicisti che raggiungono uguale distinzione nei campi del virtuosismo, della composizione, dell'insegnamento»[15]. Come si vede, Petrobelli e Jacobi puntano sull'importanza epocale di questo testo teorico (ma anche pratico). Pur non costituendo l'oggetto principale del presente intervento, non ci si può sottrarre dal darne una scorsa, se non altro a volo d'uccello.

Nicolai inizia il suo testo con le regole per le arcate: l'ornamentazione nasce tra il crine dell'arco, la pece che lo rende sonoro, e il budello delle corde che vengono sfregate. Non può essere definita senza collocarla nel luogo preciso dove avviene l'emissione sonora, lo strumento che fornisce un senso (un significante, trattandosi di musica strumentale) a ciò che il compositore scrive. Il crine dell'arco sfrega la corda, ed agisce su di essa come l'aria che passa attraverso le corde vocali facendole vibrare, causando l'emissione di un suono. Senza colpi, sforzi, fatiche di sorta, il suono è portato dal piano al forte e poi nuovamente al piano, con una *messa di voce* in tutto simile a quella descritta dai coevi trattati di canto[16].

In altri termini: cambia l'intensità sonora perché cambia la velocità dell'arco, nello stesso modo in cui viene modificata la velocità dell'aria immessa nella gola dal cantante. Si parla di ornamentazione, ma si prende l'argomento alla larga, dandone una precisa e preliminare contestualizzazione relativa alla tecnica strumentale atta ad eseguire l'ornamentazione in un certo modo. Quale? Lo stesso utilizzato dai cantanti.

La prima fattispecie esornativa descritta da Nicolai è l'appoggiatura, la più importante ornamentazione cantabile aggiunta alla nota vera, eseguita nella stessa arcata (ossia nello stesso portamento di voce). È qui che Nicolai (ossia Tartini) scrive qualcosa di fondamentale sul rapporto tra testo e ornamentazione, che va al cuore della definizione del paradigma settecentesco di cui in apertura:

> Dunque se il compositore scrive note eguali per sentimento o per tema
> della sua composizione, non dovendosi mai alterare il sentimento o tema del

---

[13]. Il lessico del trattato spiega molti aspetti di prassi violinistica con termini in tutto e per tutto mutuati dal linguaggio tecnico del canto. Per una riflessione sul lessico tartiniano del *Traité / Regole* si veda GRASSO CAPRIOLI, Leonella. 'Lessico tecnico e strutture linguistiche di Tartini didatta nelle «Regole per ben suonar il violino»', in: *Estratto offerto in occasione della presentazione di «Canto: lessico italiano del canto»*, Londra, IMS Conference, 1997.

[14]. PETROBELLI, Pierluigi. *Op. cit.* (si veda nota 11), p. 196.

[15]. JACOBI, Erwin. *Op. cit.* (si veda nota 12), p. 39.

[16]. Si veda TOSI, Pier Francesco. *Opinioni de' cantori antichi e moderni*, Bologna, Lelio Della Volpe, 1723.

compositore, le appoggiature non potranno né dovranno aver luogo; e sarà sempre vero in pratica che il loro luogo naturale è in note ineguali, la prima delle quali sia più lunga delle susseguenti, e sia o nel battere o nel levare della battuta di tempo ordinario, o nel battere della tripola[17].

Estesa, più in generale, all'ornamentazione *tout-court*, questa frase relativa alle appoggiature conferma quanto riferito dal sopra citato Petrobelli:

La funzione degli abbellimenti, e la loro applicazione al momento dell'esecuzione, parte dal presupposto che loro scopo più autentico sia quello di specificare, nei termini musicalmente più precisi, l'affetto' del movimento o del passo nel quale gli ornamenti vengono impiegati[18].

Ecco alcune risposte alle domande di cui sopra. L'ornamentazione, per Tartini, non deve tradire il senso del testo musicale, l'affetto che il compositore vuole per un dato movimento. Non si può e non si deve stravolgere quello che un compositore vuole dire. Ecco perché non solo esistono appoggiature cantabili adatte a movimenti lenti, ma anche le appoggiature brevi di passaggio, adatte a «ridurre l'espressione a vivacità e brio»[19], da utilizzarsi, quindi, nei movimenti vivaci.

Dopo le appoggiature, Nicolai parla di trillo, tremolo, mordente. La cosa che colpisce di più — per brevità si è costretti a riassumere —, è che per ogni modificazione del testo sono importanti due requisiti: il primo, che il testo sia compreso dall'esecutore nella sua forma base (ossia nel suo 'significato affettivo' originario); il secondo, che ogni trillo (tremolo o mordente) deve essere adeguato all'affetto che si deve esprimere nell'esecuzione. Non esiste cioè un trillo sempre uguale all'altro, un tremolo o un mordente che si equivalgano nella loro fisionomia. Tutto dipende dal testo di partenza, che, posto in questi termini, determina l'esito finale della modifica testuale operata dall'ornamento. Quest'ultimo ha un potere metamorfico rispetto ad una melodia di base che però, sin qui, sembrerebbe essergli comunque e sempre 'superiore'[20]. Ma torniamo a scorrere il testo del Nicolai.

Segue infine la descrizione dei modi naturali ed artificiali. I primi

procedono dalla natura e dal suo dono, comuni a chiunque sia dotato di questo dono, sebbene inesperti affatto di musica, di che vi sono mille esempi

---

17. TARTINI, Giuseppe. *Op. cit.* (si veda nota 12), p. 6.
18. PETROBELLI, Pierluigi. *Op. cit.* (si veda nota 11), p. 196.
19. TARTINI, Giuseppe. *Op. cit.* (si veda nota 12), p. 8.
20. Superiorità semantica, e, restando nell'ambito della prassi esecutiva, superiorità autoritativa, tale che il testo del compositore debba in ogni caso restare quale punto di riferimento del risultato finale proposto dall'esecutore. *Mutatis mutandis*, viene in mente il problema del diritto d'autore nell'improvvisazione: fino a che punto un testo ornato rimane di proprietà del compositore, e fino a che punto viene trasformato dal suo esecutore che ne è, in certa misura, ri-scrittore o co-compositore? Ovviamente, in questo caso si deve intendere il concetto di proprietà in maniera molto ampia.

intellegibili da chiunque, ed adattabili a qualunque cantilena[21] senza pregiudizio della medesima, o discordanza col basso posto sotto la stessa cantilena[22].

Sono modi «insegnati dalla natura stessa», per i quali Nicolai (ossia Tartini) indica il «sito preciso della cantilena» dove poterli collocare, dato che «siccome la natura non falla nel modo, così certamente non falla nel sito dove si deve adattare»[23]. Dove? Gli esempi riportati riguardano melodie che vengono paragonate a quei

periodi o sensi che non portano mai punto fermo, ma o punto e virgola o due punti e si suol dire che sono parti, membri della cantilena che non è interamente compita. Questi dunque sono li veri luoghi e siti convenienti per l'adattazione de' modi naturali[24].

I secondi, i modi artificiali «possono essere infiniti, perché dipendono principalmente dall'arte del contrappunto, quale sopra un dato basso può variare la parte acuta in quanti modi sono possibili, e la possibilità è quasi infinita»[25]. Dove si trovano?

I modi artificiali non possono né devono aver luogo in tutti que' casi ne' quali il tema della composizione o le parti della medesima siano o a soggetto, o di tal sentimento specifico, che non possa alterarsi in modo alcuno, ma debba esprimersi tale quale si trova[26].

Queste citazioni non lasciano dubbi, e forniscono una regola d'ornamentazione duplice: l'una radicata nell'istinto dell'esecutore, l'altra — più concettuale — legata all'uso della tecnica contrappuntistica. Il genio di Pirano sembra riassumere, cartesianamente, i due principali approcci all'improvvisazione 'tra le note'. In questi punti delle *Regole* è racchiusa una chiave di lettura molto interessante per la definizione del paradigma dell'ornamentazione nel Settecento.

Ma si passi ora ai testi musicali cui s'è fatto riferimento sopra, e si torni ad un'altra delle domande poste: che rapporto s'instaura tra struttura e sovrastruttura nell'ornamentazione Settecentesca? Quanto questo rapporto determina l'essenza artistica di un testo musicale?

Per rispondere si è pensato di scomporre il testo tartiniano, operando in senso contrario rispetto a quanto sin qui detto, ossia aumentando le parti già diminuite (ornate), per arrivare all'osso del pensiero musicale del Maestro.

---

[21]. Termine legato al lessico contrappuntistico, qui usato come sinonimo di *cantus firmus* (sul quale il contrappuntista aggiustava nello studio quotidiano le sue concatenazioni 'armoniche'), o, più in generale, come sinonimo di melodia.

[22]. TARTINI, Giuseppe. *Op. cit.* (si veda nota 12), p. 20.

[23]. *Ibidem.*

[24]. *Ibidem*, p. 22.

[25]. *Ibidem*, p. 29.

[26]. *Ibidem.*

Sin qui si è parlato di 'affetto originale del compositore', di 'testo di base', di 'struttura', lo stesso Tartini parla di 'scheletro' sul quale ornare. Osserviamo, in questo modo, lo scheletro da vicino. Per fare questo, si prendano in esame tre esempi dalle sonate tartiniane, in particolare la Sonata D4 in re maggiore, la Sonata G8 in sol maggiore, e la Sonata E4 in mi maggiore[27].

LA SONATA D4 IN RE MAGGIORE

Le sonate del Ms. 1888 della Biblioteca Antoniana a Padova sono autografe, in tutto 25, con il citato Petrobelli «in un manoscritto che reca evidenti i segni del lavoro di lima e di riordino del compositore, […] [le Sonate costituiscono] l'estrema fase di sviluppo del linguaggio sonatistico tartiniano»[28]. In una lettera al Conte Francesco Algarotti, del 24 febbraio 1750, è lo stesso Tartini a darne una definizione: «Le piccole sonate mie a violino solo […] hanno il basso *per cerimonia*: particolarità, che non le scrissi. Io le sono senza bassetto, e questa è la vera mia intenzione». Ancora: «La linea melodica del solista racchiude quindi l'intera manifestazione del pensiero musicale»[29].

L'ornamentazione scritta in un simile contesto, forse rappresenta quanto di più personale, quasi intimo, si possa leggere sullo stile esornativo di Tartini, forse più che nel cosiddetto trattato. Ma come si stratifica il testo? L'Esempio 1a è la trascrizione della versione ornata del terzo movimento — Aria cantabile «Alla stagione novella» — della Sonata D4 in re maggiore, così come si presenta nel manoscritto. Si è passati dalla notazione tartiniana ad una prima aumentazione, ottenendo una struttura di semiminime (Esempio 1b). Dalle semiminime si è aumentato ancora, ottenendo uno scheletro di minime (Esempio 1c).

Es. 1: Giuseppe Tartini, Sonata per violino D4, terzo movimento. (A) Parte del violino, come si presenta nel manoscritto autografo padovano. (B) La stessa parte, prima aumentazione, con una struttura di semiminime. (C) La stessa parte, seconda aumentazione, con uno scheletro di minime.

---

[27]. Le sigle delle sonate sono quelle in BRAINARD, Paul. *Le sonate per violino di Giuseppe Tartini*, Milano, Carisch, 1975 (Studi e Ricerche dell'Accademia Tartiniana di Padova).

[28]. PETROBELLI, Pierluigi. *Op. cit.* (si veda nota 11), p. 194.

[29]. Questo stralcio di lettera di Tartini all'Algarotti è trascritto *ibidem*.

Gregorio Carraro

Andando avanti di questo passo, si potrebbe ottenere una sorta di forma essenziale del testo scarnificato, all'osso del messaggio musicale del compositore. Allora: cos'è il cosiddetto scheletro? E, al contrario, cosa si intende per ornamentazione? Ogni scalino verso l'aumentazione porta ad eliminare note ottenendo una melodia a valori sempre più lati. Ogni scalino verso la diminuzione porta ad aggiungere note, ottenendo una melodia a valori sempre più piccoli. Ma si proceda all'altro esempio.

LA SONATA G8 IN SOL MAGGIORE

La Sonata G8 è un testo interessante perché collega il manoscritto 1905 di Padova a due altri luoghi tartiniani: Ancona e Berkeley[30]. Tre manoscritti hanno una versione ornata del primo movimento, l'Adagio. Ma non è questo in oggetto. Si osservi, anche in questo caso, lo *shift* tra sovrastruttura e struttura. La versione trascritta nell'Esempio 2a riporta gli ornamenti nel manoscritto padovano. Si vedono trilli, mordenti, appoggiature, tirate di biscrome. Nell'Esempio 2b si vede il testo ripulito da ogni elemento sovrastrutturale, in una semplice melodia di semiminime.

Che significato ricopre la complessità della sovrastruttura? È attinente all'affetto della struttura sopra indicata? Si torna a chiedere: che cos'è la struttura? Se avessimo aumentato ancora, ad ottenere una melodia di minime, si sarebbe trattato di uno scheletro ancor più essenziale, e quindi ancor più vicino all'idea originaria? Ancora: cosa significa diminuire un testo? Quale testo? Ma si proceda con l'ultimo esempio.

---

30. I-AN, Ms. T.62 (versione ornata del primo movimento), US-BE, It. Ms. 694/2, 742, e 988/8 (versione ornata del primo movimento).

Es. 2: Giuseppe Tartini, Sonata per violino e basso G8, primo movimento. (a) Misure 1-4, riportando gli ornamenti del Ms. 1905 a Padova. (b) Le stesse misure, aumentazione, una semplice melodia di semiminime.

LA SONATA E4 IN MI MAGGIORE

L'autografo qui in oggetto (I–Pca, Ms. 1896) è una miscellanea contenente parti di concerti e altro materiale testuale del quale non s'intende trattare qui. La sonata è presente anche nel già menzionato Ms. 1905 di Padova, nel Ms. T. 49 di Ancona e nel Ms. It. 724 di Berkeley, dove c'è un'altra versione ornata del primo movimento con sigla 998/14, come nel citato Catalogo Brainard. Ma non ci si vuole certo soffermare su questioni filologiche che porterebbero via spazio al *focus* del contributo.

Si faccia riferimento, piuttosto, alla particolare notazione in cui si presenta il primo movimento dell'autografo, del quale si riporta la trascrizione nell'Esempio 3. Come si vede, la parte del violino è scritta su tre righi, e sul quarto è notato il basso. Qual è la particolarità? Le tre righe acute riportano, in realtà, tutte la medesima *tranche* di movimento, fiorito in tre modi diversi.

Es. 3. Giuseppe Tartini, Sonata per violino e basso E4, primo movimento, come si trova nel Ms. 1896 a Padova.

È interessante perché, sul manoscritto, la mano di Tartini (la stessa per tutti e tre i righi) annota soluzioni diverse per la medesima melodia. È questa una testimonianza diretta delle infinite possibilità di cui si parlava poco sopra nel trattato. In realtà non sono infinite (ce ne sono a malapena tre), ma risulta singolare questa attitudine a lasciare il discorso aperto. Si notino anche le caselle lasciate in bianco, quasi un invito a riempirle. Va senza dire che persino in questo caso si può ragionare per aumentazione, e ottenere un testo a valori lati come negli esempi precedenti.

A quali conclusioni porta l'esercizio di *shifting* sin qui attuato?

CONCLUSIONI

Il rapporto tra struttura e sovrastruttura è del tutto arbitrario, demandato allo sguardo di chi analizza un movimento ornato, che per aumentazione può essere ridotto a poche note di riferimento.

Una nota 'tra le note' è un ornamento quando riempie intervalli di note dal valore più grande. Le minime rispetto alle semibrevi, le semiminime rispetto alle minime, e via così, fino ad arrivare alle biscrome.

È difficile pensare che basti togliere la sovrastruttura per ottenere il pensiero originale del compositore, che, a ben guardare i casi sin qui trattati, risulterebbe davvero scarno. Forse il pensiero dell'autore risiede proprio nella sovrastruttura da lui indicata per iscritto, ossia nell'ornamentazione. Di più, è proprio senza l'ornamentazione che il pensiero del compositore rischia di essere deformato, travisato, non capito.

Procedendo in questo ragionamento, si giunge ad una situazione diametralmente opposta rispetto a quanto si diceva in apertura dell'intervento. Da questo punto di vista, non solo l'ornamento arricchisce il testo, ma ne rappresenta una chiave di lettura (di comprensione) privilegiata. Senza ornamentazione l'essenza artistica del testo difficilmente si riuscirebbe ad individuare.

A questo punto, però, entra in gioco un altro fattore, a completare il puzzle: l'abilità che l'esecutore possiede nel porgere gli abbellimenti indicati, dal compositore o da chi per lui. Dove risiede? Si deve tornare all'inizio delle *Regole*, dove si parla di arcate. Anche dove la quantità di note d'ornamento risultasse notevole, l'arco dovrebbe volare sulle corde ed essere duttile al punto da non far notare la pesantezza dei passaggi impegnativi, e tutto dovrebbe rientrare in una cantabile naturalezza. La stessa che è capace di sottolineare, al contrario, i momenti più calmi, teneri e patetici.

Insomma, l'ornamentazione, così come la presenta Tartini, è una questione di prassi esecutiva intrinsecamente legata alla tecnica del violino (inteso come lui l'intendeva), della quale oggi restano soltanto le ipotesi degli studiosi, e la buona volontà dei musicisti.

Natura e arte nell'improvvisazione di Giuseppe Tartini

English Summary

Nature and Art in the Improvisation of Giuseppe Tartini

Gregorio Carraro

'Beyond Notes' can be understood as referring to that which is added to the written score. Sometimes composers expect performers to adhere assiduously to the written texts; in other situations it is assumed that the performers add much to what is written. There is a long history of these additions being notated in full. If not notated, they consist of improvisation 'within the notes' rather than 'beyond the notes'. The work of Giuseppe Tartini (1692-1770) provides excellent examples with which to study these processes, since he has left both a treatise about ornamentation and practical examples. The treatise was published in Paris posthumously in French translation as *Traité des agrémens de la musique* (1771), but is also known in various manuscript versions in Italian, of which that compiled by his pupil Giovanni Francesco Nicolai (now in I-Vc) is the most important. There are two ways to elaborate a musical composition, the natural mode and the artificial mode. The natural mode mostly retains the melody, the artificial mode may move away from the original melody but remains within the limits of harmony and counterpoint defined by the melody. The first (slow) movements of three sonatas for violin, preserved in various manuscripts in Padua, Ancona and Berkeley, may serve as examples of the various ways of realizing a musical surface on top of a basic structure. The melodies of the opening Adagios of the Sonatas in D major D8 and G major G8 can be rewritten stepwise in ever larger note values, until only basic skeletons remain. The opening Adagio of the Sonata in E major E4 is preserved in an autograph manuscript where the violin part is worked out in three different ways, with an ever-changing surface. These examples raise, but do not answer, the question of what is the most important and essential part of the composition: the skeleton or the detailed, elaborated surface structure?

«Cet art est la perfection du talent»
Chordal Thoroughbass Realization
and Improvised Solo Performance on the Viol
and the Cello in the Eighteenth Century

John Lutterman
(Walla Walla, WA)

Recent scholarship has raised significant ontological problems concerning the concept of a musical work and the meaning of notation in music composed before 1800[1]. This is an important but difficult topic, one that has generated more heat than light, and I will avoid delving very far into that particular can of worms in this essay. However, when considering early examples of music for unaccompanied viol and cello and their relation to historical improvisatory practices, I would suggest that by attempting to bracket common modern assumptions about the nature of written compositions as musical works, we may more profitably come to understand them as artefacts that offer valuable clues to the nature of the unwritten practices that played such an important role in eighteenth-century musical life. In my view, such an approach offers two important advantages. First, by seeking traces of historical improvisatory practices that may be embedded in written compositions, we should be able to effectively triangulate our understanding of such practices. But we should also be able to enrich our understanding of the ontological status of written compositions by triangulating them against what we are able to learn of their relation to historical improvisatory practices.

Since, as his nemesis Johann Scheibe so infamously complained, J. S. Bach was in the habit of writing out what other composers left to the performer, his compositions should be particularly useful in this regard. One artefact, that by Bach's own account constitutes a written record of a particular improvised performance, is the score of the three-part

---

[1]. Dahlhaus, Carl - Müller, Ruth E. - Zaminer, Friederick. *Die Musiktheorie im 18. und 19. Jahrhundert*, Darmstadt, Wissenschaftliche Buchgesellschaft, 1984; Goehr, Lydia. *The Imaginary Museum of Musical Works. An Essay in the Philosophy of Music*, New York, Oxford University Press, 1992; Taruskin, Richard. *Text and Act. Essays on Music and Performance*, New York, Oxford University Press, 1995; Treitler, Leo. 'History and the Ontology of the Musical Work', in: *The Journal of Aesthetics and Art Criticism*, 1/3 (1993), pp. 483-497.

Ricercare from *The Musical Offering*. David Schulenberg has suggested that we consider this score in the same light as contemporary engravings of opera scenes, in which the effects of gravity are ignored and the stage machinery that enables gods and heroes to fly into the heavens is nowhere to be seen[2]. Like an engraving of a favorite opera scene, the score of *The Musical Offering* would have served as a record or memento of an important performance. While an artefact such as an engraving can certainly be understood as an autonomous art work, it may also provide us with important insights into the arts that it depicts, such as the practice of opera staging, especially when we interpret what we see in terms of what we know or are able to discover about the laws of gravity, historical practices of choreography and dramaturgy, and the mechanical nature of the unseen stage machinery that may have been available at a particular historical moment. Since much of Bach's instrumental music was designed for use in his teaching, particularly the pieces for unaccompanied instruments, we should be able to deduce some of the improvisatory principles that he was illustrating for his students.

A word of caution is in order here: we should bear in mind that Bach's written music probably presents us with an idealized portrayal of his improvisatory practices. Thus, it may be useful to think of his approach to creating the written version of the three-part Ricercare as analogous to the 'post-production' editing of modern sound recordings. Nonetheless, by considering Bach's compositions in the light of what we know of contemporary improvisatory practices, we should be able to make some educated guesses about the nature of the techniques and structural frameworks that made his improvisatory practices possible, just as we can estimate the nature of the inconvenient effects of gravity and the kinds of balky stage machinery that may have shaped the operatic practices represented in engravings. In this essay, I will attempt to sketch a few of the insights that such an approach may offer to the study of eighteenth-century improvisatory practices on the viol and cello.

PRACTICES OF THOROUGHBASS REALIZATION ON THE CELLO

The title of this essay, «Cet art est la perfection du talent», is taken from the official cello treatise of the Paris Conservatoire, published c. 1804[3]. The citation refers, not as one might expect, to virtuoso solo playing, but rather to a practice of chordal realization of figured bass lines in the accompaniment of recitative, a topic accorded great importance in most of the early cello treatises, but which has received very little attention from modern scholars or performers. Yet, for a virtuoso performer of Bach's day, both solo performance

---

[2]. SCHULENBERG, David. 'Composition and Improvisation in the School of J. S. Bach', in: *Bach Perspectives*, 1 (1995), pp. 1-42.

[3]. BAILLOT, Pierre - LEVASSEUR, Jean-Henri - CATEL, Charles-Simon - BAUDIOT, Charles-Nicolaus. *Méthode de violoncelle et de basse d'accompagnement*, Paris, L'imprimerie du Conservatoire, [c. 1804].

and the art of accompanying would have depended on the development of a common set of improvisatory skills, founded on the ability to realize the harmonic implications of a bass line. Most of the late seventeenth- and early eighteenth-century composition treatises, particularly in Germany, were essentially thoroughbass methods, and it is clear from these treatises that for a professional musician improvisation was the most highly regarded form of composition. In fact, keyboard players used figured bass lines as frameworks to extemporaneously compose complete examples of all of the common instrumental genres of the day, a practice commonly referred to today as *partimento*. I will argue that eighteenth-century cellists and viol players used similar procedures in their solo improvisations.

The first published cello treatise to discuss thoroughbass realization, Johann Baptist Baumgartner's *Instructions de musique, théorique et pratique à l'usage du violoncello*, did not appear until 1774[4], but the author makes clear that he is describing practices with a long history, and we should bear in mind that his was the very first comprehensive treatise to be published by a professional cellist. We should also bear in mind that virtually all of the early instrumental methods were designed for and marketed to amateur musicians, witness the title of John Lenton's *The Gentleman's Diversion, or the Violin Explained* (1693). Until the advent of the nineteenth-century conservatories, professional musicians were most often trained as apprentices, in a guild system in which advanced techniques were regarded as trade secrets, and, as a result, were seldom expressed in writing. Thus, while useful, we should bear in mind that the early instrumental treatises can offer us only very fragmentary and indirect evidence of professional practices, that their instructions are, in effect, simplified translations of such practices for the benefit of amateur musicians.

The importance that eighteenth-century cellists accorded thoroughbass realization is reflected in the fact that Baumgartner devotes close to half of his treatise to the topic. Even cello methods that do not explicitly mention thoroughbass practice attach great importance to the skills that would be required for the chordal realization of a bass line, particularly the study of double-stops and arpeggiated chords, studies that are typically arranged in formulaic patterns of scales, sequences and cadential progressions, with fingerings designed to facilitate the proper approach and resolution of dissonance (see Ex. 1).

Ex. 1: double-stop fingerings organized for smooth resolution of dissonance. From Johann Baptist Baumgartner, *Instructions de musique, théorique et pratique à l'usage du violoncello* (1774).

---

4. BAUMGARTNER, Johann Baptist. *Instructions de musique, théorique et pratique à l'usage du violoncello*, The Hague, Monnier, 1774.

Practices of Chordal Harmonic Realization on the Viol

Earlier evidence, often in the form of complaints, shows that virtuoso viol players were also in the habit of improvising harmonic realizations of continuo lines, and the practices described in the cello treatises would appear to reflect the types of harmonic thinking and improvisatory traditions that solo viol players had developed over the previous two centuries — ways of thinking and traditions that the many eighteenth-century viol players who abandoned the viol for the cello would almost certainly have adapted to their new instrument (see TABLE 1).

TABLE 1
A CHRONOLOGICAL LIST OF TREATISES AND CONTEMPORARY ACCOUNTS
OF CHORDAL THOROUGHBASS PERFORMANCES

AUTHOR	TITLE	PLACE OF PUBLICATION LOCATION OF MANUSCRIPT DATING
Nicola Matteis	*Le false consonanse della musica* / *The False Consonances of Musick*	London, [Author], c. 1680 / John Carr, 1782
Anonymous	*Modo, ò sia Regola per acompagnare il basso continuo per la viola da gamba.*	Manuscript, XVII–XVIII? I-Bc, D.117
M. de L.T.	'Dissertation sur la musique italienne et françoise'	*Mercure Galant*, November 1713
Johann Mattheson	*Das neu-eröffnete Orchester*	Hamburg, Author, 1713
	Report of a concert by violinists G. B. Somis and J. P. Guignon, accompanied by only bassoon and viola da gamba	*Mercure [de France]*, Paris, 25 April 1725
Roland Marais	*Règles d'accompagnement pour la basse de viole*	Manuscript, Paris, XVIII NL-DHa
Ancelet	*Observations sur la musique, les musiciens, et les instruments*	Amsterdam, Compagnie, 1757, p. 24.
Johann Baptist Baumgartner	*Instructions de musique, théorique et pratique à l'usage du violoncello*	The Hague, Daniel Monnier, 1774
Christian Friedrich Daniel Schubart	*Ideen zu einer Ästhetik der Tonkunst*	Written: Vienna 1784 Vienna, J. V. Degen, 1806
Ferdinand Kauer	*Kurzgefasste Anweisung das Violoncello zu Spielen*	Vienna, Artaria, 1788
Jean-Marie Raoul	*Méthode de violoncelle*	Paris, I. Pleyel, c. 1797

Anonymous	'Einige Tonkünstler älterer Zeiten'	*Allgemeine musikalische Zeitung*, III (1799), pp. 34-38
John Gunn	*An Essay Theoretical and Practical*	Edinburgh, Preston, 1802
Pierre Baillot, and others	*Méthode de violoncelle et de basse d'accompaniment*	Paris, Magasin de Musique du Conservatoire Royal, c. 1804
Gottfried Weber	'Praktische Bemerkungen'	*Allgemeine musikalische Zeitung*, LI (1807), pp. 805-811
Franz Joseph Froehlich	*Violoncell-Schule nach den Grundsätzen der besten über dieses Instrument bereits erschienen Schriften*	Bonn, Simrock, c. 1810
Gottfried Weber	'Begleitung des Recitativs'	*Allgemeine musikalische Zeitung*, 6 (1811), p. 93-97
Johann Georg Schetky	*Practical and Progressive Lessons for the Violoncello*	London, Bremner, 1811
Bernard Stiastny (Šťastný)	*Violoncell-Schule*	Mainz, Schott, c. 1811
Justus Johann Friedrich Dotzauer	*Violonzell-Schule* [translation of Baillot, 1804]	Mainz, Schott, c. 1823
Charles-Nicolas Baudiot	*Méthode pour le violoncelle, Op. 25*	Paris, I. Pleyel, c. 1826
Frederick William Crouch	*A Compleat Treatise on the Violoncello* [translation of Baillot, 1804]	London, Chapell, 1827
Arnold Merrick	*Method for the Violoncello by Baillot, Levasseur, Catel & Baudiot, Adopted by the Paris Conservatory of Music* [translation of Baillot, 1804]	London, Robert Cocx, [1832]
Bernhard Romberg	*Méthode de violoncelle*	Berlin, Trautwein, before 1839
Ferdinand Simon Gassner	*Dirigent und Ripienist für angehende Musikdirigenten, Musiker und Musikfreunde*	Karlsruhe, C. T. Groos, 1844

Even the very earliest treatises and examples of unaccompanied solo viol music offer valuable insight into the technical means of improvised polyphonic solo playing, beginning with the sixteenth-century treatises of Sylvestro Ganassi and Diego Ortiz, and the accounts of *lira da braccio*, *lirone* and *bastarda* styles of performance. Later traditions of polyphonic solo viol playing, such as the seventeenth-century lyra-viol practices also provide important clues. One of the most tantalizing of these is the French practice known as *jeu d'harmonie*. In the preface to his *Pièces de violle* of 1685, Sieur de Machy described three primary genres of performance on the viol, and then went on to argue that *jeu d'harmonie* was an essential feature of the two most important of these practices:

> The first and most common is playing *pièces d'harmonie* [unaccompanied chordal pieces] [...] the second [...] consists of accompanying oneself, singing one part while playing the other [...]; the third is to play in consort. [...] To respond to those who want to argue that Solos of a single melody are preferable to those that are harmonized: I say that they are more wrong than they think, since by this they reveal that they are ignorant in this matter. And when they cite pieces with a single melody by some skilled man [...] they do not notice that these are made for several viols — which should be easy to recognize. A person can have a hand for playing melodies that are beautiful but single; but this must be compared to a man who might play perfectly on the Harpsichord or the Organ with one hand alone. This single playing might be very pleasant, but one would hardly call it playing the Harpsichord [or] the Organ[5].

The most thorough and sophisticated instruction in the art of improvised polyphonic solo playing on the viol came from Britain: Christopher Simpson's *The Division-Viol*, first published in 1659. *The Division-Viol* is among the most systematic and comprehensive treatises on improvisation ever written, and it offers exceptionally valuable insight into the practices of seventeenth-century British musicians, practices that had a far more widespread and longer-lasting influence than has generally been recognized. Indeed, *The Division-Viol* remained popular enough to justify the printing of a third edition as late as 1712.

Most of Simpson's examples offer rather formulaic settings over relatively short ground basses, but this simply reflects the didactic nature of his work. Indeed, several of the larger sets of divisions that he appends to the treatise make use of more complex and extended structures, especially his examples of free preludes. Simpson's conception of harmony is more advanced than has been generally recognized, anticipating Rameau by more than fifty years in demonstrating the equivalence of inverted triads. Simpson begins his treatise with instructions for 'breaking the ground' (ornamentating of the ground bass), followed by 'descanting' (improvising a new line above the bass) and concluding with 'mixt' divisions, in which the performer jumps quickly back and forth between divisions in the bass and descant, producing a texture of implied polyphony.

The organization of *The Division Viol* shares certain important features with Friedrich Erhardt Niedt's *Musikalische Handleitung*, an important treatise on *partimento* thoroughbass realization, published in three installments, that documents the influential teachings of Bach's cousin, Johann Nicolaus Bach in Jena[6]. Like Simpson, Niedt begins his instructions for *partimento* elaboration with examples of varying the bass itself, followed by variations in the right-hand realization, before giving examples in which both right and left hands are meant to improvise variations. Niedt's most valuable contribution to our understanding

---

5. MACHY, Sieur de. *Pièces de violle, en musique et en tablature*, Paris, l'auteur, 1685, as translated in KINNEY, Gordon J. 'Writings on the Viol by Dubuisson, De Machy, Roland Marais, and Étienne Loulié', in: *Journal of the Viola da Gamba Society of America*, XVIII (1976), pp. 17-55.

6. NIEDT, Friedrich Erhardt. *Musikalische Handleitung*, 3 vols., Hamburg, Benjamin Schiller, 1710-1721.

of eighteenth-century improvisatory practices is to be found in the second volume of the *Handleitung*, in which he demonstrates ways to adapt a figured bass line to serve as a framework for generating a variation suite.

Although *The Division Viol* does not give the kind of written-out examples of the more complex large-scale genres found in Niedt's treatise (Simpson complains of the cost of printing long sets of divisions), following his advice to use a longer «continued ground», such as «the *Through-Bass* of some *Motet* or *Madrigal*» would result in the same kind of structured *partimento* approach to the improvisation of large-scale genres that Niedt's treatise was intended to teach[7].

Harmonic Treatment in Early Compositions for Unaccompanied Cello

Most of the mid to late seventeenth-century manuscript collections of solo music for unaccompanied 'violone' by composers in Bologna and Modena are rather tedious sets of *partite* that, much like Ortiz's *glosas* and English collections of divisions, were apparently meant to be used in teaching simple improvisatory skills[8]. One of the most important of these collections, Giovanni Battista Vitali's *Partite sopra diverse sonate per il violone*, includes several pieces that make references to *alfabeto* chord symbols, suggesting something of the harmonic nature of Vitali's conceptual framework[9].

Harmonically conceived improvisatory skills are also implicit in the treatment of Francesco Supriani's twelve *Toccate*, which are found in a manuscript that constitutes the first surviving method written specifically for the cello. Supriani's *Toccate* are also found in a later manuscript source in an alternate version in which they are subjected to both reductive simplification and extremely virtuosic elaboration, both of which depend on an understanding of the harmonic implications of the toccatas (see Exs. 2ab)[10].

Ex. 2: (a) Francesco Supriani, Toccata No. 1, in: *Principij da imparare a suonare il Violoncello e con 12 Toccate a solo* (before 1756); (b) Same composition, in the so-called *Sonate a 2 Violoncelli e Basso*.
(a)

---

7. Simpson, Christopher. *The Division Viol*, London, W. Godbid, 1659, p. 57.

8. The term 'violone' was used in various ambiguous ways in late seventeenth-century Italy, and should not be taken as referring to an instrument precisely equivalent to a modern cello, but the early compositions for unaccompanied 'violone' do appear to have been intended for an eight-foot instrument of the violin family.

9. Vitali, Giovanni Battista. *Partite sopra diverse sonate per il violone*, Modena, before 1692, Manuscript in I-MOe.

10. Supriani, Francesco. *Principij da imparare a suonare il violoncello e con 12 Toccate a solo*, and *Sonate per 2 violoncelli e basso* (Naples, before 1756). Both manuscripts are currently housed in I-Nc.

(b)

Supriani's treatise appears to have been designed for use at one of the Naples Conservatories, which were also among the most important centers of late seventeenth- and early eighteenth-century *partimento* practices. Several important early virtuoso cellists were associated with the Naples conservatories, among them, Francesco Alborea, known as 'Francischello', Rocco Greco and Leonardo Leo. The latter two were among the authors of manuscripts containing bass lines that served as *partimento* exercises, exercises that share a number of motivic and structural similarities with early Northern-Italian compositions for unaccompanied violone or violoncello.

TRACES OF IMPROVISATORY PRACTICES IN BACH'S SUITES FOR VIOLONCELLO SOLO

Near the end of the Prelude to Bach's D Minor Suite for Violoncello solo, the predominant sixteenth-note motion comes to an abrupt halt, and the final five bars consist of a simple cadential progression over a dominant pedal, notated as a series of dotted half-note triple-stops. For a performer well-versed in eighteenth-century notational practice it should be obvious that such a passage was intended to serve as a basis for an arpeggiated realization, but until quite recently, it was common practice for performers to treat this passage literally, the result being a series of stentoriously sustained chords. Double slashes through the stems of these chords in an eighteenth-century manuscript copy of the suites found in Vienna, but which originated from a scribe associated with C. Ph. E. Bach in Hamburg, serve to verify that some kind of arpeggiated realization would have been expected.

Bach wrote simple block chords that were to be arpeggiated in performance in several of his compositions, and it seems safe to take such passages as clues to some of the simpler processes that Bach used when improvising. Perhaps the best-known example is an early version of the famous C Major Prelude from *The Well-Tempered Clavier*, Book 1. Most of this version, found in the *Clavierbüchlein für Wilhelm Friedemann Bach*, is written in block chords, and it is considerably shorter than the expanded version that Bach later created by interpolating new sequences of harmonies.

As David Schulenberg and Joel Lester have suggested, this prelude manifests a process that Bach employed in many of his compositions, and as Schulenberg points out, the vocabulary of arpeggiations that Bach employs in such preludes is similar to the much simpler examples illustrated by Niedt in his *Handleitung*:

> The significance of these figures in Bach lies in what may be called their motivicity — their emergence out of a fleeting or arbitrary usage as improvisatory embellishments and their crystallization as concrete musical ideas, valued and developed in their own right and not as ornaments of something else[11].

Joel Lester has demonstrated that Bach's preluding process may be understood as the elaboration of a general *schema* that he employed as a framework for composing or improvising in a broad variety of genres. Bach's *schemata* typically begin with a 'framing' cadential gesture to establish the key, often over a tonic pedal, followed by a passage in which sequential treatment initiates movement toward new key areas, often supported by a descending scalar bass, characterized by a gradual intensification of harmonic and/or contrapuntal activity, and eventually building to a cadential passage in the new key that marks the end of the first large section. This procedure is then reprised in one or more parallel passages, which are themselves invariably more expansive, elaborate intensifications

---

11. Schulenberg, David. 'Composition as Variation. Inquiries into the Compositional Procedures of the Bach Circle of Composers', in: *Current Musicology*, xxxiii (1982), pp. 57-87: 77. Bach's employment of such *schema* is discussed further in Schulenberg, David. 'Composition and Improvisation […]', *op. cit.* (see note 2), as well as in Lester, Joel. 'J. S. Bach Teaches Us How To Compose. Four Pattern Preludes of the Well-Tempered Clavier', in: *College Music Symposium*, xxxviii (1998), pp. 33-46; and Id. 'Heightening Levels of Activity and J. S. Bach's Parallel-Section Constructions', in: *Journal of the American Musicological Society*, liv (2001), pp. 49-96.

of the opening *schema*. In approaching the end of a movement, a dominant pedal point is usually introduced, with further sequences culminating in a final closing cadential 'frame', which, like the opening, is often over a tonic pedal.

Although J. S. Bach never wrote a manual to explain his approach, the use of such *schemata* is just the kind of process that C. Ph. E. Bach outlines in his chapter on free improvisation. As Schulenberg has argued, the implication is that Bach and his students possessed a vocabulary of flourishes and other ornamental gestures that could be inserted at appropriate points into pieces of various genres. Some formulas — Schulenberg cites examples in BWV 738a and BWV 806a — might have been favorite personal inventions. Others would have corresponded to conventional cadential and sequential patterns or to established opening and closing gestures[12].

The use of such a vocabulary of formulas and protocols would not have been restricted to the more obviously improvisatory genres like the prelude and fantasy. The *partimento* treatises show that similar *schemata* served as a foundation for improvising fugues, as well as genres with more fixed formal constraints, such as the dances that make up the majority of movements of the Suites for Violoncello solo.

C. Ph. E. Bach's recommendation that a performer should «fashion his bass of the ascending and descending scale of the prescribed key, with a variety of figured bass signatures»[13], is reminiscent of François Campion's 'Rule of the octave', a method of teaching thoroughbass realization based on the memorization of a series of common chord patterns used to harmonize scale passages, and similar exercises were staples of the eighteenth and early nineteenth-century cello treatises[14]. According to C. Ph. E. Bach's recipe, such scale passages could be chromatically altered, or expanded and varied by interpolating sequences, another common improvisatory technique, and a skill that was fostered by the emphasis that many early cello treatises placed on transposition exercises.

C. Ph. E. Bach recommends beginning and ending an improvisation with a tonic pedal, and suggests that it is effective to introduce a dominant pedal at some point before the close. Such pedal point 'frames' are found throughout the preludes of the Suites for Violoncello solo, and the Suites also feature frequent 'framing' cadential passages in the dance movements, as well as intermediary pedal points on scale degrees other than the tonic or dominant, features that C. Ph. E. Bach describes as hallmarks of more complex, extended improvisations (see TABLE 2).

---

[12]. SCHULENBERG, David. 'Composition and Improvisation […]', *op. cit.* (see note 2), p. 20.

[13]. BACH, Carl Philipp Emanuel. *Versuch über die Wahre Art das Clavier zu Spielen, Zweiter Teil, in welchem die Lehre von Accompagnement und der freyen Fantasie abgehandelt wird*, Berlin, Georg Ludewig Winter, 1762, pp. 327-328; translation by William J. Mitchell, *Essay on the True Art of Playing Keyboard Instruments*, New York, Norton, 1949, p. 431.

[14]. CAMPION, François. *Traité d'accompagnement et de composition, selon la Règle de l'octave de musique*, Paris, chez la veuve G. Adam, 1716.

Table 2
'Framing' Pedal Point Treatment
in the Preludes of J. S. Bach's Suites for Violoncello Solo

Suite	Key	Initial Tonic Pedal	Dominant Pedal	Concluding Tonic Pedal
I	G major	mm. 1-4	mm. 25-41 (cadential)	none
II	D minor	Tonic frame, but no pedal	mm. 29-35 mm. 59-62 (cadential)	none
III	C major	mm. 1-7	mm. 45-61	mm. 81-88
IV	E-flat major	mm. 1-9	none	mm. 82-91
V	C minor	mm. 1-9	mm. 10-13 mm. 171-174	mm. 209-214
VI	D major	mm. 1-4	mm. 10-15 mm. 90-93	mm. 100-104

Compositions as Inventories of Ideas for Elaboration

A common-property shared vocabulary of arpeggiated pedal points is suggested by parallels between pedal-points in the preludes of the Suites for Violoncello solo and passages in the music of other composers. The E-flat major Prelude opens with just the kind of tonic pedal suggested in C. Ph. E. Bach's treatise, and a strikingly similar passage opens C. Ph. E. Bach's own Fantasia in E-flat major, H. 348 (see Ex. 3). In fact, the opening of the Fantasia is essentially a triplet variation of the Prelude, sharing the same harmonic progression and register, and giving a virtually identical voicing for each chord.

Ex. 3: (a) J. S. Bach, Suite for Violoncello solo in E-flat major, BWV 1010, mm. 1-8, Prelude. (b) C. Ph. E. Bach, Fantasia in E-flat Major, H. 348, opening (unmeasured).

(a)

(b)

David Watkin has pointed out another arpeggiated gesture that appears to have been part of the shared vocabulary of early eighteenth-century musicians[15]: he notes a parallel between the extended barriolage sequence over a dominant pedal in the Prelude to the C major Suite for Violoncello solo, BWV 1009, and the figuration, harmonic progression and voice-leading (especially the sequences of suspensions) of a similar dominant pedal in the second movement of Corelli's Sonata for Violin and Bass in C major, Op. 5, No. 3 (See Ex. 4).

Ex. 4: motivic/harmonic concordance between (a) Arcangelo Corelli, Sonata, Op. 5, No. 3, in C Major, Second movement, mm. 46-50, and (b) J. S. Bach, Suite for Violoncello solo in C Major, BWV 1009, Prelude, mm. 45-61. For ease of comparison, the Corelli excerpt has been transposed down one octave.

(a)

[15]. WATKIN, David. 'Corelli's Op. 5 Sonatas. «Violino e Violone o Cimbalo»?', in: *Early Music*, XXIV/4 (1996), pp. 645-663.

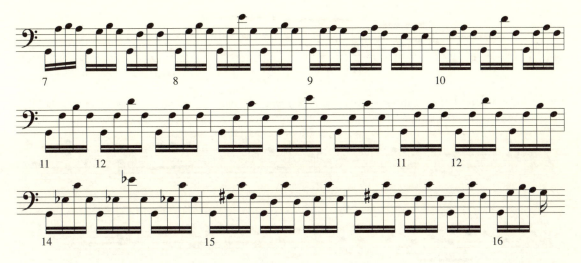

Watkin, one of the few professional cellists to have experimented with chordal thoroughbass accompaniment, has used such passages from Bach's solo music as a repertory of ideas for arpeggiated continuo realization, but it is clear from sources such as Spiridion's *Nova Instructio* (1670-1671), Niedt's *Handleitung*, C. Ph. E. Bach's *Versuch*, and Jacob Adlung's *Anleitung zu der musikalischen Gelahrheit* (1758), as well as many other eighteenth-century treatises, that similar types of continuo realization were also a foundation of improvisatory solo instrumental practices[16]. Examples of 'instrumental recitative', as found in Bach's transcriptions of Vivaldi's violin concertos and the recitative passages of the Chromatic Fantasy, are perhaps the best-known traces of this thoroughbass foundation. The third movement of Telemann's Sonata for Unaccompanied Viol is another example of a German composer's use of the expressive instrumental recitative. It consists of the speech-like melodic formulas and chordal punctuation characteristic of eighteenth-century vocal recitative (see Ex. 5). Were a cellist to perform a conflation of the vocal part and chordal realization given in the examples of thoroughbass accompaniment found in many of the early cello treatises, the effect would be strikingly similar (see Ex. 6).

Ex. 5: Georg Philipp Telemann, third movement, 'Recitatif', of a Sonata for Viol solo, in the 'Sechszehnte Lection des Music Meisters', in *Der Getreue Music-Meister* (Hamburg, s.n., 1728-1729), p. 61. (The First and Second Movements are in the 'Fünfzehnte Lection'.)

[16].   SPIRIDION. *Nova instructio pulsandis organis, spinettis, manuchordiis, etc. Pars prima*, Bamberg, Johann Jacob Immel, 1670, *Pars secunda*, Bamberg, Johann Georg Seyffert, 1671; BACH, Carl Philipp Emanuel. *Versuch über die wahre Art das Clavier zu spielen*, Leipzig, Schwickert, 1753; ADLUNG, Jakob. *Anleitung zu der musikalischen Gelahrtheit*, Erfurt, J. D. Jungnicol, 1758.

Ex. 6: Johann Baptist Baumgartner, *Instructions de musique, théorique et pratique à l'usage du violoncello* (The Hague, Monnier, 1774), example of chordal realization of a recitative. The vocal and basso parts and conflated.

It seems safe to assume that examples of instrumental recitative like Bach's and Telemann's are but the written traces of solo improvisatory traditions that were not often recorded in notation, traditions that were long established by the beginning of the eighteenth century. Indeed, while it is possible that Telemann would have been familiar with specific examples of Bach's use of instrumental recitative, imitating monodic vocal idioms had been a common practice since the early seventeenth-century, and traces can be found in many of the early violin sonatas published by musicians employed in Northern Italy and Austria, including the peripatetic Biagio Marini (1594-1663), who held posts in Venice, Brescia, Parma, Milan, Ferrara and Düsseldorf, Giovanni Pandolfi Mealli (c. 1630-c. 1670) and Giovanni Buonaventura (1638-1692), musicians active in Innsbruck, and Pietro Degli Antonii (1639-1720), who held a number of posts in Bologna[17].

The remaining movements of Telemann's Sonata offer certain motivic concordances that suggest something of the common-stock inventory of ideas that Bach and Telemann drew upon when improvising or composing. The second movement deploys motives strikingly similar to those found in two well-known examples of Bach's solo instrumental music. The head motive is reminiscent of the opening of the Two-Part Invention No. 8, in F major, and several motives have parallels in the Courante of the E-flat major Suite for Violoncello solo: (1) sixteenth-note connecting passages, (2) triplets, and (3) a prominent cadential eighth-note figure that is given a similar sequential elaboration in

---

[17]. Pietro Degli Antonii was the brother of Giovanni Battista Degli Antonii, who until recently had been credited with publishing the earliest compositions for unaccompanied violoncello, in the form of a curious set of figured bass lines, entitled *Ricercate sopra il violoncello o clavicembalo*, Op. 1, Bologna, Gioseffo Micheletti, 1687.

each work (See Ex. 7). There is also a more general correspondence in the manner in which irregular phrase lengths are constructed by stringing together these three motives in various sequences.

Ex. 7: Telemann-Bach motivic concordances. For ease of comparison, all excerpts have been arranged in bass clef and transposed to E-flat major. (a) J. S. Bach, Two-Part Invention in F Major, BWV 779, opening motive. (b) G. Ph. Telemann, Sonata for Viola da Gamba senza Cembalo in D Major, Second Movement, Vivace, opening motive. (c) J. S. Bach, Suite for Violoncello solo in E-flat major, BWV 1010, Courante.

The C minor Suite for Violoncello solo, BWV 1011, offers examples of Bach drawing on the motivic ideas of another specific musical 'other'. Here, head motives are cited from the movements of Gaspard le Roux's F-sharp minor Suite from the *Pièces de clavessin* (1705), in a manner that seems designed as a direct allusion to the world of the French *clavecinistes*, an allusion that is most easily perceived by comparing Le Roux's pieces to the lute version (BWV 995) of Bach's suite (see Ex. 8).

Ex. 8: Bach's borrowing of head motives from the Suite in F-sharp minor in Gaspard le Roux's *Pièces de clavessin* (1705). For ease of comparison, all excerpts have been transposed into C minor. A. Allemande. (a) Le Roux, Suite in F-sharp minor, Allemande. (b) J. S. Bach, Suite for Violoncello solo, in C minor, BWV 1011, Allemande. (c) J. S. Bach, Suite for Lute solo, in G minor, BWV 995, Allemande. B. 'La Favoritte' / Gigue. (a) Le Roux, Suite in F-sharp minor, 'La Favoritte'. (b) J. S. Bach, Suite for Violoncello solo, in C minor, BWV 1011, Gigue. (c) J. S. Bach, Suite for Lute solo, in G minor, BWV 995, Gigue.

A–a

A–b

A–c

B–a

B–b

B–c

CONCLUSION

The notion of a common-property vocabulary of figures presents a challenge for musicologists concerned with questions of attribution that depend on establishing the individual identifying characteristics of a particular composer. As David Schulenberg has observed:

> The idea of a *composer* in such a piece may be something of an anachronism. [...] Such pieces may belong to a *network* of related works using recurring formulas that were regarded as common property. Indeed, when we consider how many of these pieces are probably merely the visible survivals of an improvising tradition, we are faced with a situation not unlike the traditions of early chant or, for that matter, oral poetry[18].

There is evidence of a distinctly *bachische* vocabulary of motives in the collections of fragmentary musical passages made by Johann Gottfried Müthel, who studied with both J. S. and C. Ph. E. Bach, collections which appear to have served both as exercises and as inventories of ideas to be drawn upon in composing and improvising.

We should be cautious in interpreting this phenomenon in terms of a modern aesthetics of originality. The fact that seventeenth- and eighteenth-century musicians relied on a common vocabulary of figures should not be taken as a sign that they were in the habit of resorting to formulaic clichés, any more than it would for a skillful author who has mastered the allusive power of a vocabulary of common figures of speech. Indeed, as the Russian literary theorist Mikhail Bakhtin argued, competence in complex secondary verbal genres depends on just such a mastery of the more quotidian primary genres, and their deployment in more artistic genres requires a kind of dialogic discourse with ideas that, as Bakhtin put it, are already «entangled, shot through with shared thoughts, points of view, alien value judgments and accents»[19].

Bach's adaptation of other musicians' works in his written compositions is well known, and as Christoph Wolff and Laurence Dreyfus have argued, the process of adapting Vivaldi's concerti for clavier was an important influence in the development of Bach's musical thinking[20]. As an account by Theodore Pitschel, one of Bach's Leipzig townsmen shows, Bach's habit of using other composers' ideas as a source of inspiration was also an important component of his approach to improvisation:

---

18. SCHULENBERG, David. 'Composition and Improvisation [...]', *op. cit.* (see note 2), p. 26.

19. BAKHTIN, Mikhail. 'Discourse in the Novel', in: *The Novel: An Anthology of Criticism and Theory, 1900-2000*, edited by Dorothy Hale, Malden (MA), Blackwell, 2006, pp. 481-510.

20. WOLFF, Christoph. 'Vivaldi's Compositional Art, Bach and the Process of 'Musical Thinking'', in: ID. *Bach. Essays on His Life and Music*, Cambridge (MA), Harvard University Press, 1991, pp. 72-83, and DREYFUS, Laurence. *Bach and the Patterns of Invention*, Cambridge (MA), Harvard University Press, 1996.

> The famous man who has the greatest praise in our town in music, and the greatest admiration of connoisseurs, does not get into condition, as the expression goes, to delight others with the mingling of his tones until he has played something from the printed or written page, and has [thus] set his powers of imagination in motion. [...] The able man whom I have mentioned usually has to play something from the page that is inferior to his own ideas. And yet his superior ideas are the consequence of those inferior ones[21].

The elegant ways in which Bach's written compositions engage the vocabulary of his contemporaries must surely be a reflection of the kind of treatment he would have given the important musical ideas of his day when improvising. His first biographer, Johann Nicolaus Forkel, must have had something like this type of extemporaneous dialogue in mind when he reported that in the course of Bach's performances «under his hand every piece was, as it were, like a discourse»[22].

[21]. Pitschel, Theodor Leberecht. Letter of 1741, in: *Bach-Dokumente II*, edited by Hans-Joachim Schulze, Kassel, Bärenreiter, 1969, p. 397, as translated in David, Hans T. - Mendel, Arthur - Wolff, Christoph. *The New Bach Reader. A Life of Johann Sebastian Bach in Letters and Documents*, New York, Norton, 1998, pp. 333-334.

[22]. Forkel, Johann Nikolaus. *Ueber Johann Sebastian Bachs Leben, Kunst und Kunstwerke*, Leipzig, Hoffmeister & Kühnel, 1802, as translated in David, Hans T. - Mendel, Arthur - Wolff, Christoph. *Op. cit.* (see note 21), p. 435.

Improvisation into Composition
The First Movement of Johann Nepomuk Hummel's Sonata in F-sharp Minor, Op. 81[*]

Rohan H. Stewart-MacDonald
(Leominster, UK)

Hummel the Improviser: Contemporary Accounts

By speaking of the celebrated Hummel last, we wish to reserve a special place for treating of one who justly stands in the first rank of his profession. When this admirable artist took the resolution of visiting Paris, where his compositions have long been known and appreciated, the curiosity of the public was highly excited. It was expected that there would be found in his execution not only the highest degree of brilliancy, but the very excess of those difficulties which modern style so much affects. These expectations, however, were very ill founded. Chasteness, moderation, and gracefulness, are his distinguishing characteristics, and instead of charlatanism were found science and power; the delight and admiration of the audience were succeeded by astonishment; for such are the deep resources of his art, that they appear inexhaustible. *His extemporaneous playing, which is of the very highest order of excellence, produced the greatest enthusiasm in his hearers*[1].

This quotation comes from a review of the final concert given by Johann Nepomuk Hummel (1778-1837) during his concert tour to Paris in 1825. Notably, it is the «extemporaneous playing» that the reviewer singles out as the aspect of Hummel's performance that impressed the most.

---

[*]. I am indebted to Philippe Borer, Rogério Budasz, Martin Edin, Walter Kreyszig, Warwick Lister and Valerie Woodring Goertzen for their reactions and suggestions to the paper version of this chapter that proved helpful in the revision process.

[1]. Concert review translated in the *Quarterly Musical Magazine*, VII (1825), p. 313, quoted in Kroll, Mark. *Johann Nepomuk Hummel. A Musician's Life and World*, Toronto, Scarecrow Press, 2007, p. 118. Italics added.

Hummel lived at a time when the ability to improvise was central to a successful career as a virtuoso[2]. The programmes of two of the other concerts Hummel gave during the same trip to Paris are shown in Table 1. They typify the «regular format» into which Hummel's concerts fell during the tour, of «three instrumental or orchestral pieces of which two were by himself and in which he partook as a performer, interspersed with two or more smaller vocal items, and rounding the whole off with his improvisation»[3]. Hummel's reputation as an improviser was, in fact, supreme[4]. The obituary published in *The Musical World* on 27 October, 1837 recalled that «[a]s an extempore player, [Hummel's] ideas flowed in a copious and unremitting stream»[5]. A preview of a concert he was to give, again in Paris but this time in 1830, gives some indication of the attributes of Hummel's improvisations as seen at the time:

> Improvising, for [Hummel], is not a work of mechanism and memory; he is not content to take a theme, modulate it and embellish it for a few minutes, then to leave it there to recommence the same operation on a second theme, nay even on a third; no, he seeks a thought, and develops it in all its facets and formulas, without making a patch work, by an effort totally spontaneous and daring. To be sure these improvisations of the highest purity, if one may so designate them, have a celebrity in Germany that is without equal [...] It is not, I think, adding a feeble allurement to Wednesday's concert, to announce that it will be terminated with one of these beautiful improvisations[6].

Table 1

Programmes of two concerts given by Hummel in Paris in April 1825
Information taken from Kroll, Mark. *Op. cit.* (see note 1), pp. 115-116

Date	Venue	Programme
8 April 1825	Paris, Salle Érard	Concerto, composed and played by Hummel Air, sung by Mlle. [Adelaide] Schiasetti Solo for flute, composed and played by M. [Jean-Louis] Tulou Rondo brilliant, composed and played by Hummel Duet sung by Mlle. Schiasetti and M. [Carlo] Zucchelli Improvisation by Hummel

---

[2]. Derek Carew asserts that «improvisation was an accepted and necessary part of any composer/performer's attainments in the public domain during the first forty years of the nineteenth century». Carew, Derek. *The Mechanical Muse. The Piano, Pianism and Piano Music, c. 1760-1850*, Aldershot, Ashgate, 2007, p. 438.

[3]. *Ibidem*, p. 432.

[4]. *Ibidem*, p. 431, footnote 1.

[5]. Kroll, Mark. *Op. cit.* (see note 1), p. 339.

[6]. *Le Globe*, p. 139, translated into English in *The Harmonicon*'s 'Foreign Musical Rapport', May 1830. Quoted in Kroll, Mark. *Op. cit.* (see note 1), p. 126.

15 April 1825	Paris, Salle Érard	Quintette, composed by Hummel, played by him with MM. Vidal, Sina, [Louis] Norblin, Lami
		Air sung by Mm. [Giuditta] Pasta
		Solo for French horn, composed and played by M. [Louis-François] Dauprat
		Novelle sonate for piano and 'cello («encore manuscrite»), played by Hummel and Norblin
		Duo, composed by Rossini, sung by Mme. Pasta and M. [Felice] Pellegrini.
		Improvisation by Hummel

This notion of motivic development contributing to an impression of continuity and coherence perhaps departs from the automatic association of improvisation with spontaneity, disorder and the unexpected. These qualities are hardly eschewed, however: despite all the logic, the effect remains «spontaneous and daring».

The American pianist Louis Moreau Gottschalk describes what must have been one of Hummel's most impressive improvisations. Thematic processing is again prominent and is now associated with counterpoint; but the element of spontaneity now takes a positively theatrical turn:

> So exceptional was Hummel as an extemporizor [sic] that during a concert in the Erard Hall, Paris, when bells from a nearby church began ringing, he was able to switch immediately from his Polonaise 'La bella capricciosa', Op. 55, into a harmonization of the peal, which he then combined with motifs from the Larghetto Introduzione, capping the whole with a fugue improvised on the main theme of the *polacca*[7].

This incident calls to mind Ignaz Moscheles's improvisation that incorporated a storm: «with every flash of lightening I brought my playing to a pause, which allowed the thunder to make itself heard independently»[8]. A more detailed account of Hummel's improvising appears in a review of the second concert he gave during his visit to London in 1830. The conjunction between counterpoint («profound musical science») and thematic manipulation surfaces once again, and we also find Hummel requesting themes from the audience, a practice he seems to have invented[9]. In this instance the themes were a 'Swiss air' and an unidentified melody, most likely «some very inferior German Production»:

---

7. CAREW, Derek. *The Mechanical Muse* [...], *op. cit.* (see note 2), p. 438. Carew's source for Gottschalk's description is BARNUM, Marion Phillys. *A Comprehensive Project in Piano Literature and an Essay on J. N. Hummel and his Treatise on Piano Playing*, D.M.A., Performance, Iowa City (IA), The University of Iowa, 1971, p. 42.

8. MOSCHELES, Charlotte. *Life of Moscheles, with Selections from his Diaries and Correspondence; by his Wife*, 2 vols., London, Hurst & Blackett, 1873, vol. I, p. 20.

9. CAREW, Derek. *The Mechanical Muse* [...], *op. cit.* (see note 2), p. 437.

> Mr Hummel appeared somewhat discouraged by the unprofitableness
> [sic] of the materials presented to him, but, of course, did not reject them [...]
> He commenced with an introductory adagio, followed by some light and
> playful variations on the Swiss air, he modulated through a variety of keys into
> an elaborate fugue, in the progress of which he displayed all the enthusiasm
> of powerful genius, with the consummate art and refinement of the most
> profound musical science. Having submitted to the temporary restraint of the
> second theme, which he dismissed as soon as possible, he gave the reins to his
> imagination, and revelled in the mazes of melody and harmony, to the exquisite
> delight of his audience, and, we should suppose, to his entire satisfaction. During
> this most happy inspiration of talent and genius, he occasionally introduced a
> few bars of an old English song 'The Flaxen-Headed Cow-Boy', which he
> played and sported with in a manner at once so masterly and fascinating, that it
> might have been listened to for hours without a feeling of satiety[10].

These and other accounts tally closely with Derek Carew's summary of the main
criteria to be met by successful early nineteenth-century keyboard improvisations,
including heightened virtuosity[11]; motivic development[12]; a command over a range of
musical topics including counterpoint[13], and importantly, the improviser's responsiveness to
environmental factors; these included the audience's ongoing reaction to the improvisation,
coalescing around the expectation that the improvisation appear genuinely spontaneous.
The appearance of spontaneity was increasingly important «in a climate in which, in some
quarters, suspicions were gnawing about the authenticity of *impromptu* performances» and
the possibility of prior preparation[14].

One of the most famous descriptions of an improvisation by Hummel that brings
together many of those factors comes from Louis Spohr who heard Hummel at a party
around the time of the Congress of Vienna:

> I there for the first time heard Hummel play his beautiful Septett, as
> well as several other of his compositions of that period. But I was mostly
> charmed by his improvisations in which no other Pianoforte-Virtuoso ever
> yet approached him. I especially remember with pleasure one evening when
> he improvised in so splendid a manner as I never since heard him whether in
> public or in private. The company were about to break up, when some ladies,
> who thought it too early, entreated Hummel to play a few more waltzes for
> them. Obliging and galant as he was to the ladies, he seated himself at the

---

[10]. Review in *The Athenæum*, 1 May 1830, p. 301, quoted in KROLL, Mark. *Op. cit.* (see note 1), p. 131.

[11]. Carew cites contemporary accounts of Beethoven's virtuosity in this context, citing Carl Czerny's
observation that «Beethoven's virtuosity in *impromptu* performances was almost always of a higher order than
in his written-out pieces». CAREW, Derek. *The Mechanical Muse* [...], *op. cit.* (see note 2), p. 434.

[12]. *Ibidem*, pp. 438-440.

[13]. *Ibidem*, p. 435.

[14]. *Ibidem*, p. 436.

piano, and played the wished-for waltzes, to which the young folks in the adjoining room began to dance. I, and some other artists, attracted by his play, grouped ourselves round the instrument with our hats already in our hands, and listened attentively. Hummel no sooner observed this, than he converted his play into a free fantasia of improvisation, but which constantly preserved the waltz-rhythm, so that the dancers were not disturbed. He then took from me and others who had executed their own compositions during the evening a few easily combined themes and figures, which he interwove into his waltzes and varied them at every recurrence with a constantly increasing richness and piquancy of expression. Indeed, at length, he even made them serve as fugue-themes, and let loose all his science in counterpoint without disturbing the waltzers in their pleasures. Then he returned to the galant style, and in conclusion passed into a bravura, such as from him even has seldom been heard. In this finale, the themes taken up were still constantly heard, so that the whole rounded off and terminated in real artistic style. The hearers were enraptured, and praised the young ladies' love of dancing, that had conducted to so rich a feast of artistic excellence[15].

In this account, motivic development, counterpoint, galant and dance topics combine with an acute sensitivity to the demands of the occasion to form a veritable *tour de force* of improvisation of the type that underpinned Hummel's reputation as an improviser of the first rank.

Considering Hummel's improvisatory prowess, the space he devoted to improvisation in his 1828 treatise *Ausführliche theoretisch-practische Anweisung zum Piano-Forte-Spiel* is surprisingly small. Disappointment about this amongst early reviews did prompt Hummel to expand the section for the second edition, published in circa 1829[16]. Both versions include a useful account of how he himself developed the skill. Hummel wrote:

> I aimed particularly at a good connection and succession of ideas, of strictness of rythm [*sic*], at variety of character, at changes of colouring, at the avoiding of great diffusiveness [...] [I attempted] to ground my *Fantasia* on the flow of my own ideas, as also, occasionaly [*sic*] to weave among them some known *Thema* or subject [...] When by degrees the taste and judgement were correctly formed; and when [...] I ventured to extemporize before a few persons only [...] and while so doing, observed quietly how they received it [...] Lastly [...] I ventured to offer myself before the public[17].

---

[15]. Spohr, Louis. *Louis Spohr's Autobiography, Translated from the German*, London, Longman, 1865, New York, Da Capo Press, 1969, pp. 191-192. Spellings have been modernized and regularized within the quotation.

[16]. See Kroll, Mark. *Op. cit.* (see note 1), p. 273, footnote 110.

[17]. Hummel, Johann Nepomuk. *Ausführliche theoretisch-practische Anweisung zum Piano-Forte-Spiel* [...], 3 vols., Vienna, Haslinger, [1828], Part III, Section 2, Chapter 7, p. 74, quoted in Kroll, Mark. *Op. cit.* (see note 1), pp. 259-260.

Comparing this with the accounts cited above reveals considerable agreement between the ideals and aims of improvisation that Hummel professed in theory (including coherence achieved through logical thematic processing) and the nature of the end products he delivered in practice. For instance, the improvisation at the London concert of 1830 in which Hummel improvised on two themes and made reference to 'The Flaxen-Headed Cow-Boy' shows him «weave[ing] among» his own ideas «some known *Thema* or subject»; and at the party at which Spohr was present Hummel borrowed themes from compositions heard earlier that evening.

These eyewitness accounts can of course only provide indirect evidence of the exact nature of Hummel's improvisations. Thankfully, the evidence is of a fairly detailed kind and can be compared with Hummel's own testimony in the treatise. More intricate questions concern the relationship between Hummel's style as a performer-improviser and his objectives as a composer. To what extent did Hummel's approaches as an improviser infiltrate his compositional style? Implicitly, and logically, this must have taken place to a considerable degree. As the quoted material makes clear, public improvisations were frequently based on existing themes from other compositions; Hummel often carried this over into notated compositions where quotations from works by J. S. Bach, Mozart and Luigi Cherubini provided the basis for witty, sometimes flamboyant embellishments. In some cases the sources are rather recognisable — as in the impressive manipulation of several themes from the finale of Mozart's 'Jupiter Symphony' in the coda of the third movement of Hummel's Sonata in F minor, Op. 20 — in others, rather more furtive, as in the subtle yet explicit reference to the 'Goldberg Variations' in the finale of the String Quartet in G major, Op. 30, No. 2[18]. In other works Hummel seems to construe improvisation as a musical topic compatible with, but departing from, surrounding conventions — recalling Leonard Ratner's conception of fantasia making its presence felt through «unexpected, even eccentric turns of figure, texture and harmony», giving «a fresh twist and new vitality to the familiar clichés of the eighteenth-century musical vocabulary»[19]. A comparatively

---

[18]. Hummel's penchant for quotation in his larger-scale instrumental works has attracted some attention in recent years. In particular, see ROSEN, Charles. *Sonata Forms*, New York, Norton, 1980, pp. 293-294; PEARSON, Ian. 'Johann Nepomuk Hummel's «Rescue» Concerto. Cherubini's Influence on Hummel's Trumpet Concerto', in: *Journal of the International Trumpet Guild*, xv/4 (1992), pp. 14-20; RICE, John. 'The Musical Bee. References to Mozart and Cherubini in Hummel's «New Year» Concerto', in: *Music & Letters*, LXXVII/3 (1996), pp. 410-414; and STEWART-MACDONALD, Rohan H. 'The Undiscovered Flight Paths of the «Musical Bee»', in: *Eighteenth-Century Music*, III/1 (2006), pp. 7-34. Another quotation not mentioned in any of these publications and which I noticed only recently occurs in the first movement of Hummel's Sonata in C major, Op. 38: the exposition's second theme bears an unmistakable resemblance to the principal theme of the finale of Mozart's Sonata in C major, KV 330, dating from circa 1783. Hummel's initial presentation of it, in bars 60ff, modifies it slightly; but the second version of it, in bars 68-71, is virtually identical to the Mozart original, transposed to the dominant.

[19]. RATNER, Leonard G. *Classic Music. Expression, Form and Style*, New York, Schirmer, 1980, p. 314.

mild example occurs in the first movement of the Sonata Op. 20 (see Ex. 1). The exposition transition reaches the dominant of the relative major. The final approach to A-flat major is then delayed by an episode containing stops, tempo changes and doublings back, as if the performer-improviser had become distracted from the business of launching the *codetta*. The Adagio in bar 28 cogitates over an ascending figure from the previous two bars. The freely imitative exchange in bars 28-30, based loosely on the opening theme, briefly restores the tempo but only provokes a second decision to stop and consider further. A more emphatic putting-on of the brakes in bars 31-32 leads to a quasi-canonic 'improvisation' on the Allegro agitato in bars 32-34: this recalls the opening more directly and reveals its contrapuntal potential (compare bars 32-34 with bars 1-2). This example shows Hummel construing improvisation as a localised event or topic that disrupts (or digs deeper into) otherwise more conventional surroundings. Once again the emphasis seems to be on thematic processing, with an interest in exploring further the potential of a particular theme or motif. Crucially, the improvisatory effect does not emanate from the thematic processes *per se* but from their context: that is, the syntactical fragmentation generated by pauses and tempo changes, plus repetition and localised variation, create an element of digression, or the impression that something out of the ordinary is taking place. The effect can be compared with an interruption to a flow of conversation when one of the participants insists on returning to an earlier topic to engage in a more thorough, or even 'learned', exploration of it.

Ex. 1a: Johann Nepomuk Hummel, Sonata in F minor, Op. 20, first movement, bars 1-4.

Ex. 1b: Johann Nepomuk Hummel, Sonata in F minor, Op. 20, first movement, bars 28-39.

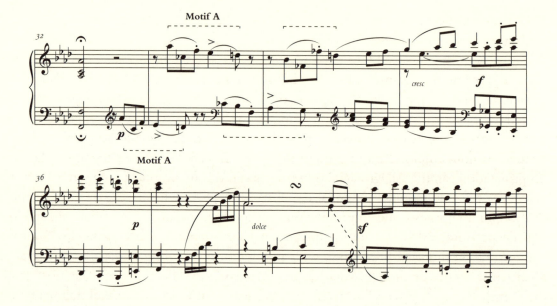

HUMMEL'S MAGNUM OPUS: THE SONATA IN F-SHARP MINOR, OP. 81 (1819)

The focus of the present discussion is the first movement of Hummel's Sonata in F-sharp minor, Op. 81, in which the spirit of improvisation is especially pervasive. Dating from 1819, this sonata is one of Hummel's most imposing works, and certainly one of his most prestigious. At the time there were speculations that Beethoven's 'Hammerklavier Sonata' had been written in direct competition with it[20]. Robert Schumann, who appears to have been practising the sonata in the late 1820s when he injured his hand and forestalled his intended career as a virtuoso pianist[21], described the sonata in a letter to Friedrich Wieck as «a truly epic, titanic work» and as a «portrait of a[n] heroic spirit, struggling but resigned»[22]. Contemporary writers are gradually rediscovering the work's importance, mediated through its influence on major figures of the following generation, including Schumann. Joel Lester has cited the first movement of Hummel's sonata as a stimulus for Schumann's Toccata Op. 7; Allegro Op. 8; and Sonata No. 1 in F-sharp minor, Op. 11[23].

---

20. SOLOMON, Maynard. *Beethoven*, London, Granada, 1980, p. 416, quoting VON LENZ, Wilhelm. *Beethoven. Eine Kunst-Studie*, 5 vols., Hamburg, Hoffman & Campe, 1860, vol. v, p. 32.
21. See CAREW, Derek. 'Hummel's Op. 81: A Paradigm for Brahms's Op. 2?', in: *Ad Parnassum. A Journal of Eighteenth- and Nineteenth-Century Instrumental Music*, III/6 (2005), pp. 133-156, p. 134 and KROLL, Mark. *Op. cit.* (see note 1), p. 280.
22. CAREW, Derek. 'Hummel's Op. 81: […]', *op. cit.* (see note 21), quoting SCHUMANN, Robert. *Jugendbriefe. Nach den Originalen mitgeteilt von Clara Schumann*, Leipzig, Breitkopf & Härtel, 1885, p. 80.
23. LESTER, Joel. 'Robert Schumann and Sonata Forms', in: *19th Century Music*, XVIII/3 (Spring, 1995), pp. 189-210. See *ibidem*, pp. 199-203 for the discussion of Hummel's Sonata Op. 81 in relation to Schumann.

Charles Rosen draws a parallel between the digressive approach taken towards the bridge passage in the first movement and what occurs in Chopin's Sonata in B minor, Op. 58: he asserts (rather baldly, perhaps) that Chopin's «model was Hummel's Sonata in F-sharp minor»[24]. Carew has put forward a more extensive case for Brahms having modelled his own F-sharp minor sonata on Hummel's Op. 81[25]. Carew suggests that an «improvisational freedom» inhabits the opening movement of Hummel's sonata. Thought provokingly, and echoing James Webster's work on Haydn's 'Farewell Symphony'[26], Carew links the key of F-sharp minor with what he describes as a «wayward and 'Romantic'» character. Other works in this mould include the 'Grande Sonate' Op. 7 (1842) by Theodor Kullak; Franz Lachner's 'Grande Sonate' Op. 2 (1824); Schumann's Sonata in F-sharp minor, Op. 11 (1832-1835); and even Wagner's Fantasia Op. 22 (1831). The prototype for all of these compositions was Ferdinand Ries's 'Grande Sonate-fantaisie intitulée L'infortunée' Op. 26 (Grand Sonata-Fantasy entitled 'The Unfortunate Woman'), written in 1808 and published seven years later[27]. Of course, the adjective 'improvisatory' is something of a commonplace in discussions of nineteenth-century music, and Carew's group of F-sharp minor works is quite diverse. The question therefore arises of what improvisatory really means in a technical sense. Is it possible to give a specific account of an improvisatory style or to offer watertight definitions of the improvisatory characteristics of a particular composition, or does applying the adjective to a piece like Hummel's Sonata Op. 81 lead only to a tautological association of the piece with the prevailing idiom of the period?

Hummel's opening, certainly, is striking (see Ex. 2). It is intensely dramatic, and the plethora of dynamic, tempo and articulation designations implies a painstakingly precise conception of the desired effect in performance. Nothing, it would appear, is left to chance, or to the discretion of the performer; and perhaps ironically, realising the improvisatory effect as Hummel implicity envisaged it demands unfailing fidelity to a highly complex musical text: a highly contrived, verisimilitude of spontaneity. Carefully graded tempo changes working in tandem with syntactical fragmentation contribute to an improvisatory act in which thematic ideas are ephemeral and logical continuity of any kind is established only gradually and with effort. The melodic dimension is highly erratic: an imposing thematic gambit in bars 1-4 with connotations of instrumental recitative[28] is followed, in bars 4-6, by non-thematic, improvisatory 'vamping' which seems to mark time until the next melodic idea emerges. Indeed, this 'vamping' texture almost qualifies as a musical type, or topic, in itself: equivalents can be found at the openings of Mozart's fragmentary

24. ROSEN, Charles. *Op. cit.* (see note 18), pp. 390-392.

25. CAREW, Derek. 'Hummel's Op. 81: [...]', *op. cit.* (see note 21).

26. See WEBSTER, James. *Haydn's «Farewell» Symphony and the Idea of Classical Style: Through-Composition and Cyclic Integration in His Instrumental Music*, Cambridge, Cambridge University Press, 1991, p. 116.

27. CAREW, Derek. 'Hummel's Op. 81: [...]', *op. cit.* (see note 21), p. 143.

28. I am indebted to Rogério Budasz for making this suggestion at the conference.

Fantasia in D minor, KV 397, and Jan Ladislav Dussek's Fantasia and Fugue in F minor, Op. 55. Hummel's implicit simulation of an improvisation in which conditions are at first chaotic but ideas then gradually coalesce is suggested by the passage beginning in bar 12 which seems to offer a corrective version or second attempt at bars 4-12. The point of departure is the same: more vamping. Instead of leading to an impasse, as in bars 7-8, things continue this time around: a sequence is formed (bars 15-21), using the two-minim rhythm derived from bar 1, and a logical harmonic direction is found, towards the relative major. This spasmodic opening establishes an expressive world of extremes in which a wide range of different types of texture, figuration and register are encountered within a short space: it sets the tone for the remainder of the movement, if not the whole sonata.

Ex. 2: Johann Nepomuk Hummel, Sonata in F-sharp minor, Op. 81, first movement, bars 1-18.

HUMMEL'S OP. 81:
IMPROVISATORY DIGRESSIONS AND THEIR SUBSEQUENT INTEGRATION

This interpretation of the opening of Hummel's sonata construes improvisation as a musical topic embodying expressive potency, fragmentation and barely controlled chaos; but it also encompasses a progression from chaos to increased order and continuity, via logical thematic processing. It should be emphasised again that «the avoiding of great diffusiveness» when improvising was one of the aims avowed by Hummel himself in the *Ausführliche theoretisch-practische Anweisung*[29] and that Hummel's success with this in his live improvisations is reflected in the comments extolling how Hummel «seeks a thought, and develops it in all its facets and formulas, without making a patch work»[30]. The implication of a «thought» being developed «in all its facets and formulas» is of a linear approach to thematic content, and this is more prominent in the first movement of Op. 81 than in the majority of Hummel's other works. Carew argues that it shares with the opening movement of Brahms's F-sharp minor Sonata «a thematic unity-in-diversity by virtue of which the opening gambit [...] behaves like a kind of *Ur-Motiv* whose various forms pervade each of the works»[31]; but his comparative approach allows space for only a cursory demonstration of Hummel's thematic techniques.

Early reactions to Hummel's sonata emphasised coherence. A review in the *Allgemeine musikalische Zeitung* dating from 16 February 1820, reads as follows:

> The thoughts [...] appear at the same time of great breadth, convincing, unusual, distinctive, and expressive. From its very first page, the expression and character are noble throughout, with just the right spirit and taste *and held together with skill and experience*, almost reaching the limits of the pathetic. The development [of the ideas] is quite masterful[32].

The behaviour of bars 1-4 as an *Ur-Motiv* is most conspicuous in the first half of the exposition. The opening segment, until the bridge passage begins in bar 22, really consists of what Carew calls the 'opening gambit' followed by an intensive, almost obsessive meditation on it (see again Ex. 2). Two out of the three pitches D-B-sharp-C-sharp of bars 3-4 are echoed in the upper bass part in bars 5-6, and all three provide the framework for the semiquaver motif introduced in bar 8 (Motif B), which is expanded sequentially in bars 9-10. The three-minim rhythm of the initial, most assertive component of the

---

[29]. HUMMEL, Johann Nepomuk. *Ausführliche theoretisch-practische Anweisung* [...], *op. cit.* (see note 17), p. 259.
[30]. KROLL, Mark. *Op. cit.* (see note 1), p. 339.
[31]. CAREW, Derek. 'Hummel's Op. 81: [...]', *op. cit.* (see note 21). See also ID. *The Mechanical Muse* [...], *op. cit.* (see note 2), p. 438.
[32]. Quoted in KROLL, Mark. *Op. cit.* (see note 1), p. 387. Italics added.

opening gambit (Motif A) is distantly echoed in bars 7-8; the motif gradually regains its vigour in its sequential expansion in bars 15-20, which provides a conduit to the start of the bridge passage in bar 22 (shown in Ex. 3). Perhaps more efficiently than any other passage in the movement, this opening paragraph illustrates the paradox between the syntactical disjunction and lack of logical continuity invoking the unpredictability of an act of improvisation being sustained, or even directly stimulated, by a motivic logic that prevents the «great diffusiveness» that in his writings Hummel implies would result from an unsuccessful improvisation.

Ex. 3: Johann Nepomuk Hummel, Sonata in F-sharp minor, Op. 81, first movement, bars 22-33.

The most regularly employed method of motivic processing seen in bars 1-21 is the sequential expansion of Motif A. This is pursued more tenaciously by the first part of the bridge passage, where contrapuntal techniques are invoked (see Ex. 3). Motif A is first discernible (although hard to project in performance) in the 'tenor' line of bars 22-27, where it is expanded into three sequential rotations; these are underpinned by the prolonged dominant that first resolves to the relative major at the start of bar 28. Thereupon, the motif assumes a more prominent position in the 'alto' voice in bars 28-33, transposing the three sequential rotations to A major. In bars 28-33 Motif A participates in an intricate, three-part texture[33] that includes a 'countersubject' in the tenor part incorporating a modified version of Motif B (compare Ex. 3, bars 28-30 with Ex. 2, bars 8-10). Motivic derivations from the opening gambit become rather less conspicuous in the central part of the extended bridge passage, where the harmony veers temporarily off course[34], but they are resurrected when the harmonic equilibrium is restored. Bars 53-55 (not shown) evoke the opening with their assertive octave sonorities and recollection of the upwardly scalar motion of Motif A, starting again from C-sharp, and in bars 70-73 (not shown) there is a direct reference to A-sharp-B-E-sharp-F-sharp from bars 2-3 of the gambit which now undergird the final stabilisation of the relative major, preceding the exposition's conclusion.

After the very intensive preoccupation with Motif A at the opening and during the early part of the bridge passage, the interest in it and its compatriot Motif B wanes as the section proceeds. The melody in bars 80-86 (not shown), *pace* Carew, has surprisingly little to do with preceding motivic events[35]. It lacks any strong connection with either Motif A or B; its retreat to stratospheric regions in the treble as the bass plumbs the depths is one distinguishing factor. Clear motivic references are equally scarce during the central, harmonically digressive part of the bridge passage. With the swerve to C major in bar 36 (see Ex. 4) the melodic content all but vanishes, as if in reaction to the harmonic shock. A strained connection could be made between the C-D-flat-D fragment in bars 40 and 42 (canonically imitated at the octave in bars 41 and 43) and the last three pitches of the opening gambit in bars 3-4, which they enharmonically reinterpret and re-order, but this is tenuous at best, and probably inconsequential. Significant motivic references remain at bay until bars 53-54 (not shown) where, as already noted, memories of the opening start to resurface. Another area in which motivic references are absent, and somewhat more disconcertingly so, is the body of the development section (bars 103-133, not shown). This

---

[33].   Hummel's notation, including periodic rests in the 'tenor' part, actually implies a four-part texture, even if only three parts ever sound simultaneously.

[34].   The harmonic digression will be discussed below.

[35].   Carew includes this melody in a diagram that is meant to show motivic derivations from the opening gambit. The (unexplained) implication is that the connection lies in the (tenuous) resemblance of the two-minim rhythm. See CAREW, Derek. 'Hummel's Op. 81: [...]', *op. cit.* (see note 21), p. 151.

consists of an upwardly chromatic sequence connecting B-flat major with the dominant of F-sharp minor. The re-use of material from bars 40-45 of the bridge passage denudes the development of significant thematic content, and this provoked an almost morally charged diatribe from Harold Truscott. In his words, the development

> turns into a technical study [...]. The fireworks add nothing to the argument and are an excrescence, so that when the recapitulation begins nothing has happened to the music. There is no increase in stature [...] The entire movement, which could have been a masterpiece, sags because of this wanton yielding to sheer technical display. It is at moments such as this that Hummel shows why he is less than Beethoven, or, for that matter, than Clementi and Dussek[36].

The apparent lack of thematic substance from Hummel's development is certainly unusual[37]. In most cases chromatic sequencing provides the framework for motivic processing, often involving the imitative exchange of a particular motive between parts. Rather than condemning the lack of motivic content in Hummel's development as evidence of a creative lapse, it seems more constructive to interpret it as part of a strategy whereby, starting with the passage in the exposition from which the development section is largely derived, there is a shift of focus away from the motivic processing of the opening gambit to an harmonically based exploration which is improvisatory in its (temporary) challenge to linear continuity.

In the *Méthode des méthodes de piano* of 1840, François-Joseph Fétis and Ignaz Moscheles make distinctions between written compositions and improvisations thus:

> To improvise [...] would be an impossible art if its products were to be judged with the rigour that applies to the appreciation of written compositions. No matter how great the talent of the improviser, there will always be some disorder, some redundancy in the premature fruit of his mind, and sometimes his sleepy imagination will allow him to wander in the indefinite[38].

Fétis and Moscheles configure 'disorder' and 'redundancy' in negative terms, as the result of natural limitations in the skill of the improviser. A more positive association might be nineteenth-century works of visual art cited by Carew in which «painters [...] took steps to narrow the gap between inspiration and finished picture». This is exemplified by

---

[36]. TRUSCOTT, Harold. 'Introduction', in: HUMMEL, Johann Nepomuk. *Complete Piano Sonatas*, 2 vols., London, Musica Rara, 1975, vol. I, pp. i-ix: vi.

[37]. It is not, of course, unheard of: an obvious example of a development section in which the harmonic progression is adorned only with quaver and semiquaver figuration occurs in the first movement of Mozart's Clarinet Quintet in A major, KV 581.

[38]. FÉTIS, François-Joseph - MOSCHELES, Ignaz. *Méthode des méthodes de piano*, Paris, Maurice Schlesinger, 1840, p. 73, quoted in GOERTZEN, Valerie Woodring. 'By Way of Introduction. Preluding by 18th- and 19th-Century Pianists', in: *The Journal of Musicology*, XIV/3 (1996), pp. 199-337: 310.

Ex. 4: Johann Nepomuk Hummel, Sonata in F-sharp minor, Op. 81, first movement, bars 35-48.

the paintings of Joseph Mallord William Turner (1775-1851) discovered in 1939 that were purportedly sketches but in fact finished products in which there had been a deliberate effort to preserve «the freedom and spontaneity of the sketch»[39]. Following this, one might argue that a natural connotation of improvisation, whether in a live product or an improvisatory composition, is «a stretching of musical conventions, in a way that would not really be acceptable to the same degree (if at all) in 'proper' compositions»; and the area in which this was seen the most frequently was harmony[40].

At least one contemporary review pays tribute to the harmonic intricacy of Hummel's improvisations; one reviewer described Hummel wandering through various keys and revelling «in the mazes of melody and harmony»[41]. That this was consciously carried over into his Sonata Op. 81 is suggested by the C-major digression in the bridge passage. C major, firmly articulated by its dominant, interrupts the confirmation of the relative major, first reached in bar 27 (see again Ex. 4). The tangential effect comes partly from the firm assertion of what is so obviously a distant, parenthetical key area. There is even an impression of having taken a wrong turning and having got stuck at a tonal impasse; this is most acute in bars 44-45 with their almost humorously directionless I-V alternation. The mere presence of a harmonic digression at the approximate mid-point of an early nineteenth-century exposition is not in itself surprising. The possibilities of multiple-key expositions were being systematically explored by Schubert during those years, and according to some accounts, had been periodically deployed from as early as the mid-eighteenth century[42]. However, the rationale for most multiple- or three-key expositions is that the onset of the secondary key (whether dominant, relative major, or minor dominant) is delayed by encounters with other keys of varying distance. In the case of Hummel's Op. 81, A major has already been tonicised when the foray to C major takes place. This makes the latter a genuine digression within what is ostensibly confirmation of the secondary key, and thus distorts the proportions of the section. The digressive effect of C major is reinforced by the elliptical method of its approach and departure. Although C major itself is approached via a normal, rather emphatic V-I cadence in bars 35-36, its dominant emerges from a diminished seventh in bars 33-34 whose initial direction is obscure and which interrupts the sequence begun in bar 28 (see again Ex. 3): the F-natural in the bass in bar 33 seems to contaminate the sequence with a flatwards tendency which gains momentum in the shift to C major a couple of bars later. The return from C major to A major in bars 46-48 (Ex. 4) creates the impression

---

[39]. CAREW, Derek. *The Mechanical Muse* […], *op. cit.* (see note 2), p. 433. The idea of an improvisation as some kind of sketch is also discussed in the contribution to this volume by Martin Kaltenecker.

[40]. *Ibidem*, p. 435.

[41]. Review in *The Athenaeum*, 1 May 1830, p. 301, quoted in KROLL, Mark. *Op. cit.* (see note 1), p. 131.

[42]. See LONGYEAR, Rey M. - COVINGTON, Kate R. 'Sources of the Three-Key Exposition', in: *The Journal of Musicology*, VI/4 (1988), pp. 448-470.

of a hurried — or improvised — correction of the harmony involving an extremely bold assertion of C major at the start of bar 46, followed by a B-flat major 6-3 (bar 46); this leads to a diminished seventh with superimposed suspension resolving onto a dominant seventh of A major (bar 47). Especially after the dogged simplicity of the harmony in bars 38-45, the harmonic pivot provides the listener with more information than can easily be assimilated; the consequent impression is of harmonic normality having been restored through obscure, confused or even forced, means.

The digression itself can either be understood as a localised event or as a continuation of the policy of expanding and examining earlier events: it could be related to flatwards tendencies near the opening. One interruption of the opening's continuity is caused by the short encounter with D major in bars 7-8 whose subdominant, G major, is the dominant of C major. This connection, tenuous in itself, is affirmed by subsequent events[43].

Another part of the movement that seems to reflect Fétis's and Moscheles's association of improvisation with latent «disorder» is the start of the development section (see Ex. 5). Even more overtly than the C-major digression, perhaps, this seems to enact the temporary loss of linear coherence that might be considered the occupational hazard (or the calculated allure) of an improvisation. The gesture that ended the exposition (bar 94) is repeated four times (bars 96-101). The harmonic coherence declines as the passage progresses so that the rhythmic full stop in bar 99 is followed by a rather oblique progression from F-sharp major (acting as the dominant of B minor) to a diminished seventh providing a very marginal dominant to the F major which then launches the body of the section in the unlikely key of B-flat major (not shown). In fact, this passage's qualities are more readily explicable in a theoretical sense, for it may be understood as the kind of short-winded introductory section to the main body of the development implied by William Caplin's distinction between a 'pre-core' and a 'core'. The core's continuity often comes, as in this case, from a sequential continuum[44]; pre-cores, according to Caplin's classification, are diverse and flexible, but often, as here, begin with the tonic of the subordinate key[45] and provide a modulatory approach to the dominant of the first key of the core[46]. Caplin does suggest that a pre-core may be «hesitant and anticipatory» in character, with «discontinuous» rhythmic motion[47], but it has to be said that the volatility of Hummel's specimen in the first movement of Op. 81 differs from any of the examples cited by this writer.

---

[43]. This topic will be explored below.

[44]. See CAPLIN, William. *Classical Form. A Theory of Formal Functions for the Instrumental Music of Haydn, Mozart and Beethoven*, New York, Oxford University Press, 1998, pp. 147-155.

[45]. *Ibidem*, p. 147.

[46]. *Ibidem*, p. 153.

[47]. *Ibidem*, pp. 147 and 151.

Ex. 5: Johann Nepomuk Hummel, Sonata in F-sharp minor, Op. 81, first movement, bars 94-103.

So far I have mainly argued that the first movement of Hummel's F-sharp minor Sonata is improvisatory in its exhaustive experimentation with the possibilities of the opening. This can lead to linear motivic processing of the type implicitly celebrated in appraisals of Hummel's actual improvisations; it can also lead to harmonic digressions and syntactical vicissitudes that challenge the coherence of the implied sonata model and directly invoke the associations of temporary, or latent, disorder inherent in a live improvisation. This paradox between normative and subversive tendencies is also played out in the rather strenuous efforts made in the development and recapitulation to resolve or subsequently explain certain earlier departures. This can either be understood as reflections of Hummel's priority of avoiding «diffusiveness» in improvisations (and, by extension, compositions informed by the spirit of improvisation) or in terms of the aesthetic requirements of the eighteenth-century sonata model to which the movement ultimately conforms.

The opening of the recapitulation considerably reworks and retrospectively regularises bars 1-20 (compare Ex. 6 with Ex. 2). The development culminates, in bars 134-141, in a recapitulation of the opening gambit, dovetailing with the retransition. This time the gambit is stated twice successively at different octaves. The direct emergence from the retransition, which has already been prolonging the dominant for ten bars, and the addition of semiquaver figuration to the initially skeletal gambit, removes any harmonic ambiguity it might initially have had[48]. The twofold presentation, coupled with the harmonisation, turns the gambit into a regular, eight-bar phrase unit. In bars 141-150 bars 4-12 are transposed to the major and reworked so that the encounter with D major in bars 6-7 is replaced with a conventional move to the dominant in bars 144-145, and the volatility of bars 8-12 is replaced with a logical continuation that confirms the dominant: what is achieved is a regular, eight-bar antecedent unit devoid of harmonic and syntactical irregularities. Bars 150-158 revert to the minor and necessarily modify bars 12-21 to bypass the original turn towards the relative major.

Ex. 6: Johann Nepomuk Hummel, Sonata in F-sharp minor, Op. 81, first movement, bars 134-157.

48.   The initial tritone, from D to G-sharp (bars 1-2), might be taken to imply A major more strongly than F-sharp minor. The tonic status of F-sharp minor does not become fully apparent until the third bar.

Hummel inserts a brief encounter with C major (bars 152-153) into the modified version of bars 12-21 in bars 150-158. Appearing at the equivalent point in the unit to the initial D major in bars 7-8, this retrospectively confirms the connection between this initial flat-wards dip and subsequent expansions of C major as well as introducing the first of several residues of C major that punctuate the recapitulation. On two further occasions Hummel alters what is generally a very literally transposed version of the exposition[49] to include brief forays into C major. In effect, this confirms a process that has already taken place; the rationale for the development appears to be the assimilation and resolution of the bridge passage's C-major digression. I have already noted that the body of the development consists almost entirely of a great sequential expansion of the heart of the bridge passage where the harmony first digressed. Hummel refashions it as an extensive medium-scale upwardly chromatic sequence that starts from the distant terrain of B-flat major and works its way to the dominant for a spacious retransition. C major, reappearing in bars 112-114, is thus assimilated into a dynamic harmonic process that ultimately connects it with the tonic; and as a sequence whose rhythmic momentum is undisturbed, the passage can also be understood as a foil to those other areas (including the very start of the development) where things proceed in fits and starts. Consequently, and despite Truscott's vituperation, the development does advance certain arguments that happen to be harmonic and syntactical rather than thematic. The development's achievement is then reinforced by the recapitulation's 'residues' of C major and related centres; these include bars 152-153 and 191-194, where Hummel replaces what would (if literally transposed) have been a VI-V-I progression into the tonic with a brief

---

49.   The literal transposition means that the bridge passage's digression — which Hummel retains in the recapitulation — reappears in A major rather than C major, a structural centre within the movement's key scheme.

tonicisation of G major, V of C. The final residue of C appears in bars 209-210 where, again, literal transposition is modified to accommodate it.

One of Hummel's priorities in the movement seems to have been to offer full compensation and subsequent resolution of all harmonic transgressions; this is the work of the development and recapitulation. The rather strict approach to the latter, whereby almost everything from the exposition is literally reproduced, almost suggests a clinical conformity to normative practice. This might in turn start to suggest that improvisatory departures are somewhat suppressed by the weight of structural convention. As already suggested, however, this movement's improvisatory aspects serve both sides of the aesthetic equation. One of the most remarkable features of the exposition is the spacious approach Hummel takes towards articulating the exposition's secondary key. A major is first reached in bar 28, but the final cadence confirming it and ending the exposition does not take place until bar 95. The spaciousness comes from a process of repeating and varying similar, successive approaches to the relative major. This can be seen as improvisatory in concept: one of the principal topics cited by Carew with which nineteenth-century improvisers were expected to be familiar was the variation technique that led some sets of variations to be entitled 'Fantasia'[50]. The first stage of the process involves a recovery from the C-major digression. This consists, firstly, of the harmonic pivot restoring A major and then a series of cadential moves which seem gradually to lose momentum. The second stage of affirming A major restores the rhythmic momentum and launches an elaborate *codetta*. This culminates in the aforementioned reference to the opening gambit within A major. Still, the process is unfinished, and the upwardly chromatic bass movement in bars 74-75 magnifies a similar progression in bars 58-61. Hummel then demonstrates yet another way of affirming the relative major, through the *cantabile* melody that is unconnected with any previous motivic events. This gives way to a final *codetta* that at last brings the section to a close.

HUMMEL'S SONATA OP. 81 IN CONTEXT

Traditionally Hummel is seen as a transitional figure between Classical and Romantic eras. Kroll, Hummel's most recent biographer, attaches the composer more firmly to the nineteenth century by putting him forward as the first true touring artist in history[51] and as composing works comparable in style with those of Schubert, Schumann, Chopin and even Liszt[52]. This counterbalances the earlier perception of him as a reactionary figure, composing works that represented little more than Mozart with frills. Interpreting the first movement of Op. 81 in terms of improvisation might look like an attempt to underpin

---

50. CAREW, Derek. *The Mechanical Muse* [...], *op. cit.* (see note 2), p. 435 and footnote 17.
51. See KROLL, Mark. *Op. cit.* (see note 1), Chapter 6.
52. See *ibidem*, Chapters 5, 19, 11 and 12.

the 'Romantic' Hummel: as Valerie Woodring Goertzen has noted «[t]he notion of improvisation accorded well with the Romantic fascination with the immediacy and intangibility of music» since «[t]he spontaneous outpouring of an artist's inspiration afforded a glimpse of genius in the very process of creating»[53]. Carew writes:

> All of the great preoccupations of the period, and those that we associated most closely with the Romantic *ethos*, were brought together in improvisation. Generally, the artists' own elevation of the instinctual over the contrived, of art over craft, of creativity over composition, and the overriding need to impress with the emotional force of his or her own personality — a personality that had to be recognisably stamped on a series of artworks of universal appeal[54].

According to this, Hummel's Op. 81 would emerge as a quintessentially 'Romantic' work. However, as I have tried to show, the improvisatory element of the first movement of Op. 81 cannot be affiliated to moments of disruption or subversion alone; it also has to encompass quite strenuously normative orientations. The paradoxical connotations of improvisation are equally inherent in the eyewitness accounts cited in the opening section of this discussion: improvisations must be coherent yet spontaneous, logical yet daring.

The notion of a tangibly improvisatory element interacting with and ultimately animating normative conventions in a work like Op. 81 might in the end imply that Hummel's overarching motive was conservative and that the aim was to rejuvenate a genre well on the way to (perceived) anachronism or even extinction. Carew quotes the famous 1839 review in the *Neue Zeitschrift für Musik*[55] in which Schumann outlines the paradox between a scarcity of new sonatas being composed in the 1830s and the persisting prestige of the genre[56]. Hummel's F-sharp minor Sonata is the only work to be specifically cited in the review[57], and it is clear that Schumann thought highly of it. We might therefore situate the sonata within the final throes of late Classicism, as standing alongside works like Beethoven's 'Hammerklavier Sonata', Dussek's Sonata in A-flat major, Op. 70 ('*Le retour à Paris*'), or even Anton Eberl's Grand Sonata in G minor, Op. 39[58], in which eighteenth-century principles hold sway but are overlaid by, or viewed through, the increasingly distorting prism of techniques or stylistic traits that came to form the bedrock of early Romanticism.

---

53. GOERTZEN, Valerie Woodring. *Op. cit.* (see note 38), p. 305.
54. CAREW, Derek. *The Mechanical Muse* [...], *op. cit.* (see note 2), p. 432.
55. SCHUMANN, Robert. *Neue Zeitschrift für Musik*, x (1839), p. 134, quoted in CAREW, Derek. 'Hummel's Op. 81: [...]', *op. cit.* (see note 21), p. 133.
56. *Ibidem.*
57. *Ibidem*, p. 134.
58. On Eberl's sonata, see WHITE, Alton Duane. *The Piano Works of Anton Eberl (1765-1807)*, Ph.D. Diss., Madison (WI), University of Wisconsin-Madison, 1971, pp. 117-128. *Cfr.* ID. 'Anton Eberl, Composer and Pianist between Vienna, Germany and Russia', in: *La cultura del fortepiano / Die Kultur des Hammerklaviers 1770-1830*, edited by Richard Bösel, Bologna, Ut Orpheus Edizioni, 2009, pp. 261-280: 276-280.

The notion that Hummel's Sonata Op. 81 is in some way special or belongs to a subset of outstanding works is reinforced by the extent to which Hummel's approaches differ from what is to be found in his other solo sonatas (see TABLE 2). This is particularly noticeable in the handling of the second halves of the expositions of the opening movements. Generally Hummel favours conventionally binary key schemes, clearly demarcated bridge passages and, most often, melodically differentiated second themes. A typical case is the first movement of the Sonata in E-flat major, Op. 13. The bridge passage is concise and business-like and is followed by a song-like second theme with a regular periodic structure and an internal variation on the initial twelve-bar paragraph. The *codetta* has a clear onset and consists of a quasi-orchestral paragraph followed by a short tailpiece of the type often cultivated by Mozart[59]. Much the same template is used for the expansive Sonata in D major, Op. 106, composed in March 1824 as Hummel's last solo piano sonata and written on a scale comparable with Op. 81[60]. The bridge passage is more elaborate than in Op. 13: it overshoots the dominant of A major, reaching V of III — but there is no digression as such, and the move to C-sharp major highlights rather than obscures the structural subdivision between the bridge passage and second theme. In fact, Hummel goes out of his way to demarcate the onset of the second theme. The bridge passage comes to a stop in bar 38 followed by a pause and an introduction based on the opening material. When it arrives, the second theme is song-like in the manner of Op. 13. A sixteen-bar antecedent unit is followed by a nineteen-bar variation that touches on the minor dominant and, as in Op. 13, introduces melodic diminutions. Although the *codetta* reaches virtuosic heights comparable with what one finds in Op. 81, the structural premise of this exposition is completely different. Whereas the impression in Op. 81 is of a continuous, if unpredictable and periodically disorientating, improvisatory continuum, Op. 106 consists more of a series of tableaux, alternating paragraphs of lyricism with virtuosity; whereas in Op. 81 everything points towards continuity, Op. 106 appears deliberately sectional. In Op. 20, as already explained, a lyrical second theme is replaced by a quasi-improvisatory reworking of fragments of the opening; but the improvisatory episode is too transient to generate serious structural ambiguity and is in any case flanked by a coherent bridge passage and *codetta*; and it introduces no harmonic complications.

---

[59]. See ALLANBROOK, Wye Jamison. 'Mozart's Tunes and the Comedy of Closure', in: *On Mozart*, edited by James Malachy Morris, Washington DC, Woodrow Wilson Center Press, 1994, pp. 169-186. In relation to *codettas* in works by Mozart, including the String Quartet in C major, KV 465 ('Dissonance'), Allanbrook defines two, successive closing formulae: «one the solid, primarily harmonic closing formula, not elaborating particular thematic material, but exuding rhythmic and harmonic conviction; the other a reflective, valedictory close, usually involving previous motivic fragments made end-oriented, often over a drone bass». *Ibidem*, p. 180.

[60]. Op. 106 is Hummel's only solo piano sonata to contain four movements.

TABLE 2
HUMMEL'S SOLO PIANO SONATAS, WITH OPUS NUMBERS
Information taken from KROLL, Mark. *Op. cit.* (see note 1), Appendix A, pp. 347-358

WORK	OPUS NUMBER	DATE OF PUBLICATION
Sonata in C major	Op. 2(a), No. 3	April 1792
Sonata in E flat major	Op. 13	Circa 1805
Sonata in F minor	Op. 20	Circa 1807
Sonata in C major	Op. 38	Circa 1812
Sonata in F sharp minor	*Op. 81*	*1819*
Sonata in D major	Op. 106	Circa 1825 (composed in March 1824)

The point of these brief comparisons is to stress the relative uniqueness of Hummel's Sonata Op. 81, in which the improvisatory element is conspicuous without being totally embedded in the surrounding idiom. The successful realisation of Hummel's implicit aim of adding immediacy and impact to what may well be considered his *magnum opus* is captured by Jean-Jacques Rousseau's characterisation of improvisation:

> It is in improvising that the great musicians, freed from that extreme bondage to rules that the eyes of the critics impose on written works, realize the bold and masterful transitions that so delight the audience. Here it is not enough to be a good composer, nor to possess a thorough knowledge of the piano, nor to have a good and well-practiced hand. One must also possess that verve, that touch of genius, and that inventive spirit that immediately finds and treats subjects that are most favourable to the harmony and most pleasing to the ear[61].

---

[61]. ROUSSEAU, Jean-Jacques. *Dictionnaire de musique*, Paris, la Veuve Duchesne, 1768, p. 383, quoted in GOERTZEN, Valerie Woodring. *Op. cit.* (see note 38), pp. 310-311.

Clara Wieck Schumann's Improvisations and Her 'Mosaics' of Small Forms

Valerie Woodring Goertzen
(New Orleans, LA)

Clara Schumann's preludes, notated in 1895, provide clues not only to her improvisatory practice but also to her engagement with other composers' music over her long career[1]. When studied together with her collection of over 1200 concert programs in the Archive of the Robert-Schumann-Haus Zwickau, the preludes help us envision the 'mosaics' of short pieces by Chopin, Mendelssohn, Bach, Beethoven, Robert Schumann, herself, and others that she performed beginning in the mid-1830s, as Clara Wieck[2]. She connected these small forms, which the public was unaccustomed to hearing in concerts, through improvised preludes and transitions, thereby creating extended musical numbers incorporating contrasting styles, characters, and keys[3]. The new approach showed her concern for large-scale design, her highlighting of relationships among pieces

---

[1]. The notated preludes consist of seven exercises, two 'Einfache Praeludien für Schüler' (Simple Preludes for Students) resembling those in her father Friedrich Wieck's *Piano Studies*, edited by Marie Wieck (1875), plus eleven introductory preludes, including preludes to Robert Schumann's 'Des Abends' and 'Aufschwung' from the *Fantasiestücke* Op. 12, 'Schlummerlied' from *Albumblätter* Op. 124, and the slow movement of the F minor Sonata Op. 14. See my edition of the introductory preludes in *Women Composers. Music through the Ages. Vol. 6: Composers Born 1800-1899*, edited by Martha Furman Schleifer and Sylvia Glickman, New York, G. K. Hall, 1999, pp. 44-104, and of the entire set in *Clara Schumann: Preludes, Exercises, and Fugues for Piano*, Bryn Mawr (PA), Hildegard, 2001. The principal autograph is in the Staatsbibliothek zu Berlin Preussischer Kulturbesitz, Musikabteilung, Ms. autogr. 9. The Robert-Schumann-Haus in Zwickau houses a handwritten copy of these items (Nr. 7486,5) and an autograph of four of the preludes (Nr. 11514-A1).

[2]. *Die große Programm-Sammlung Clara Schumanns (eigene Konzerte)*, Robert-Schumann-Haus, Zwickau, No. 10463 (hereafter 'PC'). Although titles of compositions are sometimes generic — for example, a Chopin etude or a 'Clavierstück' by Scarlatti — it is possible to identify some of these pieces by observing patterns in Clara Schumann's programming and with the help of her diary and correspondence, reviews in the press, and other sources.

[3]. See Goertzen, Valerie Woodring. 'Setting the Stage. Clara Schumann's Preludes', in: *In the Course of Performance. Studies in the World of Musical Improvisation*, edited by Bruno Nettl, Chicago, University of Chicago Press, 1998, pp. 237-260. Clara Schumann's programming and her relationship with the public is explored in Klassen, Janina. *Clara Schumann. Musik und Öffentlichkeit*, Cologne, Böhlau, 2009.

by different composers, and her desire to develop in particular directions an enduring repertory for piano that combined works of the past and present.

Improvisation was part of Clara Wieck's training from childhood, a means of mastering technique and musical styles, and of creating compositions that she could perform and publish. As was typical for pianists of her day, she improvised free fantasies in her concerts, as well as preludes before and between pieces; such preludes allowed pianists to test the instrument and to quiet the audience and, if they wished, to introduce materials of the upcoming composition[4]. In the 1830s Clara Wieck's improvisations helped her bring into her concerts three categories of pieces not yet typically heard in public concerts: a Beethoven sonata, preludes and fugues of Bach, and Romantic character pieces such as etudes and songs without words. The present study centers on one mosaic of pieces that Clara Wieck presented in different versions between December 1835 and February 1837, and occasionally later.

During a visit to Paris in March 1832, the thirteen-year-old Clara Wieck entertained at the home of Prince von Aremberg. According to her diary, she improvised a prelude to Henri Herz's Variations on Haydn's 'Emperor' hymn, also working in a Scherzo in A-flat major of her own composition, and spontaneously breaking into a statement of the Emperor hymn — the Austrian anthem — as the wife of the Austrian ambassador came through the door[5]. We may gain some notion of this improvisation from the introduction to Wieck's *Souvenir de Vienne* Op. 9, which she composed six years later in response to being named Royal and Imperial Chamber Virtuosa, and which uses the same theme (see Ex. 1). Although the piece will be in G major, Wieck begins in E-flat, and presents bits of Haydn's melody alternating with transitional passages grounded in chains of secondary dominants and diminished seventh chords. We hear the hymn's opening motive treated in sequence, then a reference to the tune's last line in m. 5, disguised somewhat by its beginning on A-flat. The tune begins again in m. 11, but soon dissolves. At the *un poco animato* in the fourth line, Wieck invents a new figure based on the head motive, which leads to a partial statement of the last phrase of the tune on G and a short transition setting up the entrance of the theme proper. The dynamic indications and expression marks leave no doubt that this introduction is to be a moment of high drama, intended to bring the audience to the edges of their seats.

[4]. See GOERTZEN, Valerie Woodring. 'By Way of Introduction. Preluding by 18th- and Early 19th-Century Pianists', in: *The Journal of Musicology*, XIV/3 (Summer 1996), pp. 299-337; HAMILTON, Kenneth. 'A Suitable Prelude', Chapter 4, in: *After the Golden Age. Romantic Pianism and Modern Performance*, Oxford, Oxford University Press, 2008, pp. 101-138.

[5]. 22 March 1832, cited in WITTKOWSKI, Désirée. 'Clara Wiecks erster Parisaufenthalt 1832', in: *Clara Schumann. Komponistin, Interpretin, Unternehmerin, Ikone*, edited by Peter Ackermann and Herbert Schneider, Hildesheim, Georg Olms, 1999, pp. 243-257: 252, based on a transcription by Martin Schoppe of an entry of an unpublished diary in the Robert-Schumann-Haus in Zwickau. The Scherzo by Clara Wieck may have been her 'Étude' in A-flat. See the works list in REICH, Nancy B. *Clara Schumann. The Artist and the Woman*, revised edition, Ithaca (NY), Cornell University Press, 2001, p. 323.

Ex. 1: Clara Wieck, *Souvenir de Vienne*, Op. 9, Vienna, Diabelli, 1838, measures 1-29.

As early as February 1834, thus by the time Clara Wieck was fifteen, she was including groups of small pieces in her programs. In Plauen she performed a nocturne and two grand etudes by Chopin, a composer whose music she especially admired, but who was not generally familiar to her audiences[6]. Improvisation seems to have been part of these groupings of pieces from the beginning: the program for her second concert in Plauen on 3 April 1834 announces «two grand etudes of Chopin, with free introduction» (*2 grosse Etuden von Chopin mit freier Einleitung*; PC #41). The fact that Clara Wieck performed from memory beginning in Paris in 1832[7], blurred the distinction between notated and non-notated portions of her programs.

Reviews from 1837 and 1838 comment on her groups of connected pieces. In Berlin she played a set of four pieces «following directly one after another and introduced by short preludes based on the themes of the solo pieces»[8]. In Prague she performed 'mosaics' of pieces, and a reviewer in Vienna described her «innovative combination of several short movements, just as in a suite», noting that this format placed each composer's style in sharp relief[9]. Also from Vienna, Josef Fischhof wrote Robert Schumann of the importance of Clara Wieck's preludes in winning admirers for Chopin's works and for herself:

> Clara's short improvised preludes, which introduced each piece in ingenious fashion, and which combined tender, melodious playing with the most brilliant bravura — bravura that she used only as a means, however, never as an end in itself, as many others do — were received enthusiastically by a public belonging to the most distinguished society and who attended in large numbers, despite the fact that it was a weekday [Thursday] and thus not an ideal day for a concert. [...] Chopin's compositions, performed in such a way, must finally succeed with the masses; may his opponents realize now *sub rosa* that the

---

[6]. Concert of 14 February 1834. PC #39. Reich (*op. cit.* [see note 5], pp. 191-194) discusses meetings of Chopin and Clara Wieck, her programming of his music, and the impact of his music on her compositional style. In the program for the February 14 concert, the nocturne and the etudes are identified as «Compositionen aus der neu-romantischen Schule».

[7]. WITTKOWSKI, Désirée. *Op. cit.* (see note 5), p. 251.

[8]. *Allgemeine musikalische Zeitung*, XXXIX/16 (19 April 1837), cols. 257-258: «unmittelbar nach einander folgend durch kurze, aus dem Thema der Solosätze entnommene Präludien eingeleitet». Clara Wieck's programs in Berlin are discussed in FERRIS, David. 'Public Performance and Private Understanding. Clara Wieck's Concerts in Berlin', in: *Journal of the American Musicological Society*, LVI/2 (Summer 2003), pp. 351-408.

[9]. *Neue Zeitschrift für Musik*, VIII/1 (2 January 1838), pp. 3-4, 8; *Allgemeine musikalische Zeitung*, XL/10 (7 March 1838), cols. 164-165: «Die originelle Zusammenstellung mehrer kurzen Sätze, gleichsam in eine Suitenreihe, zeigt schon genügend den beabsichtigten Standpunkt, von welchem die Beurtheilung auszugeben hat, die prävalirende Haupttendenz nämlich, die Eigenthümlichkeit eines jeden Meisters zur klaren Anschaulichkeit zu bringen, ihn selbst, sein innerstes Wesen mit Verstand, Gefühl und aus voller Seele wiederzugeben».

talented Henselt has translated Chopin freely into German, and that the noblest features of Thalberg's compositions are inspired by Chopin's[10].

Recordings by Ferruccio Busoni, Josef Hofmann, Wilhelm Backhaus and others document a later stage in the improvisation of preludes, a practice that remained strong throughout the nineteenth century and into the twentieth[11]. Josef Hofmann supplied brief preludes to several pieces in his Golden Jubilee concert in 1937, including a modulating transition between Chopin's Waltz in A-flat Op. 42 and the Andante Spianato in G major[12]. Wilhelm Backhaus took ill in his last recital in 1969, and replaced the finale of Beethoven's Sonata Op. 31 No. 3 with Schumann's 'Des Abends' and 'Warum?' from the *Fantasiestücke* Op. 12. He preluded for about 16 seconds, beginning with a small melodic and rhythmic figure and continuing with a progression leading to a dominant seventh chord in D-flat that then resolves into the beginning of 'Des Abends'[13].

In both of these recordings, the performers play the preludes quietly, so that they appear to be directed back towards the pianist himself rather than projecting outward across the audience. In this way, the transitional or introductory nature of preludes is made clear; they represent the musings of the performer, and have a tone that is different from the compositions they connect. Clara Wieck Schumann may have adopted such a tone for her short transitions; this would have helped listeners distinguish between her improvisations and pieces, and to keep their places within her mosaics of pieces.

Clara Schumann's more substantial notated prelude to 'Des Abends', one of the set of introductory preludes she notated in 1895, is shown in Ex. 2. Here Clara Schumann states the melody clearly at the outset, then employs techniques of fragmentation, sequence, and extension of ideas seen in the introduction of her 'Souvenir de Vienne'. The half-step appoggiatura motive that produces the poignant opening dissonance of 'Des Abends' appears repeatedly in different guises, both obvious and hidden, including in the final plagal cadence.

---

[10]. NAUHAUS, Gerd. '«Signale aus Wien». Hintergrundinformationen zum ersten Wien-Aufenthalt Clara (Wieck-)Schumanns', in: *Festschrift Otto Biba*, edited by Ingrid Fuchs, Tutzing, Hans Schneider, 2006, pp. 285-286: «Claras kurze improvisierte Präludien, die jedes Stück geistvoll einleiteten, der innige zarte schmelzende Vortrag in Vereinigung mit der glänzendsten Bravour, die sie aber nur als Mittel, nicht wie viele Andere als Zweck betrachtet, erhielt[en] enthusiastische Anerkennung bey einem Publiko, welches, der gewähltesten Gesellschaft angehörig, an einem dem Concertgeben ungünstigen Wochentage in großer Zahl zugegen war. [...] Chopin's Compositionen, auf solche Art vorgetragen, mußten endlich bey der Masse durchdringen; mögen dessen Gegner nur jetzt sub rosa erfahren, daß der talentvolle Henselt den Chopin frey ins Deutsche übersetzt hat, u. daß das Edlere in Thalberg[s] Compositionen Chopin'sche Anregung sey». Schumann published an edited version of Fischhof's report in the *Neue Zeitschrift für Musik*, VII/51 (26 December 1837), p. 204.

[11]. See HAMILTON, Kenneth. *Op. cit.* (see note 4).

[12]. *The Complete Josef Hofmann, Vol. 2: The Golden Jubilee Concert*, recorded 28 November 1937, Metropolitan Opera House. Available on VAI Audio, VAIA/IPS 1020, 1992.

[13]. *Wilhelm Backhaus: The Last Recital, Ossiach, 28 June 1969*. Available on Decca, 455 048-2, 1996.

Ex. 2: Clara Schumann, 'Prelude to 'Des Abends' by R[obert] S[chumann]', notated 1895, from GOERTZEN, Valerie Woodring. 'Clara Schumann', in: *Women Composers. Music through the Ages. Vol. 6: Composers Born 1800-1899, op. cit.* (see note 1), p. 98. © Gale, a part of Cengage Learning Inc. Reproduced by permission.

TABLE 1 shows how Clara Wieck in 1835-1837 created a context for works of Bach and Beethoven that audiences were not used to hearing in public concerts. On 20 March 1835 she had first performed the C-sharp major Fugue of Bach in Hamburg, as the first of a group of pieces including also Chopin's Nocturne in F-sharp major [Op. 15, no. 2] and her own 'Capriccio,' probably Op. 2 (PC #70). She had played the finale of Beethoven's Sonata in F minor, Op. 57 ('Appassionata'), for the first time in Halle on 24 July of the same year, followed by a mazurka, a nocturne and a 'grand characteristic etude' of Chopin (PC #78)[14]. Then on 1 December 1835 in Plauen — two months before the Dresden concert excerpted in TABLE 1 — she brought the fugue and the sonata movement together for the first time, as numbers one and two of a mosaic (PC #81), and she programmed them in this way in six out of the eleven concerts she gave over the next fourteen months. Numbers three and four of the group were new, Romantic pieces, by Chopin or Mendelssohn — number three a slow piece or dance (Chopin mazurka or nocturne, or Mendelssohn song without words), and number four a virtuosic *tour de force* etude of Chopin.

TABLE 1

GROUPING OF SHORT PIECES PLAYED BY CLARA WIECK IN DRESDEN, 1836
Concert of Clara Wieck, supported by the King's orchestra
and directed by Kapellmeister Carl Gottlieb Reissiger

DATE	VENUE	PROGRAM
30 January 1836 (PC #87)	Dresden Saale der Harmonie	End of Part 1 J. S. Bach, Fugue in C-sharp major [*Well-Tempered Clavier*, Book 1] Beethoven, Sonata in F minor, Op. 57, Finale Chopin, Notturno, F-sharp major [Op. 15, No. 2] Chopin, Grand Bass-Etude, C minor [Op. 10, No. 12, 'Revolutionary']

Clara Wieck's pairing of movements in C-sharp major and F minor probably was suggested by Beethoven's sonata itself, in which the second movement in D-flat major leads into the finale without a break. Here Beethoven provided a transition from D-flat into F minor, employing a diminished seventh chord on E in the last measures of the Second Movement and the first measures of the Third Movement. Clara Wieck easily

---

14. See DE VRIES, Claudia. *Die Pianistin Clara Wieck-Schumann. Interpretation im Spannungsfeld von Tradition und Individualität*, Mainz, Schott, 1996, pp. 361-362. In her repertoire list, De Vries identifies the C-sharp major fugue as from Book 1 of the *Well-Tempered Clavier* (p. 361). On 28 July 1835 Clara Wieck performed the C-sharp major fugue in Halle, followed by her own 'Hexenscene' (apparently Op. 5, No.1), Chopin's Etude in D-flat major, Op. 10, No. 11, transposed down a whole step from the original key of E-flat major, and Chopin's Etude in C minor Op. 10, No. 12 (PC #79). See Fischhof's report of Clara Wieck's first concert in Vienna, 14 December 1837, in NAUHAUS, Gerd. *Op. cit.* (see note 10), p. 285. Although several pianists were playing Beethoven sonatas privately at this time, public performances were rare. Felix Mendelssohn performed the 'Waldstein' and 'Moonlight' Sonatas in separate concerts at the Berlin Singakademie late in 1832. See TODD, R. Larry. *Mendelssohn. A Life in Music*, New York, Oxford University Press, 2003, pp. 268-269.

could have expanded upon this harmony to connect the Bach fugue in C-sharp with the sonata finale, perhaps even working in references to Beethoven's transition or to the upcoming movement. Factors other than key also may have played a role: the Bach fugue and sonata finale both feature a descending sixteenth-note figure of similar shape, and Beethoven's initial presentation of this figure in a single voice creates an expectation of contrapuntal treatment — or, in the context of this grouping *recalls* contrapuntal treatment.

Since Chopin's Nocturne in F-sharp begins on the dominant, Clara Wieck would have needed a transition that reversed her movement between the Bach and Beethoven pieces, and that also set up a change in mood. The middle, B section of this nocturne also is in the dominant key, and thus connects back to the key of the fugue, C-sharp. The 'Revolutionary' Etude provides a dramatic finale for the mosaic, and an opportunity for Wieck to display her power and agility. But its presence also highlights similarities with Beethoven's Op. 57 finale: the dominant seventh chord (a dominant ninth if the sixteenth-note a-flat is included) recalls the diminished seventh sonority at the beginning of the sonata movement, and both pieces continue with descending figures in sixteenth notes spanning three octaves that are at first prominent but soon assume an accompanimental role (see Ex. 3). In this set of pieces, therefore, Clara Wieck constructed an extended musical number — about 17 minutes in length that offered a range of contrasting tempos, keys, and characters, and also exhibited general and some more specific similarities among the components. Such groupings also explicitly presented the notion of a historical progression in the keyboard repertory from Bach through Beethoven to the later Romantics.

Ex. 3: (a) Johann Sebastian Bach, Prelude in C-sharp major from the *Well-Tempered Klavier*, Book 1, measure 4, uppermost voice; (b) Ludwig van Beethoven, Sonata in F minor, Op. 57, Movement 4, right hand, end measure 5 to beginning measure 7.

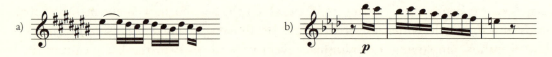

In such mosaics, Clara Wieck treated both the fugue and the sonata movement as essentially character pieces. Her performances of the F minor Sonata in Vienna in the winter of 1837-1838 led to what she called a 'press war', as one disgruntled writer responded to the publication on 9 January of Franz Grillparzer's laudatory poem, 'Clara Wieck and Beethoven' (*Clara Wieck und Beethoven*), with the observation that Wieck had reduced Beethoven's music to a feat of technical display in which the composer's spirit was entirely absent[15]. But if the finale is separated from the context of the sonata, and also from our contemporary view of these iconic works, the movement stands rather convincingly

---

[15]. Nauhaus identifies the reviewer as Baron Lannoy, composer and conductor, and member of the Board of Directors of the Conservatory of the Gesellschaft der Musikfreunde. See NAUHAUS, Gerd. *Op.*

as a character piece, with its pervasive sixteenth-note motion, its sectional structure with internal repetitions, and the at first playful, then fiery Presto ending. The start of the Presto resembles Robert Schumann's music in its alternation of brash held chords and a soft, sharply contrasting staccato passage that seems to run in circles. It is not difficult to imagine listeners constructing for themselves an underlying program for this movement — and perhaps for this entire mosaic of pieces.

In the early months of 1837 Clara Wieck began to program the fugue and the sonata movement in new ways. She incorporated both the first and second movements of the sonata into her mosaic on 25 February in Berlin (PC #103), then programmed the entire F minor Sonata as an independent work a week later in the same venue (1 March 1837, PC #105). She went on to perform other Beethoven sonatas, as well as sonatas of Schubert, Mendelssohn, and eventually Robert Schumann. She now played the Fugue in C-sharp major, which had become one of her 'hits', as an encore, by request, and to introduce unfamiliar pieces. From Spring 1837, however, her groups of short pieces consisted mainly of Romantic character pieces — that is, *new* music. Table 2 presents a sample of these groupings from the later 1830s and 1840. The first grouping cited is an isolated, early instance of Clara Wieck's programming of Robert Schumann's music in this format.

Table 2
Representative Groupings in Clara Wieck's Concerts, 1837-1840

Date	Venue	Program
13 August 1837 Morning Concert (PC #115)	Leipzig Saale der Buchhändlerbörse	End of Part 1 R. Schumann, 3 Études symphoniques with their preceding theme (from Op. 13) [first performance; C-sharp minor] Chopin, Notturno, B major [Op. 9, No. 3 or Op. 32, No. 1] Adolph Henselt, Andante und Allegro [=*Poëme d'amour*, Op. 3, B major, published 1838]
21 January 1838 Fourth concert (PC #127)	Vienna Saale der Gesellschaft der Musikfreunde	Chopin, Etude No. 10 in A-flat major [Op. 10, No. 10] Chopin, Notturno, E-flat major [Op. 9, No. 2] Clara Wieck, Mazurka in G major [Op. 6, No. 4] Henselt, Andante und Allegro [*Poëme d'amour*, Op. 3]
11 January 1840 First soirée (PC #164)	Berlin Saale der Sing-Academie	Henselt, Etude in E-flat minor [Op. 2, No. 8] Schubert-Liszt, *Ave Maria* Mendelssohn, Praeludium Scarlatti, Clavierstück

cit. (see note 10), pp. 290-291. Grillparzer's poem appeared in the *Wiener Zeitschrift für Kunst*; see Reich, Nancy B. *Op. cit.* (see note 5), pp. 1, 56-57.

In a later stage of her mosaics — and thus of her use of preludes — after Robert's hospitalization in 1854, Clara Schumann began to program his most accessible character pieces in groups on a regular basis, either as all-Schumann sets or mixed with pieces by other composers. 'Des Abends' is among the works she chose most frequently. Although it is the first number of Op. 12, she programmed this lyrical night song as the middle, 'slow' movement of a group in three-fourths of her performances of it; two instances are shown in TABLE 3. Even in the case of Robert's music, preserving the composer's ordering of pieces in a set or cycle was not as important to Clara Schumann as creating a sonic structure that would be dramatic and effective in her concerts.

TABLE 3
SAMPLE MOSAICS PERFORMED BY CLARA SCHUMANN
AND INCLUDING CHARACTER PIECES BY ROBERT SCHUMANN

DATE	VENUE	PROGRAM
14 December 1854 Musical soirée of Clara Schumann née Wieck and Joseph Joachim (PC #339)	Potsdam Saale des Palastes Barberini	Beginning of Part 2 Chopin, Impromptu in A-flat major [Op. 29] R. Schumann, 'Des Abends' and 'Traumeswirren' [from Op. 12]
15 April 1856 Concert of the Musical Union (PC #391)	London Willis's Rooms	End of concert R. Schumann, 'Des Abends' from Op. 12 Mendelssohn, two Songs without Words, including Book 6, No. 4 [Presto in C major]
16 January 1880 First concert of the Städtische Cur-Direction (PC #1189)	Wiesbaden Curhaus	Penultimate number on program R. Schumann, Novellette in F major, Op. 21 [No. 1] R. Schumann, 'Des Abends' R. Schumann, 'Traumeswirren'

As the young Clara Wieck was performing and also composing the typical showpieces in the mid-1830s, she already was developing her role as an interpreter of what she considered to be the best of European music. In mosaics that included older music, groupings held together by improvised preludes, she presented in capsule form the broad chronological sweep of European keyboard music — with special focus on the German and Austrian tradition and on Chopin. In this new format she explicitly connected Romantic composers, including Chopin, Mendelssohn, Adolph Henselt, herself and soon also Robert Schumann, with the legacy of Bach and Beethoven, engaging with these different styles in her own instrumental voice, and affirming that all of this music belonged under the umbrella of the modern Romantic aesthetic.

Cadenza Improvisation in Nineteenth-Century Solo Piano Music According to Czerny, Liszt and Their Contemporaries

Martin Edin
(Stockholm)

These embellishments in music [...] are a measure of good taste [...]. Naturally, only the performer's delicacy of feeling and extensive practice can settle the proper way to use them[1].

THIS ESSAY DEALS WITH CADENZA IMPROVISATION in nineteenth-century solo piano music, an issue that hitherto has not received enough attention. My aim is briefly to examine some ways in which the eighteenth-century tradition of embellishing fermatas was, at least by some pianists, maintained long into the next century, and was used in nineteenth-century piano repertoire. The focus of attention will be the question about where fermata improvisation was considered fitting. There will be no attempt to analyse the way these cadenzas were designed, and therefore we will not go into the specific ways in which nineteenth-century fermata embellishments were different from their eighteenth-century counterparts[2].

---

[1]. CZERNY, Carl. *Systematische Anleitung zum Fantasieren auf dem Pianoforte*, Op. 200, Vienna, Diabelli, 1829, p. 22: «Diese Verzierungen in der Musik sind [...] ein Maßstab des guten Geschmacks [...] Über deren passende Anwendung kann natürlicherweise nur der feinere Sinn des Spielers und eine grosse Übung entscheiden».

[2]. In Carl Czerny's German the words 'Cadenz' and 'Fermate' are used interchangeably. *Ibidem*, pp. 22-35. I will follow him in this respect in my text, using 'fermata' with the same meaning as 'cadenza'. When intending the graphic symbol ⌢ I will use 'fermata sign'. When I have the concluding, big cadenza of a concerto movement in mind, I will use the expression 'concerto cadenza'. Alice L. Mitchell is unfortunately misguided regarding Czerny's usage of the terms 'Fermate' and 'Cadenz' in her English translation of the *Systematische Anleitung*. This causes her problems in some instances (see note 27 below). She writes, for example: «For the most part, Czerny uses *Cadenza* and *Fermata* in their modern senses, namely as the interpolated elaboration at a pause (*Cadenza*), and as the sign designating the pause (*Fermata*) [...]. Because of Czerny's predominantly modern usage, the occasional exceptions can be confusing, as in *Schlussfermata*». See CZERNY, Carl. *Systematische Anleitung zum Fantasieren auf dem Pianoforte*; English translation by Alice L.

The fermata sign in a score means that a note, chord or rest should be extended beyond its nominal value. A number of eighteenth-century writers on the art of playing keyboard instruments, among them most famously perhaps Carl Philipp Emanuel Bach and Daniel Gottlob Türk, describe how the performer may add embellishment to a note with such a sign. Today the appropriateness of supplying cadenzas at fermata signs is universally accepted for eighteenth-century keyboard concertos, and authorities argue that cadenza improvisation is also valid in eighteenth-century solo keyboard and chamber music works by, among others, C. Ph. E. Bach, the young Joseph Haydn and the young Muzio Clementi[3]. This practice, though, is generally supposed to be irrelevant to the performance of solo piano compositions of the nineteenth century, a view that I would like to call in question.

It is true that fermata improvisation was less widely used in the nineteenth century than in the preceding one — a tendency that grew stronger as the century progressed. The following examples indicate that signs of this development may be found both in music manuals and the ways composers wrote their scores.

In the first decades of the nineteenth century fermata embellishment was frequently described in piano instruction books teaching the fundamental skills of piano playing. It is mentioned in different early editions and translations of Clementi's *Introduction to the Art of Playing on the Piano Forte*, Jan Ladislav Dussek's *Instructions on the Art of Playing the Piano Forte or Harpsichord*, Daniel Steibelt's *Méthode de piano* and Johann Baptist Cramer's *Instructions for the Piano Forte*[4]. Cramer's description from 1812 is quoted here:

Mitchell, *A Systematic Introduction to Improvisation on the Pianoforte*, New York, Longman, 1983, p. 3, note 3. This is a mistake, and it is an interpretation that makes many of Czerny's sentences in Chapter 3 difficult to comprehend. The confusion disappears if one reads 'Fermate' as equivalent to 'Cadenz'. I am grateful to Angela R. Mace for helpful comments on this essay.

3. ROSENBLUM, Sandra P. *Performance Practices in Classic Piano Music. Their Principles and Applications*, Bloomington, Indiana University Press, 1988, p. 287. HARRISON, Bernard. *Haydn's Keyboard Music. Studies in Performance Practice*, Oxford, Clarendon Press, 1997, pp. 162-163. SOMFAI, László. *Joseph Haydn zongoraszonátái: Hangszerválasztás és előadói gyakorlat, műfaji tipológia és stíluselemzés*, Budapest, Zeneműkiadó, 1979; English translation by the author in collaboration with Charlotte Greenspan, *The Keyboard Sonatas of Joseph Haydn. Instruments and Performance Practice, Genres and Styles*, Chicago, University of Chicago Press, 1995, pp. 81-83. That singers went on contributing cadenzas to written music throughout the nineteenth century is also widely commented upon.

4. See CLEMENTI, Muzio. *Einleitung in die Kunst das Piano-Forte zu spielen*, Vienna, Hoffmeister - Leipzig, Hoffmeister & Kühnel, Plate Number 104, 1802, p. 12 (the German translation); DUSSEK, Johann Ladislaus. *Pianoforte-Schule nach der englischen Ausgabe (Dussek's Instructions etc.) übersetzt, und von dem Verfasser selbst verbessert und mit vielen praktischen Beispielen vermehrt herausgegeben. Vierte Auflage*, Leipzig, Breitkopf und Härtel, Plate Number 2294, [4]1815, p. 6; STEIBELT, Daniel. *Méthode de piano, ou L'art d'enseigner cet instrument. Pianoforte-Schule*, Leipzig, Breitkopf & Härtel, Plate Number 1334, 1809, p. 16; CRAMER, Johann Baptist. *Instructions for the Piano Forte*, London, Chappell & Co, Plate Number 77, 1812, p. 26.

> This mark ⌒ is called a Pause[;] it renders the note longer at pleasure, and in certain cases the performer is to display his taste by introducing some extempore and fanciful passage[5].

However, in piano manuals of a comparable kind published later in the century the explanations of the fermata sign are normally more restricted. The instruction to introduce an improvised passage is here no longer given as part of the account of the graphic symbol. This is exemplified by Wilhelm Bauck's Swedish edition and translation of Cramer's *Instructions* published as *Praktisk piano-skola* in 1853, where the corresponding passage reads:

> The sign ⌒ is called *fermata* (pause). One dwells upon the note or rest, over which it is written, for as long as one wishes or as demanded by the character of the piece[6].

Some of the more advanced instrumental treatises from the first part of the nineteenth century — Carl Czerny's *Systematische Anleitung zum Fantasieren auf dem Pianoforte* (1829), Pierre Baillot's *L'art du violon* (1834) and Bernard Romberg's *Violoncell-Schule* (1840) — present more elaborate instruction as well as examples of embellished fermatas to be used by the student as models[7]. We will shortly explore Czerny's treatise, but, although my essay is concerned with piano music, it is worthwhile first to note one of Baillot's points in *L'art du violon*. This manual bears ample evidence that Baillot considered the improvisational practices of ornamentation, fermata embellishment and preluding to be important elements in the education of a violinist.

Baillot explains his views on when the embellishing of music is appropriate and when it is not. In Chapter 17, which deals with ornamentation, he makes a distinction between two kinds of musical notation. He describes, on the one hand, an older manner of writing where the notation is not complete in itself, where it is a skeleton that needs to be worked out by the musician. His prime examples of compositions of this kind are the Adagios of Corelli and Tartini, which are portrayed as «not only simple, but we could even say bare»[8]. On the other hand he depicts a contemporary style of notation where the composer has written the necessary embellishments into the score. In music with notation

---

[5]. CRAMER, Johann Baptist. *Op. cit.* (see note 4), p. 26. The explications found in the piano methods by Clementi, Dussek and Steibelt mentioned are very similar.

[6]. «Tecknet ⌒ kallas *fermat* (hvilopunkt.) Man dröjer vid den not eller paus, hvaröfver den står, så länge man vill eller styckets karakter erfordrar». CRAMER, Johann Baptist. *Praktisk piano-skola*, edited by W. Bauck, Stockholm, Hirsch, Plate Number 548, 1853, p. 25.

[7]. CZERNY, Carl. *Systematische Anleitung* […], *op. cit.* (see note 1), pp. 23-29. BAILLOT, Pierre. *L'art du violon*, Paris, Dépôt Central de la Musique, 1834; English translation by Louise Goldberg, *The Art of the Violin*, Evanston, Northwestern University Press, 2000, pp. 295-327. ROMBERG, Bernard. *Violoncell Schule*, Berlin, Selbstverlag (Kommission Trautwein), 1840, p. 81.

[8]. BAILLOT, Pierre. *Op. cit.* (see note 7), p. 287.

of this second type there is no room for added ornamentation. According to Baillot there are therefore many fewer opportunities for improvised elaboration in music composed in his own time than in older compositions[9].

This view is similar to those expressed by Johann Friedrich Schubert and Johann Nepomuk Hummel. In his *Neue Singe-Schule* of 1804 J. F. Schubert supports the view that written-out embellishments preclude the addition of ornamentation in singing:

> Some composers have the habit of writing melismatic embellishment
> into their compositions. In these cases the singer must withhold all additions,
> because otherwise he would accumulate embellishments upon embellishments,
> which would damage the expression and thoroughly distort the composition[10].

A few decades later Hummel similarly indicated that a new way of composing had changed the conditions for ornamentation of fermatas. He writes the following in his *Ausführliche theoretisch-praktische Anweisung zum Piano-Forte-Spiel* of 1828:

> The *Schlussfermate* (cadenza), as it is called, was formerly frequently found
> in concertos, etc., mostly towards the end of a piece, and there the performer
> strived to display his strengths; but it is rarely needed any more because the
> form of the concertos has changed and the difficulties are spread out in the
> composition itself. When such a major cadenza still sometimes occurs in sonatas
> or variation pieces the embellishment is provided by the composer himself[11].

A palpable illustration of the development of the principles guiding musical notation may be found in the sequence of editions of Clementi's Piano Sonatas Op. 2 occurring

---

[9]. *Ibidem*, pp. 278-287. Baillot's exposition of this thought belongs to Chapter 17 on ornamentation, whereas the fermata embellishments are presented in Chapter 19. But since fermata embellishment is a type of ornamentation I can see no reason to doubt that Baillot intended his reasoning about two types of notation to apply to ornamentation of fermatas as well as to ornamentation of melodies. This becomes even more plausible if we take into consideration Baillot's example in Chapter 17 of a way to ornament the second movement of a violin concerto by Giovanni Battista Viotti, which includes three cadenzas at fermata signs.

[10]. «Einige Componisten pflegen die melismatischen Verzierungen in ihre Tonstücke mit herein zu schreiben. In diesem Falle muss sich der Sänger aller Zusätze enthalten, indem er sonst Verzierungen auf Verzierungen häufen, und so dem Ausdruck schaden und die Composition gänzlich entstellen würde». SCHUBERT, Johann Friedrich. *Neue Singe-Schule oder gründliche und vollständige Anweisung zur Singkunst*, Leipzig, Breitkopf & Härtel, 1804, p. 138.

[11]. «Die sogenannte Schlussfermate (*Cadenza*, Tonfall) kam früher häufig in Konzerten etc. meist gegen Ende eines Stückes vor, und der Spieler suchte in ihr seine Hauptstärke zu entwickeln; da aber die Konzerte eine andere Gestalt erhalten haben, und die Schwierigkeiten in der Komposizion selbst vertheilt sind, so gebraucht man sie selten mehr. Kommt noch zuweilen in Sonaten oder Variazionen ein solcher Haupt-Ruhepunkt vor, so giebt der Komponist selbst dem Spieler die Verzierung». HUMMEL, Johann Nepomuk. *Ausführliche theoretisch-praktische Anweisung zum Piano-Forte-Spiel, vom ersten Elementar-Unterrichte an, bis zur vollkommensten Ausbildung*, Vienna, Haslinger, 1828, p. 65.

from 1779 to circa 1819. The differences between the various editions are of many kinds, but as far as fermatas are concerned it is interesting to note that where we find plain fermata signs over dominant chords at transitions between sections in the 1779 edition of Op. 2, No. 2, these are decorated with written-out embellishments provided by the composer in an edition from 1809[12], and even more so in the edition from circa 1819[13].

The general tendency in the beginning of the nineteenth century to write embellishments into the score is a strong argument against the relevance of fermata improvisation for nineteenth-century piano music. Eva Badura-Skoda and William Drabkin adhere to this train of thought in their article on 'Cadenza' in *The New Grove Dictionary of Music and Musicians*, in a section primarily dealing with the nineteenth-century concerto, but also mentioning solo piano music:

> Following Beethoven's lead in the Fifth Piano Concerto, 19th-century pianist-composers usually wrote their own cadenzas into the score, or they dispensed with them altogether. Significantly, Liszt rarely left a fermata sign indicating that the performer should insert a cadenza; he supplied all such material himself. Even in his transcriptions of operatic arias by Rossini, Bellini and others, Liszt wrote out cadenzas at those points where, in the original works, fermatas indicate their insertion. [...] Violinists and singers, on the other hand, consistently demanded the right to shape cadenzas according to their specific technical abilities[14].

Although this description may be fairly accurate from one point of view, it does not tell the whole story about how nineteenth-century pianist-composers dealt with fermatas. I will not dispute that in the nineteenth century, as a rule, ornamentation was written into the score by the composers. However, there are different ways of comprehending the significance of fermata improvisation for nineteenth-century piano music. It may be studied, of course, through the score, and such an approach might lead to pondering questions like: is the structure of the composition such that it needs complementary additions from the musician? It is also possible to tackle the issue by examining not how *we* interpret these scores, but how *nineteenth-century pianists* were interpreting the scores

---

[12]. CLEMENTI, Muzio. *Nouvelle édition des trois sonates Œuvre 2* [...] *avec des augmentations & améliorations considérables faites par l'auteur*, Offenbach, Johann André, Plate Number 2870, 1809.

[13]. See CLEMENTI, Muzio. *3 Sonate Op. 2 nn. 2, 4, 6 per Pianoforte o Clavicembalo*, edited by Andrea Coen, Bologna, Ut Orpheus Edizioni, 2001 (Muzio Clementi Opera Omnia, 4). See also HARRISON, Bernard. 'The Revision of Clementi's Opus 2 and the Transformation of Piano Performance Style', in: *Muzio Clementi. Studies and Prospects*, edited by Roberto Illiano, Luca Sala and Massimiliano Sala, Bologna, Ut Orpheus Edizioni, 2002 (Muzio Clementi Opera Omnia, 61), pp. 303-321. I am grateful to William Drabkin for directing my attention to these scores and Harrison's article.

[14]. BADURA-SKODA, Eva - DRABKIN, William. 'Cadenza', in: *The New Grove Dictionary of Music & Musicians, Second Edition*, edited by Stanley Sadie, 29 vols., London, Macmillan, 2001, vol. IV, p. 789.

written in their own era; which leads to questions about their attitude towards fermata signs in the pieces they were playing. This will be the focus of my essay.

In the *New Grove* quotation above one can notice a shift from the first perspective — emanating from the score — to the second — emanating from performance practice. The first portion of the quotation describes composers' way of writing, and the last sentence what violinists and singers wanted to perform. The relation between these two perspectives may be contemplated by the reader, in connection to the examples that will be presented. Although nineteenth-century piano scores may be complete in themselves in a sense, some of the pianists active in this century embellished fermatas in contemporary piano music, and, furthermore, also recommended such embellishment, as we shall see. We will first have a look at some guidelines taken from Czerny's writings, and later turn to concrete cases derived from Friedrich Wieck, Adolph Henselt and Franz Liszt.

Carl Czerny in 1829
Systematische Anleitung zum Fantasieren auf dem Pianoforte

The manual *Systematische Anleitung zum Fantasieren auf dem Pianoforte* that Czerny had published in 1829 contains instruction and models intended to teach a number of skills involved in the art of piano improvisation. Chapter 3 is about cadenzas — it first depicts fermatas of the *Eingang*-type, and then turns to concerto cadenzas[15]. Here we are interested in the first part of the chapter. Like Baillot, Czerny wants to explain when embellishment is appropriate and when it is not. Chapter 3, § 3 states that «in works of profound substance and serious character (for example Beethoven's Sonata in D minor, Op. 29 [*sic*]) every kind of addition would be most inappropriate»[16]. The fact that the illustrative example used by

---

[15].   Czerny does not himself use the term *Eingang*, but I have chosen it because it is in general usage today. It refers to an inserted, comparatively short transitional passage at a fermata, leading to a new section of the music. In Czerny's opinion such a fermata should outline a single harmony — that of the chord with the fermata sign — which in most cases is a dominant seventh chord (Czerny, Carl. *Systematische Anleitung* [...], *op. cit.* [see note 1], p. 22). In a more detailed discussion we might wish to distinguish between an embellishment of the fermata chord proper, and transitional notes leading to the beginning of the following theme. The *Eingang*-type fermata is in contrast to the concerto cadenza, which is characterized by Czerny as a free fantasia — a description quite in accordance with Heinrich Christoph Koch's account 27 years earlier (*ibidem*, p. 29. Koch, Heinrich Christoph. *Musikalisches Lexikon*, Frankfurt am Main, August Hermann der Jüngere, 1802, pp. 566-567).

[16].   «In Werken von tiefen Gehalt und ernsten Charakter (z.B. Beethovens Sonate, D mol, Op. 29 [*sic*]) wäre jede Art von Zugabe sehr übel angewendet». Czerny, Carl. *Systematische Anleitung* [...], *op. cit.* (see note 1), p. 22. The intended sonata is Beethoven's Op. 31, No. 2, which was published in Vienna with the incorrect opus number 29 by Cappi. See Mahlert's introduction and commentary in Czerny, Carl. *Systematische Anleitung zum Fantasieren auf dem Pianoforte*, Op. 200, Vienna, Diabelli, 1829, reprinted in facsimile, with an introduction by Ulrich Mahlert, Wiesbaden, Breitkopf & Härtel, 1993, p. xi.

Czerny is a piano sonata shows that the instructions in this *Eingang*-section of the chapter are not solely directed to the performance of concertos, but are supposed to apply also, even if not exclusively, to solo piano music.

The opinion expressed here, that a piece of music of «profound substance and serious character» is not a suitable arena for improvisation, is also articulated by Czerny in the preceding chapter about preludes. There he states that it is not fitting to improvise an extended prelude to a serious piece like Beethoven's F minor Sonata Op. 57[17]. In this respect Czerny's description is in agreement with expressions found in Türk's *Klavierschule* (1789) and J. F. Schubert's *Neue Singe-Schule* (1804). They both recommend less of embellishing in serious ('*ernst*'/'*ernsthaft*') music[18].

In Chapter 3, § 3 of his *Systematische Anleitung* Czerny continues:

> On the other hand, in compositions primarily intended for a glittering, delicate or sentimental manner of playing, in variations, potpourris, transcribed vocal pieces or other works in popular taste, there are abundant opportunities, where small impromptus of this kind are adequate, and in fact often required, to embellish a perhaps otherwise bare and dragging passage[19].

The *Systematische Anleitung* was published in 1829, and we know that a large portion of the piano music played in salons as well as in the theatre in the 1820s and the 1830s consisted of «variations, potpourris, transcribed vocal pieces or other works in popular taste», of compositions that were «primarily intended for a glittering, delicate or sentimental manner of playing». This is also the music Czerny recommends for young pianists making their debut[20]. This is the music that they should be able to perform in a successful way. The corollary has to be that it was quite common that pianists in the 1830s would encounter pieces of a kind where fermata improvisation would be quite appropriate, even desirable in Czerny's eyes. In compositions of this type there were «abundant opportunities» for such extemporizations, they were «in fact often required».

These guidelines mean that for Czerny it was necessary to consider the seriousness of a work when judging if an improvised addition was advisable or not; pianists must be able to assess which type of music they were playing. It is instructive to compare the quotations

---

[17]. CZERNY, Carl. *Systematische Anleitung* [...], *op. cit.* (see note 1), p. 15.

[18]. SCHUBERT, Johann Friedrich. *Op. cit.* (see note 10), p. 138. TÜRK, Daniel Gottlob. *Klavierschule oder Anweisung zum Klavierspielen für Lehrer und Lernende*, Leipzig, Schwickert, 1789, pp. 238 and 325.

[19]. «Dagegen in Compositionen, die vorzugsweise für ein glänzendes, delikates oder sentimentales Spiel berechnet sind, in Variationen, Potpourris, arrangirten Gesangstücken, oder sonstigen Produkten des herrschenden Geschmacks, giebt es häufige Gelegenheiten, wo dergleichen kleine Impromptus angemessen, ja oft Bedürfniss sind, um eine vielleicht sonst kahle und schleppende Stelle auszuschmücken». CZERNY, Carl. *Systematische Anleitung* [...], *op. cit.* (see note 1), p. 22.

[20]. ID. *Vollständige theoretisch-practische Pianoforte-Schule, Dritter Teil, Von dem Vortrage*, Op. 500, Vienna, Diabelli, ²1846, p. 63.

from Czerny's *Systematische Anleitung* with the statements about embellishment in *L'art du violon* by Baillot. There is an important difference between their ways of approaching the matter. We may say that Czerny discusses the character of the *music*, while Baillot writes about the character of the *notation*. As we will recall, Baillot's account was based on a distinction between an old and a new style of writing. Baillot might have asked: Has the composer provided a completely worked out surface structure for the music, or is the music unfinished in its details? For Czerny, on the other hand, the most relevant question seems to have been: Is this music of a character that makes improvisation appropriate? The distinction in *Systematische Anleitung* is between serious and popular music, while *L'art du violon* points to a distinction between new and old music[21]. It is also possible to state that the difference is that between a formal criterion (Baillot) and a judgment based on content (Czerny) — between an attention directed to the formal features of the notation, and one directed to the affective content of the music. For Baillot the prohibition of ornamentation in music written in the modern way is not grounded on the assumption that it would be opposed to the character of the music. It is about not intervening in a finalized musical structure. A plausible interpretation of Czerny's account is that he finds fermata improvisation to be eminently suitable for enhancing the sparkle of glittering music and for expressing delicacy and sentimentality, but not for projecting the profound content of a serious piece.

Czerny in 1846
Die Kunst des Vortrags

In 1846 Czerny seems to have developed his thinking somewhat on this matter. *Die Kunst des Vortrags der ältern und neuen Claviercompositionen* contains the following lines about the performance of Beethoven's piano music:

> When performing his [Beethoven's] works, (and more generally those by all classical authors) the performer may absolutely not allow himself to make changes, additions or cuts to the composition.
> Also in the piano pieces that in former times were written for the old instruments with five octaves, the effort to use the sixth octave, through additions, has always turned out unfavourably, as well as all embellishments,

---

[21]. It is not correct to assume that Czerny in 1829 was unaware of style differences between music composed in different eras. In the section about concerto cadenzas («Von den Schluss-Fermaten zu Concerten»), he points out that it is concertos *of an earlier date* that provide the opportunity to improvise a big fantasia at the end of the last tutti. There are no signs of this kind in the section about *Eingang*-type fermatas, restricting their application to older compositions. Czerny, Carl. *Systematische Anleitung* [...], *op. cit.* (see note 1), pp. 22-29.

mordents, trills, etc. that the composer himself has not prescribed stand out as superfluous, even if they in themselves appear perfectly tasteful[22].

A novelty here is that where the rules from 1829 speak about the *nature of a piece*, the quotation from 1846 deals with the *nature of the composer*. The relevant property of the composer to recognize is if he or she is classical or not.

Friedrich Wieck gives advice in the same vein in his *Clavier und Gesang* (1853). He points out that reverence for compositions by Beethoven, Mozart, Weber and others necessitates a more restrained attitude to the addition of embellishments in their works (but he also adds that such reverence is often exaggerated in a pedantic way); whereas in «gallant variations» («galanten Variationen») the performer may add a considerable number of ornaments[23]. So Wieck likewise chose to direct the reader's attention to certain composers, rather than to specify affective characters, as many eighteenth-century writers on music had done, when explaining which compositions were less suited to ornamentation. The expression «gallant variations», however, designates a type of music.

To Czerny 'classical' did not mean 'Viennese classical'. In the first chapter of *Die Kunst des Vortrags* Czerny gives a general definition of a classical composition as being a piece that for an extended period has stood the test of time and secured its durability for the future[24]. Exactly which composers Czerny in 1846 was assigning to the category of classical composers is difficult to know, but alongside Beethoven there are two more names to be gathered from the heading of the fourth chapter in *Die Kunst des Vortrags*, which reads: «About the Execution of the Fugues of Seb. Bach, Handel and other Classical Authors»[25]. Beethoven, Handel and J. S. Bach were obviously among the classical composers in Czerny's mind at the time; they were among the composers whose works, consequently, should be performed completely without changes and ornamentation.

Now, what does the change in Czerny's vocabulary from «works of profound substance and serious character» in 1829, to works «by all classical authors» in 1846 mean? First, the two concepts 'profound music of a serious character' and 'music composed by a classical

---

22. «Beim Vortrage seiner [Beethovens] Werke, (und überhaupt bei allen klassischen Autoren) darf der Spieler sich durchaus keine Änderung der Composition, keinen Zusatz, keine Abkürzung erlauben. | Auch bei jenen Clavierstücken, welche in früherer Zeit für die damaligen 5-octavigen Instrumente geschrieben wurden, ist der Versuch, durch Zusätze die 6ste Octave zu benützen, stets ungünstig ausgefallen, so wie auch alle, an sich noch so geschmackvoll scheinenden Verzierungen, Mordente, Triller, *etc.* welche nicht der Autor selber andeutete, mit Recht überflüssig erscheinen». CZERNY, Carl. *Die Kunst des Vortrags der ältern und neuen Claviercompositionen oder Die Fortschritte bis zur neuesten Zeit. Supplement (oder 4ter Theil) zur grossen Pianoforte-Schule*, Op. 500, Vienna, Diabelli, 1846, p. 34.

23. WIECK, Friedrich. *Clavier und Gesang und andere musikpädagogische Schriften*, edited by Tomi Mäkelä and Christoph Kammertöns, Hamburg, von Bockel Verlag, 1998, p. 167. *Clavier und Gesang* was originally published in 1853.

24. CZERNY, Carl. *Die Kunst* […], *op. cit.* (see note 22), p. 31.

25. «Über den Vortrag der Fugen Seb. Bach's, Händel's und andrer classischen Autoren». *Ibidem*, p. 122.

composer' do not have the same meaning. There are many works by classical composers that can be characterized as light and entertaining rather than serious, and, conversely, non-classical composers may well produce music of a serious character. Czerny's different choice of words in the later quotation therefore points to a development in his thinking; it is not just a restatement of the same thought in new words. The 1846 formulation is likely to be read as expanding the class of pieces where fermata embellishment should be avoided. My conjecture is namely that the new wording supplies a new thought in addition to the old ones, rather than being a replacement for the old rules (which, however, cannot be excluded as a possibility). In other words, the later Czerny is here understood as still thinking that «works of profound substance and serious character» should be performed without added ornamentation, but that he also had come to believe that all compositions by classical composers, the light-hearted ones as well, ought to be treated in this more restrained way.

Second, still with Czerny's statements regarding the classical composer taken into account, his and Baillot's analyses are strikingly dissimilar. Their respective categories of music-prohibited-from-improvised-additions are not coextensive. A fashionable, glittering and delicate set of variations from the 1820s should according to Baillot's instruction be played as written, because it already contains embellishments from the composer (which music from this decade normally does). According to Czerny, however, this is exactly the type of piece where the pianist may find it profitable to amplify the music through improvised additions. The conclusion, and the point to be emphasized, is that Czerny in his writings invites additions of fermatas in *solo piano music written in his own era*. In this he was not alone, as we shall see.

CZERNY ON WHERE TO IMPROVISE FERMATAS

A question of fundamental interest is where — in a piece of suitable character and origin — one can add an improvised cadenza. Czerny provides us with the following statement:

> Pauses over 6/4 or 7 chords quite often occur in the middle of pieces; (in the latter case especially as transition to a new motif or tempo, as well as to the main theme) where the composer either indeed prescribed: cadenza ad libitum, or where a cadenza at least would not be superfluous, or finally where a truly written out but too brief cadenza may be extended in an appropriate way[26].

---

[26]. «Sehr häufig kommen Mitten in Stücken Aushaltungen über dem Quart-Sext, oder Septimen-Accord vor; (:über dem Letzteren besonders, als Übergang in ein anderes Motiv oder Tempo, auch ins Hauptthema:) wo der Componist entweder wirklich vorschrieb: Cadenza ad libitum, oder wo wenigstens

Here, three situations are mentioned where a fermata improvisation may be added to a composition at a pause: (1) Where the composer has written «cadenza ad libitum». This instruction is fairly straightforward. A solo piece with such an inscription that easily comes to mind is Liszt's Hungarian Rhapsody No. 2. (2) Where a «cadenza at least would not be superfluous»[27]. This phrase addresses the musician's taste, and taste is a phenomenon in a state of constant change throughout history. Therefore it is difficult to judge by this rule, with the guidance of our own taste, where a fermata may have been considered tasteful in Czerny's time. The most fruitful way to do this is almost certainly by exploring examples from musicians of his era, which we are going to accomplish in the last portion of this essay. (3) Where «a truly written out but too brief cadenza may be extended in an appropriate way». This is a most noteworthy remark from Czerny, which shows the issue from a new angle. Furthermore, this part of the instruction undoubtedly appeals to the pianist's taste in judging if the notated cadenza is too short or is a satisfying length. We may observe that the idea expressed here is quite consistent with the opinion that in fashionable piano music fermata improvisation is «adequate» and «often required», which was discussed above. Such fashionable music from the 1820s and the 1830s already contains written cadenzas. For Czerny, however, this is no hindrance for improvisers to practise their art, because written embellishments may be expanded according to artistic need.

As we may surmise, such views were not uncontested. Gottfried Wilhelm Fink wrote a review of the *Systematische Anleitung* in the *Allgemeine musikalische Zeitung*, where he gives much praise to the chapter about cadenzas, but singles out exactly this third part of the last Czerny quotation for comment:

> The rules of this chapter are among the best things in the work. [...] The additional clause 'where a truly written out but too brief cadenza may be extended in an appropriate way' we would rather have seen formulated in a more duly restricted way. As a rule not every player should permit himself to replace written-out cadenzas with arbitrary ones; first of all, because today most newer compositions contain good cadenzas, even exemplary ones[28].

---

eine Fermate nicht überflüssig wäre; –oder endlich wo eine wirklich ausgeschriebene, aber allzukurze Cadenz schicklich verlängert werden kann». ID. *Systematische Anleitung* [...], *op. cit.* (see note 1), p. 22.

[27].   Alice L. Mitchell unfortunately gives a confused rendering of this clause in her English translation of the *Systematische Anleitung*. This is caused by her failing to realize that Czerny uses the word «Fermate» with the same meaning as «Cadenz». (See note 2 above.)

[28].   «Die Regeln dieses Kapitels gehören zu dem Besten, was im Werke vorkommt [...] Den Zusatz: 'wo eine wirklich ausgeschriebene, aber allzu kurze Cadenz schicklich verlängert werden kann' hätten wir lieber gehörig beschränkt gelesen. In der Regel soll sich nicht jeder Spieler erlauben, statt der ausgeschriebenen, willkürliche Cadenzen zu machen, vorzüglich da jetzt in den meisten neueren Compositionen gute Cadenzen, ja musterhafte sich vorfinden». FINK, Gottfried Wilhelm. 'Recension. *Systematische (?) Anleitung zum Fantasieren auf dem Pianoforte von Carl Czerny* [...]', in: *Allgemeine musikalische Zeitung*, No. 35 (2 September 1829), col. 578.

Fink's objection to Czerny in this instance shows a way of thinking aligned with Baillot's and Hummel's. He thinks that written-out ornamentation should normally not be changed. Fink is not, however, rejecting fermata improvisation in solo piano music *per se*.

Examples of Performance Instruction

The *Systematische Anleitung* unfortunately does not provide any samples of compositions where Czerny considered fermata improvisation to be advisable, only the negative one of the unsuitable Beethoven sonata. Instead, suitable exemplification has to be found in other sources.

Czerny asserts that in most new, brilliant compositions there is a great variety of cadenzas that may be used as models for imitation by the student[29]. It is clearly valuable to use models to study *how* fermatas may be designed in an artful way, but it is also possible to investigate models to gain knowledge about *where* in a composition musicians during the nineteenth century considered fermata embellishment to be tasteful. That is what interests us here. Every composition with a written cadenza-like transition, of course, shows where the composer considered a cadenza transition to be desirable. In the pages that follow some examples will be considered where cadenzas have been added to a piece after its publication, rather as Clementi did in his already mentioned later editions of the Piano Sonata Op. 2, No. 2.

We are going briefly to examine some cases of performance instruction from F. Wieck, Henselt and Liszt. All of them concern works written in the first half of the nineteenth century; and the early, fundamental part of the pianistic development of these three, famous pianists and piano teachers likewise belongs to the same time period. The performance instruction examples in question, though, date from after 1850.

Friedrich Wieck

Friedrich Wieck is most of all known as the eminent piano teacher of his daughter Clara. In *Clavier und Gesang* (1853) he relates four lessons where he teaches the fictitious Amalie how to play the variation piece 'Les trois graces', No. 1, 'Cavatine du Pirate', Op. 68, No. 1 by Henri Herz. A passage in the fourth lesson is of special interest here. When dealing with the theme of the work, Wieck instructs Amalie that «If another passage that deftly leads to the dominant comes to mind at the fermata in the second part, then try it out and connect it, perhaps, to the one written on the page»[30]. This is a description of

---

29. Czerny, Carl. *Systematische Anleitung* [...], *op. cit.* (see note 1), p. 29.

30. «Fällt Ihnen bei der Fermate im zweiten Theil eine andere Passage ein, welche geschickt auf die Dominante leitet, so versuchen Sie dieselbe und verbinden sie vielleicht mit der dort stehenden». Wieck, Friedrich. *Op. cit.* (see note 23), p. 167.

an improvisation that prolongs or substitutes a written embellishment. Ex. 1 shows the fermata Wieck is writing about[31]. The procedure is exactly in accordance with Czerny's rule about the possibility to expand written-out cadenzas.

Ex. 1: excerpt from the theme of Henri Herz, 'Les trois graces', No. 1, 'Cavatine du Pirate', Op. 68, No. 1.

The fermata in Ex. 1 belongs to the theme of the piece. But Herz also presents us with written-out fermata embellishments of the same type, although more elaborate, in the corresponding bars in Variations 1, 3 and 4. Given his reference to the pianist's fancy when playing the theme, is there any reason to doubt that the same type of freedom should serve as guiding principle also for the performance of the following variations, according to Wieck's taste? After all, they belong to the same composition. Musically there is little difference between the written-out cadenzas in the theme and the variations, and therefore I argue that, following Wieck, it was commendable to amplify the following fermatas as well, if one so wished.

Clavier und Gesang was published in 1853, and therefore clearly belongs to a later period than Czerny's *Systematische Anleitung* of 1829. Nevertheless, the two authors are of the same generation: Wieck was born in 1785 and Czerny in 1791. This comparative closeness of their birth dates is a factor that makes the similarities in their outlooks appear less than startling. Another piece of information that may link the musical sensibilities of these piano masters is reported by Berthold Litzmann. He reveals that Clara Wieck studied improvisation using Czerny's *Systematische Anleitung*[32]. That means that her father, in all probability, also knew this work, and his opinions on improvisation could very well have been influenced by it.

---

[31]. The edition I used was published circa 1832-1835. It is not known to me if there are earlier editions of this work. HERZ, Henri. *Les trois graces, No. 1, Cavatine du Pirate de Bellini variée pour le piano*, Op. 68, No. 1, Mainz, Schott, Plate Number 3728.1, c. 1832-1835.

[32]. GOERTZEN, Valerie Woodring. 'Setting the Stage. Clara Schumann's Preludes', in: *In the Course of Performance. Studies in the World of Musical Improvisation*, edited by Bruno Nettl with Melinda Russell, Chicago, University of Chicago Press, 1998, p. 239.

MARTIN EDIN

ADOLPH HENSELT

The pianist-composer Adolph Henselt was born in 1814 in Schwabach, Bavaria. He studied music with, among others, Hummel and Simon Sechter, and emigrated in 1838, at the age of 24, to Russia where he stayed for the rest of his life until his death in 1889. In the later part of his life he prepared a large body of editions of piano music of various kinds and by various composers. According to Henselt himself he edited more than 500 works[33]. The editions were produced with a specifically pedagogical intent, and marketed with subtitles such as «with fingering and explanatory remarks and arranged for use in the Imperial Educational Institutions by A. Henselt»[34], or «edited by Adolph Henselt for use in the Imperial Russian Educational Institutions»[35]. The pedagogical intent of Henselt's editions is also corroborated by an editorial comment in the journal *Le Nouvelliste*, where many of them were published[36].

Ex. 2: excerpt from Ignaz Moscheles, Étude Op. 70, No. 5, edited by Adolph Henselt. After MOSCHELES, Ignaz. *Studien für Pianoforte*, Op. 70, Leipzig, Kistner, Plate Numbers 5180-5191, 1879, composed 1825-1826. The top system shows Moscheles's original notation, and the system below it Henselt's embellishment of the chords with fermata signs.

---

[33]. KEIL-ZENZEROVA, Natalia. *Adolph von Henselt. Ein Leben für die Klavierpädagogik in Rußland*, Frankfurt am Main, Peter Lang, 2007, p. 143.

[34]. «Compositions classiques et modernes pour piano doigtées avec des remarques explicatives et arrangées a l'usage des établissements Impériaux d'éducation par A. Henselt», on the title page of CHOPIN, Fryderyk. *Impromptu en la♭ majeur*, Op. 29, Moscow, Gutheil, plate number A. 6078 G., c. 1874-1889. Dating according to Schiwietz, who writes that Henselt's editions of music by Chopin were probably published between 1874 and 1889. SCHIWIETZ, Lucian. 'Henselts Chopin', in: *Chopin 1849/1999. Aspekte der Rezeptions- und Interpretationsgeschichte*, edited by Andreas Ballstaedt, Schliengen, Argus, 2003, pp. 111-112.

[35]. «zum Gebrauch in den Kaiserlich Russischen Erziehungs-Instituten eingerichtet von Adolph Henselt», on the title page of MOSCHELES, Ignaz. *Studien für Pianoforte von I. Moscheles Op. 70*, Leipzig, Kistner, Plate Numbers 5180-5191, 1879.

[36]. KEIL-ZENZEROVA, Natalia. *Op. cit.* (see note 33), p. 147.

Ex. 3: excerpt from Chopin, Impromptu Op. 29, edited by Adolph Henselt. The top system presents Chopin's notation, the system below portrays Henselt's embellishment of the transition.

Excerpts from two of Henselt's editions are portrayed in Exx. 2 and 3. They present two instances of fermata signs — one in an Étude by Ignaz Moscheles, and the other one in an Impromptu by Chopin — where Henselt clearly considered the addition of a cadenza to be artistic, making for a more beautiful transition[37].

The fact that Henselt had his amplifications printed in a system that runs parallel with the original text is a sign that he considered it important to show, in a most pedagogical manner, which amendments he had made and how they relate to the original text[38]. Because of this it is easier for a pianist to learn concrete things about

---

[37]. CHOPIN, Fryderyk. *Op. cit.* (see note 34). Chopin's Op. 29 originates from 1837.

[38]. This is the case with most of Henselt's additions in his editions, but it is also true that there are some exceptions.

performance from these editions than from, for instance, Theodor Leschetizky's, where the revisions of the composers' scores are not pointed out to the reader[39]. Through printing his elaborations in an *ossia* system Henselt presents his cadenzas as alternative ways of performing the transitions rather than obligatory ones. The cadenzas are suggested to, but not imposed upon, the pianist. Given the expressly pedagogical intent of Henselt's editions it does not seem unreasonable to view his addition of fermatas to the score as an encouragement to pianists to make up their own embellishments in these spots — perhaps using Henselt's cadenzas as models — rather than to perform them as they stand. Although the supplied cadenzas, no doubt, are beautiful to play in themselves, this seems to be a sensible reading.

At first sight one might tend to think that Henselt's procedure here conforms with Czerny's 1829 rules for fermata elaboration, since both the Moscheles and the Chopin pieces could be described as «intended for a glittering, delicate or sentimental manner of playing». All the same, there exists an important difference between their attitudes concerning the reworking of written compositions. As shown above, Czerny recommended total abstinence from additions and changes in music of profound content (1829), and by classical composers (1846). Henselt, on the other hand, had no qualms about updating music he considered great — on the contrary, he seems to have done this with enthusiasm and out of veneration of the great composers, in order to make their beautiful ideas communicate in the best way possible in a new era[40]. So Henselt's idea of how to show reverence was rather different from that expressed by Wieck and by Czerny in 1846. In practice this means that there are substantial additions and revisions in, for example, Henselt's editions of Beethoven's Piano Sonatas in D minor, Op. 31 No. 2, and F minor, Op. 57; and Carl Maria von Weber's Piano Sonata in D minor, Op. 49; and these are, no doubt, serious pieces by classical composers. On the other hand there are no important elaborations to be found in his editions of Richard Wüerst's 'Intermezzo, Menuet et Gavotte' Op. 64; Hermann Adolf Wollenhaupt's Nocturne Op. 32; and Gustav Schumann's Trois Mazourkas Op. 8 and Impromptu Op. 9[41]. From

---

[39].   See different pieces published in the series *Stücke aus dem Repertoire Essipoff-Leschetizky*, edited by Theodor Leschetizky, Hamburg-Leipzig, Rahter, Plate Numbers 2245-2258, n.d.

[40].   See SCHIWIETZ, Lucian. 'Henselts Beethoven — oder: der Versuch, ein Genie zu verbessern. Untersuchungen zu Henselts Editionen Beethoven'scher Werke', in: *Adolph Henselt und der musikkulturelle Dialog zwischen dem westlichen und östlichen Europa im 19. Jahrhundert. Konferenzbericht Schwabach 25.-27. Oktober 2002*, edited by Lucian Schiwietz, Sinzig, Studio Verlag, 2004, pp. 175-201; and SCHIWIETZ, Lucian. 'Henselts Chopin', *op. cit.* (see note 34).

[41].   BEETHOVEN, Ludwig van. *Sonate (en re mineur)*, Op. 31, No 2, edited by Adolph Henselt, Moscow, Gutheil, Plate Number A. 4330 G. ID. *Sonata appassionata*, Op 57, edited by Adolph Henselt, Moscow, Gutheil, Plate Number A. 3678 G. WEBER, Carl Maria von. *III. Grosse Sonate (D moll)*, Op. 49, edited by Adolph Henselt, Berlin, Schlesinger, Plate Number S. 6682, 1874 (C. M. v. Weber's ausgewählte Werke für das Pianoforte

Czerny's perspective it would preferably be the music in this last group that would need amendments to increase its effectiveness and beauty.

FRANZ LISZT

The most famous of all the pianists who studied with Czerny was certainly Liszt. His life was by and large contemporaneous with Henselt's. We will consider a passage from a composition by Liszt, and approach it with information that has emerged from his piano teaching. This material is of a later date than Czerny's *Systematische Anleitung*, but the picture of Liszt's musical thinking arising from it seems to be in alignment with the practice outlined by Czerny.

Ex. 4: excerpt from Liszt, Concert Étude in D flat Major, 'Un sospiro', S. 144, No. 3.

Ex. 4 shows a fragment from the Concert Étude 'Un Sospiro' by Liszt, namely the transition to the last statement of the main theme[42]. There is a fermata sign over a rest after the scale-passage in the treble, and this sign may be interpreted in at least three different ways, all of them plausible.

The most frequently adopted solution, which obviously is an impeccable one, is to interpret the rest with the fermata sign as a prolonged silence before the return of the main theme. If rendered in a sensitive way such a break in the flow of the music may bring a moment of enhanced tension.

---

mit Varianten, erläuternden Vortragszeichen und Fingersatz bearbeitet und herausgegeben von Adolf Henselt. [Insbesondere für den Gebrauch an den K.K.russischen Erziehungsanstalten in Petersburg bestimmt.], No. 5). WÜERST, Richard. *Intermezzo, menuet et gavotte, op. 64. Doigté et augmenté de remarques explicatives concernant l'exécution, destine à l'usage des élèves des établissements Impériaux d'éducation des demoiselles nobles en Russie par Adolphe Henselt*, Berlin, Erler, Plate Number 147. WOLLENHAUPT, Hermann Adolf. *Nocturne, Op. 32. Doigtées avec des remarques*, edited by Adolf Henselt, Moscow, Gutheil, Plate Number 5235. SCHUMANN, Gustav: *Trois Mazourkas*, Op. 8, edited by Adolf Henselt, Berlin, Bote & Bock, Plate Number 2166. ID. *Impromptu*, Op. 9, edited by Adolf Henselt, Berlin, Bote & Bock, Plate Number 2076.

[42]. The three études s. 144 were composed 1845-1849 and published in 1849.

However, near the end of his life Liszt wrote down at least three short cadenzas to be inserted at the fermata sign before bar 53[43]. Another attractive interpretation of the sign therefore naturally consists in selecting one of Liszt's own cadenzas for this transition. This way of performing bar 52 is also quite commonly used by pianists. Ex. 5 depicts Liszt's cadenza written for Auguste Rennebaum.

Ex. 5: one of Liszt's cadenzas for 'Un sospiro', written for Auguste Rennebaum in 1875.

My suggestion, though, is to interpret Liszt's notation of the cadenza variants to be inserted at the transition to bar 53 as an invitation to pianists to improvise a cadenza of their own at this fermata sign. According to this interpretation the cadenzas are not considered to be attempts by *the composer Liszt* at presenting revisions of the composition 'Un sospiro', but rather lessons by *the pianist Liszt*, demonstrating how this passage might be rendered. Here they are seen as models with a pedagogical purpose, much in the same way as Henselt's cadenzas to works by Moscheles and Chopin may be viewed (and perhaps also the added cadenzas in Clementi's later editions of his Sonata Op. 2, No. 2).

There is, naturally, no guarantee that this is the reading of his fermatas that Liszt intended, but it seems musically convincing. Three arguments can be put forward to support the hypothesis that Liszt was not hostile to the idea of an extemporized cadenza at the fermata sign in question. The first is the fundamental one:

1. Irrespective of how Liszt intended us to understand his cadenzas, we may observe that an interpolated embellishment at this fermata sign is entirely in accordance

---

[43]. Lina Ramann published two of them in *Liszt-Pädagogium* in 1902, and the Neue Liszt-Ausgabe gives these two cadenzas plus a third one. The cadenzas in *Liszt-Pädagogium* are dated 1875 and 1885 respectively. RAMANN, Lina. *Liszt-Pädagogium*, IV Serie, Leipzig, Breitkopf & Härtel, 1902, p. 5. LISZT, Franz. *Etüden II*, edited by Zoltán Gárdonyi and István Szelényi, Kassel, Bärenreiter-Budapest, Editio Musica, 1971 (Neue Ausgabe sämtlicher Werke, Serie I, Werke für Klavier zu zwei Händen, Band 2), p. 35.

with Czerny's instructions: (a) 'Un sospiro' is a piece «intended for a glittering, delicate or sentimental manner of playing». (b) The fermata sign is located at a seventh chord leading back to the main theme[44]. (c) There is already a written cadenza flourish at the transition, but, according to Czerny, pianists may extend it if they find that the embellishment is too short.

It does not seem far-fetched to imagine an affinity between Czerny's and Liszt's musical sensibilities, given that Czerny was the only advanced piano teacher Liszt ever studied with. In the *Liszt-Pädagogium* of 1902, a collection of testimonies about Liszt's piano teaching, Lina Ramann uses a vocabulary suggesting such a kinship. Ramann labels the fermata in Ex. 5 a «cadenza extension» (*Kadenz-Verlängerung*), and we will recall that Czerny stated that a written-out fermata «may be extended in an appropriate way» (*schicklich verlängert werden kann*). They both used forms of the word '*verlängern*', and wrote as if there was such a thing as to make extensions (*Verlängerungen*) of written cadenzas. Depicting Liszt's fermatas to 'Un sospiro' in a manner that makes them reminiscent of the cadenza extensions Czerny is writing about is therefore in line with the way the Liszt confidante Ramann describes the fermatas in 1902.

There are two additional considerations:

2. That Liszt added cadenzas at this transition shows, at the very least, that he did not consider 'Un sospiro' to be a piece composed in such a way that any alteration would destroy the balance of its musical structure. On the contrary, he seems to have felt that a cadenza is *needed* to bridge the gap between the scale in the high register and the return of the main theme. One can only agree with Liszt on this point. The prolonged-silence-interpretation of the fermata sign often makes this transition in the piece stand out as problematic.

It is possible that the idea about the fermata was a second thought — that Liszt realized, at some moment after the publication of the piece, that something was missing, that a short bridge passage would make the transition work better. But it is also conceivable that Liszt always envisioned this transition to be played with an additional passage, and that he left the more precise design of it to the performer's whim.

3. Independently of the character of this particular piece and this particular fermata, our interpretation is in agreement with Liszt's general manner of perpetually adding variants to works composed by himself and by others[45].

---

[44]. The sign is really located above a rest *after* the seventh chord, but this difference was obviously of no consequence to Liszt and Henselt. As we have seen, Henselt, in Chopin's Op. 29, also added a cadenza at a place where the fermata sign belonged to a rest adjacent to a dominant seventh chord.

[45]. On variants conveyed in his piano teaching see RAMANN, Lina. *Op. cit.* (see note 43) and GÖLLERICH, August. *The Piano Master Classes of Franz Liszt 1884-1886. Diary Notes of August Göllerich*, edited by Wilhelm Jerger, translated, edited and enlarged by Richard Louis Zimdars, Bloomington, Indiana University Press, 1996. It is worth noting that Ramann and Göllerich are not two completely independent sources. Ramann relies in *Liszt-Pädagogium* partly on information from Göllerich. But she has

Conclusion

This discussion has included examples and opinions from Czerny, F. Wieck, Henselt and Liszt, musicians that could hardly be regarded as peripheral or unimportant figures in nineteenth-century musical spheres. It would, though, be possible to argue that they went on using an outdated practice — the practice of improvising fermatas — unsuited to the new piano music composed[46]. That some nineteenth-century pianists used — and even recommended — fermata improvisation in compositions of their own era, does not necessarily imply that it is a desirable ingredient in the performance of this music. In the first part of my essay I laid out two different paths to follow when investigating the relevance of fermata improvisation to nineteenth-century piano music: the study of scores and the study of contemporary performance practice respectively. Certainly, there is also a third dimension to ponder here, articulated by the question: How should this music be performed today? The stand one takes on this question may be informed by the two types of investigation mentioned, but it is not necessarily dictated by either of them.

In the end it is up to the musicians to decide which kind of interpretation they want to pursue, but I would like to append a minor after-thought to that statement. In the quotation used as motto at the outset of this essay Czerny declared that only «delicacy of feeling» in combination with «extensive practice» can bring the performer knowledge of how to apply fermata embellishment in a proper way. Most pianists today have never indulged in «extensive practice» in the realm of cadenza improvisation, and therefore, according to Czerny, cannot have developed the good taste that makes it possible to exercise artistic discrimination in this field. From this perspective some degree of resuscitation of cadenza-improvisation practice would be valuable just for the sake of exploring, or rather re-exploring, the artistic qualities intrinsic to this art — qualities that will remain concealed as long as the practice remains dormant. Nevertheless, we have seen that two musicians who were trained in an era when fermata improvisation was taught, and who used it in their own artistic practice — Baillot and Czerny — disagreed on the rules of the game. Both of

---

on the one hand collected material from a number of other sources, and on the other hand she does not report everything Göllrich tells in his book, which means that the two writers after all supplement each other. On variants in Liszt's published études see SAMSON, Jim. *Virtuosity and the Musical Work. The «Transcendental Studies» of Liszt*, Cambridge, Cambridge University Press, 2003. On variants utilized by Liszt's piano students see FAN, Wei-Tsu. *Variant Performances of Franz Liszt's Piano Music in Early Recordings. A Historical Perspective on Textual Alterations*, 2 vols., Ph.D. Diss., Evanston (IL), Northwestern University, 1991; and listen to the piano-roll recording by Bernard Stavenhagen of Liszt's Hungarian Rhapsody No. 12 with the subheading «gespielt nach persönlicher Erinnerung an Franz Liszt» in the LP box *Welte-Mignon 1905*, Teldec, SLA 25 057-T/1-5, 1971, LP 3, side 6.

[46]. Charles Rosen puts forward an argument of this type against using the piano to provide a continuo accompaniment in piano concertos by Mozart and symphonies by Haydn. ROSEN, Charles. 'Should Music Be Played "Wrong"?', in: *High Fidelity Magazine*, XXI/5 (May 1971), pp. 54-58.

them were informed and sensible musicians, and were quite capable of making distinctions between different kinds of music. They did not teach indiscriminate embellishment of fermatas, but were of the opinion that sometimes it was needed, sometimes not. The nature of their tastes differed, though.

It is hardly surprising to find different tastes and different views on performance among leading musicians within the same era. There always were and will always be. And we should not be surprised to find different views today as well, on the praiseworthiness of using cadenza improvisation in nineteenth-century solo piano music if this deserted practice was to be reconsidered, and to some degree revived.

Practical Improvisation
The Art of Louis Vierne

Steven Young
(Bridgewater, MA)

THE ART OF IMPROVISATION HAS BEEN A STAPLE of organ playing since the fifteenth century. In the eighteenth century, the great Johann Sebastian Bach would often improvise on a new instrument to 'test out its lungs', and Handel regularly fashioned impromptu cadenzas while performing his organ concertos during the intervals of his oratorios. As can be seen, the tradition continued for many centuries but it seems to have matured into a true art form during the nineteenth century, most notably in France. In fact, the French were so convinced that they had raised improvisation to an exceptional level that one organist, Alexandre Cellier, referred to improvisation as 'French art'[1]. Improvisation was a requisite skill of all catholic organists, and, according to Jacques-Nicolas Lemmens, any organist who could not properly improvise for a solemnity should be replaced[2]. However, all improvisational styles used were not necessarily appropriate for liturgical services. Louis-Alfred-James Lefébure-Wely, a contemporary of César Franck, thrilled congregations with his more popular style of improvisation which used stirring rhythms and were usually of a picturesque nature. (He often improvised 'thunder storm' pieces.) These improvisations were, most likely, better suited for concert halls. Franck, organist of the Sainte-Clothilde, approached the art with an eye toward a more worshipful experience.

A recent book on the teaching of improvisation by Odile Jutten notes that the focus of improvisation at the Paris Conservatoire had been, until recently, liturgically oriented[3]. At the Paris Conservatoire, Franck insisted on the teaching of improvisation as a mandatory part of the curriculum, changing the style of the improvisations to that which would ennoble the listener, in order to provide a more dignified and suitable atmosphere for

---

[1]. CELLIER, Alexandre. 'L'improvisation, art français', in: *Le Ménestrel*, LXXXIX/49-50 (1927), pp. 505-506, 517-518.

[2]. LEMMENS, Jacques-Nicolas. 'Du caractère religieux de l'orgue; de l'organiste catholique', in: *Musique Sacrée*, VII/1 (1908), pp. 6-7.

[3]. JUTTEN, Odile. *L'enseignement de l'improvisation à la classe d'orgue du Conservatoire de Paris: 1819-1986. D'après la thématique de concours et d'examens*, Lille, Presses Universitaires de Septentrion, 2000, p. 16.

religious services. As Franck's students began to teach others, this more dignified approach to the art of improvisation spread and began to flourish throughout the country.

This art, while often harmonically daring and technically virtuosic, has a more subtle and practical side to it as evidenced by the recorded improvisations of Louis Vierne, *organiste titulaire* of Notre-Dame-de-Paris from 1900 until his death at the organ console in 1937[4]. Vierne's mastery of the more virtuosic style of concert improvisation can be found in the reviews of his numerous performances, but little attests to his art as a church musician except for the recordings he made for the Odeon record company in the late 1920s (some documentation exists to confirm that at least two of the recordings were completed in November of 1928). For the most part, scholars and admirers of Vierne's music often lament these improvisations as being uninspired and pedantic, especially when compared with the lyricism, majesty, and excitement found in the published organ works, but closer examination reveals that Vierne, while not as dramatic or intense in these improvisations, practiced his craft artfully, infused it with musicality, and performed it admirably in the service of the church.

The history of these improvisations is somewhat unclear as it has been long believed that only three were recorded and later transcribed by Vierne's student and friend, Maurice Duruflé[5]. It was long assumed that Vierne recorded these improvisations on three separate discs that had a very limited public release. However, documentation exists that demonstrates that at least one of these improvisations, the 'Méditation', was aired on Radio France in the early 1930s. Brigitte de Leersnyder, the French musicologist, has possession of the majority of Vierne's personal estate, and she recently discovered, had transcribed and published a fourth improvisation in 2005; it is questionable as to whether or not Duruflé or the musical public was ever aware of this fourth improvisation[6].

Some background information on Louis Vierne might help in understanding him as an artist and musician, and what led him to develop a method for teaching improvisation. Vierne, being blind from birth, attended the Institution National de Jeunes Aveugles. It was here that Vierne began to study music seriously, as the institution viewed itself as a school, a studio, and a music academy. Part of his curriculum included the study of organ under the tutelage of Louis Lebel and, later, under Adolphe Marty, one of César Franck's many outstanding students. Marty undertook the task of teaching young

---

[4]. The recordings referenced are found in *Orgues et organistes français du XXᵉ siècle*, EMI Music France, 2002, on the first disc of this five-disc set. The disc contains recordings of Charles Tournemire performing several published works and improvisations, as well as Louis Vierne performing his Andantino (*Pièces de fantaisie*, Opus 51/2) and the three improvisations that were later transcribed and published. The recording date for the Vierne is 17 November 1928.

[5]. Duruflé transcribed three improvisations at the request of Madeleine Mallet-Richepin. Those transcriptions were published as VIERNE, Louis. *Trois improvisations*, Paris, Durand, 1954: I. 'Marche épiscopale', II. 'Méditation', III. 'Cortège'.

[6]. ID. *Improvisation*, reconstituted by Jean-Michel Louchart, Paris, Henry Lemoine, 2006.

organists to improvise, as the organ students who left the Institution usually worked as Catholic church musicians. Vierne's study of improvisation began under Marty and later continued for a very brief period under César Franck himself. In his organ class, Franck emphasized the importance of improvisation since it was a major component of the year-end competition. According to Vierne's memoirs, five hours of the six-hour organ class were devoted to improvisation[7]. Following Franck's untimely death, less than one month after Vierne officially entered the Paris Conservatoire, Charles-Marie Widor became professor of organ and radically changed the way organ instruction was delivered and performance was treated, creating the modern French organ school recognized world-wide. Vierne discovered that Widor's approach to the teaching of improvisation differed greatly from Franck's, and he feared that what Franck had taught would be lost. Widor certainly maintained strict standards; he felt strongly that one needed to possess sufficient technical skill before one could adequately improvise, so he insisted on upgrading the level of playing of traditional organ repertoire. A few years later, Alexandre Guilmant took charge of the organ class and his approach to teaching combined both the strict emphasis on technique that Widor used, as well as a stress on the ability to improvise in a manner that was closer to that of Franck. Vierne was appreciative that Guilmant did not ignore the practices taught by his illustrious predecessor.

Improvisation played a dual role in the liturgical service: it accompanied the plain chants sung during the various offices celebrated on feast days and was a major component in the celebration of the Mass, and it provided accompaniment during moments of the liturgy where there was no singing.

The music for the offices and masses relied heavily on Gregorian chant, requiring the organist to harmonize chants. It seems clear that this skill was an important one as there are no fewer than forty-five books and manuals on the art of accompanying chant in the holdings of the Bibliothèque nationale in Paris. Clearly, Vierne knew this skill but, as there were so many published texts, it was not an area he chose to pursue in his teaching. Instead, he focused on improvisation based on free themes. As *organiste titulaire*, he was responsible for the music for the processional, offertory, elevation, communion, and recessional. He would often alternate chant accompaniments with the choir organ during sung portions of the liturgy. Counting this as a major part of the church musician's job, Vierne focused his teaching in this area. However, in order to do this easily, practicing improvisational schemes was expected in order to develop facility and ease with the technique.

As a result of having performed at countless liturgical functions, witnessing the various approaches to the teaching of improvisation at the Conservatoire, and having taught improvisation at both the Conservatoire and at the Schola Cantorum, Vierne had ample foundation for what has been referred to as his course on improvisation. Several of

---

7. SMITH, Rollin. *Louis Vierne. Organist of Notre Dame Cathedral*, Hillsdale (NY), Pendragon Press, 1999, p. 43.

Vierne's own improvisations reveal that he likely relied on some well-established formulas, and probably incorporated many of Franck's ideas. While little has been documented concerning the way Franck taught improvisation, a treatise by Étienne-Victor-Paul Wachs (1851-1915) reveals some relevant information related to the training of organists, including approaches toward the creation of processional and recessional marches, offertories, elevations, and other useful music for the celebration of ritual services[8]. Jutten believes the Wachs treatise to be more about Wachs's approach than Franck's, but it is the only treatise on free improvisation published in the nineteenth century. It is an interesting aside that two of France's greatest organists of this period, Charles Tournemire and Alexandre Cellier both felt that improvisation could not be taught. Cellier wrote: «One could become a musician, but one is born an improviser!»[9]. As both Vierne and Wachs studied under Franck, the divergence between the two approaches provides some interest.

A brief comparison between Wachs's example of a processional march and Vierne's 'Cortège' clearly shows how each man's approach differs. While both pieces use one repetitive rhythmic idea throughout, as suggested by Wachs, Vierne creates an ABA form featuring considerable contrast in the B section differing greatly from Wach's mono-thematic prototype. This 'Cortège' is the shortest of the three recorded works and may have been the first one imprinted onto a disc. Its brevity may be due, in part, to Vierne's unfamiliarity with the recording process and his desire to not exceed the time constraints demanded by this new form of sound reproduction.

Documentation of Vierne's teaching appears in published notes from his student Jean Bouvard, professor at the Lyon Conservatoire[10]. In his teaching of improvisation, Vierne emphasized that making music was paramount, a tenet insisted upon by Franck.

In making a comparison between what Wachs relates in his treatise and what Vierne did in his teaching and playing, one sees that Vierne sought to create art that also was serviceable. He appears to have followed the admonition of Wachs, suggested in the preface to the treatise that the organist should convince the listener that what he was hearing was an actual printed musical score, rather than something that was being extemporized. In an examination of two of the recorded improvisations, one sees that Vierne combined elements drawn from the treatise as well as his own set of guidelines. While he relied on tried and true formulas, Vierne did not ever lose sight of music as a mode of communication and expression, and not just a perfunctory means to an end.

In his teaching of this highly-valued skill, Vierne relied on rules which he apparently followed fairly rigorously. Bouvard demonstrates the manner in which Vierne employed a six-part plan as follows: (1) the performer begins with an exposition of the thematic

---

8. WACHS, Paul. *L'Organiste improvisateur. Traité d'improvisation*, Paris, Schott, 1879.
9. CELLIER, Alexandre. *Op. cit.* (see note 1), p. 518.
10. BOUVARD, Jean. *Les maîtres de l'orgue et improvisation. Hommage à Louis Vierne*, Paris, Association des Amis de l'Orgue, 1984.

material using a four measure theme, followed by a commentary, a reprise of the theme with a different harmonization, and another brief commentary to conclude the first section; (2) after this, one should transition to another theme by way of three short four-measure modulatory phrases that lead to a remote key area; (3) the second theme should be placed in the tenor or bass voice, and it should consist of four measures, followed by a commentary of the same length; (4) a development based on a rhythmic element which is further extended by using a melodic idea from one of the themes; (5) next comes the preparation for the return of the original theme using two fragments based on the opening material of the initial theme that arrives on a dominant pedal point just as the theme is about to return. In the final step (6), the initial theme is then played in its entirety, followed by a commentary using a canon at the octave whenever possible. Then one should make some reference to the transitional material, use an inversion or augmentation of the theme, and conclude with a final commentary. A very detailed set of instructions, indeed. André Lambinet, writing in the *Revue Musicale de Lyon*, stated that musical improvisation itself was a game of logic and Vierne bears this out in his methodical approach to planning improvisations[11].

The 'Marche épiscopale', the first of the published improvisations, demonstrates that Vierne used much of this method in his own playing; he does what he expects his students to do. He begins with a four-measure theme followed by a four-measure commentary, cadencing on the dominant. He then reprises and reharmonizes the theme and closes out the opening section with another commentary. While Vierne's systematic approach suggests a three-phrase transition to the second theme, this recorded improvisation omits the transition and moves immediately to the second theme. Following this second theme, Vierne returns to his plan and prepares the return of the first theme with a fragment of the original theme in F major, followed by another fragment transposed to G major. He then introduces a short canonic section that leads to a dominant pedal, signifying the return to the tonic key. The reprise employs all measure of intense chromatic harmony, a trademark of the composer. While he did not employ fully his rigorous method, possibly due to limitations of time, Vierne basically practiced what he preached.

The clergy of the Catholic Church placed great emphasis on organ improvisation as a means to aid in prayer and reflection. Vierne took this to heart, being the devout man he was. However, as mentioned, Vierne valued the creation of a musical composition above anything else, and the middle work, 'Méditation', stands as the quintessential example of both these tenets. Here Vierne reveals his poetic side. Maurice Duruflé captured the essence of Vierne's improvisational skill as seen in a letter to Marie-Madeleine Chevalier:

---

11. LAMBINET, André. 'La Musique dans l'enseignment secondaire', in: *La Revue Musicale de Lyon*, III/2 (1905), pp. 33-40.

It's rapture! The music puts you in a euphoric state that you can't imagine [...] What tender emotion, what sweet melancholy in the *Méditation*. Vierne possesses more than anybody in the world the art of making the organ sing, of leading a melody, of developing it with an inexhaustible breath, of varying it to great effect, of taking it up again under another form, and all of this, which is constructed and logical, like a written piece, blossoms with abandon, with a naturalness, a rare sensitivity. And what charm, what freshness in the modulations! Vierne knows how to reconcile the two extremes, that is to say, the rigor of logic and the fantasy of imagination. He doesn't drop his theme for an instant. Nor does he forget the principal key in the course of his tonal escapes. He calls it back furtively with a delightful unexpectedness. And despite this continual presence of the intellect, he opens his heart wide[12].

As Duruflé noted, Vierne does not rely on formulas; he appears to play from the heart. One can hear the religious man and the musical artist in a perfect union. Perhaps, after hearing Vierne's own performance of this work, we can modify Cellier's statement: Indeed, one can become *an* improviser, but one is *born* a great improviser!

---

[12]. FRAZIER, James E. *Maurice Duruflé. The Man and His Music*, Rochester (NY), University of Rochester Press, 2007, p. 136.

Paganini's Virtuosity and Improvisatory Style

Philippe Borer
(Boudry, Switzerland)

Che arcata!... Che strappate! Mente eletta, lë o te l'improvvisava![1]

Improvisation was Paganini's most natural creative genre», writes Sergio Martinotti in his *Ottocento strumentale italiano*, «in him the performance did not follow, but rather instantly translated the spirit of creation as a result of immediate self-identification with the music. This was one of the strongest aspirations in Romantic art»[2].

According to countless contemporary accounts, and his own admission, Nicolò Paganini (1782-1840) improvised freely and constantly. His performing style was indeed based on improvisation and poetic licence. This clearly runs counter to our present-day precepts of interpretation and 'authentic style'. Authenticity for Paganini meant abandoning himself to the inspiration of the moment. Due to his Italian background and temperament, he was inclined to vary and embellish to the extreme the compositions he performed, his own as well as those of others, sometimes to the point of entirely modifying the original[3]. Relentlessly striving to push the boundaries and astound his listeners, he intended the performance to be a continuation of the creative process. Thus, the printed score, including that of the Twenty-Four Caprices (MS 25), represents only a limited statement of his artistry and can give us no real insight into his playing[4]. His rendering was

---

[1]. Carbone, Costanzo. *A vitta de Paganin*, Genoa, L'Italica, 1940, p. 15: «What a bow!... What chords! Predestined mind, he improvised!» (translated from the Genoese vernacular).

[2]. Martinotti, Sergio. *Ottocento strumentale italiano*, Bologna, Forni, 1972, p. 588: «L'improvvisazione era infatti il genere creativo a lui più consentaneo»; p. 276 : «in lui insomma l'esecuzione non seguiva, bensì traduceva istantaneamente lo spirito della creazione, secondo un immedesimarsi immediato eppure riflessivo che fu una delle più avvertite e forse temute aspirazioni dell'arte romantica».

[3]. See, for example, Bachmann, Alberto Abraham. 'Nicolò Paganini. Sa vie, son œuvre et son influence', in: *Mercure Musical*, IV/1 (1908), pp. 4-25; Heermann, Hugo. *Meine Lebenserinnerungen*, Leipzig, Brockaus, 1935, p. 18.

[4]. The abbreviation MS followed by Arabic numerals refers to the thematic catalogue of Paganini's works by Moretti, Maria Rosa - Sorrento, Anna. *Catalogo tematico delle musiche di Niccolò Paganini*, Genoa, Comune di Genova, 1982.

distinguished by creative freedom and virtuosity but also, most importantly, by a peculiar quality of expression that gave his violin the inflections of speech and that he referred to as the 'playing that speaks' (*suonare parlante*). Thanks to a unique articulatory quality, his playing was not infrequently compared to the delivery of an orator or actor[5]. Paganini was even credited with the uncanny ability to convey the sound of words and names with his bow. As legend has it, he sometimes said '*buona sera*' so distinctly on the strings at the close of a concert that the delighted audience replied '*buona sera!*'[6]. All this has to be considered within the context of musical, theatrical and poetic improvisation, a strain of Italian culture that Paganini cultivated with assiduity — more perhaps than any of his contemporaries. One major influence was of course the Commedia dell'Arte[7], the Italian improvised drama. The very title of his famous first opus, *24 Capricci* (see ILL. I)[8], as well as the dedication 'to the Artists'[9], link to this tradition.

«A theatrical past echoes within him», wrote Adolf Weissmann of Paganini[10]. In content and spirit the Caprices could indeed be seen as a musical counterpart of the *arte improvisation*, a 'comedy of the violin' in its own right. A theatrical vitality pervades the work — twenty-four contrasting and highly characterised musical scenarios conjuring up visions of Harlequin's virtuosic leaps and pratfalls (Caprice 1), curtain-lifting introductions (Caprices 17, 19 and 21), a love duet of the *innamorati* (Caprice 21), a bravura parade of the Capitano (Caprice 14), Pierrot's moonlight *lamento* with mandolin tremolo (Caprice 6), cascades of laughter of the *prima donna* (Caprice 13), conversational give-and-take (Caprices 7, 19), melodramatic tirades alternating with cautious retreats (Caprice 17), and so on. As may be inferred from contemporary sources, the Caprices were not concert pieces but rather impromptu compositions for friends and *cognoscenti*, created in different places and at different times «on some informal evenings when he was in the mood»[11]. According to Karol Lipiński, Paganini reconstructed them from memory «in a great hurry and frenzy»

[5]. See, for example, MATTHEWS, Henry. *The Diary of an Invalid*, Paris, Gagliani, 1825, p. 201.

[6]. This was no doubt achieved through skilful control of timbre, pitch and articulation, involving advanced bow and left-hand techniques. See 'Il suonare parlante', in: *La pagina e l'archetto. Bibliografia violinistica storico-tecnica e studi effetuati su Niccolò Paganini*, edited by Philippe Borer, Genoa, Comune di Genova, 2003, pp. 119-122.

[7]. Commedia dell'Arte was also known as *Commedia all'improvviso* (as contrasted to *Commedia premeditata*). *Arte*, short for medieval guild, or corporation, referred to the professional character of the genre.

[8]. The *Capriccii et nuove fantasie alla Venetiana*, twenty-two stage scenarios (or *pantalonades*), appeared in 1601, that is, before instrumental caprices such as Girolamo Frescobaldi's *Capricci* for keyboard of 1624.

[9]. The expression '*Agli Artisti*' — as contrasted to '*Alle Amatrici*' — implied the conventional distinction between professionals and amateurs.

[10]. WEISSMANN, Adolf. *Der Virtuose*, Berlin, Cassirer, 1918, p. 54: «eine theatralische Vergangenheit in ihm nachklingt».

[11]. STENDHAL. *Vie de Rossini* (1823), Paris, Lévy, 1854, pp. 266-267.

Ill. 1: Nicolò Paganini, *24 Capricci*, Milan, Ricordi, 1820, title page.

when Giovanni Ricordi requested them for publication[12]. The absence of preliminary sketches, revisions, or tentative drafts consolidates the suggestion that they are essentially notated improvisations[13].

---

[12]. SCHUMANN, Robert. *Gesammelte Schriften über Musik und Musiker*, 2 vols., edited by Martin Kreisig, Leipzig, Breitkopf & Härtel, 1914, vol. 1, p. 213.

[13]. Paganini's mode of structured improvisation, very different from modern 'improv', evinced ebullient inventivity developed within a strict form. Similarly, the *scenario* or framework within which action and speech could be improvised was the first and fundamental element of the *Commedia all'improvviso*.

The link with comic theatre is also evident in the *Carnaval de Venise* (MS 59) in which Paganini is reported to have, on occasion, improvised up to thirty additional variations[14]. Premiered in 1828 in Vienna, the *Carnaval de Venise* created a furore all over Europe, eliciting creative responses from Chopin, Schumann, Théophile Gautier, Heinrich Wilhelm Ernst, Félix Ziem, to mention but a few. Attempting to describe the sensational sounds coming from Paganini's violin, the critic of *Le Sémaphore* of Marseille enthused:

> This famous traditional *Carnaval* was the most entertaining, the most witty and amusingly burlesque that imagination can conceive. [...] The truth of the great artist's rendering was such that one believed to see Harlequin, Pantalon, Pierrot, Colombine parading, and last but not least... Polichinelle! The great, the incomparable Polichinelle. [...] There, Paganini was prodigious, and revealed himself entirely in one of his incomparable, indescribable bow-strokes: it was like words articulated by a human voice[15].

Another source of Paganini's creative performing style was the art of the *improvvisatori* such as Pietro Metastasio, Bernardo Perfetti, Francesco Gianni, Corilla Olimpica, Teresa Bandettini, Rosa Taddei and Tommaso Sgricci who improvised poetry in public on themes suggested by the audience. The *improvvisatori* often chanted verses accompanied by a musical instrument, after the fashion of the Greek rhapsodes. Some had prestigious musical partners, notably Gian Felice Zappi who improvised together with Alessandro Scarlatti[16] or Corilla Olimpica who performed to the violin accompaniment of Pietro Nardini[17]. Poetic improvisation demands enormous concentration and emotional exertion and was known to cause detrimental physical effects. Carried away by their enthusiasm and *furor poeticus,* the great improvisers were able to dream up a hundred verses and more, sometimes even whole tragedies[18]. Nervous disorders, fevers and even paralysis

---

[14]. BERRI, Pietro. *Paganini. Documenti e testimonianze*, Genoa, Sigla Effe, 1962, p. 84.

[15]. INZAGHI, Luigi. *Camillo Sivori. Carteggi del grande violinista e compositore allievo di Paganini*, Varese, Zecchini, 2004, p. 248: «Ce fameux *Carnaval* traditionel était un poème des plus gais, des plus amusants, des plus spirituellement bouffons que l'imagination puisse rêver. [...] La couleur de vérité imprimée au jeu du grand artiste était telle, que l'on croyait voir défiler sur la scène une mascarade au grand complet ayant en tête Arlequin, Pantalon, Pierrot, Colombine, et puis Polichinelle! le grand, l'incomparable Polichinelle. [...] Là, Paganini était prodigieux, et se révélait tout entier dans un de ces coups d'archet fabuleux dont on ne saurait se faire une idée, et qu'il est impossible de décrire, même après l'avoir souvent entendu. On eût dit une voix humaine articulant des paroles».

[16]. DI RICCO, Alessandra. *L'inutile e maraviglioso mestiere. Poeti improvvisatori di fine settecento*, Milan, Franco Angeli, 1990, p. 24.

[17]. BURNEY, Charles. *The Present State of Music in France and Italy*, London, Becket, 1771, p. 250.

[18]. This was the case of Tommaso Sgricci (1789-1836) who deeply impressed Mary and Percy Shelley in 1821 in Pisa, playing all the male and female roles in addition to a tragic chorus (the theme was *The Death of Hector*).

caused by emotional and physical stress were not uncommon among these artists. The young Pietro Metastasio nearly died of exhaustion while practising extempore poetry in the streets of Rome. As improvisation was unadvised for health reasons, he converted to writing dramas. Side-effects caused by the intensity of his playing and complete absorption were also observed in Paganini:

> After playing a long solo, he has exactly the same symptoms as a man having an epileptic fit; his skin is livid, cold, and covered by sweat; his pulse is extremely faint, and if one asks him a question he does not answer, or if he does, it is monosyllabic and almost always off the point[19].

In a letter to Luigi Guglielmo Germi, Paganini explained how he had to transcend the ordinary before performing in public. He called this higher state 'electricity' (*elettricismo*), alluding to a current of emotional energy that streamed right to his fingertips. He complained that the release of all that 'electricity' had a harmful effects on his health but saw it as the price to pay for translating emotions into sound[20].

The recent unriddling of the inscription «Madama T.» at the head of the Six Sonatas for Violin and Guitar (MS 12) has revealed a link between Paganini and Teresa Bandettini (1763-1837), one of the most celebrated poetic improvisers of the time[21]. Other poets that Paganini knew were Martin Piaggio[22], Felice Romani, the *improvvisatore* Francesco Gianni[23], Pietro Isola[24], Lazzaro Rebizzo, Lorenzo Costa[25], Arturo and Giuseppe Crocco, all of whom gravitated in the orbit of his Genoese mentor, the Marquis Gian Carlo Di Negro. He also

---

[19]. IMBERT DE LAPHALÈQUE, Georges (= L'HÉRITIER, Louis-François). *Notice sur le célèbre violiniste [sic] Nicolo Paganini*, Paris, E. Guyot, 1830, p. 53: «Après avoir achevé un grand morceau, il manifeste exactement les mêmes symptômes qu'un homme livré à un accès d'épilepsie; sa peau livide et froide est couverte d'une sueur abondante; on ne sent plus le pouls, et si on l'interroge sur un sujet quelconque, même sur l'état où il se trouve, il ne répond pas, ou s'il répond, c'est par monosyllabes et presque toujours à contre-sens de la demande».

[20]. *Paganini Epistolario*, edited by Edward Neill, Genoa, Comune di Genova, 1982, No. 169, p. 149: «L'elettricismo che provo nel trattare la magica armonia mi nuoce orribilmente»; No. 189, p. 164: «non posso esprimerti la pena che provo di vedere la difficoltà di rimettermi nell'elettricismo onde far sentire!»; No. 306, p. 253: «Cette faculté qui fait passer l'âme d'un exécutant au bout de ses doigts pour traduire en sons les émotions».

[21]. MORETTI, Maria Rosa - SORRENTO, Anna. 'Note di aggiornamento al catalogo tematico', in: *Paganini divo e comunicatore*, a cura di Maria Rosa Moretti, Anna Sorrento, Stefano Termanini and Enrico Volpato, Genoa, SerEl International-Eeditrice.com, 2007, pp. 565-589: 566.

[22]. Martin Piaggio (1774-1843), the famous Genoese vernacular poet.

[23]. Francesco Gianni (1759-1822) was a close friend of the Marquis Di Negro as well as offering him artistic guidance.

[24]. The first Italian translator of Lord Byron's works.

[25]. The author of a moving poetic tribute to Paganini in both Italian and Latin; see COSTA, Lorenzo. *A Niccolò Paganini*, Genoa, Faziola, 1837.

met Ugo Foscolo in Milan[26], Karl von Holtei in Berlin[27], and Wolfgang von Goethe in Weimar[28]. His motto 'Poetry and Music are Sisters' (*Poesia e Musica sono sorelle*) and his frequent quoting from Homer, Dante and Tasso bear witness to his fondness for poetry[29]. His stance on this matter was rather traditional, for the simple reason that string playing and poetry had always been closely associated in Italy. An episode of the life of Saint Francis of Assisi gives clues to the symbolism attached to such a relationship. According to Thomas of Celano, Francis extemporised poems and chants whenever he was inspired, often ending his improvisation in tears[30]. Thomas once saw him enact his verses picking up a piece of wood and using it like a fiddle[31]. Vasari reports that Leonardo da Vinci played on the lira da braccio while «divinely improvising lyrics over the music»[32]. Around 1533, street artists like the famous Venetian *buffone* Zuan Polo Liompardi performed *cantastorie*-style improvisations in *ottave rime* while playing on the violin (see ILL. 2)[33].

The four 'illustrative sonnets' (*sonnetti dimostrativi*) of Vivaldi's famous Four Seasons (published 1725) exemplify the almost symbiotic relationship between words and the voice of the violin. Poetic texts complementing the music appear in Giuseppe Tartini's original manuscripts, but not in the printed editions. Tartini cryptically transcribed verses of Metastasio and Tasso under the themes of his concertos for his personal use and that of a selected circle of students (see Ex. 1)[34].

Tartini's idea was to add poetic emotion to interpretations, thereby intensifying the power of expression. His views were shared by Francesco Geminiani who recommended the reading of great poetic works as a means of achieving a truly inspired musical

---

[26]. See SCHOTTKY, Julius Max. *Paganini's Leben und Treiben als Künstler und als Mensch*, Prague, J. G. Calve'schen Buchhandlung, 1830, pp. 327-329.

[27]. See VÝBORNÝ, Zdeněk. 'Paganini und *il poeta declamatore*. Eine Episode aus dem Leben des Teufelsgeigers', in: *Neue Zeitschrift für Musik*, CXXIV (1963), pp. 95-98.

[28]. Paganini's visit to Goethe took place on 29 September 1829.

[29]. See TIBALDI CHIESA, Maria. *Paganini. La vita e l'opera*, Milan, Garzanti, 1940, frontispiece; SCHOTTKY, Julius Max. *Op. cit.* (see note 26), p. 281; see also *Paganini Epistolario, op. cit.* (see note 20), Nos. 188 and 219.

[30]. TOMMASO DA CELANO. *Vita secunda Sancti Francisci Assisiensis*, Part II, Chapter 90, 127.4: «Terminabantur tota haec tripudia frequenter in lacrimas, et in passionis Christi compassionem hic iubilus solvebatur».

[31]. *Ibidem*, 127.3: «Lignum quandoque, ut oculis vidi, colligebat e terra, ipsumque sinistro brachio superponens arculum filo flexum tenebat in dextera, quem quasi super viellam trahens per lignum, et ad hoc gestus repraesentans idoneos, gallice cantabat de Domino».

[32]. VASARI, Giorgio. *Vite de' più eccellenti pittori scultori e architetti* (1550), 11 vols., edited by Guglielmo della Valle, Siena, Pazzini Carli e Comp., 1792, vol. V, p. 22: «Si risolvé a imparare a sonare la lira [...] onde sopra quella cantò divinamente all'improvviso»; p. 30: «Oltra ciò fu il migliore dicitore di rime all'improvviso del tempo suo».

[33]. See HENKE, Robert. *Performance and Literature in the Commedia dell'Arte*, Cambridge, Cambridge University Press, 2002, pp. 51-53.

[34]. Tartini's cryptograms were deciphered by Minos Dounias in 1935. See DOUNIAS, Minos. *Die Violinkonzerte Giuseppe Tartinis als Ausdruck einer Künstlerpersönlichkeit und einer Kulturepoche*, Wolfenbüttel, Möseler, 1966.

ILL. 2: the *poeta canterino* Zuan Polo Liompardi with his lion-headed fiddle (Venice 1533).

Ex. 1: Giuseppe Tartini, Violin Concerto No. 56, second movement, bar 1.

performance[35]. Such ideals of creative interpretation guided by inspiration were indeed far removed from present-day note-for-note renditions based on *Urtext* editions. Ex. 1 shows that something essential is hidden behind the notes of the printed score. This is reminiscent of the esoterism of Dante whose poetry conveyed a non-literal sense «to be detected under the veil of the strange verses»[36].

Another major influence was opera; which in light of the exclusive penchant for this art form in Italy and the emphasis placed on the cultivation of native singing talent is evident. Paganini acquired knowledge of the *bel canto* tradition from his early artistic association with Luigi Marchesi and Teresa Bertinotti, later with Girolamo Crescentini (whom he

---

[35]. GEMINIANI, Francesco. *The Art of Playing on the Violin*, London, s.n., 1751, p. 8.
[36]. DANTE. *Inferno*, IX, 63: «sotto il velame de li versi strani».

befriended)[37]. The castratos Marchesi and Crescentini were both great improvisers and were indeed genuinely concerned with extempore invention. They were, however, among the last representatives of the old tradition; after them this type of singing degenerated into ready-made formulas and written conventions which Stendhal complained about in his *Life of Rossini*:

> After the epoch of [Matteo] Babini, [Gasparo] Pacchiarotti, Marchesi, Crescentini and their contemporaries, the art of *bel canto* degenerated to such a degree of impoverishment that today nothing is left of all its former glory save the cold and literal technique of rendering an exact and inanimate note. The glories of *spontaneous inspiration* have been banished for ever from an art whose loveliest achievements have so often depended upon the individual interpreter and his genius for improvisation. [...] The whole art of adorning the melody belonged by right to the performer. [...] There is no composer on earth, suppose him to be as ingenious as you will, whose score can convey with precision these and similar infinitely minute nuances which form the secret of Crescentini's unique perfection[38].

Paganini was a great admirer of the old singing tradition and spoke highly of Babini, Pacchiarotti, Giovanni Battista Velluti and Crescentini[39]. He had acquired such an understanding of the art of *bel canto* that, even though he did not sing himself, he was able to impart his insight to singers. When he began his liaison with Antonia Bianchi, at the time a modest supernumerary chorister in Venice, he gave her special instruction «so that she could sing at concerts»[40]. Bianchi rapidly became an accomplished soprano whose *maestria* was recognised by leading music critics, notably in Vienna[41]. In relation to Stendhal's statement about the decline of the art of *bel canto*, it is quite revealing that Paganini also felt that the tradition was not being sustained. In 1823, the very year of the publication of the *Vie de Rossini*, he confided in his friend Germi after hearing the famous soprano Angelina Catalani:

> Catalani would have more soul if she had been trained by such celebrated
> masters as Crescentini, Pacchiarotti, Babini and our celebrated [Giovanni]

---

[37]. Luigi Marchesi (1755-1829) and Girolamo Crescentini (1762-1846) were two of the last great castrato singers. In 1795, Luigi Marchesi and Teresa Bertinotti had sung in a joint concert with the young Paganini at the Sant'Agostino Theatre in Genoa.

[38]. STENDHAL. *Life of Rossini*, translated by Richard N. Coe, London, Calder, 1956, pp. 326-327 and 344.

[39]. *Paganini Epistolario, op. cit.* (see note 20), Nos. 19, 22, 26, 32, 63 and 185.

[40]. *Nicolò Paganini. Epistolario 1810-1831*, edited by Roberto Grisley, Milan, Skira, 2006, p. 471: «La conobbi ch'era l'ultima delle cantanti, e l'abbilitai a figurar ne' concerti».

[41]. See *Allgemeine Theaterzeitung*, Vienna, 5 April 1828, a review of the concert of 29 March held at the Redoutensaal.

Serra[42]. [...] She made me yawn a lot. Her strong and agile voice is the most beautiful instrument; but she lacks a sense of rhythm and musical philosophy[43].

In line with Paganini's criticism, Stendhal described Catalani as «a *cantatrice* who knew no worthier ambition than to mimic and outrival the mechanical dexterity of a violin»[44]. Although she was an extraordinary vocal phenomenon, a soprano with a range of nearly three octaves and unexcelled power and flexibility, Catalani did not have a thorough grounding in the performance traditions of the great Italian school. On the other hand, Paganini, in spite of not being a singer, was considered the spiritual heir of the likes of Marchesi, Babini, Pacchiarotti and Crescentini. A most enlightening passage in Manuel Garcia (Junior)'s *Traité complet de l'art du chant* provides evidence that Paganini was an outstanding exponent of the *rubato*, a manner of tempo fluctuation specific to the true operatic tradition:

> Two artists of a very different kind, García (my father), and Paganini, excelled in the use of the *tempo rubato* applied by phrase. While the orchestra maintained the tempo regularly, they, on their part, abandoned themselves to their inspiration to rejoin the bass only at the harmony change, or even at the end of the phrase. But this technique requires before everything an exquisite feeling of the *rhythm* and an imperturbable poise[45].

The above passage may help understand Paganini's observation that «she [Angelina Catalani] lacks a sense of rhythm and musical philosophy». In spite of all her technical and vocal brilliance, Catalani failed to captivate him because she did not master the improvisatory dimension in rhythm, hence the predictable character of her delivery. The diplomat and art researcher August Kestner attended all the concerts that Paganini gave in Rome in 1819 and 1825. He, too, made reference to the great violinist's use of *tempo rubato*:

---

[42]. Giovanni Serra (1788-1876) studied the violin with Giacomo Costa. In 1828 he became the musical director of the orchestra of the Teatro Carlo Felice in Genoa.

[43]. *Paganini Epistolario*, *op. cit.* (see note 20), No. 63, p. 65: «La Catalani avrebbe più anima se la fosse stata formata da de' celebri maestri, come un Crescentini, un Pacchiarotti, un Babini ed un Serra nostro celebre. [...] Io sbadigliai moltissimo. La sua voce forte ed agile forma il più bello strumento; ma le manca la misura e la filosofia musicale».

[44]. STENDHAL. *Op. cit.* (see note 38), p. 326.

[45]. GARCIA, Manuel (Junior). *Traité complet de l'art du chant en deux parties*, Paris, 1847, Part II, p. 25: «Deux artistes d'un genre très-différent, Garcia (mon père) et Paganini, excellaient dans l'emploi du tempo rubato appliqué *par phrase*. Tandis que l'orchestre soutenait régulièrement la mesure, eux, de leur côté, s'abandonnaient à leur inspiration pour ne se rencontrer avec la basse qu'à l'instant où l'accord changeait, ou bien à la fin même de la phrase. Mais ce moyen exige avant tout un sentiment exquis du *rythme* et un aplomb imperturbable».

> This was one of the most beautiful things I have ever heard, lyrical, played in long sustained strokes of the bow, high in the fifth octave. [...] The highest degree of skill dominated his performance insofar as the master recognised the bar as the basis — covered by the leisurely flow of tones — without ever allowing its structure to come to the surface[46].

The *rubato* gives spirit and life to rhythm and melody, and the more it recognises the norm, the freer and more expressive it is. Paganini's improvisational *maestria* and the way he imparted the inflections of the voice to his instrument (which so impressed Friedrich Wieck, Felix Mendelssohn, Ole Bull and other experts) must have originated from his involvement in *bel canto*. In the words of Ole Bull:

> No one can thoroughly understand Paganini without an educated appreciation of melody and the art of giving life and expression to it. Without a knowledge of the Italian art of singing, it is impossible to properly appreciate his playing. Contemporary with [Giuditta] Pasta, [Benedetta Rosmunda] Pizzaroni, [Giovanni Battista] Rubini and [Maria] Malibran, Paganini rivalled them, singing on his violin melodies, many of which had been sung by these artists, and astonishing even *them* more than the public. Paganini especially excelled in giving life to the simplest melodies, in giving to his tone the quality of the human voice[47].

POLARITIES IN PAGANINI'S EARLY TRAINING AND PERFORMING

Paganini, as it appears from recently published data, developed a familiarity with improvisation from an early age until it became second nature. At just ten years old, he was already busy playing ballroom music with his elder brother Carlo, who was also a violinist[48]. There is evidence of the two young boys having played for the rather generous fee of 50 liras during the 1793 Genoese carnival at a very popular but controversial and even prohibited event, 'the Stick Ball' (*ballo da bastone*). The music performed on such occasions consisted mainly of improvisations based on popular

---

[46]. KESTNER, August. *Römische Studien*, Berlin, Verlag der Deckerschen Geheimen Ober-Hofbuchdruckerei, 1850, p. 41: «Dies war von den schönsten Sachen, die ich jemals gehört habe, gesangvoll, in langen Bogenstrichen in der fünften Oktave oben vorgetragen. [...] Hier herrschte der höchste Grad von gewandter Erfahrung im Vortrag, worin der Meister den Takt, als die von dem gemächlichen Gange der Töne bedeckte Grundlage anerkennt, ohne seiner Gliederung irgend ein Hervortreten zu erlauben».

[47]. BULL, Sara. *Ole Bull. A Memoir*, Boston, Houghton, Mifflin & Co., 1897, pp. 24-25.

[48]. MORETTI, Maria Rosa. 'Intorno a Paganini. Nuove acquisizioni sulla biografia e su alcuni cimeli paganiniani', in: *Paganini divo e comunicatore*, op. cit. (see note 21), pp. 23-100, pp. 24 and 52.

dances and rhythmical patterns such as *alessandrine, perigordini, scozzesi,* and *valzer*[49]. Remarkably, Paganini had spent the early, most vital phase of his apprenticeship away from the current methods and dogmatic rules prevalent at music institutions of the time. His first teacher was his father, an enthusiastic amateur mandolinist and violinist whose insight was to recognise that his son would not really benefit from outside influence at that stage, in so much as the basics of violin techniques were concerned. Paganini's rather unconventional left-hand grip (with the thumb-in-the-palm position that was depicted so well in Edward Landseer's sketches and in Eugène Delacroix's portrait) as well as other technical ploys mentioned by François-Joseph Fétis and Carl Guhr resemble those of folk fiddlers and guitarists rather than academically trained violinists. Be that as it may, the inevitable step to send the child to an official teacher was taken in 1794, just one year after the episode of the carnival ball. By that time, Paganini already held strongly individual views on the matter of bowing and fingering and the relationship with his new teacher Giacomo Costa was not without tensions[50]. Nevertheless a consensus between them was reached and Costa, who held the position of *maestro di cappella* at San Lorenzo Cathedral, organised for his pupil to play three times a week in church[51]. In later life, Paganini declared that he had greatly benefited from the rigour of this regular performance practice which demanded the constant study of new works and the necessity to improvise. Church musicians must be ready to improvise to adapt to last minute decisions and changes. Furthermore, musical improvisation bears special significance in the liturgy, with particular regard to string instruments, «because they express the joyous and sad sentiments of the soul with an indescribable power»[52]. It must be observed at this point that the art of improvisation in Italy — rhetorical,

---

[49]. See ILLIANO, Roberto. 'Paganini. A Virtuoso Composer', in: *Henryk Wieniawski and the Bravura Tradition of Style. Techniques and Performing Practice,* edited by Maciej Jabłoński, Poznań, Henryk Wieniawski Musical Society, 2011 (forthcoming), pp. 149-157.

[50]. Giacomo Costa (c. 1761-1836). His students included Francesco Gnecco, Giovanni Serra and Nicola De Giovanni.

[51]. At that time and up to about 1799, music was much present in the churches of Genoa, not only during Masses and other sacred functions, but also in concert form with the participation of famous singers and instrumentalists. Paganini performed in several churches, including the San Lorenzo Cathedral, the Oratorio San Filippo Neri and the Chiesa di Nostra Signora delle Vigne, as recorded in the local weekly journal the *Avvisi*. Among the composers and organists attached to the Genoese churches were Gaetano Isola, Luigi Cerro, and Antonio Maria Celle. Celle was the organist at San Lorenzo from 1770 to 1792 and therefore worked in collaboration with Giacomo Costa. See PODESTÀ, Francesco. 'Gli organisti del Comune di Genova', in: *Giornale Storico e Letterario della Liguria,* IX (1908), pp. 97-105; GIAZOTTO, Remo. *La musica a Genova nella vita pubblica e privata dal XIII al XVIII secolo,* Genoa, Comune di Genova, 1951, pp. 263-270; BONGIOVANNI, Carmela. *Il fondo musicale dell'archivio capitolare del Duomo di Genova,* Genoa, Associazione Italiana Biblioteche, Sezione Ligure, 1990, p. 15.

[52]. PIUS XII (Pope). *Litterae Encyclicae 'Musicae Sacrae Disciplina'* (1955), § 59: «quia seu maestos, seu laetos animi sensus ineffabili vi quadam exprimunt».

theatrical, poetic, musical — was inseparable from the Catholic culture as a whole and had its roots in the techniques of exegesis, oration and preaching as passed on by Saint Augustine and the Fathers of the Church. A fundamental principle of delivering a sermon is to diversify words and intonation whilst maintaining concepts, like in theme and variations. From the spiritual angle, the decision to improvise implies a sense of sacrifice, of 'letting go' (*lâcher-prise*). Without the protection and precautions of the written text the improviser puts himself at risk and must rely on the inspiration of the moment. Only then may he approach authenticity in expression and, as Marc Fumarolli writes, become «flame of the word»[53]. When improvisation takes place during the Elevation, a further symbolic step is attained, in particular if heard on a string instrument[54].

In 1805, Paganini found fixed employment in Lucca at the service of Princess Elisa Baciocchi, Napoleon's sister. There, improvisation became an integral part of his professional duties as he himself reported:

> The Republic of Lucca appointed me first violin of the court, in which capacity I remained three years, giving lessons to Baciocchi. Having to perform at two concerts every week, I always played an improvisation: I always wrote down a bass for the piano and on that harmonic background I improvised on a theme[55].

He continued, and perfected, this technique of elaborate improvisation with a piano or orchestral backdrop until the end of his career. During his grand concert tour of Europe 1828-1834, he captivated and amazed his audience by renewing and surpassing any previous interpretation of the same piece, reinventing much of the solo line for each performance. The fact that Paganini never repeated his interpretation of a piece in any given performance still lingers in Italian minds: it is firmly established in the collective memory that '*Paganini non ripete*'.

Significantly, the music that Paganini wrote during his stay at the Lucchese court (1805-1808) includes the Six Sonatas for Violin and Guitar (MS 12) dedicated to the

---

[53]. WAQUET, Françoise. *Rhétorique et poétique chrétiennes. Bernardino Perfetti et la poésie improvisée dans l'Italie du XVIIIᵉ siècle*, préface de Marc Fumarolli, Florence, Olschki, 1992, p. 16.

[54]. Concerning the symbolism attached to the string instruments and the violin in particular see BORER, Philippe. 'Some Reflections on Paganini's Violin Strings', in: *Proceedings of the International Conference on Violin Making 2004. Restoration and Conservation of the Violin 'Guarneri del Gesù' (1743) Known as 'Cannone'*, Genoa, City of Genoa, 2004, pp. 85-98.

[55]. CONESTABILE, Gian Carlo. *Vita di Niccolò Paganini da Genova*, edited by Federico Mompellio, Milan, Dante Alighieri, 1936, p. 535: «La repubblica di Lucca mi nominò primo violino di corte, nella quale qualità restai tre anni, dando lezioni a Bacciocchi [*sic*]. Dovendo sonare ne' due concerti che si davano settimanalmente, sonai sempre a capriccio, accompagnato dal pianoforte, per cui scrissi sempre un basso immaginandovi un tema».

famous poet Teresa Bandettini who was a native of Lucca[56]. Paganini took a friendly interest in her son Francesco who was first contrabassist of the court orchestra, teaching him new techniques for his instrument. Sources refer to Teresa Bandettini as the 'emotional improviser' (*l'improvvisatrice commossa*) who was capable of conveying her deeply felt emotions to the point of «electrifying her audience»[57]. A genuine artistic affinity thus existed between the *improvvisatrice* and the young *maestro di cappella* whose artistic credo was 'one must feel strongly in order to make others feel' (*bisogna forte sentire per far sentire*). For artists of that calibre having such lofty ideals, the audience's emotional response was an essential component of the performance. Their notions of improvisation, inspiration and emotional intensity were closely intertwined.

Many musicians, poets, painters and critics who heard Paganini play and improvise have left precious testimonies[58]. Their respective accounts — including letters, reviews, transcripts of lectures, paintings, and poems — may perhaps give us a glimpse of what the printed score could never reveal. The following 1829-1831 selection aims at uncovering historical and musical data (some quite unexpected) and comparing responses to the experience of Paganini's playing.

Berlin, 1829: Varnhagen, Rellstab, Marx, Hegel, Bardua

The highpoint of Paganini's first German tour was Berlin where he played on eleven occasions with sensational and repeated success. His first three concerts took place on 4, 13 and 19 March 1829 at the Schauspielhaus. Concurrently, on 11 and 21 March, Mendelssohn conducted his memorable performances of Bach's St. Matthew Passion at the Singakademie, which gives an idea of Berlin's ebullient musical life. The writer Rahel Varnhagen (1771-1833), a household figure in artistic and intellectual circles, attended Paganini's debut concert. His approach struck her as entirely different from that of any other violinist she knew, including great representatives of the French, German, and Italian schools like Pierre Rode (pupil of Giovanni Battista Viotti), Karl Haack (pupil of

---

[56]. The pieces were perhaps intended as musical background during the dedicatee's improvisations. Suggestive tempo and mood indications are: 'Adagio con passione', 'Andante smorfiosamente' (Sonata 1); 'Adagio con amore', 'Andante con semplicità' (Sonata 2); 'Adagio con anima', 'Andantino galante' (Sonata 3); 'Adagio con sentimento', 'Corrente con motteggio' (Sonata 4); 'Adagio con grazia', 'Allegro con brio' (Sonata 5); 'Adagio con trasporto', 'Pollonese brillante' (Sonata 6).

[57]. 'Teresa Bandettini, the Improvvisatrice', in: *Bentley's Miscellany*, xxxvi (1854), p. 491.

[58]. August Kestner, Karol Lipiński, Fryderyk Chopin, Friedrich Wieck, Clara and Robert Schumann, Adolph Bernhard Marx, Rahel Varnhagen, Heinrich Friedrich Rellstab, Caroline Bardua, Carl Guhr, Wilhelm Speyer, Friedrich Zelter, Louis Spohr, Ole Bull, Franz Liszt, Théophile Gautier, Honoré de Balzac, Heinrich Heine, Pierre Baillot, Eugène Delacroix, Manuel Garcia, François-Joseph Fétis, Pierre-Jean David, John Edmund Cox, Mary Shelley, and others.

Franz Benda), Giovanni Giornovichi (pupil of Antonio Lolli), and the technical prodigy Auguste-Frédéric Durand (pupil of Viotti). Both amazed and delighted, she wrote to her husband an appreciation of Paganini's *suonare parlante*:

> I heard Paganini on Wednesday. [...] He actually does not play the violin — he does not have the tone (or tones) of Rode, of Durand, of Haack, of Giornovichi, *he actually speaks*; he whimpers, imitates a thunderstorm, the stillness of night, birds that descend from heaven [...]; in short this is poetry. In the prayer from Rossini's *Moses*, he plays the different voices as they enter one after the other and then all together. In celestial spheres[59].

ILL. 3: Rahel Varnaghen, née Levin (1771-1833), pastel by Peter Friedel, c.1800. Berlin, Staatsbibliothek.

Similarly, Heinrich Friedrich Rellstab — the leading Berlin critic of the time — emphasised the fervour and emotional appeal of Paganini's playing. He wrote a review in the *Vossische Zeitung*, departing from his usual moderation:

> The audience was in a state of exaltation the like of which I have seldom witnessed in a theatre, and never in a concert hall. [...] *He spoke*, he wept, he

59. VARNHAGEN, Rahel. *Briefwechsel mit August Varnhagen von Ense*, Munich, Kösel-Verlag, 1967, pp. 382-383 (letter of 7 March 1829): «Ich habe Mittwoch Paganini gehört. [...] Er spielt auf diesem Instrument eigentlich *nicht* Geige. Er hat nicht Rodes, nicht Durands, nicht Haakes, nicht Giornovichs Ton, noch Töne. Aber er *spricht*, gradezu; er wimmert; er ahmt Meereswetter nach; Nachtstille; Vögel, die vom Himmel kommen, nicht die zum Himmel fliegen; kurz, Poesie. Er spielt die *Preghiera* aus Moses von Rossini; alle Stimmen, wie sie nach und nach einfallen, und dann zusammen. In Himmelssphären».

sang! I have never seen the Berliners in such a state! And this was the effect of a simple melody[60].

Adolph Bernhard Marx was at that time Professor of Music Theory at Berlin University. Hinting at the contrasting notions of technicality and creativity, he reported:

> The external elements of Paganini's playing, these tours de force that seem impossible for anybody else, this combination of rapid *arco* and *pizzicato* runs, these octave passages on one string [...] all these things are merely vehicles, they really mean nothing to him. *The inward poetry of his imagination, shaping the creations before our eyes* — this is what fascinated the listeners[61].

Georg Wilhelm Friedrich Hegel was also in the audience. As inferred from his correspondence, he attended the first or the second Paganini concert (4, 13 March), or perhaps both of them[62]. On 19 March, he dictated to his university students the famous passage about improvisation and instrumental virtuosity that appeared in the second volume of his *Aesthetics*, at the end of the chapter dedicated to music[63]. This text, clearly linked with the experience of having heard Paganini's playing, represented a turning point. Hegel had until then considered instrumental virtuosity as mere technicality and he had even expressed contempt for the so-called virtuosos, finding the display of difficulties simply tasteless. In a previous lecture he had pointed to the peculiar attraction associated with improvisation «because we have before us not simply a work of art but the actual production of one»[64]. However he was referring to vocal music, in particular to Italian opera in which the composer (he cites Rossini) leaves room for singers to improvise cadenzas. After hearing Paganini, Hegel revised his views. During the lecture of 19 March, he professed that «the highest peak of musical vitality» occurs when a virtuoso of genius

---

[60]. DE COURCY, Geraldine. *Paganini the Genoese*, 2 vols., Norman, University of Oklahoma Press, 1957, vol. I, pp. 317-318.

[61]. MARX, Adolf Bernhard. *Erinnerungen: Aus meinem Leben*, 2 vols., Berlin, Otto Janke, 1865, vol. II, pp. 77-78: «Was man äußerlich aus seinem Spiel herausnehmen und bewundern konnte, — diese allen Andern unmöglich scheinenden Spielfiguren, diese Mischung von gestrichenen und gerissenen Tönen (*coll'arco* und *pizzicato*) in einem schnell dahinrollenden Lauf, diese Oktavengänge auf Einer Saite (die tiefere Oktave in blitzschnellem, kaum merkbarem Vorschlag), das alles waren nur Mittel, bedeutete an sich für den Mann gar nichts; die innere Poesie seiner vor unsern Augen ihre Schöpfungen vollendenden Phantasie: das war es, was die Hörer gefangen nahm».

[62]. *Briefe von und an Hegel*, edited by Johannes Hoffmeister, Hamburg, Felix Meiner, 1954, vol. III (1823-1831), p. 251.

[63]. See OLIVIER, Alain Patrick. *Hegel et la musique. De l'expérience esthétique à la spéculation philosophique*, Paris, Honoré Champion, 2003, p. 80.

[64]. HEGEL, Georg Wilhelm Friedrich. *Ästhetik*, edited by F. Bassenge, 2 vols., Berlin, Das Europäische Buch, 1985, vol. II, p. 325: «Man hat nämlich nicht nur ein *Kunstwerk*, sondern das wirkliche künstlerische *Produzieren* selber gegenwärtig vor sich».

improvises not with the voice, but on an instrument, arriving at a «complete coincidence of interiority and exteriority», a «complete fusion of conception and execution» in a wonderful mystery that appears «like a flash of lightning» (*blitzähnlich*). A great virtuoso transcends the mere mechanics, his instrument ceases to be an instrument and becomes an extension of himself, «a perfectly ensouled organ». Such remarkable reflection on the adequation between subject and object is worth quoting here at length:

> Thirdly, such vitality is still more wonderful if the organ is not the human voice but an instrument. The sound of instruments is more remote from the expression of the soul and they remain, in general, an external matter, a dead thing, while music is inner movement and activity. If the externality of the instrument disappears altogether, if inner music penetrates this external reality through and through, then, thanks to this virtuosity, the foreign instrument appears as a perfectly developed organ of the artistic soul. [...] When virtuosity like this reaches its culminating point it not only evinces an astounding mastery over external material but displays its inner unbounded freedom by surpassing itself in playing with apparently insurmountable difficulties, making surprising jokes in a witty mood with interruptions and fancies, and, thanks to its original inventions, making enjoyable the baroque itself. [...] Artists of genius can overcome the restrictions of their instrument and now and again, as an audacious proof of victory, can go through the gamut of the different sorts of sounds given by instruments other than their own. In this sort of execution we enjoy the highest peak of musical vitality, the wonderful mystery of an external tool becoming a perfectly ensouled organ[65], and we have before us at the same time, like a flash of lightning, the inner conception and the execution of the imagination of genius, in a temporary and very ephemeral fusion[66].

[65]. Alain Patrick Olivier (*op. cit.*, see note 63), p. 80, mentions another version of this phrase. See HEIMAN. *Die Aesthetik nach Hegel's Vorlesungen geschrieben von Heiman. Im Wintersemester 1828-1829*, Manuscript, private collection, p. 127: «We have before our ears this wonderful mystery that an instrument *like the violin* can become an ensouled organ».

[66]. HEGEL, Georg Wilhelm Friedrich. *Op. cit.* (see note 64), vol. II, pp. 325-326: «Wunderbarer noch wird *drittens* solche Lebendigkeit, wenn das Organ nicht die menschliche Stimme, sondern irgendeines der *anderen Instrumente* ist. Diese nämlich liegen mit ihrem Klang dem Ausdruck der Seele ferner und bleiben überhaupt eine äußerliche Sache, ein totes Ding, während die Musik innerliche Bewegung und Tätigkeit ist. Verschwindet nun die Äußerlichkeit des Instrumentes durchaus, dringt die innere Musik ganz durch die äußere Realität hindurch, so erscheint in dieser Virtuosität das fremde Instrument als ein vollendet durchgebildetes eigenstes Organ der künstlerischen Seele.[...] Solche Virtuosität beweist, wo sie zu ihrem Gipfelpunkte gelangt, nicht nur die erstaunenswürdige Herrschaft über das Äußere, sondern kehrt nun auch die innere ungebundene Freiheit heraus, indem sie sich in scheinbar unausführbaren Schwierigkeiten spielend überbietet, zu Künstlichkeiten ausschweift, mit Unterbrechungen, Einfällen in witziger Laune überraschend scherzt und in originellen Erfindungen selbst das Barocke genießbar macht.[...] bei genialen Künstlern aber beweisen dieselben die unglaubliche Meisterschaft in ihrem und über ihr Instrument, dessen Beschränktheit die Virtuosität zu überwinden weiß und hin und wieder zu dem verwegenen Beleg dieses Siegs ganz andere Klangarten fremder Instrumente durchlaufen kann. In dieser Art der Ausübung genießen wir die höchste Spitze musikalischer Lebendigkeit, das wundervolle Geheimnis, daß ein äußeres Werkzeug zum vollkommen beseelten Organ wird,

ILL. 4: Hegel with his students during the winter semester 1828/29. Lithograph by Franz Kugler.

The portrait painter Caroline Bardua (1781-1864) attended Paganini's second Berlin concert, on 13 March. She was accompanied by her sister Wilhelmine who confided in her diary that «this wonderful man certainly belongs to the most unique of apparitions» and that his music was «the rarest that one can hear»[67]. By that time Caroline Bardua's sitters had already included Goethe, Caspar David Friedrich, Julius Eduard Hitzig, Carl Maria von Weber and Johanna Schopenhauer. As stated in the catalogue of the *Berliner Akademieausstellung* of 1830, Paganini's portrait was drawn from life, but the date of the sitting session was not recorded (see ILL. 5). The painting is full of symbols linked to hermetic tradition and freemasonry, not surprisingly in view of the influence of Bardua's mentor Goethe. The inclusion of particulars such as the star of the Order of the Golden Spur[68], and the angel imparting a violin lesson to a child (on the vase, just above the

---

und haben zugleich das innerliche Konzipieren wie die Ausführung der genialen Phantasie in augenblicklichster Durchdringung und verschwindendstem Leben blitzähnlich vor uns».

[67]. WERNER, Johannes. *Die Schwestern Bardua, Bilder aus dem Gesellschafts-, Kunst- und Geistesleben der Biedermeierzeit*, Leipzig, Koehler & Amelang, 1929, p. 121: «14.3.1829. Gestern haben wir einen ganz außerordentlichen Künstler bewundert: den berühmten Violinspieler Paganini, der alle Welt herbeiströmen macht, ob er gleich 2 Thaler Entrée nimmt. Dieser wunderbare Mensch gehört gewiß zu den seltensten Erscheinungen, die es gibt. Von der unglaublichen Vollkommenheit seiner Kunst kann ich nichts sagen — so was Außerordentliches läßt sich nicht beschreiben. [...] So schwer es uns erst erschien, aus unserer kleinen Kasse 4 Thaler für einen Abend zu erübrigen, so würden uns doch jetzt 4 Thaler sehr wenig erscheinen für einen nochmaligen Genuß des Seltensten, was man hören kann».

[68]. Paganini's nomination as Knight of the Order of the Golden Spur by Pope Leo XII (3 April 1827) permitted him to sign *Cavaliere Nicolò Paganini* (or *Ritter Nicolò Paganini* in Germany).

violin)[69], may have been suggested by the sitter himself. Interestingly, the bridge fitted to the violin is of the baroque type. Concurring with Balzac's perception of Paganini that «there is certainly something mysterious in this man»[70], Bardua's romantic and expressive vision of Paganini is presented as a riddle. Light falls on the violinist's forehead emphasising the development of the frontal lobe[71]. This, according to Franz Joseph Gall's theories that were in vogue at that time, denotes musical creativity. Paganini's left hand is also fully lit, relaxed and flexible, poised for an imaginary tune, his arm resting on a sphinx's back. Paganini was often perceived as an enigmatic personality, possessing a musical secret. The very word 'sphinx' conjures up the idea of an enigma: according to tradition, the Gizeh sphinx was the symbol of secret knowledge. Instead of a pyramid, Bardua chose to depict a volcano as a symbol of creative energy and incandescence of genius (this perhaps prompted Goethe's words to Carl Friedrich Zelter after the concert of 30 October 1829 in Weimar[72]). In Bardua's composition, Paganini appears to be toying with a wooden snuffbox in his right hand, a stance that suggests his fundamentally active, if not to say restless nature. This rare and remarkable portrait is now exposed in the Art Gallery of Dessau[73].

FRANKFURT, 11 APRIL 1830: SCHUMANN

On Easter Sunday 1830, Robert Schumann, at that time a law student at Heidelberg University, went to Frankfurt to hear Paganini. After the concert, he jotted in his diary: «Easter Sunday! In the evening Paganini; what a delight!»[74]. He wrote later: «In Paganini's

69. Paganini recounted that his mother had invoked divine assistance to promote her ambitions for him. Through her lively imagination «she had fancied that her guardian angel appeared to her in her sleep and she asked that her son might be a great violinist». See CONESTABILE, Gian Carlo. *Op. cit.* (see note 55), p. 34.

70. BALZAC, Honoré de. *Œuvres complètes*, 26 vols., Paris, Calmann-Lévy, 1869-1906, vol. XXIII, p. 204: «Le miracle le plus extraordinaire qui me surprenne en ce moment à Paris, est celui que Paganini sait opérer. Ne croyez pas qu'il s'agisse de son archet, de son doigté, ou des sons fantastiques de son violon… il y a sans doute quelque chose de mystérieux dans cet homme».

71. The famous physician Francesco Bennati who examined Paganini in Paris in 1831 observed that «in him the bump of melody is extremely developed at the external angle of the forehead»; see BENNATI, Francesco. 'Notice physiologique sur le célèbre violoniste Niccolò Paganini', in: *Revue de Paris*, XXVI/17 (May 1831), pp. 52-60: 53: «la bosse de la mélodie, qui est chez lui très-développée à l'angle extérieur du front».

72. GOETHE, Johann Wolfgang von. *Goethes Briefwechsel mit Zelter*, Leipzig, Wolkenwanderer Verlag, 1924, p. 415, letter of 9 November 1829: «Paganini hab ich denn auch gehört. [...] Mir fehlt zu dem, was man Genuss nennt und was bei mir immer zwischen Sinnlichkeit und Verstand schwebt, eine Basis zu dieser Flammen und Wolkensäule. [...] Ich hörte nur etwas Meteorisches».

73. Inventory No. 446. See LANGE, Andreas. 'Da Berlino', in: *Quaderni dell'Istituto di Studi Paganiniani*, XIV (2002), p. 75.

74. SCHUMANN, Robert. *Tagebücher*, edited by Georg Eismann, Leipzig, VEB Deutscher Verlag für Musik, 1971, vol. I (1827-1838), p. 282: «Ostersonntag. [...] Abends Paganini. [...] ungeheure Entzückung».

ILL. 5: Caroline Bardua, *Paganini*, 1829, reportedly painted from life, 64 x 49 cm.

hands the driest exercises flame up like Pythian pronouncements!»[75]. Schumann announced to his mother that he had decided to abandon his law studies. As a direct outcome of the Frankfurt concert, he set to the task of adapting some of the Paganini Caprices for the piano. In a first set, *6 Studien nach Capricen von Paganini*, Op. 3, of 1832, he closely adhered to Paganini's text, concentrating on the task of fitting these violin solos into the idiom of the keyboard. The preface to that opus, almost a piano method in itself, contains a theory of fingering as well as a definition of the Caprice that sheds light on the importance accorded to this genre by Romantic composers:

> To no other type of musical compositions are poetic liberties as beautifully suited as to the Caprice. But if, beyond the lightness and the humour which should characterise it, profundity and depth of study also appear, then this is really true mastery[76].

---

[75]. ID. *Gesammelte Schriften* [...], *op. cit.* (see note 12), vol. II, p. 286: «in Paganinis Hand die trockensten Übungsformeln zu Pythiasprüchen aufflammen».

[76]. SCHUMANN, Robert. *6 Studien nach Capricen von Paganini*, Op. 3 (1832), edited by E. von Sauer, Frankfurt, Peters, n. 10550, no year, p. 3: «Keiner andern Gattung musikalischer Sätze stehen poetische Freiheiten so

The second set, *6 Concert-Etüden nach Capricen von Paganini* Op. 10, of 1833, while still an attempt to translate Paganini's music from one instrumental medium to another, goes a step further, «breaking loose from the pedantry of the literal translation»[77] and «uncovering Paganini's innermost poetic dimension»[78]. The Caprices remained Schumann's companions throughout his life. Their performance and transcription by other artists always aroused his interest, and, shortly before his death, he provided the original violin part with a piano accompaniment for the practical use of concert violinists[79]. A further reference to Paganini is found in *Carnaval* Op. 9 for piano solo[80]. Here the violinist is portrayed as one of the masked characters together with Pierrot, Arlequin, Coquette, the Sphinxes, Florestan and Eusebius, Chiarina (for Clara Wieck), Estrella, and Chopin. Schumann captured a characteristic feature of Paganini's virtuoso style: a *moto perpetuo* texture of *presto* semiquavers, enhanced and dynamised by a persistent syncopation. This perhaps can be seen in relation to the linguistic concept of 'intense latching'[81]:

Ex. 2: Robert Schumann, *Carnaval*, Op. 9, 'Intermezzo', bars 1-2.

The last bars of the 'Intermezzo' are charged with symbolic overtones. After the reiteration of the F minor chord, the emergence of V7/III in harmonics creates a magical effect:

---

schön als der Caprice. Ist aber hinter der Leichtigkeit und dem Humor, welche sie charakterisieren sollen, auch Gründlichkeit und tieferes Studium sichtbar, so ist das wohl die echte Meisterschaft».

77. SCHUMANN, Robert. *Gesammelte Schriften* […], *op. cit.* (see note 12), vol. I, p. 212.

78. VALOIS, Nathaniel. 'Reviews Books', in: *The Strad* (January 2011), p. 102; see also MALVANO, Andrea. '«Il lato poetico della composizione». La recezione schumanniana dei *Capricci* di Paganini', in: *Nicolò Paganini Diabolus in Musica*, edited by Andrea Barizza and Fulvia Morabito, Turnhout, Brepols, 2010, pp. 515-526.

79. This piano accompaniment was published by Peters (Leipzig, 1941), edited by Georg Schünemann, with the addition of an *Urtext* edition of the original violin part.

80. Completed in 1835 and dedicated to Karol Lipiński.

81. The maximisation of the exploitation of discourse space.

Ex. 3: Robert Schumann, *Carnaval*, Op. 9, 'Intermezzo', bars 36-38.

This rare use of harmonics in piano literature requires a pedal technique *sui generis*. Of great interest is the instruction *messa di voce* (< >) on the final chord. This is part of a whole series of effects that Schumann experimented with after his experience in Frankfurt. However, it was in the improvisatory sphere that Schumann considered Paganini to be at his greatest. By virtue of temperament and education, Schumann recognised the ability to extemporise as a musician's most precious gift. In addition, his piano teacher Friedrich Wieck had always encouraged improvisation both as a method of creating compositions and «because it was expected of a virtuoso»[82]. It is no coincidence that Wieck's daughter Clara[83] became one of the best pianist-improvisers of her time, second only to Franz Liszt[84]. Schumann was indeed ideally placed to spot a great performer and it is significant that the greatest compliment he could ever pay to a violinist was to liken him to Paganini, making clear that the art of improvisation was the touchstone of instrumental virtuosity:

> I have heard nearly all the great violinists of the new generation, from Lipiński down to [François] Prume. [...] But Ernst, like Paganini, is able to satisfy, to win all parties whenever he pleases. *He even approaches Paganini in his genius for improvisation* — the most fascinating of virtuoso gifts[85].

---

[82]. GOERTZEN, Valerie Woodring. 'Setting the Stage: Clara Schumann's Preludes', in: *In the Course of Performance, Studies in the World of Musical Improvisation*, edited by Bruno Nettl and Melinda Russell, Chicago, University of Chicago Press, 1998, pp. 237-260: 239.

[83]. Clara Wieck (1819-1896). She married Robert Schumann in 1840.

[84]. GOERTZEN, Valerie Woodring. *Op. cit.* (see note 82), p. 240. See also the contribution about Clara Wieck by Valerie Woodring Goertzen to this volume.

[85]. SCHUMANN, Robert. *Gesammelte Schriften* [...], *op. cit.* (see note 12), vol. II, pp. 466-467: «Die Worte von Berlioz, Ernst werde wie Paganini einmal die Welt von sich reden machen, fangen an in Erfüllung zu gehen. Ich habe die großen Violinspieler der neueren Zeit fast alle gehört, von Lipinski an bis zu Prume herab. [...] Aber Ernst versteht es, ähnlich wie Paganini, allen Parteien zu genügen, alle für sich gewinnen zu können, wenn er will. Auch an improvisatorischer Kraft, der reizendsten am Virtuosen, steht er Paganini nahe».

Paris, 1831: Delacroix

Eugène Delacroix painted an extraordinary portrait of Paganini playing on the violin (see Ill. 6). The posture, the manner of holding the violin and the bow, the expression of intense involvement, all contribute to an evocative and dramatic picture. Delacroix's artistic *credo* was that technique must be perfected to the point of being unnoticeable, whilst leaving room for spontaneity. He was fascinated by Paganini's technique, developed from endless hours of practice[86]. His knowledge of the violin enabled Delacroix to recognise the true import of seemingly trivial details like the positioning of the left thumb across the fingerboard or the characteristic way Paganini used the wrist in bowing.

Delacroix heard Paganini at the Paris Opera on 9 March 1831[87], and painted his portrait a short time after, from memory. Delacroix's representation confirms that Paganini's physical appearance was quite striking at that time, in part due to illness and recent jaw surgery. He plays with his eyes closed, his right foot seeming to beat time. Light falls on his face, hands and shirt-front, like an Orpheus emerging from darkness. His melancholic expression reflects the intensity of his playing, perhaps the Adagio flebile of his Concerto No. 4 or the Adagio espressivo of the Concerto No. 1, both featuring in the programme of the Paris concerts. Willibald Gurlitt referred to this painting as the 'humanisation of the instrument' (*das Menschwerden des Instrumentes*), a perception very close to Hegel's[88]. Delacroix saw in Paganini a truly creative artist, not simply an outstanding player of written notes. Years later he wrote in his journal: «Here is the *inventor*; here is the man who is made for his art. I thought of so many artists who are just the reverse, in painting, in architecture, in everything»[89].

A violinist himself, Delacroix drew an analogy between playing the violin and painting. He saw in Paganini a sort of *alter ego*, a musical equivalent of the painter with his palette and brush. Delacroix found similarities between sketches and musical improvisations. He insisted that «the painter should always take improvisation into account»[90]. He described how he abandoned himself to improvisation to make discoveries during the painting

---

[86]. Delacroix, Eugène. *Journal*, 2 vols., edited by Michèle Hannoosh, Paris, José Corti, 2009, vol. ii, p. 373, note 264: «Paganini n'a dû son étonnante exécution sur le violon qu'en s'exerçant chaque jour pendant une heure à ne faire que des gammes. C'est pour nous le même exercice».

[87]. Among the other celebrities known to have been present at the Paris Opera that evening one can mention: Victor Hugo, Théophile Gautier, Alfred de Musset, Alfred de Vigny, George Sand, Charles de Bériot, Maria Malibran, Gioachino Rossini, Dionysio Aguado, Honoré de Balzac, Pierre Baillot, Gaetano Donizetti, Luigi Cherubini, the Baron de Rothschild, Franz Liszt.

[88]. Kókai, Rudolf. *Franz Liszt in seinen frühen Klavierwerken*, Kassel, Bärenreiter, 1968, p. 71, note 223.

[89]. Delacroix, Eugène. *Op. cit.* (see note 86), vol. ii, p. 990: «Voilà *l'inventeur*, voilà l'homme propre à la chose. Je pensais à tant d'artistes, qui sont le contraire, dans la peinture, dans l'architecture, dans tout».

[90]. *Ibidem*, p. 338: «[…] l'exécution dans la peinture doit toujours tenir compte de l'improvisation».

Ill. 6: Eugène Delacroix, *Paganini jouant du violon,* 1831, oil on cardboard, 47 x 30 cm, Washington, Phillips Collection.

process. Thus, by virtue of empathy and artistic self-identification, he portrayed Paganini in full flight, in the very act of creation[91].

NORWICH, 1831: THE REVEREND JOHN EDMUND COX

John Edmund Cox (1812-1890) was a theologian of the highest academic attainments (he was awarded Doctor of Divinity) as well as a keen and very perceptive music lover. On the whole, nothing of importance in British musical life escaped him as shown in his two-volume *Musical Recollections of the Last Half Century* that covers the period from 1817 to 1870. He acknowledged that «of all the violinists I have ever heard, from Christoph Gottfried Kiesewetter to Joseph Joachim — and their name is 'legion'— there is not one that has left such an impression upon my mind as Paganini did»[92]. His meeting with Paganini took place during the summer of 1831 as he was asked to be the great violinist's interpreter. In that capacity, he attended all the concerts Paganini gave in Norwich and Great Yarmouth, travelling with him, accompanying him to his hotel and helping him in administrative matters[93]. As a bond of mutual friendship developed, Paganini «threw off the suspicious restraint which was always apparent in his manner when he was amongst strangers»[94], and Cox had the unique privilege to hear him practising. Paganini, it appears, did not rehearse his concert programme but preferred to play passages from great composers, interpreting them in a completely unconventional and highly personal way, beyond notes as it were:

> In public Paganini confined himself almost exclusively to the performance of his own music. [...] But in private — for he had his violin constantly in his hand — he would sit and dash off by the hour together snatches from the compositions of the best masters, and give readings of such originality to passages that had been heard again and again, as apparently have never been supposed to be possible by any other player. As an instance in point, he one morning, whilst I was writing several notes for him, commenced the first *motivo* of Beethoven's magnificent violin concerto. To write was then impossible; and he, perceiving how entranced I seemed, promised, if it could be managed, that I should hear the whole of that movement before we separated. [...] On the last

---

[91]. Following more classical lines, Jean-Dominique Ingres did not show the musician in action. In his famous 1819 pencil portrait of Paganini, the violin appears merely as an inanimate object, or tool, tucked under Paganini's right arm.

[92]. Cox, John Edmund. *Musical Recollections of the Last Half Century*, 2 vols., London, Tinsley, 1872, vol. I, p. 195.

[93]. The concerts took place on 28, 29, 30 July, 1 and 3 August in Norwich and 2 August in Great Yarmouth.

[94]. Cox, John Edmund. *Op. cit.* (see note 92), vol. I, p. 196.

night of the last concert at which he had played, several persons came to take their leave of him; and one gentleman, whom I never saw before or since, on a signal from the master, sat down at a pianoforte, and began to play. Instantly I was on the alert, for I remembered the notes, and his promise rushed back upon me. Never shall I forget the smile on that sad, pale, wan, and haggard face, upon every lineament of which intense pain was written in the deepest lines, when I caught his eye — or the playing, into which a spirit and a sympathy were thrown that carried one wholly away[95].

Cox's contribution to research includes an English version of Hermann Olshausen's commentary on the Pauline Epistles[96]. As the above passage reveals, his insightful attitude to problems pertaining to interpretation extended to the musical sphere. He felt Paganini's rendering of Beethoven's Violin Concerto not only legitimate, but spirited and true, being guided by inspiration. In recollecting his experience, Cox subtly adapted Paul's «vivicat autem spiritus»[97] to «the playing, into which a spirit and a sympathy were thrown that carried one wholly away».

---

[95]. *Ibidem*, vol. I, pp. 196-197.

[96]. OLSHAUSEN, Hermann. *Biblical Commentary on St. Paul's First and Second Epistles to the Corinthians*, translated from the German, with Additional Notes, by John Edmund Cox, London, Seeley and Co. [...], 1851.

[97]. 2 Cor. 3, 6.

Charles-Auguste de Bériot
e l'improvvisazione virtuosistica per violino

Renato Ricco
(Salerno)

L A PRATICA DELL'IMPROVVISAZIONE riveste per Charles-Auguste de Bériot (1802-1870) un ruolo d'assoluta centralità, tanto nella prima parte del percorso artistico (incentrata sulla carriera solistica all'insegna del virtuosismo strumentale) quanto nella successiva fase dedicata all'insegnamento. Per quel che riguarda il primo aspetto, nel numero di *Athenæum* del primo ottobre 1836 si può leggere, all'interno di una cronaca di un concerto tenuto insieme alla cantante Maria Malibran, sua moglie, dell'estemporanea esecuzione di arpeggi descritta come disfida artistica tra marito e moglie, in un contesto di «completa leggerezza di perfetta maestranza»[1]. Non è inoltre da sottovalutare il fatto che Bériot non si sia mai sentito molto a suo agio nella classe di Pierre Baillot, che veniva considerato il difensore di uno stile 'classico' rispetto agli 'eccessi' della trascendenza paganiniana — pur dimostrando sempre una grande riconoscenza e un sincero affetto per il maestro[2], ed ereditandone alcuni principi basilari di tecnica violinistica, come ad esempio la posizione del pollice e del polso sinistri. Un dato significativo è comunque che proprio la pratica dell'improvvisazione, seppur con ogni probabilità con stili e soluzioni tecniche molto differenti, fu contemplata tanto da Baillot quanto da Paganini. Ad ogni modo, i contatti Baillot-Bériot non superarono la durata di pochi mesi, dal momento che l'insegnamento del primo fu probabilmente recepito dal secondo come «troppo sistematico e di uno spirito un po' stretto»[3].

---

[1]. Il testo della rivista è contenuto anche in *The Annual Biography and Obituary*, XXI (1837), p. 224: «very wantonness of consummate power». La più dettagliata ricostruzione della *liaison* tra Bériot e la Malibran è quella compiuta da SCHUENEMAN, Bruce. 'The Search of the Minor Composer. The Case of Charles Bériot and Maria Malibran', in: *Musical References Services Quarterly*, III/2 (1994), pp. 29-46.

[2]. Al quale dedicò anche i *Six études ou caprices pour le violon* editi tra il 1830 e il 1831 a Milano (Francesco Lucca) e Torino (Magrini).

[3]. QUITIN, José. 'Introduction', in: *Catalogue de l'exposition «L'école belge de violon»*, a cura di Bernard Huys, Bruxelles, Bibliothèque Royale Albert I, 1978, pp. xvi-xviii: «trop systématique et d'ésprit quelque peu étroit».

La capacità improvvisativa per Bériot viene a porsi come miglior garanzia di qualità artistica e soprattutto di unicità di stile esecutivo, anche secondo il consiglio ricevuto da Giovanni Battista Viotti nel 1821: «Avete uno stile bello, impegnatevi a perfezionarlo; ascoltate tutti gli uomini di talento. Approfittate di tutto e non imitate nulla»[4]. Se infatti da un punto di vista specificamente compositivo si può agevolmente riconoscere per Bériot un'autonomia di scrittura, già presente nei primi *Airs variés*, seppur con l'innegabile debito nei confronti delle innovazioni tecniche paganiniane, come dimostra[5] il Concerto n. 1 Op. 16, 'Le militaire', è proprio con il massimo esponente della scuola franco-belga che la pratica dell'improvvisazione riceve un'accurata analisi, sia di tipo estetico-stilistico che tecnico-strumentale. Fondamentali, per Bériot, sono le connessioni tra le idee di 'preludio' e di 'improvvisazione'.

L'art du prélude (Second annexe de la Méthode de violon) di Bériot viene pubblicata postuma a Magonza presso Schott's Söhne (si veda ILL. 1) nel 1875, in edizione bilingue (francese e tedesca)[6]. Nella 'Préface' (Premessa) vengono subito ribaditi alcuni concetti già espressi nella precedente *Méthode* dedicata allo strumento: la riproduzione della voce umana come fine ultimo dell'arte violinistica e la necessità di emanciparsi dalla «febbre del tecnicismo» che «negli ultimi anni» — spiega l'autore — «si è impadronita del violino» allontanandolo dalla sua «missione vera», quella «di imitare gli accenti della voce umana»[7]. Questa riflessione risulta in linea con una certa libertà di pensiero, assolutamente coerente con la pratica improvvisativa, che innerva anche diversi passaggi della *Méthode*: «il sentimento è una qualità che sfugge all'analisi»[8]. Questo perché il fine ultimo dell'arte violinistica è, per Bériot, «quello di riprodurre e di esprimere tutti i sentimenti dell'anima»[9].

---

4. *Ibidem*: «Vous avez un beau style; attachez-vous à le perfectionner; entendez tous les hommes de talent — Profitez de tout et n'imitez rien».

5. Questo fu l'unico concerto di Bériot ad esser pubblicato con Paganini ancora in vita. La prima edizione è infatti del 1837 (Magonza, B. Schott's Söhne). I restanti concerti furono editi, per la stessa casa editrice tedesca, in un arco di ventotto anni, dal 1841 (Concerto n. 2, Op. 32) al 1869 (Concerto n. 10, Op. 127).

6. Félix Huet, allievo di Eugène Sauzay a sua volta discepolo di Baillot, scrive a proposito nel suo *Étude sur les différentes écoles de violon depuis Corelli jusqu'à Baillot*, Chalons-sur-Marne, F. Thouille, 1880, p. 10: «L'auteur s'est simplement attaché à donner à l'élève, dans les tons majeurs et dans les mineurs, des examples ou formules que son imagination pourra modifier et varier ensuite à l'infini, en tenant compte de règles élémentaires qu'il a apprises dans le solfège».

7. BÉRIOT, Charles-Auguste de. *Méthode de violon*, Parigi, Schott, 1858, p. i: «fièvre du méchanisme, qui, dans ces dernières années, s'est emparée du violon, l'a souvent détourné de sa mission véritable, celle d'imiter les accents de la voix humaine».

8. *Ibidem*, p. 100: «Le sentiment musical est une qualité qui échappe à l'analyse».

9. *Ibidem*, p. ii: «celui de reprouire et d'exprimer tous les sentiments de l'âme».

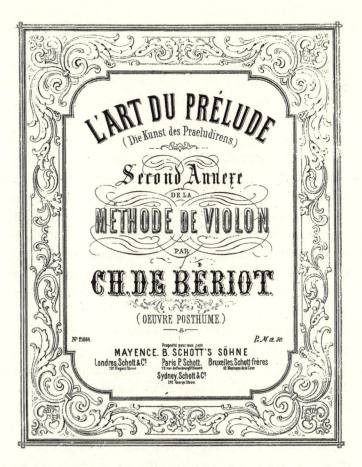

ILL. 1: frontespizio di Charles-Auguste de Bériot, *L'art du prélude (Second annexe de la Méthode de violon), Œuvre posthume*, Magonza, Schott's Söhne, 1875.

In riferimento alla pratica dell'improvvisazione, o del libero preludiare (Bériot talvolta intende in maniera quasi sinonimica le due accezioni), il virtuoso di Lovanio ribadisce che «l'eccessivo sacrificio all'algebra stanca e scoraggia»[10] e, per quel che concerne le analogie tra espressività violinistica e regole prosodiche inerenti alla costruzione fraseologica, *L'art du prélude* viene definita come «un piccolo corso di retorica musicale»[11]. 'Arte del Preludio' che sottende per Bériot una duplice finalità: se infatti deve risultare utile a tutti i violinisti per l'interpretazione dei capisaldi del repertorio dello strumento, essa — e questa è la più grande speranza dell'autore — «spalancherà le porte del tempio»[12] ai virtuosi più dotati. Il linguaggio massonico del 'fratello' appartenente

---

[10]. *L'art du prélude*, Magonza, Schott's Söhne, s.d. [1875], p. i: «Trop sacrifier à l'algèbre fatigue et rebute».

[11]. *Ibidem*: «un petit course de rhétorique musicale».

[12]. *Ibidem*: «ouvrira toutes grandes les portes du temple».

alla loggia bruxelliense degli *Amis Philanthropes* sembra indicare la pratica improvvisativa come cruciale *trait d'union* tra la perfezione propria di un'esecuzione brillante, intesa come completa conoscenza e conquista delle principali difficoltà meccaniche, e arte compositiva, tassello fondamentale nella *Weltanschauung* artistica di Bériot. In tal senso, questi dimostra quindi di essersi senza dubbio inserito nella scia di Nicolò Paganini, per il quale gli aspetti dell'interpretazione, dell'esecuzione e della composizione giungono a un livello di compenetrazione mai raggiunto prima: il fattore improvvisativo viene a fungere da collante, per intrinseche ragioni di volta in volta cangianti, tra questi tre fondamentali momenti. Di certo, il mero aspetto esecutivo, considerato in modo assoluto, viene visto da Bériot come un limite fatale: «La vera essenza dell'arte sarà sempre cosa ignota per l'artista che non è che esecutore»[13]. Bériot mette anche in rilievo la tangenza che vige tra capacità compositiva e prassi improvvisativa, di cui il preludio si prefigura quale «primo stadio della composizione»[14]; tra i due campi, considerata l'ottica specificamente violinistica, o meglio solistica propria di Bériot, sembra anzi vigere una sorta di corrispondenza biunivoca: «improvvisare è comporre rapidamente, comporre è improvvisare lentamente»[15].

Sebbene doti improvvisative siano state riconosciute già ad altri violinisti come Ole Bull e Heinrich Wilhelm Ernst (che a Parigi, non in modo sistematico, entrò in contatto proprio con Bériot[16]), oltre ovviamente a Paganini, e nonostante altri virtuosi del calibro di Karol Józef Lipiński e Louis Eller abbiano composto *Impromptus* per il proprio strumento[17], Bériot è l'unico che abbia avvertito l'esigenza di dedicare un trattato a quello che, specie nell'ambito della scuola violinistica parigina dell'Ottocento, viene ritenuto il primo livello della pratica improvvisativa.

L'art du prélude si pone dichiaratamente un duplice traguardo: fungere da perfezionamento del meccanismo tecnico-strumentale e fornire «modelli ovvero tipi di forma musicale» volti ad affinare l'originalità, che deve esser la *condicio sine qua non* di ogni virtuoso che voglia misurarsi con l'arte improvvisativa[18].

Alla 'Préface' segue una lunga e variegata serie di esempi musicali. Esattamente come altri violinisti-compositori dei secoli precedenti, ad esempio Carlo Zuccari con *The True Method of Playing an Adagio* (pubblicato a Londra tra il 1760 e il 1765) e Franz Benda con le sue Sonate per violino e basso Op. 1 (pubblicate a Parigi nel 1763), Bériot preferisce

---

[13]. *Ibidem*, p. ii: «Le vrai côté de l'art sera toujours lettre close pour l'artiste qui n'est que exécutant».

[14]. *Ibidem*: «condition première de la composition».

[15]. *Ibidem*: «improviser c'est composer vite; composer c'est improviser lentement»

[16]. Si veda ROWE, Marc W. *Heinrich Wilhelm Ernst: Virtuoso Violinist*, Farnham, Ashgate, 2008, p. 55.

[17]. Lipiński scrisse *Deux impromptus pour violon seul*, Op. 34, oltre a un altro Impromptu, sempre per violino solo, rimasto manoscritto, attualmente custodito presso la Kongelige Bibliotek di Copenaghen e datato 14 febbraio 1842. Tra le opere di Eller figura l'*Improvisation sur un chant religieux de Joseph Haydn* per violino solo nonché *Deux impromptus*, Op. 21, per violino e pianoforte.

[18]. *L'art du prélude*, p. iv: «modèles ou types de forme musicale».

fornire nella sua *Art du prélude* una nutrita serie di esempi concreti piuttosto che dilungarsi in discussioni teoriche[19].

L'opera è costituita da centocinquanta segmenti musicali di varia lunghezza per violino e pianoforte (dove il primo ha quasi sempre un ruolo di preminenza assoluta) volti a illustrare varie possibilità di ricamo melodico o di chiusura di un'esecuzione: *summa* artisticamente compiuta e autonoma dei precetti e degli esempi forniti è, in ultimo, la composizione 'Prélude ou Improvisation'[20]. Il disegno predominante rimane quello dell'arpeggio o della progressione melodica sulla base di scalette: in entrambi i casi la scrittura può essere sia a corde semplici che a bicordi. Diverse soluzioni ritmiche vengono di continuo combinate con vari espedienti tecnici relativi sia alla mano sinistra che a differenti soluzioni d'arcata. Per quel che concerne le possibilità di concludere una *performance*, Bériot consiglia ad esempio una scala ascendente e discendente, in *détaché continue*, per gradi congiunti (il suo Esempio n. 1); in alternativa, un'altra soluzione fornita prevede vari intervalli spezzati in *grand martelé* o una figurazione mista di scalette e arpeggi legati in vario modo (Esempi nn. 2-3). Come ulteriore possibilità viene suggerito lo schema ritmico di due sedicesimi legati seguiti da rapida scaletta discendente di trentaduesimi in picchettato, cui seguono passaggi di trilli e scala cromatica. Analoghi disegni ritmici vengono proposti per ritmi di tipo ternario, con rapide sestine di volta in volta sciolte, legate, picchettate o talvolta in *ricochet*.

Nella silloge che il virtuoso belga propone, ai fini di sviluppare l'arte del preludiare/improvvisare, non manca il fine più puramente tecnico, come dimostrano l'Esempio n. 39, 'Excercice du petit doigt' (Esercizio per il mignolo), dedicato a rafforzare e perfezionare le estensioni del mignolo sinistro, e il n. 42, 'Pour l'égalité des doigts' (Per l'uguaglianza delle dita), mentre il n. 60 è volto a curare i salti di corda, come dimostra l'indicazione *archet rebondi vers le talon* (arco rimbalzato al tallone). Quest'ultimo, come il n. 95, 'Léger du milieu' (leggero a metà arco; si veda ILL. 2) basato su quadricordi spezzati, per le estensioni e gli incroci di dita previsti, dimostra come Bériot possa aver talvolta condiviso l'assunto tecnico paganiniano che, già presente nelle opere di Antonio Lolli e Pierre Gaviniés e successivamente da Paganini portato ai massimi livelli, si mostra refrattario all'idea fissa e limitante di posizione: mediante il posizionamento del pollice sinistro verso il centro del manico del violino, invece che in linea con l'indice, risulta infatti più semplice coprire contemporaneamente più posizioni con velocità e agilità.

---

[19]. Si veda STOWELL, Robin. *Violin Technique and Performance Practice in the Late Eighteenth and Early Nineteenth Centuries*, Cambridge, Cambridge University Press, 1985, p. 337.

[20]. HUET, Félix. *Op. cit.* (si veda nota 6), p. 101: «Cette seconde annexe de la méthode est moins un traité complémentaire qu'un recueil de formules destiné à guider les premiers pas de l'élève dans le domaine du prélude et de l'improvisation».

ILL. 2: esempio n. 95 di Bériot, *L'art du prélude*, p. 53.

In alcuni casi (gli Esempi n. 111 e 134) una particolare indicazione di tempo designa un frammento di livello musicale superiore: nel primo, 'Tempo di Polacca', compare la figurazione ritmica (croma staccata seguita da semiminima, coppia e quartina di semicrome) molto usata nella musica violinistica brillante, come dimostrato ad esempio dal tema principale del 'Rondò ossia Polonese' del Concerto 'n. 0' in Mi minore di Paganini, mentre una certa grazia e compiutezza si riscontra per i n. 138 ('Allegro con Spirito') e n. 148 ('Tempo di Valsa'; si veda ILL. 3) di Bériot. Quest'ultimo presenta particolare interesse dal momento che Bériot fornisce tre differenti versioni della stessa idea esposta in tricordi e bicordi: sestina legata in *bariolage*, sestina di note doppie con legature prima/seconda e quinta/sesta semicroma, e terzina di semicrome in *jeté* seguita da due incisi formati da semicroma staccata/pausa di semicroma. Il virtuoso di Lovanio sembra così seguire una tradizione già ben conosciuta nel Settecento[21], consistente infatti nel fornire varie versioni, con lievi variazioni relative alle arcate o alle note di volta, di una medesima idea musicale.

---

[21]. Come ben documentato dai molteplici raffronti delle varie versioni delle Sonate Op. 5 di Corelli, senza dimenticare opere di Telemann, Christian Philipp Emanuel Bach e Franz Benda. *Cfr.* STOWELL, Robin. *Op. cit.* (si veda nota 19), p. 340.

ILL. 3: esempio n. 148 di Bériot, *L'art du prélude*, p. 95.

Da un punto di vista armonico, all'interno delle soluzioni fornite da Bériot per sviluppare l'arte del preludio e dell'improvvisazione, si nota una certa immobilità o scarsa fantasia, con rarissime modulazioni a toni vicini, limitandosi piuttosto solo a progressioni cromatiche o arpeggi di settima diminuita. In questo Bériot sembra mostrare una convergenza con quanto sostenuto da François-Antoine Habeneck, il quale (sulla scorta di Baillot) nella sua *Méthode* del 1842, dopo aver suddiviso i tipi di preludi in melodico e armonico, definisce il primo composto «da scale, accordi spezzati e altri segmenti combinati in modo da far emergere le note essenziali della tonalità principale e delle sue relative», mentre con il secondo si intende un preludio «quasi sempre basato sugli accordi della scala e su qualche modulazione ai toni relativi»[22].

A conclusione del paragrafo introduttivo in cui vengono affrontati questi aspetti, Bériot cita la frase «miscere utile dulci». Orazio scrive: «Omne tulit punctum, qui miscuit utile dulci, / Lectorem delectando pariterque monendo», ovvero: «Come fare per ottenere un consenso generale? Mescolando piacere e utilità, solleticando i pruriti del lettore e al contempo fornendogli consigli»[23]. La citazione tratta dall'*Ars poetica* viene a porsi come

---

[22]. HABENECK, François-Antoine. *Méthode théorique et pratique de violon*, Parigi, Canaux, 1842, p. 154: «Le Prélude mélodique se compose de gammes, accords brisés et autres traits combinés de manière à faire entendre les notes essentielles du ton principal et de ses relatives. Le Prélude harmonique est Presque toujours basé sur les accords de la gamme et sur quelques modulations dans les tons relatifs».

[23]. ORAZIO, *Ars poetica*, 343-344.

cardine del trattato postumo di Bériot, e se *ars* e *ingenium* sono i concetti-base su cui il poeta latino costruisce il suo impianto poetologico, il violinista belga pone l'accento su «il giudizio e il gusto», dove con il primo termine ci si riferisce alla sfera 'pratica e matematica' del suonare a preludio, mentre al secondo pertiene «la qualità del sentimento e dello spirito»[24]. Se il giudizio viene assimilato a un compasso da geometra (non a caso altra icona simbolica dei liberi muratori) capace di tracciare un cerchio all'interno del quale il genio dell'esecutore ha diritto d'esprimersi, per il gusto, in quanto «senso critico del bello», il più grande ostacolo è rappresentato dal «gusto delle masse, la moda»[25]. Secondo Bériot, nulla è più antimusicale della foga debordante e ipertecnicistica, difetto dal quale non furono talvolta immuni alcuni virtuosi dell'Ottocento. Per evitare questo nella libera improvvisazione, al giudizio deve appartenere una qualità in particolare: la sobrietà. «Ammassare note su note, difficoltà su difficoltà, sorprendere e folgorare il suo uditorio»[26] può essere infatti una tentazione che, secondo Bériot, affascina il giovane violinista brillante impegnato nell'improvvisare, ma che è di sicuro meglio evitare. Perché ciò avvenga, è necessario invece procedere gradualmente, utilizzando nell'arte del preludio (e dell'improvvisazione) i vari espedienti con parsimonia e intelligenza: solo così l'artista potrà «condurre con sé il suo ascoltatore, in linea retta ovvero attraverso le vie della fantasia, fino alle più alte vette dell'emozione»[27]. Concetti cardine nella pratica improvvisativa sono quindi *pureté* (purezza), *clarté* (chiarezza) e *convenance* (convenienza): riguardo proprio alla convenienza, Bériot discute ad esempio della giusta contestualizzazione delle fioriture. Sulla base di queste regole deve poi subentrare il fattore della *varietas*, intesa come felice coniugazione del «meccanismo e dell'idea»[28].

In riferimento all'arte dell'improvvisazione, ovvero del libero preludiare, un'altra suggestione presa da Bériot dal mondo della letteratura latina è la tripartizione in stile semplice, temperato e sublime. Se anche la *Méthode de violon* già presenta una divisione in tre parti: *difficultés élémentaires*, *difficultés transcendantes*, *style* (difficoltà elementari, difficoltà avanzate, stile), questa suddivisione — che nell'ottica sinestetica cara al virtuoso belga potrebbe avere un corrispettivo in quella ciceroniana relativa alle esigenze del *probare*, *delectare* e *movere* — è usata da Bériot a proposito della razionalità con cui, all'interno dell'ornamentazione estemporanea, devono esser distribuiti i gruppetti.

Dimostrazione concreta e artisticamente compiuta di quanto sostenuto da Bériot è il 'Prélude ou Improvisation', pubblicato in chiusa all'*Art du prélude*. A differenza di quanto fatto anni dopo da un altro grande esponente della scuola violinistica franco-

---

24. *L'art du prélude*, p. iii: «le jugement et le goût», «la qualité du sentiment et de l'ésprit».

25. *Ibidem*, p. iv: «Son plus grand écueil est le caprice des masses, la mode».

26. *Ibidem*: «Entasser notes sur notes, difficultés sur difficultés, étonner et foudroyer son auditoire».

27. *Ibidem*: «conduire avec lui son auditeur, en ligne droite ou par les chemins de la fantasie, jusqu'aux plus hautes sommets de l'émotion».

28. *Ibidem*, p. v: «du mécanisme et de l'idée».

belga, Eugène Ysaÿe, che dedicherà ciascuno dei *Dix préludes pour violon seul* Op. 35 a un particolare intervallo (dall'unisono a quello di decima), focalizzando quindi l'attenzione unicamente sul problema dell'intonazione, Bériot mostra una concezione più variegata e concertistica. Da un punto di vista strutturale, il primo dato che balza subito all'occhio è la mancanza d'indicazione di tempo e, per la maggior parte della partitura, l'assenza di divisione in battute. Esattamente come per la scrittura solistica dei dieci concerti e delle altre composizioni brillanti, l'ideale di *varietas* proprio di Bériot ha modo di dispiegarsi al meglio mediante l'utilizzo di quasi tutto il bagaglio tecnico-virtuosistico di marca paganiniana, con un sapiente gioco d'alternanza tra momenti di calma e guizzi d'energia, squarci di liricità e soluzioni trascendentali, lungo una serie di episodi concatenati — tra cui spiccano un 'Adagio Sostenuto', seguito da un 'Recitativo *ad libitum*', un 'Adagio' la cui indicazione agogica è 'Canto Sostenuto', e un 'Allegretto (Scherzando)' conclusivo.

★★★

> Il preludio è un piccolo pezzo di fantasia, breve e irregolare, che attraverso le note o gli accordi essenziali del modo, serve per così dire da introduzione al pezzo che ci si accinge a suonare[29].

> Il talento e l'arte dell'improvvisatore consistono dunque nello scegliere un'idea, sia propria sia d'altrui, e darle issofatto, senza alcuna preparazione, una forma musicale[30].

Se la prima frase definisce icasticamente la natura del preludio così come veniva inteso nell'ambito della scuola violinistica parigina ottocentesca, dove Bériot si forma, quella del virtuoso e didatta viennese — in cui a ragione Vincenzo Caporaletti individua «il principio proprio dell'improvvisazione che s'incarna all'interno dell'ideale della società romantica: il *logos* articolatorio, la proiezione della soggettività agente, del *melos*»[31] — ha il merito di focalizzare sinteticamente alcuni fattori d'assoluta importanza sia per quel che concerne l'istanza virtuosistica sia per la pratica improvvisativa. Qualsiasi discorso relativo all'improvvisazione, infatti, difficilmente può rimanere astratto o fine a se stesso, bensì deve connettersi necessariamente ad altri campi, come

---

[29]. HABENECK, François-Antoine. *Op. cit.* (si veda nota 22), p. 154: «Le prélude est un petit morceau de fantasie, irrégulier et court qui passant par les notes ou les accords essentiels du mode, sert pour ainsi dire d'introduction au morceau qu'on va jouer».

[30]. CZERNY, Carl. *L'arte di improvvisare resa all'intelligenza dei pianisti, Op. 200*, Milano, Ricordi, 1863, p. 1; tradotto dall'originale tedesco, *Systematische Anleitung zum Fantasieren auf dem Pianoforte, Op. 200*, Vienna, Diabelli, 1829.

[31]. CAPORALETTI, Vincenzo. *I processi improvvisativi nella musica*, Lucca, LIM, 2005, p. 255.

quello esecutivo o inerente alla problematica formale. L'improvvisazione acquista quindi un valore cruciale all'interno dei molteplici rapporti che legano vari fattori, tra loro eterogenei, quali il contesto dove l'esecuzione avviene e l'abilità tecnica dello strumentista, sino alla fama e al nome di quest'ultimo[32]. L'elemento improvvisativo, infatti, si presenta come qualcosa di non direttamente omologabile da un punto di vista formale, comprensivo di un *range* di soluzioni quanto mai ampio, e per sua intrinseca natura come un *quid* aleatoriamente basato sull'ispirazione del momento, i cui vincoli sembrano piuttosto indebolirsi nei confronti dell'istanza compositiva e al contempo stringersi con il momento della *performance*[33]. Una peculiarità della trattatistica relativa all'improvvisazione è che se vengono affrontati temi come l'esigenza di originalità e novità, la terza componente indispensabile a questa pratica, quella della spontaneità, viene — almeno in parte — a mancare: «Affermare di un'improvvisazione che essa da una parte è un collage di formule, dall'altra invece è avvertita come spontanea, sarebbe una formulazione linguistica sconcertante o per lo meno sorprendente, per quanto l'asserzione descriva in modo assolutamente esatto lo stato delle cose»[34].

Come rilevato anche da Bruce Ellis Benson[35], è con i primi fenomeni di grande popolarità e acclamato divismo (ossia con Paganini e Liszt) che la concentrazione dell'uditorio inizia a polarizzarsi quasi esclusivamente sul momento e sulle modalità dell'esecuzione, con una conseguente minor attenzione riservata al vero e proprio contenuto musicale delle composizioni o alle strutture formali che di queste sono alla base. Secondo tali parametri l'improvvisazione virtuosistica rimane un passaggio quasi obbligato per ogni concertista desideroso d'esibire il proprio bagaglio tecnico/virtuoso.

In un discorso relativo al virtuosismo strumentale, l'estrema libertà caratterizzante il momento performativo comporta tendenzialmente un'idea poco 'logica' di tema[36]: essendo questo tanto poco 'geometrico' quanto d'immediata presa e orecchiabilità, il risalto dato alle varie soluzioni virtuosistiche messe in atto non deve scontrarsi o

---

[32]. BERNSTEIN, Susan. *Virtuosity of the Nineteenth Century. Performing Music and Language in Heine, Liszt and Baudelaire*, Stanford (CA), Stanford University Press, 1998, p. 86.

[33]. SAMSON, Jim. *Virtuosity and the Musical Work. The Transcendental Studies of Liszt*, Cambridge, Cambridge University Press, 2003, p. 47.

[34]. DAHLHAUS, Carl. 'Che cosa significa improvvisazione?', in: *«In altri termini». Saggi sulla musica*, a cura di Alberto Fassone, Milano, Ricordi, 2009, p. 243. La pubblicazione originale è del 1979.

[35]. BENSON, Bruce Ellis. *The Improvisation of Musical Dialogue. A Phenomenology of Music*, New York, Cambridge University Press, 2003, p. 166. Da un punto di vista estetico, benché oggi sicuramente datate e di valore essenzialmente storiografico, possono comunque risultare ancor degne di un certo interesse le osservazioni fatte da Alfredo Parente in *La musica e le arti* (Bari, Laterza, 1936) in relazione alla netta distinzione tra «momento creativo, assoluto, astorico» e il «momento pratico-tecnico della sua realizzazione, […] contingente e storico». Si veda FUBINI, Enrico. *L'estetica musicale dal Settecento a oggi*, Torino, Einaudi, 2001, p. 256.

[36]. Si veda DAHLHAUS, Carl. *La musica dell'Ottocento*, traduzione di Laura Dallapiccola, Firenze, La Nuova Italia, 1990, p. 148.

esser limitato dal flusso evolutivo del discorso musicale[37]. Proprio per questo motivo, la tendenza a una conduzione del discorso fondamentalmente allergica a rigidi schemi di regole formali, a favore di una propensione per la variazione e per il piccolo pezzo, gode di grande fortuna nel repertorio del violino virtuoso, in linea con la romantica tendenza alla forma *durchkomponiert* e al frammentismo. L'improvvisazione virtuosistica, intesa come occasione di dimostrazione d'abilità tecnica, in un contesto che quasi per antonomasia si caratterizza per una piena libertà formale, si pone in linea di coerenza sia con la labilissima concezione di *Urtext*, propria appunto di Paganini e di quasi tutti i violinisti che si pongono nella sua scia, sia con le particolari scelte da questi operate in ambito formale[38]. Se è sintomatico il parere riservato da Bériot a Rossini, giudicato «uomo di un genio straordinario» nella lettera del 10 gennaio 1822 a Eugène Fontaine[39], la libertà della prassi improvvisativa sembra ben sposarsi con la scarsa simpatia mostrata da Paganini e da coloro che si dimostrarono capaci di coglierne l'eredità nei confronti dei rigidi schemi strutturali propri della forma-sonata classicamente intesa.

Non a caso, accanto all'attenzione dedicata all'arte del preludio, una forma particolarmente amata da Bériot è quella della variazione[40], come dimostrano i 15 *Airs variés* e la quasi totalità delle composizioni per violino e pianoforte. Questo, per una semplice e fors'anche ovvia ragione: lontano dalle costrizioni di tipo formale, tanto la variazione quanto il libero preludiare e il momento improvvisativo garantiscono al solista la miglior possibilità di sviscerare tutta la propria capacità tecnico-esecutiva. Ciò è ancor più valido per Bériot, il cui approccio alle varie problematiche relative alla tecnica strumentale è associato in maniera costante e attenta a un'esigenza di libera espressività, lontano da cervellotiche e astratte teorizzazioni. Questo, in linea di coerenza con la libertà improvvisativa, si riflette anche sulle innovazioni d'ordine formale che Bériot applica nei suoi dieci concerti per violino e orchestra, in cui, accanto al tradizionale impianto dei tre tempi separati, si affianca quello di un solo movimento o di un unico macromovimento, generalmente tripartito, in cui il materiale tematico rifluisce in vari momenti[41].

---

[37].   Specie per quel che riguarda questo periodo storico, l'intero sistema della storia della musica si trova di fronte e sembra reggersi su quella che Dahlhaus definisce «dicotomia» tra la «variante strumentale del virtuosismo operistico» e la «variante operistica del sinfonismo beethoveniano», in riferimento a Wagner (*ibidem*, p. 10).

[38].   Come dimostrato ad esempio anche dalla struttura dei due concerti per violino e orchestra (1834 e 1840-1841) di Ole Bull.

[39].   Bruxelles, Bibliothèque du Conservatoire, RR 32.337: «homme d'un génie extraordinaire».

[40].   Con particolare riferimento ad alcune modalità compositive proprie di Henryk Wieniawski, Renata Suchowiejko, nel capitolo 'Wariacje' della sua monografia *Henryk Wieniawski. Kompozytor na tle wirtuozowskiej tradycji skrzypcowej XIX wieku* (Poznań, Towarzystwo Muzyczne im. Henryka Wieniawskiego, 2005, p. 149) dedicata al virtuoso polacco, discute appunto delle analogie vigenti tra l'arte improvvisativa e la tecnica della variazione.

[41].   Soluzione che, a partire dal Concerto n. 8 di Louis Spohr («in modo di una scena cantante»), trova significative applicazioni in diverse composizioni da concerto di virtuosi d'area franco-belga, come Alexandre

In questo processo di allentamento dei vincoli formali, senza mai disgiungersi dall'afflato del canto, riluce l'intima essenza dell'arte e del lascito paganiniano, poiché la lezione che Paganini trasmise a Liszt e agli altri compositori — aldilà delle epocali innovazioni per quel che concerne il timbro — fu proprio «l'applicazione in prospettiva del virtuosismo come un mezzo compositivo non *per se* ma piuttosto come un mezzo al fine di acquistare maggior libertà inventiva ed espressione artistica»[42]. Non è un caso che, subito dopo la primissima composizione, probabilmente concepita sotto il diretto influsso di Francesco Gnecco — una Sonata del 1790 strutturata, a detta di Pietro Berri[43], secondo i dettami classici, ma di cui ad oggi non si sa nulla — la scelta del Paganini compositore ricada subito su quella che sarà poi la sua forma prediletta: la variazione — come dimostrano le 'Variazioni su La Carmagnola'. In questo contesto la fantasia, il libero cadenzare, come la libertà nel preludiare o l'improvvisare su un dato tema, s'inseriscono con piena e coerente ragion d'essere, a scapito di composizioni dalle architetture formali eccessivamente laboriose.

Esattamente come per la musica di Rossini, inoltre, era ben raro che la stessa composizione virtuosistica fosse eseguita ogni volta nella medesima versione. Questo dato, che quindi comporta quasi necessariamente una propensione all'improvvisazione, può dirsi valido per la quasi totalità dei violinisti virtuosi che di Paganini furono contemporanei o che ne seguirono l'esempio. In parte se ne distanziarono artisti come Pierre Baillot, ma anche i maturi Camillo Sivori e Joseph Joachim, per i quali, terminata la fase delle composizioni giovanili e dei numerosi concerti all'insegna del virtuosismo più sfrenato, poi gradatamente sostituito da una più ligia interpretazione dei classici, il rispettoso ossequio del testo scritto divenne un imprescindibile valore.

È possibile affermare che praticamente a nessun violinista — o, più in generale, strumentista — attivo in questa fase storica fu estranea la pratica dell'improvvisazione. Per quel che riguarda Paganini, una testimonianza di approccio libero nei confronti del testo musicale, con evidenti tendenze all'improvvisazione, è rintracciabile nelle pagine redatte da Pietro Lichtenthal, autore della *Autobiografia di Paganini da lui stesso dettata all'Autore di questo Almanacco, prima della sua partenza per Vienna, il giorno 28 febbraio 1828, a Milano*, dove si legge: «Cercando varietà nelle suonate eseguite alla Corte [di Lucca], una sera togliendo due corde del violino (la seconda e la terza) improvvisò una suonata intitolata Scena amorosa, figurando la quarta corda il maschio (Adone), e il cantino la femmina (Venere), ed ecco d'onde nacque in lui il suonare una sola corda»,

---

Artôt e Hubert Léonard, negli ultimi concerti di Lipiński e in qualche opera di Antonio Bazzini.

[42]. BORER, Philippe. *The Twenty-Four Caprices of Paganini and Their Significance in the Romantic Era*, Zurigo, Stiftung Zentralstelle der Studentenschaft der Universität Zürich, 1997, p. 43: «[...] the prospective application of virtuosity as a compositional tool not per se but rather as a means to achieve greater freedom of invention and artistic expression».

[43]. BERRI, Pietro. *Paganini. La vita e le opere*, Milano, Bompiani, 1982, p. 38.

ed ancora: «[Paganini] suonò sempre a capriccio, accompagnato dal pianoforte, per cui scrisse sempre un basso immaginandovi un tema musicale»[44]. Nella lettera bolognese del primo luglio 1818, indirizzata a Luigi Germi, dopo aver espresso un giudizio positivo sul violinista piemontese Felice Radicati, Paganini scrive: «L'altro ieri eseguì un quartetto di Haydn, io ne eseguij un altro come si trovava scritto ma a dirti il vero scaturì dalla mia esecuzione una certa magìa che non saprei descriverti»[45]. Quest'affermazione, se conferma l'assoluta importanza assegnata al momento performativo, evidenzia come Paganini senta il bisogno di specificare — essendo probabilmente un caso raro — la sua fedeltà al testo scritto. Paolo Luigi Raby, nella pur entusiastica recensione apparsa sulla *Gazzetta Piemontese* del 14 e 17 febbraio 1818, in cui si commentava il concerto tenuto da Paganini al Teatro Carignano, sottolineava «il lusso de' tanti ricami», ma anche l'abitudine a «non attenersi strettamente alle note»[46]; importante a tale riguardo è l'osservazione di Massimo Quarta e Francesco Fiore riguardo alle due piccole cadenze manoscritte di Paganini, concepite per l'inedito 'Adagio' in mi maggiore, quale ulteriore dimostrazione della sua pratica improvvisativa[47].

Nell'Ottocento l'arte dell'improvvisazione virtuosa fu quasi una costante nella carriera artistica di Ole Bull, il violinista norvegese che viene dichiaratamente a porsi nella scia di Paganini. Documentate, infatti, diverse sue improvvisazioni in vari concerti: in quello bolognese del 1834, sia libere che su motivi tratti da *Norma* e *I Capuleti e i Montecchi* di Bellini e *Le siège de Corinthe* di Rossini; in occasione di quello praghese del 1841 sul motivo popolare ceco 'Sil jem proso na souvrati'; durante il concerto lipsiense dello stesso anno sulle arie 'Ecco il ridente cielo', 'Son vergin vezzosa' e 'Fin ch'han dal vino calda la testa' tratte da *Il barbiere di Siviglia*, *I Puritani*, e *Don Giovanni*[48]. E se Heinrich Wilhelm Ernst, forse il vero erede di Paganini, durante l'esecuzione della cadenza del concerto mendelssohniano «triplicava le difficoltà introducendo ottave e

---

[44]. Pubblicata per la prima volta nell'*Allgemeine musikalische Zeitung*, XXXII/20 (1830), pp. 326-327, poi nell'*Almanacco storico, estetico, musicale, umoristico del Dottor Pietro Lichtenthal* (Milano, Ricordi, 1853), l'autobiografia paganiniana è riportata integralmente in NEILL, Edward. *Nicolò Paganini. Il cavaliere filarmonico*, Genova, De Ferrari, 1990, pp. 294-295.

[45]. *Niccolò Paganini. Epistolario 1810-1831*, a cura di Roberto Grisley, Milano, Skira, 2006, p. 122.

[46]. Citato in MOFFA, Rosy. *Storia della Regia Cappella di Torino*, Torino, Centro Studi Piemontesi, 1990, p. 130. A ulteriore testimonianza della diffusione della pratica improvvisativa presso i violinisti italiani di questo periodo basti vedere quel che dice Nicola Petrini Zamboni, che di Paganini fu anche amico: parlando dell'esecuzione della Sinfonia della *Lodoïska*, egli ammette tranquillamente di eseguire la sua parte «con gli armonici», variando estemporaneamente quanto scritto in partitura. Si veda PETRINI ZAMBONI, Nicola. *Memorie di un violinista cesenate (1785-1849)*, a cura di Franco Dell'Amore, Cesena, Comune di Cesena, 1995, p. 30.

[47]. Si veda KAWABATA, Maiko. 'Violinists 'Singing'. Paganini, Operatic Voices, and Virtuosity', in: *Ad Parnassum: A Journal of Eighteenth- and Nineteenth Century Instrumental Music*, V/9 (2007), pp. 7-39: 12.

[48]. Si veda HAUGEN, Einar - CAI, Camilla. *Ole Bull. Norway's Romantic Musician and Cosmopolitan Patriot*, Madison, University of Wisconsin Press, 1993, pp. 253, 296 e 300.

doppie corde che, pure preservando il carattere originale, contribuivano materialmente alla sua brillantezza»[49], anche Alexandre Boucher, il virtuoso-patriota fervido ammiratore di Napoleone, in occasione di un concerto inglese «suonò delle variazioni improvvisate sul tema di 'God save the King'»[50].

Ancora, Warwick Lister ha di recente fornito importanti testimonianze a conferma che l'arte dell'improvvisazione non era sconosciuta neanche a Giovanni Battista Viotti, maestro di André Robberechts, come dimostra tra l'altro l'autografo londinese dell''Andante Sostenuto' centrale del Concerto per violino e orchestra n. 27[51]. Un'altra testimonianza a questo riguardo è infine quella fornita da François Fayolle nel suo *Paganini et Bériot* (1831): parlando a proposito del violinista Louis-Julien Castel de Labarre, allievo di Viotti, egli scrive: «suonava magistralmente i *solo*, spesso negli Adagio, improvvisando fioriture secondo l'esempio del suo maestro»[52].

In concreto, l'arte dell'improvvisazione, il cui fine precipuo rimane sempre lo sfoggio di abilità tecniche di vario tipo, è essenzialmente connessa alla forma della variazione melodico-ornamentale: le tipologie più diffuse riguardano l'estemporaneo inserimento di abbellimenti, e l'invenzione di 'fermate' (chiamate *points d'orgue* nella trattatistica francese) o cadenze[53].

La scuola violinistica franco-belga sembra dimostrare una vivacità non indifferente, allorquando, con Rossini in ritiro e la riscoperta della *Matthäus Passion* ad opera di Mendelssohn, Paganini — anche grazie alle monografie a lui dedicate, tutte nel 1830, da Carl Guhr, Georg Harrys e Georges Imbert de Laphalèque — è promosso da conclamato fenomeno di costume a elemento fondante della storia della musica europea[54]. Nella *System der Ästhetik als Wissenshaft von der Idee der Schönheit* di

---

[49]. La testimonianza, riferita a un concerto tenuto a Manchester nel 1849, è riportata in ROWE, Marc W. *Op. cit.* (si veda nota 16), p. 172: «[…] tripled the difficulties by introducing octaves and double notes, which, while preserving its character, materially added to its brilliancy».

[50]. FÉTIS, François-Joseph. *Histoire générale de la musique depuis les temps les plus anciens jusqu'à nos jours*, 5 voll., Parigi, Didot, 1874, vol. II, p. 39: «[…] joua des variations improvisées sur *God save the King*».

[51]. LISTER, Warwick. *Amico. The Life of Giovanni Battista Viotti*, New York, Oxford University Press, 2009, pp. 109-110. Sulla base dell'edizione Sieber, del 1788, del Concerto per violino e orchestra n. 15 lo studioso dimostra sia come la pratica improvvisativa viottiana non fosse limitata semplicemente ai movimenti centrali sia quanto siano state importanti le relazioni tra improvvisazione, ornamentazione e utilizzo del *tempo rubato* per la definizione dello stile violinistico non solo direttamente di Viotti ma anche di tutti i violinisti che del Piemontese assunsero la lezione.

[52]. Citato in POUGIN, Arthur. *Viotti et l'école modern de violon*, Parigi, Schott, 1888, p. 136: «[Labarre] jouait supérieurement le solo, surtout dans l'*adagio*, en improvisant des broderies, à l'exemple de son maître»

[53]. Si veda STOWELL, Robin. *Op. cit.* (si veda nota 19), p. 337: «The incidence of improvisation can be subdivided into four main areas: the variation of melody, the decoration of fermatas and the extemporisation of both cadenzas and preludes».

[54]. GUHR, Carl. *Ueber Paganini's Kunst die Violine zu spielen*, Magonza, Schott, 1830; HARRYS, Georg. *Paganini in seinem Reisewagen und Zimmer*, Braunschweig, F. Vieweg, 1830; IMBERT DE LAPHALÈQUE, Georges (= L'HÉRITIER, Louis-François). *Notice sur le célèbre violiniste [sic] Nicolo Paganini*, Parigi, E. Guyot, 1830.

Christian Hermann Weisse, edita quest'anno, inoltre, la 'modernità' dello spirito viene caratterizzata in base al grado di indipendenza e autosufficienza che solo la musica propriamente strumentale può dare[55]. Alla triade parigina Viotti / Kreutzer / Baillot viene a sostituirsi quella di marca franco-belga, formata da Bériot / Vieuxtemps / Wieniawski, in cui è la rivoluzionaria lezione di Paganini a costituire il cruciale comune denominatore e l'elemento caratterizzante. Anche gli anni 1838-1840 possono esser visti come spartiacque nell'evoluzione della storia del violino, con la parabola artistica paganiniana ormai conclusa, il riconoscimento di Viotti quale pilastro della scuola violinistica francese (come dimostrato dal giudizio di Henri Blanchard[56]) e la fine della brillante carriera concertistica di Bériot. Questa, come quella di molti altri violinisti e più genericamente dei virtuosi, anche di altri strumenti, non sembra d'altronde risentire troppo di quella insofferenza verso l'esibizione dell'abilità tecnica che, sin dal personaggio di Pococurante del *Candide* di Voltaire, viene poi a cristallizzarsi principalmente negli scritti di Schumann, Heine e Hoffmann[57]. In particolare, è il secondo che, specie in vari passaggi dei *Reisenbilder* o delle *Florentinische Nächte*, riesce a cogliere l'esatta cifra e la peculiare natura del virtuosismo violinistico.

Per quel che concerne l'impiego da parte di Bériot delle varie soluzioni tecnico-virtuosistiche relative alla mano sinistra e ai diversi colpi d'arco è quasi ovvio parlare di eredità paganiniana, ma questa va intesa anche in senso più lato. Inserendosi nella scia del virtuoso genovese per quel che riguarda l'approccio strumentale e — seppur con una prolissità ben maggiore — le scelte formali, Bériot sembra infatti condividere e accentuare anche la romantica contraddizione che vede la *coincidentia oppositorum* tra due differenti poli: da un lato un'emancipazione/autonomia del discorso esclusivamente strumentale, dall'altro una costante ed evidente analogia, per quel che concerne le modalità di costruzione fraseologica e agogica, con il mondo dell'opera[58]. In entrambi i casi l'improvvisazione gioca un ruolo fondamentale.

Questa forma d'arte, seppur in diversi modi e sotto differenti prospettive, ha accompagnato l'evolversi di tutto il repertorio violinistico, dai primordi sino alle produzioni

---

[55]. Si veda DAHLHAUS, Carl. *The Idea of Absolute Music*, traduzione a cura di Roger Lustig, Chicago, University of Chicago Press, 1989, p. 76.

[56]. Nell'articolo 'Physiologie du violon', pubblicato sulla *Revue et Gazette Musicale de Paris* del 28 luglio 1839, p. 389, l'autore spiega anche le connessioni tra Viotti e i suoi principali discepoli: «Viotti jeta les fondements de l'école française moderne du violon. Il laissa dans Paris [...] Rode, son élève favori, qui réunissait la grâce à la pureté; Rodolphe Kreutzer, à la tête puissante, à l'archet large et vigoureux; et Baillot, faisant revivre toutes les anciennes écoles d'Italie et de France. Ce triumvirat violiniste a régné pendant près de cinquante ans sur l'Europe musicale».

[57]. Si veda CHANTLER, Abigail. *E. T. A. Hoffmann's Musical Aesthetics*, Aldershot, Ashgate, 2006, p. 88.

[58]. Sulle interazioni tra i due campi, anche con riferimenti alle diverse percezioni delle 'vocalità' pianistiche di Sigismond Thalberg, Fryderyk Chopin, Johann Baptist Cramer e John Field, si veda KAWABATA, Maiko. *Op. cit.* (si veda nota 47), p. 14.

più recenti[59]; ma è con Paganini, e con la metabolizzazione del suo lascito, che sembra ricevere piena dignità estetica. Ancora, l'istanza improvvisativa acquista, nell'architettura strutturale del concerto solistico di marca viottiana, un'importanza ben diversa e maggiore rispetto agli schemi formali del concerto d'area tedesca: se in quest'ultimo caso, infatti, la libera cadenza si trova quasi sempre verso la fine del primo movimento, nel concerto maturato in area parigina la fermata, sovente intesa come invito a un'estemporanea improvvisazione, è posizionata all'interno dello sviluppo, come secondo episodio solistico[60].

Il dato emozionale, che deve esser la *condicio sine qua non* del momento improvvisativo, come ben dimostrano varie affermazioni fatte nella *Préface* de l'*Art du prélude*, rimane la pietra angolare della teoria del virtuoso belga, sia per quel riguarda in generale l'approccio alle varie problematiche tecnico-strumentali sia nel particolare della pratica improvvisativa: «Dal momento che la musica è prima di tutto una lingua di sentimento, la sua melodia contiene sempre in sé un senso poetico»[61]. Se questo appare assolutamente coerente con il pensiero musicale dell'Ottocento a livello generale, nello specifico del campo violinistico basterà ricordare il motto paganiniano «Bisogna forte sentire per far sentire!». Inoltre, Bériot sembra condividere in pieno il pensiero di Baillot, il quale, nella sua opera pedagogica principale, definisce come fine principale della musica appunto quello di «commuovere, di parlare all'anima recando piacere all'orecchio, di fare nascere un'immagine nello spirito, e più sovente ancora, un sentimento nel cuore»[62]. L'arte improvvisativa, inoltre, in nome della sua implicita libertà e propensione alla *variatio*, ben si coniuga con i costanti richiami di Bériot alla sfera della lingua parlata, come dimostrano i vari accenni alle convenzioni ritmiche e prosodiche che di questa stabiliscono le regole basilari: «Quando si tratta di distribuire le arcate al fine di fare parlare la melodia [...] si deve necessariamente seguire la varietà delle inflessioni del linguaggio reale o finto che ci impongono le leggi della

---

[59]. Secondo David Boyden la prima relazione diretta tra il violino e l'improvvisazione è stabilita negli *Harmonicarum libri* di Marin Mersenne del 1636. Si veda BOYDEN, David. *The History of Violin Playing from its Origins to 1761*, London, Oxford University Press, 1965, p. 89.

[60]. Seguendo questo esempio, applicato in diversi concerti da Rode e Kreutzer, si muove ad esempio Wieniawski nell''Allegro moderato' del Concerto per violino e orchestra, Op. 14, n. 1. Si veda LEHER, Charles-David. *The Nineteenth-Century Parisian Concerto*, Ph.D. Diss., Los Angeles (CA), University of California, 1990, pp. 123-124, e SZYMAŃKA, Alicja. 'The Issue of the Sonata Form in the Concertos of Henryk Wieniawski', in: *Henryk Wieniawski. Composer and Virtuoso in the Musical Culture of the XIX and XX Centuries*, a cura di Maciej Jabłoński & Danuta Jasińka, Poznań, Rhytmos, 2001, pp. 83-101: 89.

[61]. BÉRIOT, Charles-Auguste de. *Méthode de violon, op. cit.* (si veda nota 7), p. ii: «La musique étant, avant tout, une langue de sentiment, sa mélodie renferme toujours en elle un sens poétique». Un primo compiuto antecedente di questo modo d'intendere la musica si potrebbe rintracciare in Geminiani, del quale *The Art of Playing the Violin* (1751) si apre appunto con la frase: «The Intention of Musick is not only to please the Ear, but to express the Sentiments, strike the Imagination, affect the Mind, and command the Passions».

[62]. BAILLOT, Pierre. *L'art du violon. Nouvelle méthode*, Parigi, Imprimerie du Conservatoire, [1834], p. 163: «[...] émouvoir, de parler à l'âme en charmant l'oreille, de faire naître une image dans l'esprit, et plus souvent encore, un sentiment dans le coeur».

melodia»[63]. Questi ricorrenti accostamenti tra la musica e la lingua parlata sono d'altronde assolutamente coerenti con un certo gusto salottiero che, nel periodo di attività del virtuoso belga, godette di enorme fortuna[64]. A conferma della diffusione dello *style dialogué*, come testimoniato dal titolo *Six simphonies ou quatuors dialogués* dato all'Op. 1 di Joseph Haydn o anche dal *Quatuor dialogué* di Michel Woldemar, Jérôme-Joseph Momigny consiglia ai musicisti di essere «continui e conseguenti nei loro discorsi e proposizioni, floridi nelle loro espressioni, capaci di contrasto nell'impiego dei loro colori, graduati nei loro effetti»[65].

Ancora, per quel che concerne l'improvvisazione, Castil-Blaze, dopo aver ribadito l'ovvia necessità di una grande competenza strumentale e il bisogno di unità e d'insieme — inteso come un'esposizione coerente e dosata delle idee — che non deve mai venir meno nel momento improvvisativo, pone l'accento sul «cuore facile da riscaldare e da commuovere»[66].

L'attenzione dedicata al preludio, in linea con quanto già scritto nella *Méthode*, primo livello dell'improvvisazione, a sua volta primo passo verso l'arte della composizione, viene a inserirsi quindi con coerenza all'interno della concezione estetica e artistica di colui che può senza dubbio esser annoverato come uno dei più importanti virtuosi dell'Ottocento. Questo anche in ragione del suo ruolo congiunturale: nello stile di Bériot, infatti, le innovazioni proprie della 'lezione' paganiniana si innestano su un sostrato stilistico di chiara marca parigina. Esattamente come per Baillot, e in generale per ogni virtuoso, la composizione era considerata «quale il perfetto complemento del talento dell'esecuzione»[67]. È proprio a quanto scrive Baillot sulla pratica del libero preludiare o dell'improvvisare *ex abrupto* che è necessario guardare per capire l'impostazione e il fine dell'*Art du prélude* di Bériot. Il francese, dopo aver specificato infatti quali differenze vi siano tra i vari *point de repos*, si sofferma sulla tipologia dei *points d'orgue*, distinguendone ben dieci categorie di massima.

---

[63]. Bériot, Charles-Auguste de. *Méthode de violon, op. cit.* (si veda nota 7), p. 213: «Lorsque il s'agit de distribuer les coups d'archet de façon à faire parler la mélodie […] il faut de toute nécessité suivre la variété des inflexions de la parole réelle ou fictive qui nous imposent les lois de la mélodie».

[64]. Si veda Hanning, Barbara R. 'Conversation and Musical Style in the Late Eighteenth-Century Parisian Salon', in: *Eighteenth-Century Studies*, xxii/4 (1989), pp. 512-528.

[65]. Momigny, Jérôme-Joseph. *Cours complet d'harmonie et de composition*, Parigi, Autore, 1808, p. 678: «Soyez suivis et conséquents dans vos propos ou propositions, fleuris dans vos expressions, contrastés dans l'emploi de vos couleurs, gradués dans vos effects». In ambito violinistico, Habeneck scrive a riguardo: «Dans la mélodie comme dans le discours, il y a des periods, des phrases et des memebres ou dessins». Si veda Habeneck, François. *Op. cit.* (si veda nota 22), p. 107.

[66]. Castil-Blaze [François-Henri-Joseph Blaze]. 'Improviser', in: *Dictionnaire de musique moderne*, Parigi, La Lyre Moderne, 1825, pp. 298-299: «coeur facile à échauffer et à émouvoir».

[67]. Suchowiejko, Renata. 'Virtuoso - An Incarnation of God or Devil? Some Thoughts about Violin Virtuosity in the 19th Century', in: *Instrumental Music and the Industrial Revolution*, a cura di Roberto Illiano e Luca Sala, Bologna, Ut Orpheus Edizioni, 2010, pp. 99-106: 100: «as the perfect complement of the talent to perform».

L'attenzione di Baillot si sofferma in particolare — con maggiore precisione rispetto al suo mancato successore Bériot — sulla divisione tra *Préludes mélodiques* e *Préludes harmoniques*, come anche sulla differenza vigente tra *Prélude écrit* e *Prélude improvisé*, che è quello che «permette al virtuoso di abbandonarsi completamente alle sue ispirazioni»[68]. Nelle 'Règles générales' poste alla fine del discorso, l'autore anticipa concetti sui quali anche Bériot si soffermerà nella sua *Art du prélude*: il bisogno di *varietas* e la necessità di mantenere sempre una giusta misura. Infine, già in Baillot è riscontrabile una certa labilità terminologica tra *improvisation* et *prélude*: «Il preludio improvvisato […] si può chiamare *preludio di fantasia* o *improvvisazione*; è libero nel suo procedere, nelle sue forme, nella sua durata: onore a colui che, seguendo l'impulso del suo genio, può allo stesso tempo impiegare tutte le risorse dell'arte in questo genere di fantasticheria che gli permette di raggiungere il sublime!»[69].

Secondo il concetto d'improvvisazione brillante proprio del virtuoso belga, le soluzioni tecnico-stilistiche devono esser sempre impiegate *cum grano salis*, in relazione al contesto e al tipo di musica che si sta eseguendo: la validità e l'importanza di questi precetti risultano chiare e funzionali quindi non solo nel nuovo stile virtuosistico del musicista belga, ma soprattutto per quel che riguarda la stragrande maggioranza della produzione concertistica ottocentesca per violino. In maniera differente rispetto all'impiego più diretto e massiccio della tecnica avanzata da parte di solisti del calibro di Lipiński, Ernst, Vieuxtemps e Wieniawski, nelle opere di Bériot, insieme a un più attento e dosato utilizzo dei vari artifici virtuosistici, centrale rimane sempre la riflessione sul *caractère*[70], sulla differenziazione agogica e quasi 'spirituale', centro nevralgico dell'arte improvvisativa. Passaggio obbligato volto a sostanziare e nobilitare l'approccio con qualsivoglia difficoltà di tipo tecnico-strumentale, all'interno della concezione artistica di Bériot tale peculiarità si pone, più in generale, come pietra di volta di ogni discorso relativo all'espressività musicale. Questo perché l'improvvisazione, ancor di più quella con forte matrice virtuosistica, è direttamente connessa con la sfera della mera 'intenzionalità' espressiva propria di ciascun esecutore[71].

---

[68]. BAILLOT, Pierre. *Op. cit.* (si veda nota 62), p. 183: «[…] permet au virtuose de se livrer entièrement à ses inspirations».

[69]. *Ibidem*, p. 184: «Le *Prélude improvisé* […] peut être appelé *prélude de fantasie* ou *improvisation*; il est libre dans son allure, dans ses formes, dans sa durée: honneur à qui, suivant l'impulsion de son génie, peut en même temps déployer toutes les ressources de l'art dans ce genre de rêverie qui lui permet d'atteindre jusqu'au sublime!».

[70]. Una cui ottima dimostrazione consiste nelle singole spiegazioni del 'carattere' riferito a ogni singolo capriccio delle *12 Scènes ou caprices*, Op. 109, dedicate a François-Joseph Fétis.

[71]. DAHLHAUS, Carl. *Op. cit.* (si veda nota 34), p. 246: «In ogni caso il concetto di "ciò che non è fissato con la notazione", con il quale opera la teoria dell'improvvisazione, designa primariamente fenomeni situati non soltanto al di là di una notazione che esprime per mezzo di simboli ciò che è acusticamente "reale", ma anche al di là di un testo che include, inoltre, il momento musicale "intenzionale" — e i mezzi per renderlo in tutta chiarezza».

Mentre il pianoforte, per intrinseche ragioni meccaniche, può esser considerato come ideale mezzo d'espressione del virtuosismo romantico, al violino viene demandato l'altrettanto fondamentale compito dell'espressione della più appassionata liricità: questo assunto è valido anche in riferimento alla pratica improvvisativa, come dimostrano le costanti e puntuali analogie evidenziate da Bériot tra voce del violino e voce umana, e le sue avvertenze a frenare gli eccessi di sterile virtuosismo. Anche per quel che concerne i criteri informanti l'arte del libero preludiare, Bériot s'inserisce coerentemente nel corso della storia della musica, riprendendo concetti già espressi. Gli avvertimenti relativi al *jugement* e al *goût* riprendono infatti in maniera analoga i consigli alla moderazione espressi del *Versuch einer Anweisung die Flöte traversiere zu spielen* di Johann Joachim Quantz, in particolare nel Paragrafo 27 del Capitolo 12, 'Von der Art das Allegro zu spielen' (Della maniera di suonare l'Allegro). La critica di Bériot nei confronti di quei virtuosi incapaci di controllare la propria foga suona inoltre, *mutatis mutandis*, simile a quanto osservato da Quantz nei paragrafi conclusivi dell'ultimo capitolo, 'Wie ein Musikus und eine Musik zu beurtheilen sey' (Come un musicista e una musica siano da giudicare), circa gli 'eccessi' di Giuseppe Tartini e dei concerti di Vivaldi tecnicamente più impegnativi[72]. Anche in questo Bériot sembra raccogliere la lezione di Baillot, il quale a proposito dell'improvvisazione di ornamenti pone tra le regole basilari una giusta proporzione e attinenza al pezzo che si sta eseguendo, specificando anche in quali casi è preferibile non aggiungere nulla al testo scritto[73]. L'arte del libero preludiare, inoltre, viene già presentata da L'Abbé *le fils* improntata a una forte istanza didattica[74], e sia Baillot che Bériot mantengono ferma tale prerogativa.

La centralità del momento improvvisativo, su cui Bériot sofferma la sua attenzione, risulta ancor più importante alla luce dell'assunto principale della musica virtuosistica dell'Ottocento: che il contesto sia quello della *Hausmusik* o dei pubblici concerti, la relazione tra testo e *performance* conserva molta di quella fluidità che, usualmente e giustamente, viene associata alle prassi esecutive del secolo precedente. Ma se questo è un dato inconfutabile, altrettanto innegabile è che la mancanza di rispetto per il testo scritto e un'eccessiva, debordante libertà esecutiva iniziavano ormai a esser sempre meno tollerate. Eloquente è a riguardo anche il giudizio di Wagner, secondo cui la vera natura del virtuoso

---

[72]. Si veda Boyden, David. *Op. cit.* (si veda nota 59), p. 458. Giustamente tale affermazione di Quantz viene dallo studioso inglese connessa con quanto sarcasticamente osservato da Leopold Mozart nel suo *Versuch einer gründlichen Violinschule* (Augusta, 1756) all'interno della Sezione n. 3 del Capitolo d'apertura, p. 50: «Diese Notenwürger legen dadurch ihre schlechte Beurtheilungskraft zu Tage, und zittern, wenn sie eine lange Note aushalten oder nur ein paar Noten singbar abspielen sollen, ohne ihr angewöhntes, ungereimtes und lächerliches Fick Fack einzumischen». (Questi assassini di note portano alla luce il loro cattivo giudizio, e tremano quando devono sostenere una nota lunga o suonare solo poche note alla volta, senza inserire i loro abituali irragionevoli e ridicoli fronzoli.)

[73]. Baillot, Pierre. *Op. cit.* (si veda nota 62), p. 162.

[74]. L'Abbé *le fils* [Joseph-Barnabé Saint-Sévin]. *Principes du violon pour apprendre la doigté de cet instrument et les différentes agréements dont il est susceptible*, Parigi, Lauries, 1761, pp. 68-71.

consiste proprio nell'esatta realizzazione del pensiero del compositore: all'appropriazione e all'intima adesione verso i dettami del compositore deve corrispondere una totale rinuncia, da parte dell'esecutore, del proprio estro inventivo[75].

D'altronde, esattamente come la pratica dell'improvvisazione nasce quasi in contemporanea con lo strumento stesso del violino, per raggiungere uno dei picchi massimi durante l'età romantica, così anche le raccomandazioni di fedeltà al testo e all'idea del compositore — contrappeso e freno della libertà improvvisativa — si possono già trovare nella *Regola Rubertina* di Sylvestro Ganassi[76]. Per Rossini, Paganini e Liszt, il testo viene comunque sempre concepito «in un senso di 'compimento' dall'esecutore»[77], con l'implicita considerazione del fattore improvvisativo: sintomatico che anche Baillot si soffermi espressamente sul *génie d'éxécution* (genio d'esecuzione)[78]. Tale assunto risulta ancora valido per Bériot. Più che a problematiche di tipo formale, l'attenzione quindi è sempre e comunque rivolta alla brillantezza dell'esecuzione, ed è esattamente in questo senso e a tal fine che va considerato il trattato, e quindi l'idea stessa di improvvisazione, del virtuoso di Lovanio. Questo, poco prima del definitivo declino e del quasi inevitabile scadimento della pratica improvvisativa a mera pratica trivializzata, dove alla mancanza d'originalità subentra un estenuante e quasi circense esibizionismo di acrobazie tecniche[79]. L'improvvisazione virtuosistica tende poi a tramontare definitivamente quando il rispetto e l'osservanza del testo scritto diventano patrimonio acquisito e indiscutibile[80].

---

[75]. WAGNER, Richard. 'Über das Dirigieren', in: *Gesammelte Schriften und Dichtungen*, a cura di Karl Ferdinand Siegel, 10 voll., Lipsia, Fritsch, 1897, vol. I, pp. 169-170.

[76]. GANASSI, Sylvestro. *Regola Rubertina*, Venezia, l'Autore, 1542, Parte II, Capitolo 16, 'Raggionamento dil natural del Violon & il modo di pratticarlo in tal effeto': «non accrescere ne mancare di quello chel compositore l'hauera ordinada». Come ricordato da BOYDEN, David. *Op. cit.* (si veda nota 59), p. 89, sia in questo trattato che ne *La Fontegara* viene comunque discussa la pratica dell'improvvisazione.

[77]. SAMSON, Jim. 'The Musical Work and the Nineteenth-Century History', in: *The Cambridge History of Nineteenth-Century Music*, a cura di Jim Samson, Cambridge, Cambridge University Press, 2002, p. 26: «in a sense of 'completion' by the performer».

[78]. BAILLOT, Pierre. *Op. cit.* (si veda nota 62), p. 266.

[79]. SAFFLE, Michael. 'Czerny and the Keyboard Fantasy. Traditions, Innovations, Legacy', in: *Beyond the Art of Finger Dexterity. Reassessing Carl Czerny*, a cura di David Gramit, Rochester (NY), University of Rochester Press, 2008, pp. 202-228: 223: «Today, improvisation is largely the province of church organists and of jazz and popular musicians; few 'classical' musicians, for instance, invent even their own cadenzas. As publication replaced spontaneity and hit tunes replaced 'hidden' harmonic secrets, virtuosity itself became the province of men and women trained to play what was put before them rather than invent it themselves». All'interno del repertorio violinistico, la pratica improvvisativa troverà poi — in tutt'altro contesto e con ben altri presupposti — valida e credibile ragion d'essere grazie all'integrazione e alla metabolizzazione in alcune strutture formali di natura rapsodica, come diverse composizioni di Jean Sibelius, Béla Bartók, Karol Szimanowski e Ernst Bloch ben dimostrano.

[80]. Si veda anche NOVEMBER, Nancy. 'Off-String in Beethoven. Re-examining the Evidence', in: *Ad Parnassum: A Journal of Eighteenth- and Nineteenth Century Instrumental Music*, VII/14 (2009), pp. 129-153: 153.

Charles-Auguste de Bériot e l'improvvisazione virtuosistica per violino

English Summary

Charles-Auguste de Bériot and Virtuoso Improvisation for Violin

Renato Ricco

For the nineteenth-century violinist Charles-Auguste de Bériot (1802-1870), improvisation was a vital element of his career, both as a performer and as a teacher. Although trained in a classical manner by Pierre Baillot, his style of performance accords more with the expressive and sometimes extravagant style of Paganini, in which improvisation is absolutely indispensable. Improvisation is amply discussed in Bériot's *L'art du prélude*, published posthumously in 1875, at a time when it was practiced progressively less by violin virtuosos, due to the increasing wishes of composers that performers adhere to written text. Bériot emphasises that a good performer must be both a good improviser and composer. In his *L'art du prélude* Bériot provides a comprehensive series of examples of what preludes can entail: upward and downward scales in many varieties, broken chords, all kinds of bowing. All these figures can be part of improvisations. The last example of *L'art du prélude* is a 'Prélude ou Improvisation'. In the second part of the essay connections are made with the performance practice of Paganini and other contemporaries, and it is shown that Bériot's practice of varying and ornamenting existing material is a late example of a centuries-old tradition, which is actually waning during the second half of the nineteenth century.

The Advantages and Drawbacks of Notation, or How to Face Improvisatory Elements in Nineteenth-Century Hungarian Popular Music

Csilla Pethő-Vernet
(Paris)

The corpus which determined nineteenth-century Hungarian music and which influenced to a great extent the country's whole musical life was a specific one, including instrumental dance pieces. They emerged from the last decades of the eighteenth century, absorbing various — Hungarian and non-Hungarian — musical elements but, as their style crystallized into a homogenous musical language, they were rapidly perceived as the manifestations of a genuine national style. This style, like the repertoire itself, was called later *verbunkos*. Although *verbunkos* music was present in everyday musical life, functioning mainly as music for entertainment, it made a profound impact on the artistic achievements of those who tried to establish a particular Hungarian musical language in the field of art music. In spite of this, it retained its popular context for a long time. It was present both in the very first Hungarian operas and at the balls, political events, vintages, in the village pubs or in the restaurants and cafés of the towns. Its public came from the most varied social classes.

In the emerging phase of the *verbunkos*, before 1800, pieces came to existence often without the creative act of a specific composer. The creation of *verbunkos* music was rooted in an oral, or, more precisely, in an instrumental performing tradition (as we are basically talking about an instrumental repertoire). In spite of this, a considerable number of these early anonymous pieces were published in publications also containing Hungarian dances composed by several, lesser known composers of the time. Thus, the individual creation and the traditional, 'handcrafted' creation lived together, side by side, and certainly influenced each other. Later on, in the first decades of the nineteenth century, the individualization of the act of composing came into prominence: the published pieces were more often the creations of one or another composer. From this period, we have to mention three composers-musicians whose musical activity played a large part in the elaboration and crystallization of the *verbunkos* style: János Bihari, János Lavotta and Antal Csermák. The case of one of them is especially worth examining. Whereas Lavotta and Csermák were composers in the strict sense of the word, noting down their own compositions, Bihari was different. He was a well-known Gypsy violinist of his time, renowned for his great talent, and having his own Gypsy band. There is nothing special about this, considering the fact that in Hungary, for centuries, the profession of the entertaining musician was reserved for the Gypsies. Therefore, also during the nineteenth century, the unique performers of the popular dance repertoires, such as the *verbunkos* and later on the *csárdás*, were Gypsy orchestras. The best ones achieved a high artistic level and considerable technical skill. Bihari's orchestra was only one of the best Gypsy orchestras. The interesting thing about Bihari is rather that, as were his fellow musicians, he was, in the musical sense of the word, illiterate. In other words, he did not know musical notation, and he was unable to write or read a score, or even a few notes of music. This is more than surprising in case of someone who is nevertheless considered by Hungarian historiography as one of the main *verbunkos* composers.

On the other hand, musical illiteracy was a general phenomenon amongst the Gypsy musicians, who learned the pieces by ear, and played them without score, by heart. This was quite normal, a usual practice at least until the mid-nineteenth century when, due to the growing demands of a larger public (in Hungary and abroad) in terms of repertoire, some of the musicians undertook a more serious musical training[1]. Until this point, playing music was a natural, instinctive activity for the Gypsy musicians. Accordingly, in Bihari's case, the compositional process was far from the usual one. He composed directly on his violin, and presumably, improvisation played an important role in the musical creation. His pieces existed only in his memory, on his violin, and they did not have a definitive form (as he was absolutely free to change anything in every moment of the execution), until the moment when a listener, amateur or professional musician, noted it down to be remembered and to make its publication possible.

Considering all these historical data, it is quite obvious that improvisation was an essential element of the *verbunkos* music, and even in the 'compositional' phase, as demonstrated by the example of Bihari. Moreover, we may suppose that the genesis of the early pieces was similar: the musicians played and replayed, varied and transformed more or less fixed elements, to bring them together, more frequently within the frame of a two- or three-period structure, in an improvisatory manner. Improvisation had an important role in performance practice too. Already existing dance pieces could be performed with various ornamental passages, slight or more visible changes could occur during the various performances of the pieces, partly due to the lack of a fixed version during the rehearsals, and in the performing process, partly due to the known predilection of Gypsy musicians for improvised virtuoso solo passages and freely introduced, rich embellishments.

---

[1]. SÁROSI, Bálint. *Gypsy Music*, translated by Fred Macnicol, Budapest, Corvina, 1978, p. 139.

The ornamental practice of Gypsy musicians was omnipresent in a specific case, which consisted in performing a vocal melody (often requested by a listener) freely, in an improvisatory way, enriched by a series of instrumental passages and overwhelming ornamentation. This practice is described in several written reports of the period. A particularly interesting source is quoted by Bálint Sárosi, in his article on the first Gypsy bands[2]. It is a description which appeared in a German newspaper entitled *Aehrenlese zur Belehrung und Unterhaltung*, in 1829. It is quite amusing to be confronted with the fact that the author of the article, obviously a person who likes precision and order, is totally upset by the performing tradition of the Gypsies. Actually, he complains that the musicians never play the pieces in their original form, they always add to them specific elements. He tells about how he tried to convince the Gypsies to play the melody (a melody which the reporter himself taught them) in the 'right' way, with precision. However, his efforts were in vain. Even years after that, he found the same additional elements in the interpretation by the same musician. Moreover, his pupils added new elements and omitted others, and in the end the melody became unrecognizable. The disappointed reporter compared these musicians to thrushes and he gave up trying to change their improvisatory practices.

The same phenomenon is described thirty years later by Liszt in his book on the music of the Gypsies in Hungary (which rightly provoked much criticism because of his erroneous view of 'Gypsy' music) which confirms that the method of elaborating vocal songs in an instrumental manner (or instrumental dance tunes with rich ornamentation) remained for several decades a very important element in the performance practice of Hungarian Gypsy orchestras[3]. It is worth noting that Liszt, unlike the unknown writer of the German article, praises and admires the improvisatory technique of the Gypsy musicians. He wrote:

> The Gypsy artist is he who accepts a song or dance motive only as a subject of a discourse, or as a motto of a poem, and who roams and roves, with in his mind this idea, which he never let go totally, during an endless improvisation. The person who is admired is the one who enriches his theme with such a profusion of figures, appoggiaturas, scales, tremolos, arpeggios, diatonic or chromatic passages, turns and other ornaments, that under this luxuriant embroidery the original thought hardly appears any more prominent than the fabric of his brown garment appears upon his sleeve[4].

---

[2]. *Aehrenlese zur Belehrung und Unterhaltung*, December 1829, p. 409. Quoted in: SÁROSI, Bálint. 'Híradások az első cigánybandákról', in: *Muzsika*, XLIII/12 (2000), pp. 15-19. A Hungarian translation of the German article is on pp. 17-18.

[3]. LISZT, Franz. *Des Bohémiens et de leur musique en Hongrie*, Paris, A. Bourdillat, 1859.

[4]. *Ibidem*, p. 229: «L'artiste bohémien est celui qui ne prend un motif de chanson ou de danse que comme un texte de discours, comme une épigraphe de poëme, et qui sur cette idée qu'il ne perd jamais tout à fait de vue, vague et divague durant une improvisation sempiternelle. Celui qu'on admire, c'est celui qui enrichit son sujet d'une telle profusion de traits, d'appogiatures, de gammes, de trémolos, d'arpèges, de

and:

> Almost always, these inventions of the moment have something in them
> that surprises. [...] They have no motivation at all, nor rules or preparations, so
> that they remind of the rustle of young birds who fly up in all directions, with
> no other aim than to try their wings[5].

When Robert Franz gave a description of the performance of Hungarian Gypsy musicians in the *Revue des Deux Mondes* of 1874, the same improvisatory practice is evoked. The parallel between the texts of Liszt and that of Franz is obvious:

> Suddenly, a strange sustained note made me prick up my ears. [...] A rest
> followed it and then a divine, sweeping and dark song emerged with majesty. [...]
> Another rest, and a music with a frenetic joy started. We still recognized the main
> phrase, but as a flower, coming off its stem under the myriad of winged notes, of
> misty sound-groups, of long, spiral, transparent, nearly prismatic fiorituras[6].

As this phenomenon belongs to the field of the free interpretation of a melody and the improvisation during the performance, there is hardly any sign of this technique in the musical sources. That is why Liszt criticizes the publication of these pieces. However, his negative opinion is a bit exaggerated and unfair. Even if he speaks about the fact, praising the Gypsy performance, that «their thoughts [that is, the thoughts of Gypsy musicians] were probably mutilated», and even if he rejects «the infidelities of the publications»[7], we have to admit that the existence of these publications of the period is crucial to the understanding of this specific repertoire and to the overall knowledge we can have of it today. Yet, Liszt was not wrong to declare that there is a palpable contrast between the 'dead' notation and the lively performance of these pieces by Gypsy musicians. Regarding the printed versions of the pieces (let us note that Liszt speaks in general, without mentioning any concrete example or publication), he remarks that

---

passages diatoniques et chromatiques, de groupes et gruppetti de sons, que sous ce luxe de broderie la pensée primitive ne paraît guère davantage que le drap de sa houppelande brune ne perce sur sa manche».

5. *Ibidem*, p. 230: «Presque toujours ces inventions du moment ont quelque chose en elles qui surprend. [...] N'ayant absolument pas de motivation, de règles, ni de préparations, elles rappellent le frou-frou de jeunes oiseaux qui s'élancent de ci et de là sans autre but que d'essayer leurs ailes».

6. FRANZ, Robert. 'La musique tzigane en Hongrie', in: *Revue des Deux Mondes*, XLIV/5 (1874), pp. 940-952. «Soudain une note étrange, longuement soutenue, me fit dresser l'oreille. [...] Une pause survint, et un chant divin, large et sombre, se développa avec majesté. [...] Une nouvelle pause, et des strophes d'une allégresse effrénée éclatèrent. On retrouvait encore la phrase principale, mais se détachant comme une fleur de sa tige sous des myriades de notes ailées, des touffes de sons vaporeux, de longues spirales de fioritures transparentes et comme prismatiques» (*ibidem*, p. 945).

7. LISZT, Franz. *Des Bohémiens et de leur musique* [...], *op. cit.* (see note 3), pp. 253-254: «on a sans doute mutilé leurs pensées», «les infidélités des publications».

they were deprived […] of their more savage inspirations […] the *dead letter*, which we meet at every footstep or rather in every publishing house of our country, can hardly give an idea of the *brio* of the Gypsy virtuoso's interpretation, of the constant modifications of their rhythms, of the eloquence of their phrases, of the accent of their declamation. One can only have an idea of all these things after hearing the orchestras[8].

It is true that a few richly ornamented, printed instrumental pieces are available, in which the ornamentations are really abundant and are present nearly in an exaggerated way. This is contrary to most of the dance pieces appearing in print, in which the use of the ornamental passages is more well-balanced, having their place at strategic points of the musical process, before the cadences, for example. The notation of the richly ornamented instrumental pieces can help us to imagine how these endless improvised embellishments described by the above-mentioned sources could have sounded in reality. One rare example can be seen in Ex. 1. Even here, we cannot exclude the possibility that in some places, for example at the fermata in bar 40, additional ornaments or virtuoso passages were added by the performer.

Ex. 1: Bandi Angyal, 'Bátskai magyar' [Hungarian Dance from Bátska], Vienna, c. 1826-1827, First part: Slow, bars 33-48.

---

[8]. *Ibidem*, p. 254: «on les privait […] de leurs plus sauvages inspirations. […] la *lettre morte* qu'on rencontre à chaque pas, ou plutôt à chaque magasin d'éditeur dans notre pays, ne peut-elle guère donner l'idée du *brio* de l'exécution des virtuoses bohémiens, des modifications constantes de leurs rhythmes, de l'éloquence de leurs phrases, de l'accent de leur déclamation. On n'en peut juger qu'après avoir entendu les orchestres». In addition to the lacking traces of the improvisatory practice, Liszt also criticizes the publications because of their incapability to reproduce the nuances (dynamics, tempo changes, and so on) of the live performance. These features can be brought in parallel with improvisation, because they really exist only at the very moment of the interpretation (as the improvised musical materials) and they can hardly be fixed precisely by the tools of notation.

While on the one hand notation fails to reproduce the very essence of an important aspect of Gypsy playing, namely the technique of improvised ornaments, on the other hand it is essential to get an idea of how improvisation can function in the phase of the creation of the pieces. Actually, as I have mentioned before, it is quite possible that, during the emerging period of the *verbunkos*, their creation was closely linked with an instrumental tradition, in which the transmission of its musical elements was carried out in an oral-practical way. An examination of the early *verbunkos* reveals that these elements, that is melodic figurations, often in conjunction with certain rhythmic patterns, became decisive for the entire material. A collection of *verbunkos* music edited by the Hungarian musicologist Géza Papp in 1986 gives an overall picture of this early repertoire[9]. Seventeen sets of dances contain 234 pieces by both known and anonymous composers. Regarding the pieces with certified authorship, they are represented by works of minor composers of the period such as József Bengráf, Anton Zimmermann and Franz Paul Rigler. The anonymous pieces include, among others, those in the four books of *Originelle ungarische Nationaltänze* and a dance collection known as the *Ausgesuchte Ungarische Nationaltaenze im Clavierauszug von verschiedenen Zigeunern aus Galantha*, which include the pieces notated after the guest performance of the Galánta Gypsies in Vienna in 1787. The pieces published confirm that in the early *verbunkos* repertoire the musical material filling the formal frames (often two- or three-period structures) was nothing but a set of some typical distinct melodic turns, melodic building blocks or patterns in the narrow sense of the phrase. This technique for creating and recreating little dance pieces was necessary for Gypsy musicians who, as we know, played without score, improvising a great deal. It is interesting to note that even those who can be called 'composers' (in the strict sense of the word) imitated this process of creation.

---

[9]. PAPP, Géza. *Hungarian Dances 1784-1810*, Budapest, MTA Zenetudományi Intézet, 1986 (Musicalia Danubiana, 7).

This phenomenon, however, seems to be common in musical cultures rooted in oral tradition. Jeff Pressing draws attention to the fact that the pattern-like thinking, according to an existing musicological position, can determine the improvisatory practices of a great number of repertories, from Gregorian chant to jazz:

> The relevance of formulaic composition to specific types of musical improvisation has recently been discussed by several writers. Treitler (1974) has argued that Gregorian chant was composed and transmitted in an analogous process to that used in the oral epics. Smith (1983) has used the process to describe the constraints imposed on the song-based jazz performer, and has gone on to analyse piano improvisations by Bill Evans. Kernfeld (1983) has examined how far formulas may be used to describe the music of saxophonist John Coltrane. Reck (1983) has produced the evocative idea of a musician's 'tool-kit', in a mammoth study of five performances by South Indian musician Thirugokarnam Ramachandra Iyer. The tool-kit is considered to be piece-specific and to contain both individually chosen and culturally determined formulas, musical habits, models of improvisational and compositional forms, aesthetic values, and social attitudes. The application of Parry-Lord theory to musical improvisation is thus a clear contemporary trend[10].

In this case, as explained by the example of the Indian musician, the elements of improvisation did not really function as the means of a freely expressed flow of individual artistic fantasy. This 'compositional' process rather lay midway between the use of defined and free elements. Often a great part of the elements was already at hand, and the main question was how to fit them together. It is not as easy as it seems to be: this improvisatory technique rooted in tradition requires creative fantasy, ability in the field of variation and a good knowledge of the vocabulary of the specific, instrumental language. We have good reason to assume that the performers of *verbunkos* music, that is Gypsy musicians, had a similar approach to music-making. As early as in 1800, an article in the *Allgemeine musikalische Zeitung* of Leipzig, presenting the Hungarian music of the period, reported on this specific improvisatory technique:

> Nearly every piece played among Hungarian people is the momentary product of fantasy. It often occurs that a man, if he dislikes the pieces played by the musicians, puts himself in front of them and he trills the notes just coming to his mind or the notes which he heard from other musicians, before them for

---

[10]. PRESSING, Jeff. 'Improvisation: Methods and models', in: *Generative Processes in Music. The Psychology of Performance, Improvisation, and Composition*, edited by John A. Sloboda, Oxford, Clarendon press, 1988, pp. 129-178. The quoted text is on pp. 146-147. Let us note that Pressing seems to be hesitating to accept this theory without criticism. For him «the limits of its validity and usefulness are still open questions, and are probably linked to whether a satisfactory agreement can be reached on the principles to be used to define musical 'formulas'». *Ibidem*, p. 147.

so long, and he makes the musicians one by one re-play them for so long, until the virtuosos can create a whole piece out of the same notes. This explains the uniformity which characterizes every Hungarian dance. From this practice one can also understand why one and the same piece, played by different orchestras, may have very different appearances[11].

Ex. 2 represents this early period and illustrate clearly what is described in the last phrases of the quotation.

Ex. 2: Hungarian dance in two variant versions. From *Originelle Ungarische Nationaltänze*, vol. II, Vienna, c. 1807, Nos. 19 and 22. Published as Nos. [164] and [167] in PAPP, Géza. *Op. cit.* (see note 9), pp. 246-248.

11. 'Ueber die Nationaltänze der Ungarn', in: *Allgemeine musikalische Zeitung*, II/35 (28 May 1800): «Fast alle Stücke, die in den Zirkeln der N[ation] Ungarn gespielt werden, sind das augenblickliche Produkt der Phantasie. Da stellt sich nicht selten ein Mann, wenn ihm die Stücke der Musiker nicht gefallen, vor die Musiker hin und trillert ihnen die Töne, die ihm gerade einfallen, oder die er von andern Musikern hörte, so lang vor, und lässt sie sich einzeln so lange nachfiedeln, bis die Virtuosen aus denselben ein Ganzes heraus zu fiedeln vermögen. Hieraus kann man sich auch das Einförmige erklären, welches allen ung[arischen] Tänzen eigen ist. Man sieht daraus aber auch, woher es komme, dass ein und dasselbe Stück, von verschiedenen Gesellschaften gespielt, sehr verschiedenartige Modulationen hat». Quoted in: PAPP, Géza. *Op. cit.* (see note 9), pp. 15, 30. The article is anonymous, but Papp suggests, following another Hungarian musicologist, Ervin Major, that its author is Heinrich Klein of Pozsony (now Bratislava).

It is even more interesting to note that the vestiges of this compositional process, which is closely related to improvisation, can be found even in a later phase, during the 'golden age' of the *verbunkos*, when composing became a more individual affair (as I pointed out earlier). Actually, in some cases — less frequently than before, to be precise — the presence of thematic-motivic interchanges, as well as some melodies existing in many varied forms prove that the composers of this period were not totally detached from the principle of creation as improvisation determined by the use of patterns. Borrowing was not a personal affair, and it did not lead to copyright problems either; actually, it was not really borrowing, but rather a free use of a common treasury, a kind of semi-popular vocabulary. This is less surprising if we keep in mind what we mentioned before: one of the composers of the so-called '*verbunkos* triad', Bihari, was a musically illiterate, improvising composer. Even the others could take some material from the common stock without being embarrassed, because the individual character of a piece was less important than its national taste, partly based on pre-existing elements of the common musical language, partly created gradually, as these composers continued composing new musical materials more or less in the same idiom. Exs. 3 and 4 clearly demonstrate how themes and motives could wander quite freely in this repertoire[12].

Ex. 3: different versions of the same opening motive. (a) János Bihari, 'Lassú Magyar' [Hungarian Slow Dance], in: *Magyar Nóták Veszprém Vármegyéből* [Hungarian Tunes from the Veszprém Region], vol. IV, Pest-Buda, 1825, No. 29, bars 1–8; (b) János Lavotta, Andante, bars 1–8, Dance No. 2 of *Nemzeti Magyar Tántzok* [Hungarian National Dances], edited by Ágoston Mohaupt, Pest-Buda, 1823; and (c) Antal Csermák, 'Lassú Verbunk' [Slow Verbunk], in: *Magyar Nóták Veszprém Vármegyéből* [Hungarian Tunes from the Veszprém Region], vol. VII, no. 54, Pest-Buda, 1826, bars 1–8.

---

12. We cannot exclude the possibility that the publications were imprecise regarding the attribution of the authorship of the pieces. A piece by a certain composer could be published under the name of another one. This, however, does not change, but on the contrary confirms, the fact that these pieces preserved to some extent the traces of an oral tradition, in which musical materials existed in freely varied forms.

The dance published as no. 29 in volume IV of *Magyar Nóták Veszprém Vármegyéből* [Hungarian Tunes from the Veszprém Region] — one of the most important nineteenth-century publications of *verbunkos* music[13] — is a *Lassú Magyar* [Hungarian Slow Dance] by

---

13. It contains 136 *verbunkos* pieces published in 15 volumes from 1823 to 1832, edited by Ignác Ruzitska. Among the composers of the dances we can find the most important ones of the mature *verbunkos*, such as Bihari, Lavotta, Csermák, Ruzitska and Rózsavölgyi.

Ex. 4: recurring motive. (a) János Bihari, 'Friss Magyar' [Hungarian Fast Dance], bars 1-4, in: *Magyar Nóták Veszprém Vármegyéből* [Hungarian Tunes from the Veszprém Region], vol. V, Pest-Buda, 1826, No. 32; (b) Unknown composer, 'Friss Magyar' [Hungarian Fast Dance], bars 1-4, in: *Magyar Nóták Veszprém Vármegyéből* [Hungarian Tunes from the Veszprém Region], vol. IX, Pest-Buda, 1826, No. 73; (c) János Árvay, 'Friss' [Fast Dance], closing section, bars 1-4, in: *Pannónia*, vol. II, Vienna, 1826, No. 2; and (d) Joseph Haydn, motive from Piano Trio in G major, Hob, XV:25, Finale, bars 1-4.

Bihari (see Ex. 3a). A variant of this piece can be found in Ágoston Mohaupt's publication called *Nemzeti Magyar Tántzok* [Hungarian National Dances] (1823), as Dance no. 2. The piece is attributed to Lavotta here (see Ex. 3b). The beginning of the theme is the same as in Bihari's dance, and then the melody continues in a different way. However, both have the same simple harmonic plan. The third dance, published under the name of Csermák as no. 54 in volume VII of *Magyar Nóták Veszprém Vármegyéből*, is a remote variant of the same theme. It uses the same opening motif, although in a major key, and transposes the second motif to the fourth degree of the scale, instead of keeping it on the second, as in the other pieces, a solution which considerably modifies the harmonic plan. In spite of this, a memory of the original theme comes back, for example if we look at the beginning of the second half of the period in Ex. 3c, and the parallel remains recognizable.

The next example shows that even pieces published during the second period of *verbunkos* can preserve earlier material showing the processes of the transmission by oral tradition, that is improvisation and variation. In fact, as can be seen in Ex. 4, the variability of some pieces can be attributed to the fact that the composers drew on an earlier stratum of the repertoire which was naturally characterized by variation. No. 32 of volume V of *Magyar Nóták Veszprém Vármegyéből* (by Bihari; Ex. 5a) and no. 73 of volume IX (anonymous; Ex. 4b), as well as no. 2 of volume II of *Pannónia*[14] (by János Árvay; Ex.

---

14. *Pannónia* is another well-known *verbunkos* collection of the same period. Volume II was published in 1826.

4c) can probably be retraced to one and the same early *verbunkos* movement whose first notation is known from the finale of Haydn's Piano Trio in G major (1795, Hob. xv:25; Ex. 4d). It is not known if it had an earlier *verbunkos* source or later *verbunkos* composers adopted its rondo theme as typical early *verbunkos* material. One thing is certain, however: the melody, which was either rooted in popular tradition or emanating from Haydn's *all'ongarese* style, which is very faithful to the original vernacular idiom, based on various instrumental figurations was really suitable to appear in several variants.

On the one hand, we must be grateful that we have a great number of publications of the period, and that from the noted version of the pieces we can detect the mechanism of the 'handcrafted' creation, which was closely linked with improvisation, as well as the specific nature of some of the musical material used in the improvisatory or improvisation-like processes existing in several varied forms without any 'definitive version'. On the other hand, we have to admit that the notation in general does not reveal — more precisely: cannot reveal — every aspect of a repertoire the pieces of which were constantly enriched by additional elements, originating from the performers' creative power. In addition to the problem of the improvised ornaments, there is another example which clearly shows the discrepancy between the notation and the living musical practice.

When talking about nineteenth-century Hungarian music, writers on music and musicologists often evoke a characteristic which is presented as a very important melodic element, an emblematic Hungarian (Hungarian-Gypsy) interval. Liszt was the first to write about the abundance of the augmented second in this repertoire, in his 1859 book on Gypsy music. Moreover, he did not hesitate to declare that the interval was downright indispensable to express the specific 'Gypsy' character of the music. (Actually, he should have said 'Hungarian', but he thought incorrectly that this distinct repertoire, as presented in the introduction of the present article, was the popular music of the Romani people[15].) In the twentieth century, several Hungarian musicologists, among them Bence Szabolcsi and Bálint Sárosi, mentioned this element as a very important feature of Hungarian music. The problem is that the musical sources do not confirm this statement. The interval in question (which can be present between the third and the fourth, as well as the sixth and the seventh degrees of a minor scale) does not appear in the publications as often as

---

[15]. This is totally wrong, and unfortunately, his ideas create a constant misunderstanding even nowadays. However, we cannot enter here into an inevitably long discussion on this topic, scarcely linked with our main issue, that is improvisation versus notation. Several musicologists — mostly Hungarians but also non-Hungarians — have already tried to clarify this seemingly problematic (in reality, not so complicated) question. Many passages and the whole conception of Sárosi's book serve to shed a clear light on it. See SÁROSI, Bálint. *Gypsy Music, op. cit.* (see note 1). See also Bartók's article partly on this topic in *Ethnographia* (1931), available in English as: BARTÓK, Béla. 'Gipsy Music or Hungarian Music?', in: *Béla Bartók Essays*, translated by Richard Tószeghy and others, edited by Benjamin Suchoff, London, Faber & Faber, 1976, pp. 206-223 (for this specific question, see pp. 206-207, 221-222), or BELLMAN, Jonathan. *The Style Hongrois in the Music of Western Europe*, Boston, Northeastern University Press, 1993, pp. 11-12, 16, 20.

one might expect after reading the above-mentioned sources. Consequently, from this statement we could deduce that the augmented second is not as crucial in this repertoire as it seems to be.

It would be impossible to draw up precise statistics concerning this question, in view of the huge quantity of pieces which ought to be examined. In spite of this difficulty, we can present some data based on the above-mentioned collections which offer a reliable and firm sample, in order to have an idea about the quantitative aspects of the question. In the *Magyar Nóták Veszprém Vármegyéből* we find this interval in a certain quantity which does not go unnoticed but its importance remains limited. Less than twenty per cent of the pieces contain the augmented second, normally only once or twice a piece, rarely three times. However, this percentage is quite high if we compare it with that of the collection published by Papp. There the use of the augmented second occurs in less than ten per cent of the dances. Of course, one cannot deny that an element which is present with a certain regularity in a repertoire (approximately in every fifth or tenth piece) can already be considered as one of the characteristics of this repertoire. It would however be exaggerating to affirm that its presence is obligatory to create a specific Hungarian character (as Liszt did, for example). The augmented second is not omnipresent in the sources, neither is it omnipotent in the musical characterization of the Hungarian idiom.

The observation that the interval is scarcely represented in the publications can be explained in several ways. According to Liszt, it would be due to the purifying efforts of the publishing houses and musical editors who banished this harmonically unusual element from the written sources because they took it for an error[16]. Now, as the publications came in most cases from Hungarian publishing houses (so Liszt is talking primarily about Hungarian editors), we can wonder why these Hungarian people could have been so shocked by this element, and so reluctant to reproduce it in print while hearing it every day. If we believe Liszt, the augmented second was inseparable from the music played by Hungarian Gypsies, so, as this music was present in everyday life, every Hungarian was familiar with it. Certain people might have disliked it, but this is a question of taste and not a question of ignorance or misreading. (Liszt's opinion would be more applicable to a foreign public, but this is yet another question.) Moreover, if the editors had been so dissatisfied with the augmented second, they would have omitted it from every single dance piece, which was, as we could see, not the case.

Another possible hypothesis might be to imagine that in the publishing process this interval was handled as a sort of 'modern *musica ficta*'. There was no point in indicating it in the score, because in any case, everybody knew about its existence and its presence in the sounding reality. But why was it reproduced then from time to time? Once again, it would have been more logical not to do it at all.

---

[16]. LISZT, Franz. *Des Bohémiens et de leur musique* […], *op. cit.* (see note 3), p. 254.

An important idea of Sárosi reminds us of the fact that notation does not necessarily have to reveal this element of the musical language, for a specific reason which has something to do with interpretation and with the presence of improvised elements during the performance. He confirms that «the extra spice which counts as virtually obligatory in the instrumental music played by gypsy musicians since the *verbunkos* period [is] the augmented second. [...] the augmented second is not an organic part of the melodies but an element in the performing style»[17]. Now, as long as this element behaves like an additional colour, functioning nearly as an ornament within a melodic line, any attempt to determine the place and the role of it in the repertoire with exactitude remains illusory. If the augmented second is introduced in the musical material only in the phase of the performance (instead of being a product of the creation already during the conception of a piece), it can be treated in an absolutely free manner by the performing artists. Evidently, we are free to believe that the use of this interval was general (as Sárosi and the others suggest). To tell the truth, we are obliged to admit that we have no proof of it either.

We do, however, have very interesting and valuable information from the period which suggests exactly the contrary. According to this information, the augmented second was not a general musical phenomenon, but something determined by chronological questions and socio-cultural factors linked also with the function of the music and with the behaviour of the (improvising) artists and the public. The author of the book which contains the passage in question is Sámuel Brassai. His book is a very critical reaction to Liszt's above-mentioned book on Gypsy music. He disagreed with Liszt on nearly every statement of his work; so, it is not surprising at all that he was far from being satisfied with what Liszt wrote about the preponderant role of this specific interval. According to Brassai «the present-day gypsy uses this piquant little spice more than is necessary — and, with our compatriot Liszt's permission, more than is desired by good taste»[18].

This remark reveals two things. The first is that this specific interval in the repertoire was used with especial frequency at the end of the 1850s and at the beginning of the 1860s. The second one is that this had not been the case at all before. This element became a fashionable effect only by 1860, without being really justified by the so-called 'classical' corpus of the *verbunkos*. So, Brassai's text suggests too that the interval in question was not a substantial and essential element of the repertoire, but rather an additional one (as Sárosi also pointed out). As such, it belonged to the field of improvisation and it was evidently an improvised element. Consequently, its presence in every single case was linked to different factors, such as the instrumentalists' freedom during the performance, which was traditionally enriched by a series of improvised elements; the changing fashion and the

---

[17]. SÁROSI, Bálint. *Gypsy Music*, op. cit. (see note 1), p. 96.

[18]. BRASSAI, Sámuel. *Magyar vagy czigány-zene?*, Kolozsvár, s.n., 1860, p. 44: «ezzel a kis piquant fűszerezéssel [...] a mostani czigány a kelleténél — s L[iszt] h.[azánkfia] engedelmével a jó ízlés kívánalmánál — többször él». Quoted in English by SÁROSI, Bálint. *Gypsy Music*, op. cit. (see note 1), p. 147.

public's momentary taste; and finally, the musicians' urge to satisfy the needs of the public. The latter is a very important factor[19], and it shows us that the act of improvising, instead of being an exclusive affair of the performing artist to add his own contribution freely to the existing musical materials, can be influenced by more pragmatic commercial-artistic factors. Behind it one can detect the musicians' desire to be appreciated (and remunerated!) and for this, to offer the listener what he wants to hear. This is less surprising if we consider the fact that the repertoire in question was basically a functional one, it was designed for everyday use and 'consumption', and its performers, the Gypsy musicians, considered themselves (and were considered) as musical 'entertainers', even if they were, at the same time, praised, admired and honoured like real artists, for their natural artistic talent. An interesting description provided by Sárosi reveals this aspect of the Gypsy musicians' behaviour. Regarding the instrumentalist playing the first violin in the Gypsy orchestra, the *prímás*, he confirms that

> every leader is a separate *individual*. In his playing he determines the proportion between the expressive means of the style himself — with particular regard for the 'customer' and his desires. In the nineteenth century, for example, they were much more liberal in spicing their playing with augmented seconds than today — and they were reprimanded for it, too, although it was obvious that they were trying to please their audience with it; and the average public certainly did want it this way. The gypsy musician wants the song to be 'tasty' for the customer in the way he 'cooks' it. It happened with one of our folklorists that when he was collecting from a village gypsy musician, the gypsy came to realize that it was mainly the melodies with a *Phrygian* cadence which pleased the collector [...]. From then onwards, whenever it was at all possible, he brought even the commonest melody to an end with a Phrygian cadence — while his companion obligingly observed the effect on the face of the listener: «Just as the customer likes it — I can do it *kuruc* style, too...»[20].

---

[19].   This behaviour characterizes to a great extent the Gypsy musicians' behaviour in general. However, in many other cultures, as Jean Düring points out, improvisation is determined by the performer's relation with its public; by the fact that the musician is far from being independent from what the public wants to hear. «Improviser, c'est d'abord s'adapter aux auditeurs, aux circonstances. C'est une manière de s'adresser au public, de tenir compte de lui, de refléter ces sentiments, puis de les diriger. [...] Le musicien attend en retour un assentiment, une confirmation de son jeu [...]». DÜRING, Jean. 'Le jeu des relations sociales: Éléments d'une problématique', in: *L'improvisation dans les musiques de tradition orale*, edited by Bernard Lortat-Jacob, Paris, Selaf, 1987, pp. 17-23. The quoted text is on p. 20. For the same topic, see also BAILEY, Derek. *Improvisation. Its Nature and Practice in music*, New York, Da Capo, 1993; French translation by Isabelle Leymarie, *L'improvisation. Sa nature et sa pratique dans la musique*, Paris, Éditions Outre Mesure, 1999, Part III, the chapter on the public (in the French version, pp. 60-64).

[20].   SÁROSI, Bálint. *Gypsy Music, op. cit.* (see note 1), pp. 246-247. The *kurucs* were Hungarian soldiers fighting against the Hapsburg army during the Hungarian Independence War of 1703-1711, led by Ferenc Rákóczi II. The term '*kuruc* style' used by the Gypsy musician with a certain freedom refers to some melodies

As we can see, in a repertoire rooted in the oral tradition, harmonic-melodic elements can be improvised more or less freely, often on demand, without being subsequently preserved by notation. The case of the augmented second in nineteenth-century Hungarian popular music is a good example for this phenomenon. The difficulties in determining its role are due to its unfixed character and to the fact that its real existence was in close relation to live performance.

The performance of a piece is an affair of the moment; if it can be fixed nowadays thanks to recordings, it was not the case at all in the nineteenth century. So, the missing link cannot be restored. One can only suppose that it will be more realistic to imagine this specific element as a fluctuating one in the musical context. Its flexibility and its free use (or free omission) in every single performance is much more probable than its obligatory presence as a fixed 'Hungarian' symbol. But one thing is sure: there is something which is beyond the limits of our current scholarly perception. Improvisation will be keeping inevitably its share of mystery.

---

from this period, possibly having a Phrygian cadence. The Phrygian cadence can be found in a great number of Hungarian folksongs.

Improvvisazione e ornamentazione nell'opera francese e italiana di primo Ottocento

Damien Colas
(Parigi)

Nel suo trattato *L'étude du chant*, pubblicato a San Pietroburgo nel 1881, Henriette Nissen-Saloman indicava che

> In Italia o in altri luoghi, dove la stessa opera è ripetuta ogni sera per un lungo periodo […] o anche in occasione della ripresa di un'aria di bravura, durante la rappresentazione, è raro che una cantante di primo piano ripeta le stesse variazioni. Ne sceglierà spesso altre, più nuove, che inventerà ella stessa, o che prenderà nella collezione presentata in questa sede[1].

Il lettore non può non notare la similitudine con un famoso passo di Pier Francesco Tosi, che la cantante svedese probabilmente non conosceva:

> Quegli che sono nel numero degli ottimi antichi s'impegnavano *di sera in sera* di cangiar nell'opere non solo tutte le arie patetiche, ma qualchedun delle allegre ancora[2].

La capacità di cambiare variazione da una sera all'altra appartiene all'arte dell'improvvisazione e ne costituisce uno degli aspetti possibili. È, in ogni caso, una delle descrizioni più precise dell'attività dell'improvvisazione che si possa trovare nella letteratura teorica. Manuel Garcia (junior), nel suo *Traité complet de l'art du chant* (1840), utilizza

---

[1]. Nissen-Saloman, Henriette. *L'étude du chant* [Генризтта Ниссень–Саломань, *Школа пънія*], San Pietroburgo, B. Bessel, [1881], Cap. xii, 'Changements. Variantes': «En Italie et dans d'autres lieux, où le même opéra est répété chaque soir pendant longtemps, presque jusqu'à satiété, — ou même — à l'occasion du bis (Da Capo) d'un air de bravoure (pendant une représentation), il est rare qu'une cantatrice distinguée le répète toujours avec les mêmes changements; elle en choisira plutôt souvent d'autres, des plus nouveaux, qu'elle inventera elle-même, ou qu'elle empruntera à la collection communiquée ici».

[2]. Tosi, Pier Francesco. *Opinioni de' cantori antichi e moderni, o sieno Osservazioni sopra il canto figurato*, Bologna, Lelio dalla Volpe, 1723, Cap. 'Dell'arie', p. 60. Il corsivo è mio.

l'espressione antica di 'cantar alla mente', vecchia eredità della pratica del contrappunto del Quattro e Cinquecento:

> Poiché lo studio degli ornamenti esige molto esercizio e deve condurre l'artista ad improvvisare variazioni (*cantar alla mente*), merito distintivo del cantante eminente, il maestro non saprà mai troppo esercitare l'allievo a variare egli stesso i pezzi[3].

Stando alle testimonianze dei pedagoghi, sembra dunque che la tradizione dell'improvvisazione sia perdurata, nel campo dell'opera italiana, almeno per un secolo e mezzo. Non c'è motivo di mettere in dubbio tale capacità, caratteristica dei bravi cantanti, benché simile longevità sia sorprendente. Ci si può invece chiedere perché nella prassi esecutiva odierna, anche quando si ha a che fare con il repertorio del Settecento, non si assista più spesso a tali cambi di variazioni da un'esecuzione all'altra, così come descritti da Tosi e da Nissen-Saloman. Al contrario, sono numerose le produzioni, tanto concertistiche quanto sceniche, in cui gli interpreti riprendono i medesimi ornamenti utilizzati per una precedente incisione discografica. Questa situazione, diametralmente opposta alla variabilità dell'ornamentazione sostenuta dai pedagoghi nel Sette e Ottocento, è purtroppo frequente oggi[4].

Le testimonianze di Garcia e di Nissen-Saloman sollevano domande che questo studio intende affrontare, benché non sia possibile rispondere compiutamente: (1) poiché le 'tradizioni', cioè la trasmissione di una stessa variazione ornamentale da un cantante all'altro, sono comparse a metà Ottocento circa, come è possibile che la pratica più antica dell'improvvisazione sia coesistita con la pratica più recente della tradizione? (2) In cosa consisteva precisamente l'atto improvvisativo? Si svolgeva in tempo reale, nel momento dell'esecuzione, o era invece preparato prima? (3) Tenendo conto dell'evoluzione delle forme liriche, quali parti dell'opera e quali parti dell'aria sono oggetto d'improvvisazione?

ANNOTAZIONI E ARTEFATTI

Le fonti musicali e teoriche del Settecento sono povere di esempi musicali annotati per quanto riguarda l'ornamentazione della musica vocale italiana. Dell'arte dei castrati restano solo poche tracce. Di recente, sono stati pubblicati gli ornamenti del castrato

---

[3]. GARCIA, Manuel (junior). *Traité complet de l'art du chant*, Parigi, Garcia, 1840, vol. II, § III, 'Des changements': «Comme l'étude des ornements exige beaucoup d'exercice et qu'elle doit conduire l'artiste à improviser des variantes (*cantar alla mente*), mérite distinctif du chanteur éminent, le maître ne saurait trop exercer l'élève à varier lui-même les morceaux».

[4]. Numerosi sono gli studi sulla relazione tra industria discografica e prassi esecutiva. Circa il caso specifico delle *historically informed performances*, si rinvia a HAYNES, Bruce. *The End of Early Music. A Period Performer's History of Music for the Twenty-First Century*, Oxford, Oxford University Press, 2007.

Marchesini per il rondò 'Rendi, o cara' di Giuseppe Sarti; lo stato del manoscritto, conservato alla Bibliothèque nationale de France, non ci permette di dire quanto questa versione dell'aria corrisponda a ciò che il cantante ha effettivamente eseguito[5]. Molto più numerose sono invece le testimonianze scritte sull'ornamentazione dei cantanti dell'Ottocento, che si tratti di arie edite, di esempi forniti nei trattati di canto o ancora di manoscritti utilizzati dagli interpreti.

Nella sua tesi di dottorato sul canto rossiniano (1935), Hedwig Faller vide in questa abbondanza di tracce scritte il segno stesso del declino dell'arte dell'improvvisazione:

> In realtà, le abbondanti annotazioni di ornamentazioni aggiunte ci dicono che l'arte dell'improvvisazione spontanea non fece più parte della cultura comune dei cantanti. Una prova ancor più convincente è costituita da questi passaggi, dove le note indicano chiaramente come si è cercato di arrivare alla forma giusta. Sono attestate tre, quattro, o addirittura cinque versioni. E quando si trovava la linea fondamentale delle ornamentazioni, allora si ricominciava di nuovo a perfezionare un solo motivo[6].

Non sono pienamente convinto dall'analisi di Faller, anche se certi elementi confermano quello che ho potuto osservare e analizzare nel mio studio sull'ornamentazione delle opere rossiniane a Parigi[7]. L'abbondanza delle tracce scritte nell'Ottocento, in contrasto con la rarità di quelle scritte nel Settecento, non è indizio sufficiente di un ipotetico declino dell'improvvisazione. Vi sono altre ragioni di cui bisogna tener conto:

---

[5]. COLAS, Damien - DI PROFIO, Alessandro. 'Le rondò «Rendi, o cara, il Prence amato» de Sarti et les variations de Luigi Marchesi', in: *D'une scène à l'autre. L'opéra italien en Europe*, vol. I: *Les pérégrinations d'un genre*, a cura di Damien Colas e Alessandro Di Profio, Wavre, Mardaga, 2009, pp. 157-187. Gli studi dei filologi specialisti del Sei e Settecento, in particolare quelli di Hendrik Schulze, invitano d'altra parte a essere prudenti circa la lettura dei manoscritti, in particolare di quelli a funzione mnemonica, appartenenti alle collezioni di ricchi collezionisti e non corrispondenti necessariamente ad uno stadio della partitura mai realmente eseguito. Si veda SCHULZE, Hendrik. 'Cavalli Manuscript Scores and Performance Practice', in: *Francesco Cavalli. La circolazione dell'opera veneziana nel Seicento*, a cura di Dinko Fabris, Napoli, Turchini, 2005, pp. 39-58.

[6]. FALLER, Hedwig. *Die Gesangskoloratur in Rossinis Opern und ihre Ausführung*, tesi di dottorato, Berlino, 1935, p. 115: «Schon die vielfach gefundenen Eintragungen der willkürlichen Verzierungen sagen uns, daß die Kunst der freien Improvisation nicht mehr Allgemeingut der Sänger war. Einen noch schlagenderen Beweis liefern einige Stellen in jenen Noten, die ein klares Bild vermitteln, wie man nach der richtigen Form zu suchen begann. Drei, vier, ja sogar fünf verschiedene Fassungen werden ausprobiert. Und scheint man wirklich die Grundlinie einer Verzierung gefunden zu haben, dann wurde nochmals begonnen und ein einzelnes Motiv gefeilt». Il lavoro di Faller è citato e discusso da LIPPMANN, Friedrich. 'Per un'esegesi dello stile rossiniano', in: *Nuova Rivista Musicale Italiana*, II (1968), pp. 813-856: 819n.

[7]. COLAS, Damien. *Les annotations des chanteurs dans les matériels d'exécution des opéras de Rossini à Paris (1820-1860). Contribution à l'étude de la grammaire mélodique rossinienne*, 4 voll., tesi di dottorato, Tours, Université François Rabelais, 1997; ID. 'Melody and Ornamentation', in: *The Cambridge Companion to Rossini*, a cura di Emanuele Senici, Cambridge, Cambridge University Press, 2004, pp. 104-123.

nel sistema di produzione italiano, esteso a tutta l'Europa ad eccezione della Francia, i teatri non conservavano le particelle dei cantanti. Non si può dunque escludere che i cantanti si siano serviti di documenti scritti per elaborare e memorizzare le loro variazioni, la cui traccia si è persa verosimilmente poco tempo dopo la produzione. Per quanto riguarda i trattati, invece, sono i limiti della tipografia musicale che hanno ristretto il numero di esempi musicali nella letteratura teorica e pedagogica dell'epoca, come notò Tosi stesso, mentre l'esplosione, perfino eccessiva a volte, di testi dedicati all'insegnamento del canto a partire dei primi decenni dell'Ottocento approfittò precisamente della banalizzazione della tipografia musicale[8].

Una grande prudenza s'impone dunque nell'interpretazione di queste 'tracce scritte' ottocentesche, come rivelano i due esempi seguenti. Nel suo metodo di canto del 1849, il soprano francese Laure Cinti-Damoreau, prima interprete dei principali ruoli femminili delle opere francesi di Rossini a Parigi, pubblicò una cadenza per l'aria alternativa della contessa, 'Ah, plaignez ma misère' (N. 4a) ne Le comte Ory (1828)[9]. Questa cadenza (si veda Es. 1), situata alla fine del cantabile, immediatamente prima dell'attacco della cabaletta, comincia con una serie di trilli su un arpeggio spezzato ascendente, cui segue un passaggio in semicrome culminante in un Do acuto e concluso, dopo il trillo finale piazzato sulla sensibile, da una nota tenuta alla quinta superiore[10].

Es. 1: cadenza per l'aria 'Ah, plaignez ma misère' ne Le comte Ory di Rossini. CINTI-DAMOREAU, Laure. Op. cit. (si veda nota 10), p. 98, No. 21.

[8]. Si veda CRUTCHFIELD, Will. 'The 19th-century. Voices', in: Performance Practice. Music after 1600, a cura di Howard Mayer Brown e Stanley Sadie, Londra, Norton, 1989, pp. 424-458; ID. 'Early Vocal Ornamentation', in: ROSSINI, Gioachino. Il barbiere di Siviglia, a cura di Patricia B. Brauner, Kassel, Bärenreiter, 2008, pp. 362-420; BEGHELLI, Marco. I trattati di canto italiani dell'Ottocento. Bibliografia, caratteri generali, prassi esecutiva, lessico, tesi di dottorato, Bologna, Università degli Studi di Bologna, 1995.

[9]. L'aria è un contrafactum dell'aria di Matilde 'Sento un'interna voce' nell'Elisabetta regina d'Inghilterra (1815).

[10]. CINTI-DAMOREAU, Laure. Méthode de chant composée pour ses élèves du Conservatoire, Parigi, Ménestrel, 1849.

Nella biblioteca dell'Opéra di Parigi sono conservate due particelle utilizzate da Laure Cinti-Damoreau ne *Le comte Ory*[11]. Una di queste non contiene alcuna annotazione. L'altra presenta una cadenza di tutt'altro tipo, come ci mostra l'Es. 2.

Es. 2: cadenza (inserita a lapis) per l'aria 'Ah, plaignez ma misère' ne *Le comte Ory* di Rossini. F-Po, Particella Comtesse.

La cadenza comincia direttamente con una diminuzione introdotta da un gruppetto iniziale, e l'originalità è che l'apice di questo passaggio è oggetto di un gioco cromatico tra il Sol bemolle e il Sol naturale — del tutto frequente nella musica di Rossini. Un'altra particolarità è la fine della cadenza, senza trillo, ma l'arrivo alla quinta superiore si fa con un passaggio in *saltus duriusculus*, altrettanto frequente secondo lo stile dell'epoca. In poche parole, si tratta di una bellissima cadenza, di certo, ma né così sviluppata né così spettacolare quanto quella che l'interprete pubblicò venti anni dopo e che probabilmente non è mai stata eseguita in scena. Si constata dunque che la cadenza pubblicata, più ardua e pure più elegante sulla carta, corrisponde a un artefatto, scritto dall'interprete in vista della pubblicazione, come promemoria o con fini didattici, come esercizio proposto agli allievi.

Ancora più eloquente è la trasformazione subita dalla cadenza effettivamente cantata da Laure Cinti-Damoreau, nel ruolo di Mathilde di *Guillaume Tell*, rispetto a quella pubblicata successivamente da Duprez ne *L'art du chant* (1845) e alle cinque pubblicate dalla stessa Cinti-Damoreau (si veda Es. 3)[12]. Più ci si allontana cronologicamente dalla rappresentazione scenica, più la cadenza diventa complessa. Si noterà in particolare, nell'ultima, gli acrobatici intervalli di quinta diminuita, sottolineati dalle corone, che costituiscono per l'interprete una sfida temeraria per l'intonazione. Si tratta di un rischio che la cantante non aveva assunto in scena.

---

[11]. Pubblicata in Rossini, Gioachino. *Le comte Ory*, a cura di Damien Colas, Kassel, Bärenreiter, in fase di stampa, commento critico, N. 4a.

[12]. Cadenza pubblicata in Rossini, Gioachino. *Guillaume Tell*, a cura di M. Elisabeth C. Bartlet, Pesaro, Fondazione Rossini, 1992, Commento critico, pp. 147-149; Duprez, Gilbert-Louis. *L'art du chant*, Parigi, Heugel, 1845; Cinti-Damoreau, Laure. *Op. cit.* (si veda nota 10).

Es. 3: cadenze per la *romance* di Matilde in *Guillaume Tell* di Rossini. (a) F-Po, Particella Mathilde; (b) Duprez, Gilbert-Louis. *Op. cit.* (si veda nota 12); e (c) Cinti-Damoreau, Laure. *Op. cit.* (si veda nota 10).

Varianti multiple

Questi due esempi ci esortano alla prudenza nella valutazione degli ornamenti dell'opera italiana, in particolare dell'Ottocento, ed evidenziano il valore particolare delle annotazioni manoscritte sui documenti utilizzati dagli interpreti per studiare la loro parte, a differenza delle versioni pubblicate e conseguentemente migliorate.

L'esempio che Hedwig Faller fornisce, come illustrazione della sua tesi sul declino dell'arte dell'improvvisazione, a vantaggio del lavoro di preparazione messo per iscritto, sembra a riguardo molto interessante (si veda Es. 4). Si tratta della trascrizione diplomatica di un estratto de *La donna del lago*, tratto dalla cabaletta 'Fra il padre e fra l'amante' del rondò finale[13]. Nel sistema a sinistra riconosciamo sul secondo pentagramma partendo dall'alto,

---

13. Trasposto in Fa, mentre la tonalità originale è Mi bemolle.

in chiave di soprano, la linea del canto che corrisponde alle parole «[felici-]tà, tanta», cui manca una nota. Sopra la linea del canto si trova uno schizzo che indica semplicemente la nota estrema del passo preso in considerazione, cioè un Si bemolle acuto. Sotto la linea del canto si trovano tre varianti, che esplorano ciascuna una formula melodica particolare, costituita da quattro semicrome e ripetuta su ogni tempo.

Es. 4: ornamentazioni per la cabaletta 'Fra il padre e fra l'amante' ne *La donna del lago* di Rossini. Secondo Hedwig, Faller. *Op. cit.* (si veda nota 6), p. 115.

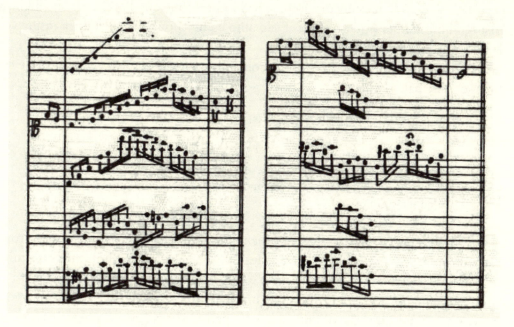

Questa disposizione, abituale per coloro che praticano l'analisi paradigmatica, si osserva di frequente, tanto nelle particelle quanto nei trattati di canto. La troviamo spesso, per esempio, nella raccolta di variazioni riunite da Nissen-Saloman e destinate ai suoi allievi[14]. Nelle variazioni per l'inizio dell'aria 'Una voce poco fa' de *Il barbiere di Siviglia*, la cantante propone non meno di sei variazioni di una difficoltà crescente nella misura corrispondente al testo «Sì, Lindoro mio sarà» (si veda Es. 5). Come mostrano gli esempi di Cinti-Damoreau esaminati sopra, queste variazioni devono essere lette con cautela: non è da escludere che una parte sia 'artefatta', destinata cioè ad abbellire la pubblicazione. Nondimeno, si riconoscono facilmente dei procedimenti all'epoca frequenti[15]. Nel terzo

---

[14]. Nissen-Saloman, Henriette. *Op. cit.* (si veda nota 1).

[15]. Colas, Damien. *Les annotations* [...], *op. cit.* (si veda nota 7), Cap. II, 'Cadences', vol. I, pp. 169-264 e vol. III, pp. 91-144.

pentagramma a partire dal basso, per esempio, si trova il passaggio ascendente con una *échappée* inferiore, figura che veniva qualificata di *subsumtio* nel Seicento, e che è correntemente utilizzata da Rossini nelle linee melodiche[16]. La troviamo d'altra parte come variazione nel passaggio de *La donna del lago* trascritto da Faller. Si tratta dunque di una variazione perfettamente plausibile. Lascia invece perplessi il diluvio di biscrome della sesta variazione, che non può essere correttamente interpretato senza un 'a piacere' dell'interprete, e un 'colla parte' dell'orchestra. Lo stesso vale per la misura precedente, in cui Nissen-Saloman propone l'interpolazione di un ampio passo su «contenta», sottolineato da una corona su «re-[sterò)]»[17]. Vedendo queste variazioni, si ha l'impressione che l'orchestra sia obbligata a fermarsi ogni misura per poter seguire il cantante e che la pulsazione ritmica originale del pezzo sia completamente sfasata (Es. 5).

Inserire questi esempi a fianco alle raccomandazioni che la stessa cantante pone come condizione principale rischia di far sorridere:

> [gli ornamenti] non siano troppo sovraccarichi e non appaiano esclusivamente calcolati allo scopo di servire alla virtuosa a sviluppare tutte le risorse d'agilità e che l'impiego troppo frequente o maldestro non soffochi la melodia primitiva o non ne snaturi il carattere, in modo da rendere più o meno irriconoscibile l'intenzione del compositore — ciò che sfortunatamente accade spessissimo[18].

Si deve dunque constatare che tali ornamentazioni e cadenze, come quella proposta per l'aria d'Amina 'Come per me sereno' de *La Sonnambula* di Bellini, non costituivano affatto dimostrazioni gratuite di virtuosismo e restavano nei limiti del buon gusto (si veda Es. 6). È certo che non siamo più abituati a una tale prolissità nell'ornamentazione vocale; eppure ciò non vuol dire che queste cadenze, iperboliche ai giorni nostri, non possano essere state eseguite in modo convincente e stilisticamente appropriato per il pubblico di fine Ottocento.

Di fronte ai vocalizzi ipertrofici della Nissen-Saloman, si può in primo luogo pensare a un artefatto finalizzato alla pubblicazione. Ma, con il beneficio del dubbio, si può pure considerare che gli eccessi dei cantanti, vituperati in ogni epoca dai critici di ogni tendenza e di ogni paese, siano una realtà sonora di cui non abbiamo probabilmente la minima idea

---

[16]. *Ibidem*, vol. I, pp. 195, 254.

[17]. È interessante paragonare queste variazioni a quelle per la stessa aria trovate in un manoscritto torinese e discusse nel contributo di Laura Moeckli in questo volume.

[18]. NISSEN-SALOMAN, Henriette. *Op. cit.* (si veda nota 1), Cap. XXII, p. 65, 'Changements. Variantes': «[les ornements] ne fussent pas surchargés et ne parussent pas exclusivement calculés dans le but de servir à la virtuose à développer toutes ses ressources d'agilité et que l'emploi trop fréquent ou maladroit n'étouffât pas la mélodie primitive ou n'en dénaturât pas le caractère, de façon à rendre plus ou moins méconnaissable l'intention du compositeur — ce qui malheureusement est très souvent le cas».

Es. 5: variazioni per l'aria 'Una voce poco fa' ne *Il barbiere di Siviglia* di Rossini. Nissen-Saloman, Henriette. *Op. cit.* (si veda nota 1), p. 410.

e che vada ben oltre la complessità e la prolissità degli esempi forniti dalla Nissen-Saloman. È utile ricordare che la nozione di gusto dell'interprete — nozione cui la maggior parte dei teorici e pedagoghi di canto, da Tosi a Duprez[19], accorda un'importanza fondamentale — resta per l'uditore variabile e sottomessa alle rivoluzioni della moda, come notavano

---

[19]. Tosi, Pier Francesco. *Op. cit.* (si veda nota 2), pp. 60-61; Reicha, Antoine. *Traité de la mélodie, abstraction faite de ses rapports avec l'harmonie*, Parigi, [Autore], 1814, p. 65; Garcia, Manuel (junior). *Op. cit.* (si veda nota 3), p. 36; Lablache, Luigi. *Méthode complète de chant*, Parigi, Canaux, 1840, p. 84; Duprez, Gilbert-Louis. *Op. cit.* (si veda nota 12), p. 206; Nissen-Saloman, Henriette. *Op. cit.* (si veda nota 1), p. 65.

Es. 6: variazioni per l'aria 'Come per me sereno' ne *La Sonnambula* di Bellini. NISSEN-SALOMAN, Henriette. *Op. cit.* (si veda nota 1), p. 422.

già Diderot e, all'epoca di Rossini, Jean-François Gail[20]. È difficile assumere una posizione netta e dire se le variazioni proposte dalla Nissen-Saloman siano di per sé eccessive. Mi sembrerebbero, alcune, difficili da interpretare sulla scena ai giorni nostri, innanzitutto a causa della sfida che costituirebbero per l'interprete, e poi perché sarebbero talmente distanti dall'attesa del pubblico da finire per essere respinte. Ma non ho difficoltà a credere che, alla fine dell'Ottocento, simili interpretazioni lussureggianti, proposte da interpreti che le padroneggiavano, possano essere state apprezzate dal pubblico senza sembrare incongrue.

Nelle due misure dell'aria di Rosina presentate in precedenza si vede chiaramente la convergenza di due elementi stilistici appartenenti a epoche diverse. La formulazione melodica fa parte del vocabolario di Rossini: le volatine ribattute che troviamo su «[Lin]-doro mio sa-[rà]» sono ricorrenti[21]. Lo stesso vale per il passo congiunto annotato con notine e interpolato su «contenta»[22]. Al contrario, la moltiplicazione delle possibilità metriche non esisteva all'epoca di Rossini. Una testimonianza del direttore d'orchestra Alberto Mazzuccato, nota agli storici dell'orchestra, ci permette di precisare in quale momento siano apparse nel corso dell'Ottocento queste distorsioni della linea melodica. Il testo, pubblicato nel 1846 nella *Gazzetta musicale di Milano*, descrive la partecipazione di Bellini alle prove d'orchestra delle sue opere e il modo in cui, dopo la sua morte, i cantanti moltiplicarono a piacimento gli effetti di rallentando e accelerando, derogando variamente e ulteriormente al rigore ritmico, senza parlare delle corone introdotte a migliaia[23]. È proprio questa 'tradizione', che in realtà tradisce la scrittura di Bellini, osservata nella proliferazione di passaggi fuori misura, che attesta l'ornamentazione proposta dalla Nissen-Saloman.

In ogni caso, le variazioni multiple non figurano unicamente nelle pubblicazioni, ma si riscontrano pure nei documenti che i cantanti utilizzavano per preparare le loro interpretazioni di scena. L'Es. 7 è tratto dall'aria 'Quelle horrible destinée' di Anaï, nel *Moïse* francese di Rossini[24]. Come per il passaggio trascritto da Hedwig Faller, le misure variate precedono l'accordo di quarta e sesta che indica la risoluzione cadenzale. Per la prima delle due misure in oggetto l'interprete (sempre Laure Cinti-Damoreau) ha proposto una sola variazione consistente in una semplificazione della linea originale. Ne indica invece quattro diverse per la seconda misura, cui aggiunge un ritocco della linea originale sul medesimo pentagramma. Si tratta, in questo caso, di figure di sostituzione, un meccanismo

[20]. DIDEROT, Denis. *Essai sur la peinture* [1765], Parigi, Buisson, Anno IV [1795]; GAIL, Jean-François. *Sur le goût musical en France*, Parigi, Paulin, 1832, pp. 4-5: «Nous n'examinons pas dans ce moment si le goût du public s'est parfois jeté dans des aberrations, et si la mode qui exerce son empire sur tout et amène d'éternelles fluctuations, ne met pas successivement en faveur certaines choses qui seront un ridicule de l'époque».

[21]. COLAS, Damien. *Op. cit.* (si veda nota 7), vol. III, pp. 388-396.

[22]. *Ibidem*, vol III, pp. 351-367.

[23]. MAZZUCATO, Alberto. 'Critica melodrammatica. *Roberto il diavolo*', in: *Gazzetta musicale di Milano*, III/21 (1846). Ripubblicato in DELLA SETA, Fabrizio. *Italia e Francia nell'Ottocento*, Torino, EDT, 1993, pp. 332-337.

[24]. Ripubblicato in COLAS, Damien. *Op. cit.* (si veda nota 7), vol. III, p. 390.

di variazione completamente diverso rispetto all'interpolazione[25]. Anziché inserire tra le note della linea originale un passaggio in diminuzione, l'interprete toglie le note di Rossini per sostituirle con le proprie. Questa tecnica è resa possibile dal carattere formulare della linea melodica: è sufficiente che l'interprete sostituisca una formula equivalente a quella originale e segua la progressione melodica, rispettando ovviamente allo stesso tempo il movimento del basso. È quanto si osserva nelle quattro variazioni proposte.

Secondo Hedwig Faller, la trascrizione di più variazioni per un medesimo passaggio testimonia il lavoro preparatorio del cantante alla ricerca della linea da scegliere in ultima istanza. Tale notazione attesta il processo genetico e permette di seguire le diverse tappe che conducono alla comparsa di una linea definitiva, destinata a sostituire la linea originale del canto. Non è escluso che i cantanti abbiano lavorato in questo modo. Di fatto, le particelle dei cantanti dell'Opéra o del Théâtre-Italien contengono alcune figure iterate che non sono prolungate perché la concatenazione armonica non lo permetteva[26]. Altri passaggi, spesso nelle cadenze, lasciano apparire ripensamenti: le idee provate dai cantanti, ma che non si confacevano al pezzo, e le formule adatte allo schema armonico unicamente su alcuni tempi della misura, ma che non potevano essere continuate, sono state scartate[27]. È quanto si osserva nelle cadenze non accettate dell'aria della contessa 'En proie à la tristesse' ne *Le comte Ory* o ancora del duetto 'Ah, quel respect, madame' nella stessa opera (si veda Es. 8)[28].

Ma si può pure constatare la traccia materiale di questo cambiamento di variazioni, da una sera all'altra, di cui parlano Tosi e Nissen-Saloman. È del tutto possibile per un interprete memorizzare versioni alternative di un medesimo passaggio grazie al procedimento della sostituzione, premessa dell'aspetto formulare della melodia. In queste circostanze, si può facilmente immaginare che un interprete scelga, al momento dell'esecuzione, quale formula di diminuzioni utilizzare. In questo modo tutto funziona perfettamente, come se l'interprete avesse memorizzato un'opera aperta, cioè contenente diverse potenzialità, fissata solo al momento della realizzazione sonora. L'improvvisazione consiste dunque nella scelta di una versione piuttosto che di un'altra, e non nella creazione, in senso letterale, della linea melodica.

La scrittura di variazioni multiple, sovrapposte secondo un asse 'paradigmatico', è il punto di contatto tra l'attività dei cantanti in scena e la loro formazione durante gli anni di studio. L'apprendimento di formule reiterate faceva parte della formazione dei cantanti e ne troviamo numerosi esempi nei trattati. La tavola presentata nell'Es. 9, estratta dai *Modi generali* di Antonio Calegari (1836), propone ventuno 'maniere' d'ornare ciò che si chiamava la 'cadenza superiore', cioè la seconda discendente dalla

---

[25]. *Ibidem*, vol. III, pp. 282-284; e vol. I, pp. 116-120.
[26]. *Ibidem*, vol. I, pp. 48-51.
[27]. *Ibidem*.
[28]. *Ibidem*, vol. I, pp. 136-137 e 155-156.

Es. 7: variazioni per l'aria 'Quelle horrible destinée' nel *Moïse* di Rossini. (a) F-Po, Particella Anaï. (b) Trascrizione.

Es. 8: parte dell'aria 'En proie à la tristesse' ne *Le Comte Ory*. F-Po, Particella Comtesse.

sovratonica alla tonica[29]. Gli interpreti memorizzavano tali formule che diventavano così veri automatismi. Senza che fosse necessario rifletterci, venivano naturalmente in mente ai musicisti ogni volta che si presentava un concatenamento melodico-armonico tipico. L'indicazione 'Qualora il tempo lo permetta', precisata per le ultime nove maniere, merita alcune considerazioni. Negli anni Trenta dell'Ottocento si considerava che i passaggi più lunghi potevano essere eseguiti solo *a tempo*, senza la proliferazione di quelle corone che Mazzucato avrebbe descritto più tardi. Un'altra tavola 'piramidale', con diminuzioni sempre più dense, si trova negli esercizi di canto di Manuel García (senior), il primo interprete del ruolo di Almaviva ne *Il barbiere di Siviglia*, dove si possono osservare molteplici procedimenti equivalenti, del tutto frequenti nel linguaggio melodico dell'epoca, per una progressione cadenzale del tipo I →IV → V → I[30].

---

[29]. CALEGARI, Antonio. *Modi generali del canto premessi alle maniere parziali onde adornare o rifiorire le nude semplici melodie o Cantilene giusta il metodo di G. Pacchiarotti*, Milano, Ricordi, 1836.

[30]. GARCÍA, Manuel (senior). *Exercises and Method for Singing*, Londra, Boosey, 1824.

Es. 9: CALEGARI, Antonio. *Op. cit.* (si veda nota 29), Part II, Chapter I, p. 10.

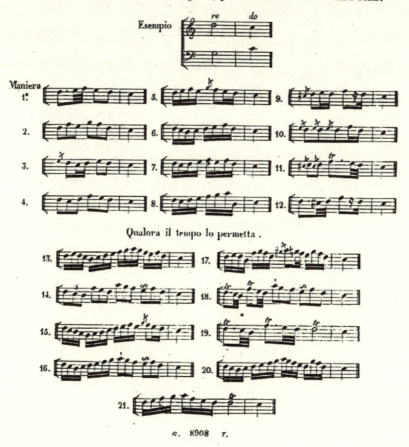

Ci si può dunque chiedere come fosse stata interpretata l'ottava variazione del tema 'Sul margine d'un rio' proposta da Gesualdo Lanza nei suoi *Studi elementari di canto* (1809), anche se l'autore ha preso la precauzione di precisare '[a] piacere del cantante' per l'accompagnamento (si veda Es. 10)[31].

---

[31].   LANZA, Gesualdo. *Studi elementari di canto*, Londra, Chappell, 1809.

Es. 10: Lanza, Gesualdo. *Op. cit.* (si veda nota 31), p. 166.

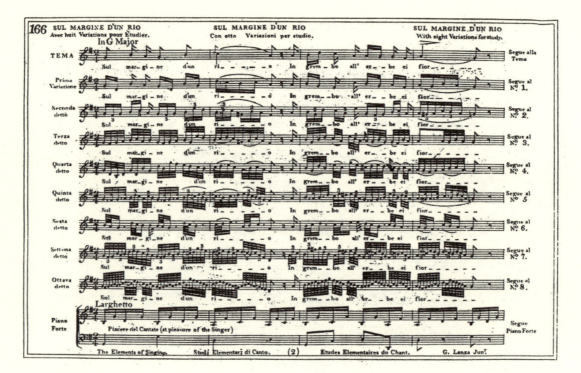

Sono da anni convinto che pubblicazioni del genere rientrino nella categoria dell'artefatto, perché mi sembra poco verosimile che un medesimo accompagnamento regolare di semicrome possa essere abbinato a linee vocali tanto diverse quanto la prima variazione (in semicrome) e l'ottava (in semibiscrome)[32]. Ma, è vero che questi metodi di canto avevano in realtà un duplice obiettivo: parallelamente all'acquisizione di un repertorio di formule di sostituzione, l'allievo cantante sviluppava a poco a poco la flessibilità vocale. In un'epoca in cui l'uso del metronomo non era generalizzato, il passaggio dalla prima all'ottava variazione equivaleva a eseguire la coloratura sempre più rapidamente, ma in modo progressivo, come se fosse aggiunta ogni volta una tacca di metronomo, ciò che praticano oggi tanto gli strumentisti quanto i cantanti che si esercitano nello stile della coloratura. Troviamo ancora diversi esempi di queste variazioni, che potremmo qualificare come 'piramidali' o 'logaritmiche', nel trattato di Johann Friedrich Schubert, la *Neue Singschule* (1804)[33]: si tratta della famosa aria 'Nel

---

[32]. Giambattista Mancini, nelle sue *Riflessioni pratiche sul canto figurato* (Milano, Galeazzi, 1777), precisa che i numerosi sedicenti maestri di canto sono in realtà clavicembalisti o violinisti, cosa che spiega il carattere strumentale di numerose formulazioni melodiche indicate nei loro manuali di canto.

[33]. Schubert, Johann Friedrich. *Neue Singschule, oder gründliche und vollständige Anweisung zur Singkunst in 3 Abtheilungen, mit hinlänglichen Übungsstücken*, Lipsia, Breitkopf & Härtel, 1804.

cor più non mi sento' de *La Molinara* di Paisiello. Le variazioni da 4 a 6 permettono in ogni modo di prendere atto che questo Andantino era molto più lento del tempo abitualmente osservato ai giorni nostri.

Un altro modo d'improvvisazione?

Per quanto riguarda le variazioni multiple è già stata ricordata l'importanza del procedimento di sostituzione e del suo legame con la natura formulare della linea melodica nelle diminuzioni, cioè una struttura fondata sull'iterazione regolare della medesima cellula melodica e su uno schema armonico semplice. La tecnica di sostituzione è per questa ragione impiegata innanzitutto negli Allegro dell'aria, cioè le riprese di cabaletta; tuttavia, benché l'aspetto formulare della melodia non sia sempre regolare, la incontriamo pure nei passaggi diminuiti delle sezioni rapide delle arie con da capo del Settecento. In queste arie, i cantanti potevano dunque improvvisare allo stesso modo, avendo precedentemente memorizzato diverse versioni alternative, optando per una scelta piuttosto che per un'altra solo all'ultimo momento.

Nella descrizione dei cambiamenti da parte del cantante da un'esecuzione all'altra, Tosi torna sulla distinzione che gli sta a cuore tra i due stili opposti dell''aria patetica' e dell''aria allegra'[34], distinzione fondamentale del canto italiano che si osserva, nel trattamento della formula melodica, fino a Donizetti e Verdi, e nei teorici fino a Garcia[35]. È importante tenere presente questa distinzione tra i due stili di canto e le loro implicazioni in materia d'improvvisazione. L'impiego di figure semplici, reiterate regolarmente con omogeneità di valori ritmici (per esempio, diminuzioni in sequenza di semicrome), è una caratteristica dell'allegro, che si distingue radicalmente dal cantabile (che Tosi chiama 'il patetico'), caratterizzato invece da ritmi fioriti in cui coesistono diversi valori ritmici e dall'assenza di schemi regolari o 'geometrici'. La sostituzione, legata all'aspetto formulare della melodia, è dunque solo raramente utilizzata nel Cantabile, in cui il principale procedimento di variazione è al contrario l'interpolazione, che consiste nell'inserire note d'ornamento tra le note originali della melodia. Tramite esempi rilevati nelle parti dei cantanti, in questa tabella è presentata la differenza tra i due procedimenti di variazione: in basso, si riconosce una delle figure di sostituzione che abbiamo dell'aria di Anaï nel *Moïse*, mentre sopra si trova un esempio d'interpolazione tratto dall'aria alternativa della contessa ne *Le comte Ory* (si veda Es. 11).

---

34. Tosi, Pier Francesco. *Op. cit.* (si veda nota 2).

35. La dicotomia tra i due stili di canto è espressa in Lanza, Gesualdo. *Op. cit.* (si veda nota 31), Garcia, Manuel (junior). *Op. cit.* (si veda nota 3), e implicitamente Duprez, Gilbert-Louis. *Op. cit.* (si veda nota 12).

Es. 11: interpolazione e sostituzione. (a) Interpolazione in 'Ah, plaignez ma misère' de *Le Comte Ory* di Rossini; (b) Sostutizione in 'Quelle horrible destinée' nel *Moïse* di Rossini.

Preme sottolineare che le note d'interpolazione non sono state provviste, dall'interprete, di una notazione ritmica completa. Questo dettaglio è interessante: spesso, gli interpreti si limitavano a scrivere l'altezza della nota, senza mettere aste (cosa che accade proprio in questo esempio) né riunire le note d'abbellimento sotto un'unica barra di valore, senza specificare così se si tratti di semicrome, biscrome o semibiscrome. Questo tipo di notazione è spesso utilizzato nelle opere di Chopin e di Liszt, dove lunghi arabeschi si presentano sotto forma di notine, senza indicazione ritmica precisa; tale notazione permette di differenziare immediatamente l'ornamentazione dalle note principali della melodia. Nell'Es. 12 figura un estratto dallo Studio Op. 25 No. 7 di Chopin, in cui si può riconoscere il tema 'Teneri figli' dell'inizio del secondo atto della *Norma* di Bellini, tessitura di violoncello. Questo tema è preceduto da un ampio motivo ornamentale affidato alla mano sinistra, che nell'opera italiana è l'omologo del passaggio vocale che porta alla ripresa. È molto probabile che questo tipo di notazione provenga dalla notazione vocale.

Es. 12: estratto dallo Studio Op. 25 n. 7 di Chopin, misure 53-55.

Lanza insiste sulla differenza di temporalità che separa i due tipi di ornamenti[36]. Tutti gli abbellimenti introdotti nelle arie vengono chiamati ornamenti e sono di due specie: nella prima le note sono cantate a tempo; nella seconda le note sono cantate *ad libitum*. Quest'ultimo ornamento consiste nell'aggiunta, operata dal cantante, di più note che devono essere cantate con gusto.

Gli esempi d'interpolazione che ho potuto trovare nei manoscritti dei cantanti sono considerevolmente meno numerosi di quelli di sostituzione. Non credo però che i cantanti variassero le loro parti cantabili meno di quelle brillanti. La mia opinione è che l'annotazione di questi ornamenti fosse meno necessaria. In effetti, nella misura in cui il tempo lento non era sottoposto a una pulsazione metrica implacabile e meccanica, il rubato era fortemente incoraggiato in questo stile di canto, e le interpolazioni poggiavano su figure contrappuntistiche, cioè essenzialmente congiunte o fondate sugli intervalli dell'armonia del basso: un cantante aveva tutta la libertà di lanciarsi in un passo più o meno sviluppato, senza rischiare di perdersi. Anche nel caso in cui il cantante si lasciasse trascinare dall'improvvisazione e rischiasse di essere condotto da essa verso una nota estranea all'armonia nel momento della ripresa dell'orchestra, la natura profondamente irregolare, tanto ritmicamente quanto melodicamente, del passo interpolato gli permetteva di aggiungere tante note quante fossero necessarie per ritrovare una nota consonante. Ed è questa la differenza fondamentale con la logica della sostituzione, in cui il numero di note variate corrisponde rigorosamente al numero di note della linea originale, e non è possibile alcun passo falso. Sono dunque convinto che un'improvvisazione del secondo tipo, fondata su una realizzazione fatta al momento, fosse praticata tramite la tecnica d'interpolazione nei movimenti lenti, mentre l'improvvisazione nei movimenti rapidi necessitava in precedenza della memorizzazione di una combinazione di possibilità.

La differenza tra le due tecniche d'improvvisazione è riassunta nella tabella seguente:

TEMPO RAPIDO	TEMPO LENTO
contingenza ritmica forte	– debole o inesistente
memorizzazione delle formule necessaria	– non necessaria
notazione necessaria	– non necessaria
restrizione dei gradi di libertà	numerosi gradi di libertà
SOSTITUZIONE	INTERPOLAZIONE

Non credo dunque, come Hedwig Faller sostiene, che la traccia scritta sia il segno di un declino dell'improvvisazione. Le tracce scritte dei cantanti possono essere confrontate ai *generici* degli attori della commedia dell'arte, spesso messi per iscritto, grazie ai quali gli attori memorizzavano un arsenale di repliche che impiegavano, da uno scenario all'altro, per la propria interpretazione[37].

---

[36]. LANZA, Gesualdo. *Op. cit.* (si veda nota 31).

[37]. HENKE, Robert. *Performance and Literature in the Commedia dell'arte*, Cambridge, Cambridge University Press, 2002.

È certo che la notazione di variazioni multiple e la loro trasmissione, per esempio quella da professore ad allievo, abbia contribuito alla selezione di un certo numero di varianti ornamentali. Ma questo è un allontanamento della funzione principale della notazione delle versioni alternative, che era essa stessa un prolungamento della formazione del cantante nell'arte della variazione. Lo testimoniano, per esempio, le cadenze proposte da Mathilde Marchesi nelle sue *Variantes et points d'orgue* (1886), tra le quali si possono riconoscere certe formule che vengono ancora utilizzate ai giorni nostri[38].

Questa trasmissione della tradizione pone un duplice problema: sono stati numerosi i teorici del canto che, sin dal Settecento, hanno sostenuto che l'ornamentazione vocale, per essere convincente e riuscita, non dovesse essere scritta dal compositore, ma lasciata alla discrezione dell'interprete. Anton Reicha dichiarava a tale riguardo:

> un compositore non è un cantante; ciò che comporrà per la sua voce, o con la sua voce, non andrà bene né al talento né alla voce del cantante abile. I ricami *prescritti* sono poi quasi sempre interpretati male. La maggior parte delle volte un cantante di talento li fa per ispirazione, che in questo caso è sempre meglio rispetto alla ricerca del compositore. Il cantante li sistema secondo la natura della sua voce e del suo diapason, e li modifica spesso; di tutto questo non resta nulla, se il compositore li prescrive[39].

Se un cantante deve appropriarsi di un linguaggio melodico per formare a suo modo uno stile vocale, questo significa che non può prendere per modello lo stile di un altro interprete. È quanto ricordava Anna Maria Pellegrini-Celoni che, pur fornendo esempi di variazioni, indicava di non imitarla, poiché «ciò facendo, non formarebbesi stile, e la cosa sarebbe pedantesca»[40]. Inoltre, il rispetto cieco di una tradizione e la trasmissione, da un cantante all'altro, delle medesime variazioni — come accade ancora oggi con i volumi di Luigi Ricci — giunge a conferire alle varianti d'interprete un'autorità superiore a quella del testo originale del compositore, cosa che contraddice la stessa idea di variazione vocale.

Sarebbe dunque d'importanza cruciale riportare in vigore, nella formazione dei giovani cantanti, la pratica dei *generici*, ossia delle figure di sostituzione impiegate tanto nell'improvvisazione degli allegri quanto nella fabbricazione delle cadenze. Solo una

---

[38]. MARCHESI, Mathilde. *Variantes et points d'orgue pour les principaux airs du répertoire*, Parigi, Heugel, 1886.

[39]. REICHA, Antoine. *Op. cit.* (se veda nota 17), p. 69: «un compositeur n'est pas un chanteur; ce qu'il composera pour sa voix, ou avec sa voix, ne conviendra ni au talent ni à la voix du chanteur habile. Les broderies *préscrites* sont ensuite presque toujours mal exécutées. Un chanteur de talent les fait le plus souvent par inspiration, ce qui vaut toujours mieux dans ce cas que la recherche du compositeur. Le chanteur les arrange d'après la nature de sa voix et de son diapason, et les modifie souvent; tout cela est perdu, si le compositeur le prescrit».

[40]. PELLEGRINI-CELONI, Anna Maria. *Grammatica o sieno regole di ben cantare*, Roma, Piale & Martorelli, 1810.

familiarità quotidiana con i passaggi melodici più frequenti, in un repertorio preciso, può conferire all'interprete ciò che Schulz chiamava la 'pratica corrente della lingua' e che considerava come una qualità essenziale dell'interprete, nella sua funzione di 'traduttore', di 'messaggero' o ancora di 'ambasciatore' del pensiero del compositore[41]. Solo questa pratica corrente della lingua rende il cantante atto a esprimersi con le sue parole, ad assimilare il pensiero del compositore e a riformularlo, a piacere, per mezzo di espressioni equivalenti o di sinonimi, tutte operazioni che sono tante manifestazioni della capacità d'improvvisazione.

---

[41]. Schulz, Johann Abraham Peter. 'Vortrag', in: *Allgemeine Theorie der schönen Künste*, a cura di Johann Georg Sulzer, Lipsia, Weidmann, 1792: «eine hinlängliche Geläufigkeit in der musikalischen Sprache».

DAMIEN COLAS

ENGLISH SUMMARY

IMPROVISATION AND ORNAMENTATION IN FRENCH AND ITALIAN OPERA
OF THE FIRST HALF OF THE NINETEENTH CENTURY

Damien Colas

Nineteenth-century treatises on singing such as those of Garcia (Junior, 1840) and Nissen-Saloman (1881) describe the elaborate and ever changing variations and ornamentations that opera singers added in their performances. Written-out examples are found in the treatises by Duprez (1845), Cinti-Damoreau (1849) and Nissen-Saloman (1881) and in the notebooks left by Cinti-Damoreau, and those of the Paris opera. To some extent they repeat formulae published earlier by Lanza (1809) and Calegari (1836). Important aspects to study are (1) whether or not this practice diminished or even disappeared during the second half of the nineteenth century; (2) to what extent these embellishments were really improvised or rather prepared beforehand; and (3) which parts of the aria were considered particularly apt for embellishment. The question also remains of whether the examples in the treatises represent actual practice or rather a repertory to be studied. Both the theoretical and the practical sources often provide multiple embellished lines, suggesting that the singer had a choice before him or her when he had to sing the particular aria. There are two fundamental ways to construct these variations: substitution, when longer note values are substituted with shorter ones, and interpolation, when larger melodic intervals are filled by stepwise progressions. Substitution can be linked to the faster tempi, interpolation to the slower. Substitution mostly retains the metrical structure of the aria. In the case of interpolation, a *rubato* performance is often necessary, which necessitates a careful collaboration between singer and orchestra. The article discusses passages from *Il barbiere di Siviglia*, *La donna del lago*, *Moïse*, *Le comte Ory* and *Guillaume Tell* by Rossini and *La sonnambula* by Bellini.

«Abbellimenti o fioriture»
Further Evidence of Creative Embellishment in and beyond the Rossinian Repertoire[1]

Laura Moeckli
(Bern)

Though by no means a free form of improvisation, early nineteenth-century vocal ornamentation of Italian opera is an area of musical practice where singers were expected to contribute extensively to the musical parameters of an operatic performance. Composers provided space for singers to demonstrate their expressive virtuosity, while singers made each opera performance a creative and unique event. *Diminution*, *roulade*, *gruppetto* and *appoggiatura* are some of the terms one finds in nineteenth-century sources describing the musical elements that could be used to transform written arias and recitatives within the conventions of the genre. Due to the long and ongoing tradition of Italian opera, this repertoire is an ideal field in which to observe the gradual historical shifts in composition and performance practices. Generally speaking, the parameters remained more traditional in Italian opera than in other genres of the time: «Opera, and Italian opera in particular [...] remained bound longer than other nineteenth-century genres to eighteenth-century traditions concerning the relationship between composer and performer»[2]. Throughout the first half of the nineteenth century, singers acted as collaborative artists of a work rather than performers of a fixed composition.

Ornamentation conventions were generally transmitted orally from generation to generation, through a combination of teaching, imitation and cultural exchange. Even today, some aspects of nineteenth-century singing technique continue to be taught by singers who studied with students of singers who were active as far back as the 1850s[3].

---

[1]. My special thanks go to Anselm Gerhard, Kai Köpp and Giuliano Castellani for their helpful feedback regarding this article.

[2]. Gossett, Philip. *Divas and Scholars: Performing Italian Opera*, Chicago, University of Chicago Press, 2006, p. 293.

[3]. For a discussion of the oral transmission of nineteenth-century Italian singing techniques, see Berne, Peter. *Belcanto. Historische Aufführungspraxis in der italienischen Oper von Rossini bis Verdi. Ein praktisches Lehrbuch*

Another means of oral transmission emerged by the end of the nineteenth century with the new possibilities of sound recording. A few singers born in the 1830s, and many born in the 1840s, 50s and 60s, recorded ornamented versions of arias, some of which have survived until today and these offer valuable insight into nineteenth-century ornamentation practice[4].

Although some musicians and scholars have taken an interest in such sources in recent years, many universities, music schools and theatres continue to ignore the evidence of singers' improvisational freedom, expecting performances to adhere to the written scores or to some famous ornamented versions of the twentieth century. Today, literal reading of scores, fixed interpretations of works and unadorned renditions of melodic lines have become the aesthetic norm, while improvised individual ornamentation is no longer a commonly accepted practice for classical and romantic opera performance. However, the historical evidence shows that many works which are a part of today's standard opera repertoire could well (and perhaps should) be performed very differently than they are today. In any case, vocal ornamentation of some kind is clearly more than a simple option for performance; in Italian opera of this time, individual ornamentation is a structural element of the works themselves. By studying the various performance sources in addition to the original scores, one can understand and master the conventions of ornamentation so obvious to the contemporaries of Rossini. In what follows, I shall focus on the written material available and more particularly on the examples of vocal ornamentation found in a manuscript which is kept in the Biblioteca Nazionale Universitaria di Torino under the signature Foà-Giordano 631 and unpublished so far[5].

WRITTEN EVIDENCE OF NINETEENTH-CENTURY VOCAL ORNAMENTATION

In its very essence, ornamentation tends to resist notation. Written traces of ornamental practice are therefore both valuable documents and historical anomalies, since they present unusual evidence of an otherwise orally transmitted tradition. Luckily some such traces have survived for early nineteenth-century repertoire, enabling us to access an aspect of operatic performance that has been neglected in recent years. The conventions

---

für Sänger, Dirigenten und Korrepetitoren, Worms, Wernersche Verlagsgesellschaft, 2008, Part 1, Chapter 4: 'Antonio Cotogni, Luigi Ricci und die mündliche Überlieferung', pp. 51-68.

4. For an example of how these sound sources can be used to gain precise information about nineteenth-century ornamentation see CRUTCHFIELD, Will. 'Vocal Ornamentation in Verdi. The Phonological Evidence', in: *Nineteenth-Century Music*, VII (1983-1984), pp. 3-54.

5. The contents of the manuscript will be published in a critical transcription in 2011 as the first volume of a new series on interpretation research at the Bern University of Applied Sciences edited by Kai Köpp. See our project webpage at <http://www.hkb.bfh.ch/> under the headings 'research'; 'interpretation'; 'publications'.

and variations of ornamentation were favoured topics among the early nineteenth-century opera audience. Accordingly, the first half of the century produced a rich selection of documents describing vocal technique, interpretation and ornamentation of Italian opera: composers wrote explicit ornaments and variations for their own compositions; singing teachers included chapters on ornamentation in their pedagogical treatises; performers kept written records of their own ornaments, while critics discussed both the necessity and the excesses of ornamentation.

Composers such as Rossini, Donizetti and Verdi increasingly wrote explicit ornaments for the repetitions and cadenzas of their compositions where they could otherwise have left room for professional singers' creativity. This development is the result of a complex series of socio-cultural paradigm shifts which emerged during the nineteenth century, and dictate many of our conscious and unconscious aesthetic judgments even today. To put it simply: composers became 'geniuses', singers became 'divas', the sublime replaced the beautiful, and 'ornamental' came to mean accessory rather than complementary. Yet the fact remains that, well into the second half of the nineteenth century, Italian opera composers continued to write ornamented versions of their compositions, while praising those singers who proposed elegant and expressive variations of their own. Surviving autograph variations provide an ideal starting point of access to some stylistically appropriate ornaments for arias and recitatives of this period.

The study of contemporary pedagogical treatises presents another valuable source of information for historical ornamentation practice. Founded in 1794, the Paris Conservatoire became the primary model for institutionalized musical education throughout nineteenth-century Europe. In this context of pedagogical standardisation, many theorists sought to capture and redefine the precepts for lyric education and to transmit their methods to future generations. Written collectively under the direction of the Italian singer Bernardo Mengozzi, the first *Méthode de chant du Conservatoire* presents a general singing method based on «the principles drawn from the school of the famous Bernachi», that is to say the orally transmitted Italian tradition[6]. In a footnote to the chapter entitled 'On the Various Characters of Singing' (*Des divers caractères du chant*), the authors explain how teachers must choose appropriate ornaments for their students. They insist on the importance of using ornamental variations that can be easily improvised rather than learnt by heart, so that these can be integrated effectively and effortlessly into a piece:

> Experience shows us that not all voices are adequate for performing
> all figures without distinction; therefore an experienced singing master [...]
> must have a complete knowledge of the character, the strength, the flexibility

---

[6]. [Mengozzi, Bernardo (et al.)]. *Méthode de Chant du Conservatoire*, Paris, Imprimerie du Conservatoire de Musique, [1803], in the '*Avertissement*' following the title page: «les principes qu'il avait puisé dans l'école du célèbre Bernachi».

and ultimately of all the qualities of [a student's] voice, in order to give him to perform, among the various figures, only those which he will be able to grasp and render, if not immediately, then at least after a minimal amount of work, so that these figures do not lose their characteristic neatness and expression. A figure that has been studied for a long time, always bears the imprint of the work and trouble it has cost to learn, which spoils the qualities it must have to produce a good effect[7].

Nearly half a century later Manuel Garcia junior's *Traité complet de l'art du chant* describes the rhetorical function of ornamentation in the case of textual repetitions: «One must vary a thought every time it is repeated, either entirely or partially; this is indispensable and serves to give the thought new charm and retain the listener's attention»[8], and then explains how a series of progressing variations can be used to build-up the meaning and impact of a phrase within a particular section:

> These changes must follow an increasing progression in their disposition. At first one uses effects sparingly, and the motif exposition retains all its simplicity; then, in the first repeat, one incorporates some embellishments or accents different from the first ones; finally one increases and varies the embellishments and accents more and more with every new repetition[9].

These two sources are among the most detailed and prominent nineteenth-century singing treatises; they were read and translated widely throughout Europe. Many other treatises contain important information on ornamentation which confirms and nuances the statements presented here[10].

---

7. *Ibidem*, p. 66: «L'exemple nous montre que toutes les voix ne sont pas propres à exécuter indistinctement tous les traits; par conséquent un maître de chant expérimenté [...] doit avoir une entière connaissance du caractère, de la force, de la flexibilité et enfin de toutes les qualités de sa voix, afin de ne lui donner à exécuter, parmi les traits choisis, que ceux qu'il saura saisir et rendre, sinon à l'instant même, du moins avec peu de travail, sans que ces traits perdent de la netteté et de l'expression qui leur sont particulières. Un trait qui a été étudié longtems se ressent toujours du travail et de la peine qu'il a couté à apprendre, ce qui nuit aux qualités qu'il doit avoir pour produire un bon effet».

8. GARCIA, Manuel (junior). *Traité complet de l'art du chant*, 2 vols., Paris, Auteur, 1847, vol. II, Chapter 3, 'On Variation' (*Des changements*), p. 36: «On doit varier une pensée chaque fois qu'elle se répète, soit en totalité, soit en partie; cela est indispensable et pour donner un nouveau charme à la pensée et pour soutenir l'attention de l'auditeur».

9. *Ibidem*: «Ces changements, dans leur disposition, doivent suivre une progression croissante. On ménage d'abord les moyens d'effet, et on conserve à l'exposition du motif toute sa simplicité; puis on mêle à la première reproduction quelques fioritures ou quelques accents différents des premiers; enfin, on augmente et on varie de plus en plus, à chaque nouvelle répétition les ornements et les accents».

10. For a list of nineteenth-century singing treatises containing information on ornamentation, see CRUTCHFIELD, Will. 'Chapter XXI. Voices', in: *Performance Practice. Music after 1600*, edited by Howard Mayer Brown and Stanley Sadie, London, Macmillan Press, 1989, p. 425.

Besides composers and teachers, the most direct sources of information concerning ornamentation practice are the singers themselves. In the case of Garcia's treatise, his transcriptions of ornaments by leading singers of the time, such as his father Manuel Garcia Senior and his sisters Pauline Viardot and Maria Malibran, provide illustrative examples of the principles he describes. The French soprano Laure Cinti-Damoreau is a well-known case of a singer whose notebooks and singing method, both containing suggestions for ornamentation, have survived until today[11]. Many other singers of the time wrote their ornaments in notebooks or annotated their scores, but these sources were usually kept as personal reminders or didactic material rather than for publication or posterity[12]. The Manuscript Foà-Giordano 631 of the Biblioteca Nazionale Universitaria di Torino is a surviving notebook similar to those of Laure Cinti-Damoreau in that it contains numerous detailed and elaborate examples of ornamentation for works by Rossini, Donizetti, Bellini, Verdi and their contemporaries.

The Manuscript Foà-Giordano 631

The Raccolta Foà-Giordano of the Biblioteca Nazionale Universitaria in Turin contains a miscellaneous assortment of printed and manuscript musical materials. Its name is misleading since most of the documents it contains have nothing to do with the industrial families Foà or Giordano. Two generous patrons, Roberto Foà and Filippo Giordano, did in fact acquire and donate an important collection of seventeenth and eighteenth-century music — most famous are the Vivaldi autograph manuscripts — to the Biblioteca Nazionale Universitaria of Turin in the 1930s, but their donations are kept in two distinct collections named after and dedicated to their respective sons: the Raccolta Mauro Foà and Raccolta Renzo Giordano[13]. Although the miscellaneous Raccolta Foà-Giordano contains a few of Filippo Giordano's later donations, most of its content was assembled haphazardly later in the century. Completed in 2001, Annarita Colturato's *Catalogo della musica a stampa* offers detailed information concerning the more than one thousand printed sources dating

---

[11]. For an introduction to the singing method and notebooks of Laure Cinti-Damoreau, see CASWELL, Austin. 'Mme Cinti-Damoreau and the Embellishment of Italian opera in Paris', in: *Journal of the American Musicological Society*, XXVIII/3 (1975), pp. 459-492. Cinti-Damoreau's detailed notebooks are housed in the Lilly Library at Indiana University in Bloomington (Indiana). A selection of these ornaments has been transcribed and published in *Embellished Opera Arias*, edited by Austin Caswell, Madison, A-R Editions, 1989 (Recent Research in the Music of the Nineteenth and Early Twentieth Centuries, 7-8).

[12]. For a comprehensive study of singers' annotations in Parisian performance parts, see COLAS, Damien. *Les annotations des chanteurs dans les matériels d'exécution des opéras de Rossini à Paris (1820-1860). Contribution à l'étude de la grammaire mélodique rossinienne*, Ph.D. Dissertation, 4 vols., Tours, Université de Tours, 1997.

[13]. For a detailed account of these collections see BASSO, Alberto. *Raccolta Mauro Foà, Raccolta Renzo Giordano*, Rome, Torre d'Orfeo, 1987.

from the eighteenth, nineteenth and twentieth centuries, some of which are valuable unique or first editions[14]. However, there is no catalogue describing the collection's almost two hundred manuscripts. The Manuscript Foà–Giordano 631 is one of these unidentified, unsigned and undated manuscripts. Though it probably made its way into the miscellaneous collection at some point during the twentieth century, there is no acquisition record in the Turin Library confirming this assumption.

The notebook measures 36.5 cm by 27 cm and consists of 21 folios, or 42 pages, with sixteen staves on each page. On the front page, a title is inscribed in small letters and underlined: 'Raccolta di abbellimenti, o fioriture di Cavatine, Arie, Duetti di varii autori'. The document contains 58 separate entries headed by the title of an aria, a recitative or a duet, and the name of the opera from which it is taken, or the name of the composer. Each entry consists of ornamented vocal lines with the corresponding text underneath. In some cases the entire melodic line of an aria is transcribed with ornaments added in appropriate places; more often, however, the ornaments are fragments that apply to specific bars of a piece and are separated from each other by vertical lines. In some cases the text enables an unambiguous attribution of a fragment to a particular location in a certain opera; in other cases this attribution remains ambiguous. TABLE 1, containing a diplomatic transcription of the autograph table of contents, offers an overview of the manuscript's scope.

TABLE 1

DIPLOMATIC TRANSCRIPTION OF THE TABLE OF CONTENTS, FOL. 18V,
OF THE MANUSCRIPT FOÀ–GIORDANO 631, BIBLIOTECA NAZIONALE UNIVERSITARIA DI TORINO

Sapienza –	Cav^{na}: dell'Audacia - Pag:		1
Pacini –	Cav.^{na} nel Barone di Dolsheim - fortunata rivale –		1
Bellini.	Cav.^{na} nella Sonnamb: come per me sereno –		2.
Donizetti.	Cav.^{na} nell'Anna Bolena: Vivi tu –		2
Rossini.	Cav^{na} nella Matilde di Shabran –	come alla pag:	3
	10		
idem	Cav.^{na} nella pietra del paragone –		3.
idem	Duetto nel Tancredi - m'abbraccia Argirio –		4.
idem	Duetto nella Matilde –		4.
idem	Cav.^{na} nel Tancredi per Contr: –		5
idem	Cav.^{na} nella donna del lago: - mura felici	si veda anco alla pag: 6	9
			e 10
idem	Duetto - perché mai le luci aprimmo		6

14. COLTURATO, Annarita. La raccolta Foà-Giordano della Biblioteca Nazionale Universitaria di Torino. Catalogo della musica a stampa, Milan, Electa, 2001.

idem	Cav.^{na} ~~per~~ Come dolce all'alma mia	6
idem	Cav.^{na} nel Torvaldo, e dorliska: <u>Tutto è vano</u>	7
<u>Conti</u> -	Aria negli Arragonesi in Napoli: non t'involar così	7.
Rossini	Cav:^{na} nel barbiere di Siviglia - Una voce poco fa	8
idem	Cav.^{na} nel <u>Ciro</u> = t'abbraccio, ti stringo	8, e 20
idem	Duetto nell'<u>Armida</u>: Amor, possente nume	9
idem	Cav.^{na} nella donna del lago; mura felici	9
Pacini:	Scena e rondò nel Barone di Dolsheim: ah per me l'avversa sorte	10
Rossini	Cav.^{na} nella Matilde di Shabran; piange il mio ciglio	10
idem	Duetto nella Semiramide - Ebben a te ferisci	11, e 16
Donizetti -	Cavatina nell'Anna Bolena - Come innocente giovane	12
Rossini -	Duetto nella Semiramide - Bella imago	12
Mercadante -	Duetto nell'Andronico -	12, e 13
Rossini -	Cavatina - nella Gazza ladra -	13, e 17-18
idem -	Cavatina nel barbiere di Siviglia - una voce poco fa -	13
Mercadante*-	Duetto nel Zadig ed Astartea - Deh! lascia ch'io respiri.	14
Rossini -	Duetto nell'Otello - Vorrei che il tuo pensiero	14
Rossini -	Rondò nella Zelmira - Se serbai la vita, il trono	14
Garaudé -	Duetto	16
Pacini -	Duetto	16
Rossini -	Cavatina, nella Bianca e Faliero - della rosa il bel vermiglio	19.
Bellini -	Cavatina, nella Sonnambula - Come per me sereno	19
idem.	Cavatina, od aria nei Puritani - Qui la voce sua soave	20
Rossini.	Cavatina nel barbiere di Siv: Una voce poco fa	20 e 21
idem.	Duetto, nel barbiere di Siviglia - Dunque io son.	21
idem	Seguito della parte della p.^a donna nella Cenerentola con parte del Introduzione, e Duetto: io vorrei saper perché.	22
idem -	Seguito del Duetto, e Quintetto a pag:	25 -
idem -	Sestetto, ed aria della med.^{ma}	26
idem		27
idem	Aria nel Tancredi = come dolce all'alma mia	28, e 29
idem	Cavatina nella Semiramide, a soprano	29.
Pacini -	Cavatina nella <u>Niobe</u>: il soave e bel contento	30
Donizetti	Cavatina nella Lucia	30, e 31

	Alcune cadenze	31
Rossini	Cavatina: Ah quel giorno ognor rammento	31, e
		32
	Varie cadenze	32, e
		33

* This opera is by Nicola Vaccai, not by Mercadante.

The notebook contains 58 different entries with suggestions of ornamentation for Italian opera arias, recitatives and duets. TABLE 2 lists the operas represented in the manuscript in chronological order. The number of entries and bars dedicated to each opera are listed as well in order to give an approximate indication of their relative importance within the notebook.

TABLE 2

THE OPERAS FOR WHICH THE MANUSCRIPT FOÀ-GIORDANO 631 CONTAINS ORNAMENTS

COMPOSER	OPERA	DATE	ENTRIES	BARS
Mozart	*Le nozze di Figaro*	1786	3x	144
Rossini	*Ciro in Babilonia*	1812	1x	24
Rossini	*La pietra del Paragone*	1812	1x	12
Rossini	*Tancredi*	1813	3x	170
Rossini	*Aureliano in Palmira*	1813	1x	8
Rossini	*Torvaldo e Dorliska*	1815	1x	68
Rossini	*Il barbiere di Siviglia*	1816	4x	171
Rossini	*Otello*	1816	1x	10
Rossini	*La Cenerentola*	1817	6x	236
Rossini	*La gazza ladra*	1817	3x	132
Rossini	*Armida*	1817	1x	38
Pacini	*Il barone di Dolsheim*	1818	3x	63
Rossini	*La donna del lago*	1819	2x	78
Rossini	*Bianca e Faliero*	1819	1x	37
Mercadante	*Andronico*	1821	1x	54
Rossini	*Matilde di Shabran*	1821	3x	36
Rossini	*Zelmira*	1822	1x	29
Rossini	*Semiramide*	1823	6x	230
Sapienza	*L'Audacia fortunata*	1824	1x	40
Vaccai	*Zadig et Astartea*	1825	1x	18
Pacini	*Niobe*	1826	1x	40
Conti	*Gli Aragonesi in Napoli*	1827	1x	52
Donizetti	*Anna Bolena*	1830	2x	48
Bellini	*La sonnambula*	1831	4x	99

Donizetti	*Lucrezia Borgia*	1833	IX	10
Donizetti	*Rosamunda d'Ingliterra*	1834	IX	28
Bellini	*I puritani*	1835	IX	18
Verdi	*Macbeth*	1847	IX	8

Though the manuscript is undated, the chronological spectrum of the works included gives a rough indication of its temporal situation. Most of the repertoire was composed between 1812 and 1835; only Mozart's *Le Nozze di Figaro* (1786) and Verdi's *Macbeth* (1847) extend beyond these limits. Since there is no chronological coherence in the order of the entries, one can assume that they were all written around 1835, and not gradually assembled over a longer period of time. The unified style of writing from fol. 3r to fol. 18v further confirms this idea. The last pages of the manuscript (including the short entry with ornaments for Verdi's *Macbeth* found on fol. 19r) are less uniform and were probably added at a later date since they are not included in the table of contents.

The hand has not yet been definitely identified, but a series of hypotheses have lead to the conclusion that he or she was active both in Italy and in France during the first half of the nineteenth century, was most probably a singer or singing teacher, and definitely a professional musician. The most likely function of this notebook seems to have been a didactic one, where the various entries may have served as suggestions for individual singing students. In what follows, I have chosen two prominent examples in order to contextualise and highlight the material contained within this manuscript.

'Una voce poco fa'

In the recent critical edition of Rossini's *Il barbiere di Siviglia*, various appendices provide performers with additional music and information concerning ornamentation[15]. There is, for example, an appendix containing Rossini's variations for 'Una voce poco fa', 'Dunque io son' and 'Ah qual colpo'. An additional appendix in the commentary volume presents a broad selection of ornaments used by singers during the first fifty years of the opera's history. In his introduction to this material, Will Crutchfield insists that such examples are not meant to prescribe how singers should ornament their parts, but only indicate the kinds of variations singers actually introduced during Rossini's lifetime. The same obviously applies for the variations found in the Manuscript Foà-Giordano 631, which confirm and complement the material already known.

---

[15]. ROSSINI, Gioachino. *Il barbiere di Siviglia*, edited by Patricia B. Brauner, Kassel, Bärenreiter, 2008 (*Works of Gioachino Rossini*, 2).

Rosina's cavatina 'Una voce poco fa' is an ideal ornamentation piece, with numerous repeated figures and a light and fiery character inviting virtuoso embellishment[16]. The manuscript contains three separate entries for 'Una voce poco fa', on fols. 5v, 8r and 11v respectively. The suggestions on fols. 5v and 8r are practically identical fragmentary versions, highlighting key moments of the aria such as the central cadenza and the repetitions in the Andante and the Allegro sections.

The entry on fol. 11v is a rare example where the embellisher has transcribed most of the aria, adding ornaments when required, thus allowing an overview of the piece, and a relatively easy localisation of the various changes (see Ex. 1).

Ex. 1: transcription of the embellishments for 'Una voce poco fa' from Rossini's *Il barbiere di Siviglia*, as found in the Manuscript Foà-Giordano 631, fol. 11v.

---

[16]. See also the ornamentations to this cavatina in Henriette Nissen-Saloman, *L'étude de chant* (Saint Petersbrug, B. Bessel, 1881), discussed in the contribution of Damien Colas to this volume.

«Abbellimenti o fioriture»

In the first section of the cavatina (bars 1-42), one particular phrase is repeated four times: 'Sì, Lindoro mio sarà | lo giurai, la vincerò'. With each repetition the ornamentations are varied and elaborated in order to add new flavours to the expression of victory. In the embellished version, one can observe how Garcia's principle of progressive ornamentation is applied in an exemplary way: the first occurrence of the phrase includes only a few minor embellishments in the second part (Ex. 1, bars 22-24); the second occurrence elaborates upon Rossini's already quite florid first line and then introduces a fermata followed by a lavish series of ascending and descending figures (bars 26-28); after an intermediary parlante section, the third occurrence reuses Rossini's original descending line but then moves into an elaborate embellishment for the second half of the phrase (bars 35-37); finally, the fourth

288

occurrence coincides with the aria's central cadenza for which two different possibilities are proposed (bars 38-42). The fragmentary version presents an even longer and more elaborate cadenza for this section, which explores two full octaves (a-a'') of the mezzo-soprano voice range. In this same section, the detailed continuous version illuminates some interesting and often forgotten aspect of ornamentation: for example the slight changes of rhythm and minor embellishments which are inserted freely at the beginning of the cavatina (see Ex. 1, bars 13-22), the expressive shifts of emphasis in the parlante section (bars 30-34), or the personal indications 'con espr.' and 'con malizia', inserted above the line, giving additional information about the interpretation of this particular phrase (bars 21 and 31 respectively).

In the second section (bars 43-120), the vocal line is hardly embellished before the typical cabaletta repetitions begin in bar 67. As the textual and musical repetitions increase, they are progressively varied, again demonstrating the structural and rhetorical function of ornamentation. Obviously, if this had been his aesthetic aim, Rossini could have composed arias which fit the exact number of words in the text and thus avoided the numerous repetitions so typical of this repertoire. If interpreted correctly, these repetitions are not redundant, but create vast improvisational spaces for singers to insert their variations. In the case of Italian opera, dating from well into the nineteenth century, the singers' opportunities for ornamentation and rhetoric emphasis go far beyond nuance. They include variation of dynamics and phrasing, but also extend to rhythmical changes and, most impressively, considerable melodic ornamentation and improvisation. Some of the ornamentation passages in this manuscript are similar to those found in other sources, but many are completely original renditions which provide new material for musicians to experiment with when creating their own stylistically appropriate ornaments for each piece.

'VOI CHE SAPETE': MOZART IN ROSSINIAN GARB

The only examples of eighteenth-century repertoire found in the Manuscript Foà-Giordano 631 are three pieces from Mozart's *Le nozze di Figaro*. This is by no means an unusual exception, since Mozart and Da Ponte's masterpiece is one of the first operas to have attained canonical status in the western canon, and is often included in nineteenth-century singers' collections.

Ornamenting Mozart is a highly controversial affair, and there are many important reasons why this controversy continues to fuel debate and stimulate new interpretations today[17]. There are of course eighteenth-century examples of ornamentation for Mozart's

---

[17]. For a general introduction to ornamentation in Mozart see SEEDORF, Thomas. *Notation und Aufführung*, in: *Das Mozart-Handbuch*, edited by Dieter Borchmeyer and Gernot Gruber, Laaber, Laaber Verlag, 2005-2009, vol. III/1: *Mozarts Opern*, pp. 138-147. For a more conservative approach see NEUMANN, Frederick. *Ornamentation and Improvisation in Mozart*, Princeton (NJ), Princeton University Press, 1986.

operas, including autograph cadenzas and the very detailed variations by Domenico Corri[18]. By comparison the status of the examples presented here, taken from an anonymous nineteenth-century manuscript, is more problematic since these ornaments are historically and aesthetically removed from their original context. However, the historiographic interest of such a document is undeniable if we ask ourselves not what Mozart would have wanted, but what a performance of *Le nozze di Figaro* around 1835 may have entailed. In what follows I shall focus on the suggestions for Cherubino's arietta 'Voi che sapete che cosa è amor', found on fol. 13r of the manuscript (see Ex. 2).

For section A of the arietta (bars 1-20) no changes are suggested; in fact, the original vocal melody is inserted unchanged at the bottom of the page seeming to underline the importance of its unadorned rendition. The rest of the aria, however, is continuously ornamented with various changes, ranging from minor shifts and graces to elaborate embellishments and cadenzas. The changes in section B (bars 21-61) begin with a slight rhythmic shift of the semiquavers (bar 22) allowing more room for the culminating *f'*, which is further highlighted by the accent mark showing the main emphasis within the phrase. The movement then gradually accelerates with a series of varying diminutions: a *gruppetto* sign inserted between the first two notes (bar 23), followed by semiquaver triplets leading into a lower (instead of the habitual upper) appoggiatura of the F major cadence (bar 24); then simple diatonic passage notes (bar 26); and a final flourish of virtuosic large interval triplets (bar 27). The second phrase of this section is dominated by an ambitious embellishment of twelve demisemiquavers expressing the protagonist's intense and confusing desire (bar 31). This is the first ornament that clearly requires metrical adaptation and coordination with the orchestra, although all the more elaborate ornaments tend to profit from a flexible metrical treatment.

Ex. 2: transcription of the embellishments for 'Voi che sapete' from Mozart's *Le nozze di Figaro*, as found in the Manuscript Foà-Giordano 631, fol. 13r.

---

18. CORRI, Domenico. *The Singer's Preceptor*, London, Chappell, 1810.

31

pien di de — — sir ch'o — ra è di - let — to

vam — par

35 *pp*

ch'o - ra è mar - tir ge - lo e poi sen - to l'al - ma av — vam - par

41 *p*

e in un mo — men-to tor - no a ge - lar Ri - cer-co un be — ne

47

fuo — ri di me non so chi'l tie — ne non so cos' è So-spi-ro e

53

ge - mo sen - za vo - ler pal - pi - to e tre — mo sen - za sa - per Non tro - vo

57

pa — ce not-te ne ma pur mi pia — ce lan - guir_____ co - sì Voi che sa -

63

pe — te che co - sa__ è a - mor don - ne, ve - de — te s'io l'ho nel

69

cor don — ne ve - de — te_____ s'io l'ho nel cor don — ne ve -

oppure   ritard:

te_____

75

de — — — — — — te_____

291

The third phrase of section B — in A-flat major — begins with a dynamic indication *pp* and two lightly diminished bars (bars 37-38), followed by a second extravagant flourish underpinning the protagonist's sensation of a burning soul (bar 39). This time, however, the embellishment is crossed out in the manuscript and replaced by a more simple diminution, showing the ornamentor's hesitation to include this figure so near the similar one in bar 31[19]. Since both ornaments are not only alike in form, but also express analogous sentiments they are indeed redundant, making a choice of one of them advisable. The changes in bars 41-42 include a rare example of augmentation, where the last syllable of the word 'momento' becomes a crotchet rather than two quavers. The ligature in bar 43 probably indicates an extended vocal portamento, while the rhythmic accelerations reflect and render the nervous palpitations of a young and uncertain heart. The two next phrases continue with simple diminutions of the kind already seen, always varied and adapted to the musical context of the original composition.

Section A' (bars 62-79) returns to the musical and textual material of A; but now that Cherubino has revealed the emotions of his heart, he cannot simply fall back into his earlier, hesitant mood; this time the melody is enhanced in the manuscript through a rich selection of changes, flourishes, passage notes and gruppetti. For the final cadenza, the embellisher proposes three alternative suggestions of varying length, difficulty and vocal range: the first is a continuous series of demisemiquaver embellishments leading up to *B-flat''* before ending with a relatively simple cadenza; the second is an alternative suggestion beginning in the second half of bar 75 with a much longer chromatic embellishment for bar 76, but a slightly lower range (*g'-a''*); the third proposition is a simpler version of bar 76 with a fermata on *f''-sharp* and an even lower range (*e'-g''*). These alternative propositions give a good impression of the countless possibilities for variation.

If one compares this embellished version of 'Voi che sapete' to the changes proposed for 'Una voce poco fa', one finds both similarities and differences in their ornamental treatment: the changes for Rosina's aria begin, though subtly, in the very first bars of the vocal part, whereas Cherubino's first section remains untouched. The ornaments for

---

[19]. Despite the embellisher's correction, all the notes of the original embellishment in bar 39 are legible. I have therefore included both this and the simpler ornament in the transcription.

Mozart's arietta only rarely exceed the set metre of the piece, while those for Rossini's aria regularly trespass the metric norm with elaborate ornaments. These different treatments obviously reflect the unique formal structures of each piece. In her *Méthode de chant* Mme Cinti-Damoreau explains the importance of adapting ornaments to the musical contexts in which they are sung:

> The fermatas, figures and entries deployed to embellish a piece must above all reflect the style of the piece for which they are destined, that means they must have its character and its movement. In order to achieve this one must take care to change the kind of figures used for each movement even within the same piece, for example when shifting from the Andante to the Allegro[20].

Rossini's aria has two distinct sections with two different tempos and styles, requiring two series of repetitions and cadenzas. Mozart's short arietta on the other hand is composed in one style throughout, with very few textual repetitions and a single final cadenza. Beyond these formal differences, it is above all regarding the characters of the pieces and the protagonists under consideration that these compositions diverge: the provocative and fiery Rosina versus the naïve and shy Cherubino. Garcia insists that appropriate ornamentation is not only a question of musical form; rather each ornament is intimately connected to the dramatic expression of the phrase it embellishes:

> As one cannot determine in advance categories of embellishments that are adapted to the requirements of certain feelings, the pupil must consider the ornaments not in themselves, but in relation to the feeling that they express. This feeling will obtain its character, not only through the choice of notes and the form of the figures, but more through the expression that the singer puts into them. Therefore the particular intention of the words and the music must constantly be consulted in the search for embellishments[21].

In other words the youthful and naïve quality of 'Voi che sapete' simply excludes heavy or overly assured effects, which the bravura quality of 'Una voce poco fa' specifically

---

[20]. Cinti-Damoreau, Laure. *Méthode de chant*, Paris, Au Ménestrel, 1849, p. 93: «Les Points d'Orgue, Traits et Rentrées consacrés à embellir un morceau doivent avant tout porter le cachet du morceau auquel ils sont destinés, c'est-à-dire en avoir le caractère et le mouvement. Dans ce but on devra dans le même morceau, en passant de l'Andante à l'Allegro par exemple, avoir soin de changer le genre de traits consacrés à chacun de ces mouvements».

[21]. Garcia, Manuel (junior). *Op. cit.* (see note 8), vol. II, Chapter 3: *Des changements*, p. 36: «Comme on ne peut d'avance établir des catégories de fioritures adaptées au besoin des divers sentiments, l'élève doit considérer les ornements, non en eux-mêmes, mais par rapport au sentiment qu'ils expriment. Ce sentiment tiendra son caractère, non pas seulement du choix des notes et de la forme des traits, mais plutôt encore de l'expression que leur communique le chanteur. C'est donc l'intention particulière des paroles et de la musique qu'il faut incessamment consulter dans la recherche des fioritures».

invites. If one goes a step further, one may imagine that the embellisher's 'careful' treatment of certain passages in Mozart's arietta is not only a matter of good taste and dramaturgy but also a reflection of historical consciousness. Indeed, the desire to distinguish between the ornamentation of a contemporary opera and that of a temporally more distant composition seems to prefigure authenticity debates of the present day. Nevertheless, this version of the arietta is richly ornamented throughout, and the embellisher has not shied away from including virtuosic flourishes where they are required by the dramatic context of a word or phrase. Some of the more extravagant embellishments and ornaments, particularly those involving large intervals, do not resemble surviving eighteenth-century examples of ornamentation, but are more likely the result of an elegant nineteenth-century wardrobe draped onto the structure of an older composition.

Is this example therefore a nineteenth-century version of an eighteenth-century piece, or a nineteenth-century singer's historically based rendition of Cherubino's arietta? In my opinion, the embellisher has achieved a fine balance between the melodic simplicity appropriate for the piece, the rhetorical conventions common to both classical and romantic ornamentation, and the Rossinian virtuosity of his or her time. In practice, the twelve-hemidemisemiquaver embellishments and the seemingly extravagant cadenzas — provided they are sung easily and with naïve conviction — do not stand in the way of an aesthetically compelling rendition of Mozart's chef-d'œuvre. When singers use such examples as a basis for creating their own ornaments, the expressive potential of improvisational ornamentation becomes apparent[22]. Indeed such performances suggest that nineteenth-century ornamentation practice may be much closer to the standards of Mozart's time than we have been inclined to believe so far. However, this is a question which deserves further reflection and examination, in a larger context than is possible for this paper. Meanwhile, our understanding of ornamentation practice is deepened and refined as we gradually rediscover and reassess sources of historical interpretation like the Manuscript Foà-Giordano 631.

---

[22]. Performances based on ornaments from Ms. Foà-Giordano 631 have taken place on two occasion: on 12 September 2008 at the 'Journées de la Musique Sacrée et Improvisée' organised by the HEMU Lausanne, and on 26 September 2009 at the musicology institute of the University of Fribourg in honour of Luigi Ferdinando Tagliavini's eightieth birthday.

MANACLED FREEDOM
NINETEENTH-CENTURY VOCAL IMPROVISATION
AND THE FLUTE-ACCOMPANIED CADENZA
IN GAETANO DONIZETTI'S *LUCIA DI LAMMERMOOR*[1]

Naomi Matsumoto
(LONDON)

IN THE FINAL ACT OF GAETANO DONIZETTI's *Lucia di Lammermoor*, Lucia is forced to marry Arturo, and then she murders him and promptly goes insane[2]. In modern traditions, as famously exemplified in performances by Maria Callas and Joan Sutherland, the mad Lucia then sings a cadenza accompanied by an echoing flute, in which the instrument takes on the mantle of a ghostly *Doppelgänger*. The flute-cadenzas of Callas and Sutherland have been praised highly by many critics as significations, not only of the psychological state of the heroine, but also of the improvisatory 'freedom' of the character and of the power of the female voice[3]. Although somewhat different, their cadenzas have in common the fact that: (1) they are 'double cadenzas' in which two musical agents (voice and flute) are in dialogue with each other in a concerted manner; and (2) they have a multi-sectional form consisting of several musical ideas, including a reminiscence of a theme previously heard in the opera, namely the main melody of Lucia and Edgardo's love duet, 'Verranno a te sull'aure', from Part I, Scene 5[4].

---

[1]. My thanks to Roger Parker (London) and José Antonio Bowen (Dallas, Texas) for their insightful and encouraging comments upon an earlier version of this article.

[2]. Part II, Act II, Scene 5. In this study, I have followed the original scene divisions as found in the original printed libretto: CAMMARANO, Salvadore. *Lucia di Lammermoor, dramma tragico in due parti* [...] *da rappresentarsi nel real teatro S. Carlo*, Naples, Esansia, 1835. The Ricordi score follows the original division but many other publications of music do not, and neither does the description of the opera by Ashbrook in the *New Grove Opera*. See: ASHBROOK, William. 'Lucia di Lammermoor', in: *The New Grove Dictionary of Opera*, 4 vols., edited by Stanley Sadie, London, Macmillan, 1994, vol. III, pp. 69-72.

[3]. Callas's performances of Lucia have been discussed in, for example, WISNESKI, Henry. *Maria Callas. The Art behind the Legend*, New York, Doubleday, 1975, especially pp. 119-122. Sutherland's first appearance as Lucia was reviewed in, for example, RUTLAND, Harold. 'Music in London', *Musical Times*, C/1394 (April, 1959), p. 211.

[4]. A transcription of Callas's cadenza (sung by others before her) is found in *Variazioni, cadenze, tradizioni*, edited by Luigi Ricci, 3 vols., Milan, Ricordi, 1937, vol. I, pp. 50-51; of Sutherland's, in *The Art*

These characteristics are somewhat outside our usual understanding of what constitutes a cadenza. Usually, 'cadenza' is defined as «a virtuoso passage inserted near the end of a concerto movement or aria; [...] cadenzas may either be improvised by a performer or written out by the composer»[5]. However, Lucia's flute-cadenza, as we will see, has little to do with improvisation and nothing to do with Donizetti. On the other hand, owing to its complex nature, it rather is a predetermined composition which performers were and are required to learn in advance as if it were a 'text'. Thus, the clichéd implications of an equation between psychological abandon and improvisational liberty hardly do justice to the complex traditions that feed into this particular expressive but constrained moment: the manacled freedom, indicated by the title of this article.

What the flute-cadenza does offer, however, is an opportunity to discuss the real nature of operatic vocal 'improvisation' in the nineteenth century, and to explain how the textual constraints of that cadenza arose and became established. Once those investigations are complete, we can begin to unravel the transmission lines of the various versions of the flute-cadenza through the different schools of singing, mainly by examining historical aspects of performance practice as encoded in early recordings of the work and tracing each singer's pedigree. As we shall see, the first attempt at a flute-cadenza in *Lucia di Lammermoor* dates back further than has hitherto been assumed. Moreover, the restricted nature of the subsequent performance traditions will certainly cast doubt on the supposedly free nature of vocal ornamentation. Furthermore, those traditions suggest that the spontaneity we hear in such vocal moments may be a learned effect rather than a creative cause.

THE FIRST LUCIA AND HER CADENZAS

Donizetti's *Lucia di Lammermoor*, based on a libretto by Salvadore Cammarano[6], was premiered at the Teatro di San Carlo in Naples on the 26 September 1835. Despite some naïve expectations that a mad scene ought to be madly unstructured, Lucia's scene, along with other such scenes in nineteenth-century operas, actually followed what had become a standard formal scheme: recitative (Lucia, 'Il dolce suono...'), *cantabile* (Lucia, 'Ardon gl' incensi'), *tempo di mezzo* (Raimondo, 'S'avanza Enrico'), and *cabaletta* (Lucia,

---

of Joan Sutherland, edited by John Sutherland and Richard Bonynge, 10 vols., London, Josef Weinberger, 1985-1998, vol. I: *Famous Mad Scenes*, pp. 11-12.

⁵. BADURA-SKODA, Eva - JONES, Andrew V. - DRABKIN, William. 'Cadenza', in: *The New Grove Dictionary of Music & Musicians*, Second Edition, edited by Stanley Sadie, 29 vols., London, Macmillan, 2001, vol. IV, p. 783.

⁶. CAMMARANO, Salvadore. *Op. cit.* (see note 2).

'Spargi d'amaro pianto')[7]. The flute-cadenza is sung customarily at the end of the 'Ardon gl'incensi' section — that is, as a bridge between the *cantabile* and the *tempo di mezzo*.

However, what Donizetti left us in his autograph at the point where the cadenza is now sung is very simple and brief. Ex. 1 is a transcription of the cadenza in question from the composer's autograph, now in the possession of the Biblioteca Angelo Mai in Bergamo[8]. Donizetti's cadenza is little more than a short ornament to be sung in one breath on the dominant chord, and is hardly likely to have exploited the vocal armoury of the original singer to the full.

Ex. 1: cadenza in Lucia's mad scene in Donizetti's original score.

The first Lucia, Fanny Tacchinardi-Persiani, in all probability devised in performance her own versions using the skeletal guide provided by the composer. At least one of Persiani's cadenzas for this scene is transcribed (or, at least, adumbrated in style and outline) in Henri Brod's Oboe Fantasy Op. 57, if the full descriptive title of that work can be taken at face value[9]. A transcription of the cadenza found in Brod's fantasy is shown as Ex. 2. Persiani's version as preserved by Brod is fundamentally an extension of Donizetti's original cadenza, which is now to be sung not in one breath but two. The first (descending-ascending)

---

[7]. A typical example based upon this formal structure is Amina's sleepwalking scene ('Ah! Non credea mirarti' - 'Ah! Non giunge uman pensiero') in Bellini's *La Sonnambula* (1831).

[8]. I-Bgc, Cassaforte 6/12. For a facsimile of this score, see DONIZETTI, Gaetano. *Lucia di Lammermoor*, edited by Guido Zavadini, Milan, Ricordi, 1941. It should be noted that Donizetti originally wrote Lucia's mad scene in F major but the scene was transposed down to E-flat major in the first Ricordi edition. It is now customarily sung in E-flat major.

[9]. BROD, Henri. *Fantasie sur l'air de Mme Persiani dans Lucie de Lammermoor de Donizetti pour haubois avec acc. de piano ou de harpe*, Paris, B. Latte, 1841; cited in PUGLIESE, Romana Margherita. 'The Origins of *Lucia di Lammermoor*'s Cadenza', in: *Cambridge Opera Journal*, XVI/1 (Spring, 2004), pp. 23-42: 28.

section, ending with a pause on *e'*, is almost identical to Donizetti's original cadenza indication, and the second (ascending-descending) section is a different arpeggiation and decoration of the same dominant ninth chord.

Ex. 2: the flute-cadenza after Henri Brod, *Fantaisie sur l'air de Mme Persiani dans Lucie de Lammermoor de Donizetti*, for oboe and piano (Paris, 1841).

THE EMERGENCE OF A *LUCIA* CADENZA WITH FLUTE

At some point during the second half of the nineteenth century, however, a new way of executing this cadenza appeared: as a cadenza with *obbligato* flute. This practice must have drawn upon the composer's use of an obbligato instrument during the moments leading up to the cadenza, which faithfully follows the soprano in thirds and sixths (see Ex. 1). Donizetti had originally indicated in the score the eerie sounds of the glass harmonica here but, owing to a dispute between the theatre and the intended glass harmonica player, he had to recast the line for flute[10]. Interestingly, for Donizetti, the glass harmonica was almost certainly more suggestive of madness than the flute[11].

Identifying the musician (singer or otherwise) who deserves the credit for initiating the practice of having a flute-accompanied cadenza in the mad scene of *Lucia di Lammermoor* has always been somewhat problematic. Prior to the present study, there were two theories. Guglielmo Barblan suggested in his 1948 book on Donizetti that Teresa Brambilla (1813-1895), the soprano who created the role of Gilda in Verdi's *Rigoletto* (1851), initiated the practice, but he does not give any evidence for it[12], and no document containing a flute-cadenza for Brambilla is known to have survived. By contrast, in 2004, Romana Pugliese attributed the creation of the flute-cadenza to Mathilde Marchesi (1821-1913),

---

[10]. ASHBROOK, William. *Donizetti*, London, Cassell, 1965, p. 417. For Donizetti's decision to replace the glass harmonica with the flute, see GOSSETT, Philip. *Divas and Scholars: Performing Italian Opera*, Chicago, University of Chicago Press, 2006, pp. 434-436.

[11]. For an interesting discussion of the association of women with the glass harmonica, see HADLOCK, Heather. 'Sonorous Bodies: Women and the Glass Harmonica', in: *Journal of the American Musicological Society*, LIII/3 (Autumn, 2000), pp. 507-542.

[12]. BARBLAN, Guglielmo. *L'opera di Donizetti nell'età romantica*, Bergamo, Edizione del Centenario, 1948, p. 125: «[…] una dilettevole quanto vana costumanza teatrale li ha definitivamente consacrati, fin dai lontani esperimenti della Brambilla».

who composed a version for her protégé Nellie Melba (1861-1931) at some time in late 1886 or early 1887[13]. Although it is true that Marchesi played a vital role in disseminating the flute-cadenza, as we shall see, my own investigations demonstrate that the first flute-cadenza for Lucia must have preceded Marchesi's version by at least two decades. There were at least three singers who executed their own flute-cadenzas before the Marchesi/Melba attempt in the late 1880s: Christina Nilsson (1843-1921), Ilma de Murska (1834-89) and Emma Albani (1847-1930).

The earliest of the three was the Swedish soprano Christina Nilsson. Her performance of Lucia at Her Majesty's Theatre, London, in the spring season of 1868 was reviewed in *The Pall Mall Gazette* as follows:

> Mdlle Nilsson's vocalization is always perfect and was never more so than in an elaborate cadenza *written to* [my italics] the melody in question by Signor Arditi, with an obbligato accompaniment in which the notes of a fine-toned flute serve to set off the superior beauty of Mdlle Nilsson's voice, and the skill of the player, her superior skill[14].

This reveals not only that Nilsson performed a flute-cadenza but also that it was written by the composer Luigi Arditi (1822-1903), who also conducted the performance. Regrettably, however, there seems not to be a surviving notation of the Arditi/Nilsson cadenza, and neither Arditi's autobiography nor any modern study of Nilsson even refers to their apparent innovation[15].

After Nilsson, but still prior to Melba, both De Murska and Albani seem to have sung some version of a flute-cadenza. Ilma de Murska, a Croatian pupil of Mathilde Marchesi and another associate of Arditi[16], presented her version in the Autumn seasons of 1868 and 1869[17]. Then, at Covent Garden, in the Spring season of 1875, the Canadian-born Albani sang a *cadenza a due* where the flute «echoes the voice, phrase by phrase»[18].

---

[13]. PUGLIESE, Romana. *Op. cit.* (see note 9), pp. 32-35.

[14]. 'Mdlle Nilsson as Lucia', in: *The Pall Mall Gazette*, 6 June 1868, [unpaginated].

[15]. There is no reference to this cadenza in ARDITI, Luigi. *My Reminiscences*, edited by the Baroness Marie Antoinette von Zedlitz, London, Skeffington & Son, ²1896; nor in BJÖRKLUND, Ingegerd. *Den Oemotståndliga. En Christina Nilsson Biografi*, Västerås, Författarhuset, 2000. Furthermore, my research at the Covent Garden Archive turned out to be of no avail and there seems no archive either at Crescentino (the composer's birth place) or at Hove, Sussex (where he died). Arditi in collaboration with Luigi Yotti (his friend at the Conservatory of Milan) wrote a work for two violins and pianoforte published as *Souvenir de Donizetti. Scherzo brillante*, Milan, G. Ricordi, [c. 1861]. Although this music is based upon motifs from Donizetti's operas *Lucia* and *Betly* (1836), it does not include the 'Ardon gl'incensi' section.

[16]. It might have been De Murska who first reported Arditi's flute-cadenza to Marchesi, with whom she had studied during the early 1860s.

[17]. See, for example, 'Music', in: *The Daily News*, 10 November 1868, [unpaginated], and 'Music', in: *The Daily News*, 9 November 1869 [unpaginated].

[18]. 'Royal Italian Opera', in: *The Times*, 26 April 1875, p. 9.

Interestingly, regarding this performance by Albani, another reviewer for *The Daily News* wrote that «the climax of [this performance] was attained in the great *scena* of delirium, commencing 'il dolce suono' and comprising frenzied reminiscences of previously heard phrases»[19]. This implies that Albani's flute-cadenza included a recapitulation of musical material heard earlier in the opera, just as in the versions by Callas and Sutherland. However, we know nothing for certain about the ingredients of Albani's version, since she did not produce a recording of *Lucia*, and, apparently, no authenticated notation of her cadenza survives. In fact, there is a cadenza intriguingly bearing the name of Albani in a book of cadenzas well-known to singers, the *Variazioni-cadenze tradizioni* edited by Luigi Ricci[20]. Ricci, who had worked as an assistant for Puccini and Mascagni, published this collection of cadenzas in 1937, seven years after Albani's death; notoriously, his publication provides no information on sources whatsoever, and the connection with Albani remains unsubstantiated. The cadenza Ricci that claimed to be Albani's includes an uncommonly long *trillo*, the technique for which her singing teacher, Francesco Lamperti expressly praised her — so much that he dedicated to Albani his publication on that particular technique[21]. Regrettably, though, the cadenza in Ricci's collection attributed to Albani contains no «reminiscence of previously heard phrases».

The situation of Adelina Patti (1843-1919), Albani's older colleague in London, is even more nebulous. Patti made her European debut singing Amina in Bellini's *La sonnambula* at Covent Garden in 1861 and sang Lucia within the same season (on 14 May)[22]. At some point during her career, Patti also seems to have devised and executed her own 'flute-cadenza'. Ricci, again with no presentation of evidence, claimed in his *Variazioni, cadenze, tradizioni* a particular version of the flute-cadenza to be Patti's[23], but we do not know exactly when Patti introduced her own flute-cadenza.

The introduction of a flute-accompanied cadenza seems to have marked a very important shift in the performance history of Donizetti's opera, since the duet aspect of the cadenza meant there could no longer be a spontaneous display of vocal acrobatics, due to the need to work with the flute. The cadenza needed to be a preconceived and well-rehearsed collaboration, which, in turn, enabled the cadenza to be in a more complex form, and to incorporate previously presented musical material in a carefully prescribed manner. However, these apparently new features, at least in type and outline, were in fact drawing on traditions of cadenza production that even predated Donizetti's *Lucia*, and it is those traditions that we now need to understand.

---

19. 'Royal Italian Opera', in: *The Daily News*, 26 April 1875, [unpaginated].
20. *Variazioni, cadenze, tradizioni, op. cit.* (see note 4), pp. 54-55.
21. LAMPERTI, Francesco. *Osservazioni e consigli sul trillo*, Milan, Ricordi, 1878.
22. This performance was advertised in *The Times* on the previous day. See 'Music, Sacred and Secular', in: *The Times*, 13 May 1861, p. 12.
23. *Variazioni, cadenze, tradizioni, op. cit.* (see note 4), p. 56.

THE FLUTE-CADENZA IN *LUCIA DI LAMMERMOOR* AS
A CONFLUENCE OF PRE-EXISTING TRADITIONS

The flute-cadenza in *Lucia di Lammermoor* belongs to the category of 'double cadenzas', and such cadenzas were already present in certain eighteenth-century repertoires, including arias where a wind instrument not only played the ritornello but also accompanied the singer in an *obbligato* manner[24]. 'Sweet Bird' from Handel's oratorio *L'Allegro, il Penseroso ed il Moderato* (1740) provides a famous example of such a type. The concerting cadenza with voice and instrument was heard in opera houses as well, and apparently more often than some critics liked, as Francesco Algarotti indicated when he criticized the excessive use of instruments in opera:

> Nowadays, one of the most favorite practices, and which makes the theatre resound is to form in an aria a contest between the voice and an oboe or between the voice and a trumpet, and to make a competition, as if a duel, between the two forces exchanging endlessly thrusts and parries with the utmost exertion on either side[25].

During the nineteenth century, some of the eighteenth-century obbligato arias with double cadenzas remained in the regular repertoire of singers. For example, both Albani and Melba have left recordings of 'Sweet Bird', both of which contain extended voice-flute-cadenzas[26]. Moreover, during the mid-nineteenth century when the flute-cadenza of *Lucia di Lammermoor* was in formation, quite a number of operas contained arias featuring the soprano and the flute. Examples include 'Jours de mon enfance' from Ferdinand Hérold's *Le pré aux clercs* (1832); 'Chason du Mysoli' from Félicien David's *La perle du Brésil* (1852); 'L'air du Rossignol' from Victor Massé's *Les noces de Jeannette* (1853); 'C'est bien l'air' (with two flutes) from Meyerbeer's *L'étoile du Nord* (1854); 'Ombra leggera' (the shadow song) from Meyerbeer's *Dinorah* (originally *Le pardon de Ploërmel*, 1859); 'O riante nature!' from Charles Gounod's *Philémont et Baucis* (1860); and 'À vos jeux, mes amis' (Ophelia's mad scene) from Ambroise Thomas's

---

[24]. For eighteenth-century performance practice of obbligato arias, see SPITZER, John. 'Improvised Ornamentation in a Handel Aria with Obbligato Wind Accompaniment', in: *Early Music*, XVI/4 (1988), pp. 514-522.

[25]. ALGAROTTI, Francesco. *Saggio sopra l'opera in musica*, Livorno, M. Coltellini, 1763, p. 32: «[...] Una delle più care usanze al dì d'oggi, e che leva il Teatro a romore [*sic*], è il far prova in un'aria di una voce, e di un'oboe, di una voce, e di una Tromba; e far tra loro seguire con varie botte, e risposte una gara senza fine, e quasi un duello a tutto fiato».

[26]. Melba's recording: Mauve G & T, London, No. 03021, recorded in March 1904; and Albani's: Red G & T, London, no matrix number given, IRCC 3131, recorded in 1904.

Hamlet (1868)[27]. Each of these arias became associated with the idea of the flute-cadenza at some time during its performance history, thus illustrating the liveliness with which the various cadenza traditions came together during the second half of the nineteenth century.

If a double cadenza between voice and instrument was executed in collaboration between the two performers, it would seem plausible that the explanation for that practice must lie not only in the traditions of vocal performance, but also in those of instrumental practice. The lengthy flute-cadenzas of Sutherland and Callas both employ a melodic reminiscence taken from the duet 'Verranno a te sull'aure', a practice which may date back to 1875 and Albani, as we have seen above. But the use of structural expansion and melodic reminiscence was clearly established in instrumental cadenzas of the eighteenth century, if not earlier.

It is well-known that the cadenzas that Mozart left for his own concertos are multi-sectional and often recapture the melodic material from the main body of the movement. Examples are those in his Piano Concertos K. 246, 271 and 414, to name but a few[28]. In their writings eighteenth-century musician-theorists — including Johann Joachim Quantz (1752) and Daniel Gottlob Türk (1789) — encouraged such a practice as a means of devising good concerto cadenzas[29]. Quantz wrote that «cadenzas must stem from the principal sentiment of the piece, and include a short repetition or imitation of the most pleasing phrase contained in it»[30].

Both Türk and Quantz seem to have been summing up practices that had existed for some time. In the early eighteenth century, there was a so-called 'capriccio' section — a series of extended, unaccompanied and virtuosic passages — which was used as an alternative to the concluding *tutti* of the movement[31]. The capriccio in essence constituted an extensive precomposed cadential prolongation (which itself could even include an improvised cadenza left at the performer's discretion) and within it material reminisced from earlier in the movement can sometimes be found. Examples of these procedures are

---

[27]. Examples of double-cadenzas for all of these pieces appear in a cadenza album edited by a pupil of Mathilde Marchesi: LIEBLING, Estelle. *The Book of Coloratura Cadenzas*, New York, G. Schirmer, 1943.

[28]. For a recent discussion about Mozart's improvisation, see LEVIN, Robert. 'Improvising Mozart', in: *Musical Improvisation. Art, Education and Society*, edited by Gabriel Solis and Bruno Nettl, Urbana, University of Illinois Press, 2009, pp. 143-149.

[29]. For Türk's discussion on the matter, see TÜRK, Daniel Gottlob. *School of Clavier Playing or Instructions for Teachers and Students* [*Klavierschule*, 1789], translated by Raymond H. Haggh, Lincoln, University of Nebraska Press, 1982, p. 298.

[30]. QUANTZ, Johann Joachim. *On Playing the Flute* [*Versuch einer Anweisung die Flöte traversiere zu spielen*, 1752], translated by Edward R. Reilly, London, Faber, ²1985, p. 182.

[31]. About the 'capriccio' aspect see WHITMORE, Philip. *Unpremeditated Art. The Cadenza in the Classical Keyboard Concerto*, Oxford, Clarendon Press, 1991, pp. 41-46; and ID. 'Towards an Understanding of the Capriccio', in: *Journal of Royal Musical Association*, CXIII/1 (1988), pp. 47-56.

found in the capriccios for the first and third movements of Locatelli's Violin Concerto Op. 3 No. 9 (1733)[32]. Although capriccio and cadenza began as fundamentally different musical entities, the mid-eighteenth century saw the cadenza more and more extended and developed, and, as a result, the distinction between the two began to fade. In fact, during the 1750s, Tartini described the changing practices thus:

> This kind of cadence [the artificial cadenza[33]] is at present rather a 'capriccio' than a cadenza because nowadays every singer or instrumentalist permits himself to lengthen it so much, and with such very different expressions, that it is not reasonable to call it 'cadenza' any longer but rather should one call them 'capriccio', since the capriccio can be lengthened as much as one wants and can be composed of different sections and sentiments, with a variety of time signatures[34].

Thus, long before the mid nineteenth century, multi-sectional and thematically reminiscent cadenzas are likely to have been exploited in double cadenzas involving the voice.

It is important to note, however, that the use of melodic reminiscence in nineteenth-century opera not only drew on established traditions but also raised a new aspect of dramaturgy. This is because cadenzas with such devices were now used in the service of characterisation. In the case of the flute-cadenza in *Lucia di Lammermoor*, which contains melodic fragments associated with Lucia's happier times, we are given a glimpse — musically as well as dramaturgically — of her private thoughts and her reactions to them. Perhaps it is no coincidence that such expressively varied cadenzas begin to appear when psychological theories start to produce a kind of interior, inward-looking approach to characterisation. On the other hand, even this tradition grew partly out of the practice of implying in the orchestral part of an opera a thought not overtly expressed in the text that a character is singing.

---

[32]. LOCATELLI, Pietro Antonio. *L'Arte del violino*, Amsterdam, Michel-Charles le Cène, 1733, pp. 64-65 and 70-71.

[33]. Tartini refers here to «cadences by which any piece of music, either slow or fast, is brought to a close». See TARTINI, Giuseppe. *Traité des agréments de la musique*, Paris, Chez l'auteur [=the translator, Pierre Denis], 1771, edited by Erwin R. Jacobi, Celle, Hermann Moeck Verlag, 1961, p. 117: «Cadences artificielles qu'on appelle en françois point d'Orgue. On appelle cadences artificielles celles par lesquelles on termine entièrement toute sorte de pièces de Musique, soit celles dont la mesure est grave, soit celles dont la mesure est gaie. En un mot ce terme exprime les cadences finales, sur lesquelles le chanteur ou le joueur d'instrument s'arrête à volonté et sans avoir égard à la mesure, pour le faire durer autant qu'il le vent et qu'il le peut».

[34]. *Ibidem*, pp. 117-118: «Cette sorte de cadence est à present plutôt un caprice qu'une cadence, parce qu'à présent, tout chanteur, ou joueur d'instrument, se permet d'allonger tant et avec des expressions si différentes, qu'il n'est pas raisonable d'appeler cela cadence, mais qu'on est forcé de l'appeler caprice, le caprice pouvant s'allonger autant qu'on le veut, et pouvant être composé de morceaux et de sentimens differens avec variété de mesure».

The Dissemination of the Flute-Cadenza in *Lucia di Lammermoor* and the Apprenticeship of Singers

Performing a flute-cadenza in Lucia's mad scene did not become standard practice immediately after Arditi's version was executed by Nilsson in 1868. Up to the turn of the century, many singers seem to have stayed with a vocal solo cadenza, without the addition of a flute[35].

It was Mathilde Marchesi's version of the flute-cadenza, devised for Melba in 1886/1887, as we have seen above, that did eventually supplant the single-voice versions. This becomes obvious when we survey early recordings of Lucia's mad scene between c. 1900 and c. 1925 listed in TABLE 1[36]. Variation in the flute-cadenza in those recordings is very rare; rather, a certain prototype became widely disseminated and with it a standardised practice. The prototype is none other than the Marchesi-Melba version. Thus, the importance of Marchesi's flute-cadenza does not lie in its purportedly being the first flute-cadenza as such, but rather in its role in producing the standardisation of that particular cadenza, through Marchesi's rigid control over her singer-pupils, and by its publications in cadenza collections and singing methods, as we shall see shortly.

TABLE 1

The Flute-Cadenza of *Lucia di Lammermoor* in Early Recordings (1900 to c. 1925)

For explanation of the cadenza types C1, C2, and C3, see p. 307.

Year	Singer (Dates) [Education]	Label	Cadenza Type
1900	Sophie Heymann (1874 Amsterdam - ?) [Mathilde Marchesi and Pauline Viardot in Paris; later Amalie Joachim in Berlin]	Berliner Record, 43050	Elaborate and original antiphonal passages + C1: (2) + (3c variant) + (5) + (6)

---

[35]. For example, Carlotta Marchisio (1835-1872) seems to have sung a solo-voice cadenza for Lucia's mad scene throughout her career. Her cadenza seems to have been used as guidance for the following generations of singers, since it is contained in the manuscript cadenza collection *Cadenze e variante composte e eseguite dalle sorelle Marechisio*, now US-NYom, M317. C 122, vol. II, fol. 16. This collection, dated 27 June 1900, was donated by Carlotta's sister Barbara Marchisio, a famous contralto, to Rocco Pagliara, the Director and Chief Librarian of the Conservatorio di Musica S. Pietro a Majella in Naples.

[36]. For those early recordings the author is indebted particularly to Nicole M. Rodriguez and the Collection of Mr. and Mrs. Laurence C. Witten II, the Yale Collection of Historical Sound Recordings, Music Library of Yale University. Also the recordings in the possession of the British Library, Sound Archive, were consulted. For information relevant to this study regarding early recordings see BAUER, Robert. *The New Catalogue of Historical Records 1898-1908/9*, London, Sidwick and Jackson, 1947; and GIRARD, Victor - BAMES, Harold M. *Vertical-Cut Cylinders and Discs / A Catalogue of All 'Hill-&-Dale' Recordings*, London, British Institute of Recorded Sound, 1964.

YEAR	SINGER (DATES) [EDUCATION]	LABEL	CADENZA TYPE
1902	Maria Alexandra Michailowa (1864 Kharkov, Russia – ?) [Saint-Yves Bax in Paris, Rauzzoni in Milan]	Black G & T, St Petersburg, 23172	[In Russian] Original antiphonal passages + C1: (2) + (3c) + (5) + (6)
1902	Gertrude Sylva (New York? – 1907 Brussels) [Frieda Ashforth in New York]	Pathé Cylinders, Paris, 2844 [also issued in disc form]	[In French without flute] C1: (1), (2) (3ab) + original decoration + C2 (4) [Arpeggiated 'accompaniment' for 'Verrano a te'] + C1: (3)c + (5) + (6)
1903	Maria Michailowa	Pathé Cylinders & Discs, St. Petersburg, 27391	Same as Michailowa 1902
1904	Nellie Melba (1859 Burnley, Australia – 1931 Sydney) [Mathilde Marchesi]	Mauve G & T, London, 03020	C1 [(1) slightly 'contracted'] [Flautist: Philippe Gaubert]
1904	Maria Michailowa	Gramophone, Black G & T, St Petersburg, 23448 [Victor 61129]	Same as Michailowa 1902
1905	Elise Elizza (1870 Vienna – 1926 Vienna) [Adolf Limley in Vienna]	Brown Odeon, Vienna , 33082/ 38037	C1
1905	Grete Forst (1880 Vienna – ?) [Hermine Granichstätten in Vienna]	Black G & T, Vienna, 43661	C1
1905/06	Lucette Korsoff (Russian, 1876 Genoa – 1955 Brussels) [Frédéric Boyer in Paris]	Dark Green Zonophone, Paris, 83144/41	[In French] Very elaborate, original beginning + a phrase reminiscent of C1: (3c) + (2) + C2 (4) +C1 (3)c variant + (5) + original ending
1906	Marcella Sembrich (1858 Wie niewcyk – 1935 New York) [Viktor Rokitansky in Vienna, Giovanni Battista Lamperti in Milan]	Red Victor, 88021	Original antiphonal passages + C1: (2) + (3abc) + (5) + (6)
1907	Aida Gonzaga (1879 Florence – 1972 Milan) [Vellani in Lisbon]	Fonotipia, Odeon, 62127	C3
1907	Selma Kurz (1874 Biala, Silesia, Austria – 1933 Vienna) [Mathilde Marchesi in Paris]	Red G & T, Vienna, 43897	C1: (1) + (2) + (3a) + (3b) + (3c first half) + original passage + (5) + (6)
1907	Nellie Melba	Victor, Camden, 88071	C1 [(1) slightly 'contracted'] [Flautist: Charles K. North]
1907/08	Graziella Pareto (1889 Barcelona ~ 1973 Rome) [Melchiorre Vidal in Milan]	Red Pre-Dog, Milan, 053153	Original antiphonal passages + C1: (2) + (3abc) + (5) + (6) + variation which reaches f''' in the final section

YEAR	SINGER (DATES) [EDUCATION]	LABEL	CADENZA TYPE
1907/08	Ellen Beach Yaw (1869 Boston - 1947 Covina, USA) [Theodore Björksen in New York, Mathilde Marchesi in Paris]	Red Victor, Unpublished	C1
1908	Maria Galvany (1878 Granada - 1944 Rio de Janeiro) [Lázaro Maria Puig at the Madrid Conservatory]	Gramophone, Red Pre-Dog, Milan, 053181	C3
1908	Giuseppina Finzi-Magrini (1878 Turin - 1944 Turin)	Fonotipia, Odeon, 92289	C3 but with a variant ending
1908	Luisa Tetrazzini (1871 Florence - 1940 Milan) [Carlo Ceccherini at the Liceo musicale in Florence]	Gramophone, London, 053144	Beginning antiphonal passages [similar to RICCI, Luigi. *Op. cit.* (see note 2), p. 50, first system] + C3: section (2) onwards
1910	Nellie Melba	Victor, Camden, 88071	C1 [(1) slightly 'contracted'] [Flautist: John Lemmone]
1910	Selma Kurz	Edison 4-minute Cylinders, London, 35009	Same as Kurz 1907
1911	Lucette Korsoff	Gramophone, 133142	Same as Korsoff in 1905/6
1911	Luisa Tetrazzini	Victor, 88299	Same as Tetrazzini in 1908
1912	Margarethe Siems (1879 Breslau - 1952 Dresden) [Anna Maria Orgeni, pupil of Marchesi and Viardot]	Pathé Etched-Label Discs, Berlin, 55631	Beginning antiphonal passage similar to Sembrich. C1 (2) + original decoration + C1 (3c) + C2 (4) + Original decorative ending
1913	Isabella de Frate (daughter of Inez de Frate (1854-1924))	Fonotipia, Odeon, 69115	Antiphonal passages based upon arpeggiated V^7 chord [see RICCI, first system, p. 54] + C3 (2) onwards
1916	Maria Barrientos (1884 Barcelona ~ Ciboure, Basses-Pyrénées) [Francesco Bonet at the Barcelona Conservatoire]	Columbia, 48627	C3 (1) + Original decoration + C3 (2) onwards
1917	Amelita Galli-Curci (Milan 1882 - La Jolla CA, 1963) [Carlo Carignani and Sara Dufes in Milan]	Victor, 74509	Antiphonal passages similar to de Frate + C3 (2) onwards
1917/18	Anna Case (1889 Clinton, New Jersey - 1984 NY) [Mme Ohrström-Renard in New York]	Edison Diamond Discs, USA, 82136	Beginning antiphonal passages original but similar to Sembrich + C1 (2) + (3abc) + C3 (5) + C1/3 (6)

YEAR	SINGER (DATES) [EDUCATION]	LABEL	CADENZA TYPE
1918	Helen Yorke (1890? American) [Details unknown]	Pathé Paper-Label Discs, London, 025067 [needle-cut version]	Beginning 'antiphonal' passages original but similar to Tetrazzini + C3 (2) onwards
1920	Stella Power (1897 Melbourne – ?) [Weidemann in Melbourne, Melba's protégé]	Gramophone, D-54	C1
1924	Toti Dal Monte (1893 Mogliano, Veneto – 1975 Treviso) [Barbara Marchisio in Venice]	Victor, Milan (?), 6466	Antiphonal passages based upon arpeggiated V⁷ chord [see RICCI, first system, p. 54] + C3 (2) + (3abc) + C2 (4) [but Sop = melody; Fl = accompaniment] + a little extension of (4) + new ending [= 'Callas cadenza']
1926	Toti Dal Monte	Camden, New Jersey, 6611	Ditto
1928	Elda di Veroli (1892 Rome – 1981 Rome) [Elvira Ceresoli-Salvatori in Rome]	Columbia D-5754	Same as Tetrazzini

Although so far we have called this cadenza the 'Marchesi-Melba' version, during the course of its formation there was a flautist whose contribution was almost equally important: Paul Taffanel. This distinguished flautist not only assisted in its composition — in fact, Melba later recalled that «this cadenza [...] was composed by Madame Marchesi and Taffanel»[37] — but he also played the flute part when Melba sang this very cadenza for the first time in an opera production at the Paris Opéra in 1889[38]. A surviving manuscript source connected to this production includes a notated version of the cadenza[39]; we will henceforth call this version of the cadenza C1. Later, Marchesi printed C1 along with two other cadenzas for the mad scene, in her collection of cadenzas published in Paris c. 1900[40]. Ex. 3 provides a transcription of C1 taken from that print.

---

[37]. MELBA, Nellie. *Melodies and Memories*, New York, Liberty, 1926, p. 177.

[38]. BLAKEMAN, Edward. *Taffanel. Genius of the Flute*, New York, Oxford University Press, 2005, p. 116. Taffenel also participated in some of Melba's subsequent performances of *Lucia*. In fact, Melba seems to have valued the flautist's contribution and approach highly; when she recorded Lucia's mad scene for the first time with this cadenza in March 1904 in London, she took the trouble to invite from Paris a pupil of Taffanel, Philippe Gaubert, to perform the flute obbligato with her.

[39]. Now F-Po, Ms. A. 549. See PUGLIESE, Romana. *Op. cit.* (see note 9), pp. 34-35.

[40]. MARCHESI, Mathilde. *Variantes et points d'orgue, composés pour les principaux air du répertoire par Mathilde Marchesi pour les élèves de ses Classes de Chant*, Paris, Heugel & Co., [c. 1900], p. 51. The two other cadenzas appear on pp. 52 and 53 respectively.

Ex. 3: the flute-cadenza of *Lucia di Lammermoor* by Marchesi and Taffanel, as published in *Variantes et points d'orgue, composés pour les principaux airs du répertoire par Mathilde Marchesi* (Paris, c. 1900).

The two additional cadenzas (henceforth C2 and C3) are very closely related to C1. C2 is of particular interest because there do we find for the first time the 'Verranno a te sull'aure' reminiscence theme. Nowadays we often find this theme sung by the voice in the cadenza supported by the accompanying flute (as in the versions by Callas and Sutherland), but in C2, the theme is played by the flute to the arpeggiated accompaniment of the voice (see Ex. 4).

Ex. 4: the 'Verranno a te sull'aure' theme in the *Lucia* flute-cadenza No. 2 as published in *Variantes et points d'orgue, composés pour les principaux airs du répertoire par Mathilde Marchesi* (Paris, c. 1900).

Structurally speaking, the skeletal form of Marchesi's cadenzas consists of six sections, counting the 'Verranno a te sull'aure' section as well. They are indicated as Sections (1) to (6) in Ex. 3, although in this example, which presents the C1 cadenza, Section (4), 'Verranno a te sull'aure', is missing. As shown in TABLE 1, all the cadenzas sung on those early recordings are based upon Marchesi's versions in one way or another. They usually follow Sections (2) to (5) as they appear in C1, with some slight variations. The beginning, Section (1), where the soprano unfolds a 'dialogue' with the echoing flute in an antiphonal manner varies a good deal, and the last phrase, Section (6), also varies, but to a lesser degree. This is understandable, since the intermediate Sections (2) to (5) require a good ensemble between the voice and the flute and offer little scope for *ad libitum* performance. TABLE 2 summarises by way of comparison the structure of C1 and the variants of several singers.

TABLE 2
STRUCTURAL ELEMENTS OF THE VARIOUS TYPES OF THE FLUTE–CADENZA

TYPE	SINGER	(1)	(2)	(3a)–(3b)
C1	Marchesi No. 1 for Melba Composed early 1887?, performed 1889, published c. 1900	Interval steps with trills. Antiphonal: soprano then flute	Descent by chromatic roulades; soprano + flute	Arpeggio-based ascent; then triplet-based descent
C2	Marchesi No. 2 Published c. 1900	Same as C1	Same as C1	Same as C1
C3	Marchesi No. 3 Published c. 1900	Chromatic ascent; antiphonal: flute then soprano	Rhythmic variant of C1	Omitted
C1 + C3	Michailowa (sung in Russian; recorded in 1905)	Slight variant of C1; reaches c'''	Same as C3	Omitted
C4	Pinkert/ Tetrazzini [Variant of C3]	Arpeggiated V_7; antiphonal: soprano then flute	Same as C3	Omitted
C4'	Dal Monte/ Pagliughi/ Callas	Slight variant of C4; antiphonal: soprano then flute	Rhythmic variant of C3	Omitted
C1 + C2'	Sutherland	Same as C1 but without initial third leap	Slight variant of C1	Slight variant of C1

TYPE	(3c)	(4) "VERRANNO A TE" THEME	(5)	(6)
C1	Scale ascent, repeated g'', then b-flat''. Scale descent	Not present	Triadic figure with trills	Fermata and trill on the penultimate b-flat''
C2	Scale ascent, arpeggio descent	Flute = melody; soprano = arpeggio accompaniment	Variant of C1	Soprano: fermata on the penultimate d'''
C3	Variant of C1; b-flat'' and a-flat'' repeated	Not present	Variant of C1	Same as C1
C1 + C3'	Slight variant of C3	Not present	Same as C1	Same as C1

C4	Same as C3	Not present	Slight variant of C3	Same as C1
C4'	Rhythmic variant of C3	Soprano = melody; flute = arpeggio accompaniment. Curtailed with tonic plus decorated tonic ending	Omitted	Scale decoration of dominant B♭
C1 + C2	Variant of C1	Same as C2 but soprano = melody and flute = accompaniment. No final three repeated notes.	Variant of C1: decorated arpeggio	Chromatic decoration of dominant; reaches B", then fl's section to B♭

The similarities among the cadenzas on early recordings strongly reflects the ways in which singers were trained in the late nineteenth and early twentieth centuries. The period from the late 1830s onwards witnessed extensive and rapid changes in vocal techniques along with the expansion of auditoriums and subsequent performance demands — this was the era of more powerful and more voluminous voices. At the same time, professional singers began to emerge widely from the thriving middle-classes and not any longer from particular families which, by producing many singers, had previously dominated the scene and had preserved the secrets of beautiful singing as if it were a kind of mysticism. This process also resulted in an increasing number of vocal teachers both private and institutional[41]. Fierce competition amongst them spurred each tutor to advertise his or her own unique method which was pursued rigidly at the expense of an individually tailored approach[42]. The wide dissemination of Marchesi's cadenza seems to be evidence of the importance of her singing method for the *bel canto* repertoire, which derived from Manuel García (senior) via her teacher Manuel Garcia junior[43]. Singers who studied directly with Marchesi such as Ellen Beach Yaw and Selma Kurz sang C1 with slight variations, while others associated indirectly with the Garcia-Marchesi school sang remote variants of C1 and C2. However, it is interesting to note that a Russian soprano, Maria Michailowa who sang Lucia in Russian, still basically followed C1. Although the detail of her training is unknown, she reportedly studied with Zelma Gröning-Wilde at the Saint-Petersburg Conservatory before studying further with Saint-Yves Bax in Paris and with Rauzzoni in

[41]. RUTHERFORD, Susan. *The Prima Donna and Opera, 1815-1930*, Cambridge, Cambridge University Press, 2006, pp. 90-92.

[42]. *Ibidem*, pp. 96-97.

[43]. For García senior, see RADOMSKI, James. *Manuel García (1775-1832)*, Oxford, Oxford University Press, 2000.

Milan[44]. If that apprenticeship history is correct, then, it is also interesting to note that Saint-Yves Bax was a colleague to Marchesi's collaborator Taffanel at the Paris Conservatoire throughout the last twenty years of his life[45].

We still hear variants of the Marchesi-Taffanel cadenza today, and the importance of the Garcia-Marchesi school is still apparent among singers of our time. Joan Sutherland's famous version is none other than a variant of C1, though it incorporates the 'Verranno a te sull'aure' theme from C2, which appears, in the modern manner, in the voice part[46].

Likewise, Callas's cadenza drew upon precedents developed in vocal institutions in Northern Italy. Although the Callas cadenza has become the most famous version, it was not tailor-made for her. Before Callas, it had been sung by several divas such as Toti dal Monte (1893-1975) and Lina Pagliughi (1907-1980), and it is not dissimilar to the version that Amelita Galli-Curci (1882-1963) sang. Moreover, the model of this version dates back to the turn of the twentieth century when it was sung by Regina Pinkert (1869-1931) and Luisa Tetrazzini (1871-1940). All of these singers had active singing and teaching careers in Northern Italy, particularly focusing on the Teatro della Scala in Milan.

We should then understand Callas's version as a Northern-Italian or Milanese cadenza. It bears strong similarities with Marchesi's C3. This may at first seem to indicate an influence of Marchesi in Northern Italy, although Marchesi never taught Italian singers directly and her only connection to Italy was that her husband, Salvatore Marchesi, was taught by Francesco Lamperti (1813-1892). This indirect association may have been more important than it first appears, since Lamperti became an important figure in Northern-Italian conservatoires where many of the singers associated with La Scala had studied[47]. The lack of evidence[48], both in notations and in reviews, for a flute-cadenza in *Lucia di Lammermoor* in Italian theatres suggests that the Italians lagged behind at least London (with the Arditi/Nilsson cadenza in 1868) if not also Paris (with the Marchesi/Melba

---

[44]. *Großes Sängerlexikon mit einer Anhang, Verzeichnis vom Opern und Operetten*, edited by Karl Joseph Kutsch and Leo Riemens, Bern, Francke, 1987, vol. II, p. 1967.

[45]. [UNSIGNED]. 'Music in Paris', in: *Musical Times*, XXXVIII/650 (April 1897), pp. 260-261.

[46]. Perhaps, in this way, Sutherland unconsciously pays tribute to her compatriot Melba, as well as to Marchesi with whose textbooks she was brought up. BRUDER, Harold. 'Manuel García the Elder. His School and His Legacy', in: *Opera Quarterly*, XIII/4 (1997), p. 42.

[47]. Tetrazzini studied singing at the Istituto Musicale in Florence and Galli-Curci at the Conservatory of Milan, while Pagliughi studied with Gaetano Bavagnoli who had graduated from the Conservatory of Parma. Pinkert and Dal Monte were associated with Arturo Toscanini who had studied also at the Conservatory of Parma. Callas's interpretation of *bel canto* roles resulted from her close collaboration with Tullio Serafin (1878-1968) who had studied at the Conservatory of Milan and had been assistant-conductor to Toscanini. The information about singers is based mainly upon: *Großes Sängerlexikon [...], op. cit.* (see note 44) and *The New Grove Dictionary of Music & Musicians, op. cit.* (see note 5). When discrepancies occur, I have followed *Grove*.

[48]. This may be partially because much source-material originally preserved in Milan was most likely destroyed during the Second World War. I am grateful to Roger Parker (London) for this information.

in 1886/1887) in this regard. However, it is clear that the flute-cadenza did become established in Northern-Italian theatres after the turn of the twentieth century, perhaps through Marchesi's cadenza publication of c. 1900 or through the connection with Arditi who himself had studied at the Conservatory of Milan. It was a local variant of Marchesi's C3 that became especially favoured.

As was indicated above, in the mid to late nineteenth century various music schools, modelled upon the Paris Conservatoire (founded in 1795), gained ground as an alternative to the old system of singing apprenticeships under the control of particular masters. In Italy, Milan became a progressive centre for that new kind of training[49], and out of this system of education came many successful singers, including Giuseppina Strepponi (the second wife of Verdi) and also Teresa Brambilla (the soprano who, as we saw, was said by Barblan to have initiated the flute-cadenza)[50].

In the conservatoire system, the traditional, patriarchal transmission of knowledge may first seem to have weakened, but, in fact, the authority of a master remained within such institutions almost intact as methods of vocal training became more systematically organised and rigidly followed. Consequently, the nineteenth century saw numerous publications of textbooks for singers as well as vocal exercises, studies and cadenzas[51]. In such a climate, the purpose of printing cadenzas was no longer simply the innocuous preservation of the otherwise ephemeral practices of great singers. Cadenzas now became hurdles set for young singers to overcome, in order to win over others and impress their masters as well as future employers.

CONCLUSION: TOWARDS A BETTER UNDERSTANDING OF IMPROVISATION

This study of the flute-cadenza in Donizetti's *Lucia di Lammermoor* has uncovered several important issues in relation to the place of the cadenza within the whole history

---

[49]. ROSSELLI, John. *Singers of Italian opera. The History of a Profession*, Cambridge, Cambridge University Press, 1992, § 'Training', pp. 91-113; and RUTHERFORD, Susan. *Op. cit.* (see note 41), pp. 103-109.

[50]. ROSSELLI, John. *Op. cit.* (see note 49), p. 110.

[51]. Both Mathilde Marchesi and Francesco Lamperti published several vocal etudes. Marchesi, after teaching at the Vienna Conservatory from 1854 to 1861 and from 1868 to 1878, set up her own singing school in Paris in 1881. Her pedagogical publications include MARCHESI, Mathilde. *Perfectionnement du mécanisme de la voix. 24 Vocalises pour soprano*, Paris, s.n., 1863; *Exercices élémentaires gradués pour le développement de la voix*, Paris, s.n., 1864; *L'art du chant. 30 Vocalises pour mezzo-soprano ou soprano*, Paris, s.n., 1884; and *École Marchesi. Méthode de chant théorique et pratique*, 3 vols., Paris, s.n., 1886. Lamperti taught at Conservatorio di Milano between 1850 and 1875, and published among others *Guida teorico-practica-elementare per lo studio del canto*, Milan, Ricordi, 1864; *8 Solfeggi secondo lo stile moderno: edizione per soprano e mezzo soprano*, Milan, Ricordi, 1877; *Prime lezioni di canto per lo studio degli intervalli secondo lo stile moderno*, Milan, F. Lucca, 1886; and *Esercizi giornalieri di canto*, Milano, Ricordi, [c. 18..].

of improvisation. The first point to make is that, within the rather restricted practices of Lucia's mad-scene flute-cadenza, singers did not introduce entirely new cadenzas but variants based upon a shared prototype. Such variants can be seen particularly in Sections 1, 5 and 6 of the Marchesi prototype, as this article has demonstrated. Secondly, however, these variants themselves do not necessarily indicate a practice of improvised composition, a practice that the *Oxford Encyclopaedia of Aesthetics* defines as «production on the spur of the moment»[52]. They may not have been written down, but they were certainly constructed in advance and prepared in rehearsal.

The cadenza as an improvised practice has often been discussed in terms of its unwritten nature as opposed to composed music. For example, in a music dictionary published by Castil-Blaze in 1825, there was an attempt to distinguish between 'cadenza' and 'point d'orgue': the former is described as an «unwritten *point d'orgue*, which the composer leaves to the discretion of those who perform the principal role»[53], whereas the *point d'orgue* proper is written down. However, as this study has made clear, the essential criterion for recognising improvisation is not that it was unwritten, but that its precise content was unprepared. In the various traditions of the flute-cadenza in *Lucia di Lammermoor*, however, nothing the singers did on stage or on recordings was in fact unprepared.

This may be a picture rather different from that which we may naïvely expect from vocal ornamentation of the nineteenth century in general. However, the flute-cadenza of *Lucia* is not an isolated phenomenon, and many singing teachers of that time left arias annotated with various ornaments and cadenzas, while celebrated singers did the same in the form of 'notebooks'[54]. Some singers went so far as to treat their cadenzas as their 'signature displays' or even literal signatures — for example, Pauline Viardot gave to Sir George Grove «my cadenza in the *aria di bravura* in [Gluck's] *Orpheé*» as a souvenir[55]. It was in such ways that certain cadenzas became fixed texts, whereas, in reality, they were not always as unique or personal as a real signature might be.

It is reported that Manuel García Senior once asserted that «a real singer must be able to improvise ten or even twenty [cadenzas] if he so desires»[56]. Likewise, the first

---

[52]. ALPERSON, Philip A. 'Improvisation. An Overview', in: *Encyclopedia of Aesthetics*, 4 vols., edited by Michael Kelly, New York, Oxford University Press, 1998, vol. II, p. 478.

[53]. CASTIL-BLAZE [François-Henri-Joseph Blaze]. *Dictionnaire de musique moderne*, Paris, Magasin de Musique de la Lyre Moderne, ²1825, vol. I, pp. 80-81: «[…] un point d'orgue non éscrit, et que l'auteur laisse a la volonté de celui qui execute la partie principale […]».

[54]. As we have seen, Marchesi's *Variantes et points d'orgue* is one such example. Also see GARCIA, Manuel (junior). *Traité complet de l'art du chant*, Paris, Auteur, 1851, which contains several annotated arias in Part II. Singers from this period who left manuscript 'notebooks' include Laure Cinti-Damoreau, who sang various heroines of Rossini's French operas (US-BLl); Pauline Viardot (US-Wc); and Adelaide Kemble, the first Scala Lucia (private collection).

[55]. GB-Lcm, Ms. 2224, a single-sheet music manuscript.

[56]. LEGOUVÉ, Ernest. *Soixante ans de souvenirs*, Paris, J. Hetzek, 1886, vol. I, pp. 241-242. Cited in RADOMSKI, James. *Op. cit.* (see note 42), pp. 266-267.

Lucia, Tacchinardi-Persiani was praised by, among others, the English critic Henry Chorley[57], for the great variety of her ornaments, which made her execution seem so spontaneous. However, we should take into account the fact that the repertoire written up to the 1830s had in general a comparatively simple harmonic structure, which enabled singers to prepare, before the performance, numerous cadenzas (usually over a long-held six-four chord) and keep them 'in stock'. And perhaps this custom of 'stocking up' allowed the performer to select a suitable embellishment for a given aria melody at the moment of performance, as long as the harmonic structure of music was simple and standardised. In the later nineteenth-century practices of vocal ornamentation began to respond to the more constraining contexts of their application. First, the more developed harmonic structure of music limited the ways in which ornamentation could be added. Second, there is abundant evidence that, as the century progressed, composers and singers became more aware of stylistic appropriateness in such matters, and would sanction only what they thought to be 'stylistically right'. Finally there were the 'patriarchal' constrictions of apprenticeship under singing masters and conservatoire-based schools of singing. As a result, not only cadenzas but also melodic embellishments could become standardized[58].

Finally, although the madness of Lucia is seemingly represented by the freedom of her extravagant vocal embellishments, it is ironic that the paradigm moment of the display of her 'liberty through lunacy' is manacled by the formal, technical and social demands of collaboration and composition, and by the authoritarian teacher-pupil relationship, probably one of the most patriarchal apprenticeship systems in society. Yet, the fixed nature of the melodic sections and some of their internal decorations do not prevent the display of other, more individualistic and subtle elements of vocal performance. For example, in early recordings we find different tempos, articulations and vocal timbres among those singers who are ostensibly performing the same cadenza. Furthermore, as their differing reputations as to stage presence bear witness in the constrained, formalised world of operatic singing, new significations are not to be achieved by mere vocal techniques alone. Rather, it is through unique performative meanings, characterizations, embodiments and insights that Lucia's singers are likely to reveal new and individual depths, and make their claims to be truly free spirits[59]. The iron hand of tradition may govern the notes that singers sing, but it cannot yet govern

---

[57]. CHORLEY, Henry F. *Thirty Years' Musical Recollections*, London, Hurst & Blacket, 1862, pp. 149-150.

[58]. For a discussion of the restricted practices of melodic embellishment, see BOWEN, José Antonio. 'Performers Interpreting History. Finding «Una voce poco fà» (forthcoming). I am grateful to José Antonio Bowen (Dallas) for allowing me access to his as yet unpublished work.

[59]. For feminist studies of Lucia's mad scene see CLÉMENT, Catherine. *Opera, or The Undoing of Women* [1988], London, I. B. Tauris, 1997, pp. 88-91; McCLARY, Susan. *Feminine Endings*, Minnesota, University of Minnesota Press, 1991, Chapter 4; and SMART, Mary Ann. 'The Silencing of Lucia', in: *Cambridge Opera Journal*, IV/2 (July, 1992), pp. 119-141.

their flair for characterisation, nor their sensitivity towards appropriate dramaturgy and convincing presentation. In that sense, in much operatic singing the term 'improvisation' is more an indication of the style of display or the freedom of theatrical spirit, than of compositional spontaneity. We may hear cadenzas as spontaneous creations, but only because they are taken to be metaphorical exemplifications of uncontrollable human emotions. The fact that the notes themselves may be carefully prepared is only another indication that, in art, intensive expression rarely makes sense without the support of adroitly arranged structures.

Improvvisazione popolare e urbana a Napoli nel primo Ottocento
Dai canti del molo a «Io te voglio bene assaje»

Raffaele Di Mauro
(Roma)

L'inizio dell'Ottocento a Napoli era stato, come sappiamo, caratterizzato da profondi e continui mutamenti politici: c'era stata la breve esperienza della Repubblica napoletana del 1799 finita nel sangue dopo la reazione 'sanfedista' che aveva riportato sul trono i Borboni ma solo per pochi anni perché, nel 1806, i francesi erano tornati a Napoli prima con Giuseppe Bonaparte e poi con Gioacchino Murat, restandovi fino al 1815, in quel 'decennio francese' caratterizzato secondo gli storici da grandi riforme[1]. Di questo periodo, cioè del primo ventennio del secolo e fino al 1824 (anno di inizio, come vedremo, della pubblicazione dei *Passatempi musicali*) per quanto riguarda la musica popolare e urbana napoletana, non abbiamo molte fonti dirette[2]. Fanno eccezione i cosiddetti fogli volanti (similari ai *broadsides* del mondo anglosassone) che si stampavano a Napoli sicuramente anche nei primissimi anni dell'Ottocento ma che ebbero un grande boom soltanto dal 1840 in poi, dopo il clamoroso successo di 'Io te voglio bene assaje', di cui parleremo diffusamente più avanti.

Attraverso varie fonti letterarie, si può dire quasi con certezza che la vita musicale popolare cittadina della Napoli del primo Ottocento girasse essenzialmente intorno a un luogo della città ben preciso, ovvero il molo, dove si raggruppavano diverse figure legate allo spettacolo e all'intrattenimento (ciarlatani, pulcinella, ecc.), e, in particolare, alcune figure di musici ambulanti e cantori girovaghi come i cantastorie, i cosiddetti viggianesi e, quelli che maggiormente ci interessano in questa sede, ovvero gli improvvisatori[3]. Una

---

[1]. Galasso, Giuseppe. *Napoli capitale. Identità politica e identità cittadina. Studi e ricerche 1266-1860*, Napoli, Electa, 1998, pp. 235-236.

[2]. Sulla musica colta a Napoli durante il periodo francese si veda invece: Maione, Paologiovanni. 'Organizzazione e repertorio musicale della corte nel decennio francese a Napoli (1806-1815)', in: *Fonti Musicali Italiane*, XI (2006), pp. 119-173.

[3]. Per una più completa comprensione di cosa fosse il Molo di Napoli in quegli anni, si veda anche: Bidera, Emmanuele. *Passeggiata per Napoli e contorni*, 2 voll., Napoli, All'insegna di Aldo Manuzio, 1844, vol. I, pp. 75-88.

delle testimonianze più preziose sulla centralità popolare del molo è quella di Karl August Mayer che tra il 1840 e il 1842 pubblica in Germania due volumi nei quali narra dei suoi lunghi soggiorni a Napoli durante la prima parte dell'Ottocento[4]. Mayer dice che «chi vuol imparare a conoscere i divertimenti giornalieri del popolo, deve frequentare innanzi tutto la strada del molo, dove, soprattutto di sera, svariati artisti e virtuosi [...] si producono davanti ai lazzaroni e ai barcaioli»[5], descrive quindi i vari tipi di personaggi che si possono incontrare in questo luogo straordinario soffermandosi ad esempio sui cantastorie, i quali declamavano versi dell'Ariosto o del Tasso, o cantavano «con voce melodiosa» servendosi scambievolmente «ora della lingua italiana, ora del dialetto napoletano»[6].

Oltre ai cantastorie, intorno al molo gravitavano anche altre categorie di musici ambulanti di particolare interesse, tra questi i viggianesi, così chiamati perché provenienti da Viggiano, un paese della Basilicata. Di questi ultimi ci dà notizie invece Giuseppe Regaldi in un articolo del 1848 dal titolo appunto 'Il Viggianese'[7]. Regaldi narra un episodio accaduto sulla riviera di Santa Lucia, dove egli dimorava (siamo sempre nei pressi del molo), quando un giorno, dopo aver udito dalla sua stanza provenire dalla strada il suono di un'arpa, chiamò il suonatore, il quale, accompagnato da due giovani che suonavano il violino, salì nella sua abitazione e prese a narrargli la sua vita. Si chiamava Francesco Pennella, era nato a Viggiano e da diciassette anni viaggiava con la stessa arpa con cui il nonno aveva già suonato i canti di Cimarosa e Jommelli e il padre quelli di Rossini e Mercadante. Il loro repertorio era costituito, però, oltre che da canti del teatro d'opera italiano anche da brani dei loro 'pastori' e infine da canzoni napoletane che il Pennella stesso, dopo averne eseguita una al Regaldi (la famosa 'Lo cardillo'), disse di acquistare al prezzo di un grano ciascuna da venditori che «con un fascio di tali canzoni schiamazzando fanno il giro di tutta Napoli», riferendosi, com'è intuibile, ai venditori dei già citati fogli volanti.

IMPROVVISATORI A NAPOLI ALL'INIZIO DELL'OTTOCENTO: DUE TIPOLOGIE

Ma veniamo agli improvvisatori, a questi dedica una grande attenzione sempre Mayer che ci dice che

---

4. MAYER, Karl August. *Neapel und die Neapolitaner, oder Briefe aus Neapel in die Heimat. Mit einem Plane der Umgegend Neapels und einer Musikbeilage*, 2 voll., Oldenburg, Schulze, 1840-1842. Questi volumi sono stati parzialmente pubblicati in traduzione italiana da Lidia Croce, *Vita popolare a Napoli nell'età romantica*, Bari, Laterza, 1948. Citiamo da questa traduzione italiana.

5. *Ibidem*, p. 144.

6. *Ibidem*, p. 148.

7. REGALDI, Giuseppe. 'Il Viggianese', in: *Poliorama Pittoresco*, XII/2 (1848), pp. 326-327 e 334-335. Sempre sui viggianesi segnaliamo anche un articolo apparso sulla stessa rivista più di dieci anni prima di quello del Regaldi: MALPICA, Cesare. 'Costumi - I viggianesi', in: *Poliorama Pittoresco*, I/2 (1836), pp. 405-406.

un maggior documento del talento poetico napoletano, e soprattutto degli italiani, è fornito dall'improvvisazione, questo splendido dono di cui il cielo ha provvisto la bella penisola più di ogni paese. Esso si trova nelle più infime classi, e si manifesta in svariatissimi modi, nella declamazione di versi trovati sull'istante, di canti e di racconti, che in verità non sono per sé stessi di un significativo valore poetico, ma fanno il loro effetto come prodotti del momento[8].

Dal racconto di Mayer è intuibile chiaramente che vi fosse, a quei tempi, un doppio livello di improvvisatori. Il primo livello appartiene agli strati sociali più umili e si esibisce per strada:

al tempo di Ferdinando I vi erano qui due improvvisatori fissi che, come i cantanti sul molo, si esibivano pubblicamente davanti al popolo. Erano due contadini di Lecce e di Ischia, che quotidianamente si provocavano in gare poetiche, e gareggiavano l'un contro l'altro cantando in versi. Sovente invitavano anche i circostanti, a proporre i loro temi, che essi poi trattavano con grande sottigliezza[9].

Non è facile, date le poche notizie forniteci da Mayer, indicare con esattezza il tipo di repertorio vocale attraverso il quale questi contadini 'improvvisatori' si sfidavano, ma alcuni elementi — l'idea di 'gara poetica', i temi proposti dal pubblico astante — ci fanno immediatamente pensare al canto estemporaneo in ottava rima assai diffuso all'epoca (l'esplosione era avvenuta in particolar modo nel Settecento) non solo in Toscana, che ne è la patria da tutti riconosciuta, ma anche in altre regioni e città italiane[10]. Ad esempio a Venezia, come testimoniatoci da Goethe che nel 1786 ascolta il canto dell'ottava da alcuni gondolieri veneziani[11], più o meno lo stesso udito pochi anni prima da Giuseppe Baretti, il quale se ne fa trascrivere il testo e la melodia pubblicandoli col titolo di 'Tasso alla veneziana'[12]. Ma il canto estemporaneo era diffuso ad esempio anche nel Lazio, tanto da ispirare, nel 1835, dopo un lungo soggiorno in Italia, un romanzo allo scrittore danese Hans Christian Andersen (noto soprattutto per le fiabe) dal titolo 'L'improvvisatore', in cui si narrano le gesta di Antonio, un giovane improvvisatore che, formatosi prima nella 'campagna romana', finirà per esibirsi al Teatro di San Carlo di Napoli[13].

---

[8]. Mayer, Karl August. *Op. cit.* (si veda nota 4), pp. 311-312.

[9]. *Ibidem*, p. 316.

[10]. Sull'*ottava rima* si veda Kezich, Giovanni. *I poeti contadini. Introduzione all'ottava rima popolare: immaginario poetico e paesaggio sociale*, con il saggio 'Cantar l'ottava' di Maurizio Agamennone, Roma, Bulzoni, 1986.

[11]. Goethe, Johann Wolfgang von. *Viaggio in Italia*, a cura di Eugenio Zaniboni, 3 voll., Firenze, Sansoni, 1911-1924, vol. I, pp. 94-96.

[12]. Baretti, Giuseppe. *An Account of the Manners and Customs of Italy*, 2 voll., Londra, T. Davies & L. Davis, 1769, vol. II, pp. 153-154.

[13]. Andersen, Hans Christian. *Un racconto romano. L'improvvisatore* (1835), Napoli, Guida, 1984.

Non bisogna però dimenticare che a Napoli vere e proprie sfide vocali popolari si effettuavano adoperando anche altre forme di canto, senza accompagnamento, tipicamente partenopee e cioè le cosiddette 'fronne 'e limone' o i 'canti a figliola', spesso confusi l'uno con l'altro ma che, pur muovendosi su uno stile abbastanza omogeneo, hanno caratteristiche e funzioni diverse[14]. Alcune di queste gare, che spesso vedevano coinvolti personaggi della malavita napoletana, cioè della camorra, potevano finire anche in modo tragico, vale a dire con accoltellamenti e ferimenti vari, così come testimoniato da Abele De Blasio[15]. La sfida più importante di canti a figliola si teneva annualmente, al ritorno dalla festa di Montevergine, in piazza del Duomo a Nola, dove diversi cantatori gareggiavano cantando da balconi e terrazze, con il pubblico sottostante che poteva acclamarli o fischiarli[16].

È possibile quindi che l'improvvisazione popolare a Napoli nel primo Ottocento si muovesse su un 'doppio binario': da un lato gare di canti cosiddetti 'a poeta' o 'a braccio', sul modello dell'ottava rima, crediamo in lingua italiana (o meglio: toscana), ma probabilmente anche in napoletano, e dall'altro sfide di 'fronne' e 'canti a figliola' rigorosamente in dialetto. In ciascuno dei due casi ci riferiamo comunque a repertori riconducibili a quella che l'etnomusicologo Diego Carpitella chiamava fascia 'agro-pastorale', relativa cioè alla musica dei contadini e dei pastori[17].

Dal racconto di Mayer è identificabile però anche un secondo livello di improvvisatori, appartenenti a ceti più elevati, che si esibivano o da soli in 'accademie di poesia estemporanea', così come venivano chiamate allora, oppure in vere e proprie gare organizzate in luoghi chiusi, vale a dire salotti o, addirittura, teatri. A tal proposito Mayer narra di una gara a cui egli stesso assistette al Teatro dei Fiorentini (tra i più antichi teatri di Napoli e uno dei 'templi' dell'opera buffa) in cui vennero estratti a sorte dodici temi su cui i concorrenti dovevano improvvisare[18]. Nella gara si distinse un noto avvocato di

---

[14]. La *fronna* è un'espressione musicale tipica ed esclusiva della Campania. Si tratta di una particolare forma di canto eseguito a distesa, senza accompagnamento strumentale, le cui tematiche si riferiscono in genere all'amore, al sesso e alla morte. Il *canto a figliola* è anch'esso un particolare tipo di canto campano eseguito senza accompagnamento strumentale e legato principalmente al culto della Madonna di Montevergine (detta anche *Madonna nera* o *Mamma schiavona*). La denominazione *a figliola* è proprio in riferimento alla Madonna. Su *fronne* e *canti a figliola* si veda DI MAURO, Raffaele. 'Canzone napoletana e musica di tradizione orale: dalla canzone *artigiana* alla canzone *urbana* d'autore', in: *Musica/Realtà*, XCIII (novembre 2010), pp. 131-151: 138.

[15]. DE BLASIO, Abele. *Usi e costumi dei camorristi*, Napoli, Luca Torre, 1993 (prima edizione Napoli, Pierro, 1897), pp. 141-143.

[16]. *Ibidem*, pp. 143-148. Sulla sfida di *canti a figliola* che si teneva a Nola al ritorno da Montevergine si veda anche BIDERA, Emmanuele. 'Le feste della Madonna di Montevergine', in: *Usi e costumi di Napoli* (Napoli, 1857-1866), a cura di Francesco De Bourcard, 2 voll., La Spezia, Polaris, 1990, vol. I, pp. 197-215. Oppure la ricostruzione fornitaci, in chiave teatrale, da Viviani nel secondo atto della sua commedia *La Festa di Montevergine*: VIVIANI, Raffaele. *Teatro*, a cura di Antonia Lezza e Pasquale Scialò, 6 voll., Napoli, Guida, 1987-1994, vol. V, pp. 124-149.

[17]. CARPITELLA, Diego. *Musica e tradizione orale*, Palermo, Flaccovio, 1973, p. 53.

[18]. Si veda MAYER, Karl August. *Op. cit.* (si veda nota 4), p. 313.

allora, tal Bindocci di Siena[19] (indicata dal Mayer come 'la città degli improvvisatori'), che diede il meglio di sé improvvisando sul primo tema proposto, ovvero 'Sulla tomba di una giovinetta', a partire da una 'melodia semplicissima' suonata da un maestro sul pianoforte a coda che stava sulla scena accanto a un seggio sul quale si alternavano gli sfidanti. Bindocci

> aveva una potente voce di baritono, e sebbene fosse solo un mediocre cantante, la sua declamazione vivace faceva una gradevole impressione [...] ora lui, ora il pubblico dava la rima [...] in alcune poesie egli si faceva accompagnare dal piano solo nei punti rilevanti [...] una volta, turbato dalla melodia nel corso dei pensieri, ne chiese un'altra che si dimostrò più fruttuosa [...] nella poesia *L'arte in Italia* si dimostrò uno schietto patriota [...] era in ottava rima e cominciava con le parole: 'Solo sotto il cielo azzurro le Muse...'[20].

Il fatto che Mayer specifichi, solo per quest'ultima poesia, che Bindocci utilizzasse l'ottava rima da una parte testimonia indubitabilmente quale fosse il principale modello di riferimento ma dall'altra ci fa capire che non tutte le improvvisazioni utilizzavano la struttura metrica canonica dell'ottava rima ovvero quella di una strofa di otto endecasillabi, formati da tre distici a rima alternata e un distico finale a rima baciata che fornisce anche l'obbligo di rima per l'ottava successiva, secondo lo schema abababcc, poi cdcdcdee, e così via. Sul fatto che gli improvvisatori si esercitassero, «in vari metri, tra cui naturalmente l'ottava rima, accompagnati talora da un violone o una spinetta» abbiamo diverse testimonianze anche relative al Settecento, riportate nel lavoro di Giovanni Kezich[21]. La presenza degli improvvisatori nei teatri napoletani (in particolare in quello dei Fiorentini) fin dal Settecento è confermata anche da Benedetto Croce che, nella prima e più ampia edizione del suo lavoro su *I teatri di Napoli*, ci racconta che

> nel 1780 un poeta, Angelo Talassi ferrarese, voleva improvvisare di giorno ai Fiorentini, «sopra quei soggetti, che gli daranno, tacendo per tale effetto un

---

[19]. Si tratta sicuramente di Antonio Bindocci, avvocato di Siena, tra i più celebri e acclamati improvvisatori dell'epoca, che tenne, spesso accompagnato da un pianista, numerose 'accademie di poesia estemporanea' sia in tutta Italia che all'estero (in Portogallo, Francia ecc.). Riportiamo a tal proposito un avviso apparso su un giornale francese: «Aujourd'hui, 20 octobre, aura lieu la seconde séance d'*Improvisation italienne*, par M. Bindocci, avocat de Sienne. Le poète, encouragé par l'accueil bienveillant des amateurs, chantera avec accompagnement de piano, ou déclamera sur des sujets proposés par messieurs les assistans, improvisant en vers intercalaires, de mesure variée, et avec rimes obliges. Prix d'entrée: premières 8 francs, seconds 5 francs. On commencera à 8 heures précises». *L'Aigle, Journal de la Liberté politique et Littéraire*, n. 294 (20 Ottobre 1830). Bindocci era talmente noto all'epoca da essere stato scelto, grazie anche all'intercessione di Felice Romani, in un primo momento come librettista per 'Il Bravo' di Mercadante che tuttavia, dopo varie vicissitudini, fu portato a termine nel 1839 da Gaetano Rossi. Il Bindocci volle però lo stesso pubblicare la 'sua' versione: *Il Bravo, tragedia lirica dell'avv. Antonio Bindocci poeta estemporaneo*, Torino, Gianini e Fiore, 1839.

[20]. MAYER, Karl August. *Op. cit.* (si veda nota 4), pp. 313-315.

[21]. KEZICH, Giovanni. *Op. cit.* (si veda nota 10), p. 117.

pubblico invito venale» [...] nel 1788 un altro improvvisatore, un Luigi Massari, che per quindici anni aveva scorso tutta l'Europa improvvisando, e s'era fatto sentire a varie Corti, specie in Russia, in Germania, in Francia [...] fece una pubblica accademia ai Fiorentini [...] ma «il pubblico che l'intese, ne fece il carattere di sciocco e saltimbanco, sicché meritò, invece di lode, fischiate!»[22].

La testimonianza di Croce conferma la fama che gli improvvisatori italiani avevano oltralpe, così come attestato anche dallo stesso Mayer che ci informa che «maggior fama di Bindocci possedeva il napoletano Grizzi[23], che negli anni 1827, 28, 29 attraversò l'Italia e la Francia»[24]. Questo secondo livello di improvvisatori, a differenza del primo riferibile al mondo contadino, è invece per certi versi riconducibile alla fascia che Carpitella definiva 'artigiano-urbana'[25], ma possiamo estenderlo fino a raggiungere anche quegli esponenti delle classi medio-alte dell'epoca (non a caso Bindocci era un avvocato e Raffaele Sacco, di cui parleremo più avanti, era uno stimato ottico) molto spesso capaci di muoversi a loro agio sia con la 'piccola tradizione' che la 'grande tradizione'[26], in questo caso quindi sia con forme riconducibili alla musica di tradizione orale sia invece con repertori colti, di cui erano sicuramente conoscitori e frequentatori[27].

Ricostruito il contesto degli improvvisatori a Napoli nel primo Ottocento, in base esclusivamente a fonti letterarie, restava da trovare qualche fonte musicale diretta da analizzare per comprendere meglio il fenomeno, facendo un'analisi delle strutture musicali oltre che testuali. Fortunatamente ci è venuta in soccorso, a tal scopo, quell'autentica 'miniera' di tesori ancora da esplorare che è la raccolta dei *Passatempi musicali*.

---

[22]. CROCE, Benedetto. *I teatri di Napoli. Secoli XV-XVIII*, Napoli, Pierro, 1891, pp. 619-620.

[23]. Non siamo riusciti a trovare alcuna notizia riguardante il Grizzi citato da Mayer. Riteniamo probabile che egli abbia commesso un errore e si riferisca a Sgricci (che di nome si chiamava Tommaso), poeta estemporaneo che conobbe il successo in quegli anni proprio in Italia e Francia. Sgricci era però aretino (essendo nato a Castiglion Fiorentino nel 1788) e non napoletano. CORNIANI, Giambattista. *I secoli della letteratura italiana dopo il suo risorgimento*, Torino, Unione tipografico-editrice torinese, 1856, vol. VIII, pp. 112-113.

[24]. MAYER, Karl August. *Op. cit.* (si veda nota 4), p. 316.

[25]. CARPITELLA, Diego. *Op. cit.* (si veda nota 17), p. 53.

[26]. Per i concetti di 'piccola tradizione' e 'grande tradizione' si veda BURKE, Peter. *Cultura popolare nell'Europa moderna*, Milano, Arnoldo Mondadori, 1980.

[27]. Oltre al caso di Bindocci, come abbiamo visto librettista 'mancato' per un'opera di Mercadante, ricordiamo ad esempio la figura di Niccola Sole, altro famoso poeta improvvisatore dell'epoca, avvocato anch'egli, lucano di nascita ma napoletano di adozione, il quale ebbe grandi rapporti di amicizia con Giuseppe Verdi che soleva accompagnarlo privatamente al piano nei suoi canti estemporanei oppure lo «ispirava» suonandogli un'aria dal *Nabucco* o dai *Vespri*. Secondo una testimonianza, Verdi scrisse per Sole anche una melodia sulla quale avrebbe potuto improvvisare in ottava rima. Si veda a tal proposito: DE CLEMENTE, Achille. 'Della vita e delle opere di Niccola Sole', in: *Il Paese*, 1/42 (28 Gennaio 1860).

Canzoni di improvvisatori nei *Passatempi* di Guglielmo Cottrau

Durante il già menzionato decennio francese era arrivato a Napoli Giuseppe Cottrau, chiamato a ricoprire importanti cariche politiche, e con lui il figlio Guglielmo che, nato nel 1797 a Parigi, era stato cresciuto ed educato nella città partenopea fin da piccolo[28]. Guglielmo, dopo un primo tentativo di seguire le orme paterne dedicandosi alla politica, aveva deciso di occuparsi a tempo pieno della sua passione, la musica, accogliendo nel 1824 l'invito di Bernardo Girard a dirigere la casa editrice musicale che questi aveva fondato fin dal 1809 nella centralissima via Toledo[29]. Una delle idee vincenti del Guglielmo editore era stata la pubblicazione, a partire proprio dal 1824, dei *Passatempi musicali*, una raccolta di brani vocali per canto e pianoforte (più altri solo strumentali)[30], destinati, per la loro semplicità, a coloro che si dilettavano con la musica, appartenenti per lo più ai salotti nobil-borghesi[31]. La grande novità dei *Passatempi* era che per la prima volta venivano trascritte, anche se rielaborate secondo i gusti musicali dell'epoca, alcune canzoni popolari napoletane che probabilmente, se lasciate alla sola trasmissione orale, non sarebbero giunte a noi col passare dei secoli.

In base a diversi indizi possiamo dire che una delle principali fonti cui Cottrau attingeva per le proprie trascrizioni era proprio costituito dai brani eseguiti sul molo (chiamati 'storie 'e copp' 'o muolo'[32]) oppure in giro per la città dalle figure di musici e cantori ambulanti di cui abbiamo già parlato, cioè cantastorie, viggianesi e appunto improvvisatori. A dimostrazione di quanto detto portiamo alcune prove: tra le 68 canzoncine della terza edizione dei *Passatempi* (del 1829) troviamo un brano dal titolo 'Storia di Angelo del

---

[28]. Lylircus (pseudonimo di Edoardo Cerillo). *Ricordi biografici napoletani dal 1820 al 1850, Guglielmo Cottrau*, Napoli, Marghieri, ²1881, pp. 6-7.

[29]. Seller, Francesca. 'Girard; Cottrau; Stab. musicale partenopeo', in: *Dizionario degli editori musicali italiani 1750-1930*, a cura di Bianca Maria Antolini, Pisa, Edizioni ETS, 2000, pp. 173-178; De Mura, Ettore. *Enciclopedia della canzone napoletana*, 3 voll., Napoli, Il Torchio, 1969, vol. I, pp. 460-461.

[30]. La denominazione precisa era *Passatempi musicali o sia Raccolta di Ariette e duettini per camera inediti, Romanze francesi nuove, Canzoncine Napoletane e Siciliane, Variazioni pel canto, piccoli Divertimenti per pianoforte, Contraddanze, Walz, Balli diversi etc.* La raccolta uscì tra il 1824 e il 1829 in due serie di fascicoli misti e in tre edizioni divise invece in *parti* che riprendevano sostanzialmente i brani già pubblicati nei fascicoli misti. Fecero poi seguito diversi *Supplementi*, i primi tre curati tra il 1843 e il 1845 sempre da Guglielmo Cottrau prima della sua morte avvenuta nel 1847.

[31]. Si vedano a tal proposito le liste degli *associati* alla prima serie di sei fascicoli dei *Passatempi* del 1824-1825 poste all'inizio dei fascicoli stessi. Vi ritroviamo gran parte della nobiltà dell'epoca, in particolar modo rappresentanti del gentil sesso che più si dilettavano con questo tipo di repertorio ritenuto semplice: principesse, duchesse, baronesse, marchese ecc. In testa alla lista generale della prima serie troviamo come prima associata addirittura 'S. M. la Regina del Regno delle due Sicilie'.

[32]. Si veda Martorana, Pietro. *Notizie biografiche e bibliografiche degli scrittori del dialetto napolitano*, Napoli, Chiurazzi, 1874, pp. 57-59.

Duca, come si canta sul molo di Napoli'[33], e un altro ancora intitolato significativamente 'Aria d'improvisatore'. Quest'ultimo, nel catalogo della Girard, viene riportato con un titolo diverso, cioè 'Soavemente ombrosa' (che è l'incipit testuale), e con un'indicazione aggiuntiva tra parentesi assai chiara, vale a dire 'canzone d'improvvisatore'[34].

Analizziamo proprio questa 'Aria d'improvisatore' (si veda ILL. 1). Il testo è formato da quattro ottave, ciascuna divisa in due quartine composte da quattro settenari di cui l'ultimo tronco, con rime abbc/abac[35]; l'«etc.» posto alla fine della quarta strofa lascia intendere che sulla stessa musica si cantavano probabilmente altre strofe, oltre alle quattro riportate, e ciò naturalmente è in pieno accordo con una canzone o aria definita 'd'improvisatore'.

ILL. 1: la partitura di 'Aria d'improvisatore' pubblicata nei *Passatempi Musicali*, terza edizione, Parte II, Fascicolo VI, del 1829.

---

33. Anche nel catalogo generale delle edizioni Girard pubblicato nel 1847 il brano viene indicato come «storia di brigante che si canta sul molo di Napoli». GIRARD E CO. *Catalogo di musica pubblicata a tutto luglio 1847*, Napoli, Stabilimento tipografico di Gaetano Nobile, 1847, Parte I, p. 29.

34. *Ibidem.*

35. Fa eccezione la quarta ottava con rime abac/babc.

ILL. 2: lo spartito di 'Barcarola popolare. Ahi che l'affetto mio', pubblicato nella prima serie dei *Passatempi Musicali*, nel Fascicolo VI, del 1825.

Il brano musicalmente si presenta come un andante in 4/4; la struttura melodica è di tipo abac/dd'ac su complessive 16 battute (due per ciascuna frase melodica), un *ambitus* di nona, un profilo melodico tendenzialmente ad arco che si muove su una scala maggiore con presenza del secondo grado aumentato, la linea melodica è essenzialmente sillabica (da notare però la presenza di tre gruppetti), procede principalmente per gradi congiunti con alcuni salti di terza e due salti di ottava quasi in chiusura di ciascuna delle due quartine. L'accompagnamento armonico si muove essenzialmente sull'appoggio degli accordi in modo da privilegiare il canto, non vi è inoltre alcuna introduzione o coda pianistica.

Oltre all''Aria d'improvisatore - Soavemente Ombrosa', abbiamo anche un altro pezzo del 1825 che nei *Passatempi* viene proposto col titolo di 'Barcarola popolare'[36], ma

---

[36].   Il brano appare la prima volta nel 1825 nel fascicolo n. 6 della prima serie dei *Passatempi* del 1824-1825.

che nel catalogo Girard viene indicato con l'incipit 'Ahi che l'affetto mio' e anch'esso con la dicitura tra parentesi di 'canzone d'improvvisatore'. Analizziamo anche quest'ulteriore brano (si veda ILL. 2).

Il testo è formato anche qui da quattro ottave, ciascuna divisa in due quartine formate da 4 settenari di cui l'ultimo tronco, con rime stavolta abbc/deec. La musica è un andantino in 4/4, con una struttura melodica di tipo abac/dd'ab' (quasi la stessa del brano precedente) sempre in 16 battute, un *ambitus* di ottava, un profilo melodico tendenzialmente ad arco che si muove su una scala maggiore con presenza del secondo e quarto grado aumentato, una linea melodica prevalentemente sillabica (da segnalare però anche qui la presenza di vari gruppetti), procedente principalmente per gradi congiunti con salti di terza ma alcuni anche di quarta e di sesta; l'accompagnamento armonico si muove anche in questo caso essenzialmente appoggiando gli accordi in modo da far risaltare la melodia.

Dall'analisi di questi due brani ricaviamo alcune prime considerazioni. Per quanto riguarda la struttura dei testi, non ci sorprende affatto l'uso di metri differenti (settenari in questo caso) da quello canonico dell'ottava rima basato, com'è noto, sugli endecasillabi, perché, come appreso da diverse fonti e anche dalla gara dei Fiorentini raccontata da Mayer, diversi erano i metri e le rime adoperate dagli improvvisatori per la 'creazione' delle loro poesie e canti estemporanei.

La cosa è invece più complessa per ciò che riguarda la musica che, come abbiamo visto nella *performance* di Bindocci, poteva dare un piccolo spunto con una semplicissima melodia[37], seguire tutto il canto o soltanto i punti rilevanti, fare da mero accompagnamento a un'esecuzione recitata o, addirittura, tacere del tutto. Diventa quindi assai arduo riuscire a capire, nel caso dei due brani analizzati, quale delle succitate scelte musicali era stata compiuta in origine per accompagnare l'improvvisazione e poi, cosa assolutamente da non trascurare, quanto ci abbia messo di suo Cottrau, che spesso non si limitava semplicemente a trascrivere i brani (probabilmente in questo caso ascoltati in qualche esecuzione o gara salottiera piuttosto che teatrale) ma li rielaborava aggiustandoli prima

---

37. Secondo Carl Ludwig Fernow gli improvvisatori avevano per ogni sorta di metro un'appropriata melodia (sulla quale per metà cantavano e per metà recitavano) e questa era talmente semplice e gradevole da adattarsi a qualsiasi materia. Anche perché era la musica a doversi subordinare, come nei tempi antichi, alla poesia e a servire solo come adornamento del canto e riempimento dei vuoti tra una 'stanza' e l'altra. Molte di queste melodie erano, a suo avviso, opera degli stessi improvvisatori. FERNOW, Carl Ludwig. 'Über die Improvisatoren', in ID. *Römische Studien*, Zurigo, H. Gessner, 1806, pp. 315-316. Quanto affermato da Fernow è per certi versi confermato da una testimonianza di Croce che, parlando di un altro improvvisatore napoletano operante sin dalla fine del Settecento, tal Nicola Nicolini (anch'egli giureconsulto), ci informa di aver trovato e posseduto un suo manoscritto dal titolo *Musiche per poesie estemporanee ad uso di Nicola Nicolini* «confacenti ciascuna al genere dei versi, endecasillabi, decasillabi, ottonarii, settenarii, senarii, quinarii». CROCE, Benedetto. 'Gl'improvvisatori', in: *Quaderni della Critica*, VI (novembre 1946).

della pubblicazione[38]. Bisogna però sottolineare che, fatte le dovute differenze, i due brani hanno una struttura musicale molto simile sotto diversi aspetti (struttura melodica, *ambitus*, profilo, accompagnamento armonico ecc.) e la cosa, probabilmente, non è casuale.

'IO TE VOGLIO BENE ASSAJE':
CANZONE IMPROVVISATA ATTRIBUITA A GAETANO DONIZETTI

Ci occupiamo, in conclusione, della famosa 'Io te voglio bene assaje', cercando di argomentare il nostro parere sulla 'data di nascita' della canzone, sulla paternità sia letteraria che musicale, e sulla modalità compositiva di questo brano sul quale già molti studiosi si sono espressi con pareri talvolta contrastanti. Innanzitutto partiamo dalla data: alcuni hanno proposto come anno di creazione il 1835, in particolare Salvatore Di Giacomo, che lo collegava alla festa di Piedigrotta dello stesso anno, in base a una testimonianza di un non meglio identificato amico di Raffaele Sacco[39], indicato come autore del testo. L'ipotesi del 1835 di Di Giacomo serviva probabilmente ad avvalorare l'attribuzione della musica a Donizetti che in quell'anno era sicuramente a Napoli. L'attribuzione del brano a Donizetti è avallata, pur senza alcuna prova documentale, da alcuni biografi e studiosi donizettiani. Il primo in ordine temporale è Filippo Cicconetti che nella sua biografia del compositore bergamasco, attribuendogli senza dubbio la canzone, dice:

> Fior di eleganza, di semplicità e di grazia, è quella comunemente conosciuta con le parole 'Io te vojo bene assaje, e tu non piense a me'. Improvvisata sopra una poesia del Sacco svegliò il mal talento di alcuni a gloriarsene siccome autori, non avendo voluto porvi il suo nome Gaetano, il quale ogni qualvolta udiva quelle boriose menzogne, lungi dallo sdegnare, ne rideva coll'amico Ghezzi, che sapeva a cui dovesse attribuirsi quella invenzione[40].

---

[38]. Non a caso la versione di 'Barcarola popolare. Ahi che l'affetto mio' pubblicata nella terza edizione dei *Passatempi* del 1829 presenta alcuni aggiustamenti sia per la linea melodica che per l'accompagnamento pianistico.

[39]. DI GIACOMO, Salvatore. *'Te voglio bene assaie!...'*, in: ID. *Napoli. Figure e paesi*, Roma, Newton Compton, 1995, pp. 45-49. Questo breve articolo ebbe tre versioni: la prima (ID. *Celebrità napoletane*, Trani, V. Vecchi, 1896) e la terza (ID. *Napoli: figure e paesi*, Napoli, Perrella, 1909, che è quella poi riprodotta dalla Newton Compton) sono identiche e basate su un'anonima ricostruzione di un ipotetico amico del Sacco. Nella seconda invece (ID. *Piedigrotta for ever*, Napoli, Melfi & Joele, 1901) si sostiene la stessa ipotesi ma narrata in 'prima persona' dal Di Giacomo senza l'espediente del racconto anonimo. Sulla differenza tra le versioni riportate da Di Giacomo si veda STAZIO, Marialuisa. *Osolemio. La canzone napoletana - 1880/1914*, Roma, Bulzoni, 1991, pp. 226-227. Un'altra versione narrata per 'conto terzi' è quella riportata dal Costagliola (il quale data il brano sempre nel 1835 attribuendone la musica a Donizetti) per bocca di 'tal Federico Polizzi, di mestiere barbitonsore' che avrebbe assistito alla nascita della canzone. COSTAGLIOLA, Aniello. *Napoli che se ne va. Il Teatro, la canzone*, Napoli, Berisio, 1967 (prima edizione Napoli, Giannini, 1918), pp. 202-205.

[40]. CICCONETTI, Filippo. *Vita di Gaetano Donizetti*, Roma, Tipografia Tiberina, 1864, p. 120.

Esattamente dieci anni dopo Pietro Martorana, probabilmente a conoscenza del passo di Cicconetti, in una nota biografica dedicata al sacerdote Francesco Saverio Casularo avalla l'ipotesi donizettiana dicendo che «nel 1835 Raffaele Sacco improvvisava una canzona, con l'intercalare *Te voglio bene assaje, E tu non pienze a me*, la quale fu messa in musica dal celebre Donizetti»[41]; oppure parlando di un certo Carlo De Crescenzi, che aveva scritto una risposta alla canzone, diceva «conserviamo una sua poesia scritta nel 1836 epoca in cui Raffaele Sacco aveva improvvisato il 'Te voglio bene assaie'»[42]. Sulla scia di Cicconetti e Martorana, anche altri studiosi riporteranno l'attribuzione a Donizetti ma senza aggiungervi alcun elemento per comprovarla[43].

La tesi di Di Giacomo è stata quella prevalente fino all'apparizione dell'enciclopedia di Ettore De Mura che indicava invece come data il 1839 sulla base di tre elementi precisi[44]: una testimonianza dal carcere di Luigi Settembrini[45], una lettera di Raffaele De Rubertis[46] e la stampa che l'editore Girard aveva fatto del brano, presentandolo come 'Nuova canzone del 1840'. De Mura ipotizzava che la canzone, nata nel 1839, fosse stata diffusa prima su foglio volante quell'anno per la Piedigrotta (la cui festa, ricordiamo, cadeva l'8 Settembre) e poi stampata da Girard l'anno successivo. Diciamo subito che l'ipotesi di datazione di De Mura ci sembra più circostanziata rispetto a quella di Di Giacomo (il cui unico appoggio è dato dalle notizie del Martorana che non sappiamo però quanto siano attendibili in quanto non ne conosciamo le 'fonti') e cercheremo di aggiungere nuovi elementi per corroborarla, ricostruendo innanzitutto in successione le prime pubblicazioni a stampa del brano.

---

[41]. MARTORANA, Pietro. *Op. cit.* (si veda nota 32), p. 101.

[42]. *Ibidem*, p. 177.

[43]. Si vedano a tal proposito: DONATI-PETTENI, Giuliano. *Donizetti (1930)*, Milano, Garzanti, ²1945, p. 202, oppure BARBLAN, Guglielmo. *L'opera di Donizetti nell'età romantica*, Bergamo, Banca popolare di Bergamo, 1948, p. 236. Anche nel catalogo del museo donizettiano il brano viene attribuito a Donizetti: *Il museo donizettiano di Bergamo*, a cura di Valeriano Sacchiero, Bergamo, Centro studi donizettiani, 1970, p. 152. Dubbi sull'attribuzione vengono invece espressi da Ashbrook che elenca il brano con la dicitura «spesso attribuita a Donizetti»: ASHBROOK, William. 'Donizetti', in: *The New Grove Dictionary of Music and Musicians*, a cura di Stanley Sadie, 20 voll., Londra, ⁶1980, vol. V, p. 568.

[44]. DE MURA, Ettore. *Op. cit.* (si veda nota 29), vol. I, pp. 158-161.

[45]. Settembrini durante la sua detenzione nel carcere di Santa Maria Apparente sentendo cantare una bella melodia chiese al carceriere Liguoro quale fosse il titolo di questa canzone nuova e questi gli aveva risposto 'Te voglie bene assaie'. Settembrini poi afferma «Tre cose belle furono in quell'anno [riferendosi al 1839]: le ferrovie, l'illuminazione a gas e 'Te voglie bene assaie'». SETTEMBRINI, Luigi. *Ricordanze della mia vita*, vol. I, Napoli, Morano, ²1879, p. 159.

[46]. In questa lettera, indirizzata a Scalinger, De Rubertis indicava il 1839 come data di nascita di 'Te voglio bene assaie', che secondo il suo racconto era nata dopo una polemica scherzosa del Sacco con «una signorina molto ben voluta da esso». Si veda *La Lega del Bene*, II/38 (Settembre 1887).

Cronologia delle versioni di 'Io te voglio bene assaje' per canto e piano

(1)
Io te voglio bene assaje. Nuova canzone napoletana, Girard e Co. n. 4825, 1840.
Anonima, in Si bemolle maggiore, testo di quattro strofe

Escludendo le probabili stampe precedenti su fogli volanti, è questa la prima versione della canzone pubblicata per canto e pianoforte (si veda Ill. 3). Marcello Sorce Keller in un suo saggio sul brano[47], cercando di smentire la tesi di De Mura, aveva detto che «la canzone apparve nel 1835 in *Passatempi musicali*»[48], ma non ci risulta alcuna edizione dei *Passatempi* nell'anno da lui indicato e 'Io te voglio bene assaje', dopo la stampa come brano sciolto nel 1840, fu ripresa sì in raccolta ma soltanto nel 1843, nel primo *Supplimento a Passatempi musicali*, così come risulta anche dal catalogo Girard del 1847. La data del 1840, peraltro chiaramente indicata su una versione 'per piano solo', è confermata ulteriormente da un avviso comparso sul *Giornale del Regno delle Due Sicilie* nell'Agosto del 1840, in cui si annuncia la pubblicazione della «nuova canzone popolare in dialetto napoletano 'Io te voglio bene assaje'» in diverse versioni: per voce di basso, con accompagnamento di chitarra e così via[49]. Ci sembra improbabile, anche se in teoria non impossibile, che la canzone fosse circolata con enorme successo per cinque anni, cioè dal 1835 al 1840, su fogli volanti prima di essere stampata da Girard come 'nuova canzone' e poi, cosa crediamo non casuale, le fonti in cui si parla della canzone che abbiamo al momento ritrovato sono tutte successive al 1839.

Inoltre c'è una testimonianza precisa del Regaldi del 1848, quindi assai vicina all'epoca dei fatti, il quale racconta che «apparve nel 1839 una canzoncella musicata con facile e grata melodia — 'Io te voglio bene assai' — della quale dice nelle sue istorie l'illustre C. Cantù ignorarsi l'autore; ma volgarmente si sa in Napoli esserne stato estemporaneo creatore Raffaele Sacco Napolitano, lodato improvvisatore nel suo patrio dialetto»[50]. Guglielmo Cottrau nel 1840 pubblica il brano anonimo, quindi non è affatto vero che se ne attribuisce la paternità così come sostenuto tra gli altri anche da De Simone[51].

---

[47]. Sorce Keller, Marcello. "Io te voglio bene assaje', celebre canzone napoletana attribuita a Donizetti', in: *Nuova Rivista Musicale Italiana*, iv (1985), pp. 642-653.

[48]. *Ibidem*, p. 652.

[49]. Ecco la parte del testo delle 'Ultime novità pubblicate da Girard e Comp., strada Toledo n. 111' dedicata alla canzone: «La nuova canzone popolare in dialetto napoletano *Io te voglio bene assaje* col canto in chiave di violino per voce di mezzo-soprano e baritono gr. 15. La stessa calata di tono col canto in chiave di basso gr. 15. La stessa con accompagnamento di chitarra gr. 15. La stessa per pianoforte solo, ma con le parole, onde potersi a volontà cantare o suonare gr. 15». *Giornale del Regno delle Due Sicilie*, n. 172 (8 Agosto 1840).

[50]. Regaldi, Giuseppe. 'I canti popolari di Napoli 1847', in: *Poliorama Pittoresco*, xii/2(1848), p. 338.

[51]. De Simone, Roberto. *Disordinata storia della canzone napoletana*, Napoli, Valentino Editore, 1994, p. 44.

ILL. 3: la partitura della prima versione per canto e piano di 'Io te voglio bene assaje. Nuova canzone napoletana' pubblicata anonima da Girard e Co. (n. 4825) nel 1840.

Ecco una breve analisi di questa prima versione. Il testo è composto da quattro ottave, ciascuna divisa in due quartine formate da quattro settenari con quello finale tronco, con rime abbc/deec[52] e con la ripetizione di ec che forma il cosiddetto *'ntercalare*[53] che oggi chiameremmo ritornello, ma non è proprio la stessa cosa poiché il brano ha una struttura essenzialmente strofica (AA'A'') e non quella canonica strofa/ritornello (cioè ABA'B ecc.). La musica è costituita da un Moderato in 6/8 con una struttura

---

[52]. Fa eccezione la seconda ottava con rime abcb/aded e ripetizione di ed corrispondente allo *'ntercalare*.

[53]. Lo *'ntercalare* che nelle prime tre strofe è il famoso 'Io te voglio bene assaje / ma tu non pienz'a me', in conclusione della quarta strofa diventa 'N'auto maie non asciarraje / 'nnammorato comm'a me'. Per comprendere cosa si intende per 'intercalare' riportiamo un passo da un volume settecentesco: «Versi intercalari si dicono i versi, che si vanno di tratto in tratto ripetendo ne' componimenti [...] L'intercalare si può mettere in principio della composizione [...] ma per lo più si costuma di accomodarlo [...] quasi conseguenza didotta, nel fine di certo periodo di versi sofficiente a conchiudere [...] l'ultima volta, che dovrebb'essere replicato, alcuni Latini, e Volgari si hanno preso la libertà di ripeterlo alquanto diversamente dall'altre volte, facendo che servisse, come di chiusa al canto di quella persona che s'introduceva a cantare». QUADRIO, Francesco Saverio. *Della storia e della ragione d'ogni poesia*, 4 voll., Bologna, per Ferdinando Pisarri all'insegna di S. Antonio, 1739, vol. I, pp. 224-228.

melodica di tipo abac/dd'ef con ripetizione di ef' (corrispondenti allo 'ntercalare del testo) per complessive 20 battute (due per ciascuna frase melodica), un *ambitus* che non supera l'ottava, un profilo melodico tendenzialmente ad arco, scala maggiore con presenza del secondo e quarto grado aumentato, linea melodica essenzialmente sillabica che procede per gradi congiunti con pochi salti di terza e quarta; l'accompagnamento armonico è essenziale, fatto di semplici arpeggi sugli accordi, con una temporanea modulazione in Sol minore (relativa di Si bemolle maggiore) corrispondente alle frasi melodiche dd' che preparano lo 'ntercalare. Le ultime quattro battute (in totale quindi 24) sono rappresentate da una coda strumentale pianistica (con un breve accenno alla melodia de lo 'ntercalare seguito da una scala discendente di quasi due ottave), la quale probabilmente veniva utilizzata anche come introduzione oltre che come interludio tra una strofa e l'altra.

(2)

Te voglio bene assaje. Canzone napoletana, Clausetti n. 43, 1848 ca.
Anonima, in Si bemolle maggiore, testo di sette strofe

Questa seconda versione a stampa del brano (si veda ILL. 4) risale probabilmente al 1848[54] e fu poi ripresa qualche anno dopo nella *3ª Raccolta di canzoncine napoletane* pubblicata dall'editore Clausetti, così come risulta dai cataloghi del 1852[55] e del 1860[56]. Anche questa è anonima, come la precedente di Girard, ma il testo è qui composto non più da quattro bensì da sette strofe, soltanto in parte simili alla versione del 1840, ma che mantengono però inalterata la struttura metrica e delle rime. Dal punto di vista musicale, la tonalità è sempre Si bemolle maggiore ma la linea melodica differisce in alcuni punti: mancano ad esempio i *fa* della quarta e sesta battuta e, cosa ben più evidente, nella undicesima battuta sulla frase 'lo juorno che t'amaje', mentre nella versione Girard trovavamo sul battere due terzine di crome sulle note *mi-re-do-do-si-la* qui troviamo una figurazione croma/semiminima/croma/ semiminima/croma, che inizia sul levare della battuta precedente, sulle note *re-mi-re-mi-re*, ripetendo esattamente la frase già presentata nella nona battuta. L'accompagnamento armonico è anche qui semplice e abbastanza simile a quello della prima versione, cambia invece la parte strumentale finale che occupa sempre quattro battute ma riprende qui interamente la melodia della ripetizione dello 'ntercalare (ef'), suonata per ottave dal piano.

54. Per la datazione delle edizioni Clausetti si veda: CAFIERO, Rosa. 'Le edizioni musicali Clausetti: 1847-1864', in: *Fonti musicali italiane*, v (2000), pp. 97-248; ID. 'Clausetti', in: *Dizionario degli editori musicali italiani 1750-1930, op. cit.* (si veda nota 29), pp. 129-132.

55. *Catalogo della musica pubblicata dagli editori Clausetti e C. in Napoli*, Napoli, 1852, p. 8.

56. *Catalogo delle opere pubblicate dallo Stabilimento Musicale dei fratelli Pietro e Lorenzo Clausetti in Napoli. Con magazzino per la vendita dirimpetto al Real Teatro S. Carlo n. 18*, Napoli, 1860, p. 13.

ILL. 4: la partitura della 'Canzone napoletana 'Te voglio bene assaje' pubblicata dall'editore Clausetti (n. 43) verso il 1848 e ripresa poi nella 3ᵃ *Raccolta di canzoncine napoletane*.

(3)

Io te voglio bene assaje. Nuova canzone napoletana, Girard e Co. n. 8062_54, 1848 ca.
Attribuita a G. Cottrau, in Si bemolle maggiore, testo di quattro strofe

Questa terza versione è stata da molti datata 1865 perché facente parte della ristampa di una raccolta dal titolo *Passatempi musicali - Raccolta completa delle canzoni napoletane composte da Guglielmo Cottrau* registrata, in seguito ad una legge, proprio nel 1865[57]. In realtà, considerando il numero di edizione della raccolta che è il n. 8062 ('Io te voglio bene assaje' è il brano n. 8062_54), essa risale a nostro avviso al 1848 circa o comunque a subito dopo la morte di Guglielmo avvenuta nell'ottobre del 1847[58]. Questa versione, che riprende integralmente quella pubblicata nel 1840 (con la sola aggiunta della traduzione,

---

[57].   La legge del 25 Giugno 1865 consentiva il deposito nell'archivio dell'allora Ministero di agricoltura, industria e commercio «per la riserva dei diritti d'autore», come si evince dal timbro apposto sulla copia della raccolta da noi vista alla biblioteca del Conservatorio di Santa Cecilia a Roma, ove tra l'altro si legge che la stessa fu «registrata nel Settembre del 1865».

[58].   La conferma di tale datazione è ricavabile anche dal sottotitolo della raccolta che recita «Collezione periodica delle 110 canzoni pubblicata dal 1827 al 1847». Era probabilmente una raccolta delle *canzoncine* pubblicate in vita da Cottrau, per rendergli omaggio dopo la sua scomparsa.

o meglio interpretazione, in italiano), è importante perché per la prima volta il brano viene attribuito a Guglielmo Cottrau[59]. Però, come abbiamo già dimostrato in altra sede per 'Fenesta che lucivi'[60], ciò avviene soltanto dopo la morte di Guglielmo, per volere del figlio Teodoro che in quegli anni inizia a prendere le redini delle edizioni Girard e per ragioni probabilmente legate a interessi economico-editoriali. Quindi, giova ribadirlo ancora una volta, Guglielmo Cottrau non si è mai attribuito alcuna delle cento e passa canzoni napoletane pubblicate dal 1824 al 1847, pur essendone, non solo il trascrittore e l'arrangiatore, ma, in alcuni casi, anche l'autore, così come specificato in una lettera alla sorella Lina[61].

(4)
Te voglio bene assaie. Canzone popolare napoletana, Stab. Mus. Partenopeo n. 11228, 1853 ca.
Anonima, in La bemolle maggiore, testo di quattro strofe

Questa quarta versione, databile tra la fine del 1853 e l'inizio dell'anno successivo, era contenuta in *Le Napolitane*, una scelta di 24 canzoni popolari napoletane già pubblicate in precedenza da Guglielmo Cottrau ma presentate in questa raccolta (che fu ristampata qualche tempo dopo da Ricordi) con l'accompagnamento pianistico di Francesco Florimo e l''interpretazione italiana' di Achille De Lauzières. La versione Florimo riprende sostanzialmente lo stesso testo e la stessa melodia della prima stampa del 1840, limitandosi soltanto a cambiare la tonalità (trasportata da Si bemolle maggiore a La bemolle maggiore), a fornire un accompagnamento pianistico un po' più elaborato rispetto a quello di Cottrau e a spostare all'inizio la parte di solo piano, che diventa quindi un'introduzione a tutti gli effetti[62]. Questa versione del brano, anche grazie ad alcune ristampe recenti della Ricordi che la riprendono[63], è tra le più diffuse in commercio, seconda forse solo alla versione De Meglio di cui parleremo fra poco.

---

[59]. Presso la biblioteca del Conservatorio di San Pietro a Majella di Napoli abbiamo ritrovato anche una versione per solo piano di 'Io te voglio bene assaje' pubblicata da Girard col n. 8074, quindi di poco successiva alla versione per canto e piano col n. 8062 di cui stiamo parlando, e anch'essa attribuita a Guglielmo Cottrau.

[60]. Di Mauro, Raffaele. 'Il caso 'Fenesta che lucive': enigma 'quasi' risolto', in: *Studi sulla canzone napoletana classica*, a cura di Enrico Careri e Pasquale Scialò, Lucca, LIM, 2008, pp. 195-240

[61]. Nella lettera alla sorella del 6 Maggio 1833 Guglielmo dice «Io sono non soltanto l'arrangiatore, l'unico trascrittore delle canzoni nazionali di Napoli, ma l'autore, come tu sai, di quelle che modestia a parte, sono più in voga, cioè 'Fenesta vascia', 'La festa di Piedigrotta', 'Aizaie l'uocchie 'ncielo' e venti altre...». *Lettres d'un mélomane pour servir de document à l'histoire musicale de Naples de 1829 à 1847, avec préface de F. Verdinois*, Napoli, Morano, 1885, p. 19.

[62]. Ci sono delle piccole modifiche ortografiche, la più evidente è la seguente: 'ma tu non pienz'a me' diventa 'e tu non piense a me'. In questa versione, a differenza di quella del 1840, lo 'ntercalare rimane sempre lo stesso anche nella quarta strofa.

[63]. Si veda Donizetti, Gaetano. *Le canzoni napoletane per canto e pianoforte*, a cura di Riccardo Allorto, Milano, Casa Ricordi, 1999, pp. 28-32. Allorto pone qui il brano alla fine del volumetto parlando di una falsa

(5)

Te voglio bene assai. Canzone napoletana, Stabilimento Musicale T. Cottrau n. 16286, 1872
ca. Attribuita a R. Sacco - G. Cottrau, in Sol maggiore, testo di quattro strofe.

Questa versione che crediamo apparsa pochi anni dopo il 1870, visto il numero di
edizione 16286, fa parte della raccolta *Eco del Vesuvio, Scelta di celebri canzoni napoletane*,
curata da Teodoro Cottrau[64], il quale riprende integralmente il testo e la musica della
versione Girard 1840 trasportandola stavolta nella tonalità di Sol maggiore[65]. La novità di
questa edizione è che, non solo la musica del brano viene attribuita di nuovo dal figlio
a Guglielmo, ma per la prima volta il testo viene ascritto, con la dicitura 'parole di', a
Raffaele Sacco, forse per accogliere quella che era una consapevolezza diffusa a livello
popolare, cioè che la primogenitura del testo spettasse all'ottico improvvisatore.

(6)

Te voglio bene assaje, R. Stabilimento Ricordi, n. 44980, 1877 ca.
Anonima, in Si bemolle maggiore, testo di sette strofe

È questa l'ultima versione importante del brano e fu pubblicata nel primo volume,
databile intorno al 1877[66], della raccolta *Eco di Napoli* curata da Vincenzo De Meglio[67],
ancora oggi assai diffusa sia nell'edizione ufficiale della Ricordi in tre volumi (ciascuno
contenente 50 brani) sia in una ristampa napoletana dell'editore Luca Torre, acquistabile
su tutte le bancarelle della città partenopea, che la riporta quasi integralmente. La versione
De Meglio riprende (anche nel titolo) sostanzialmente quella pubblicata da Clausetti nel
1848: il testo di sette strofe e la melodia (che, ricordiamo, aveva delle piccole differenze
rispetto alla versione Girard 1840, in particolare per quanto riguarda la battuta 11) sono
praticamente gli stessi. Anche la tonalità è la stessa, cambia esclusivamente il disegno
dell'accompagnamento del pianoforte e la coda strumentale che funge da interludio
tra una strofa e l'altra. Stranamente è proprio questa versione, e non la prima del 1840
pubblicata da Cottrau, a essere la più popolare e la più usata come riferimento per le varie

---

attribuzione a Donizetti. Oppure: *Canti napoletani d'autore dell'ottocento per voce e pianoforte (1835-1898)*, a cura
di Riccardo Allorto e Francesca Seller, Milano, Ricordi, 2003, pp. 24-26.

[64]. Si tratta di una raccolta di 100 brani divisi in 16 album, ciascuno dedicato a una località napoletana o
campana ('Te voglio bene assai' è nell'album *Capodimonte*). Dal catalogo delle edizioni di T. Cottrau si apprende
che si trattava di una «collezione fatta pe' forestieri colla versione italiana in quasi tutte le canzoni». *Edizioni Musicali
T. Cottrau*, Napoli, Stabilimento T. Cottrau, s.d. [1872 ca.], p. 32.

[65]. Pure in questa versione lo 'ntercalare rimane sempre lo stesso anche nella quarta strofa.

[66]. ANTOLINI, Bianca Maria. 'Ricordi', in: *Dizionario* [...], *op. cit.* (si veda nota 29), pp. 286-313.

[67]. Il titolo completo è *Eco di Napoli: 100 celebri canzoni popolari napoletane per canto e pianoforte / raccolte dal
maestro Vincenzo De Meglio*.

interpretazioni del brano date, ad esempio, da celebri cantanti come Roberto Murolo o Luciano Pavarotti[68].

Le versioni di 'Io te voglio bene assaje' su fogli volanti

Tutti gli studiosi che si sono occupati del brano riconoscono la paternità di Raffaele Sacco quantomeno dell'idea letteraria della canzone mentre quasi tutte le testimonianze dell'epoca dicono con grande evidenza che Sacco aveva improvvisato e non composto[69] il brano. La fama di improvvisatore del Sacco è confermata anche da un altro brano, 'La Morena, Aria 'mprovvisata da lo cavaliere D. Rafaele Sacco'[70], che, come si dice sul foglio volante stampato da De Marco che ne riporta il testo oltre che la musica ad opera del maestro Luigi Biscardi, «nel mentre che l'editore chiedeva al Cav. D. Raffaele Sacco una canzone sopra la Morena, egli là per là ce la improvvisò» (si veda Ill. 5).

Ma, tornando a 'Io te voglio bene assaje', il testo che oggi ancora si canta è quello originariamente scritto o, meglio, improvvisato da Sacco? Nutriamo a tal proposito forti dubbi suffragati dall'analisi di diversi fogli volanti con il testo del brano, alcuni anonimi e due firmati dallo stesso Sacco.

(1)-(2)
Due fogli volanti anonimi.
Testo di sette e quattordici strofe

Max Vajro, tra i pochi studiosi di canzone napoletana a dedicare attenzione alle canzonette napoletane del primo Ottocento, in due diversi lavori trascrive due fogli volanti anonimi di 'Te voglio bene assaje' (entrambi custoditi dalla biblioteca Lucchesi

---

[68]. Ciascun interprete non canta però mai tutte le sette strofe scegliendone solo tre o al massimo quattro: le più 'gettonate' sono la seconda, la terza, la quarta e la settima.

[69]. C'è un'unica fonte coeva in cui Sacco viene indicato come 'compositore' e non 'improvvisatore' del brano. Vi riportiamo il passo: «nel popolo ha preso grandissima voga una canzone, composta da Raffaele Sacco: è tenera e passionata. Intitolasi 'il Rimprovero'. Fra le altre quartine, queste sono le più belle, passionate e caratteristiche. 'Recordate lo juorno, che stive a me vicino…'» ecc. Mastriani, Raffaele. *Dizionario geografico-storico-civile del Regno delle Due Sicilie*, Napoli, Tipografia all'insegna del Diogene, 1839-1843, Tomo separato per la capitale Libro I, pp. 162-163.

[70]. Il testo di questo brano è costituito da tre strofe composte ciascuna da tre quartine di quinari, di cui le prime due con le classiche rime abbc/deec e l'ultima, che forma in questo caso l'intercalare o ritornello che dir si voglia, con rime fcgc e con il secondo e il quarto quinario tronchi. Per quanto riguarda la musica, firmata da Biscardi, è difficile capire se sia stata composta prima o dopo che il Sacco abbia improvvisato il testo, ovvero se abbia fornito lo spunto melodico per l'improvvisazione oppure sia una trascrizione di quanto cantato dall'ottico improvvisatore.

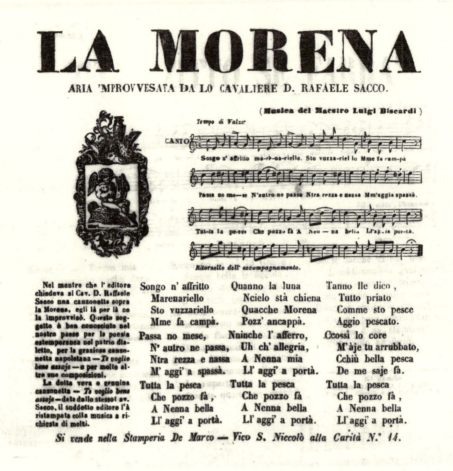

ILL. 5: il foglio volante con *La Morena* di Raffaele Sacco stampato da De Marco. Si ringrazia Maria Luisa Stazio per averci fornito una riproduzione del foglio.

Palli di Napoli[71]), uno di sette strofe[72] e l'altro di quattordici[73]. Non è semplice stabilire la datazione dei due fogli che non solo sono anonimi ma non recano neanche l'indicazione della stamperia che li ha pubblicati. A nostro avviso, ma siamo nel campo delle pure supposizioni non suffragate da alcun riscontro, è probabile che quello di quattordici strofe sia precedente a quello di sette che ne riprende integralmente la metà delle strofe (precisamente la prima, seconda, terza, quinta, settima, ottava, quattordicesima) che sono poi esattamente quelle pubblicate nella versione per canto e piano da Clausetti nel 1848 e,

---

71. Non siamo riusciti al momento a vedere le copie originali dei *fogli volanti* trascritti da Vajro. In assenza di un riscontro diretto, ci fidiamo dunque della sua, crediamo, fedele trascrizione.

72. VAJRO, Massimiliano. *La canzone napoletana dall'origini all'Ottocento*, Napoli, Vajro, 1957, pp. 150-151.

73. ID. *Canzonette napoletane del primo Ottocento*, Napoli, Pironti, 1954, pp. 9-12.

trent'anni dopo, nella versione De Meglio per la Ricordi. Il testo dell'edizione per canto e piano pubblicata da Girard nel 1840 è invece solo in parte simile a quello riportato dal foglio volante di quattordici strofe. Vengono riprese soltanto quattro strofe (nell'ordine la seconda, la settima, la sesta e la quattordicesima) peraltro modificate.

(3)

Foglio volante Tramater. Di Raffaele Sacco, testo di sette strofe

C'è poi un altro foglio volante, trascritto sempre da Max Vajro[74], stavolta firmato da Raffaele Sacco, in cui questi pubblica la sua versione 'autentica' del brano dopo che, come spiega in un'annotazione che lo accompagna, aveva acquistato dalla strada un foglio volante (probabilmente uno dei due anonimi trascritti da Vajro) con «no intercalare mio 'mpruvvesato a la casa de no forestiero ricco, dotto e putente, che me l'hanno stroppiato cchiù de no ciuccio dinto a la carriola» ('un mio intercalare improvvisato nella casa di un forestiero ricco, storpiato più di un asino nella carriola'). Sacco corre quindi da uno stampatore per pubblicare la sua versione, con «lo vero intercalare comme fuje sfurnato llà pel là» ('il vero intercalare come fu sfornato lì per lì'[75]). Il testo è qui formato da sette strofe che, manco a dirlo, sono assai diverse da quelle che noi oggi conosciamo e cantiamo, sia dalla versione Girard che da quella Clausetti e poi Ricordi.

(4)

Foglio volante De Marco. Parole del Cav. R. Sacco, musica del M. Battista

L'ultimo foglio volante del quale ci occupiamo è quello che fu messo in commercio dalla stamperia De Marco, una delle più raffinate dell'epoca rispetto, ad esempio, alla più 'rozza' stamperia Azzolino (si veda Ill. 6). Esso è stato già riprodotto nel 1964 in una pubblicazione della Fabbri editori[76], ed è stato poi ripreso e analizzato per la prima volta da Sorce Keller[77]. Tale foglio riporta, con l'indicazione 'parole del Cav. R. Sacco', il testo che è stavolta di dieci strofe e soltanto in parte simili al foglio di Tramater[78]. Questa è l'unica versione su foglio volante su cui appare anche la melodia del brano con l'attribuzione 'musica del M. Battista'. Sorce Keller non è riuscito a identificare chi fosse 'l'ignoto M. Battista'; noi pensiamo possa trattarsi quasi con certezza di Vincenzo Battista autore anche

---

[74]. Id. *La canzone napoletana* […], *op. cit.* (si veda nota 72), pp. 152-154.

[75]. Da sottolineare come in questo caso Sacco intenda per 'intercalare' non una parte ma l'intero brano.

[76]. *Storia della musica: Folklore e musica leggera*, 13 voll., a cura di Dino Fabbri e Ettore Proserpio, Milano, F.lli Fabbri editori, 1964, vol. XI, p. 128.

[77]. Sorce Keller, Marcello. *Op. cit.* (si veda nota 47), p. 652.

[78]. Unicamente le strofe prima, quinta, settima e decima di De Marco riprendono con variazioni la prima, sesta, quarta e settima di Tramater, le altre sono totalmente nuove.

di altre canzoni napoletane stampate tra gli altri da Clausetti, e che l'indicazione 'musica del M. Battista' sia da intendersi quindi semplicemente 'musica del Maestro Battista'[79]. Non è un caso che la melodia riportata da questo foglio volante è la stessa di quella della versione per canto e piano pubblicata proprio da Clausetti, editore per cui Battista lavorava e che probabilmente chiese al maestro di arrangiare per loro una versione del brano che a quei tempi, siamo alla fine degli anni Quaranta, era già molto famoso e lo diverrà sempre più non soltanto a Napoli e in Italia[80].

ILL. 6: il foglio volante con la 'Vera Canzona Te voglio bene assaie', pubblicato dalla Stamperia De Marco.

---

79. Una breve nota biografica di Vincenzo Battista (Napoli 5 Ottobre 1823 - 14 Novembre 1873) è in DE MURA, Ettore. *Op. cit.* (si veda nota 29), vol. I, p. 197.

80. La celebrità a Napoli del brano è confermata anche dalla citazione in un racconto, dal titolo 'Pascalotto', di Gaetano Somma pubblicato nel 1847: LOMBARDI, Mariano. *Napoli in miniatura ovvero Il popolo di Napoli e i suoi costumi*, ristampa dell'unica e rara edizione del 1847, Napoli, Arturo Berisio editore, 1965, p. 383. Ma abbiamo numerose testimonianze anche sulla sua diffusione all'estero: il brano viene pubblicato a Londra, in una versione «ridotta per pianoforte solo, colle parole in dialetto napoletano», edita da R. Clay che appare in WHITESIDE, James. *Italy in the Nineteenth Century, Contrasted with Its Past Condition*, 3 voll., Londra, Richard Bentley, 1848, vol. III, pp. 443-444. Si ha poi notizia che già precedentemente, nella stessa città inglese, il brano venisse eseguito in concerti all'Hanover Square Rooms, si veda *The Literary Gazette. Journal of the belles lettres, sciences, & C.*, No. 1430 (Saturday, June 15, 1844) e in Francia era abbastanza famoso da essere parodiato nel 1843 da un certo D. Tagliafico per la sua 'Nina La Marinière'. Si vedano LAMBOSSY-DE FUYENS, M. *Souvenirs d'Italie*, Friburgo, Marchand, 1857, p. 5, e *Chansons nationales et populaires de France accompagnées de notes historiques et littéraires*, a cura di Dumersan e Noël Ségur, Parigi, Garnier Frères, 1866, pp. 173-174.

Corollario

In una pubblicazione recente è riportata la trascrizione di una *copiella* dal titolo 'Canzone napoletana', anche questa custodita presso la Lucchesi Palli, con tredici strofe in versione 'maschile' che sono praticamente le stesse del foglio trascritto da Vajro (quello in quattordici strofe) stranamente però con una strofa in meno (quella che inizia con 'Saccio ca nun vuò scennere | La grada quann'è scuro'). Ma la vera novità è che sempre su questa *copiella* troviamo anche cinque strofe di una interessante versione 'femminile' del brano, con la prima ottava che inizia così: "Nzomma so' io la fauza | Pecché ca so majesta"[81].

In una fonte francese dell'epoca si parla poi di una versione del brano cantata per strada dai 'lazzaroni' composta addirittura da 23 strofe e di un'altra cantata da donne. L'autore traduce alcune strofe («quelques couplets de cette interminabile chanson») in francese, dove il celebre *intercalare* napoletano diventa 'Pour vous mon amour est extrême | Et vous ne pensez plus à moi!', oltre a riportarne quattro strofe in napoletano. L'ultima di queste è tratta da una versione femminile ed è quasi identica alla prima delle cinque strofe 'femminili' della *copiella* conservata alla Lucchesi Palli di cui sopra; anche due delle strofe tradotte in francese sembrano l'adattamento dal dialetto napoletano della prima e della quinta strofa della versione femminile[82].

Conclusioni

A nostro avviso il brano nasce, così come sostenuto dallo stesso Sacco nella postilla al foglio volante Tramater sopra citato, come brano improvvisato in una casa di un ricco straniero (forse lo stesso Cottrau?) durante una di quelle riunioni salottiere assai frequenti che prenderanno poi il nome di 'periodiche'. Raffaele Sacco, ottico di mestiere, apparteneva a quella categoria di poeti improvvisatori di area urbana appartenenti a ceti abbastanza elevati, come l'avvocato Bindocci citato da Mayer[83]. Il testo in tutte le pur diverse versioni da noi analizzate (quelle su fogli volanti e quelle per canto e piano) ha sempre la stessa struttura, identica a quella della 'canzone d'improvvisatore' 'Ahi che l'affetto mio', e cioè ottave divise in due quartine di settenari (di cui l'ultimo tronco)

---

[81]. Porpora Anastasio, Antonio. *Te voglio bene assaje. Musica, parole, storie*, Campobasso, Libreria antiquaria Editrice Filopoli, 2009, pp. 55-58.

[82]. Maricourt, Le Comte L. de. *Mes heures de paresse à Naples*, Parigi, Goujon et Milon, 1842, pp. 249-253.

[83]. Per maggiori notizie sulla vita di Raffaele Sacco si rimanda alle pagine del Martorana dove tra le altre cose si dice «se si potessero raccogliere tutte le sue poesie improvvisate, se ne farebbe un grosso volume. Il Sacco ha in mente farne una raccolta e darla alla stampa». Al momento, però, non abbiamo alcuna notizia su un'eventuale raccolta a stampa delle poesie del Sacco. Martorana, Pietro. *Op. cit.* (si veda nota 32), pp. 362-364.

con rime abbc/deec. Questo schema metrico e di rime, tipico della canzonetta arcadica e metastasiana, era presumibilmente uno dei più usati all'epoca (insieme all'ottava rima) come modello per le improvvisazioni di canto estemporaneo accompagnato da strumenti. Il brano fu probabilmente improvvisato a partire da una 'melodia semplicissima' la cui struttura è simile a quella delle due 'canzoni d'improvvisatori' dei *Passatempi* da noi analizzate ma con la novità dell'intercalare. Tale melodia accennata al pianoforte o dal maestro Campanella (indicato da De Rubertis e che De Mura ha ipotizzato essere un tal Filippo Campanella, compositore minore dell'epoca) o da Battista o da Cottrau o da Cammarano[84] o da un qualsivoglia pianista poco importa, perché, in quel momento, il musicista aveva fornito a Sacco solo lo spunto melodico, forse improvvisando su motivi operistici dell'epoca di Donizetti o di Bellini[85]. Anche in questo caso è difficile capire se il pianista aveva accennato l'intera melodia, solo quella del punto rilevante (in questo caso lo 'ntercalare[86]) o aveva semplicemente accompagnato con un sottofondo armonico l'improvvisazione. Resta poi da capire, così come abbiamo già detto per le due canzoni d'improvvisatore dei *Passatempi*, quanto di suo ci abbia messo Cottrau, o chi per lui, nella trascrizione su pentagramma del brano. Il risultato di queste considerazioni è che in ogni caso 'Io te voglio bene assaje' può essere difficilmente indicata, come spesso

---

[84]. In una pubblicazione di quegli anni dello scrittore francese Paul de Musset (fratello del più noto Alfred) vengono riportate due voci secondo le quali la canzone sarebbe opera o di Luigi Cammarano, compositore e fratello del celebre librettista Salvatore, o, in alternativa, di un galeotto di Castellammare. Ecco il passo originale: «Dans ce moment l'Italie entière répète une chansonette dont l'auteur n'est pas précisément connu. Les uns l'attribuent à M. Cammerano, frère de l'ecrivain de libretti; d'autres m'ont assuré qu'elle était d'un galérien de Castellamare. Les paroles sont en dialecte napolitain, moitié comiques, moitié sentimentales. Le refrain dit: 'Te voglio ben' assaie, e tu non pienzi a me!' — Je t'aime passionnément, et tu ne penses pas à moi'. L'air, quoique simple, suit dans ses petites proportions la marche d'une cavatine. En un instant, tout le monde l'apprit». MUSSET, Paul de. *Course en voiturin (Italie et Sicilie)*, Parigi, Victor Magen, 1845, pp. 158-159.

[85]. È da leggere proprio in tal senso l'attribuzione di questa canzone spesso a Donizetti ma anche a Bellini. Michele Scherillo ha infatti ravvisato una certa somiglianza tra l'incipit melodico di 'Te voglie bene assaie' e quello dell'aria 'Vi ravviso o luoghi ameni' della *Sonnambula* di Bellini che il pianista del salotto, dove Sacco «improvvisò» la canzone, probabilmente conosceva molto bene. SCHERILLO, Michele. 'Bellini e la musica popolare', in: *Giambattista Basile*, III/4 (1885). Il raffronto tra le due melodie è riportato in VAJRO, Massimiliano. *La canzone napoletana* [...], *op. cit.* (si veda nota 72), p. 165.

[86]. Per avere un'idea del ruolo che poteva giocare l'intercalare in un'esecuzione improvvisata riportiamo un significativo episodio narrato nelle sue memorie da Angelo Brofferio, il quale ebbe modo di assistere a un«accademia di poesia estemporanea» tenuta al Teatro Apollo di Roma da Rosa Taddei, altra celebre improvvisatrice dell'epoca. Ad un certo punto la Taddei, dopo aver avuto un tema dal pubblico sul quale improvvisare, promise di trattarlo «in versi settenari con intercalare obbligato» e chiese al pubblico stesso di «favorirle» un'intercalare ma riuscì a ottenere soltanto una rima e poi una strofa ('Far l'amore io vorrei sempre / Con te sola, o bella Rosa / È la gloria una gran cosa / Ma il salame è meglio ancor'). A ciò lei, senza scomporsi, disse: "Questa è una strofa non un intercalare; tuttavia riterrò i due ultimi versi e me ne servirò di ritornello". Ciò detto, con voce abbastanza bella, abbastanza intuonata cominciò a cantare con facile vena». BROFFERIO, Angelo. *I miei tempi. Memorie*, 20 voll., Torino, Tipografia nazionale di G. Biancardi, 1861, vol. XX, pp. 250-262.

è accaduto, quale prima canzone napoletana 'd'autore' dell'Ottocento. Innanzitutto perché, pur nascendo in ambienti colti, è figlia di modalità tipiche di questa fase della canzone napoletana a metà strada tra l'"oralità" e la 'scrittura', e poi perché prima di essa ci sono altre canzoni napoletane, della Malibran, di Florimo, di Donizetti stesso, ecc., di cui invece la paternità è certa e che devono essere quindi indicate, queste sì, come prime canzoni napoletane d'autore dell'Ottocento. Proponiamo quindi che per le interpretazioni future il brano sia indicato in questo modo: 'Io te voglio bene assaje', canzone improvvisata da Raffaele Sacco nella versione di… Guglielmo Cottrau, Francesco Florimo, Vincenzo Battista, Teodoro Cottrau, o Vincenzo De Meglio, a seconda dell'edizione presa come riferimento.

Bisognerebbe in conclusione indagare ancora più a fondo sul peso, fino a questo momento mai considerato, avuto dal canto estemporaneo accompagnato da strumenti musicali (piano, chitarra ecc.)[87], sulla nascita e lo sviluppo della canzone napoletana, perché è assai probabile che 'Io te voglio bene assaje' non rappresenti l'unico caso. Il percorso di questo brano è l'esempio chiaro dello scambio bidirezionale allora assai frequente tra mondo colto e mondo popolare urbano[88]: nasce improvvisato in un salotto borghese, da qui si diffonde per le strade per via orale e stampato attraverso fogli volanti, da uno di questi, quasi sicuramente spurio, o da un'esecuzione salottiera, viene trascritto e rielaborato dal Cottrau e ridestinato agli stessi salotti in cui era nato, chiudendo così il cerchio. La cosa indubbia è che 'Io te voglio bene assaje' fu la prima canzone napoletana ad avere un successo incredibile — Regaldi parla di 180.000 *copielle* vendute — grazie soprattutto al suo orecchiabile *'ntercalare*, o ritornello che dir si voglia, paragonabile soltanto ai 'tormentoni' della musica odierna. La fortuna commerciale del brano (testimoniata anche dalle innumerevoli *risposte*[89]) fu una specie di detonatore che provocò l'esplosione parallela sia dei fogli volanti

---

[87]. Abbiamo, nel corso di questa nostra relazione, più volte usato il termine 'improvvisazione' o 'improvvisatore', limitandoci a riportare fedelmente le indicazioni delle fonti dirette da noi consultate e analizzate (come ad esempio le canzoni d'improvvisatori contenute nei *Passatempi*) ma forse per questo tipo di repertorio, volendo accogliere la distinzione suggerita da Vincenzo Caporaletti tra 'estemporizzazione' e 'improvvisazione', sarebbe forse più corretto parlare appunto di 'estemporizzazione' più che di 'improvvisazione' vera e propria. CAPORALETTI, Vincenzo. *I processi improvvisativi nella musica. Un approccio globale*, Lucca, LIM, 2005, pp. 98-170. Si veda anche il saggio di Vincenzo Caporaletti in questo volume.

[88]. Lo scambio era favorito anche da una particolare vicinanza abitativa, tra ceti nobili e classi artigiane e popolari, che si era creata nell'800 a Napoli così come testimoniato dallo storico Giuseppe Galasso: «Nel corso dell'800 […] al piano nobile abitava la famiglia o le famiglie più importanti […] al primo piano e terzo piano abitavano le famiglie della media borghesia […] negli ammezzati e negli appartamenti ricavati fra un piano e l'altro, si incontravano artigiani […] il popolo più povero abitava al piano terreno, negli scantinati […] alla promiscuità sociale corrispondeva […] una frequenza di rapporti quotidiani che influiva profondamente sullo spirito delle relazioni sociali». GALASSO, Giuseppe. *Intervista sulla storia di Napoli*, a cura di Percy Allum, Bari, Laterza, 1978.

[89]. Davvero numerose furono le 'risposte' (o le parodie) di 'Io te voglio bene assaje'. Ben dieci sono elencate in AMALFI, Gaetano. *La canzone napoletana*, Napoli, Priore, 1909, pp. 37-42. Soltanto di tre ci son

che delle raccolte di canzoni per canto e pianoforte, e la comparsa sulla scena di nuovi autori, compositori, stampatori ed editori. Questi ultimi, fiutando l'affare, si lanciarono sul mercato della canzone napoletana, tracciandone forse il percorso che porterà verso fine del secolo all'esplosione del fenomeno e facendo sì, come ha acutamente sottolineato Roberto Leydi, che «la canzone napoletana moderna» rappresentasse «un caso tipico» — forse tra i primi, aggiungiamo noi — «di musica artigiana-urbana che diviene industria»[90], cioè quella che viene comunemente definita 'musica leggera' e che a livello scientifico viene indicata con il termine anglosassone *popular music* o ancora con la denominazione, adottata recentemente anche dai conservatori italiani, di musica audiotattile[91].

---

pervenute le partiture con i testi e le musiche sulle quali si cantavano, poiché sono state raccolte nel primo *Supplimento a Passatempi Musicali*, terminato nel 1843 e curato da Guglielmo Cottrau. La prima è 'La risposta dell'innamorata. Nennì tu sì 'mpazzuto' del 1840 (Girard n. 5029) la cui musica è attribuita al maestro Paolo Fabrizi; la seconda è 'Sfogo di un galantuomo stanco di udire la canzone napoletana Io te voglio bene assaje' (con l'incipit 'Addio mia bella Napoli') pubblicata anonima sempre nel 1840 (Girard n. 5032); la terza e ultima è la 'Risposta a dispetto della donna. 'Nzomma sentì m'attocca' stampata sempre anonima nel 1842 (Girard n. 5532). Sia i testi che le musiche di queste tre risposte sono diversi dal brano 'originario', pur avendo strutture metriche e melodiche simili, e solo in un caso (nello *Sfogo*) viene adoperato il famoso *intercalare*, ripreso integralmente sia nella melodia che nel testo.

90. LEYDI, Roberto. 'Diffusione e volgarizzazione', in: *Storia dell'opera italiana. Vol. VI: Teorie e tecniche immagini e fantasmi*, a cura di Lorenzo Bianconi e Giorgio Pestelli, Torino, EDT, 1988, , p. 323

91. La definizione di 'musica audiotattile' è stata coniata da Vincenzo Caporaletti, sulla scia del pensiero e delle teorie del sociologo canadese Marshall McLuhan, per quei generi musicali (jazz, rock, *popular music* ecc.) in cui il *medium* (in questo caso la *registrazione e riproduzione fonografica* che attiva il canale 'tattile' della membrana uditiva piuttosto che quello 'visivo', come accadeva invece con il *medium* della pagina tipografica della partitura) condizioni fortemente il 'messaggio' o meglio diventi esso stesso il 'messaggio' (secondo il noto motto mcluhaniano 'il medium è il messaggio'). Per ulteriori approfondimenti sull'argomento si rimanda a: CAPORALETTI, Vincenzo. *La definizione dello swing. I fondamenti estetici del jazz e delle musiche audiotattili*, Teramo, Ideasuoni, 2000, oppure ID. *I processi improvvisativi nella musica. [...], op. cit.* (si veda nota 87), pp. 69-86.

Improvvisazione popolare e urbana a Napoli nel primo Ottocento

English Summary

Popular and Urban Improvisation in Naples in the First Half of the Nineteenth Century
From Songs of the Pier to 'Io te voglio bene assaje'

Raffaele Di Mauro

This article begins with a sketch of the context of popular and urban music in early nineteenth-century Naples. At this time there were different kinds of itinerant musicians, especially in a particular zone of the city: the Pier. The phenomenon of the *improvvisatori* in Naples during that period is then analyzed from an ethnomusicological point of view. Taking into account both literary and musical sources, two levels of *improvvisatori* are identified. One level can be considered as 'popular' and corresponds to the socio-cultural level identified by Carpitella as 'rural-pastoral'. It is characterized by repertoires which are still alive today in the music of oral tradition in Campania, in, for example, *fronne* and *canti a figliola*. The second level of *improvvisatori* corresponds to the socio-cultural level defined by Carpitella as 'artisan-urban', with more influences from Western art music. These singers engaged in real challenges organized in salons and theatres, particularly in the famous Teatro dei Fiorentini in Naples. A musical and textual analysis of two songs contained in the *Passatempi musicali* published by Guillaume Cottrau from 1824 to 1829 and defined there as 'canzoni d'improvvisatore' follows. The second half of the article attempts to reconstruct the genesis of the famous song 'Io te voglio bene assaje', through a comparison of the different versions which were published in nineteenth-century anthologies and on several *broadsides*. This song was, albeit mistakenly, considered by many historians of Neapolitan song to be the first 'composed' Neapolitan song, and was often erroneously attributed to Donizetti. The origin of the song, however, is rather an improvised performance by Raffaele Sacco, optician by trade. Sacco was indeed one of the most important representatives of the urban improvisers described above.

«GHOST NOTES»
ISSUES OF INAUDIBLE IMPROVISATIONS

Vincenzo Caporaletti
(Rome)

1. INTRODUCTION

IN THE TAXONOMY ELABORATED BY HEINER SCHULTZ in his study on the history of concepts various structural positions are foreseen which define the relations between concept and object, measured on the axis of diachronic change[1]. Were we to apply such a criterion to the developments of the notion of musical improvisation in the last three centuries, we would obtain a line of dialectic tension between notional change and object transformation, probably biased towards the first option.

One of the theses that I intend to uphold in this study is that the concept of improvisation, according to our contemporary notion of it, defines a semantic field which does not coincide with the corresponding one of the eighteenth and nineteenth centuries (to limit ourselves to this chronological period). Such an observation, apparently intuitive, needs to be thematized because in the literature, even the most recent, there are examples of little awareness of this assumption, for instance with the implicit or explicit use of criteria and representations of jazz improvisation to categorize real-time creative practices of the past centuries[2]. Here come into play, on the methodological

---

[1]. SCHULTZ, Heiner. 'Begriffsgeschichte und Argumentationsgeschichte', in: *Historische Semantik und Begriffsgeschichte*, edited by Reinhart Kosellek, Stuttgart, Klett-Costa, 1978, pp. 43-74.

[2]. See for instance LEVIN, Robert. 'Improvising Mozart', in: *Musical Improvisation. Art, Education and Society*, edited by Bruno Nettl and Gabriel Solis, Urbana, University of Illinois Press, 2009, pp. 143-149. Illustrating Mozart's musical action in the orchestral *tutti*, the author asserts (p. 146): «The situation is not all that different from the swing bands of Duke Ellington or Count Basie, where the presence of the piano in the band need not require a lot of figuration, but merely a well-chosen riff or passage provoking delight». Or, talking about the acquisition of improvisational expertise related to the Classic repertoire, he resorts to the supposed formular jazz style and to his *licks* (p. 148): «A budding jazz musician learns a variety of normative figures, practiced in all keys, which provide a safety net [...] Such figures exist in the music of all styles, and never is the formulaic so evident as in the classical period». But the reference to jazz is generalized and pervasive in this article, as shows the exemplification of the processes that operate in it as an implicit epitome of ex tempore creativity per se assumed in a universalistic sense (*ibidem*, p. 143). Even

level, long debated issues of anthropological and ethnomusicological research, like the relation between the emic/etic categorization of intercultural processes[3]. It is clear that retroactively projecting contemporary knowledge is certainly a methodological error, because it does not take into account the conceptual reference models of the culture which is historically observed. The outlines of the issue do not obviously concern only a nominalistic distinction, as they assign to the current notion of improvisation some distinctive traits that pertain to the morphosyntactic plane and to the conceptualization of the phenomenon in its ideological reverberations. As a consequence a search for some criterion that focuses the conceptual nature of the cultural unit of historically attested 'improvisation'[4] is needed, identifying its semantic traits both in relation to aesthetic speculation and to the concrete praxis of sign production. In this article I will not only conduct an exercise limited to a *Begriffsgeschichte*, but I intend to put forward a formalization of these musical practices during the eighteenth and nineteenth centuries in the light of the theoretical model of audiotactile formativity — being well aware of the intimate universal vocation peculiar to this approach — from a comparative viewpoint as regards the dynamics of oral tradition music and of the audiotactile contemporary ones[5]. In the light of this systematic intention some specific issues could be highlighted, as a prerequisite for further elaborations in historiographical reflection.

How can the contemporary notion of improvisation be circumscribed in the first place? I have listed below at least the main distinctive features, deriving them right from the attested praxes of audiotactile music: primary linguistic value attributed to energized formal components and to suprasegmental elements (whose gestalt outcomes

---

more biased, in this sense, appears Robert S. Hatten's contribution in the same volume (HATTEN, Robert S. 'Opening the Museum Window. Improvisation and Its Inscribed Values in the Canonic Works by Chopin and Schumann', in: *Musical Improvisation.* [...], *op. cit.*, pp. 282-295). Here even the presumed values of improvisation — meant in itself, as an operative universal concept — which he programmatically uses for the analysis of Chopin's and Schumann's works are precisely those indebted with the jazz conception. For a reading of the eighteenth-century *freie Fantasie* in the light of improvisational criteria used in jazz and rock see also SCHLEUNING, Peter. 'Ordentlich chaotisch... Zur freien Klavierfantasie', in: *Musica*, XXXVIII/1 (1984), pp. 14-18.

    3.   We are referring to the etic/emic categorial opposition, introduced by Kenneth Pike (see *Language in Relation to a Unified Theory of the Structure of Human Behavior*, The Hague, Mouton, [1954], ²1967) in order to distinguish between the analysis based on the concreteness of the elements from the one based on their function and pertinence. In the anthropological perspective the etic point of view is, as a rule, referred to the outsider, while the insider uses the emic one.

    4.   For the notion of 'cultural unit', see ECO, Umberto. *Trattato di semiotica generale*, Milan, Bompiani, 1975, p. 98ff.

    5.   For the theoretical model related to audiotactile music, see at least CAPORALETTI, Vincenzo. *La definizione dello swing. I fondamenti estetici del jazz e delle musiche audiotattili*, Teramo, Ideasuoni, 2000; ID. *I processi improvvisativi nella musica. Un approccio globale*, Lucca, LIM, 2005. For a synthetic description of this theoretical model, see *infra*, Section II.

on the perceptional level assume the local denominations of *swing* and *groove*); in-depth motivic-thematic elaboration; centrality of interaction between musicians, with a constant interactive transformation — which also includes contextual instances of relation with the audience — of the material (meant as the cognitive figural model of the harmonic-motivic kind which acts as a catalyst and as a regulator of performing alterities)[6]; little incidence of improvisational modalities based on *ex novo* creations of a non-conventionalized formal model. I will not expand on the stylistic traits, like the presence of a continuous pulse which activates the function of agogic and energetic control and other features.

From an aesthetic slant, for contemporary improvisation, the burden of the search for original solutions to formal problems is instead to be noted: historically, this is a distinctive feature of written composition. This is so because of another fundamental feature on the phenomenological level: the openness of improvisational practices towards a textualizing access, towards an objectification, in the sense of the constitution of an *opus*, allowed and guaranteed by the ontological condition of phonofixation through phonographic recording. The cognitive model, the musical conceptualization unit that serves as a control panel and as an organizational principle of real-time creative praxis, through such phonofixation entrusts to technology, and not to the evanescence of mnemonic mediation, the function of the preservation of its formal features, thus allowing to detach from them more easily, to overcome them dialectically, prearranging the conditions to produce new material and not one that is pre-programmed by the limitation of its own code[7].

As we will see, these are not aspects that concern all of the processes of *ex tempore* creativity of written-tradition Western music from the eighteenth and nineteenth centuries, outlining for them an alternative profile in conceptual representation. Before getting to the heart of the matter, let us briefly review some assumptions of audiotactile formativity theory.

---

[6]. For the notion of 'model' see Lortat-Jacob, Bernard. 'Improvisation. Le modèle et ses réalisations', in: *L'improvisation dans les musiques de tradition orale*, edited by Bernard Lortat-Jacob, Paris, Selaf, 1987, pp. 45-59. See also the more recent Id. 'Forme e condizioni dell'improvvisazione nelle musiche di tradizione orale', in: *Enciclopedia della musica*, directed by Jean-Jacques Nattiez, 5 vols., Turin, Einaudi, 2001-2005, vol. v: *L'unità della musica*, pp. 717-736. For Lortat-Jacob, the model «[…] come il lessico di una lingua, è composto da elementi formali debitamente memorizzati e di numero finito nonché da regole combinatorie organizzate in una grammatica»; Id. 'Forme e condizioni dell'improvvisazione […]', *op. cit.* (see *supra*), p. 719. Obviously Lortat-Jacob does not mean too strict a sense of such a notion, as it would derive from a literal interpretation of this definition. The formalization of the model, indeed, can be constituted through various possibilities, as «[…] mode mélodique ou rythmique […] elle peut également prendre en compte des rapports de tonalité (conduites harmoniques obligées, grille de jazz, etc.) ou des structures mélodiques; ou encore, dans la musique de danse par exemple, ne concerner que de simples formules métrico-rythmiques»; Id. 'Improvisation. […]', *op. cit.* (see *supra*), p. 46.

[7]. See Caporaletti, Vincenzo. *La definizione dello swing* […], *op. cit.* (see note 5), p. 98ff.

II. AUDIOTACTILE FORMATIVITY

One of the main achievements of audiotactile formativity theory is the individuation of a taxonomic model of musical systems and experiences, as a function of the perceptive/cognitive implications of their anthropological determinants and modalities of cultural mediation. This taxonomy provides a systemic ordering essentially polarized on three different anthropological-musical realities, relating to the factors of production/representation of the cultural organization of the sound sphere and of its communication.

In the first place there are the so-called traditional cultures, where the creative/formative medium which controls the musical praxis is the psycho-somatic plexus of the performer. The musical communicational mediation is established on a mnemonic basis on the diachronic level and with evanescent performativity patterns on the synchronic one, without any chance of an objectified textualization.

In the second place there is Western art music, of written tradition — in the chronological articulation after the seventeenth century[8] — where the corporeal creative/formative determinant (as regards the process of conceptual production/representation of sound forms and not of their performance reproduction) is absorbed and filtered by the rational/abstractive structures inherent in the technological medium of notation. This semiographic medium becomes at the same time a formative and communicational intermediary of musical structures, determining their objectified textualization by writing and their operational logic.

Finally, audiotactile music of contemporary electronic culture, together with jazz and the so-called popular and world music (that is, the universe of music created and disseminated in the context of industrial and mass-mediated production). Here the creative/formative determining factor of musical praxis is once more the psycho-somatic plexus of the performer, but with a pre-eminent communicational mediation carried out by the video-phonographic recording (with the possibility of an inscription, in the sound recording, of psycho-corporeal formativity, with the function of poietic energy as a structuring factor of musical form, which in turn is crystallized as an objectified textualization).

One of the key aspects of audiotactile-music theory, which distinguishes it from analogous projects which try to model the musical cultural experience, is the particular idea of the mediological factor[9], in the general picture of the research on sensorial and

---

[8]. With a particular reference to the era when the nomological statute of the score becomes apparent, with the ideal of adherence to the written text (*werktreues Ideal*) from the middle of the nineteenth century up to the modernistic currents.

[9]. Thus meeting with the methodological needs posed by Bruno Nettl still in 2005: «Do oral and aural transmission and oral creation affect the forms of pieces and repertories? No doubt they must, but we have no theory to explain just how». See NETTL, Bruno. *The Study of Ethnomusicology. Thirty-One Issues and Concepts*, Champaign, University of Illinois Press, 2005, p. 296. And with specific reference to the effects

cognitive outcomes induced by the means (media) through which the culture is produced and communicated. In such a theoretical infrastructure the formative and communicational functions of the medium are intended as constituent of the perceptive and cognitive arrangements, in line with the outcomes of contemporary epistemology well depicted in the following assertion by Norwood Russell Hanson[10]: «Observation of x is shaped by prior knowledge of x. Another influence on observations rests in the language or notation used to express what we know, and without which there would be little we could recognize as knowledge»[11]. Relating this perspective — for which a theoretical model or a communicational channel/code is hypostatized predetermining the very synthesis of the negotiated data, in line with its own epistemic working logic — to the area of musical, the psycho-corporeal function, in its not only material identity but, precisely, the one of a medium which influences and guides the perceptive and cognitive outcomes, is identified by the 'audiotactile principle' (ATP); the homologous one carried out by modern musical notation and by its ideational correlative, given by Western music theory (a factor which Hanson, generalizing, calls 'theory ladenness'), we define it as 'visual function'[12].

It must be remembered that this cognitive/perceptive predetermination function is promoted by the medium following the guidelines of its specific 'operative system', of the working logic of its intrinsic internal 'program'. For instance, the visual logic of notation, in the first place, can be considered as a compositional poietics of the generative-combinatorial kind which controls a mechanistic immanent quality of the Western theoretical system

---

of phonographic recording on forms and repertoires: «[…] the field has not developed much by way of a generalised theory» (*ibidem*, p. 292).

[10]. In the horizon of thought to which we refer (for instance Marshall McLuhan's and Derrick De Kerkhove's socio-anthropology) plays a decisive role the specific conception of the formative/communicative 'medium', as conceptual supporting model, and considered not neutral for the purpose of message configuration and reception. As a consequence, prominence is given to the dynamic function which epistemic principles included into the medial structure — inherent in the working logic of the medium through which the cultural construct are produced and communicated — carry out on the structuration of the constructs themselves, besides on the reconfiguration of the perceptive structure and on the conceptual pattern of whoever produces or receives them.

[11]. HANSON, Norwood Russell. *Patterns of Discovery*, Cambridge, Cambridge University Press, 1958, reprinted 1975, p. 19.

[12]. Mediological functions identified by notational visuality and by the audiotactile principle are to be intended, on the anthropological level, as founders of cultural cycles, in the sense of pre-eminence and pervasiveness imposed by their operational logic on the cognitive processes in a given era or cultural context (respectively, for European art music after the seventeenth century and the contemporary repertoires of jazz, rock, popular, world music). It goes without saying that the culture of visuality should also comprise ATP-mediated practices (among which improvisational experiences) just like contemporary audiotactile music benefits from the massive resort to written scores. The issue is just in the 'mediological subsumption' of these allogenic practices under the aegis of the culturally leading function, which gives them a stigma of epistemic minority on the phenomenological level and perverts and hybridizes their internal logics in the functional order.

already pointed out by Adorno as «the rational and mechanical principle that pervades the entire history of Western music»[13]. It can also be represented by the epistemological principles, inherent in the written medium, of linearity, sequentiality, segmentation of the experience, uniform repeatability, inside an abstractive and mathematized order[14]. The coherence of motivic integration and the rules of voice leading in a polyphonic context or inside the structuration of numerical relations of learned harmony are but the more evident epiphenomena of these deep epistemic structures.

In the context of a visual/audiotactile dichotomy the notion of an *audiotactile principle* (ATP) assumes a central role in the determination of the *autographic* character (borrowing a concept from Nelson Goodman, though with a different meaning[15]) of a quite peculiar kind of musical experience. The particular form of inscription of the sound material on technological devices adopted by the musical communication and textualization processes of such a singular experience, in the context of the technological developments of the phonographic recording medium, is likewise traced back in its aesthetic and cognitive effects — in the context of audiotactile music theory — to the mediological notion of 'neo-auratic encoding' (NAE)[16]. It is in the interactions between

---

[13]. ADORNO, Theodor Wiesengrund. 'Vers une musique informelle', in: ID. *Quasi una fantasia. Essays on Modern Music* (1963), London, Verso, 1998, p. 305.

[14]. This quantitative reduction of holistic qualities of sound reality promoted some elements and processes as creatively feasible and expunged others which instead are free to exist inside a cognitive audiotactile order. For instance, the feasibility of the constitution of formal plexuses provided with meaning and important relevance in the context of 'good rhythmic conduct' based on energy modulation of temporal micro-entities has been compromised, which in ATP-based music go under the name of 'swing' or 'groove' — in jazz — or *laya* in southern Indian music. See CAPORALETTI, Vincenzo. *La definizione dello swing* [...], *op. cit.* (see note 5).

[15]. Nelson Goodman relates the 'autographic' quality to painting, while he considers music an 'allographic' art, where the identity of the work is independent from the (re)production history of the work itself (See GOODMAN, Nelson. *The Languages of Art*, New York, Bobbs-Merrill, 1968, p. 113ff.). More precisely, Goodman asserts that «What distinguishes an allographic work is that identification of an object or event as an instance of the work depends not at all upon how or when or by whom that object or event was produced» (ID. *Of Mind and Other Matters*, Cambridge [MA], Harvard University Press, 1984, p. 140). Now this perspective can stand up only if we consider Western music of written tradition (where the processes of musical reproduction of a text written in notation, presuming a diversification of roles between composer and performer, are particularly pertinent), but it is not valid for audiotactile music or, simply, for improvisational praxes. In this case I suggest a reversal of Goodman's criterion, with reference to the action of the audiotactile principle on musical formativity that carries itself out typically in musical 'autographicity'. From this point of view, the history of the production of the sign itself which objectifies the compositional/creative idea — for audiotactile music, the realization of material-syntactic values of sound in its phenomenological actuality then crystallized by phonographic recording — turns out to be a decisive factor.

[16]. In the phenomenology of some music based on the audiotactile formative medium, text 'processing' (be it a performance of a scriptural plan — with an 'open' encoding or at least considered as such — or something of an exclusively performative nature) operated by the phonographic recording plays a crucial role. From that a definitive textual statute ensues a phonofixation, which acts in a way which is analogous (even though here is firmly attached to the evenemential/audiotactile performative dimension) in many respects

ATP and NAE, therefore, in the specific form of cognitivity which is promoted by these mediations, that contemporary audiotactile music (the traditions of jazz, rock, the so-called popular music and world music) acquires a distinctive and specific epistemological statutes. The other typologies of musical repertoires based only on the ATP, but not on the NAE, remain in the domain of music of traditional cultures, with the related series of implications on the cultural and stylistic level.

This is not the place to explore the implications of this theoretical horizon. At least some of the consequences for the notion of improvisation, however, must be noted here. Our theoretical model sees the improvisational function as a phenomenon which is electively indebted to the intrinsic dynamics of audiotactile music, whose aesthetic values can be fully expressed just because the ATP can be inscribed in the phonofixation process. The ideological reverberation is given by the effects in the aesthetic area (in terms of NAE) of performance textualization — a phenomenon which completely eludes oral cultures

---

to notational crystallization of long-span planning, typical of 'written' composition, with an individualized authoriality, of Western art tradition. The possibility to use the phonographic recording medium as a creative tool gives rise, in audiotactile music, to consequences of cognitive nature (which do however exist also in performances which are not recorded): such effects reverberate on their aesthetic picture as distinctive features compared to the music of traditional/oral cultures. The repertoires of oral tradition, based on the ATP as well, did not develop in their historical course through the formative medium of phonographic recording, which intercepts them only a posteriori, as an ethnomusicological documental factor. Audiotactile music, which includes the so-called urban popular traditions, is permeated, instead, from its very musical conceptualization up to its phenomenological manifestations, by the influx of the phonographic recording medium. The theoretical whole which derives from these dynamics has been traced back by the present writer to the notion of 'neo-auratic encoding' (NAE). See CAPORALETTI, Vincenzo. 'Stratificazione metrica e modularità costruttiva in *Straight, No Chaser* di Thelonious Monk', in: *Musica Theorica Spectrum*, II-III (2002), pp. 32-51: 33; ID. 'Musica audiotattile e musica di tradizione orale', in: *Musica Theorica Spectrum*, VII (2004), pp. 2-19: 10ff; ID. *La definizione dello swing* [...], *op. cit.* (see note 5), p. 121ff., in a way which differs from the idea of the loss of aura for the work of art in the era of technical reproducibility, as theorized by Walter Benjamin in 1936 (see *Das Kunstwerk im Zeitalter seiner technischen Reproduzierbarkeit*, Frankfurt/Main, Suhrkamp, 1955). If it is indubitable, indeed, that technical reproducibility forces us to renounce the *hic et nunc* of the work, it is as well true that the aspects which can be traced back to the audiotactile principle find in the phonographic recording the means for a fixation of some significant indexes of the processual/phenomenal qualities, which is enough to build, for these musical formations, a new model of 'auraticity' through the technological means. Such objectified textualization, rescuing the musical form from the evanescence which is typical in oral cultures, makes audiotactile music available to the categories of Western modern aesthetics — creative originality, autonomy of the work, 'disinterested' reception — thus canceling *de facto* the opposition between 'low' and 'high' culture. The technological 'transcription' of the ATP, therefore, its phonographic fixation in connection with the processes of NAE — or the 'inherent' possibility of such crystallization, which also shapes the artistic awareness in non-recorded performances — limits the phenomenological and cognitive area in which the elective instances of audiotactile music in the strict sense of the world are projected. The issue which contemporary musicology is now to face is that in information/electronic technological globalization oral traditions are disappearing permanently, and are acquiring the features of audiotactile music.

characterized by performance evanescence — and by the consequent transition from the oralistic ontology of evenementiality to that of objectuality[17], even though meant as an objectuality of the performance, reified in a technological reproduction. In the light of NAE, the real-time creative action — which does not reproduce a set text — reaches an aesthetic status that assimilates the outcomes of the idiosyncratic formativity of the ATP to the works objectified in texts (written in notation) of Western music of written tradition, thus benefitting from the categories of creative originality, autonomy of the artistic text and disinterested contemplation of the reception (in other terms, the foundation of modern aesthetics). This condition of phonic objectification eludes *ex tempore* formative practices that do not allow the possibility of a phonofixation, including the ones of Western written music up to the twentieth century[18].

Among the improvisational processes the systemic notion of 'extemporization' emerges, which in audiotactile music theory is distinctively opposed to that of 'improvisation' in the strict sense of the word. Such notion is defined as the «form of the constitutive process of textual encoding in music in which the Audiotactile Principle is active»[19]. The phenomenological essence of extemporization is related, in the terms of information theory,

> to the level of informativity which is present in the performance process, that is to the *potential degree of possible choices*. This set of virtualities is different in degree and in substance from the one which is conditioned by the adhesion to the *control object* of the score in written/art music tradition: *extemporization* is not simply an expressive variable of the text, as the interpretation in western art music of the last three centuries, but has the function to constitute the text, through the ATP[20].

Operatively extemporization takes the form of the process of immediate instantiation of an imaginative figural model[21], of an actualization of a musical conceptualization unit

---

[17]. For a discussion of the musicological implications of the notions of 'objectual' and 'evenemential ontology', see MOLINO, Jean. 'Expérience et connaissance de la musique à l'âge des neurosciences', in: *Le temps et la forme*, edited by Étienne Darbellay, Genève, Droz, 1998, pp. 253-277: 259ff.

[18]. The implications of stylistic, aesthetic and phenomenological nature of this assumption, in relation to improvisational praxes of the eighteenth and nineteenth century in Western music of written tradition, will be examined in the following section.

[19]. CAPORALETTI, Vincenzo. *La definizione dello swing* [...], *op. cit.* (see note 5), p. 109: «forma del processo costitutivo di codifica testuale nelle musiche in cui agisce il Principio audiotattile».

[20]. *Ibidem*, p. 111: «al tasso d'informatività presente nel processo esecutivo, ossia al *grado potenziale di scelte possibili*. Quest'insieme di virtualità è differente nel grado e nella sostanza rispetto a quello condizionato dall'adesione al *control object* della partitura nella musica occidentale di tradizione scritta; l'*estemporizzazione* non è semplicemente una variante espressiva del testo, come l'interpretazione nella musica eurocolta degli ultimi tre secoli, ma ha funzione costitutiva, attraverso il PAT, del testo».

[21]. For the notion of model and its implementation in creative dynamics of oral cultures see Bernard Lortat-Jacob's articles (*op. cit.* [see note 6]).

which assumes the features of a harmonic pattern or a melodic profile, of a morphological path on a modal or tonal basis, and so forth. In an analogical sense we can understand it as 'interpretation' of a piece of which the textual unity fixed through notation does not exist, but is substantiated as a 'model' or 'matrix' in the consciousness of the performer. It is the notion which represents the processes of musical production at work in traditional cultures, which actually from an objective viewpoint perform music 'in real time', instantiating an ideal virtuality, culturally active, in a concrete sound form. Therefore, following common sense, we define an Indian *rāga* or an Arab *taqsîm* as 'improvising': but they constiue processs where the cultural constraints do not include the function of the search for the new, or of the elaboration of the compositional material towards an implementation of aesthetic originality. Just this secondary elaboration feature, a trait of negation of the conventional aesthetic norm through the discovery and innovation from the extemporization level — a process which is allowed and authorized by a cultural horizon which advances creative-performative evenementiality to the rank of an objectified text, which is able to trigger a dialectic dynamism in the phenomenology of style — seems instead to outline the traits of what we categorize as 'improvisation' in the strict sense of the word[22].

The practice of extemporization, pervasive in oral cultures, does not meet, on the phenomenological level, the requirements of improvisation, inasmuch as it does not have the ontological value of — nor the reverberations on the cognitive level induced by — the phonofixed text. The issue is not much in the terms of the articulation of the *niveau neutre*[23], the morphosyntactic elements in play, but rather in the terms of the current anthropological concept of music. For instance, in the European culture of modern music notation — after the seventeenth century, and with a focus in the era of the 'ideal of adherence to the written text' (*werktreues Ideal*), the middle of the nineteenth century — the absence of a phonographic recording medium did not make possible the search for innovative formal originality and the structuration on an aesthetically-progressive large scale to be constituted as an epistemological object[24]. For *ex tempore* creativity these options have not been anthropologically grounded, proving, as a consequence, impracticable, and are, perhaps, conceptual instances not even relevant in the semantic/cultural system. With

---

[22]. See Caporaletti, Vincenzo. *La definizione dello swing* […], *op. cit.* (see note 5), in particular pp. 135ff and p. 191.

[23]. We are referring to the 'semiological triad' proposed by Jean-Jacques Nattiez, with the distinction between *poietic*, *neutral* and *aesthesic* level related, respectively, to the levels of production, of immanent form, and to the receptive level of a musical sign. Nattiez, Jean-Jacques. *Fondements d'une sémiologie de la musique*, Paris, Union Générale d'Édition, 1975.

[24]. As we will see in the following section, in particular in the work of Carl Czerny, just the attempt to attribute these faculties of aesthetic research to *ex tempore* creation processes, invalidated nevertheless from its very bases by the mediological contingencies of the historical period and the cultural cycle, will cause an incompatibility between aesthetic, stylistic and phenomenological values which will create the conditions for the eclipse of such practices in the European culture.

this purpose only those mediologically processed — and actionable — praxes and planning devices through notation's theory ladenness have instead been delegated, selecting them by means of the long-span creation linked to the written practice of composition. The latter, moreover, allowed the unavoidable adhesion to objectual ontology, even though filtered through its own epistemological assumptions that sacrifice a considerable number of 'secondary qualities' to the work textualized by writing: timbral-dynamical, material and energetic/agogic aspects, essential for the real-time creation act. Notation practice historically implemented mental/cognitive patterns in agreement with its internal 'operative system' and deeply underlying the changeability of the stylistic intentions on the surface, thus making pertinent on the level of expression only the traits which are coherent with such patterns. In a historical perspective, this scenario sanctioned an unavoidable aesthetic and epistemic minority of the improvisational practice in the culture of musical writing of Modern Age, all the more marked the more we near the age of the *werktreue Ideal*, in the middle of the nineteenth century.

On the morphosyntactic level extemporization tends to be configured for the elements of conventional formularity, sequential parataxis and coordinating phraseology often carried out in cyclical forms, while improvisation is preferably implemented with the developmental variation, motivic-thematic elaboration, subordinating phraseology to a projection of the creative *telos* on the large formal scale. In jazz, for instance, where phenomena of improvisation and extemporization coexist, on the melodic level the latter can assume the traits of a theme paraphrase, or can be realized, on the harmonic level, in the structure of the metric-chordal substratum with a comping function. Otherwise it manifests itself in real-time arrangement and re-orchestration and in the delineation of architectonical variants. At any rate, it must be stressed that in improvisation in the strict sense of the word aesthetical factors of projection of the individual *melos* and the search for new formal identities are predominant over purely technical traits of morphological organization — beyond the mere development of the thematic idea, which it is, however, a determining factor as well.

Before devoting ourselves to a detailed analysis of these dynamics in the historical context of music from the eighteenth and nineteenth centuries, a final remark is appropriate about the relation between the phonofixation function of sound recording and the processes of aesthetic individuation. It is essential to understand the role of NAE processes in the foundation of the contemporary notion of improvisation and its epistemic statute, remembering that phonographic recording acted historically and functionally in a similar way to photography. This latter, roughly in the same period of Edison's experiments and his first attempts to record/reproduce sounds, made it possible for painting, in the last third of the nineteenth century, to be exempted from the burden of being adherent to — and reproducing the — reality, and to direct itself towards the unpredictability of new styles, first impressionist and then abstract, with the creation of unwonted materials and codes.

Phonographic recording, analogously, released *ex tempore* creative practices in oral cultures from the burden of the adhesion to the mnemonic figural model, actualized in the practice of extemporization. It thus prearranged the opportunity to explore other formal regions and the creation of innovative material: aesthetical processes of NAE, in this picture, as we saw, identify the coordinates for the transition from oral praxes to audiotactile ones. It is in this sense that improvisation is configured as a musical practice typical of the contemporary era, crossing the 'sacred enclosure' of conditionings and conventional constraints imposed on *ex tempore* creativity by traditional cultures.

The sound recording medium, in the moment when it lifted from the memory the burden — at the same time practical and moral — to hold the information concerning the cultural model to be actualized in the performance, freed it from the conditionings imposed by the 'sign dispersion field'[25] and by the need not to go beyond it. Roman Jakobson and Piotr Bogatyrëv noted already in 1929 that in traditional oral cultures the practices, and not only the musical ones, are subject to specific constraints and to a 'preventive censorship', just in order to preserve the integrity of the musical message deposited in the collective memory[26]. The mnemonic cultural unit is flexible, but the system cannot be forced beyond a given threshold, otherwise there is the risk of rendering the message unrecognizable. A musical conceptualization unit can be subject to regional variants, which can in turn be subject to personal variations, but these infringments of the system cannot be pushed beyond the limits imposed by cultural recognizability for the insiders. With sound recording, instead, the conditions are set for the rise of improvisation in the contemporary meaning, just because it is established by dialectically negating the limits (actually or only potentially: reserving to itself, that is to say, the possibility) imposed by the 'dispersion field', which can now be violated inasmuch as the cultural intangibility of the model, imposed by the risk of dissolution which is intrinsic to its condition of impermanence, is no longer in play.

III. Creative and Extemporary Practices in Western Music of the Eighteenth and Nineteenth Centuries

How can this theoretical picture be reconfigured in relation to extemporary creation practices in Western art music? In this section we will direct our discussion towards two distinct levels. Firstly, in III.1, we will examine the heuristic perspectives and the

---

[25]. Field of sign variability, beyond which its cultural recognizability for the insiders is not guaranteed anymore.

[26]. Jakobson, Roman - Bogatyrëv, Piotr. 'Die Folklore als eine besondere Form des Schaffens', in: *Donum Natalicium Schrijnen*, Nijmegen-Utrecht, N. V. Dekker & Van de Vegt, 1929, pp. 900-913; reprinted in Jakobson, Roman. *Selected Writings.*, 8 vols., The Hague, Mouton, 1962-1988, vol. IV (1966): *Slavic Epic Studies*, pp. 1-15.

methodological criteria commonly used in the literature, highlighting critical factors and suggesting possible operational adaptations and conceptual revisions. Secondly, in III.2, we will investigate just the distinctive phenomenological and structural attributions of such praxes, from the viewpoint of comparative musicology, relating them to the similar ones belonging to oral cultures or to audiotactile contemporariness. We will thus verify if it is feasible to apply to them the notions of 'model' (in III.2.1.) and the categorial grid of extemporization/improvisation (in III.2.2.) in the light of the theoretical perspective on audiotactile formativity, suggesting at the same time an explicative theory on the disappearance of creative performativity traditions in the middle of the nineteenth century.

III.I. RESEARCH PERSPECTIVE

We can trace back the research models in the literature on improvisational practices of Western musical culture of written tradition of the eighteen and the nineteenth centuries to three basic, variously interconnected perspectives: (a) the search for 'improvisational values' in written works, with the associated attempt to reconstruct performative-creative practices starting from the traits which are present in the compositions; (b) the individuation and definition of supplementing practices relating to textual indeterminations; and (c) the survey of morphologically constituted improvisational plans on a medium/large formal scale. Let us examine the methodological features in detail.

The detection of improvisational traits in a composition is a ubiquitous standard in the literature and it takes the form of a rarely challenged methodological attitude[27]. The ideological presupposition is based on a system of assumptions which is well depicted by the following assertion made by Lydia Goehr «by 1800, when composition was defined as involving the predetermination of as many structural elements as possible, the notion of extemporization acquired its modern understanding. For the first time it was seen to stand in strict opposition to composition 'proper'»[28]. Goehr refers to this phenomenon in terms of the 'Beethoven paradigm', crediting the composer with the merit of having ushered in this momentous revolution. This view implies, however, some predetermination with respect to the theoretical idea of improvisational processes. Within such representation, as a matter of fact, the 'improvisational value', intended in itself, is characterized by its traits of formal indefiniteness as opposed to the cohesion and cogency of the building connections of the written *opus*. By analogy, we could identify this particular conceptualization of the improvisational process, based on the semantic opposition between the structured and the

---

[27]. For a recent example of this methodological orientation, see KINDERMAN, William. 'Improvisation in Beethoven's Creative Process', in: *Musical Improvisation*. […], *op. cit.* (see note 2), pp. 296-312.

[28]. GOEHR, Lydia. *The Imaginary Museum of Musical Works. An Essay in the Philosophy of Music*, Oxford, Clarendon, 1991, p. 324.

indefinite, as the 'Goehr paradigm'. This paradigm does not appear to have an absolute validity. It must be noted that the criteria of imaginary externalization and spontaneity, realized in the indefinite as a metaphor of temporal and existential dispersion, emerge as more general dialectic outcomes compared to the pre-Romantic conception, not being integral to the representation of the processes of extemporaneous creativity regarded in themselves (as a matter of fact, in Baroque praxes they are not contemplated in this form). They are Romantic aesthetic values which are reflected in the creative *ex tempore* practices and the modality of a categorization with regard to the improvisational aspect constitutes an *emic* interpretative standard, which is specific to a well-defined ethos and which cannot be hypostatized and extended to other cultural climate, as the Baroque or the contemporary era. It is necessary to thematize this aspect on the methodological level or else we are likely to run into a theoretical misunderstanding, also owing to the persistence of attitudes and values of Romanticism in the realm of common sense. It is a misrepresentation of the opposite kind as the widespread retrospective projection of those improvisational criteria and values typical of contemporary music which I stigmatized in the introduction to this contribution. It is just the improvisational practices that proved to us how the constructivist operating model and those of a structured formal elaboration, in contrast to a mechanistic interpretation of the 'Goehr paradigm', can be completely supported and are actually implemented by the audiotactile performative formativity[29].

A related problematic crux, a mirror image of the former, regards the representation of improvisational processes — for instance those carried out in the realization of preludes — by inferring them from the corresponding written versions of the same musical genre[30]. The problem here is caused by the lack of mediological media awareness about the formative specifics of communication channels and media in general in the determination of cultural processes[31]. In other words, the ambiguity arises when a message composed in a written medium is considered as a reflection of an orally mediated text, which might even

---

[29].   See for instance the music of Charlie Parker or Lennie Tristano. On these constructivist aspects and of intentional formal structuration in jazz improvisation, see MARTIN, Henry. *Charlie Parker and Thematic Improvisation*, Lanham (MD), Scarecrow, 1996, or, from a more general perspective, LARSON, Steve. A*nalyzing Jazz. A Schenkerian Approach*, Hillsdale (NY), Pendragon, 2009.

[30].   We can define Nicholas Temperley's position with regard to this methodological option as 'open to possibilities', even if through the conscious knowledge of the issue's subtleness, as one can infer from the following assertion relating to a discussion on the *24 Preludes* Op. 28 by Chopin: «The manner of improvised preluding in the early 19th century cannot be exactly recovered, even if it were desirable to attempt such a thing. We have only printed examples, which were not in themselves improvised and were likely to be more structured and polished, and probably also more conservative, than the practice that they claimed to represent. Yet, after all, *the difference may be less than it appears*», p. 339. [our italics]. TEMPERLEY, Nicholas. 'Preluding at the Piano', in: *Musical Improvisation*. [...], *op. cit.* (see note 2), pp. 323-341: 339.

[31].   This mediological repudiation is completely offbeat with the theoretical perspective of audiotactile music theory and with the underlying epistemological infrastructure, which is typical of a theoretical front — going from Dewey to McLuhan and to De Kerkhove, up to Hanson, including even the Heidegger

be reconstructed by simply inverting the direction of the encoding process. Now then, this mediological incompatibility is largely shared within a horizon of thought that dates back, concerning folklore studies, at least to the seminal intuitions of Jakobson and Bogatyrëv in 1929 on the irreducibility between the mediological media arrangements that can be now defined of audiotactile and visual-scriptural kind, a differential field in which the opposition, in their own respective terms, between folklore and literature is encompassed:

> Without doubt the transfer of methods and concepts developed for the study of subject matter from the history of literature to the field of folklore has often influenced the analysis of folklore art forms. Especially the important distinction between a literary text and a record of a work of folklore was underestimated, which already by and for itself inevitably distorts the work and transposes it to a different category[32].

Consequently, it is possible to assume reasonably that between a prelude 'written' by Chopin[33] and another one which he created on the spot, perhaps even during a public performance, there should be a substantial difference, which cannot even be measured, just because the basic and relevant values of the distinct experiences, of audiotactile/contextual and scriptural/planning kinds are ontologically divergent, even when the 'plan' aims to replicate the chaotic fuzziness of irrational urges of energy. Such experiences would be compatible only by risking a loss of specificity which would invalidate irrevocably, whatever the polarity was on which to build the phenomenological priority, the stylistic integrity of the message, unless one is interested in experimentalism and in code crossbreeding (but these are precisely values of our times).

Concerning the detection and definition of practices that integrate textual indeterminations, the problem is to distinguish between the element of decoding relating to a notation system which differs from the conventional one[34] and the processes of performative creativity proper on a larger formal scale, notably in preludes and fantasias. (We will note *infra* the distinctions between the said practices in the music between eighteenth and nineteenth century.) In Baroque music particularly, the phenomenological

---

of the *Die Frage nach der Technik* — who reconsiders the role attributed to technological mediality in the anthropological structuration of cognitive and perceptive instances.

[32]. JAKOBSON, Roman - BOGATYRËV, Piotr. *Op. cit.* (see note 26), pp. 11-12: «Ohne Zweifel hat die Übertragung der bei der Bearbeitung des literarhistorischen Stoffes gewonnenen Methoden und Begriffe auf das Gebiet der Folkloristik des öfteren die Analyse der Folklore-Kunstformen beeinträchtigt. Insbesondere wurde der bedeutende Unterschied zwischen einem Literaturtexte und der Aufzeichnung eines Folklore-Werkes unterschätz, die schon an und für sich dieses Werk unvermeidlich entstellt und es in eine andere Kategorie transponiert».

[33]. CHOPIN, Fryderyk. *24 Préludes*, Op. 28, Paris-Leipzig, Catelin-Breitkopf & Härtel, 1839.

[34]. I thus define the technology of semiographic encoding — and the linked epistemological and aesthetic values — which asserted itself in the middle of the nineteenth century and is still used today.

sense of the implied praxis can be traced back more to the domain of *interpretation* than to that of improvisation, with its obvious reference to a text written on the basis of epistemological criteria which differ from those connected with the current Western conventional notation. In this sense, semiography would allow for more open and less binding decodings, which can nevertheless be ascribed to the criterion of musical interpretation, more than improvisation.

This theoretical perspective, which cannot be evaded regarding seventeenth-century music, highlights the cognitive implications engendered on the mediological level by the various encoding systems of the sound material. The Baroque culture, in connection with semiographic encoding, had not yet established the epistemic principles — with a symbolical formalization which is only abstract and with an acoustic/mathematizing reference — which are fully active in the notational encoding of the following centuries. Some cases of articulatory/gestural references lingered in the notation, as a typical consequence of an audiotactile mind-set. If we do not take into account the brainframe generated by the conventional notational encoding medium, the subliminal systems of cognitive and perceptive acquisition that it entails on the basis of the 'theory ladenness' of modern music theory, we run the risk of distorting the sense of musical production of the Baroque era and of the practices this writing formalized.

An audiotactile mind-set constantly refers to the gestural-motor contextuality of performativity, shunning abstractive systems. The case of basso continuo is emblematic in this sense. At first glance, inside a cognitive model founded on score functionality as a control panel, as a code of instructions to be implemented with a bi-univocal criterion in musical reproduction, founded on a visual culture that became fully apparent in the era of the 'ideal of being true to the work' (*das werktreue Ideal*), in the mid-nineteenth century, the basso continuo can appear to be an improvisational praxis, and as such it is actually classified in many a study[35]. However, a change in perspective and a comparison with historical and anthropological criteria will allow us to see how the basso continuo was in fact the current method to encode a praxis which was normalized on the level of poietics with a relevant audiotactile functionality, and from the aesthetic point of view, an interpretation criterion of a formalization system in writing that had not yet completely drawn on the principles of the 'universe of precision' (*l'univers de la précision*)[36]. What appears even more remarkable is that in Baroque culture this praxis did not define the semantic area of improvisation: the historiographical distortions arisen from this situation can be easily imagined.

---

[35]. Among the most recent examples, see MOERSCH, Charlotte. 'Keyboard Improvisation in the Baroque Era', in: *Musical Improvisation* [...], *op. cit.* (see note 2), pp. 150-170. In this article on late baroque improvisation on keyboard instruments, pp. 164-167 are dedicated to basso continuo practice.

[36]. KOYRÉ, Alexandre. 'Du monde de l'à-peu-près à l'univers de la précision', in: *Critique*, XXVIII (1948), pp. 806-823.

The same can be said, in the domain of 'real-time' Baroque creative practices, for ornamentation, both for the various French practices and the Italian free embellishments. The very notion of ornamentation derives from aprioristic assumptions founded on a nomological conception of the score. For those, and for the implied theoretical system, there is a central element, the nuclear concept of musical note — which stands out particularly in ornamentation procedures of the French School — around which revolve, with a subsidiary function, the secondary elements. We must think about this presumed substantial nuclear function of the note: a conception on which analytical methodologies are built that find their theoretical glorification in Schenker's reductionist theory, so that it is possible to trace the improvisational melodic core just by pruning the accidents from the substance, as illustrated in various writings.

We must in the first place affirm that the intuitive nature of the notion of ornamentation is culturally induced altogether. In this regard it is sufficient to notice that there are cultures, whose musical practices are based on an audiotactile experience, which simply do not know the dissociating notion of ornamentation in terms of a subsidiary *addendum* to a substantive nucleus (and I think this rationale could also suit perfectly the audiotactile *ex tempore* practices in baroque musical culture). An interesting example is given by Arthur Henry Fox Strangways, who, while he was studying in 1914 Hindustani music with the brainframe — the 'conceptual predetermination' — induced by the medium of Western semiography/music theory, found himself in the position to draw a sharp distinction between the Western concept of ornamentation and the seemingly corresponding practice of the Hindustani *gamak*: «Indian grace is different in kind. There is never the least suggestion of anything having been added to the note which is graced. The note with its grace makes one utterance»[37].

One could object that these remarks, when interculturally transposed to the Baroque context, could render equally problematic the reproduction of music composed with a written mediality, where the various modalities of ornamentation are of course present. In the light of this objection, however, the mediological issue of cultural formalizations through different medialities comes into play. One thing is, as a matter of fact, to think and to compose music through the cognitive function promoted by the medium of notational encoding, which imbues of its own epistemic logic the formal outcomes, conforming them to its operative system based on linear-syntactic structures of the quantitative-combinatorial kind, and another is — as it happens in improvised praxes — to prescind from this theoretical mediation and to rely on the psycho-corporeal medium of the audiotactile principle (whose phonic results might in turn be subsequently subject to a notational formalized encoding, for instance with a didactic purpose). It is just in the transition from audiotactile mediation to notational formalization that there is a substantial

---

37. FOX STRANGWAYS, Arthur Henry. *The Music of Hindostan* (1914), London, Oxford University Press, 1965, p. 182.

loss of informational data: and it is around this differential of informational dispersion (and on its reintegration method, which corresponds to parametrical quantifications of which we have at the present time lost the key) that the present discussion revolves. In the light of that, it is possible to see the lines of a critical rethinking, at least for the creative praxes of performative implementation, the reconstruction of procedures, particularly baroque, inferred from ornamentation models transcribed in notation.

The survey/reconstruction of *ex tempore* creative praxes as plans of morphological constitution on a medium/large formal scale leads us directly into the area of complete fulfillment of historicized improvised processes. To the class of phenomena having a statute of formal autonomy belongs the eighteenth-century free fantasy (*freie Fantasie*), of which a famous exemplification is given by Carl Philipp Emanuel Bach in the last chapter of the second volume of his *Versuch über die wahre Art das Clavier zu spielen* (1753; 1762)[38], along with the examples that Carl Czerny illustrates in his Op. 200[39]. In this regard it is interesting to notice how Czerny distinguishes the realization of cadences and preludes[40] (in the three kinds of short and medium extent and in the style of recitative) from the typologies of improvisation proper in the *fantasia* — thematic, multi-thematic, in the legato and fugato styles —, in the *pot-pourri*, in the *variations*, in the *capriccio*[41]. These improvisational praxes raise several problems related to the categorization of the actual modality of *ex tempore* action operated and to their specific phenomenological constitution, issues that are now to be systematically classified.

III.2. The Phenomenology of *ex tempore* Practice

We saw in Section II how creative/performative practices of audiotactile music in our times contemplate both extemporizational and improvisational processes, while oral cultures only allow extemporizational ones, linked to cultural constraints related to the dispersion field of the improvisational model/referent. We now must apply the theoretical infrastructure based on the notion of *model* and the paradigm identified by the systemic opposition *improvisation/extemporization* to the *ex tempore* creative practices

---

[38]. Bach, Carl Philipp Emanuel. *Versuch über die wahre Art das Clavier zu spielen, Zweiter Theil, in welchem die Lehre von dem Accompagnement und der freien Fantasie abgehandelt wird*, Berlin, Georg Ludwig Winter, 1762, pp. 325-341.

[39]. Czerny, Carl. *Systematische Anleitung zum Fantasieren auf dem Pianoforte*, Op. 200, Vienna, A. Diabelli, 1829.

[40]. As for the prelude, however, one must not be deceived by the introductory functional nature of the work, because it becomes *de facto* an autonomous genre in the nineteenth century. See Goertzen, Valerie Woodring. 'By Way of Introduction. Preluding by 18th- and Early 19th-Century Pianists', in: *The Journal of Musicology*, XIV (1996), pp. 299-337: 303.

[41]. Czerny, Carl. *Op. cit.* (see note 39), p. 3.

in Western notation (and in Western music theory which constitutes its doctrinal basis) in order to verify its theoretical practicability in the categorization of the implied improvisational processes.

III.2.I. Model Functionality

In the perspective of a further specification and closer examination of the 'model/ referent theory' of real-time creative practice, we propose a double qualification of such notion with respect to the concepts of extemporization and improvisation. In the first case, which can be defined as Process A, there is the normative criterion of the figural model — of the conceptual map that controls the explication of the *ex tempore* praxis — which is instantiated in a double articulation, in Levels 1 and 2, which correspond respectively to the processes of extemporization and improvisation we were referring to in Section II. In this case, the implied processes of extemporaneous creativity can be defined as 'creation on the model'. In Process B, instead, we can identify a model of a different nature, where it is not configured as a conceptual map but rather as a direct creative precipitate, thus coinciding with Level 1 of the concrete sound instantiation. This is the case where the extemporizational act in itself does not refer to a model which is culturally determined or predetermined in the consciousness, but it's a creation of the form in its own actualization regardless of a structural antecedence, analogous to the criteria of some aspects of primeval compositional inspiration. In this case it is possible to talk about 'creation of the model'. Naturally, this kind of model also, if 'collapsed', so to speak, on the extemporization, can be subject to a second-level elaboration, coherently with artistic/aesthetic principles treated in Section II, giving rise to a specific improvisational implementation, in the context of aesthetic processes of neo-auratic encoding[42]. These concepts are schematized in Table 1.

With relation to the notion of model — which, it must be remembered, inherits its conceptual matrix from the studies on oral traditions — it is worth to clarify some specific and distinctive questions for *ex tempore* practices of Western musical civilization of semiographic mediality, in the eighteenth and nineteenth centuries. Let us consider the criterion of the model's dispersion field[43], as a codified and conventional bond, which assumes different values in relation to oral dynamics. In the case in point, it pertains to the generative model of the tonal kind and not to the figural model — the musical conceptualization unit — which in art music is authorial and thus is fungible and can be articulated *ad libitum*, although inside given stylistic conventions, unlike what happens in oral cultures.

---

[42]. See *supra*, Section II.

[43]. See note 25.

Table 1

	Process A (Creation on the Model)	Process B (Creation of the Model)
Figural Model	Musical Conceptualization Unit ↓	Model Ex novo ⇕
Level 1 Extemporization	Concrete Instance ↓	Concrete Instance ↓
Level 2 Improvisation	Creative Elaboration	Creative Elaboration

In *ex tempore* Western written-tradition musical practices a coexistence of creative/ *authorial* and repertorial/*cultural* models takes place, unlike the preponderance of the latter in traditional music[44]. The reason is to be found in the individualistic creative ideology, promoted and historically consolidated by the written medium; the mnemonic model, on the contrary, is in many cases formalized in writing, as it can be noted in Ex. 2 (see *infra*).

In consequence, the practices which are only apparently oral — in their performative phenomenology — are permeated by authorial spirit, not being based on the reproduction of a determined collective heritage(although it is dynamical inside)[45]. As a consequence, the aesthetic quality of the improvisational model is implemented, for instance, in the music of the mid-eighteenth century, in technical and theoretical adherence to the principles

---

[44]. The relations between these two instances in the context of the same cultural traditions are however the subject of a debate in contemporary ethnomusicology, and identify respectively the more recent 'authorialist' positions (for instance, by Jean-Jacques Nattiez) and the conception of 'collective anonymity', which is typical of the tradition of the folklore studies represented by Piotr Bogatyrëv, Philipp Barry or Costantin Brăiloiu.

[45]. In the traditional societies an index of variability and cultural innovation exists, and is activated in specific transformation processes studied in anthropology and ethnomusicology. We have a stylistic mutation with (slow) phases of cultural transformation characterized by specific modalities of actuation (intracultural, by acculturation, hybridization, etc.). Differently from the aesthetic processes of Western modern art where those are an end in themselves and are consciously sought in search of the new, these stylistic mutations, however, instantly crystallize in a koine which lingers for a new period as a stabilized phase, because the aesthetic value of innovation and of creative originality is meant differently.

of musical erudition and in the application of tonal theory's legacy, with an operational specificity centered on building expertise of the material artifact, while in Romanticism it mostly manifests itself in the explication of acting subjectivity through imaginative features and traits of original creativity.

But let us now proceed to the reformulation, on the basis of the structuration fixed in TABLE I, of the taxonomy of improvisational processes we described in Section III.1[46]. Concerning the supplementing devices referred to the semiographic dictate, the practice of basso continuo will be attributed to Process A, as an instantiation of a scriptural model given by the figured bass, and similarly the ornamentations, the free embellishments, the lead-in or the varied repeats.

As for the cadences the specifics of thematic elaboration must be told apart. If references to the composition's themes are not made, as in the typology exemplified by the autograph cadence by Mozart in his own Piano Concerto K 488, the formative phenomenology can be traced back to Process B. Thematic cadences, instead, and at any rate any elaboration organized according to conventional formal construction modalities, can be definitely ascribed to Process A.

Concerning the plans of morphological constitution on a medium/large formal scale which we referred to, described by Czerny in his *Systematische Anleitung zum Fantasieren auf dem Pianoforte*, Op. 200, the theme and variations and *pot-pourris*, are to be ascribed to Process A, as well as the double preludial praxis to which Johann Nepomuk Hummel refers[47], respectively with the elaboration of the main or of a secondary theme belonging to the piece it introduces. The realization of the structure of a fugue reveals a Process A while mono- and multi-thematic fantasias described by Czerny are oriented towards Process B, though this categorization obviously depends on the concrete form the fantasia assumes in each particular case. In this connection an important distinction must be drawn between the model functionality in eighteenth-century *freie Fantasie* and in the *fantasia* of the Romantic period. In the first case it takes the form of a harmonic grid, even prescribed starting from the bass to which the figures are added, as C. Ph. E. Bach suggests, to be 'prolonged' in the transition from *Hintergrund* to *Vordergrund*, in the terms of Schenker's theory. In the nineteenth-century fantasia, in coexistence with the externalization of the fantastic inspiration and a subjective poietic *vis*, formal control structures seem to be active, usually on a framework involving a slow introduction, a thematic development and a brilliant final[48]. In this sense a dialectic of a considerable aesthetic reach is established between the

---

46. It must be underlined how, in the following systematization, between Process A and B there is a *continuum*, of which such determinations represent the polarities in order of tendency.

47. HUMMEL, Johann Nepomuk. *Ausführliche theoretisch-practische Anweisung zum Piano-Forte-Spiel*, Vienna, Tobias Haslinger, ²1829, pp. 466-468.

48. Czerny enumerates various formal settings and structural arrangements, like the sonata allegro, the adagio, the allegretto grazioso, the scherzo, the rondo, the polka, the theme with variations, the fugue, the waltz, the march. CZERNY, Carl. *Op. cit.* (see note 39), p. 36.

processes A and B, where instead of before the *freie Fantasie* we find us before a true Process A. We can on the other hand find that a variety of Process B is active in Czerny's Capriccio[49], just because of the freedom that its 'artistic principles' assumes.

Regarding the attribution of these different forms of real-time creation to Levels 1 and 2 (see Table 1), a further theoretical step is now necessary, with the examination of the development of creative phenomenology, carrying out an investigation on historical, aesthetic and stylistic levels. For this reason we must now delve into the creative dynamics which were active in the eighteenth and nineteenth centuries, detecting trend lines and stylistic outcomes.

III.2.2. The Extemporization/Improvisation Dichotomy

A central assumption of our theoretical model on improvisational processes is that the determining factor to apply the improvisational quality in the strict sense of the word, as opposed to the extemporizational process — as extensively examined elsewhere[50] and recalled in Section 1 — is not based on the mere articulation of sound matter, but rather on the specific ideological manner through which praxes are interpreted in the reference culture (that is, it depends on the concept of music that is culturally in force). Particularly, in order to determine the specificity of improvisation, the aesthetic processes of the neo-auratic encoding play a fundamental role, from the twentieth century onwards. These are implemented through the phonographic recording/reproduction medium, which enables aesthetic research, traditionally delegated to the notational textualization of written composition, to be moved to a new level — realized through audiotactile formativity and determined by the coordinates of an objectual ontology. The correlatives of choice on the formal level of this semantic and ideological core are the elaboration procedures we defined to be of Level 2, among which motivic-thematic developments play a significant, albeit not exclusive, role, in conducting the performative text beyond both structural bonds and the elements which predetermine the model.

The attribution to the extemporizational regime of the ways of real-time creation which are historically attested in Western art music in the eighteenth and nineteenth centuries is a consequence of this preamble, mainly because of the fact that these

---

[49]. *Ibidem*, p. 105: «Capriccio ist, im eigentlichen Sinne, die freyeste Art des Fantasieren; nämlich ein willkührliches Aneinanderreihen eigener Jdeen, ohne besondere Durchführung». On the capriccio see Sità, Maria Grazia. 'Modi dell'improvvisazione per tastiera tra Sette e Ottocento. Il 'principio artistico' del capriccio', in: *Sull'improvvisazione*, edited by Claudio Toscani, Lucca, LIM, 1998, pp. 63-85.

[50]. Caporaletti, Vincenzo. *La definizione dello swing* [...], *op. cit.* (see note 5).

practices — except for some examples which we will evaluate one by one later on — were not charged with the aesthetic duty of searching for 'new', of finding an original solution to formal problems. Instead such practices served a creative plan whose aesthetic outcomes were delegated to ways to organize the complexity which were independent from real-time action. The values of the audiotactile principle, which are fully at work in the *ex tempore* creative undertaking, tend as a matter of fact to direct formal values towards regions which are unrelated to the traditional melodic-harmonic syntactic dimensions. They rather insert a 'vertical gradient' hinged on sound aspects of the suprasegmental kind, which cannot be traced back to the syntagmatic linearity, which is subject to a notational spelling, and characterized by a psychically syntonic contextuality, with reference to other performers that might be playing along (interplay) and to the receivers of the musical communication[51]. Moreover, the artistic minority of real-time creation, as we saw, inside culturally dominant values, devalued irrevocably these experiences on the aesthetic level, forcing them into the heteronomous domain of mediumistic phenomenology, of mere virtuosity or learned ostentation.

Let us now pinpoint some concrete references of this speculative perspective, on the morphosyntactic linguistic level, in the concrete ways of musical sign production of historically attested praxes. Let us examine the eighteenth-century *freie Fantasie*, more precisely the example offered by C. Ph. E. Bach in his *Versuch über die wahre Art das Clavier zu spielen* (see Ex. 1). Given the intrinsic nature of improvisational virtuality, this annotated version is obviously only one of the many which could proceed from the model — the conceptual map — which Bach himself has offered us (see Ex. 2)[52]. The harmonic analysis in Roman numerals, which is included in the transcriptions, is that of Heinrich Schenker, as a token of how the conceptual structure of the improvisational model can exist in many ways, depending on the cognitive references that were taken into consideration[53].

---

[51]. The realization of a written composition requires the transcended presence of the audience, as a pure reflection of the composer's conscience. In the improvisational public act, instead, creative strategies are conditioned by the feedback that the public institutes with the performer. This contextual sensitivity was consciously thematized by the great improvisers of the past and considered a distinguishing competence. See on this aspect Hummel, Johann Nepomuk. *Op. cit.* (see note 47), p. 462.

[52]. See Bach, Carl Philipp Emanuel. *Op. cit.* (see note 38), p. 341.

[53]. See Schenker, Heinrich. 'The Art of Improvisation', English translation by Sylvan Kalib, in: Id. *Thirteen Essays from the Three Yearbooks 'Das Meisterwerk in der Musik'. An Annotated Translation*, Ph.D. Diss., Evanston, Northwestern University, 1973, pp. 21 and 28-29.

Ex. 1: exemplification of a *freie Fantasie*, from the *Versuch über die wahre Art das Clavier zu spielen* by C. Ph. E. Bach, Berlin, ²1762, p. [343]. In the transcription the original notation has been standardized to follow modern practice. Bach's original version uses soprano and bass keys. The dotted-line slurs are those indicated by Heinrich Schenker for his analysis (see text for reference), in order to highlight the large-scale design. The numbers within square brackets are from Bach's model/referent (Ex. 2).

Ex. 2: model/referent for the *ex tempore* realization of the *freie Fantasie* by C. Ph. E. Bach, from the *Versuch über die wahre Art das Clavier zu spielen* , Berlin, ²1762, p. 341. The figuring of the basso continuo is Bach's. The transcription includes Heinrich Schenker's harmonic analysis (see text for reference).

In the actualization of the model, annotated in Ex. 1, we find ourselves confronted with technical solutions that essentially belong to two different music-theoretical categories: scalar efflorescences and arpeggio patterns. It must be said that Bach strongly maintains in his *Versuch* that it is useful not to treat the arpeggio mechanically, but that it is better to insert some graceful appoggiaturas with the aim of enlivening the purely intervallic substratum that forms it. At any rate, it is the action linked to the formula that we find here: a realization which grasps in pure and animated gestuality, guided by clear rational-mathematical directions by which the frame of the precomposed model is substantiated, the key of its own interpretation.

No melodic articulation, and little motivic-thematic elaboration are present in this pattern of model treatment, and no rhythmical interest can be highlighted which acquires a figural identity; harmonic structures do not give rise to a distinct rhythmic-diastematic linearity. Furthermore, we do recognize the traits of extemporization in this typology of creation-performance modality just because of this audiotactile adhesion to ways of realization of the sound material linked to devices which do not depend on the visual epistemic matrix, linear-combinatorial, but are permeated with an acoustic effusiveness whose intimate legality is to be found in the instrumental *jeu* and in the phenomenology of the gesture which creates it. Bach's realization is a mere projection of the model[54], without the development of a second-level creative elaboration. We linger in a genre of conventional formularity, of sequential parataxis, even with a scarce incidence of that

---

[54]. Regarding this cogency of the model in Bach's *Fantasie*, with its deep teleological structure oriented towards the tonic we concur with RINK, John Scott. 'Schenker and Improvisation', in: *Journal of Music Theory*, XXXVII (1993), pp. 1-54.

phraseology of the coordinative kind which identifies one of the most characteristic indicators of extemporizational functionality[55] (just to limit ourselves to the resultants on the *niveau neutre*, aside from any consideration linked to the conceptual specifics of the particular form of 'humanly organized sound')[56]. A fundamental trait of the *freie Fantasie* is the erudite harmonic implementation, which is favoured by the non-measurability, by the release from time-metre structures. This *stilus phantasticus*-like effusiveness frees its formative outcomes not only from rhythmical constraints, but also from harmonic rhythm itself, with the possibility to pursue the creative efflorescence beyond the limits enforced by geometrical symmetry, in order to realize those «ingenious deceptions» (*vernünftige Betrügereyen*) by which style is substantiated[57].

What are then the intrinsic values of this *ex tempore* praxis? Should we scale down its aesthetic sense? That could only be if we were to measure the value indexes in a single direction, perhaps with the cognitive-literate brainframe. Actually, compared to the economy of melodic-linear means, in this specific typology of musical action we assist to what could be defined as a compensatory factor, given by the 'vertical gradient' to which we already referred, through which the idiosyncratic acquisitions of the audiotactile principle (ATP) are electively commeasured. Now, this phonic-timbral and micro-rhythmically expressive suprasegmental dimension carries out electively the mediological perspective offered by the ATP, as widely testified by the audiotactile music of our times.

In these last ones, the determinations of originality performed on the syntactic-syntagmatic level, which can be mediologically learned and represented, roughly, with the notation, can carry — and they undoubtedly do — a great weight. But more often, and chiefly in less theory-laden genres, these values of aesthetic research are distributed on the suprasegmental 'vertical gradient' (sound, timbre, attack, articulation, or the energy values having the local denominations of 'drive', 'swing', 'groove'). Similarly, the compensating factor promoted, in praxes referable to the *freie Fantasie*, epistemological features connatural with the ATP, which crossed only tangentially the visual linear-combinatorial values which are consubstantial with the semiographic-notational mediality (it must be remembered that the transcribed example is exactly a formalization of an instantaneously-created performative praxis). With these processes, just in the ostension of essentially harmonic-

---

55. Temperley points out how C. Ph. E. Bach declares, introducing the neophytes to the realization of the *Fantasie*, which «is exceptionally well suited to stirring and stilling the passions», thus betraying the change of attitude introduced by the *empfindsamer Stil* compared to baroque aesthetics. Nevertheless, he underlines how such didactic-pedagogic suggestions «contain no trace of the idea that they [the musicians] should follow their fancy». Temperley, Nicholas. *Op. cit.* (see note 30), p. 326. This conventionality of the eighteenth-century *Fantasie* on the syntactic level causes it phenomenologically to belong, in our terms, to the area of extemporization.

56. See Blacking, John. *How Musical is Man?*, Seattle, University of Washington Press, 1973.

57. Bach, Carl Philipp Emanuel. *Op. cit.* (see note 38), p. 330.

based procedures, of the scalar/arpeggial kind, a shifting of the aesthetic weight was created on nuance and suprasegmental expressive traits.

In confirmation of this, Pamela Fox asserts[58] that in the *freie Fantasie* the harmonic variety must be supported by the change of the other sound dimensions, particularly dynamics and agogics. One must not underestimate the function of those performative imponderabilities, which contributed to outline an important role of the *empfindsamer Stil* in his contemporaries' perception — which was of the emic kind. These aspects have been subjected to a notational encoding, in written compositions, sometimes at the cost of a considerable twisting of the semiographic system. Such a reductionist trend on the level of melodic development would carry on in early nineteenth-century preluding[59], which was subject to the same compensatory factor of suprasegmental values in relation to syntagmatic ones. Now, the issue with this audiotactile option, in a historical perspective, is that the time was not right yet. Its intrinsic limit on the socio-anthropological and phenomenological level, just because it was a practice indexed on the 'vertical gradient', is that the elements of musical form involved, as 'secondary qualities' of sound, are constituted in the eighteenth- and nineteenth-centuries as Kantian *noumena*, not having, in the particular cultural cycle and in the absence of a phonographic recording medium, the status of epistemological object. They cannot be encoded by the technologies of their cultural cycle. That makes this research line sterile, the more it is confronted with the notational formalization — mediologically winning in this historical phase — which highlights its phenomenological limits, by encoding its non-afferent elements, or at least those which are not substantial.

Parallel to this line of research, in the domain of improvisational processes, runs a second one, which moves in the opposite direction. We find the more complete outcome in Carl Czerny's work. This option reverted, with regard to *ex tempore* creative praxes, to the intensification of syntagmatic values of melodic-rhythmic articulation incorporated into the notational medium, with an overload of linear and building data. In relation to our model, we can recognize the features of a Level 2 elaboration.

With Czerny, particularly in his *Systematische Anleitung*[60], the improvisational criterion is resolutely oriented towards thematic-motivic elaboration modules, which subsume the values intrinsically linked to the ATP, establishing at the same time the framework of the apogee of nineteenth-century improvisation. This last one, however, forgoing the exploitation of its peculiar resources — whose formation rules are in ATP's phenomenology — and placing the stigma of their legality in a planning-visual conformation, ended up assuming the form of a 'derived composition', a pale reflection of the canonical written ones (which, it must be remembered, as mediological archetypes were

---

58. See Fox, Pamela. 'The Stylistic Anomalies of C. P. E. Bach's Nonconstancy', in: *C. P. E. Bach Studies*, edited by Stephen L. Clark, Oxford University Press, 1988, p. 126.

59. At least in short preludes, as well as in cadenzas or in the ornamentation of fermatas.

60. CZERNY, Carl. *Op. cit.* (see note 39).

a genuine expression of the *Zeitgeist*, of the 'visual' historical-anthropological phase). In the creation of written music, as opposed to improvisation, the visual principle could well radiate on the basis of notational mediality and in accordance with the long-span criteria linked with compositional practice. The technology of notation, in fact, was the ideal means in order to carry its consubstantial logical-combinatorial 'visual' epistemic values[61], with a homologous but opposite function with respect to that medium, connatural to the evenemential processuality, which improvisational phenomenology would have found only in the phonographic recording-reproducing medium. Just at the time of maximum proximity to the constitutive principle of improvisation the foundations were laid for it to be overcome, with the definitive decline of this ancient practice in Western music.

With Czerny the assimilation of improvisational procedures to the criteria of written composition becomes programmatic, following the lesson of Viennese classicism. Here is his introductory statement of his *Systematische Anleitung*:

> Therefore the talent and the art of improvising (*Fantasieren*) consists in elaborating on the spot (*aus dem Stegreif*), without any particular immediate preparation, every idea of one's own or of someone else, during the performance itself, into some kind of musical composition[62].

At the roots of this idea to which Czerny is referring we find the principle peculiar to improvisation, embodied in the spirit of Romantic individuality: the articulatory *lógos*, the projection of the *mélos* through the acting subjectivity, thus identifying the feature which we set as a condition for the concept of improvisation in itself. We already noticed that Czerny makes, de facto, a distinction between *Preludieren* and *Jmprovisieren*: a remarkable criterion, which seems to prefigure our dichotomy between the categories of extemporization and improvisation. After referring to preludes and cadenzas, the Viennese pianist, sure enough, notes that «These two kinds must be, apart from their own partial necessity, also considered as preliminary exercises and elements of true improvising»[63],

---

[61]. Without the possibility of long-span systematic elaboration, allowed by the visual and planning use of notation, the constructive criteria of Western music could not have been attained, from the achievements of serialism going back to the practices of the medieval *musica mensurata* (Johannes Boen, in 1355, with reference to the epistemic visual features of the written compositional procedures, already asserts that «color plus visui obicitur quam auditui». (BOEN, Johannes. 'Ars Musicae' [I, 30], in: *Corpus scriptorum de musica*, vol. XIX, edited by Franco Alberto Gallo, Rome, American Institute of Musicology, 1972, pp. 15-42.

[62]. CZERNY, Carl. *Op. cit.* (see note 39), p. 3: «Demnach besteht das Talent und die Kunst des Fantasierens darin, aus dem Stegreif, ohne besondere unmittelbare Vorbereitung, jede eigene, oder auch fremde Jdee, während dem Spielen selbst, zu einer Art von musikalischer Composition auszuspinnen».

[63]. *Ibidem*, p. 4: «Diese 2 Arten sind, abgesehen von ihrer eigene partiellen Notwendigkeit, auch als Vorübungen und Bestandteile des wirklichen Fantasierens zu betrachten».

introducing shortly afterwards, as a contrast, the «true and independent improvisation»[64]. This theoretic statement finds its foundation in the concept of *Durchführung*[65], in motivic-thematic elaboration, as a distinct activity from the realization of preludes and cadences (which, as a matter of fact, in the light of our theoretical paradigms, would have been ascribed by Czerny to the category of extemporization).

This theoretical passage is of the utmost importance for our argument. The visual factors which the pianist and composer connects to the improvisational praxis can be essentially traced back to three classes: (a) thematic elements with a structuring function; (b) motivic-thematic elaboration as a feature of processual conduct; and (c) building/architectural organization by means of structured forms. Those aspects mark the abandonment of formative strategies indebted to an electively audiotactile operativeness, realized in the gesturality of *Spielfiguren*, extemporized through harmonic-contrapuntal patterns, towards a formal conception introducing the epistemological legacy of constructivist visuality with a cohesive sequential elaboration inside the improvisational praxis.

In the historical process that we are analyzing, we thus assist to the transition of musical improvisation towards the full acquisition of visual epistemological models. The formal conception as an architectural pattern and as an outcome of the coherent planning of cellular elaborations is, in fact, to be traced back to an abstractive-rational-visual epistemic model, while, on the contrary, the true sense of the audiotactile form, which is processual, can be detected a posteriori, as a result of contextual transactions mediated by the audiotactile form. The issue of Czerny's creative option, on the mediological level, is linked, as a general rule, to the fact that the structure of the message can be more or less connatural with the logic of the medium. The visual logic towards which such formal research is oriented did not fully harmonize with the needs of an intrinsically audiotactile process such as improvisation, whereas it was perfectly in tune with the technology of writing.

This involved some concrete consequences from the point of view of psycho-social processes. It is realistic to suppose that the nineteenth-century creative performer, facing Czerny's paradigm, if oriented towards the «improvisation in the strict sense of the word»[66], would feel too heavy a burden for a marginal practice such as improvisation, and that in the long run he could not — or would not be motivated to — control the considerable amount of data and constructive procedures involved. Such a creative undertaking showed an intrinsic disparity between ends and means, between

---

64. *Ibidem*: «wirkliche, selbstständige Fantasieren (Jmprovisieren)». The verb *Jmprovisieren* was rendered as «improvvisazione propriamente detta» («improvisation in the strict sense of the word») in the Italian translation of Czerny's treatise (ID. *L'arte di improvvisare resa all'intelligenza dei pianisti*, Milan, Ricordi, 1863, p. 2), just in order to point out the completely distinctive sense that the term carved out in the semantic field.

65. CZERNY, Carl. *Op. cit.* (see note 39), p. 4.

66. See note 64.

psychophysical energy mobilized — both in the phase of procedure learning and in the strictly operational one — and the actual results of musical action (which took the shape of a presence in the dispersion, without being able to form into an ontology, as it was the case, instead, for written works, and as it would be the case in the following century for phonographically recorded works). The phenomenological and aesthetic minority held in this historical phase by the improvisational act interfered negatively with the care and the energy investment which the 'improvisation in the strict sense of the word' required, thus putting motivation to the test during training. The excess of parametric integration and proliferation, in this phenomenological horizon, thus turned into its opposite, the entropic annihilation of the system.

In this scenario the causal nexuses of historical dissolution of *ex tempore* creative practices in Western art music begin to take shape, through a twofold series of instances. On the one hand we have the 'compensatory principle', which is active in the class of phenomenons to which belong the eighteenth-century *freie Fantasie* and the proto-Romantic short prelude, which historically paid for the limits of a formal control mainly founded on 'secondary qualities', on the vertical gradient (an operational option which could not yet be formalized, technologically apprehensible, with the goal of a textualization which could lend it an aesthetic legality). The paradox which Czerny symbolizes, on the other hand, found its natural outcome in the mediality of the written composition, to whose syntactic-linear and analytical-combinatorial principles it ended up conforming, reaching at the same time a paralysis because of the accumulation of parameters. These two diverse and opposite procedural criteria found a common destiny in the eclipse of real-time creative praxes, just because of the double and converging stall imposed, on the mediological level, by historical-technological limits and by the pervasive annexationism of the ideology of writing.

It will be in the era of 'neo-auratic encoding', in the twentieth century, that improvisational practices, hinged on audiotactile formativity, will have access to an objectual ontology. Thus the foundations will be laid for a redemption of structural operational criteria pioneered by the great figures of improvisers of the past, while the compensatory suprasegmental process and the *ex tempore* developing variation finally became phenomenologically documentable and aesthetically rewarding thanks to phonofixation.

Translated by Paolo Del Lungo

CONTRIBUTORS

CARMELA BONGIOVANNI is Music Librarian at the Conservatory in Genoa and Lecturer in Music, Librarianship and Bibliography at the University of Genoa. She has published many essays and papers on musical sources and the history of music from the late sixteenth and to the nineteenth century. She has devoted herself to music bibliography and has published among other things the Catalogue of the music collection of the cathedral of Genoa. She is on the editorial staff of the annual periodical *Fonti Musicali Italiane*.

PHILIPPE BORER, born in Neuchâtel, Switzerland, studied the violin with Max Rostal, Ruggiero Ricci and Jan Sedivka. He took his Doctorate of Philosophy in Australia in 1995. Publications include *The Twenty-Four Caprices of Niccolò Paganini* (1997). He has contributed to a number of publications, including *Nuova Rivista Musicale Italiana*, *Revue Musicale de Suisse Romande*, *Starinnaya Muzyka*, *The Strad*, and *Nicolò Paganini Diabolus in Musica* (2010). He is Professor of Violin at the Société Suisse de Pédagogie Musicale. Current research projects include the theorisation and elaboration of the 'Violin Slide-Rule' for the calculation and the visualisation of musical intervals. Since 1998 he has played with a curved bow (Bach-bow) and his repertory of polyphonic violin music includes works by Marini, Westhoff, Bach, Paganini, Baillot, Boucher, Michael Bach Bachtischa.

ROGÉRIO BUDASZ is Associate Professor of Musicology at the University of California Riverside. He received his Ph.D. from the University of Southern California, Los Angeles, in 2001. His studies focus on early and traditional Luso-Brazilian music as the result of centuries of contact and colonization, exploring issues of cultural circularity between written and unwritten traditions, ethnicity, power, and the representation of Luso-Brazilians in eighteenth- and nineteenth-century literature. In addition, he has studied and taught lute and early plucked string instruments and traditional Brazilian music.

VINCENZO CAPORALETTI, musicologist, musician and composer, teaches Analysis of Compositional Forms at the Conservatory of Music 'Santa Cecilia' in Rome and Ethnomusicology at the University of Macerata. His research spans the fields of improvisation, analysis and the transcription of non-written music in particular, and the history of Western art music. His most important works are *La definizione dello swing* (2000); *I processi improvvisativi nella musica* (2005); *Esperienze di analisi del jazz* (2007); and *Jelly Roll Morton, the "Old Quadrille" e "Tiger Rag"* (2011). He is involved in critical editions of musical works from Western art music of the eighteenth and nineteenth centuries up to jazz. He is the general editor of the book series 'Grooves' published by LIM Edizioni in Lucca. His research on aesthetics and musical anthropology, which led to the theoretical model of 'audiotactile formativity', constitute the pedagogic-didactic framework of the Nuovi Ordinamenti Didattici (2007) of the Italian conservatories.

GREGORIO CARRARO graduated *cum laude* in Musical Philology at Padua University. His musicological studies began with a thesis about the pre-Corellian sonata, in particular, Angelo Berardi's violin sonatas. At present he is a Ph.D. student at Padua University, his research centring on the violin sonatas of Giuseppe Tartini. As a recorder player, he has performed under the baton of some of the most renowned, historically informed conductors, including Ottavio Dantone, Giovanni Antonini, Christopher Hogwood and Michael Radulescu, in well-known venues such as the Theatre des Champs Elyseées in the Paris, the Barbican in London, the Kölner Philarmonie in Cologne and the Teatro alla Scala in Milan.

Contributors

SIMONE CIOLFI is a doctoral student at the University of Rome 'Tor Vergata'. He obtained his M.A. (*Laurea*) with Pierluigi Petrobelli at the University 'La Sapienza' in Rome. He has written articles on early nineteenth-century music and on Dallapiccola, on the programming of nineteenth-century Italian musical organizations and in the contemporary period. His fields of interest are the evolution of the concept of tradition in the music of the eighteenth and nineteenth centuries and the relations between music theory and composition around 1700. Since 2006 he has been Secretary of the Editorial Board of the periodical *Rivista Italiana di Musicologia*. He writes for various organisations, among them the Accademia di Santa Cecilia, the Filarmonica della Scala and the Festival Pianistico di Brescia e Bergamo. Since many years he has worked on the artistic management of the Accademia Filarmonica Romana and has collaborated with the *Concerto Italiano*, under the direction of Rinaldo Alessandrini.

DAMIEN COLAS, musicologist, works as a researcher for the Centre National de la Recherche Scientifique. In 1998 he joined the Institut de Recherche sur le Patrimoine Musical en France in Paris, where he works on nineteenth-century opera. His research fields are Italian opera in France, vocal and orchestral performance traditions and musical philology. In 2007, he organized with Alessandro Di Profio an international conference about the relations between French and Italian opera, of which the proceeding were published by Mardaga in 2009, entitled *D'une scène à l'autre*. The research on French opera orchestras by his team was published by Berlin-Verlag in 2008, edited by Niels Martin Jensen and Franco Piperno. Forthcoming is his critical edition of *Le Comte Ory* by Rossini, to be published by Bärenreiter.

MARIATERESA DELLABORRA is the author of one book and several scholarly articles on Italian music the eighteenth and nineteenth century, for example, on Sammartini, Viotti, Clementi and Mercadante. She has been involved in critical editions of instrumental music (by Paganini, Viotti, Rolla, Mercadante) and opera (by Sammartini, Traetta, Jommelli, Portugal da Fonseca, Stradella). She is a member of the scientific committee of the Arcadia Foundation (Milan) and of the series *Monumenti musicali* of the *Società Italiana di Musicologia*. She teaches History of Music at the Conservatorio 'G. Verdi' of Turin.

RAFFAELE DI MAURO obtained his M.A. (*Laurea specialistica*) in Musicology and Musical Heritage at the University of Rome 'Tor Vergata', with a thesis in Ethnomusicology entitled *From Oral Tradition to Songwriters. New Hypotheses on the Birth of Neapolitan Song (1824-1880)*. On this subject he has also published a number of articles. At present he is conducting research for a Ph.D. on the same subject at the University of Rome 'Tor Vergata'. Since 2008 he has been affiliated to the University 'Suor Orsola Benincasa' in Naples, whilst lecturing in Ethnomusicology at the University of Rome 'Tor Vergata'.

MARTIN EDIN is a doctoral student in Musicology at Örebro University (Sweden), and a Lecturer in Performance Practice at the Royal College of Music in Stockholm. Currently, he is working on a thesis on nineteenth-century piano improvisation, centred on Carl Czerny. He has published essays on music in *Artes* (Swedish Journal for Literature, Art and Music, published by the Swedish Academy) and reviews in the *Swedish Journal of Musicology* (*Svensk Tidskrift för Musikforskning*). During 2005 he was on the editorial board of *Artes*. Martin Edin is also a pianist and has a M.A. in Fine Arts from Malmö Academy of Music.

VALERIE WOODRING GOERTZEN is Associate Professor of Music History at Loyola University New Orleans. Her research has focussed on music and musical life of nineteenth-century Europe and the United States, including the practice of improvising preludes to piano pieces, and the piano transcriptions of Johannes Brahms. Her edition of a volume of the *Johannes Brahms Gesamtausgabe* including Brahms's arrangements for piano, four hands, and two pianos of works of other composers, is forthcoming from G. Henle Verlag.

Contributors

MARTIN KALTENECKER has studied musicology and French literature at the Sorbonne (Paris), where he received his Ph.D. and his *habilitation*. He has co-edited the review for contemporary music *Entretemps* (1985-1992). Since 2006 he is associated researcher of the Centre de Recherches sur les Arts et le Langage of the École des Hautes Études en Sciences Sociales in Paris. He has been fellow of the Wissenschaftskolleg zu Berlin in 2006/2007. His publications include *La Rumeur des Batailles. La musique au tournant des XVIIIᵉ et XIXᵉ siècles* (Paris, 2000), *Avec Helmut Lachenmann* (Paris, 2001), and *L'Oreille divisée. Les discours sur l'écoute musicale aux XVIIIᵉ au XIXᵉ siècles* (Paris, 2011). He co-edited the volume *Penser l'œuvre musicale au XXᵉ siècle. Avec, sans, contre l'histoire?* (Paris, 2006).

Musicologist, cellist and viol player JOHN LUTTERMAN is currently Johnston Visiting Professor at Whitman College, Walla Walla, Washington. He has also served on the faculty of the San Francisco Conservatory, the University of California Davis, the University of the Pacific, Stockton, California, and Lawrence University, Appleton, Wisconsin. He holds a Ph.D. in historical musicology from the University of California Davis and a D.M.A. in cello performance from Stony Brook University, Stony Brook, New York. Articles by him have appeared in *Early Music America*, *Strings*, and the *San Francisco Classical Voice*. Dr. Lutterman's teaching and research interests include the history of theory, the history of improvisation, and the historical development of the modern concept of a musical 'work'.

NAOMI MATSUMOTO trained as a singer at the Aichi Prefectural University of Fine Arts and Music in Nagakute, Japan, the Liceo Musicale 'G. B. Viotti' in Vercelli, Italy, and the Trinity College of Music in London. After singing in various concerts, she commenced her musicological studies and gained M.Mus. and Ph.D. degrees from the University of London in 2000 and 2005 respectively. She has received several awards, including the Overseas Research Scholarship, the British Federation of Women Graduates National Award, and the Gladys Krieble Delmas Foundation British Award. She is currently an Associate Lecturer at Goldsmiths College, University of London, and is working on Italian opera of the seventeenth and nineteenth centuries.

LAURA MOECKLI studied musicology, English literature and philosophy in Fribourg (Switzerland) where she obtained her M.A. degree in 2009 with a thesis on vocal ornamentation. She is currently writing her Ph.D. Thesis on nineteenth-century recitative with Anselm Gerhard in Bern. In 2009-2010 she was visiting research assistant at the Gutenberg University in Mainz and taught two seminars on French and Italian opera. In the context of an interdisciplinary research project funded by the Bern University of Applied Sciences, Laura Moeckli is investigating singers' movements, gestures and expression on the nineteenth-century Paris opera stage. She has presented various aspects of her research at musicological conferences in Fribourg, York, La Spezia, Bern and Kent.

CSILLA PETHŐ-VERNET obtained her degree in musicology at the Liszt Ferenc Academy of Music (Budapest) in 1998. She worked as a researcher at the Institute of Musicology (Budapest) until 2003, before leaving for Paris, where in 2005 she began a Ph.D. on the Hungarian style in nineteenth-century French stage music. Starting in 2000, she has published several articles in Hungarian, French and German journals and other publications on Hungarian influences in Western music (see, among others, her article on the *style hongrois* in *Studia Musicologica*, XLI, 2000), as well as on nineteenth- and twentieth-century Hungarian music. Her study on György Ránki was published in English in 2004 (in Budapest), as volume XVIII of the series Hungarian Composers.

RUDOLF RASCH studied musicology in Amsterdam with Karel Philippus Bernet Kempers and Joseph Smits van Waesberghe. He wrote a dissertation on polyphonic carols in the Spanish Netherlands in the seventeenth century (Utrecht, 1985) and was affiliated to the Institute of Musicology of Utrecht University from 1977 until 2010. His main research interests are the musical history of the Netherlands, tuning and temperament, and the works of composers such as Corelli, Vivaldi, Geminiani and Boccherini. He has published articles, books and editions in these fields, including *Music Publishing in Europe 1600-1900* (a collection of essays edited, 2005), *Driehonderd brieven over muziek* (letters about music written by and to Constantijn Huygens, 2007), and critical editions of the *Duetti per 2 Violini Opus 3* and the *Sonate per tastiera e violino Opus 5* by Luigi Boccherini (2007, 2009).

After obtaining a first-class diploma in violin, RENATO RICCO graduated *summa cum laude* in liberal arts with a thesis on the evolution of the violin concerto in the period 1900-1940, supervised by Renato Di Benedetto. Since 2008 he has been pursuing doctoral studies at the Faculty of Arts of the University of Salerno. In addition to his research on Italian literature (with publications on Metastasio, Verga, D'Annunzio and Moravia), his musicological interests are centred chiefly on the instrumental music of the nineteenth century, with particular attention to virtuoso violin music influenced by Paganini.

ROHAN H. STEWART-MACDONALD was born in 1975 in Solihull, England. In 1993 he matriculated as a Choral Scholar at St Catharine's College, Cambridge, where he gained a B.A. in 1996, an M.Phil. in 1997, an M.A. in 2000 and a Ph.D. in 2001. Since completing the Ph.D. he has continued to specialise in British music of the eighteenth and nineteenth centuries with a particular emphasis on the music of Muzio Clementi (1752-1832). His book on Clementi's keyboard sonatas, *New Perspectives on the Keyboard Sonatas of Muzio Clementi*, was published in 2006 by Ut Orpheus Edizioni as volume II of the series *Quaderni Clementiani*. Between 2004 and 2009 he was Director of Music, Director of Studies in Music and more recently Bye-Fellow of Murray Edwards College, Cambridge and is now an Independent Scholar. Current projects include the book *Jan Ladislav Dussek. A Bohemian Composer «En Voyage» Through Europe*, volume IV of the *Quaderni Clementiani* series, which he is co-editing with Roberto Illiano, and he is developing an interest in Italian symphonic music of the eighteenth century.

STEVEN YOUNG, D.M.A., is Professor of Music at Bridgewater State University, Massachusetts. He serves as Director of Choral Activities and teaches courses in music theory. He is also Music Director/ Organist at the Old South Union Church in South Weymouth, Massachusetts. He is a frequent reviewer for various choral and organ journals, and also acts as a choral clinician and adjudicator.

Index of Names*

A

Abbado, Michelangelo 9
Abbatini, Antonio Maria 90
Abreu, *composer* 70
Addison, Joseph 24
Agricola, Johann Friedrich 23
Aguado, Dionysio 212
Albani, Emma 299-302
Alborea, Francesco 118
Algarotti, Francesco 56, 64, 103, 301
Alighieri, Dante 196-197
Allorto, Riccardo 333
Ancelet, *author* 114
Andersen, Hans Christian 319
Appiani, Giuseppe, known as 'Appianino' 57
Aprile, Giuseppe 59
Arditi, Luigi 299, 304, 312-313
Artôt, Alexandre 228
Ashbrook, William 328
Ashforth, Frieda 305
Azzolino, *publisher* 337

B

Babini, Matteo 198-199
Bacchelli, known as 'Mignatrice' 40
Bach, Carl Philipp Emanuel 18, 25-27, 30-31,
    119-121, 123, 127, 164, 222, 361, 364,
    366-369
Bach, Johann Sebastian 32, 111-112, 116, 118-128,
    134, 153-154, 158-162, 171, 185
Bach, Wilhelm Friedmann 31
Baciocchi, Elisa 202
Backhaus, Wilhelm 157

Badura-Skoda, Eva 167
Bailleux, Antoine 9-10, 13
Baillot, Pierre-Marie-François de Sales 13, 115,
    165-166, 168, 170, 172, 174, 182, 217-218,
    223, 228, 231-236
Bakhtin, Mikhail 127
Balzac, Honoré de 203, 208, 212
Bandettini, Teresa 36, 194-195, 203
Barblan, Guglielmo 298, 313
Bardua, Caroline 203, 207-209
Bardua, Wilhelmine 207
Baretti, Giuseppe 319
Barrientos, Maria 306
Barros, Denis de 70
Barry, Philipp 363
Bartók, Béla 236, 250
Basie, Count [William] 345
Bassano, Giovanni 97
Battista, Vincenzo 337-338, 340-341
Bauck, Wilhelm 165
Baudiot, Charles-Nicolas 115
Baumgartner, Johann Baptist 113-114, 124
Bavagnoli, Gaetano 312
Bax, Saint-Yves 305, 311-312
Bazzini, Antonio 227
Beethoven, Ludwig van 3, 29, 31-33, 43, 83, 132,
    136, 142, 150, 153-154, 157-162, 167-171,
    174, 178, 215
Bellini, Vincenzo 167, 229, 262, 264-265, 272,
    281-285, 300, 340
Benatti, Vincenzo 63
Benda, Franz 204, 220, 222

---

*. Not included in this index are the names of authors, editors, translators, etc. mentioned in bibliographical references.

BENGRÁF, József 244
BENNATI, Francesco 208
BENSON, Bruce Ellis 226
BÉRIOT, Charles-Auguste de 212, 217-236
BERNACCHI, Antonio Maria 279
BERRI, Pietro 228
BERTINI, Giuseppe 36, 41, 43
BERTINOTTI, Teresa 197
BIANCHI, Antonia 198
BIGATI, *violoncellist* 41, 43
BIHARI, János 239-240, 247-249
BINDOCCI, Antonio 321-322, 326, 339
BISCARDI, Luigi 335
BJÖRKSEN, Theodore 306
BLANCHARD, Henri 231
BLASCO, *violinist* 43
BLOCH, Ernst 236
BOCCHERINI, Luigi 2, 9-14, 41
BOGATYRËV, Piotr 355, 358, 363
BONAPARTE, Joseph, King of Naples and Sicily 317
BONET, Francesco 306
BORDONI, Faustina 40
BOTTESINI, Giovanni 47
BOUCHER, Alexandre 230
BOUVARD, Jean 188
BOVICELLI, Giovanni Battitsa 97
BOYDEN, David 232
BOYER, Frédéric 305
BRAHMS, Johannes 139
BRĂILOIU, Costantin 363
BRAMBILLA, Teresa 298, 313
BRANDENBURG, Sophia Charlotte Electress of 4
BRASSAI, Sámuel 252
BREMNER, Robert 9
BRICEÑO, Luis de 73
BROD, Henri 297-298
BROFFERIO, Angelo 340
BROSCHI, Carlo, known as 'Farinelli' 40
BROSSES, Charles de 19, 22, 27
BULL, Ole 200, 203, 220, 227, 229
BUONAVENTURA, Giovanni 124
BURKE, Edmund 31
BURMEISTER, Joachim 28
BURNEY, Charles 22, 30, 36, 39-41, 46
BUSONI, Ferruccio 157
BYRON, Lord 195

C

CALEGARI, Antonio 266
CALLAS, Maria 295, 300, 302, 307, 309-310, 312
CALVI, Carlo 77
CAMBINI, Giuseppe Maria 29
CAMMARANO, Luigi 340
CAMMARANO, Salvadore 295-296
CAMÕES, Luis de 72
CAMPAGNOLI, Bartolomeo 53, 59, 65
CAMPANELLA, Filippo 340
CAMPION, François 120
CAMPIONI, Giuseppe 57
CAMPRA, André 75-76
CANTÙ, Cesare 329
CAPLIN, William 145
CAPORALETTI, Vincenzo 89, 225, 341-342
CAREW, Derek 130-132, 136-137, 139, 141-142, 149-150
CARIGNANI, Carlo 306
CARNEYRO Tavares, Joseph *see* TAVARES, Joseph Carneyro
CARPITELLA, Diego 320, 322
CASE, Anna 306
CASTEL DE LABARRE, Louis-Julien 230
CASTIL-BLAZE, François-Henri-Joseph 233, 314
CASULARO, Francesco Saverio 328
CATALANI, Angelina 198-199
CATALISANO, Gennaro 64
CECCHERINI, Giuseppe 306
CELLE, Antonio Maria 201
CELLIER, Alexandre 185, 188, 190
CENCI, Giuseppe 76
CERESOLI-SALVATORI, Elvira 307
CERRO, Luigi 201
CHAULIEU, Charles 34
CHERUBINI, Luigi 27, 134, 212
CHEVALIER, Marie-Madeleine 189
CHOPIN, Fryderyk 39, 137, 149, 153, 156-157, 159-162, 176-178, 180-181, 194, 210, 231, 272, 346, 357-358
CHORLEY, Henry 315
CHRYSANDER, Friedrich 7
CICCONETTI, Filippo 327-328
CIMAROSA, Domenico 318
CINTI-DAMOREAU, Laure 258-261, 265, 281, 293
CLAUSETTI, *publisher* 331-334, 336-338
CLEMENTI, Muzio 31, 83, 142, 164-166, 174, 180

COLTRANE, John 245
COLTURATO, Annarita 281
CONDILLAC, Étienne de 18
CONTI, Carlo 283-284
CORBETTA, Francesco 70-71
CORELLI, Arcangelo 2, 4-9, 70, 88, 122, 165, 222
CORILLA OLIMPICA see MORELLI, Maria Maddalena
CORRI, Domenico 290
COSTA, Giacomo 201
COSTA, Lorenzo 195, 201
COSTAGLIOLA, Aniello 327
COTTRAU, Giuseppe 323
COTTRAU, Guglielmo 323, 326, 329, 332-334, 339-342
COTTRAU, Teodoro 334, 341
COTUMACCI, Carlo 63
Cox, John Edmund 203, 214-215
CRAMER, Johann Baptist 164-165, 231
CREED, J. 22
CRESCENTINI, Girolamo 197-199
CRESCIMBENI, Giovan Mario 89
CROCCO, Arturo 195
CROCE, Benedetto 321-322, 326
CROUCH, Frederick William 115
CRUTCHFIELD, Will 285
CSERMÁK, Antal 240, 248
CZERNY, Carl 17, 31-33, 132, 163, 165, 168-175, 178-179, 181-182, 225, 353, 361, 364-365, 370-373

D

DAHLHAUS, Carl 83
DALLA CASA, Filippo 63
DALLA CASA, Girolamo 97
DAL MONTE, Toti 307, 312
DANTE see ALIGHIERI, Dante
DA PONTE, Lorenzo 289
DAUPRAT, Louis-François 131
DAVID, composer 70
DAVID, Félicien 301
DE BLASIO, Abele 320
DE CRESCENZI, Carlo 328
DE FRATE, Inez 306
DE FRATE, Isabella 306
DE GIOVANNI, Nicola 201
DEGLI ANTONII, Giovanni Battista 124
DEGLI ANTONII, Pietro 124
DE KERKHOVE, Derrick 349, 357

DELACROIX, Eugène 201, 212-213
DE LAUZIÈRES, Achille 333
DE LEERSNYDER, Brigitte 186
DE MARCO, publisher 335, 337-338
DE MEGLIO, Vincenzo 333-334, 337, 341
DE MURA, Ettore 328-329, 340
DE MURSKA, Ilma [Ema Pukšec] 299
DENIS, Pierre 99
DEPANIS, Giuseppe 47
DE RUBERTIS, Raffaele 328, 340
DE SIMONE, Roberto 329
DEWEY, John 357
DIDEROT, Denis 23
DI GIACOMO, Salvatore 327-328
DI NEGRO, Gian Carlo 36, 196
DI VEROLI, Elda 307
DOIZI DE VELASCO, Nicolau see VELASCO, Nicolau Doizi de
DOLMETSCH, Arnold 7
DONIZETTI, Gaetano 212, 271, 279, 281-285, 295-300, 313, 327-329, 334, 340-341
DORIA, Diogo 70
DOTZAUER, Justus Johann Friedrich 115
DRABKIN, William 167
DREYFUS, Laurence 127
DUFES, Sara 306
DUPREZ, Gilbert-Louis 259-260, 263, 271
DURAND, Auguste-Frédéric 204
DÜRING, Jean 253
DURUFLÉ, Maurice 186, 189-190
DUSSEK, Jan Ladislav 138, 142, 150, 164-165

E

EBERL, Anton 150
EGGEBRECHT, Hans Heinrich 23
ELIZZA, Elise 305
ELLER, Louis 220
ELLINGTON, Duke [Edward Kennedy] 345
ERNST, Heinrich Wilhelm 194, 211, 220, 229, 234
EVANS, Bill [William John Evans] 245

F

FABRIZI, Paolo 342
FALLER, Hedwig 257, 260-262, 265-266, 273
FARINELLI see BROSCHI, Carlo
FAYOLLE, François 230
FERDINAND I, King of Naples 319

Fernow, Carl Ludwig 326
Fétis, François-Joseph 34, 142, 145, 201, 203
Feuillet, Raoul-Auger 71, 75
Field, John 231
Finzi-Magrini, Giuseppina 306
Fiore, Francesco 229
Fischhof, Joseph 156-157, 159
Florimo, Francesco 333, 341
Foà, Mauro 281
Foà, Roberto 281
Fontaine, Eugène 227
Forkel, Johann Nikolaus 29-30, 128
Forst, Grete 305
Foscolo, Ugo 196
Fox, Pamela 370
Fox Strangways, Arthur Henry 360
Francis ii Rákóczi, Prince of Transylvania 253
Francis of Assisi, Saint 196
Franck, César 185-188
Franz, Robert 242
Freitas, Roger 83, 92
Frescobaldi, Girolamo 192
Friedel, Peter 204
Friedrich, Caspar David 207
Froehlich, Franz Joseph 115
Fuenllana, Miguel de 68
Fumarolli, Marc 202

G

Gail, Jean-François 265
Galasso, Giuseppe 341
Galeazzi, Francesco 37-38, 46, 49, 53-54, 56, 59-61, 64
Gall, Franz Joseph 208
Galli-Curci, Amelita 306, 312
Galvany, Maria 306
Ganassi, Sylvestro 97, 115, 236
Garcia, Manuel (junior) 199, 255-256, 271, 280-281, 288, 293, 311-312
García, Manuel (senior) 199, 268, 281, 311, 314
Garelli, Giovanni 57
Gasparini, Francesco 87-88
Gassner, Ferdinand Simon 115
Gaubert, Philippe 305
Gautier, Théophile 194, 212
Gaviniés, Pierre 221
Geminiani, Francesco 5, 29, 61, 64, 196, 232

Genlis, Mme de 43
Gerber, Ernst Ludwig 33
Germi, Luigi Guglielmo 195, 198
Gervasoni, Carlo 88, 94
Gesualdo, Carlo, Prince of Venosa 90
Gherardeschi, Domenico 63
Giamberti, Giuseppe 76
Gianni, Francesco 194-195
Giannotti, Pietro 64
Giardini, Felice 41, 97
Giordano, Filippo 281
Giordano, Renzo 281
Giorgis, Domenico 42
Giornovichi, Giovanni 204
Girard, Bernardo 323-324, 326, 328-334, 337, 341
Gnecco, Francesco 201, 228
Goehr, Lydia 356-357
Goertzen, Valerie Woodring 150
Goethe, Johann Wolfgang von 38, 196, 207-208, 319
Gomes, composer 70
Gonzaga, Aida 305
Goodman, Nelson 350
Gottschalk, Louis Moreau 131
Gounod, Charles 301
Granichstätten, Hermine 305
Greco, Rocco 118
Grillparzer, Franz 160
Grisley, Roberto 44
Grizzi see Sgricci, Tommaso
Gröning-Wilde, Zelma 311
Guglielmi, author 63
Guhr, Carl 201, 203, 230
Gunn, John 115
Gurlitt, Willibald 212

H

Haack, Karl 203-204
Habeneck, François-Antoine 223, 233
Handel, George Frideric 41, 301
Hanslick, Eduard 28
Hanson, Norwood Russell 357
Harrys, Georg 230
Hasse, Johann Adolf 39-40
Hässler, Johann Wilhelm 27
Hatten, Robert S. 346
Haydn, Joseph 29, 41, 154, 164, 182, 229, 233, 249-250

Index of Names

HEGEL, Georg Wilhelm Friedrich 203, 205, 207, 212
HEIDEGGER, Martin 357
HEINE, Heinrich 231
HENSELT, Adolph 157, 161-162, 168, 174, 176-182
HERDER, Johann Gottfried 24, 28, 31
HÉROLD, Ferdinand 34, 301
HERTEL, Johann Wilhelm 29
HERZ, Henri 34, 154, 174-175
HEYMANN, Sophie 304
HITZIG, Julius Eduard 207
HOFFMANN, Ernst Theodor Amadeus 28, 33, 231
HOFMANN, Joseph 157
HOHLFELD, Johann 22
HOLTEI, Karl von 196
HOMER [Homerus] 196
HOMOLYA, István 9
HORACE [Quintus Horatius Flaccus] 223
HUET, Félix 218
HUGO, Victor 212
HUME, David 18
HUMMEL, Johann Julius 9
HUMMEL, Johann Nepomuk 30, 33, 129-152, 166, 174, 176, 364
HÜNTEN, Franz 34
HUTCHESON, Francis 23

I
IMBAULT, Jean-Jerôme, 9
IMBERT DE LAPHALÈQUE, Georges see L'HÉRITIER, Louis-François
ISOLA, Gaetano, 201

J
JACOBI, Erwin 99-100
JAKOBSON, Roman 355, 358
JANET & COTELLE, publishers 9
JENSEN, Gustav 7
JOACHIM, Amalie 304
JOACHIM, Joseph 162, 214, 228
JOÃO, Frei 70
JOMMELLI, Niccolò [Nicolò] 41, 97, 318
JOUBERT, Joseph 28
JUTTEN, Odile 185, 188

K
KALKBRENNER, Frédéric 33-34
KALLBERG, Jeffrey 39

KANT, Immanuel 19-20, 24-25, 27-28, 32
KAUER, Ferdinand 114
KELLNER, Johann Christoph 27, 31
KEZICH, Giovanni 321
KIESEWETTER, Christoph Gottfried 214
KINTZLER, Catherine 23
KLEIN, Heinrich 246
KLEIST, Heinrich von 30
KOCH, Heinrich Christoph 19, 21, 26, 168
KORSOFF, Lucette 305-306
KREUTZER, Rodolphe 231-232
KUGLER, Franz 207
KULLAK, Theodor 137
KURZ, Selma 305-306, 311

L
L'ABBÉ LE FILS [Joseph-Barnabé Saint-Sévin] 235
LACHNER, Franz 137
LAFONT, Charles-Philippe 44
LAFONT, Pierre 44
LAMBINET, André 189
LAMPERTI, Francesco 300, 305, 312-313
LANDSEER, Edward 201
LANNOY, Baron 160
LANZA, Gesualdo 269-271, 273
LAVOTTA, János 239, 248
LE ROUX, Gaspard 125-126
LEBEL, Louis 186
LEFÉBURE-WELY, Louis-Alfred-James 185
LEMMENS, Jacques-Nicolas 185
LEMMONE, John 306
LENTON, John 113
LEO, Leonardo 118
LEO XII, Pope 207
LÉONARD, Hubert 228
LEONARDO DA VINCI 196
LEONE, Pietro 64
LÉSBIO, Antonio Marques 70
LESCHETIZKY, Theodor 178
LESTER, Joel 119
LESURE, François 35
LEYDI, Roberto 342
L'HÉRITIER, Louis-François 230
LICETE, Pepo 70
LICHTENTHAL, Peter 26, 30, 50-51, 56, 228
LIMLEY, Adolf 305
LIOMPARDI, Zuan Polo 196-197

LIPIŃSKI, Karol Józef 45, 192, 203, 211, 220, 228, 234
LISZT, Franz 83, 161, 163, 167-168, 173-174, 179-182, 203, 211-212, 226, 228, 236, 241-243, 250-252, 272
LITZMANN, Berthold 175
LIVERANI, Giuseppe 94
LOCATELLI, Pietro Antonio 303
LOLLI, Antonio 43, 221
LORENZONI, Antonio 53-54, 57-58, 64
LÜTTEKEN, Laurenz 24, 29

M

MACHY, Sieur de 115
MAEDER, Costantino 83
MAJOR, Ervin 246
MALIBRAN, Maria 200, 212, 217, 281, 341
MANCINI, Giambattista 54, 59, 64, 270
MANFREDINI, Francesco 52, 60, 64-65
MANFREDINI, Vincenzo 27
MARAIS, Roland 114
MARCHESI [MARCHESINI], Luigi 197-199, 257
MARCHESI, Mathilde 274, 298-299, 302, 304-314
MARCHESI, Salvatore 312
MARCHISIO, Barbara 307
MARINI, Biagio 124
MARPURG, Friedrich Wilhelm 18, 22
MARQUES Lésbio, Antonio see LÉSBIO, Antonio Marques
MARTINI, Giovanni Battista 45, 53, 63
MARTINOTTI, Sergio 191
MARTORANA, Pietro 328, 339
MARTY, Adolphe 186-187
MARX, Adolph Bernhard 203, 205
MASCAGNI, Pietro 300
MASCARELLI, Cavagliero 70, 78
MASSARI, Luigi 322
MASSÉ, Victor 301
MASSIMINO, Federico 35
MATTEIS, Nicola 114
MATTHESON, Johann 17, 26, 28, 31, 114
MATTOS, Manuel de 70
MAYER, Karl August 21, 318-322, 326, 339
MAZZUCCATO, Alberto 265
MCLUHAN, Marshall 342, 349, 357
MELANI, Atto 83
MELBA, Nellie 299, 301, 304-307, 310, 312
MENDELSSOHN, Moses 25

MENDELSSOHN BARTHOLDY, Felix 153, 159, 161-162, 200, 203
MENGOZZI, Bernardo 279
MERCADANTE, Saverio 283-284, 318, 321-322
MERRICK, Arnold 115
MERSENNE, Marin 232
METASTASIO, Pietro 36, 194-196
MEYERBEER, Giacomo 301
MICHAELIS, Christian Friedrich 25
MICHAILOWA, Maria 305, 310-311
MILÁN, Luys de 68
MILIOLLI, Giuseppe 43
MITCHELL, Alice L. 163, 173
MOMIGNY, Jérôme-Joseph 233
MONDONVILLE, Jean-Joseph Castanéa de 21
MONTEIRO, composer 70
MONTEVERDI, Claudio 90
MONTI, Umberto 36
MOOSBAUER, Bernhard 9
MORELLI, Maria Maddalena, known as Corilla Olimpica 36, 194
MOSCHELES, Ignaz 33, 131, 142, 145, 176-178, 180
MOZART, Leopold 45, 97, 235
MOZART, Wolfgang Amadeus 27, 41, 83, 134, 137, 142, 149, 151, 171, 182, 284-285, 289-290, 293-294, 302, 345, 364
MUFFAT, Georg 87
MURAT, Gioacchino 317
MUROLO, Roberto 335
MUSSET, Alfred de 212, 340
MUSSET, Paul de 340
MÜTHEL, Johann Gottfried 27, 127

N

NARDINI, Pietro 36, 194
NATTIEZ, Jean-Jacques 353, 363
NEEFE, Christian Gottlieb 31
NETTL, Bruno 348
NICOLAI, Giovanni Francesco 99-102
NICOLAI, Otto 44
NICOLINI, Nicola 326
NIEDT, Friedrich Erhardt 116-117, 119, 123
NILSSON, Christina 299, 304, 312
NISSEN-SALOMAN, Henriette 255-256, 261-266
NORBLIN, Louis 131
NORTH, Charles K. 305
NOVALIS 28

O

Ogilvie, John, 28
Ohrström-Renard, Mrs 306
Olshausen, Hermann 215
Orgeni, Anna Maria 306
Ortiz, Diego 97, 115, 117

P

Pacchiarotti, Gasparo 198-199
Pacini, Giovanni 282-284
Paer, Ferdinando 35
Paganini, Carlo 200
Paganini, Nicolò 38-39, 42-46, 191-215, 217-218, 220-222, 226-232, 236
Pagliughi, Lina 310, 312
Paisiello, Giovanni 271
Paixão Ribeiro, Manuel da *see* Ribeiro, Manuel da Paixão
Pandolfi Mealli, Giovanni 124
Papp, Géza 244, 246, 251
Parente, Alfredo 226
Pareto, Graziella 305
Parker, Charlie 357
Pasquini, Bernardo 88
Pasta, Giuditta 131, 200
Patti, Adeline 300
Paul, Apostle 215
Paumgartner, Bernhard 9
Pavarotti, Luciano 335
Pécour, Louis-Guillaume 75
Pellegrini, Domenico 70, 77-78
Pellegrini, Felice 131
Pellegrini-Celoni, Anna Maria 274
Pena, Peixoto da 68
Penna, Lorenzo 87-88
Pennella, Francesco 318
Perfetti, Bernardo 194
Petri, Johann Samuel 30
Petrini Zamboni, Nicola 39, 42-43, 229
Petrobelli, Pierluigi 99-101, 103
Philips V, King of Spain 40
Piaggio, Martin 195
Pietrasanta, Gasparo 4
Piggot, George 7
Pike, Kenneth 345
Pinelli, Ettore 7-8
Pinkert, Regina 310, 312

Pisaroni [Pizzaroni], Benedetta Rosmunda 200
Pitschel, Theodore 127
Pixis, Johann Peter 34
Platen, August von 20
Polizzi, Federico 327
Polo, Enrico 7
Power, Stella 307
Pressing, Jeff 245
Prume, François 211
Puccini, Giacomo 300
Pugliese, Romana 297-298
Puig, Lázaro Maria 306

Q

Quantz, Johann Joachim 29, 45, 97, 235, 302
Quarta, Massimo 229
Quintilian [Marcus Fabius Quintillianus] 31

R

Raby, Paolo Luigi 44, 229
Rafaele, Alessandro 63
Rameau, Jean-Philippe 116
Rangoni, Giovanni Battista 52, 64
Raoul, Jean-Marie 114
Ratner, Leonard G. 134
Rauzzoni, *singer* 305, 311
Rebizzo, Lazzaro 195
Regaldi, Giuseppe 318, 329, 341
Reissiger, Carl Gottlieb 159
Rellstab, Heinrich Friedrich 203-204
Rennebaum, August 180
Resende, Garcia de 72
Reynolds, Joshua 23
Reynosa, Rodrigo de 72
Ribeiro, Manuel da Paixão 68-70
Ricci, Luigi 274, 295, 300, 306-307
Ricordi, *publisher* 333-334, 337
Ricordi, Giovanni 193
Ries, Ferdinand 32-33, 137
Rigler, Franz Paul 244
Robberechts, André 230
Rode, Pierre 203-204, 231-232
Roger, Estienne 5-6
Rognoni, Francesco 97
Rokitansky, Viktor 305
Romani, Felice 321
Romberg, Bernhard 115, 165

ROSEN, Charles 137, 182
ROSSI, Gaetano 321
ROSSINI, Gioachino 45-46, 167, 204-205, 212, 227-230, 236, 257-267, 272, 277-279, 281-286, 288-289, 293, 318
ROTHSCHILD, Baron de 212
ROUSSEAU, Jean-Jacques 23, 26, 50-51, 55-56
RÓZSAVÖLGYI, Márk 248
RUBINI, Giovanni Battista 200
RUZITSKA, Ignác 248

S

SACCO, Raffaele 322, 327-329, 334-335, 337, 339-341
SALIMBENI, Felice 57
SAND, George 212
SANTIAGO DE MURCIA 72-73
SANZ, Gaspar 69-70, 76-78
SAPIENZA, Antonio 282, 284
SÁROSI, Bálint 241, 250, 252-253
SARTI, Giuseppe 63, 257
SAUZAY, Eugène 218
SCARLATTI, Alessandro 83-95, 194
SCARLATTI, Domenico 70, 81, 153, 161
SCHEIBE, Johann 111
SCHENKER, Heinrich 360, 364, 366-368
SCHERILLO, Michele 340
SCHETKY, Johann Georg 115
SCHIASETTI, Adelaide 130
SCHLEGEL, Friedrich 28
SCHLEUNING, Peter 17, 25
SCHOPENHAUER, Johanna 207
SCHUBART, Christian Friedrich Daniel 114
SCHUBERT, Franz 27, 144, 149, 161
SCHUBERT, Johann Friedrich 166, 169, 270
SCHULENBERG, David 112, 119-120, 127
SCHULTZ, Heiner 345
SCHULZE. Hendrik 257
SCHUMANN, Clara see WIECK, Clara
SCHUMANN, Gustav 178
SCHUMANN, Robert 28, 136-137, 149-150, 153-154, 156-157, 161-162, 194, 203, 208-211, 231, 346
SECHTER, Simon 176
SEIXAS, Carlos 81
SEMBRICH, Marcella 305-306
SERAFIN, Tullio 312

SERRA, Giovanni 199, 201
SETTEMBRINI, Luigi 328
SGRICCI [SGRIZZI], Tommaso 20, 194, 322
SHELLEY, Mary 194
SHELLEY, Percy 194
SIBELIUS, Jean 236
SIEMS, Margarethe 306
SIEVERS, Georg 20
SIGNORETTI, P. 64
SIMPSON, Christopher 116-117
SITÀ, Maria Grazia 27
SIVORI, Camillo 228
SOLE, Niccola 322
SOMMA, Gaetano 338
SORCE KELLER, Marcello 329, 337
SPAGNA, Arcangelo 90
SPEYER, Wilhelm 43
SPOHR, Louis 43, 132-134, 227
STAVENHAGENS, Bernard 181
STEIBELT, Daniel 164-165
STENDHAL 198-199
STIASTNY, Bernard 115
STREPPONI, Giuseppina 313
STROHM, Reinhard 84
SULZER, Georg Friedrich 22-23
SUPRIANI, Francesco 117-118
SUTHERLAND, Joan 295, 300, 302, 309-310, 312
SYLVA, composer 70
SYLVA, Gertrude 305
SZIMANOWSKI, Karol 236

T

TACCHINARDI PERSIANI, Fanny 297-298, 315
TADDEI, Rosa 20, 194
TAFFANEL, Paul 307-308, 312
TAGLIAFICO, D. 338
TALASSI, Angelo 321
TALBOT, Michael 83
TARTINI, Giuseppe 56-58, 63-64, 97-108, 165, 196-197, 235, 303
TASSO, Torquato 196
TAVARES, Joseph Carneyro 68
TELEMANN, Georg Philipp 123-125, 222
TEMPERLEY, Nicolas 357, 369
TESSARINI, Carlo 64
TETRAZZINI, Luisa 306-307, 310, 312
THALBERG, Sigismond 157, 231

Thirugokarnam, Ramachandra Iyer 245
Thomas, Ambroise 301
Thomas of Celano 196
Thurn und Taxis, Anton 40
Tomášek, Václav Jan Křitel 32
Tomeoni, Florido 55, 60, 65
Tomeoni, Pellegrino 54, 64
Tonelli, Antonio 53-54, 63
Toni, Alceo 7
Torre, Luca 334
Toscanini, Arturo 312
Tosi, Pier Francesco 57, 255-256, 258, 263, 266, 271
Tournemire, Charles 186, 188
Tramater, *publisher* 337, 339
Tristano, Lennie 357
Truscott, Harold 142
Tulli, Pietro 63
Tulou, Jean-Louis 130
Türk, Daniel Gottlob 164, 169, 302
Turner, William 144

V

Vaccai, Nicola 283-284
Vajro, Max 335-337, 339-340
Vallotti, Francescantonio 53-54, 63
Valls, Francisco 69
Varnhagen, Rahel 203-204
Vasari, Giorgio 196
Velasco, Nicolau Doizi de 67-69
Vellani, *singer* 305
Verdi, Giuseppe 271, 277-279, 281, 285, 298, 313, 322
Viardot, Pauline 281, 304, 306, 314
Victoria, Luiz de 68
Vidal, Melchiorre 305
Vierne, Louis 185-190
Vieuxtemps, Henri 231, 234
Vigny, Alfred de 212
Viotti, Giovanni Battista 44, 166, 203-204, 218, 230-231
Visée, Robert de 70, 78-79

Vitali, Giovanni Battista 117
Vivaldi, Antonio 123, 127, 196, 235, 281
Voltaire 19, 28, 231

W

Wachs, Étienne-Victor-Paul 188
Wagner, Richard 137, 227, 235
Walsh, John 5
Weber, Carl Maria von 171, 178, 207
Weber, Gottfried 115
Weber, Max 83
Weidemann, *singer* 307
Weisse, Christian Hermann 231
Weissmann, Adolf 192
Widor, Charles-Marie 187
Wieck, Clara 153-162, 210
Wieck, Friedrich 136, 168, 171, 174-175, 178, 182, 200, 211
Wieniawski, Henryk 227, 231-232, 234
Woldemar, Michel 233
Wolf, Ernst Wilhelm 27
Wolff, Christoph 127
Wollenhaupt, Hermann Adolf 178
Wüerst, Richard 178

Y

Yaw, Ellen Beach 306, 311
Yorke, Helen 307
Yotti, Luigi 299
Young, Edward 24
Ysaÿe, Eugène 225

Z

Zanetti, Gasparo 76
Zappi, Gian Felice 89, 194
Zelter, Carl Friedrich 38, 203, 208
Ziem, Félix 194
Zimmermann, Anton 244
Zuccari, Carlo 220
Zuccari, Pietro 64
Zucchelli, Carlo 130